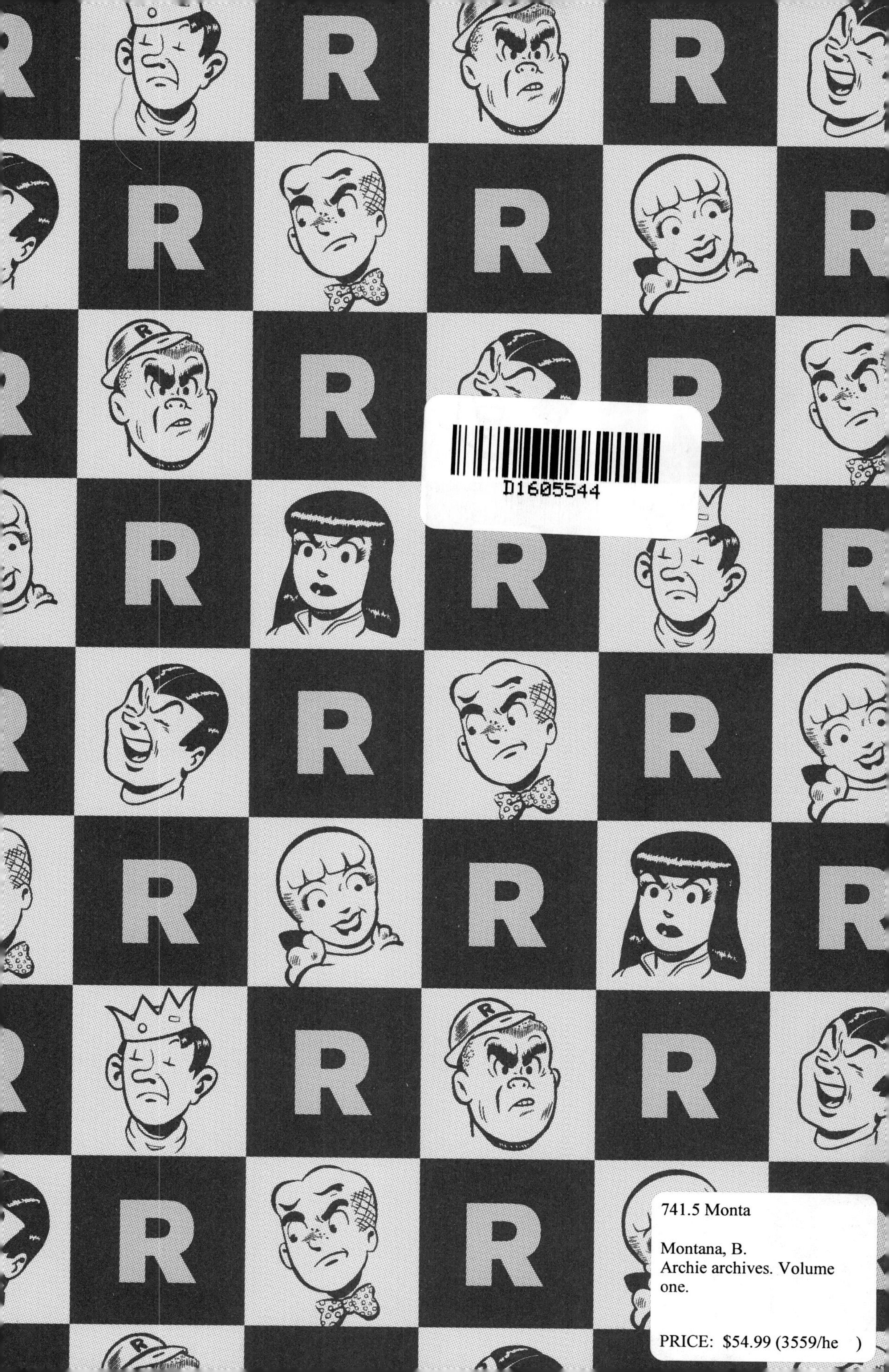

Archie

Archie Archives

VOLUME ONE

DARK HORSE BOOKS®

Publisher
MIKE RICHARDSON

Collection Editor
SHAWNA GORE

Assistant Editor
BRENDAN WRIGHT

Book Design
JOSHUA ELLIOTT
TINA ALESSI

Published by Dark Horse Books
A division of Dark Horse Comics, Inc.
10956 SE Main St.
Milwaukie, OR 97222

DarkHorse.com

This book collects all the *Archie* stories from selected stories from *Pep Comics* #22–#38, *Jackpot Comics* #4–#8, and *Archie Comics* #1–#2, all originally published by *MLJ Magazines* between December 1941 and April 1943.

First edition: May 2011
ISBN 978-1-59582-716-6

1 3 5 7 9 10 8 6 4 2

Printed by 1010 Printing International, Ltd.,
Guangdong Province, China.

Introduction

BY JON GOLDWATER

Archie. Whenever I hear the name it resonates deeply within my core. As luck would have it I grew up with Archie because my father, John L. Goldwater, along with artist Bob Montana, created Archie and the gang from Riverdale.

As a young boy, I have vivid memories of my father coming home with the new issues of *Archie* and leaving them in the same spot every time for my brother and me. It seemed as if these issues were direct from the printer, the ink on the paper so fresh you could smell it. I would lose myself in the adventures of Archie, Betty, Veronica, Jughead, and Reggie and couldn't wait for the new issues to arrive at home. I always hear wonderful stories from various people who tell me they learned to read by reading the Archie comics, and each time I hear that story I smile inside, as that truly was the case with me.

I remember going to the office on First Avenue in Manhattan and spending hours and hours in the art department, bothering a young Victor Gorelick to draw a favorite character or color something for me. What a magical place that was and full of great people—a group of young and talented artists at the top of their game creating all those classic *Archie* books. I would spend time with my father and his partner, Louis Silberkleit, and was thrilled when they invited me to have lunch with them in their private conference room. Every day there was an adventure, a miracle, to see the staff producing the comics.

Fast-forward to today, and I can say that being part of the Archie family is a dream come true. The future has never been brighter, with many exciting new platforms available to make Archie and the gang accessible to everyone. The staff we have today, our talented artists and writers, are as good as at anytime in the history of Archie Comics. I am proud to be part of this legacy, and I am grateful to all our readers and fans for the incredible support and inspiration they provide. Archie will continue to publish the high jinks of the gang from Riverdale as we move forward to the next seventy years. We are just beginning!

Jon Goldwater
Co-CEO, Archie Comics

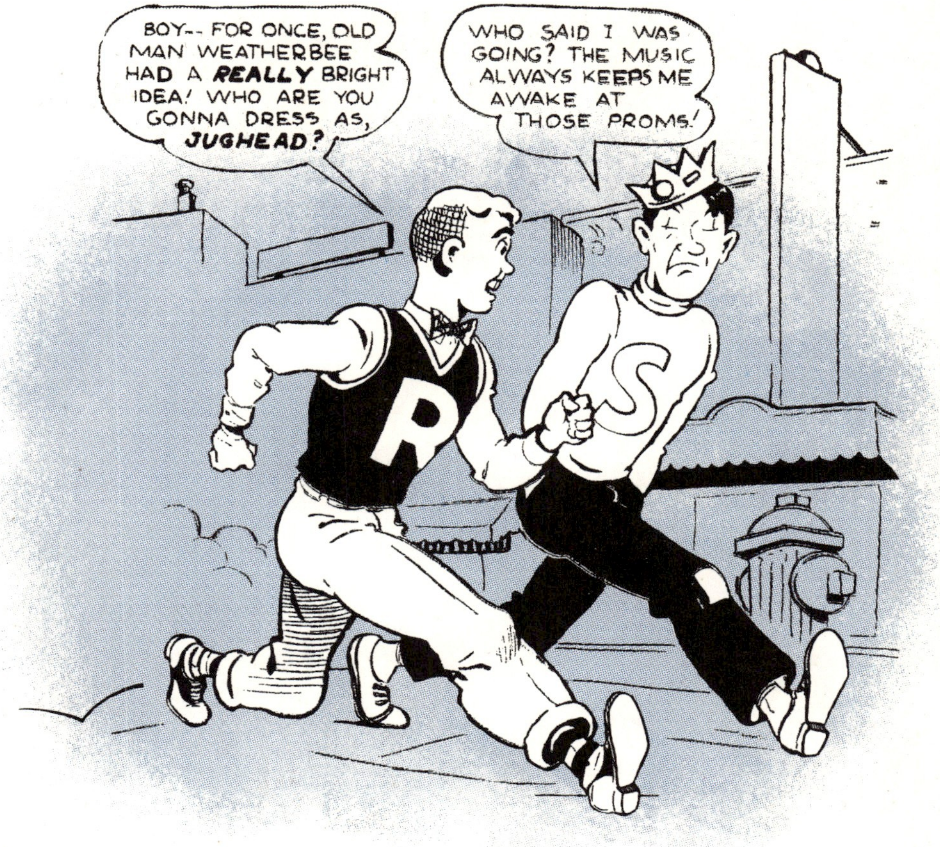
BOY-- FOR ONCE, OLD MAN WEATHERBEE HAD A REALLY BRIGHT IDEA! WHO ARE YOU GONNA DRESS AS, JUGHEAD?
WHO SAID I WAS GOING? THE MUSIC ALWAYS KEEPS ME AWAKE AT THOSE PROMS!

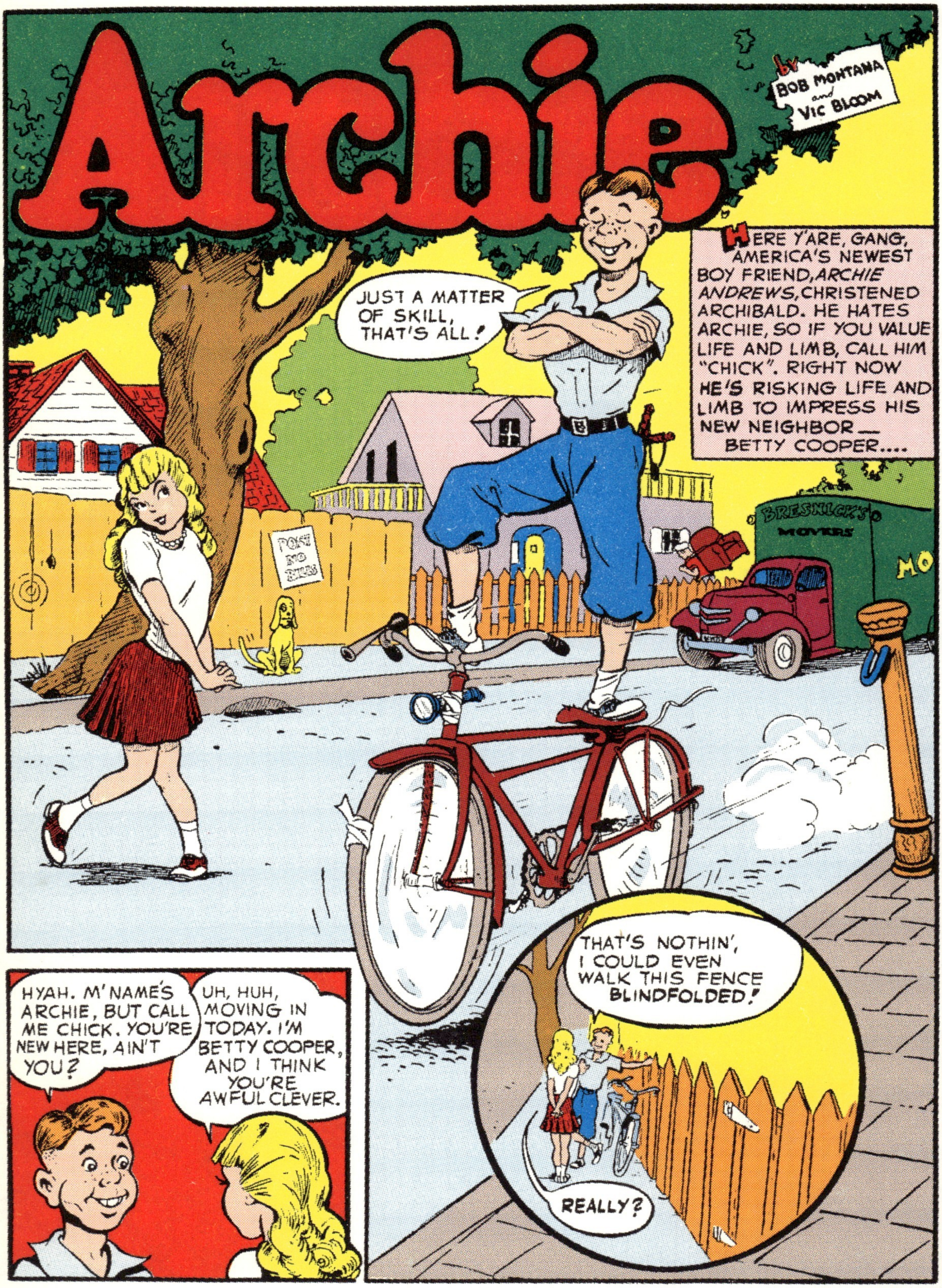
Archie
by Bob Montana and Vic Bloom
HERE Y'ARE, GANG, AMERICA'S NEWEST BOY FRIEND, ARCHIE ANDREWS, CHRISTENED ARCHIBALD. HE HATES ARCHIE, SO IF YOU VALUE LIFE AND LIMB, CALL HIM "CHICK". RIGHT NOW HE'S RISKING LIFE AND LIMB TO IMPRESS HIS NEW NEIGHBOR — BETTY COOPER....
JUST A MATTER OF SKILL, THAT'S ALL!
BRESNICK'S MOVERS
HYAH. M'NAME'S ARCHIE, BUT CALL ME CHICK. YOU'RE NEW HERE, AIN'T YOU?
UH, HUH, MOVING IN TODAY. I'M BETTY COOPER, AND I THINK YOU'RE AWFUL CLEVER.
THAT'S NOTHIN', I COULD EVEN WALK THIS FENCE BLINDFOLDED!
REALLY?

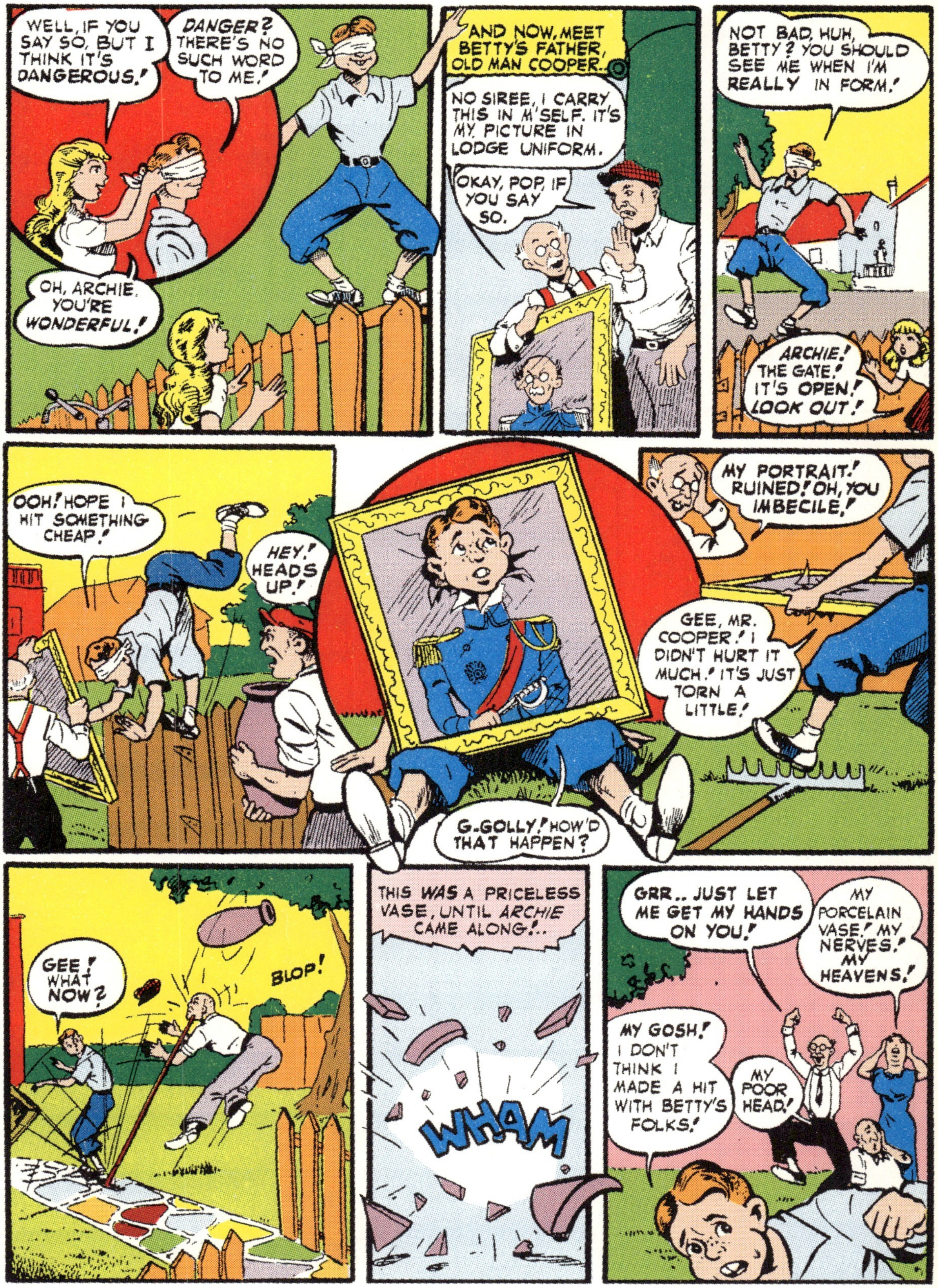
WELL, IF YOU SAY SO, BUT I THINK IT'S DANGEROUS!
DANGER? THERE'S NO SUCH WORD TO ME!
OH, ARCHIE, YOU'RE WONDERFUL!
AND NOW, MEET BETTY'S FATHER, OLD MAN COOPER...
NO SIREE, I CARRY THIS IN M'SELF. IT'S MY PICTURE IN LODGE UNIFORM.
OKAY, POP, IF YOU SAY SO.
NOT BAD, HUH, BETTY? YOU SHOULD SEE ME WHEN I'M REALLY IN FORM!
ARCHIE! THE GATE! IT'S OPEN! LOOK OUT!
OOH! HOPE I HIT SOMETHING CHEAP!
HEY! HEADS UP!
G-GOLLY! HOW'D THAT HAPPEN?
MY PORTRAIT! RUINED! OH, YOU IMBECILE!
GEE, MR. COOPER! I DIDN'T HURT IT MUCH! IT'S JUST TORN A LITTLE!
GEE! WHAT NOW?
BLOP!
THIS WAS A PRICELESS VASE, UNTIL ARCHIE CAME ALONG!..
WHAM
GRR.. JUST LET ME GET MY HANDS ON YOU!
MY PORCELAIN VASE! MY NERVES! MY HEAVENS!
MY GOSH! I DON'T THINK I MADE A HIT WITH BETTY'S FOLKS!
MY POOR HEAD!

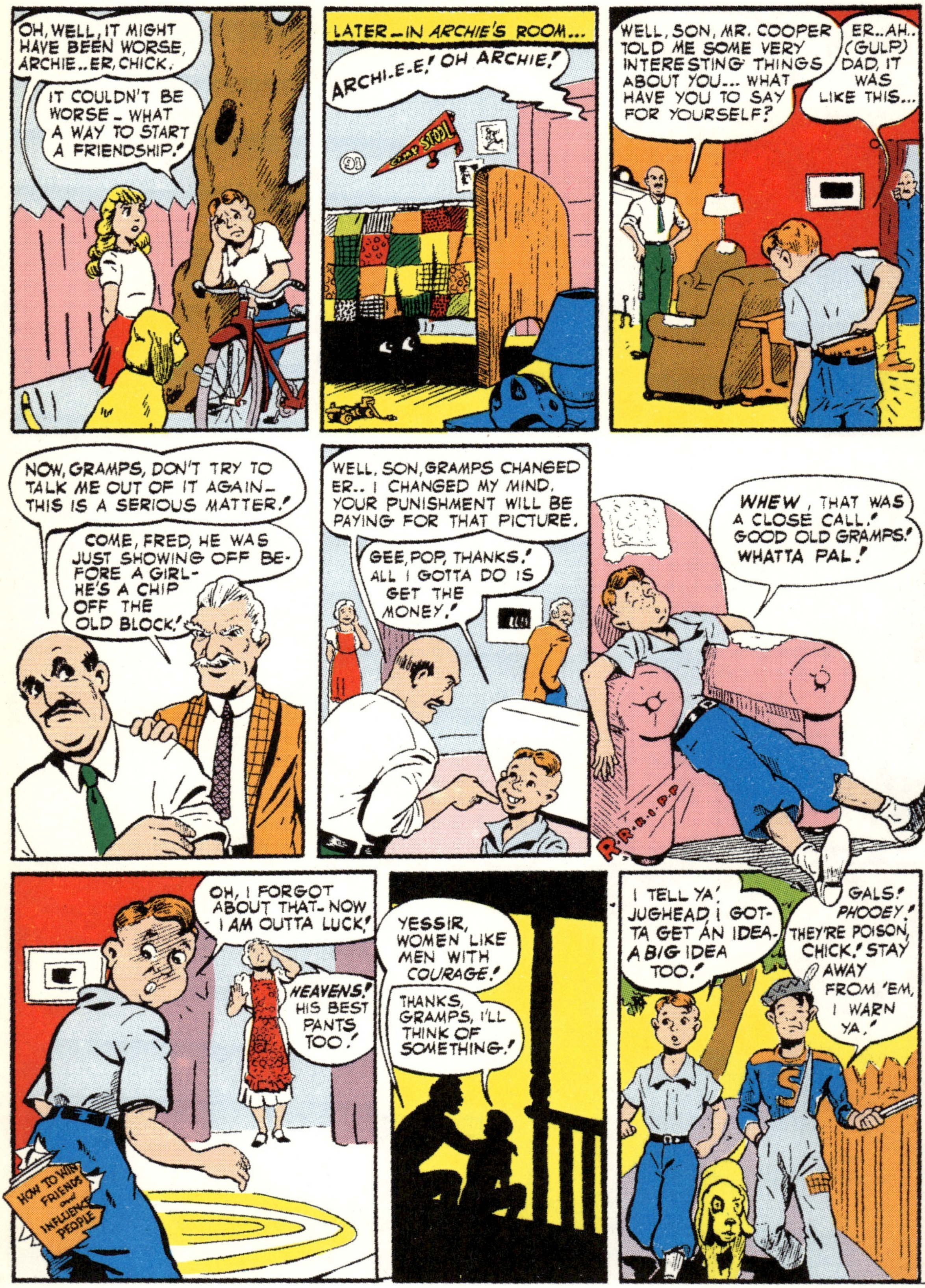
OH, WELL, IT MIGHT HAVE BEEN WORSE, ARCHIE..ER, CHICK.
IT COULDN'T BE WORSE - WHAT A WAY TO START A FRIENDSHIP!
LATER - IN ARCHIE'S ROOM...
ARCHI-E-E! OH ARCHIE!
WELL, SON, MR. COOPER TOLD ME SOME VERY INTERESTING THINGS ABOUT YOU... WHAT HAVE YOU TO SAY FOR YOURSELF?
ER..AH.. (GULP) DAD, IT WAS LIKE THIS...
NOW, GRAMPS, DON'T TRY TO TALK ME OUT OF IT AGAIN - THIS IS A SERIOUS MATTER!
COME, FRED, HE WAS JUST SHOWING OFF BEFORE A GIRL - HE'S A CHIP OFF THE OLD BLOCK!
WELL, SON, GRAMPS CHANGED ER.. I CHANGED MY MIND. YOUR PUNISHMENT WILL BE PAYING FOR THAT PICTURE.
GEE, POP, THANKS! ALL I GOTTA DO IS GET THE MONEY!
WHEW, THAT WAS A CLOSE CALL! GOOD OLD GRAMPS! WHATTA PAL!
R-R-R-I-P-P
OH, I FORGOT ABOUT THAT - NOW I AM OUTTA LUCK!
HEAVENS! HIS BEST PANTS TOO!
HOW TO WIN FRIENDS and INFLUENCE PEOPLE
YESSIR, WOMEN LIKE MEN WITH COURAGE!
THANKS, GRAMPS, I'LL THINK OF SOMETHING!
I TELL YA! JUGHEAD I GOTTA GET AN IDEA - A BIG IDEA TOO!
GALS! PHOOEY! THEY'RE POISON, CHICK! STAY AWAY FROM 'EM, I WARN YA!

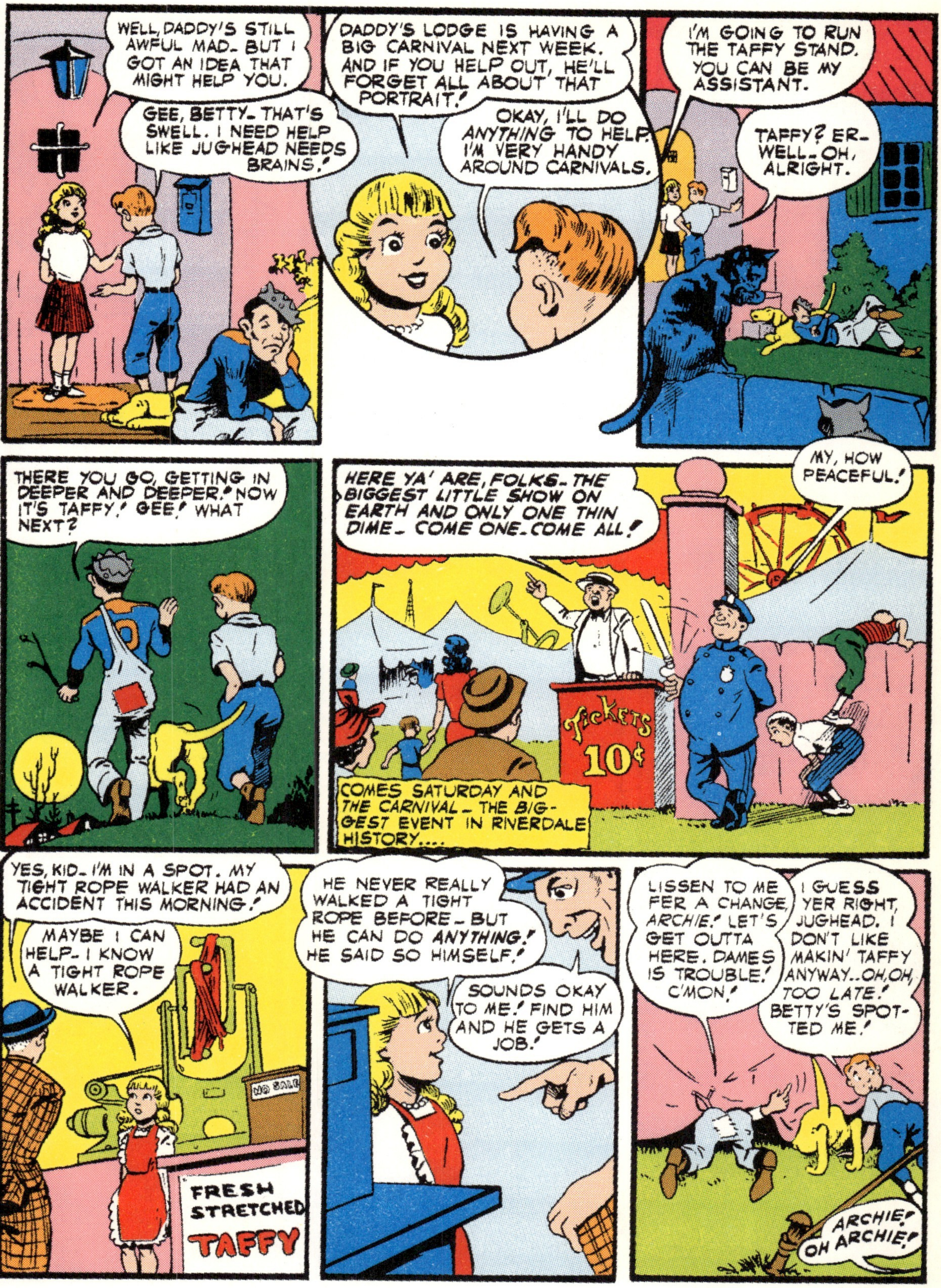
WELL, DADDY'S STILL AWFUL MAD- BUT I GOT AN IDEA THAT MIGHT HELP YOU.
GEE, BETTY- THAT'S SWELL. I NEED HELP LIKE JUGHEAD NEEDS BRAINS!
DADDY'S LODGE IS HAVING A BIG CARNIVAL NEXT WEEK. AND IF YOU HELP OUT, HE'LL FORGET ALL ABOUT THAT PORTRAIT!
OKAY, I'LL DO ANYTHING TO HELP. I'M VERY HANDY AROUND CARNIVALS.
I'M GOING TO RUN THE TAFFY STAND. YOU CAN BE MY ASSISTANT.
TAFFY? ER- WELL- OH, ALRIGHT.
THERE YOU GO, GETTING IN DEEPER AND DEEPER! NOW IT'S TAFFY! GEE! WHAT NEXT?
HERE YA' ARE, FOLKS- THE BIGGEST LITTLE SHOW ON EARTH AND ONLY ONE THIN DIME- COME ONE- COME ALL!
MY, HOW PEACEFUL!
TICKETS 10¢
COMES SATURDAY AND THE CARNIVAL - THE BIGGEST EVENT IN RIVERDALE HISTORY....
YES, KID- I'M IN A SPOT. MY TIGHT ROPE WALKER HAD AN ACCIDENT THIS MORNING!
MAYBE I CAN HELP- I KNOW A TIGHT ROPE WALKER.
NO SALE
FRESH STRETCHED TAFFY
HE NEVER REALLY WALKED A TIGHT ROPE BEFORE- BUT HE CAN DO ANYTHING! HE SAID SO HIMSELF!
SOUNDS OKAY TO ME! FIND HIM AND HE GETS A JOB!
LISSEN TO ME FER A CHANGE, ARCHIE! LET'S GET OUTTA HERE. DAMES IS TROUBLE! C'MON!
I GUESS YER RIGHT, JUGHEAD. I DON'T LIKE MAKIN' TAFFY ANYWAY.. OH, OH, TOO LATE! BETTY'S SPOTTED ME!
ARCHIE! OH ARCHIE!

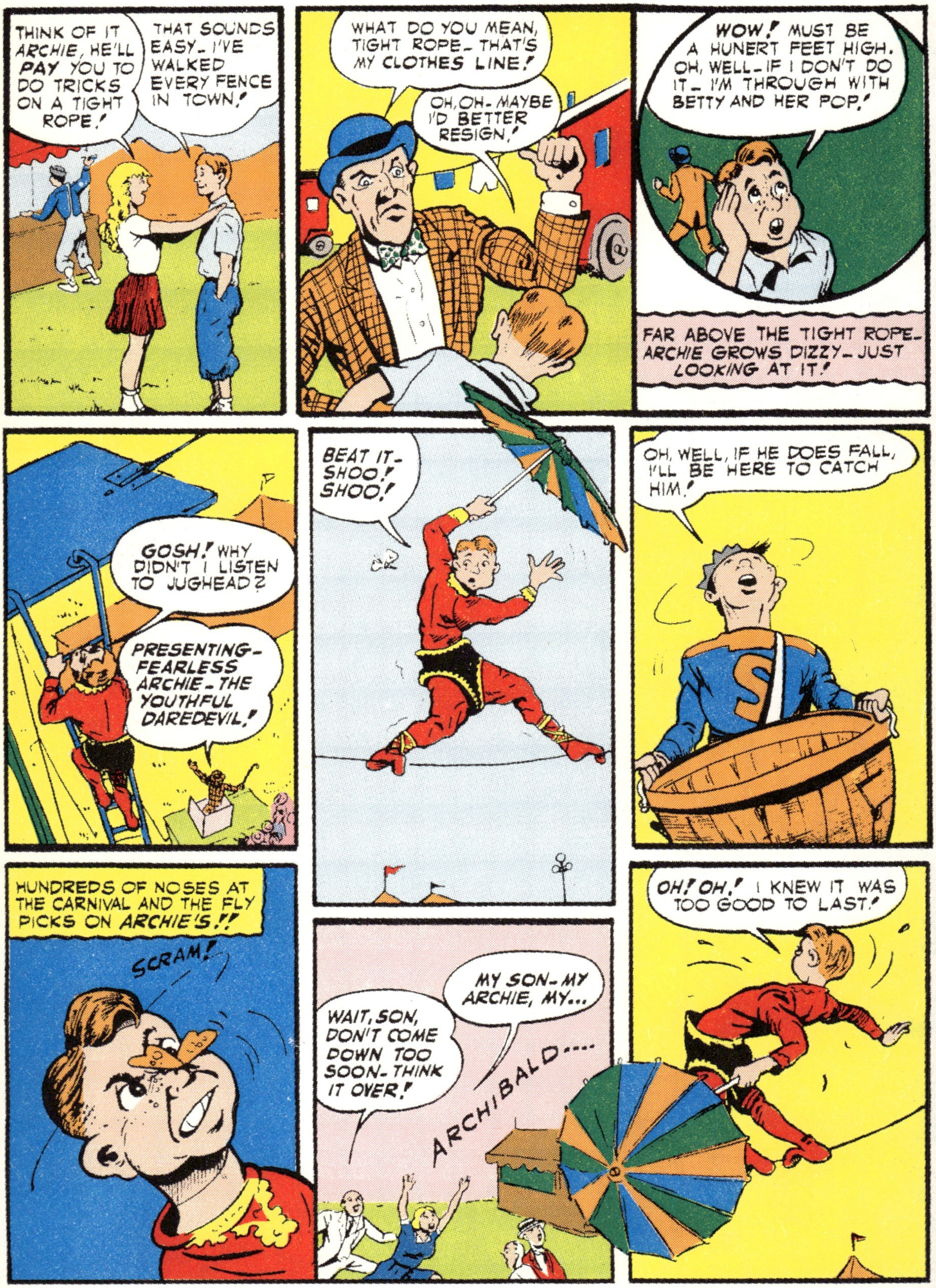
THINK OF IT ARCHIE, HE'LL PAY YOU TO DO TRICKS ON A TIGHT ROPE!
THAT SOUNDS EASY- I'VE WALKED EVERY FENCE IN TOWN!
WHAT DO YOU MEAN, TIGHT ROPE- THAT'S MY CLOTHES LINE!
OH,OH- MAYBE I'D BETTER RESIGN!
WOW! MUST BE A HUNERT FEET HIGH. OH, WELL- IF I DON'T DO IT- I'M THROUGH WITH BETTY AND HER POP!
FAR ABOVE THE TIGHT ROPE- ARCHIE GROWS DIZZY- JUST LOOKING AT IT!
GOSH! WHY DIDN'T I LISTEN TO JUGHEAD?
PRESENTING- FEARLESS ARCHIE- THE YOUTHFUL DAREDEVIL!
BEAT IT- SHOO! SHOO!
OH, WELL, IF HE DOES FALL, I'LL BE HERE TO CATCH HIM!
HUNDREDS OF NOSES AT THE CARNIVAL AND THE FLY PICKS ON ARCHIE'S!!
SCRAM!
MY SON- MY ARCHIE, MY...
WAIT, SON, DON'T COME DOWN TOO SOON- THINK IT OVER!
ARCHIBALD....
OH! OH! I KNEW IT WAS TOO GOOD TO LAST!

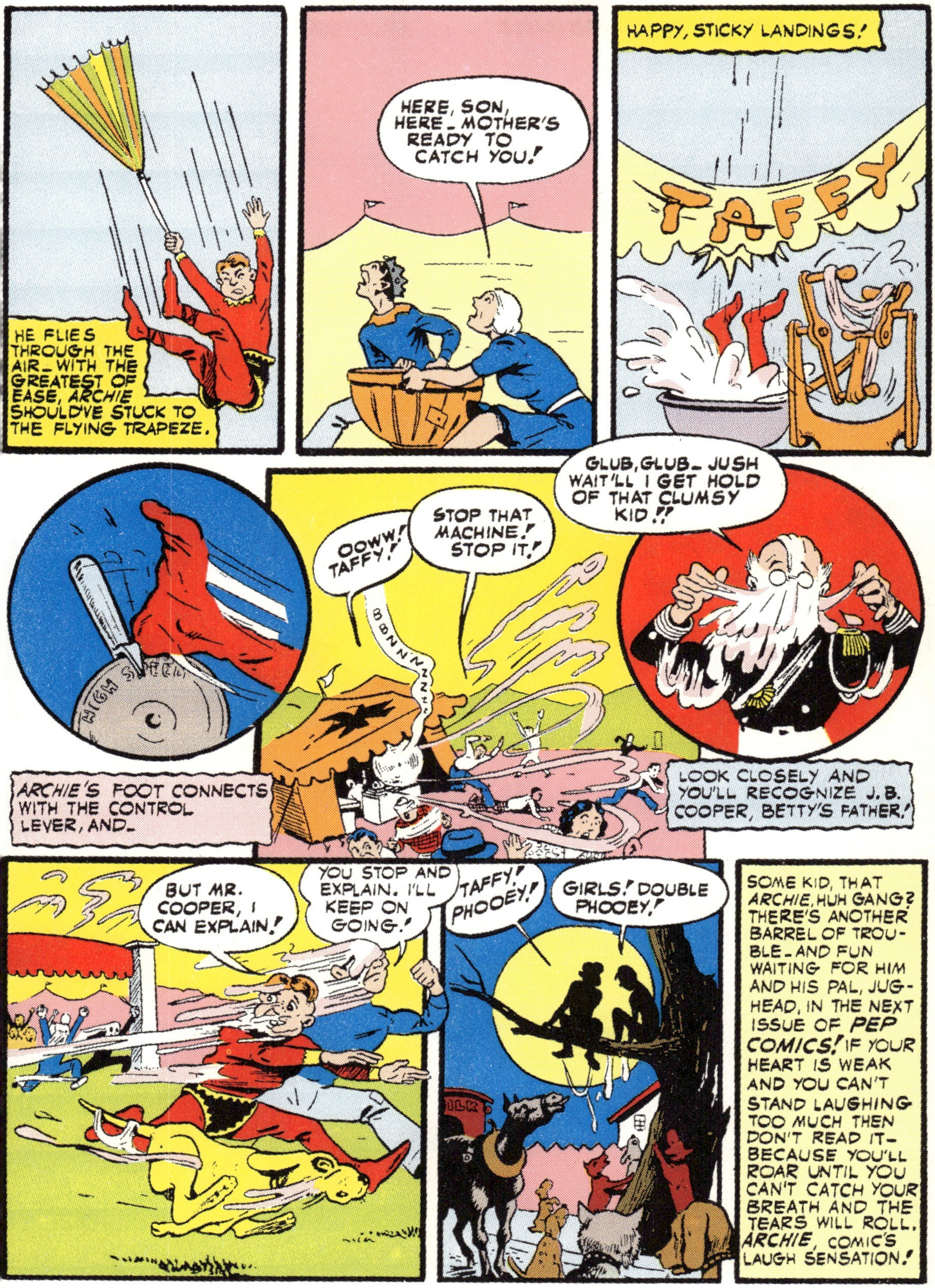
HE FLIES THROUGH THE AIR—WITH THE GREATEST OF EASE, ARCHIE SHOULD'VE STUCK TO THE FLYING TRAPEZE.
HERE, SON, HERE—MOTHER'S READY TO CATCH YOU!
HAPPY, STICKY LANDINGS!
TAFFY
ARCHIE'S FOOT CONNECTS WITH THE CONTROL LEVER, AND—
OOWW! TAFFY!
STOP THAT MACHINE! STOP IT!
BONNNZZZ
GLUB, GLUB—JUSH WAIT'LL I GET HOLD OF THAT CLUMSY KID!!
LOOK CLOSELY AND YOU'LL RECOGNIZE J. B. COOPER, BETTY'S FATHER!
BUT MR. COOPER, I CAN EXPLAIN!
YOU STOP AND EXPLAIN. I'LL KEEP ON GOING!
TAFFY! PHOOEY!
GIRLS! DOUBLE PHOOEY!
SOME KID, THAT ARCHIE, HUH GANG? THERE'S ANOTHER BARREL OF TROUBLE—AND FUN WAITING FOR HIM AND HIS PAL, JUGHEAD, IN THE NEXT ISSUE OF PEP COMICS! IF YOUR HEART IS WEAK AND YOU CAN'T STAND LAUGHING TOO MUCH THEN DON'T READ IT—BECAUSE YOU'LL ROAR UNTIL YOU CAN'T CATCH YOUR BREATH AND THE TEARS WILL ROLL. ARCHIE, COMIC'S LAUGH SENSATION!

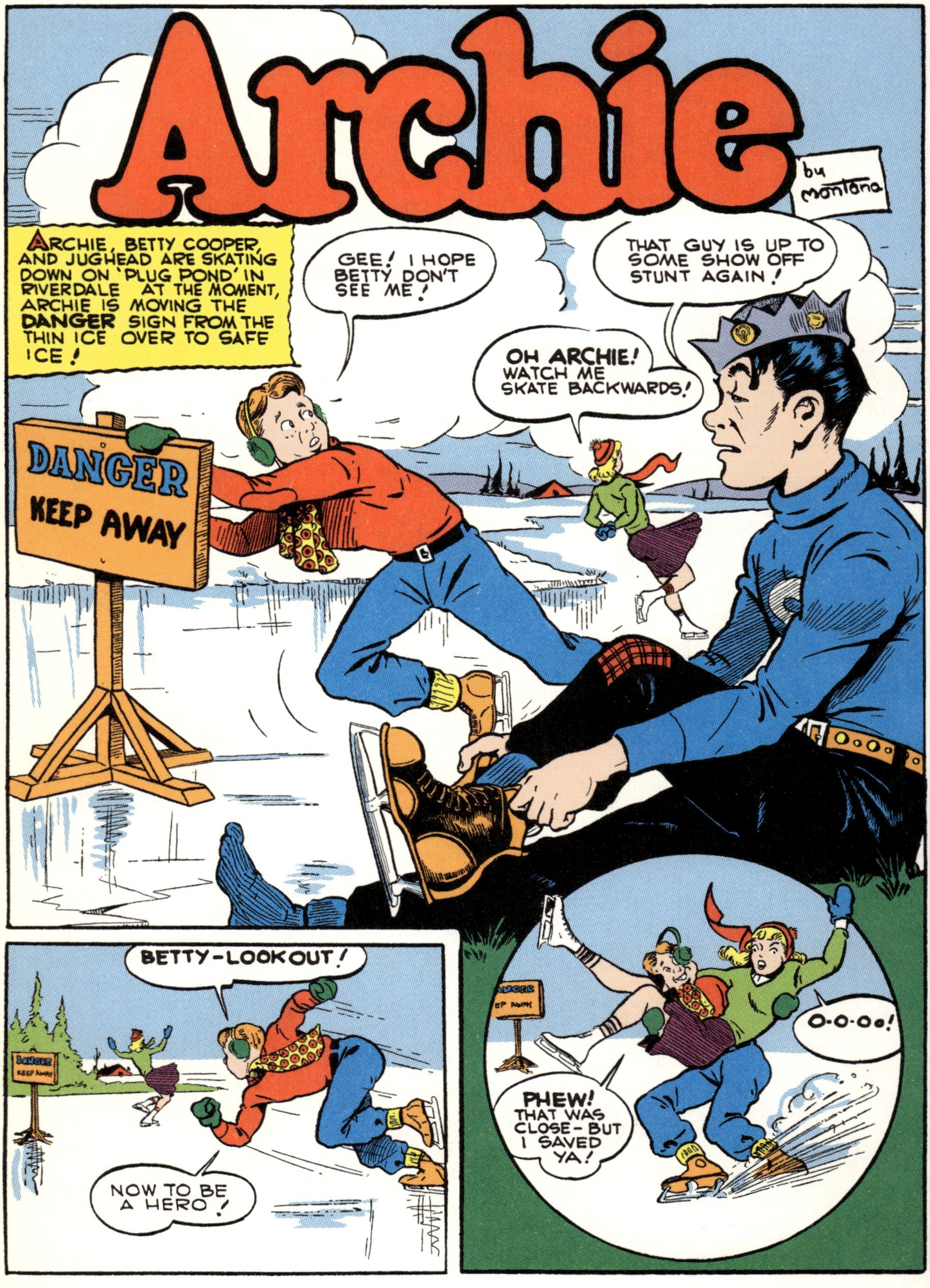
Archie
by montana
ARCHIE, BETTY COOPER, AND JUGHEAD ARE SKATING DOWN ON 'PLUG POND' IN RIVERDALE AT THE MOMENT, ARCHIE IS MOVING THE DANGER SIGN FROM THE THIN ICE OVER TO SAFE ICE!
GEE! I HOPE BETTY DON'T SEE ME!
THAT GUY IS UP TO SOME SHOW OFF STUNT AGAIN!
OH ARCHIE! WATCH ME SKATE BACKWARDS!
DANGER
KEEP AWAY
BETTY-LOOKOUT!
NOW TO BE A HERO!
O-O-Oo!
PHEW! THAT WAS CLOSE-BUT I SAVED YA!

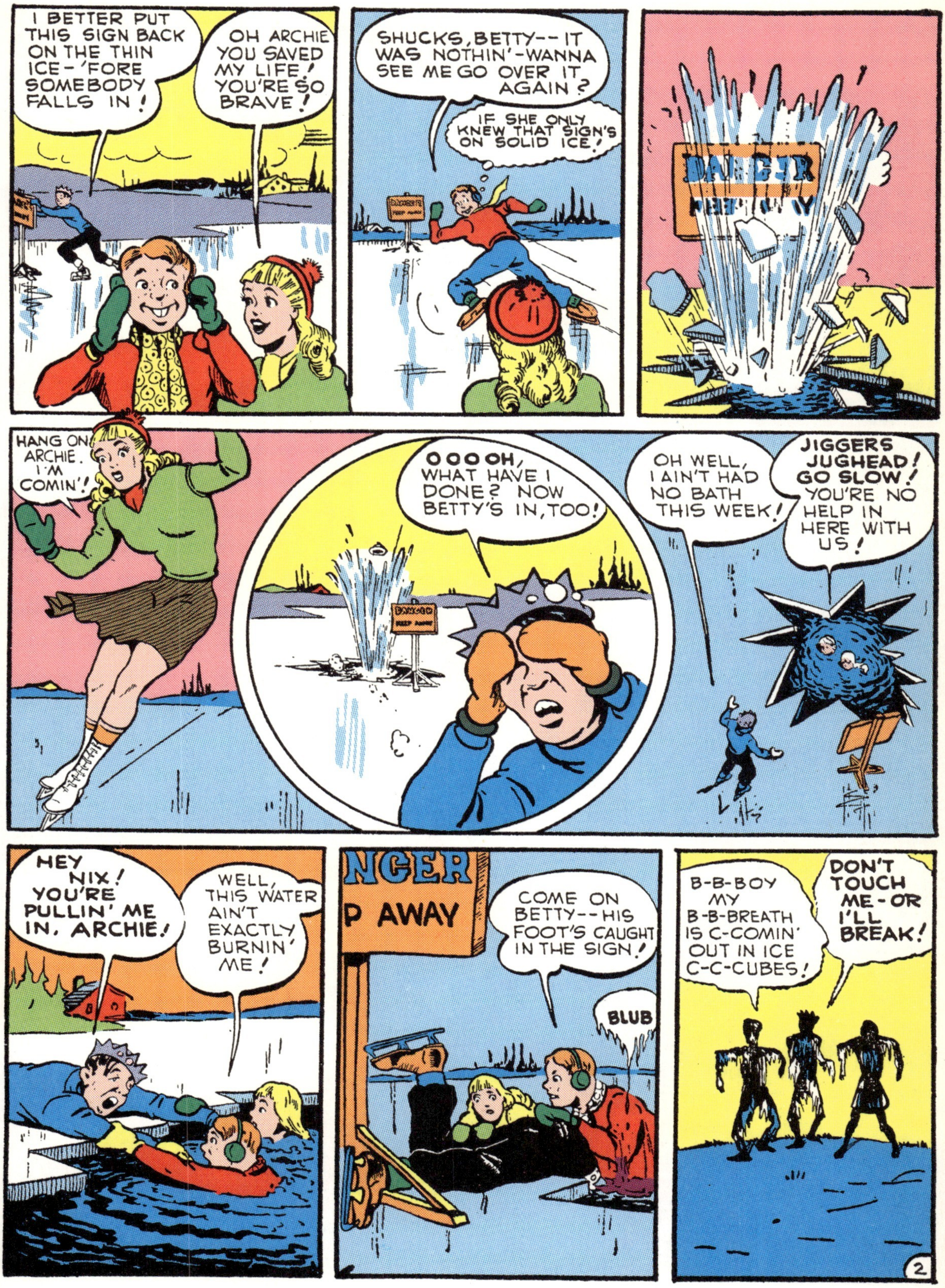
I BETTER PUT THIS SIGN BACK ON THE THIN ICE-'FORE SOMEBODY FALLS IN!
OH ARCHIE YOU SAVED MY LIFE! YOU'RE SO BRAVE!
SHUCKS, BETTY-- IT WAS NOTHIN'-WANNA SEE ME GO OVER IT AGAIN?
IF SHE ONLY KNEW THAT SIGN'S ON SOLID ICE!
HANG ON, ARCHIE. I'M COMIN'!
OOOOH, WHAT HAVE I DONE? NOW BETTY'S IN, TOO!
OH WELL, I AIN'T HAD NO BATH THIS WEEK!
JIGGERS JUGHEAD! GO SLOW! YOU'RE NO HELP IN HERE WITH US!
HEY NIX! YOU'RE PULLIN' ME IN, ARCHIE!
WELL, THIS WATER AIN'T EXACTLY BURNIN' ME!
NGER
P AWAY
COME ON BETTY--HIS FOOT'S CAUGHT IN THE SIGN!
BLUB
B-B-BOY MY B-B-BREATH IS C-COMIN' OUT IN ICE C-C-CUBES!
DON'T TOUCH ME-OR I'LL BREAK!
2

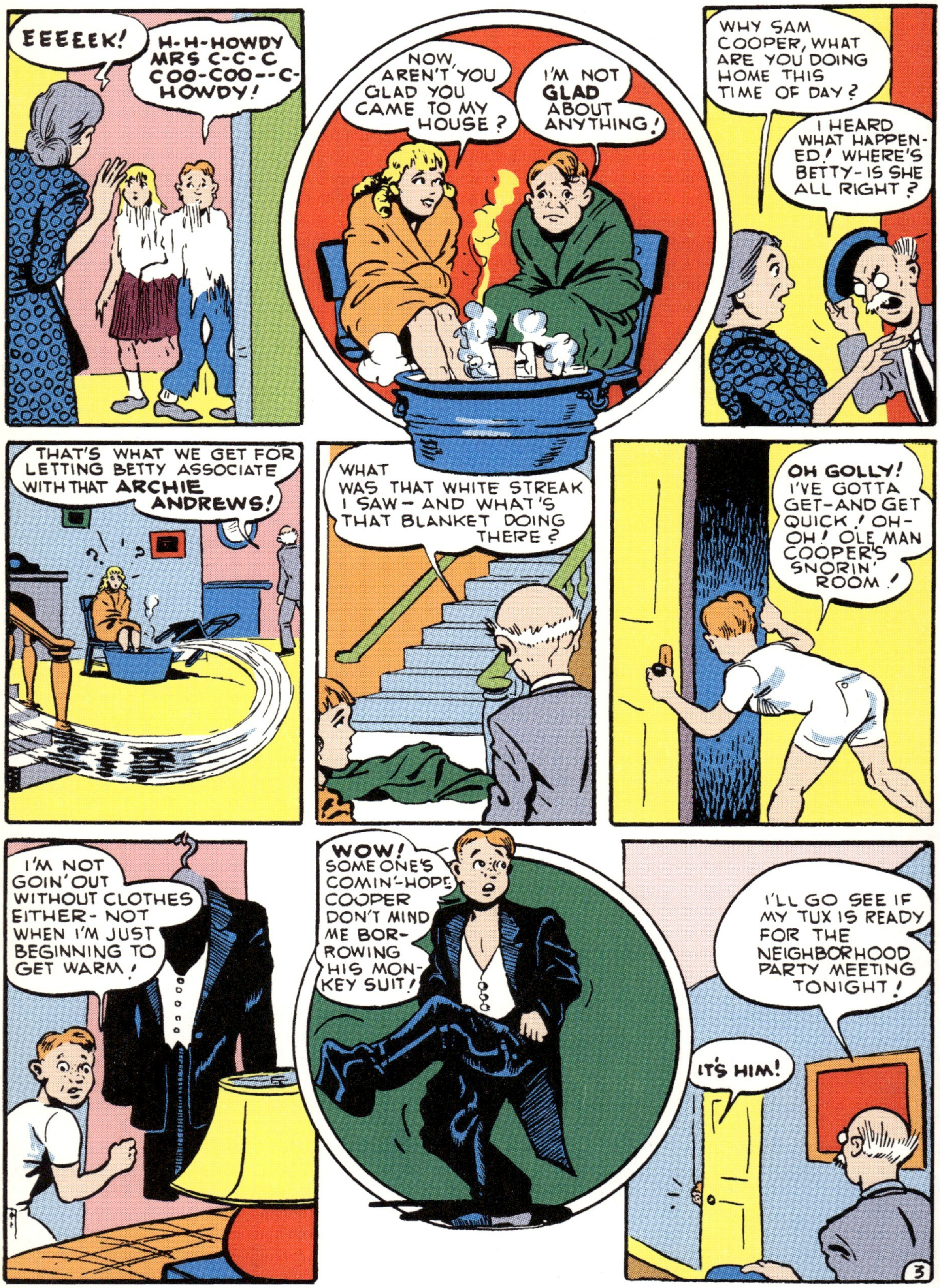
EEEEEK!
H-H-HOWDY MRS C-C-C COO-COO--C-HOWDY!
NOW, AREN'T YOU GLAD YOU CAME TO MY HOUSE?
I'M NOT **GLAD** ABOUT ANYTHING!
WHY SAM COOPER, WHAT ARE YOU DOING HOME THIS TIME OF DAY?
I HEARD WHAT HAPPENED! WHERE'S BETTY- IS SHE ALL RIGHT?
THAT'S WHAT WE GET FOR LETTING BETTY ASSOCIATE WITH THAT **ARCHIE ANDREWS!**
WHAT WAS THAT WHITE STREAK I SAW- AND WHAT'S THAT BLANKET DOING THERE?
OH GOLLY! I'VE GOTTA GET- AND GET QUICK! OH-OH! OLE MAN COOPER'S SNORIN' ROOM!
I'M NOT GOIN' OUT WITHOUT CLOTHES EITHER- NOT WHEN I'M JUST BEGINNING TO GET WARM!
WOW! SOME ONE'S COMIN'-HOPE COOPER DON'T MIND ME BORROWING HIS MONKEY SUIT!
I'LL GO SEE IF MY TUX IS READY FOR THE NEIGHBORHOOD PARTY MEETING TONIGHT!
IT'S HIM!
3

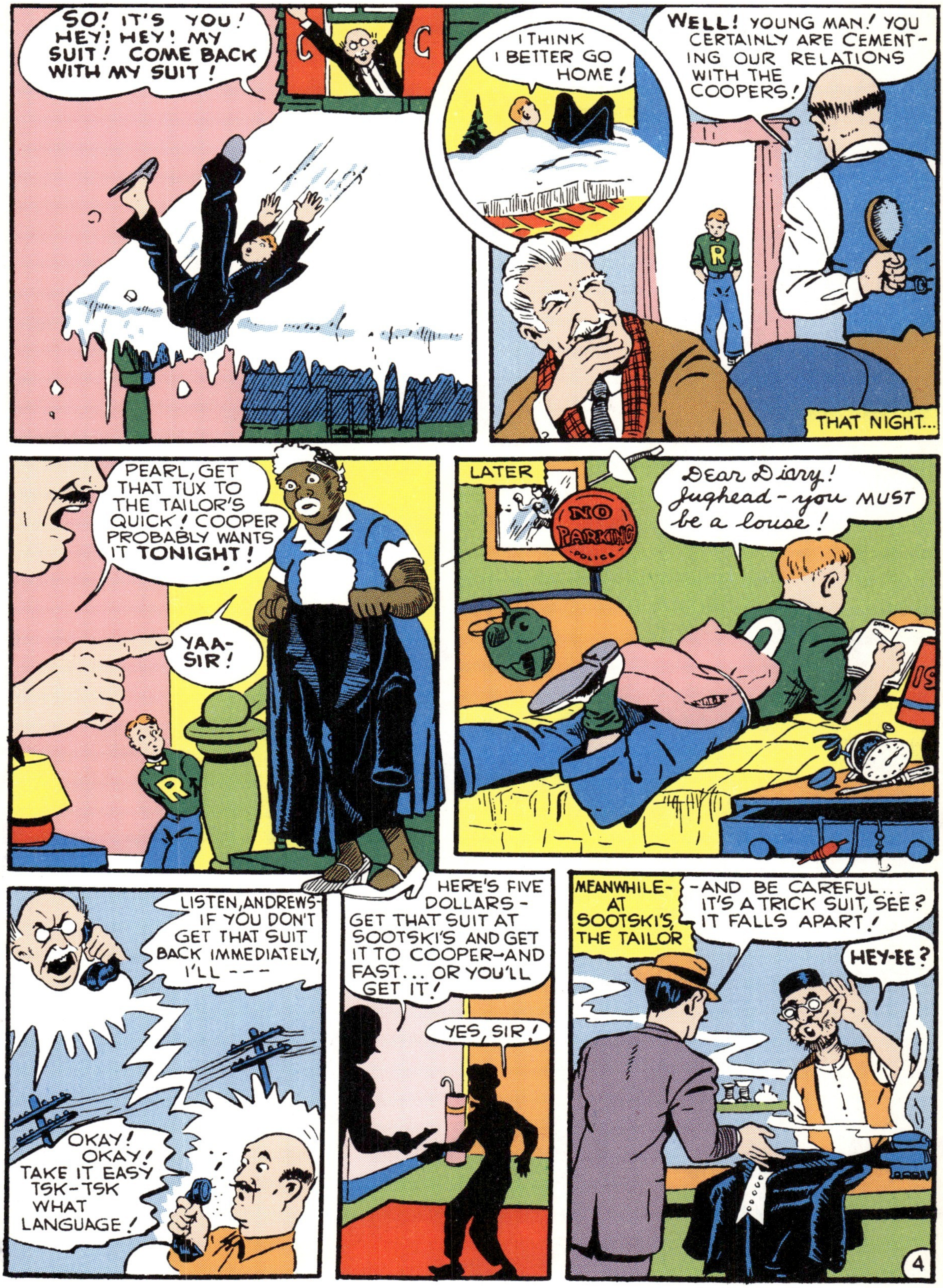
SO! IT'S YOU! HEY! HEY! MY SUIT! COME BACK WITH MY SUIT!
I THINK I BETTER GO HOME!
WELL! YOUNG MAN! YOU CERTAINLY ARE CEMENTING OUR RELATIONS WITH THE COOPERS!
THAT NIGHT...
PEARL, GET THAT TUX TO THE TAILOR'S QUICK! COOPER PROBABLY WANTS IT TONIGHT!
YAA-SIR!
LATER
NO PARKING POLICE
Dear Diary! Jughead - you MUST be a louse!
LISTEN, ANDREWS - IF YOU DON'T GET THAT SUIT BACK IMMEDIATELY, I'LL ---
OKAY! OKAY! TAKE IT EASY TSK-TSK WHAT LANGUAGE!
HERE'S FIVE DOLLARS - GET THAT SUIT AT SOOTSKI'S AND GET IT TO COOPER--AND FAST... OR YOU'LL GET IT!
YES, SIR!
MEANWHILE- AT SOOTSKI'S, THE TAILOR
-AND BE CAREFUL... IT'S A TRICK SUIT, SEE? IT FALLS APART!
HEY-EE?
4

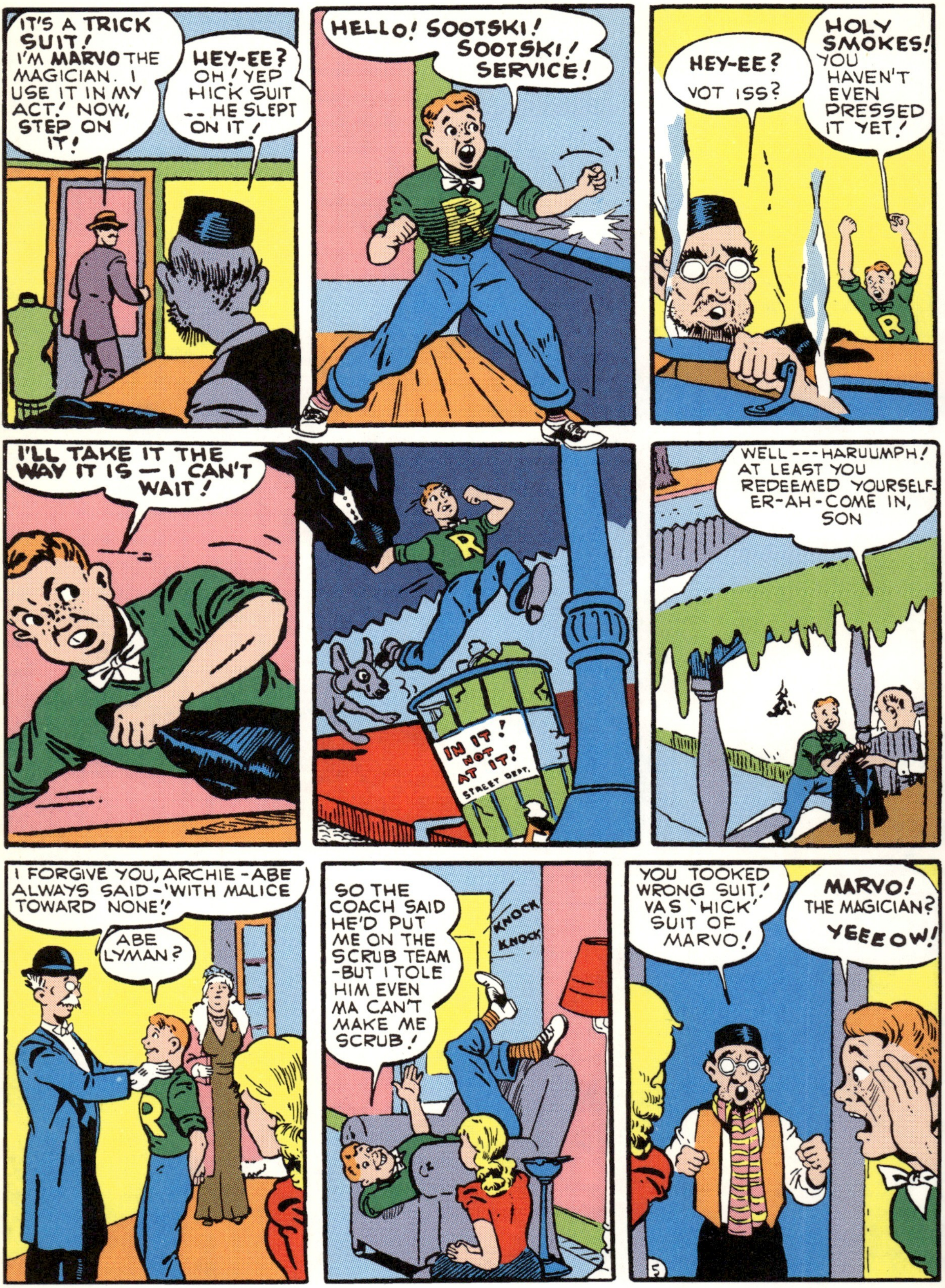
IT'S A TRICK SUIT! I'M MARVO THE MAGICIAN. I USE IT IN MY ACT! NOW, STEP ON IT!
HEY-EE? OH! YEP HICK SUIT -- HE SLEPT ON IT!
HELLO! SOOTSKI! SOOTSKI! SERVICE!
HEY-EE? VOT ISS?
HOLY SMOKES! YOU HAVEN'T EVEN PRESSED IT YET!
I'LL TAKE IT THE WAY IT IS — I CAN'T WAIT!
IN IT! NOT AT IT! STREET DEPT.
WELL --- HARUUMPH! AT LEAST YOU REDEEMED YOURSELF- ER-AH-COME IN, SON
I FORGIVE YOU, ARCHIE - ABE ALWAYS SAID - 'WITH MALICE TOWARD NONE'!
ABE LYMAN?
SO THE COACH SAID HE'D PUT ME ON THE SCRUB TEAM -BUT I TOLE HIM EVEN MA CAN'T MAKE ME SCRUB!
KNOCK
KNOCK
YOU TOOKED WRONG SUIT! VAS 'HICK' SUIT OF MARVO!
MARVO! THE MAGICIAN?
YEEEOW!
5

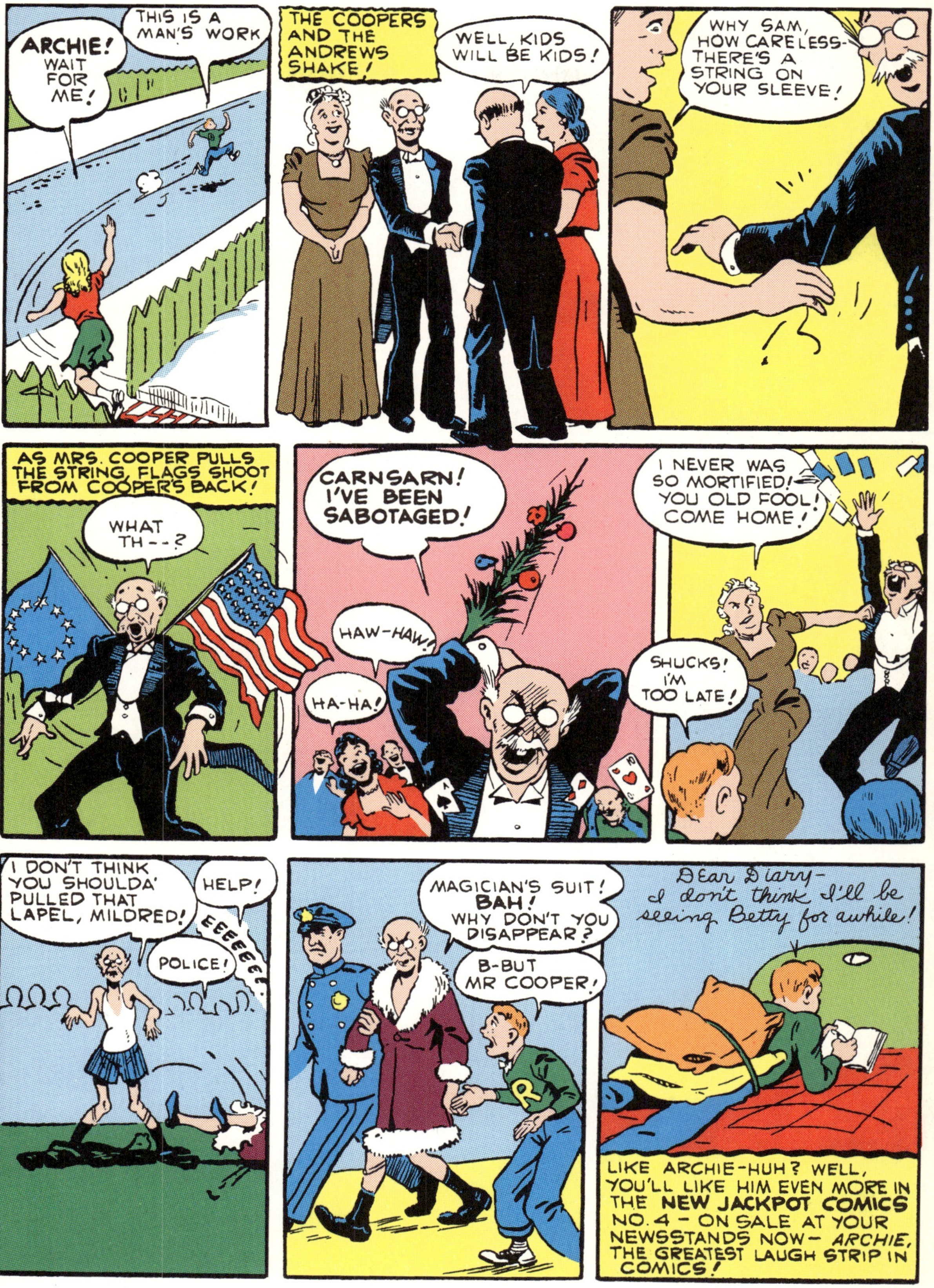

ARCHIE! WAIT FOR ME!
THIS IS A MAN'S WORK
THE COOPERS AND THE ANDREWS SHAKE!
WELL, KIDS WILL BE KIDS!
WHY SAM, HOW CARELESS-THERE'S A STRING ON YOUR SLEEVE!
AS MRS. COOPER PULLS THE STRING, FLAGS SHOOT FROM COOPER'S BACK!
WHAT TH--?
CARNSARN! I'VE BEEN SABOTAGED!
HAW-HAW!
HA-HA!
I NEVER WAS SO MORTIFIED! YOU OLD FOOL! COME HOME!
SHUCKS! I'M TOO LATE!
I DON'T THINK YOU SHOULDA' PULLED THAT LAPEL, MILDRED!
HELP!
EEEEEEE!
POLICE!
MAGICIAN'S SUIT! BAH! WHY DON'T YOU DISAPPEAR?
B-BUT MR COOPER!
Dear Diary-
I don't think I'll be seeing Betty for awhile!
LIKE ARCHIE-HUH? WELL, YOU'LL LIKE HIM EVEN MORE IN THE NEW JACKPOT COMICS NO. 4 - ON SALE AT YOUR NEWSSTANDS NOW- ARCHIE, THE GREATEST LAUGH STRIP IN COMICS!

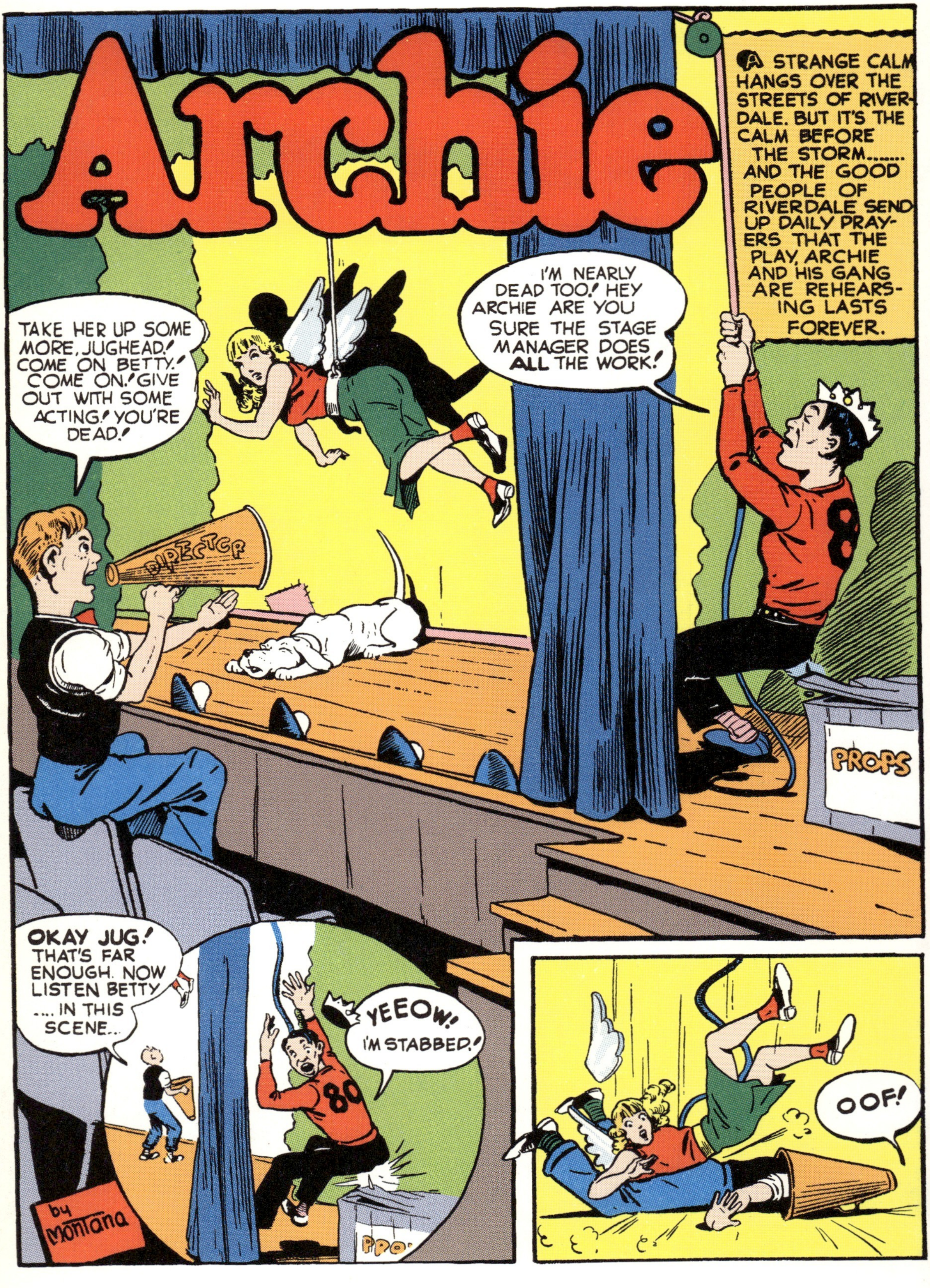

Archie
A STRANGE CALM HANGS OVER THE STREETS OF RIVERDALE. BUT IT'S THE CALM BEFORE THE STORM....... AND THE GOOD PEOPLE OF RIVERDALE SEND UP DAILY PRAYERS THAT THE PLAY, ARCHIE AND HIS GANG ARE REHEARSING LASTS FOREVER.
TAKE HER UP SOME MORE, JUGHEAD! COME ON BETTY! COME ON! GIVE OUT WITH SOME ACTING! YOU'RE DEAD!
I'M NEARLY DEAD TOO! HEY ARCHIE ARE YOU SURE THE STAGE MANAGER DOES ALL THE WORK!
PROPS
OKAY JUG! THAT'S FAR ENOUGH. NOW LISTEN BETTY .... IN THIS SCENE...
YEEOW! I'M STABBED!
by Montana
OOF!

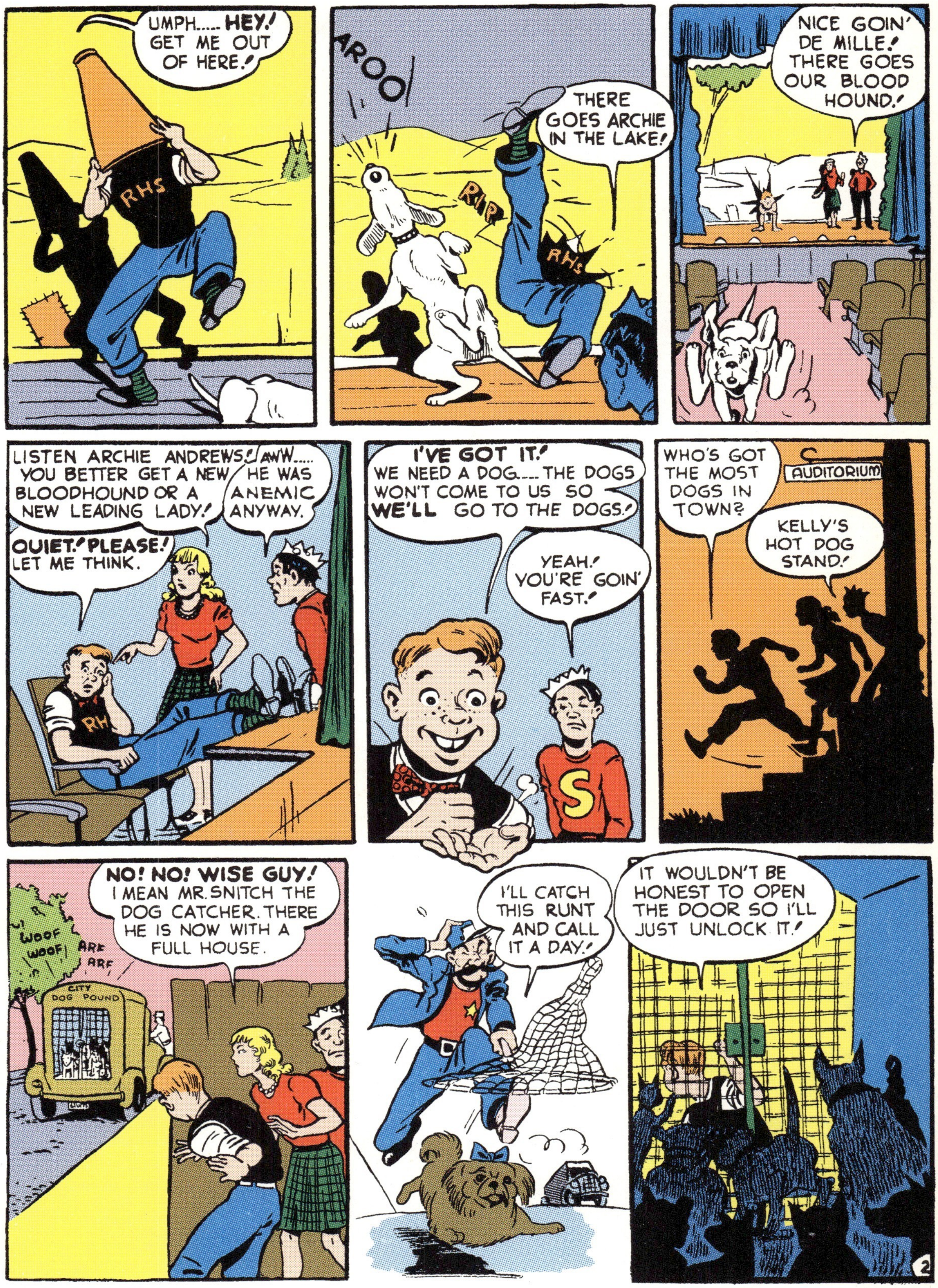
UMPH..... HEY! GET ME OUT OF HERE!
AROO
RIP
RHS
THERE GOES ARCHIE IN THE LAKE!
NICE GOIN' DE MILLE! THERE GOES OUR BLOOD HOUND!
LISTEN ARCHIE ANDREWS! YOU BETTER GET A NEW BLOODHOUND OR A NEW LEADING LADY!
AWW..... HE WAS ANEMIC ANYWAY.
QUIET! PLEASE! LET ME THINK.
I'VE GOT IT! WE NEED A DOG.... THE DOGS WON'T COME TO US SO WE'LL GO TO THE DOGS!
YEAH! YOU'RE GOIN' FAST!
WHO'S GOT THE MOST DOGS IN TOWN?
AUDITORIUM
KELLY'S HOT DOG STAND!
NO! NO! WISE GUY! I MEAN MR. SNITCH THE DOG CATCHER. THERE HE IS NOW WITH A FULL HOUSE.
WOOF WOOF!
ARF ARF
CITY DOG POUND
I'LL CATCH THIS RUNT AND CALL IT A DAY!
IT WOULDN'T BE HONEST TO OPEN THE DOOR SO I'LL JUST UNLOCK IT!
2

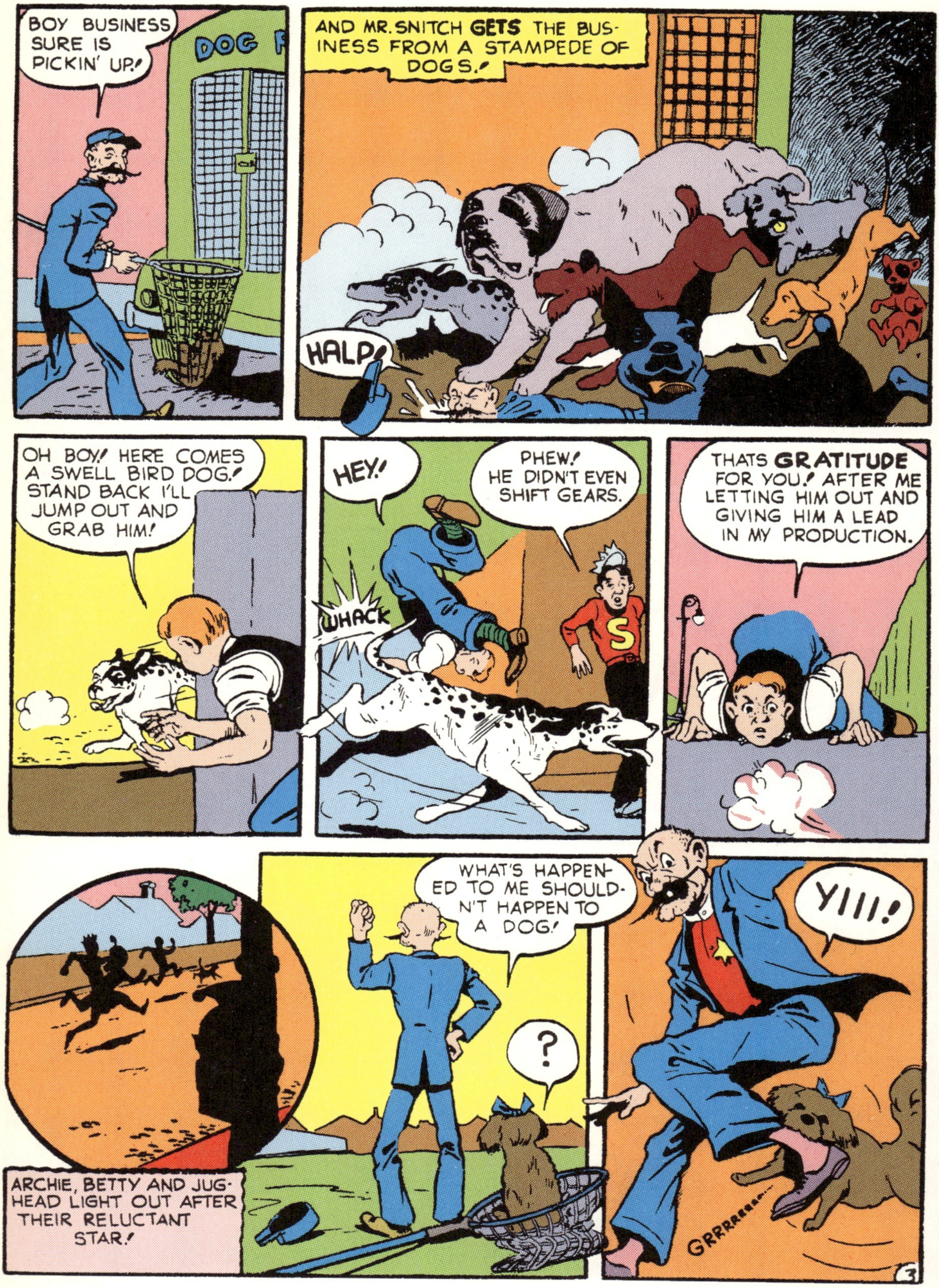
BOY BUSINESS SURE IS PICKIN' UP!
DOG
AND MR. SNITCH GETS THE BUSINESS FROM A STAMPEDE OF DOGS!
HALP!
OH BOY! HERE COMES A SWELL BIRD DOG! STAND BACK I'LL JUMP OUT AND GRAB HIM!
HEY!
PHEW! HE DIDN'T EVEN SHIFT GEARS.
WHACK
THATS GRATITUDE FOR YOU! AFTER ME LETTING HIM OUT AND GIVING HIM A LEAD IN MY PRODUCTION.
ARCHIE, BETTY AND JUGHEAD LIGHT OUT AFTER THEIR RELUCTANT STAR!
WHAT'S HAPPENED TO ME SHOULDN'T HAPPEN TO A DOG!
?
YIII!
GRRRRRR...
3

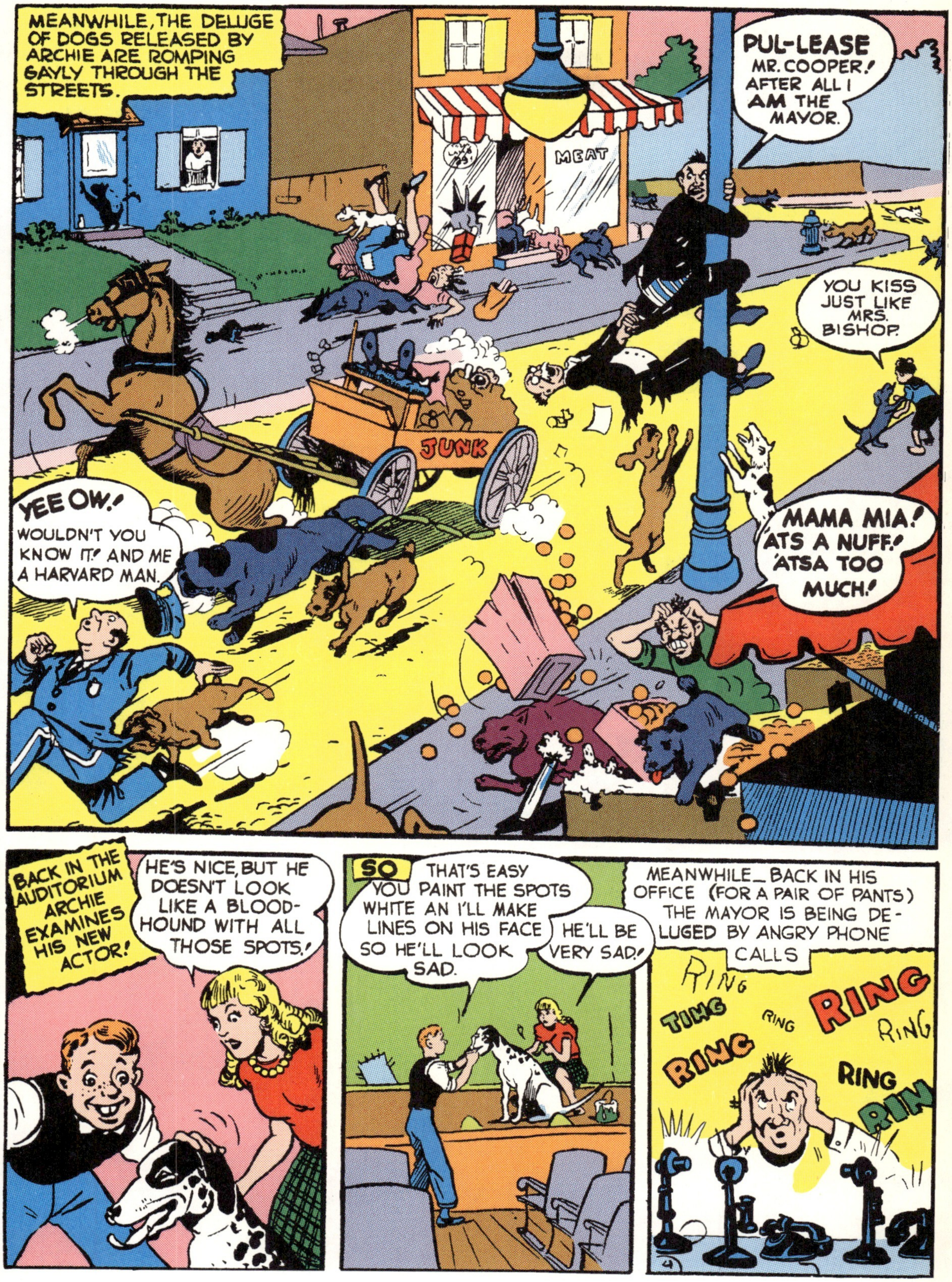
MEANWHILE, THE DELUGE OF DOGS RELEASED BY ARCHIE ARE ROMPING GAYLY THROUGH THE STREETS.
PUL-LEASE MR. COOPER! AFTER ALL I AM THE MAYOR.
MEAT
JUNK
YOU KISS JUST LIKE MRS. BISHOP.
YEE OW! WOULDN'T YOU KNOW IT! AND ME A HARVARD MAN.
MAMA MIA! ATS A NUFF! ATSA TOO MUCH!
BACK IN THE AUDITORIUM ARCHIE EXAMINES HIS NEW ACTOR!
HE'S NICE, BUT HE DOESN'T LOOK LIKE A BLOOD-HOUND WITH ALL THOSE SPOTS!
SO
THAT'S EASY YOU PAINT THE SPOTS WHITE AN I'LL MAKE LINES ON HIS FACE SO HE'LL LOOK SAD.
HE'LL BE VERY SAD!
MEANWHILE_ BACK IN HIS OFFICE (FOR A PAIR OF PANTS) THE MAYOR IS BEING DE-LUGED BY ANGRY PHONE CALLS
RING
TING
RING
RING
RING
RING
RING

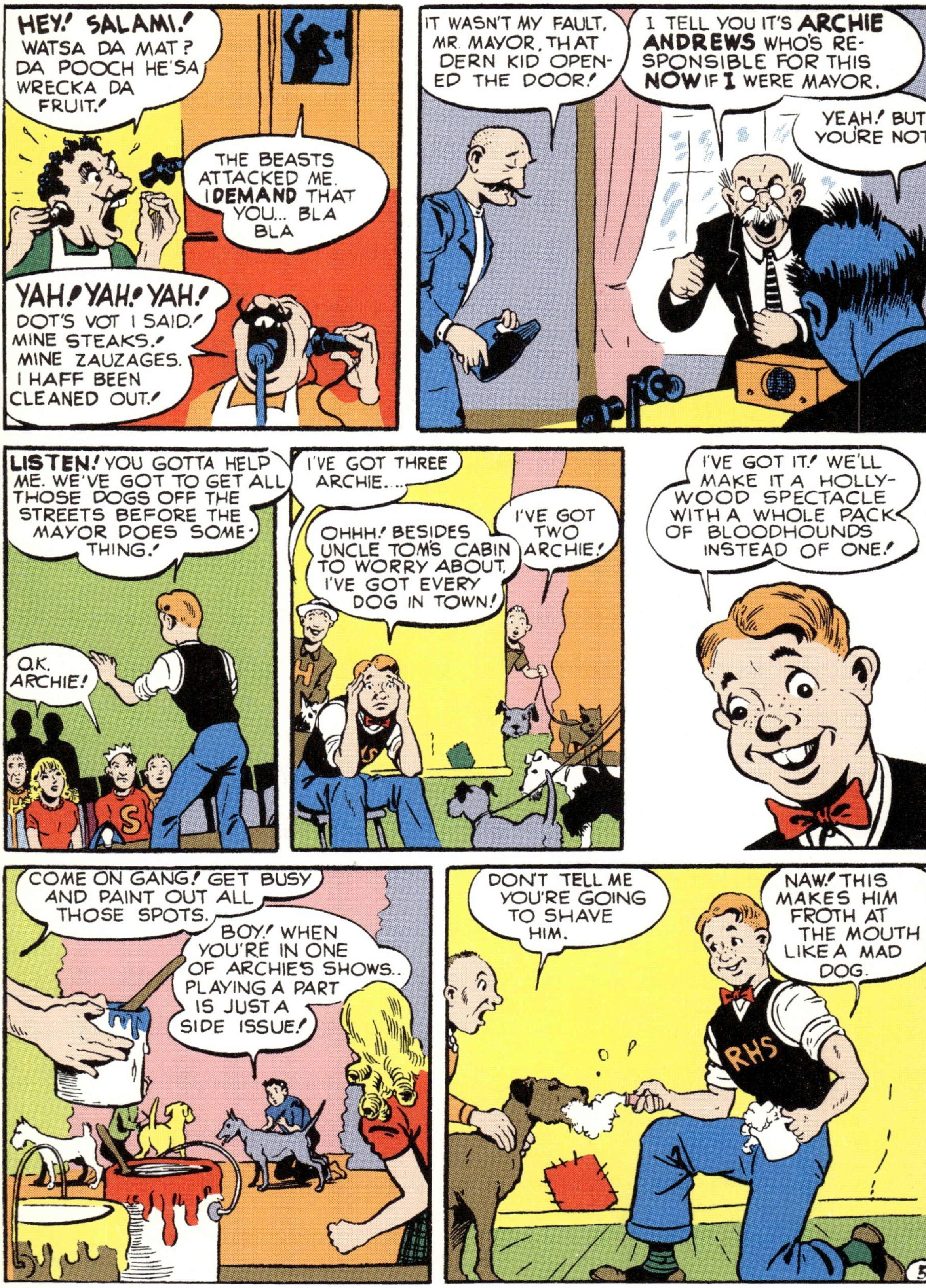

HEY! SALAMI! WATSA DA MAT? DA POOCH HE'SA WRECKA DA FRUIT!
THE BEASTS ATTACKED ME. I DEMAND THAT YOU... BLA BLA
YAH! YAH! YAH! DOT'S VOT I SAID! MINE STEAKS! MINE ZAUZAGES. I HAFF BEEN CLEANED OUT!
IT WASN'T MY FAULT, MR. MAYOR, THAT DERN KID OPENED THE DOOR!
I TELL YOU IT'S ARCHIE ANDREWS WHO'S RESPONSIBLE FOR THIS NOW IF I WERE MAYOR.
YEAH! BUT YOU'RE NOT!
LISTEN! YOU GOTTA HELP ME. WE'VE GOT TO GET ALL THOSE DOGS OFF THE STREETS BEFORE THE MAYOR DOES SOMETHING!
O.K. ARCHIE!
I'VE GOT THREE ARCHIE....
OHHH! BESIDES UNCLE TOM'S CABIN TO WORRY ABOUT, I'VE GOT EVERY DOG IN TOWN!
I'VE GOT TWO ARCHIE!
I'VE GOT IT! WE'LL MAKE IT A HOLLYWOOD SPECTACLE WITH A WHOLE PACK OF BLOODHOUNDS INSTEAD OF ONE!
COME ON GANG! GET BUSY AND PAINT OUT ALL THOSE SPOTS.
BOY! WHEN YOU'RE IN ONE OF ARCHIE'S SHOWS.. PLAYING A PART IS JUST A SIDE ISSUE!
DON'T TELL ME YOU'RE GOING TO SHAVE HIM.
NAW! THIS MAKES HIM FROTH AT THE MOUTH LIKE A MAD DOG.
RHS
5

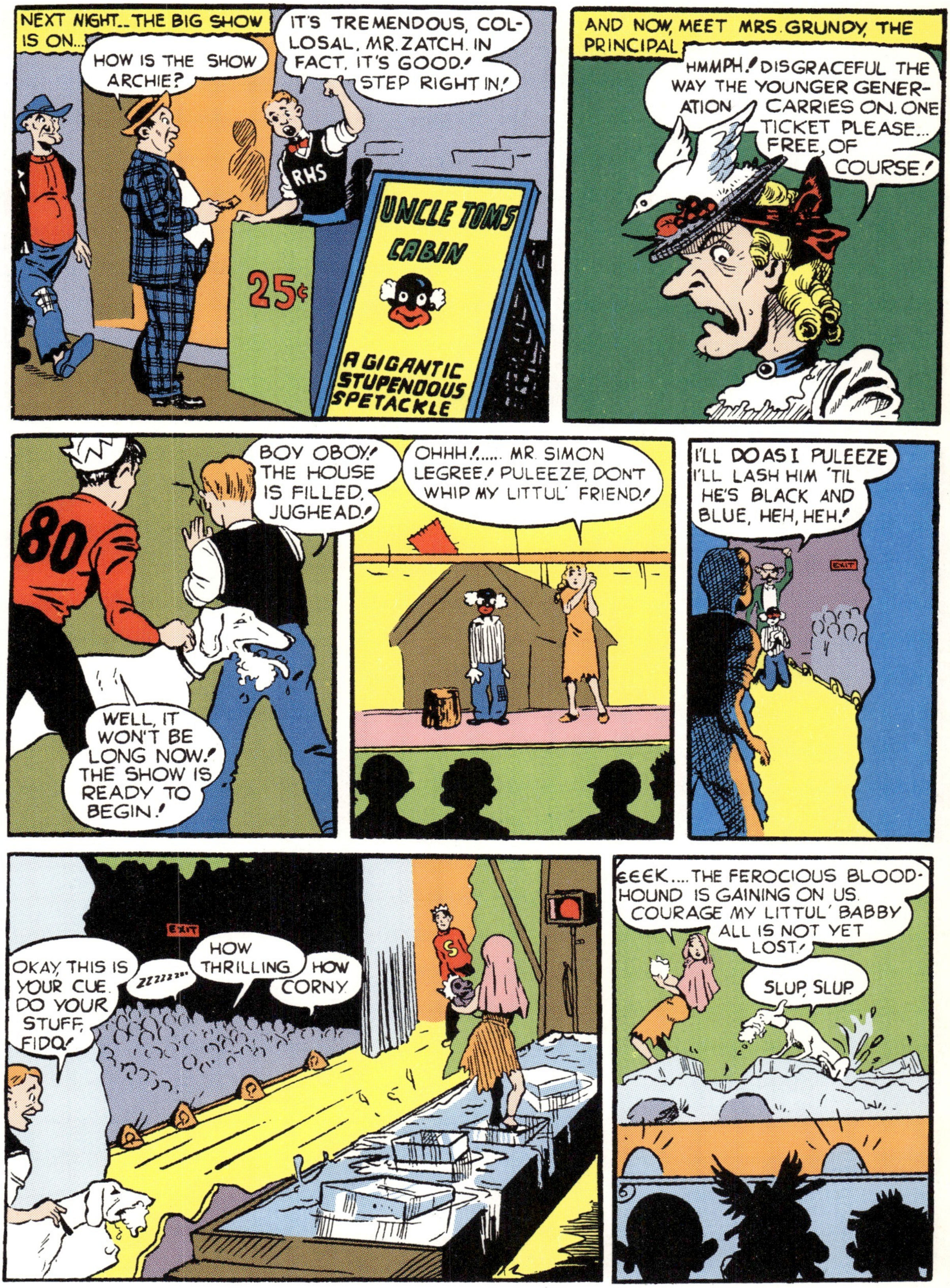

NEXT NIGHT... THE BIG SHOW IS ON...
HOW IS THE SHOW ARCHIE?
IT'S TREMENDOUS, COLOSAL, MR. ZATCH. IN FACT, IT'S GOOD! STEP RIGHT IN!
RHS
25¢
UNCLE TOMS CABIN
A GIGANTIC STUPENDOUS SPETACKLE
AND NOW, MEET MRS. GRUNDY, THE PRINCIPAL
HMMPH! DISGRACEFUL THE WAY THE YOUNGER GENERATION CARRIES ON. ONE TICKET PLEASE... FREE, OF COURSE!
80
BOY OBOY! THE HOUSE IS FILLED, JUGHEAD!
WELL, IT WON'T BE LONG NOW! THE SHOW IS READY TO BEGIN!
OHHH!..... MR. SIMON LEGREE! PULEEZE, DON'T WHIP MY LITTUL' FRIEND!
I'LL DO AS I PULEEZE I'LL LASH HIM 'TIL HE'S BLACK AND BLUE, HEH, HEH!
EXIT
EXIT
OKAY, THIS IS YOUR CUE. DO YOUR STUFF, FIDO!
ZZZZZZ...
HOW THRILLING
HOW CORNY
S
EEEK.... THE FEROCIOUS BLOODHOUND IS GAINING ON US. COURAGE MY LITTUL' BABBY ALL IS NOT YET LOST!
SLUP, SLUP

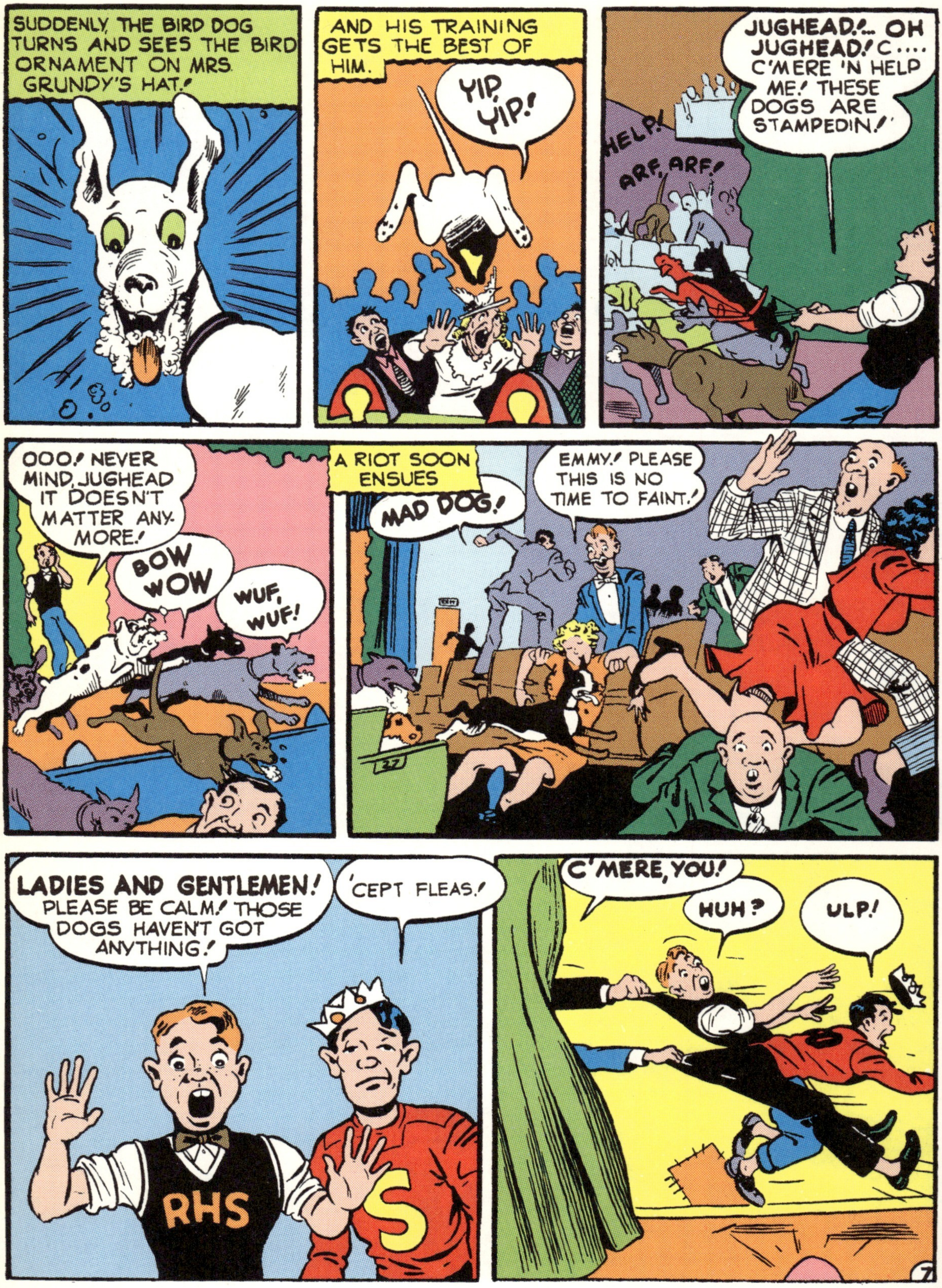

SUDDENLY, THE BIRD DOG TURNS AND SEES THE BIRD ORNAMENT ON MRS. GRUNDY'S HAT!
AND HIS TRAINING GETS THE BEST OF HIM.
YIP, YIP!
JUGHEAD!... OH JUGHEAD! C.... C'MERE 'N HELP ME! THESE DOGS ARE STAMPEDIN'!
HELP!
ARF, ARF!
OOO! NEVER MIND, JUGHEAD IT DOESN'T MATTER ANY-MORE!
BOW WOW
WUF, WUF!
A RIOT SOON ENSUES
MAD DOG!
EMMY! PLEASE THIS IS NO TIME TO FAINT!
LADIES AND GENTLEMEN! PLEASE BE CALM! THOSE DOGS HAVEN'T GOT ANYTHING!
'CEPT FLEAS!
RHS
S
C'MERE, YOU!
HUH?
ULP!
7

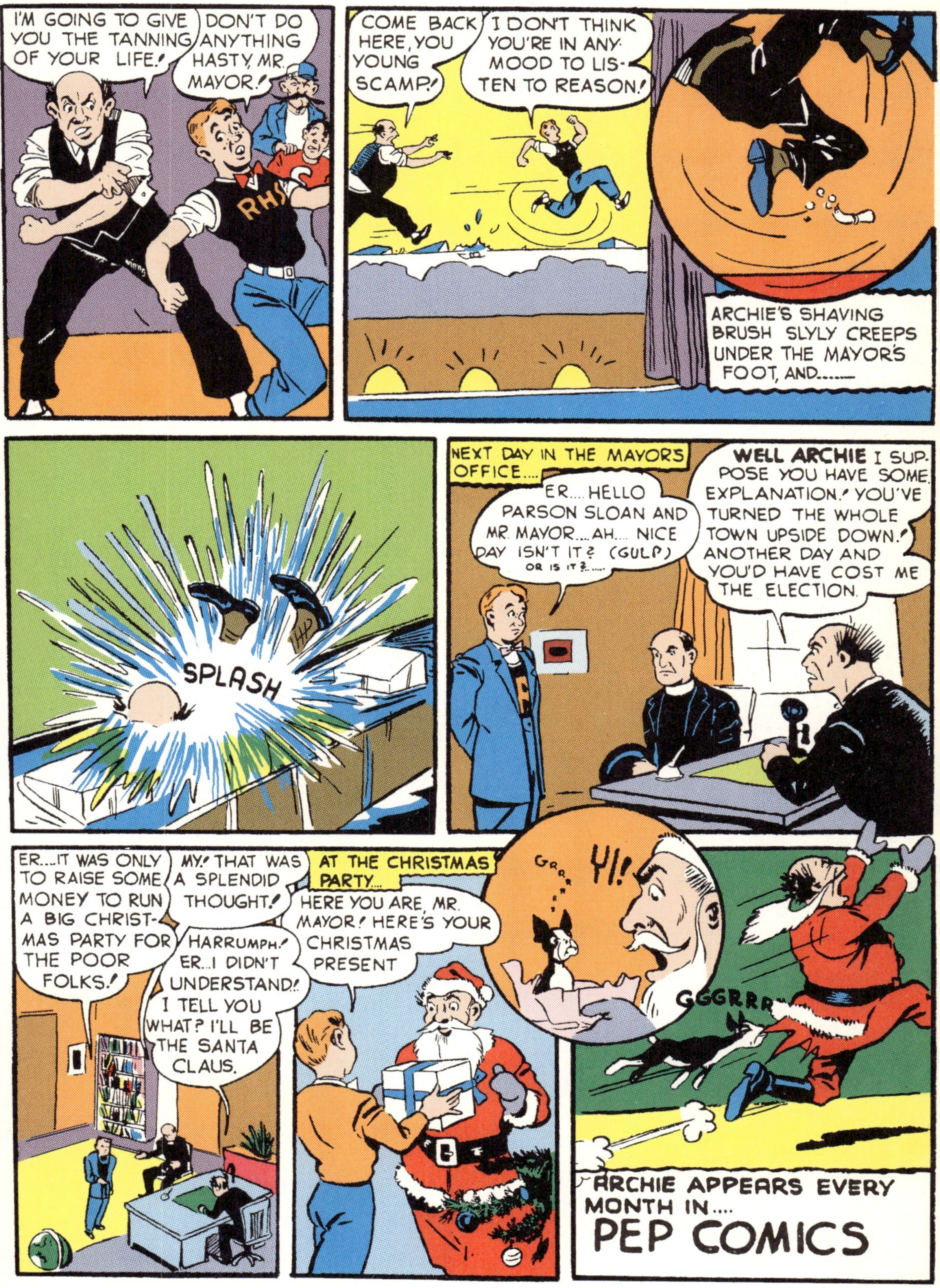
I'M GOING TO GIVE YOU THE TANNING OF YOUR LIFE!
DON'T DO ANYTHING HASTY, MR. MAYOR!
COME BACK HERE, YOU YOUNG SCAMP!
I DON'T THINK YOU'RE IN ANY MOOD TO LISTEN TO REASON!
ARCHIE'S SHAVING BRUSH SLYLY CREEPS UNDER THE MAYOR'S FOOT, AND......
SPLASH
NEXT DAY IN THE MAYORS OFFICE....
ER.... HELLO PARSON SLOAN AND MR. MAYOR... AH... NICE DAY ISN'T IT? (GULP) OR IS IT?.....
WELL ARCHIE I SUPPOSE YOU HAVE SOME EXPLANATION! YOU'VE TURNED THE WHOLE TOWN UPSIDE DOWN! ANOTHER DAY AND YOU'D HAVE COST ME THE ELECTION.
ER...IT WAS ONLY TO RAISE SOME MONEY TO RUN A BIG CHRISTMAS PARTY FOR THE POOR FOLKS!
MY! THAT WAS A SPLENDID THOUGHT!
HARRUMPH! ER...I DIDN'T UNDERSTAND! I TELL YOU WHAT? I'LL BE THE SANTA CLAUS.
AT THE CHRISTMAS PARTY....
HERE YOU ARE, MR. MAYOR! HERE'S YOUR CHRISTMAS PRESENT
GRRR
YI!
GGGRRR
ARCHIE APPEARS EVERY MONTH IN....
PEP COMICS

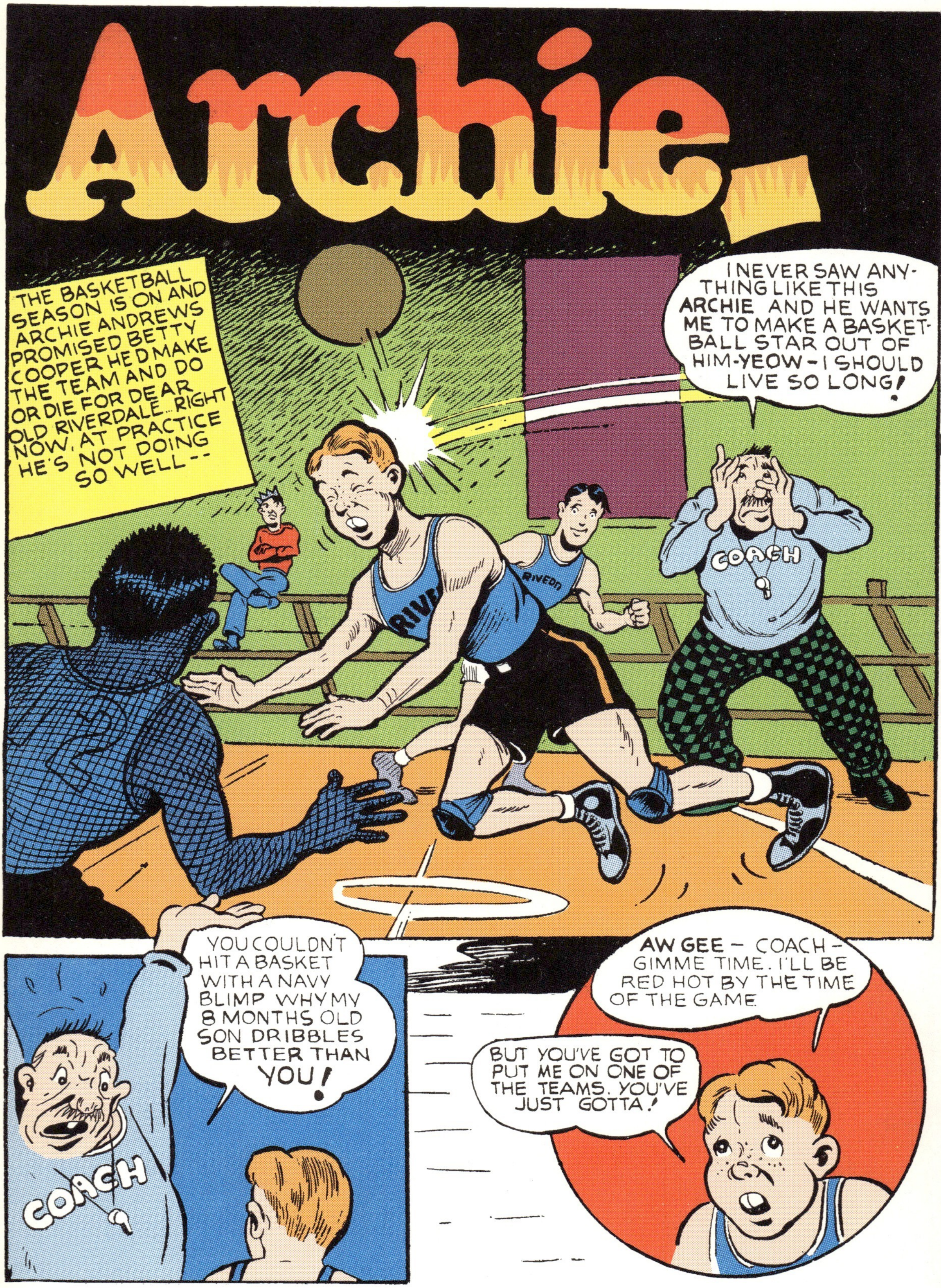
Archie
THE BASKETBALL SEASON IS ON AND ARCHIE ANDREWS PROMISED BETTY COOPER HE'D MAKE THE TEAM AND DO OR DIE FOR DEAR OLD RIVERDALE... RIGHT NOW, AT PRACTICE HE'S NOT DOING SO WELL--
I NEVER SAW ANYTHING LIKE THIS ARCHIE AND HE WANTS ME TO MAKE A BASKETBALL STAR OUT OF HIM-YEOW-I SHOULD LIVE SO LONG!
COACH
YOU COULDN'T HIT A BASKET WITH A NAVY BLIMP WHY MY 8 MONTHS OLD SON DRIBBLES BETTER THAN YOU!
COACH
AW GEE - COACH - GIMME TIME. I'LL BE RED HOT BY THE TIME OF THE GAME.
BUT YOU'VE GOT TO PUT ME ON ONE OF THE TEAMS. YOU'VE JUST GOTTA!

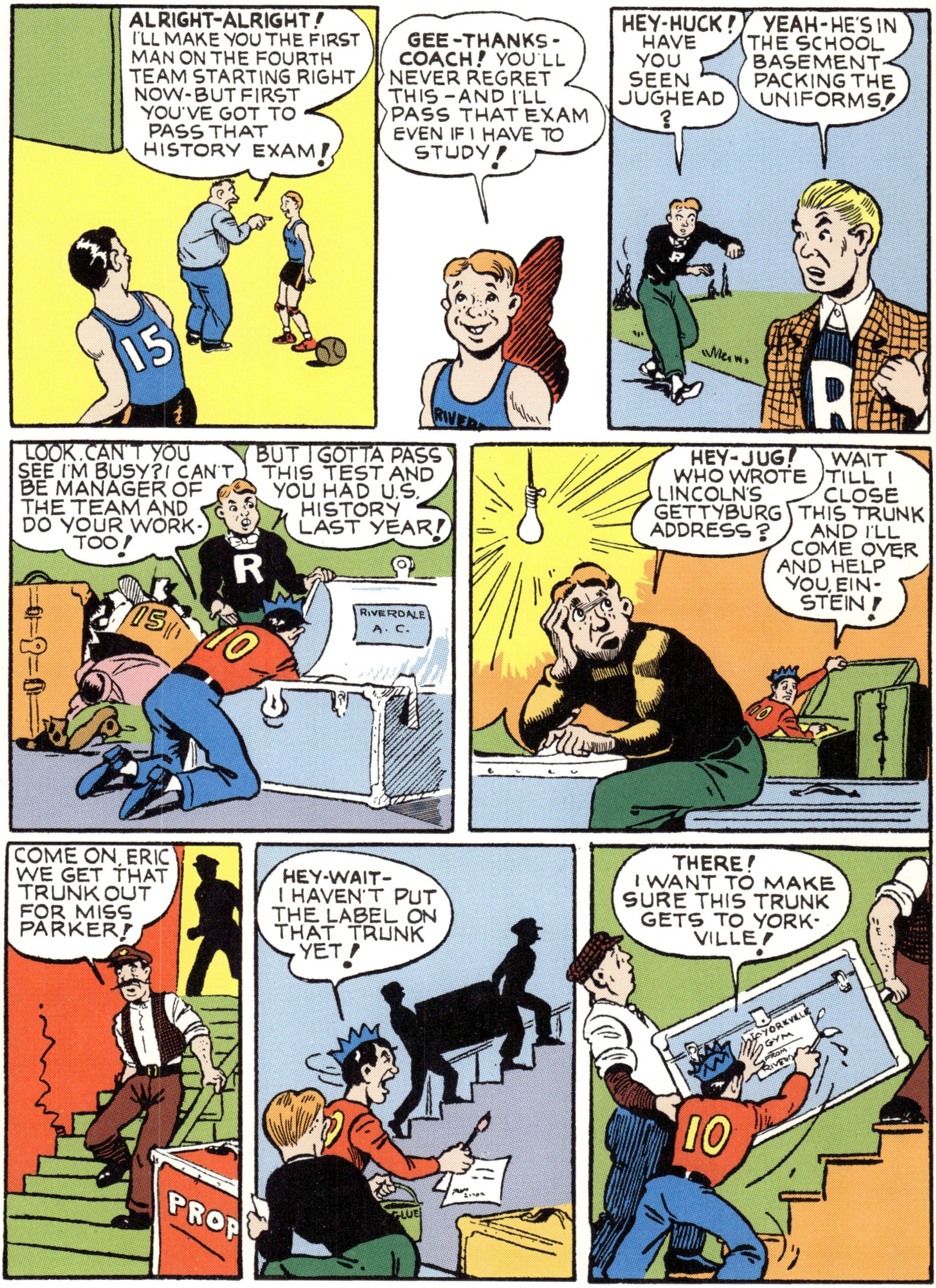
ALRIGHT-ALRIGHT! I'LL MAKE YOU THE FIRST MAN ON THE FOURTH TEAM STARTING RIGHT NOW-BUT FIRST YOU'VE GOT TO PASS THAT HISTORY EXAM!
GEE-THANKS-COACH! YOU'LL NEVER REGRET THIS-AND I'LL PASS THAT EXAM EVEN IF I HAVE TO STUDY!
HEY-HUCK! HAVE YOU SEEN JUGHEAD?
YEAH-HE'S IN THE SCHOOL BASEMENT-PACKING THE UNIFORMS!
LOOK, CAN'T YOU SEE I'M BUSY?! CAN'T BE MANAGER OF THE TEAM AND DO YOUR WORK-TOO!
BUT I GOTTA PASS THIS TEST AND YOU HAD U.S. HISTORY LAST YEAR!
RIVERDALE A. C.
HEY-JUG! WHO WROTE LINCOLN'S GETTYBURG ADDRESS?
WAIT TILL I CLOSE THIS TRUNK AND I'LL COME OVER AND HELP YOU, EIN-STEIN!
COME ON, ERIC WE GET THAT TRUNK OUT FOR MISS PARKER!
PROP
HEY-WAIT-I HAVEN'T PUT THE LABEL ON THAT TRUNK YET!
THERE! I WANT TO MAKE SURE THIS TRUNK GETS TO YORK-VILLE!

WELL. ARCHIE ANDREWS, YOU GOT 65 1/10 %! THAT'S JUST PASSING-AND THIS APPLE HAD NOTHING TO DO WITH IT!
GEE. THANKS, MISS SCOTT!
SMACK
IT MUST BE THAT NEW DEPILATORY I'M USING!
HEY- BETTY!
OOF!
I'M AWFUL SORRY, BETTY. I WAS HURRY-ING TO TELL YOU THAT I MADE THE TEAM!
THAT'S OKAY- ARCHIE -I LIKE HAVING YOU FALL FOR ME!
HUH? OH SAY, ARE YOU COMING TO SEE ME PLAY TONIGHT?
GOLLY- ARCHIE - I'D GIVE ANYTHING TO - BUT I'M IN THE SCHOOL BALLET AND WE'RE PUTTING ON "PET-ROUCHKA" TONIGHT AT HAMSTEAD!
NOW-AT THE YORK-VILLE GYM WHERE AN EAGER CROWD AWAITS THE TWO TEAMS' ENTRANCE-
WILL YOU FELLAS GET OUT HERE ON THE FLOOR- AND GET THAT NIGHT-INGALE OUT OF THE SHOWER!
OKAY- COACH!

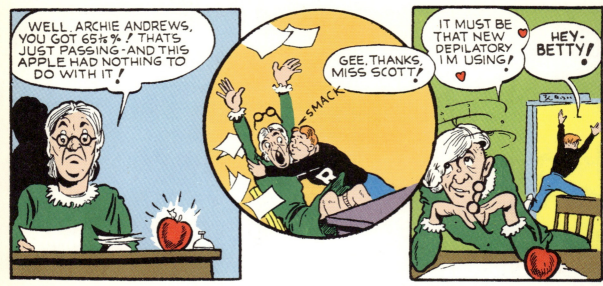

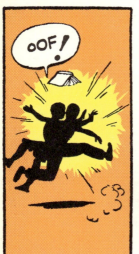

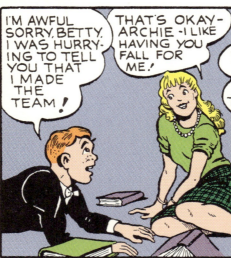

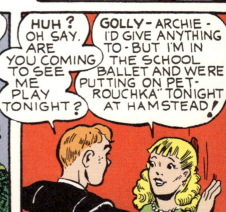

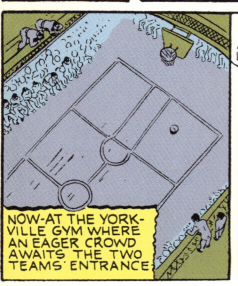

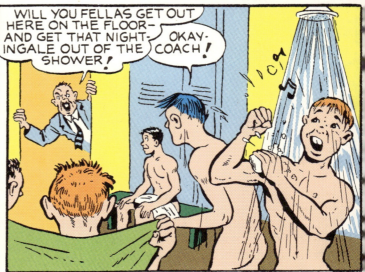

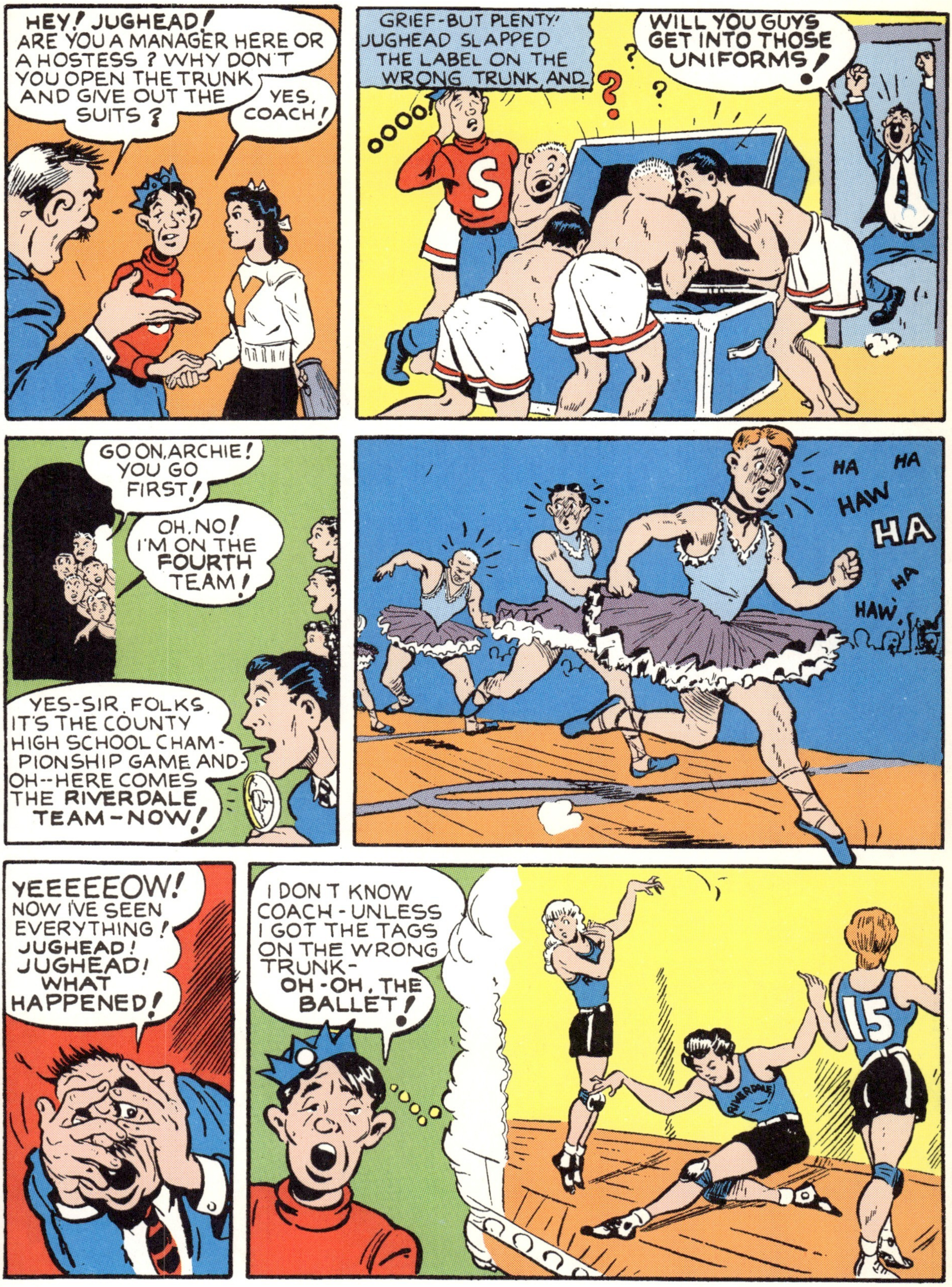
HEY! JUGHEAD! ARE YOU A MANAGER HERE OR A HOSTESS ? WHY DON'T YOU OPEN THE TRUNK AND GIVE OUT THE SUITS ?
YES, COACH!
GRIEF-BUT PLENTY! JUGHEAD SLAPPED THE LABEL ON THE WRONG TRUNK, AND
WILL YOU GUYS GET INTO THOSE UNIFORMS!
OOOO!
GO ON, ARCHIE! YOU GO FIRST!
OH, NO! I'M ON THE FOURTH TEAM!
YES-SIR, FOLKS, IT'S THE COUNTY HIGH SCHOOL CHAMPIONSHIP GAME AND--OH--HERE COMES THE RIVERDALE TEAM - NOW!
HA HA HAW HA HA HAW.
YEEEEEOW! NOW I'VE SEEN EVERYTHING! JUGHEAD! JUGHEAD! WHAT HAPPENED!
I DON'T KNOW COACH - UNLESS I GOT THE TAGS ON THE WRONG TRUNK- OH-OH, THE BALLET!
RIVERDALE
15

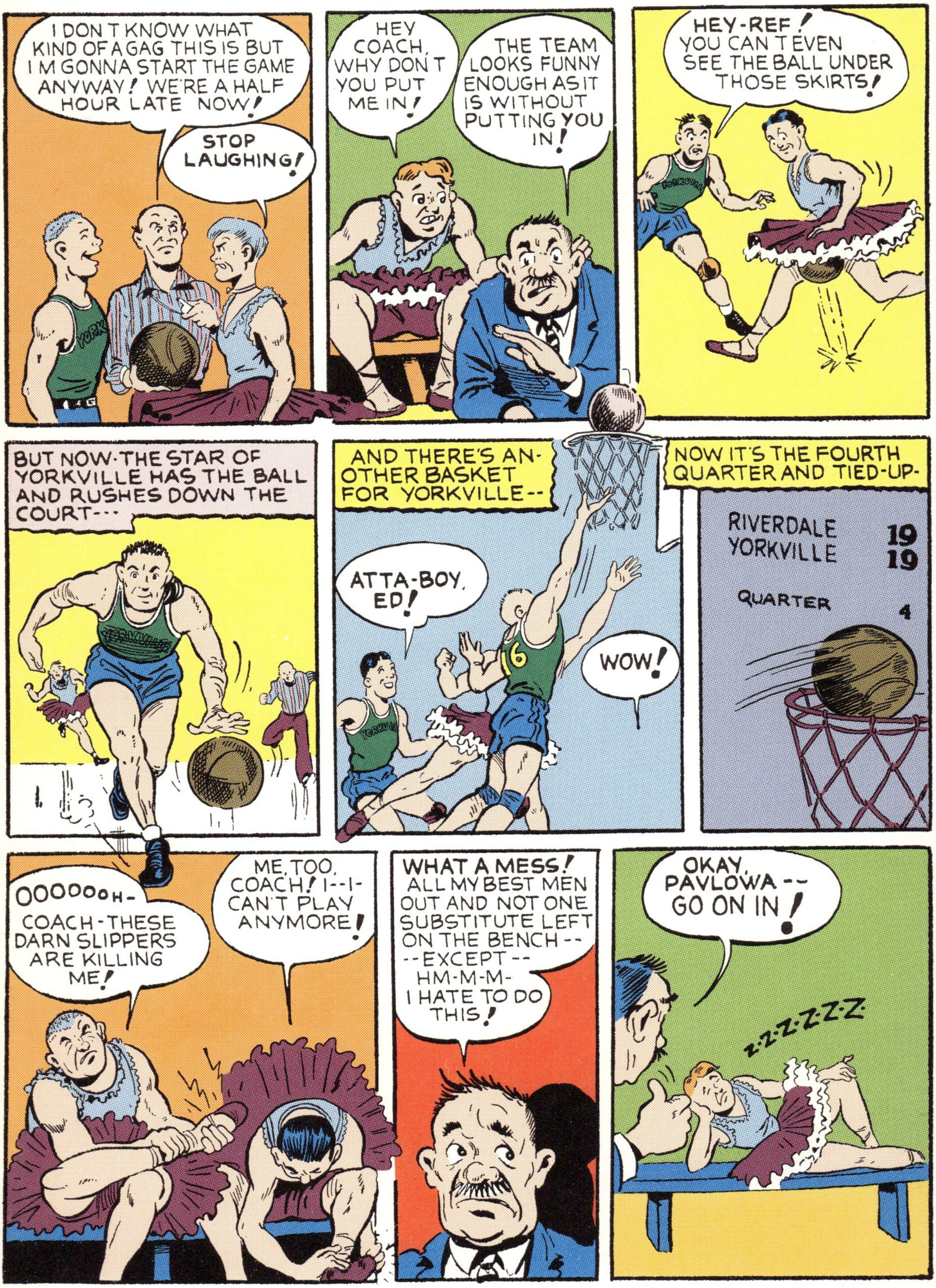

I DON T KNOW WHAT KIND OF A GAG THIS IS BUT I M GONNA START THE GAME ANYWAY! WE'RE A HALF HOUR LATE NOW!
STOP LAUGHING!
HEY COACH, WHY DON T YOU PUT ME IN!
THE TEAM LOOKS FUNNY ENOUGH AS IT IS WITHOUT PUTTING YOU IN!
HEY-REF! YOU CAN T EVEN SEE THE BALL UNDER THOSE SKIRTS!
BUT NOW-THE STAR OF YORKVILLE HAS THE BALL AND RUSHES DOWN THE COURT---
AND THERE'S ANOTHER BASKET FOR YORKVILLE--
ATTA-BOY, ED!
WOW!
NOW IT'S THE FOURTH QUARTER AND TIED-UP-
RIVERDALE 19
YORKVILLE 19
QUARTER 4
OOOOOOH- COACH-THESE DARN SLIPPERS ARE KILLING ME!
ME, TOO, COACH! I--I- CAN'T PLAY ANYMORE!
WHAT A MESS! ALL MY BEST MEN OUT AND NOT ONE SUBSTITUTE LEFT ON THE BENCH -- --EXCEPT -- HM-M-M- I HATE TO DO THIS!
OKAY, PAVLOWA -- GO ON IN!
Z-Z-Z-Z-Z-Z

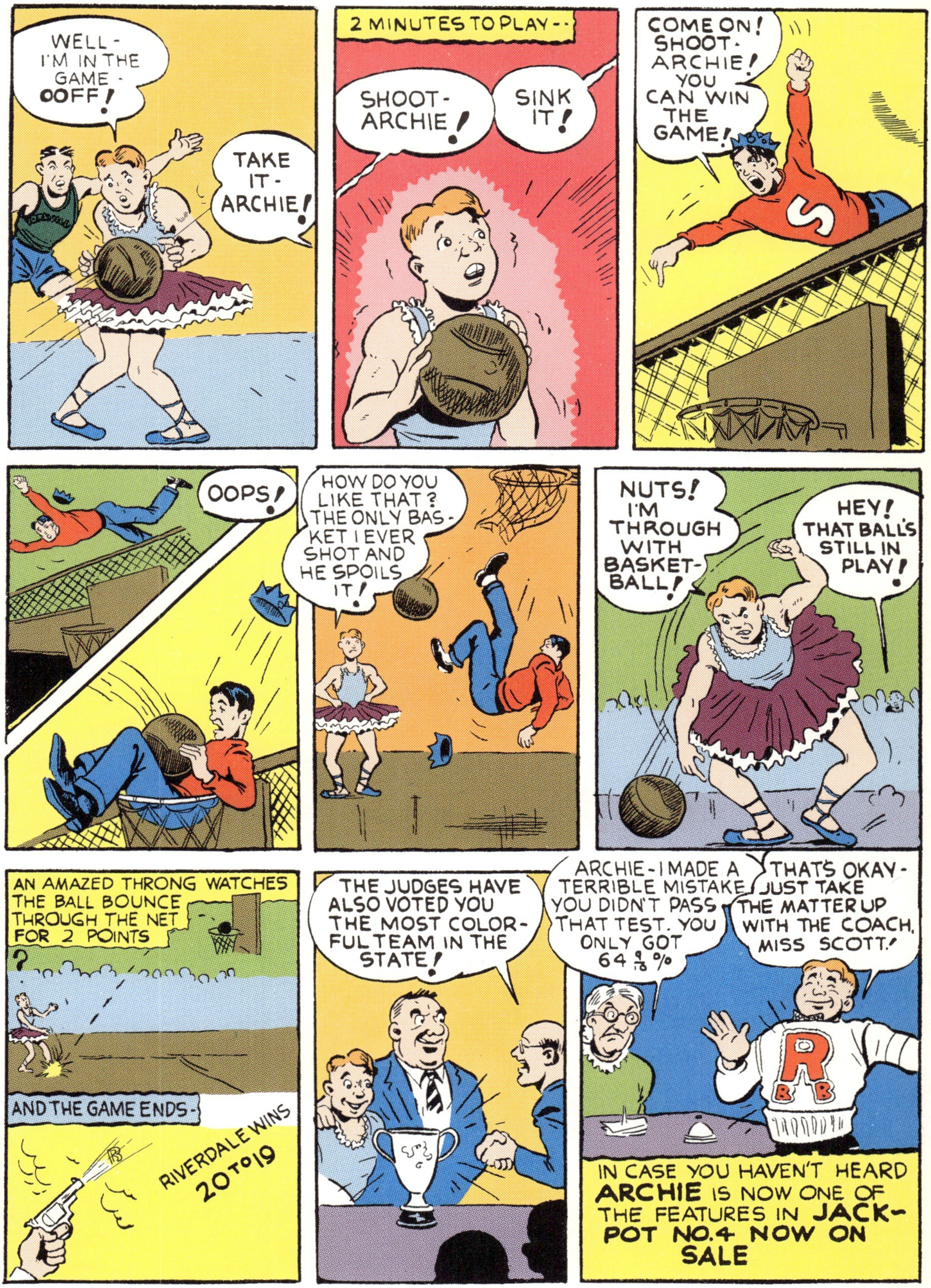
WELL - I'M IN THE GAME - OOFF!
TAKE IT - ARCHIE!
2 MINUTES TO PLAY - -
SHOOT - ARCHIE!
SINK IT!
COME ON! SHOOT - ARCHIE! YOU CAN WIN THE GAME!
OOPS!
HOW DO YOU LIKE THAT? THE ONLY BAS-KET I EVER SHOT AND HE SPOILS IT!
NUTS! I'M THROUGH WITH BASKET-BALL!
HEY! THAT BALL'S STILL IN PLAY!
AN AMAZED THRONG WATCHES THE BALL BOUNCE THROUGH THE NET FOR 2 POINTS
AND THE GAME ENDS -
RIVERDALE WINS 20 TO 19
THE JUDGES HAVE ALSO VOTED YOU THE MOST COLOR-FUL TEAM IN THE STATE!
ARCHIE - I MADE A TERRIBLE MISTAKE! YOU DIDN'T PASS THAT TEST. YOU ONLY GOT 64 9/10 %
THAT'S OKAY - JUST TAKE THE MATTER UP WITH THE COACH, MISS SCOTT!
IN CASE YOU HAVEN'T HEARD ARCHIE IS NOW ONE OF THE FEATURES IN JACK-POT NO.4 NOW ON SALE

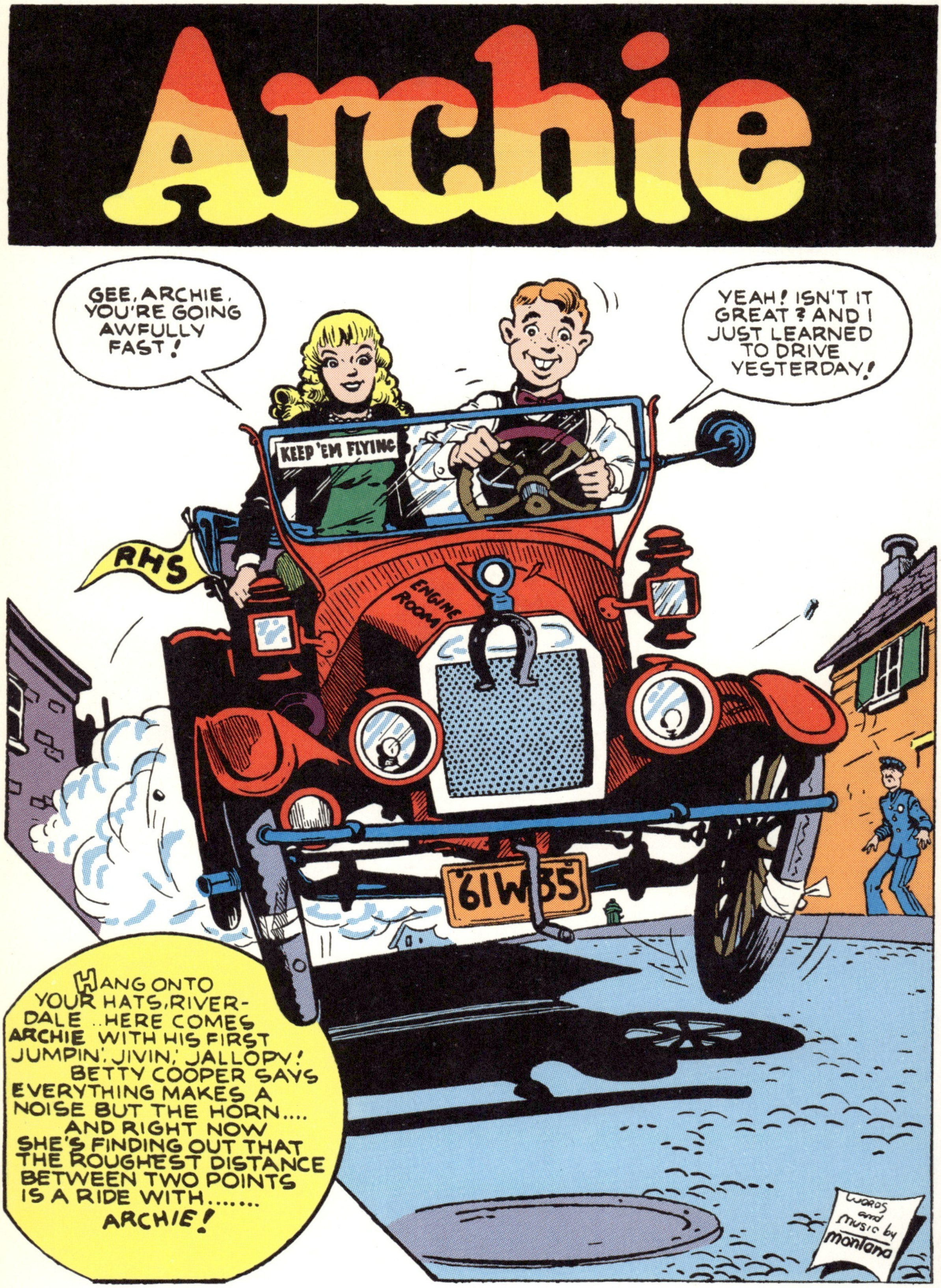
Archie
GEE, ARCHIE, YOU'RE GOING AWFULLY FAST!
YEAH! ISN'T IT GREAT? AND I JUST LEARNED TO DRIVE YESTERDAY!
KEEP 'EM FLYING
RHS
ENGINE ROOM
61W35
HANG ONTO YOUR HATS, RIVERDALE ..HERE COMES ARCHIE WITH HIS FIRST JUMPIN', JIVIN', JALLOPY! BETTY COOPER SAYS EVERYTHING MAKES A NOISE BUT THE HORN.... AND RIGHT NOW SHE'S FINDING OUT THAT THE ROUGHEST DISTANCE BETWEEN TWO POINTS IS A RIDE WITH....... ARCHIE!
words and music by montana

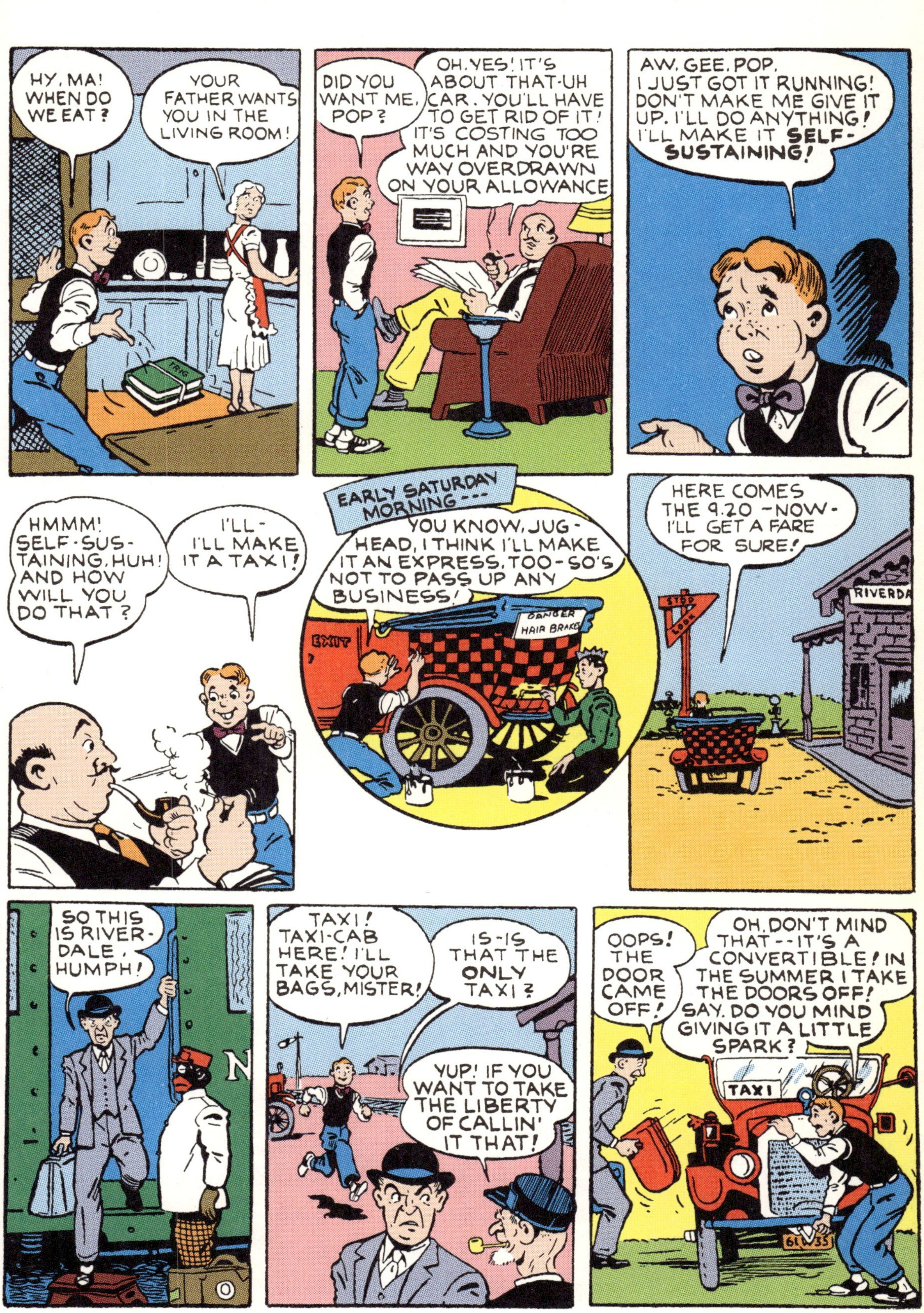
HY, MA! WHEN DO WE EAT?
YOUR FATHER WANTS YOU IN THE LIVING ROOM!
TRIG
DID YOU WANT ME, POP?
OH, YES! IT'S ABOUT THAT-UH CAR. YOU'LL HAVE TO GET RID OF IT! IT'S COSTING TOO MUCH AND YOU'RE WAY OVERDRAWN ON YOUR ALLOWANCE
AW, GEE, POP, I JUST GOT IT RUNNING! DON'T MAKE ME GIVE IT UP. I'LL DO ANYTHING! I'LL MAKE IT **SELF-SUSTAINING!**
HMMM! SELF-SUSTAINING, HUH! AND HOW WILL YOU DO THAT?
I'LL- I'LL MAKE IT A TAXI!
EARLY SATURDAY MORNING---
YOU KNOW, JUGHEAD, I THINK I'LL MAKE IT AN EXPRESS, TOO-SO'S NOT TO PASS UP ANY BUSINESS!
EXIT
DANGER HAIR BRAKES
HERE COMES THE 9.20 -NOW- I'LL GET A FARE FOR SURE!
STOP LOOK
RIVERDA
SO THIS IS RIVERDALE. HUMPH!
N
TAXI! TAXI-CAB HERE! I'LL TAKE YOUR BAGS, MISTER!
IS-IS THAT THE **ONLY** TAXI?
YUP! IF YOU WANT TO TAKE THE LIBERTY OF CALLIN' IT THAT!
OOPS! THE DOOR CAME OFF!
OH, DON'T MIND THAT--IT'S A CONVERTIBLE! IN THE SUMMER I TAKE THE DOORS OFF! SAY, DO YOU MIND GIVING IT A LITTLE SPARK?
TAXI

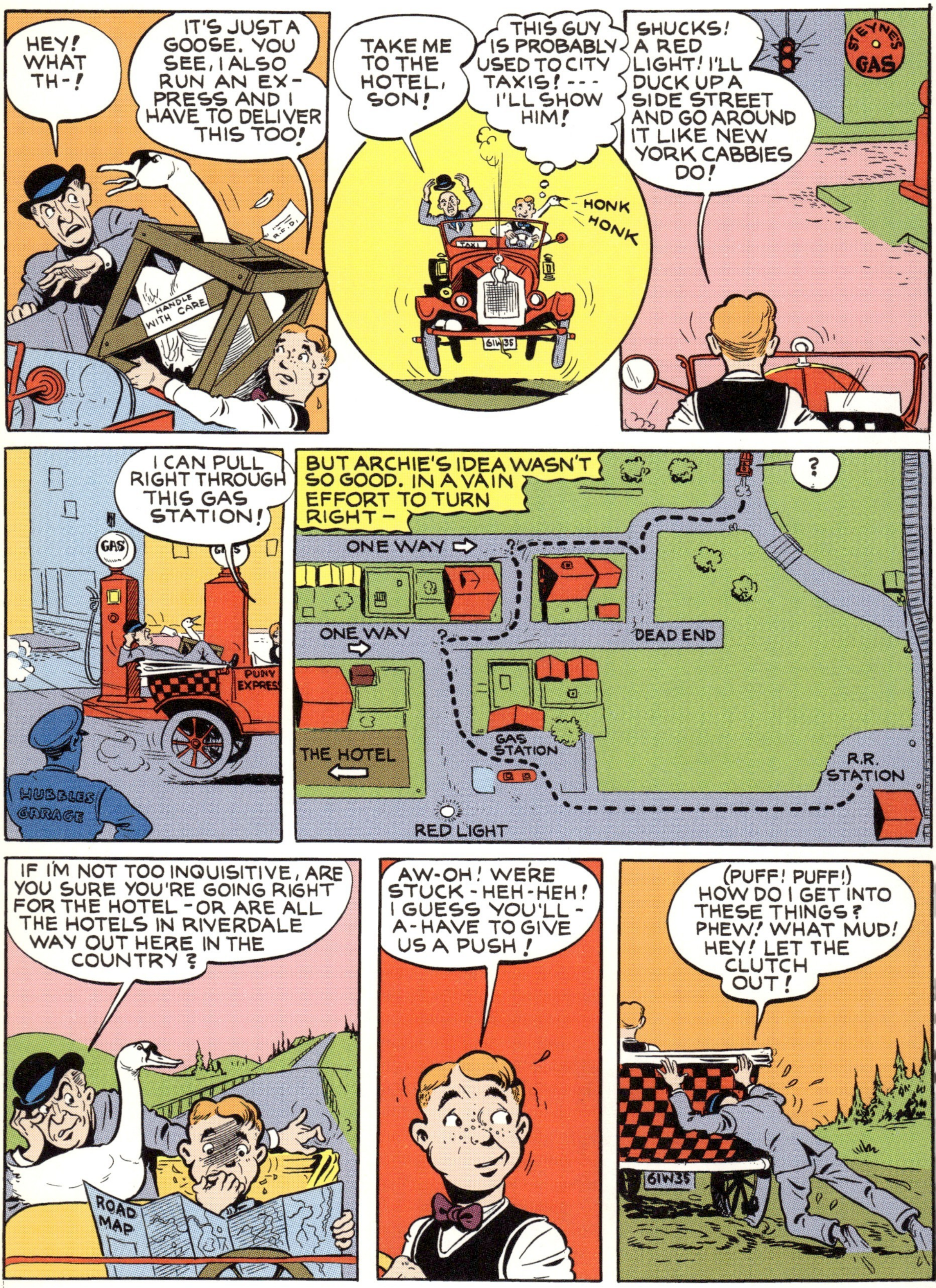
HEY! WHAT TH-!
IT'S JUST A GOOSE. YOU SEE, I ALSO RUN AN EX-PRESS AND I HAVE TO DELIVER THIS TOO!
HANDLE WITH CARE
TAKE ME TO THE HOTEL, SON!
THIS GUY IS PROBABLY USED TO CITY TAXIS! --- I'LL SHOW HIM!
HONK
HONK
61W35
SHUCKS! A RED LIGHT! I'LL DUCK UP A SIDE STREET AND GO AROUND IT LIKE NEW YORK CABBIES DO!
STEYNE'S GAS
I CAN PULL RIGHT THROUGH THIS GAS STATION!
GAS
PUNY EXPRESS
HUBBLES GARAGE
BUT ARCHIE'S IDEA WASN'T SO GOOD. IN A VAIN EFFORT TO TURN RIGHT –
?
ONE WAY
?
ONE WAY
?
DEAD END
THE HOTEL
GAS STATION
R.R. STATION
RED LIGHT
IF I'M NOT TOO INQUISITIVE, ARE YOU SURE YOU'RE GOING RIGHT FOR THE HOTEL – OR ARE ALL THE HOTELS IN RIVERDALE WAY OUT HERE IN THE COUNTRY?
ROAD MAP
AW-OH! WE'RE STUCK - HEH - HEH! I GUESS YOU'LL - A - HAVE TO GIVE US A PUSH!
(PUFF! PUFF!) HOW DO I GET INTO THESE THINGS? PHEW! WHAT MUD! HEY! LET THE CLUTCH OUT!
61W35

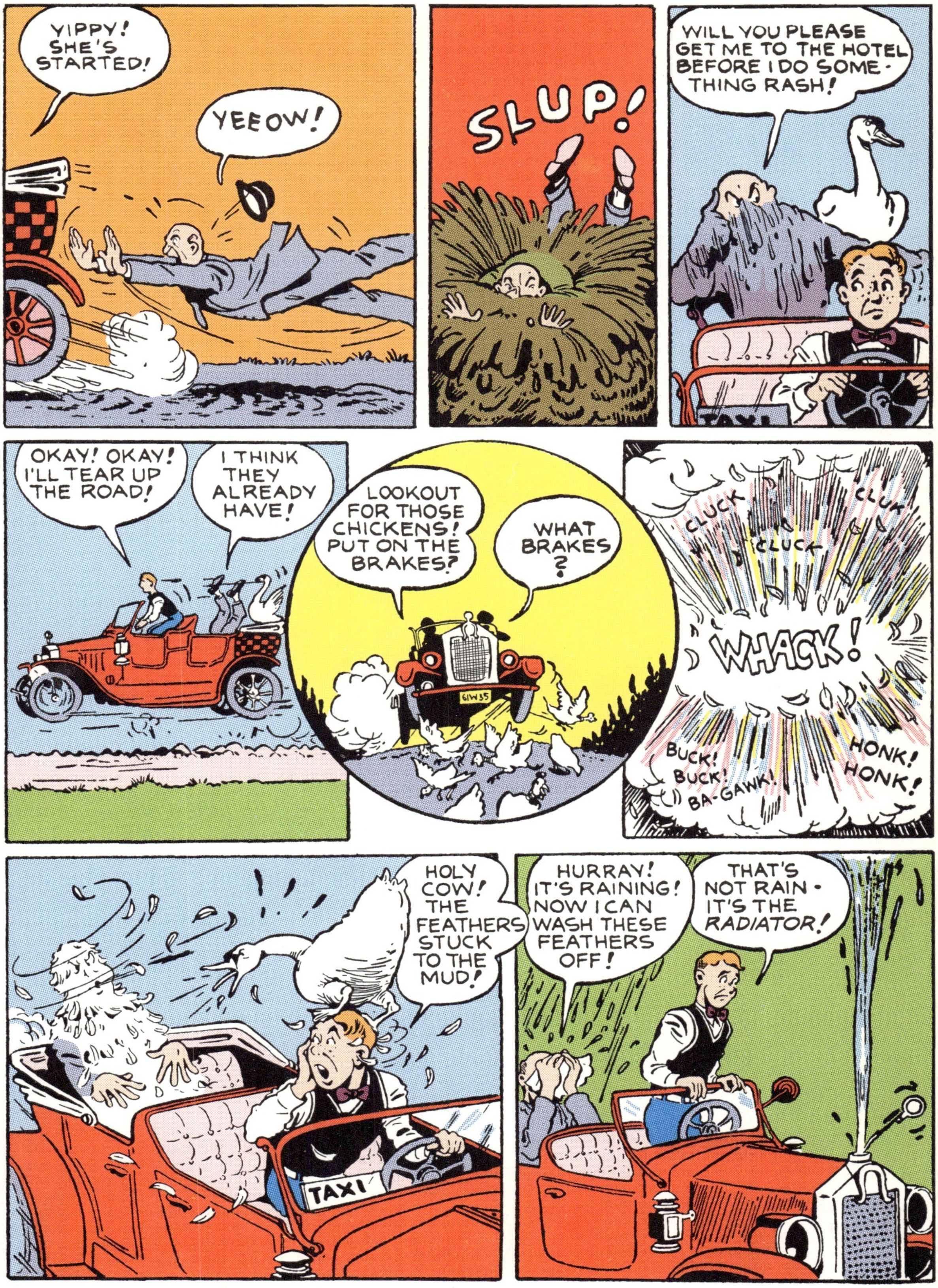
YIPPY! SHE'S STARTED!
YEEOW!
SLUP!
WILL YOU PLEASE GET ME TO THE HOTEL BEFORE I DO SOME-THING RASH!
OKAY! OKAY! I'LL TEAR UP THE ROAD!
I THINK THEY ALREADY HAVE!
LOOKOUT FOR THOSE CHICKENS! PUT ON THE BRAKES?
WHAT BRAKES ?
CLUCK
CLUK
CLUCK
WHACK!
BUCK! BUCK! BA-GAWK!
HONK! HONK!
HOLY COW! THE FEATHERS STUCK TO THE MUD!
TAXI
HURRAY! IT'S RAINING! NOW I CAN WASH THESE FEATHERS OFF!
THAT'S NOT RAIN - IT'S THE RADIATOR!

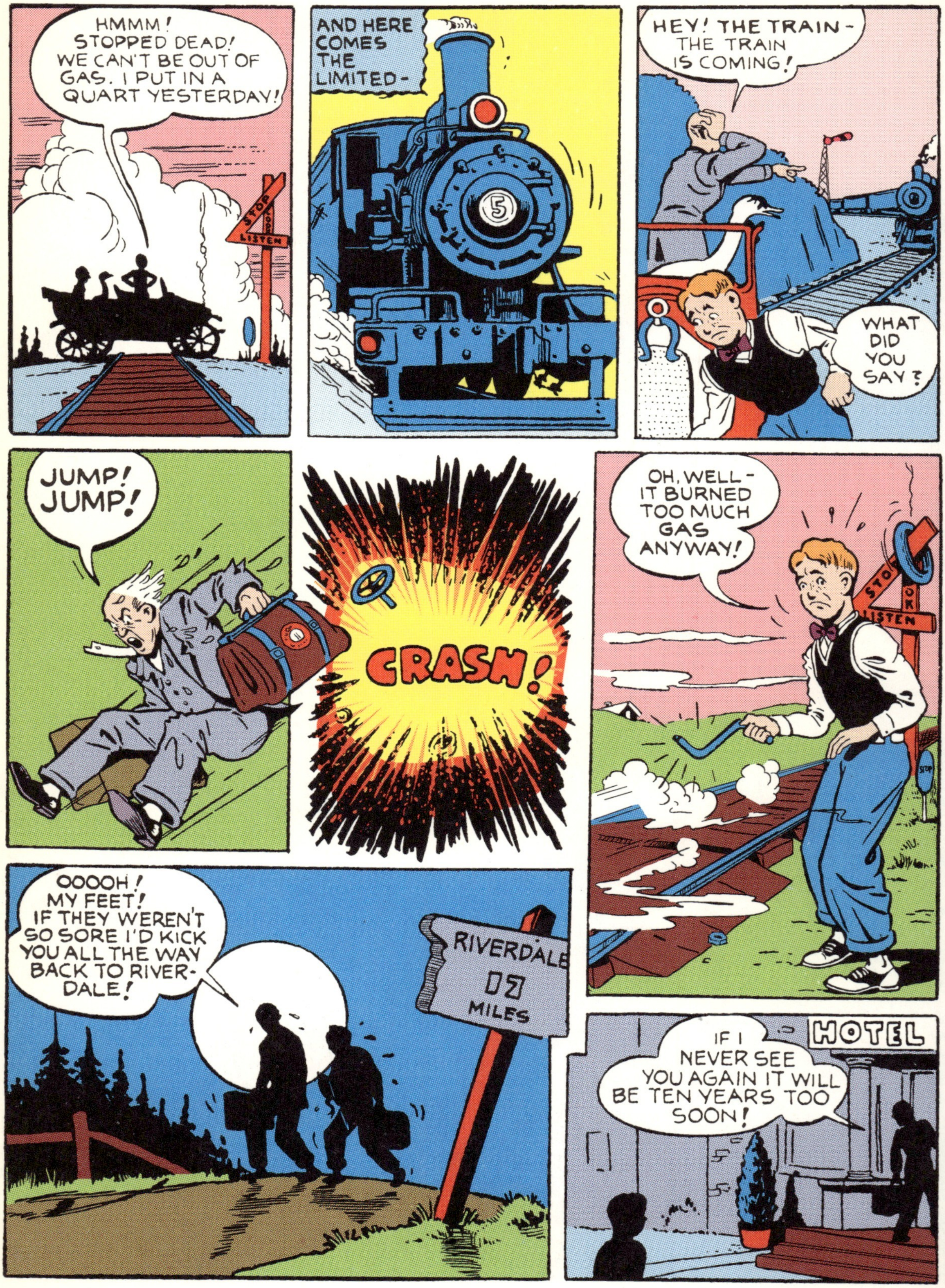
HMMM! STOPPED DEAD! WE CAN'T BE OUT OF GAS. I PUT IN A QUART YESTERDAY!
STOP
LISTEN
AND HERE COMES THE LIMITED-
5
HEY! THE TRAIN- THE TRAIN IS COMING!
WHAT DID YOU SAY?
JUMP! JUMP!
CRASH!
OH, WELL- IT BURNED TOO MUCH GAS ANYWAY!
STOP
LOOK
LISTEN
OOOOH! MY FEET! IF THEY WEREN'T SO SORE I'D KICK YOU ALL THE WAY BACK TO RIVER-DALE!
RIVERDALE
17
MILES
HOTEL
IF I NEVER SEE YOU AGAIN IT WILL BE TEN YEARS TOO SOON!

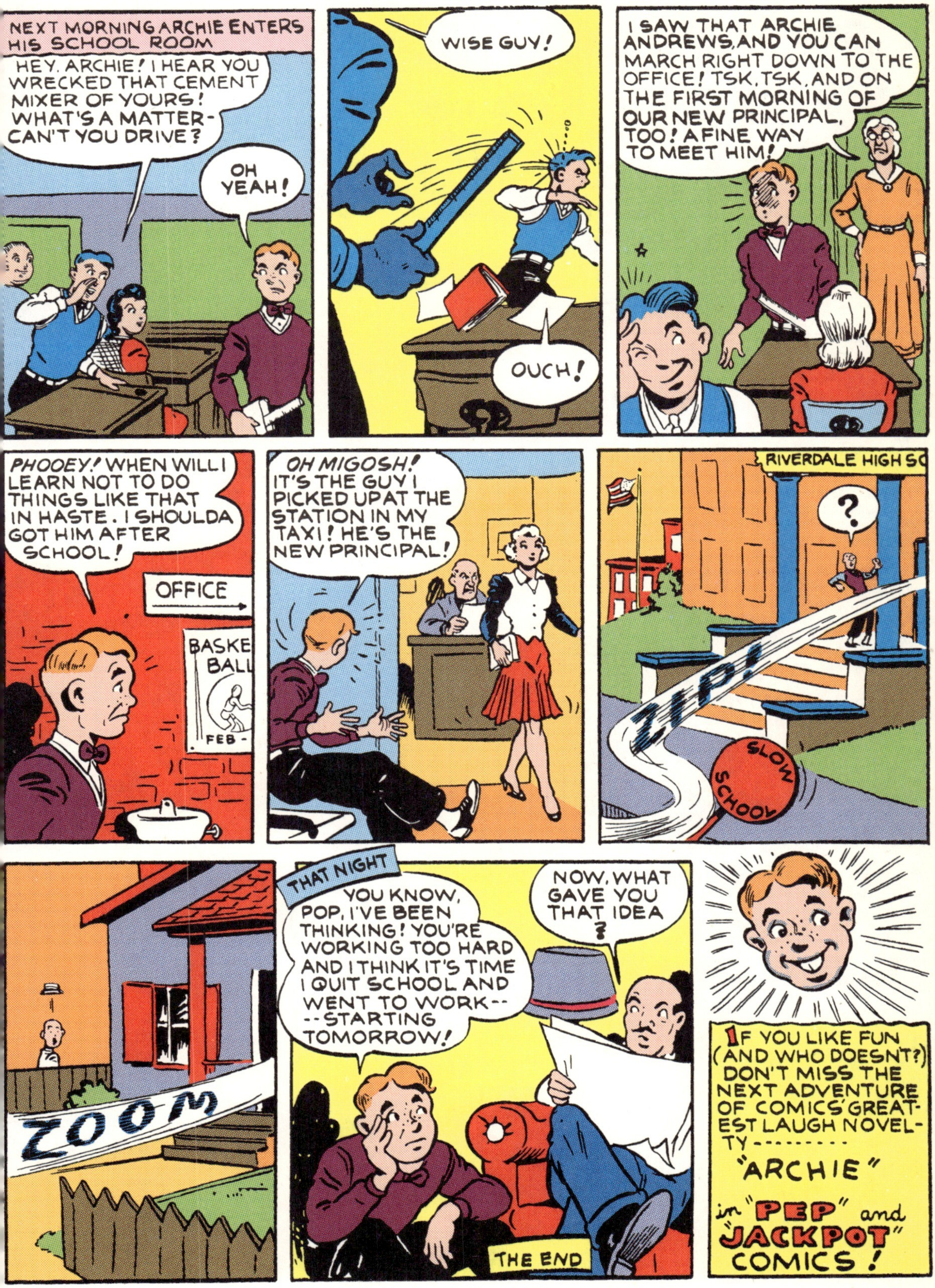
NEXT MORNING ARCHIE ENTERS HIS SCHOOL ROOM
HEY. ARCHIE! I HEAR YOU WRECKED THAT CEMENT MIXER OF YOURS! WHAT'S A MATTER-CAN'T YOU DRIVE?
OH YEAH!
WISE GUY!
OUCH!
I SAW THAT ARCHIE ANDREWS, AND YOU CAN MARCH RIGHT DOWN TO THE OFFICE! TSK, TSK, AND ON THE FIRST MORNING OF OUR NEW PRINCIPAL, TOO! A FINE WAY TO MEET HIM!
PHOOEY! WHEN WILL I LEARN NOT TO DO THINGS LIKE THAT IN HASTE. I SHOULDA GOT HIM AFTER SCHOOL!
OFFICE
BASKE BALL
FEB -
OH MIGOSH! IT'S THE GUY I PICKED UP AT THE STATION IN MY TAXI! HE'S THE NEW PRINCIPAL!
RIVERDALE HIGH SC
?
ZIP!
SLOW SCHOOL
ZOOM
THAT NIGHT
YOU KNOW, POP, I'VE BEEN THINKING! YOU'RE WORKING TOO HARD AND I THINK IT'S TIME I QUIT SCHOOL AND WENT TO WORK-- --STARTING TOMORROW!
NOW, WHAT GAVE YOU THAT IDEA ?
THE END
IF YOU LIKE FUN (AND WHO DOESN'T?) DON'T MISS THE NEXT ADVENTURE OF COMICS' GREATEST LAUGH NOVELTY---------
"ARCHIE"
in "PEP" and "JACKPOT" COMICS!

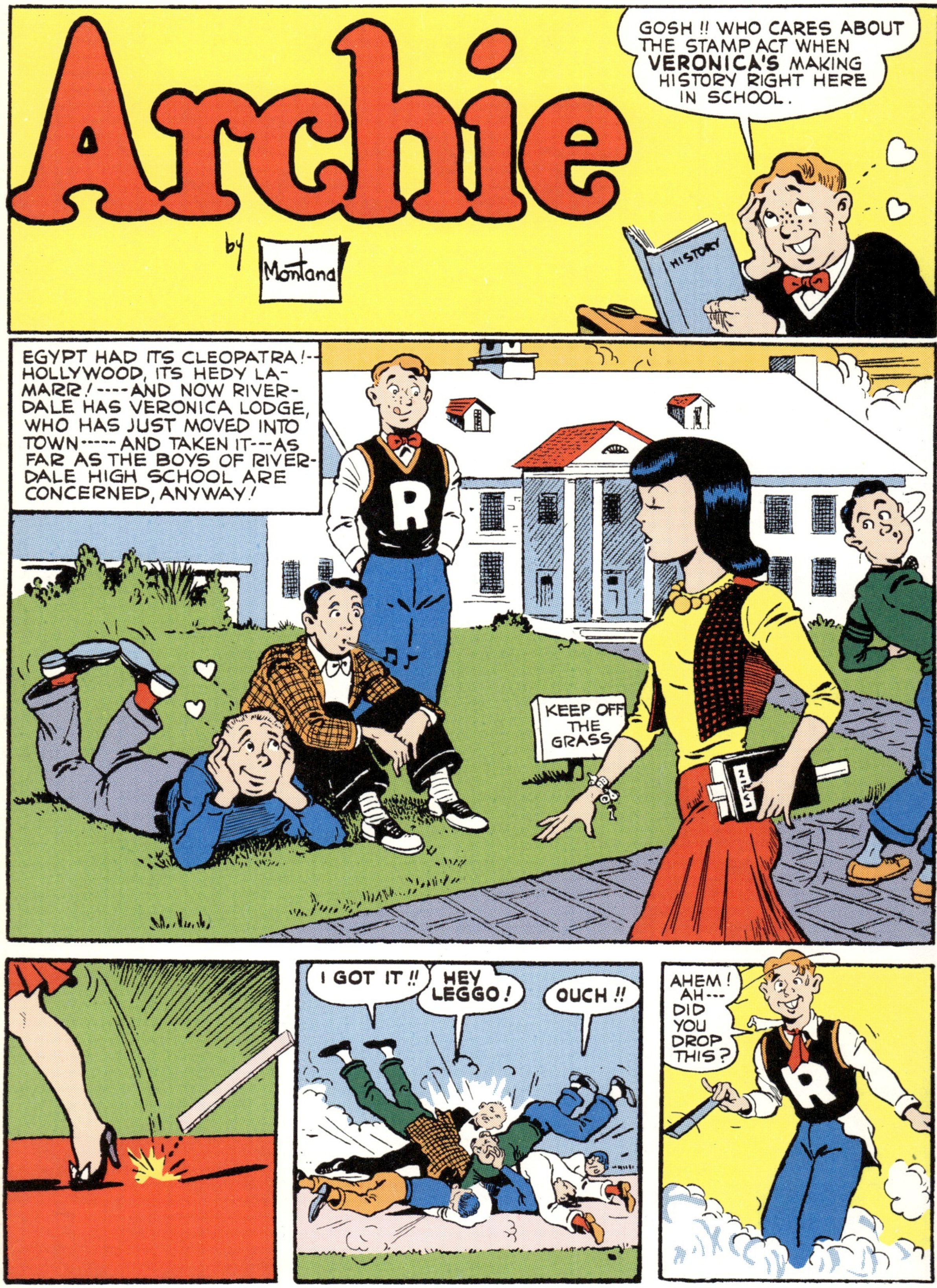
Archie
by Montana
GOSH !! WHO CARES ABOUT THE STAMP ACT WHEN VERONICA'S MAKING HISTORY RIGHT HERE IN SCHOOL.
HISTORY
EGYPT HAD ITS CLEOPATRA!-- HOLLYWOOD, ITS HEDY LAMARR! ----AND NOW RIVERDALE HAS VERONICA LODGE, WHO HAS JUST MOVED INTO TOWN----- AND TAKEN IT---AS FAR AS THE BOYS OF RIVERDALE HIGH SCHOOL ARE CONCERNED, ANYWAY!
KEEP OFF THE GRASS
I GOT IT!!
HEY LEGGO!
OUCH!!
AHEM! AH--- DID YOU DROP THIS?

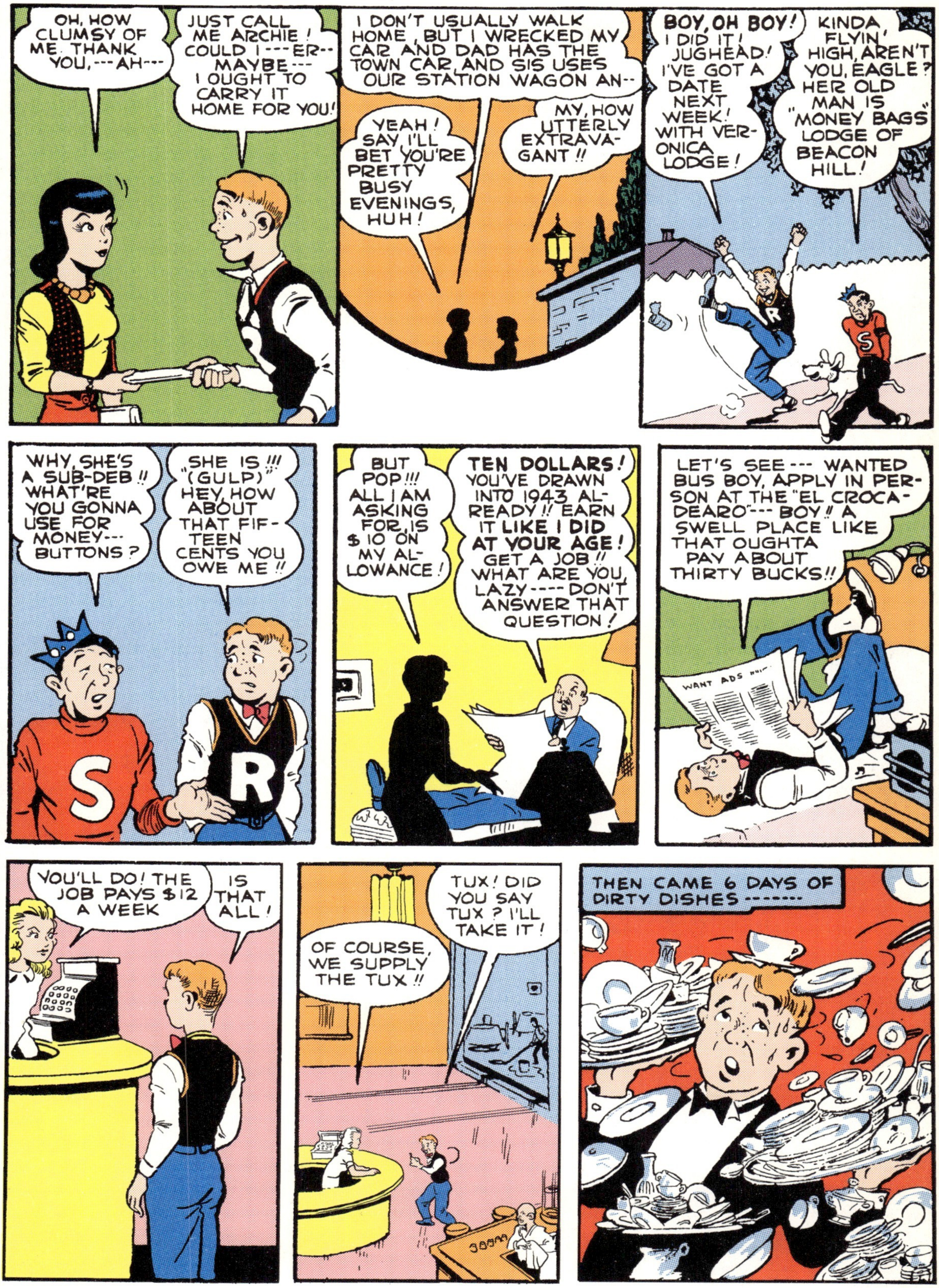
OH, HOW CLUMSY OF ME. THANK YOU,---AH---
JUST CALL ME ARCHIE! COULD I---ER-- MAYBE--- I OUGHT TO CARRY IT HOME FOR YOU!
I DON'T USUALLY WALK HOME, BUT I WRECKED MY CAR AND DAD HAS THE TOWN CAR AND SIS USES OUR STATION WAGON AN--
YEAH! SAY, I'LL BET YOU'RE PRETTY BUSY EVENINGS, HUH!
MY, HOW UTTERLY EXTRAVAGANT!!
BOY, OH BOY! I DID IT! JUGHEAD! I'VE GOT A DATE NEXT WEEK! WITH VERONICA LODGE!
KINDA FLYIN' HIGH, AREN'T YOU, EAGLE? HER OLD MAN IS "MONEY BAGS" LODGE OF BEACON HILL!
WHY, SHE'S A SUB-DEB!! WHAT'RE YOU GONNA USE FOR MONEY--- BUTTONS?
SHE IS!!! "(GULP)" HEY, HOW ABOUT THAT FIFTEEN CENTS YOU OWE ME!!
BUT POP!!! ALL I AM ASKING FOR, IS $10 ON MY ALLOWANCE!
TEN DOLLARS! YOU'VE DRAWN INTO 1943 ALREADY!! EARN IT LIKE I DID AT YOUR AGE! GET A JOB!! WHAT ARE YOU, LAZY---- DON'T ANSWER THAT QUESTION!
LET'S SEE--- WANTED BUS BOY, APPLY IN PERSON AT THE "EL CROCADEARO"--- BOY!! A SWELL PLACE LIKE THAT OUGHTA PAY ABOUT THIRTY BUCKS!!
WANT ADS
YOU'LL DO! THE JOB PAYS $12 A WEEK
IS THAT ALL!
OF COURSE, WE SUPPLY THE TUX!!
TUX! DID YOU SAY TUX? I'LL TAKE IT!
THEN CAME 6 DAYS OF DIRTY DISHES-------

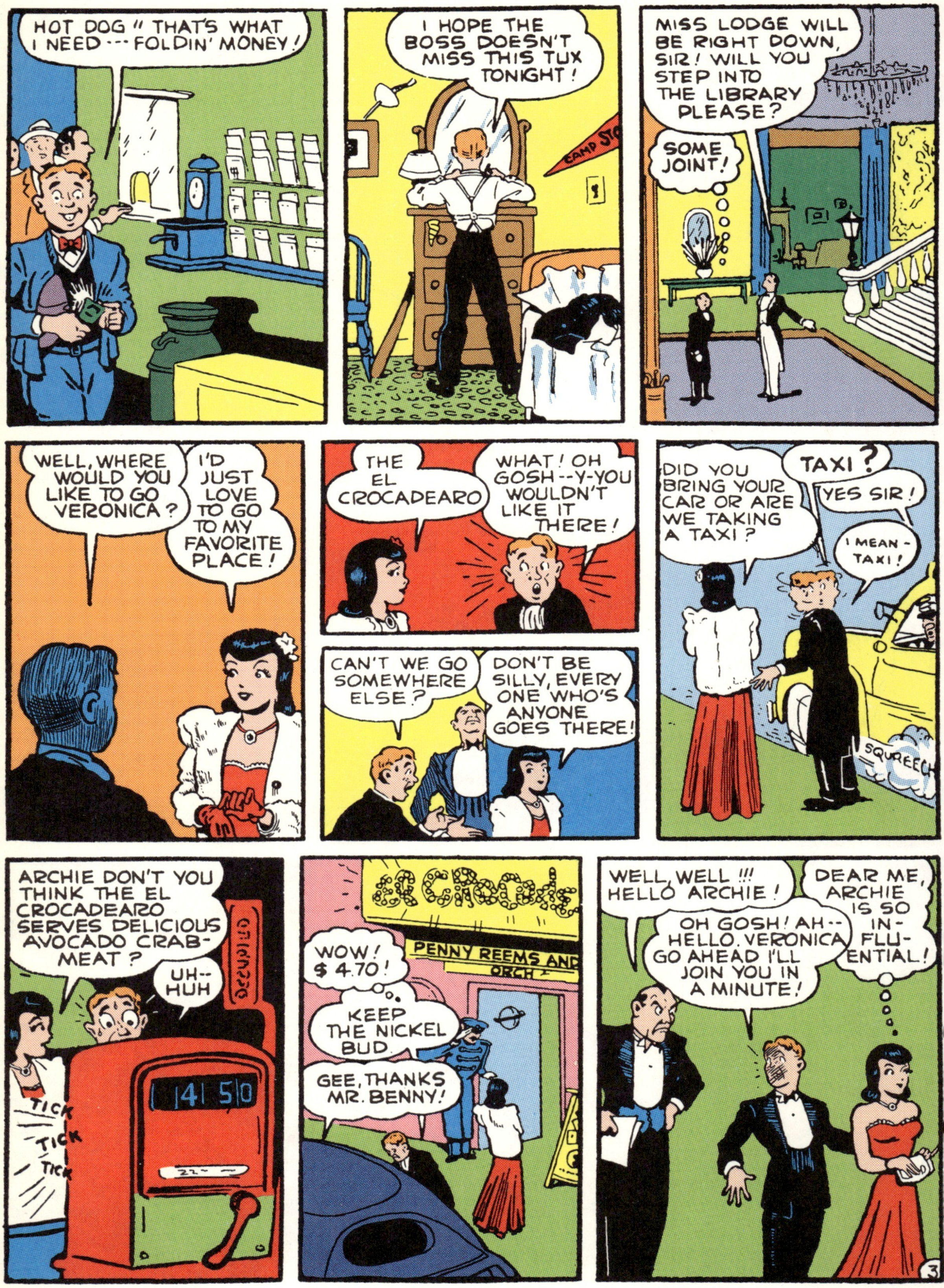
HOT DOG !! THAT'S WHAT I NEED --- FOLDIN' MONEY!
I HOPE THE BOSS DOESN'T MISS THIS TUX TONIGHT!
MISS LODGE WILL BE RIGHT DOWN, SIR! WILL YOU STEP INTO THE LIBRARY PLEASE?
SOME JOINT!
WELL, WHERE WOULD YOU LIKE TO GO VERONICA?
I'D JUST LOVE TO GO TO MY FAVORITE PLACE!
THE EL CROCADEARO
WHAT! OH GOSH --Y-YOU WOULDN'T LIKE IT THERE!
CAN'T WE GO SOMEWHERE ELSE?
DON'T BE SILLY, EVERY ONE WHO'S ANYONE GOES THERE!
DID YOU BRING YOUR CAR OR ARE WE TAKING A TAXI?
TAXI?
YES SIR!
I MEAN - TAXI!
SQUREECH
ARCHIE DON'T YOU THINK THE EL CROCADEARO SERVES DELICIOUS AVOCADO CRAB-MEAT?
UH--HUH
1450
TICK
TICK
TICK
PENNY REEMS AND ORCH
WOW! $4.70!
KEEP THE NICKEL BUD.
GEE, THANKS MR. BENNY!
WELL, WELL !!! HELLO ARCHIE!
OH GOSH! AH-- HELLO, VERONICA GO AHEAD I'LL JOIN YOU IN A MINUTE!
DEAR ME, ARCHIE IS SO IN-FLU-ENTIAL!
3

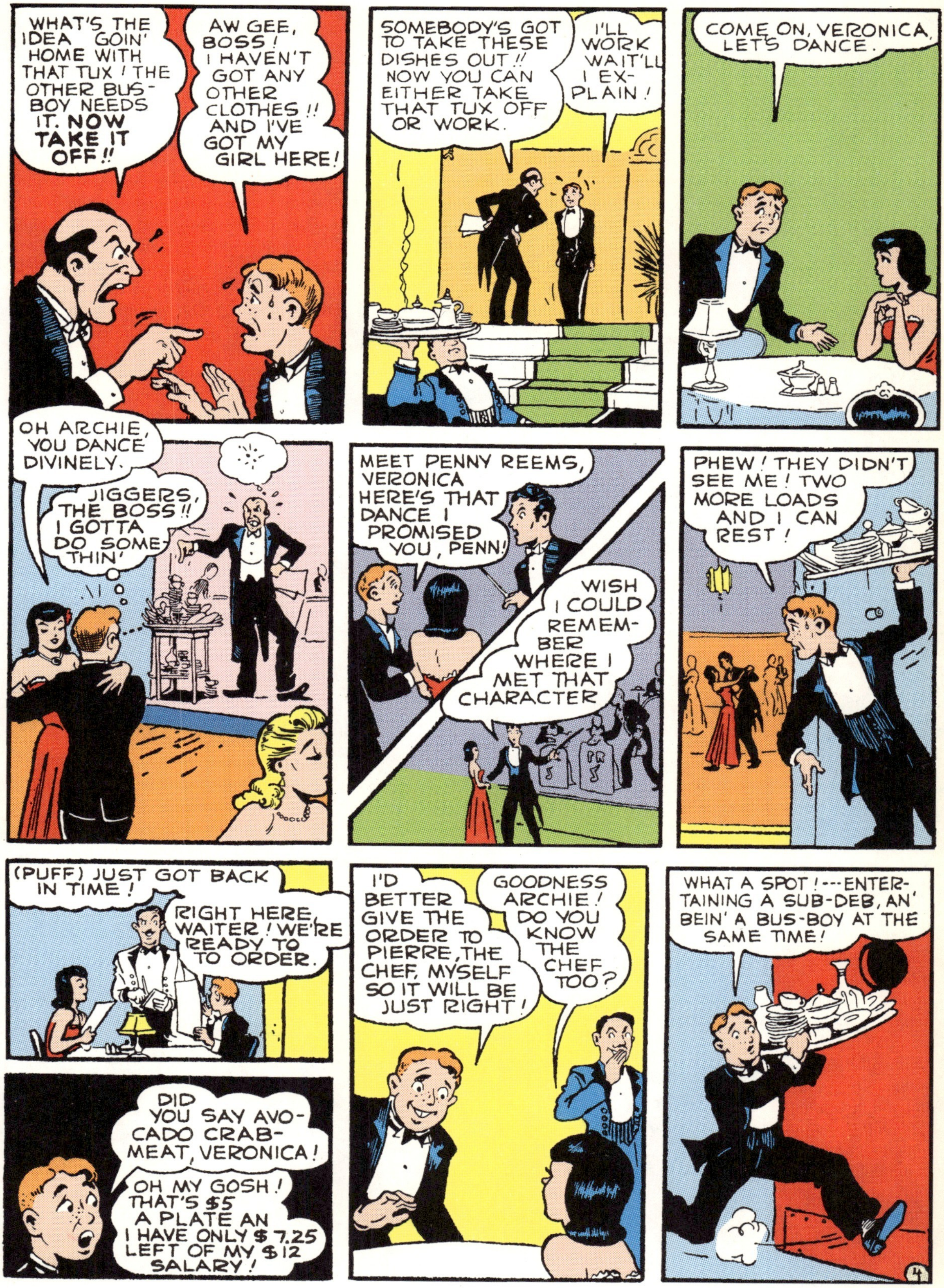
WHAT'S THE IDEA GOIN' HOME WITH THAT TUX! THE OTHER BUS-BOY NEEDS IT. NOW TAKE IT OFF!!
AW GEE, BOSS! I HAVEN'T GOT ANY OTHER CLOTHES!! AND I'VE GOT MY GIRL HERE!
SOMEBODY'S GOT TO TAKE THESE DISHES OUT!! NOW YOU CAN EITHER TAKE THAT TUX OFF OR WORK.
I'LL WORK WAIT'LL I EX-PLAIN!
COME ON, VERONICA, LET'S DANCE.
OH ARCHIE, YOU DANCE DIVINELY.
JIGGERS, THE BOSS!! I GOTTA DO SOME-THIN'
MEET PENNY REEMS, VERONICA HERE'S THAT DANCE I PROMISED YOU, PENN!
WISH I COULD REMEM-BER WHERE I MET THAT CHARACTER
PHEW! THEY DIDN'T SEE ME! TWO MORE LOADS AND I CAN REST!
(PUFF) JUST GOT BACK IN TIME!
RIGHT HERE, WAITER! WE'RE READY TO TO ORDER.
DID YOU SAY AVO-CADO CRAB-MEAT, VERONICA!
OH MY GOSH! THAT'S $5 A PLATE AN I HAVE ONLY $7.25 LEFT OF MY $12 SALARY!
I'D BETTER GIVE THE ORDER TO PIERRE, THE CHEF, MYSELF SO IT WILL BE JUST RIGHT!
GOODNESS ARCHIE! DO YOU KNOW THE CHEF TOO?
WHAT A SPOT!---ENTER-TAINING A SUB-DEB, AN' BEIN' A BUS-BOY AT THE SAME TIME!
4

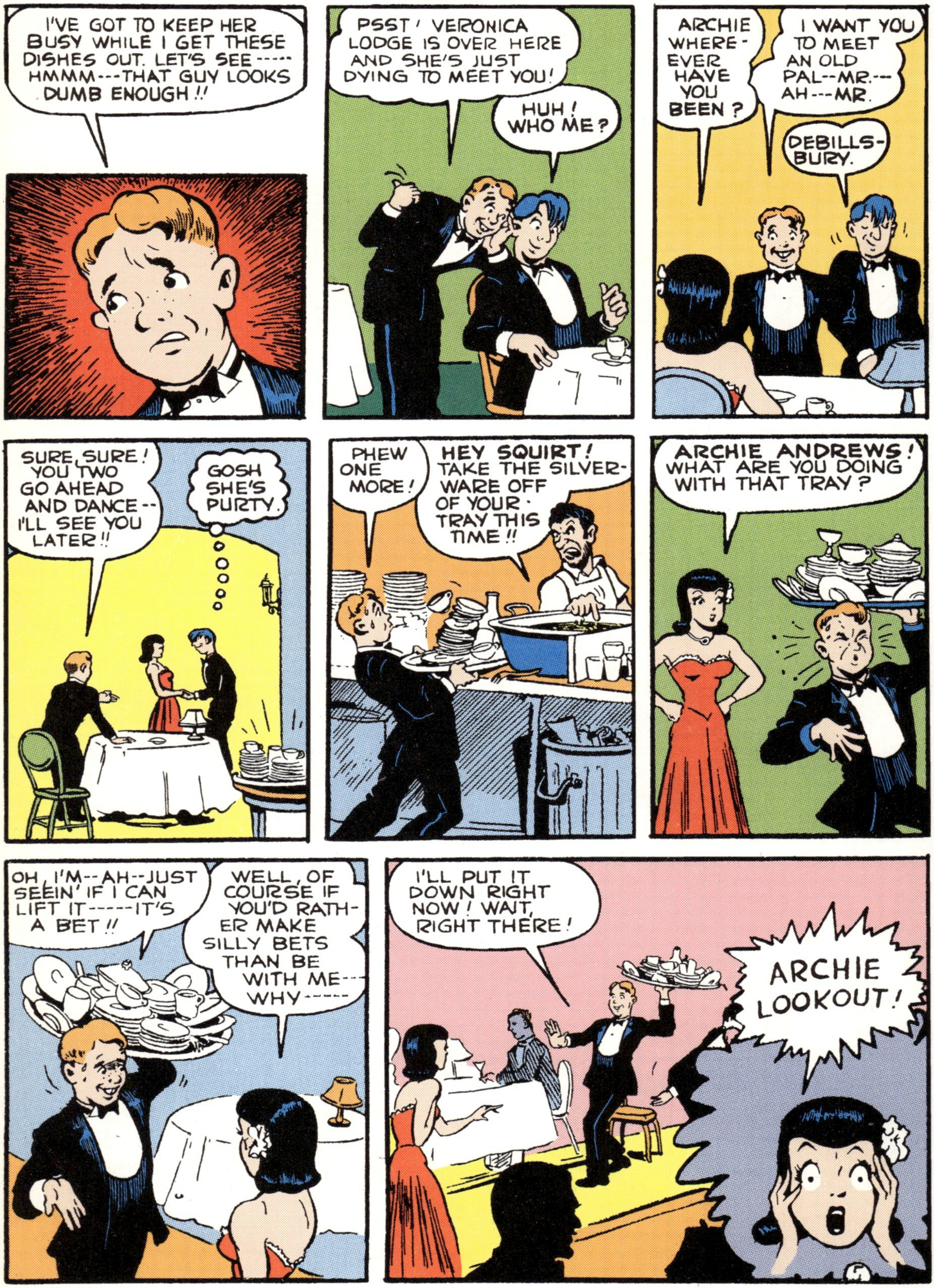
I'VE GOT TO KEEP HER BUSY WHILE I GET THESE DISHES OUT. LET'S SEE ----- HMMM---THAT GUY LOOKS DUMB ENOUGH !!
PSST! VERONICA LODGE IS OVER HERE AND SHE'S JUST DYING TO MEET YOU!
HUH! WHO ME?
ARCHIE WHERE-EVER HAVE YOU BEEN?
I WANT YOU TO MEET AN OLD PAL--MR.--- AH---MR.
DEBILLS-BURY.
SURE, SURE! YOU TWO GO AHEAD AND DANCE-- I'LL SEE YOU LATER!!
GOSH SHE'S PURTY.
PHEW ONE MORE!
HEY SQUIRT! TAKE THE SILVER-WARE OFF OF YOUR TRAY THIS TIME!!
ARCHIE ANDREWS! WHAT ARE YOU DOING WITH THAT TRAY?
OH, I'M--AH--JUST SEEIN' IF I CAN LIFT IT-----IT'S A BET!!
WELL, OF COURSE IF YOU'D RATH-ER MAKE SILLY BETS THAN BE WITH ME--- WHY-----
I'LL PUT IT DOWN RIGHT NOW! WAIT, RIGHT THERE!
ARCHIE LOOKOUT!
5

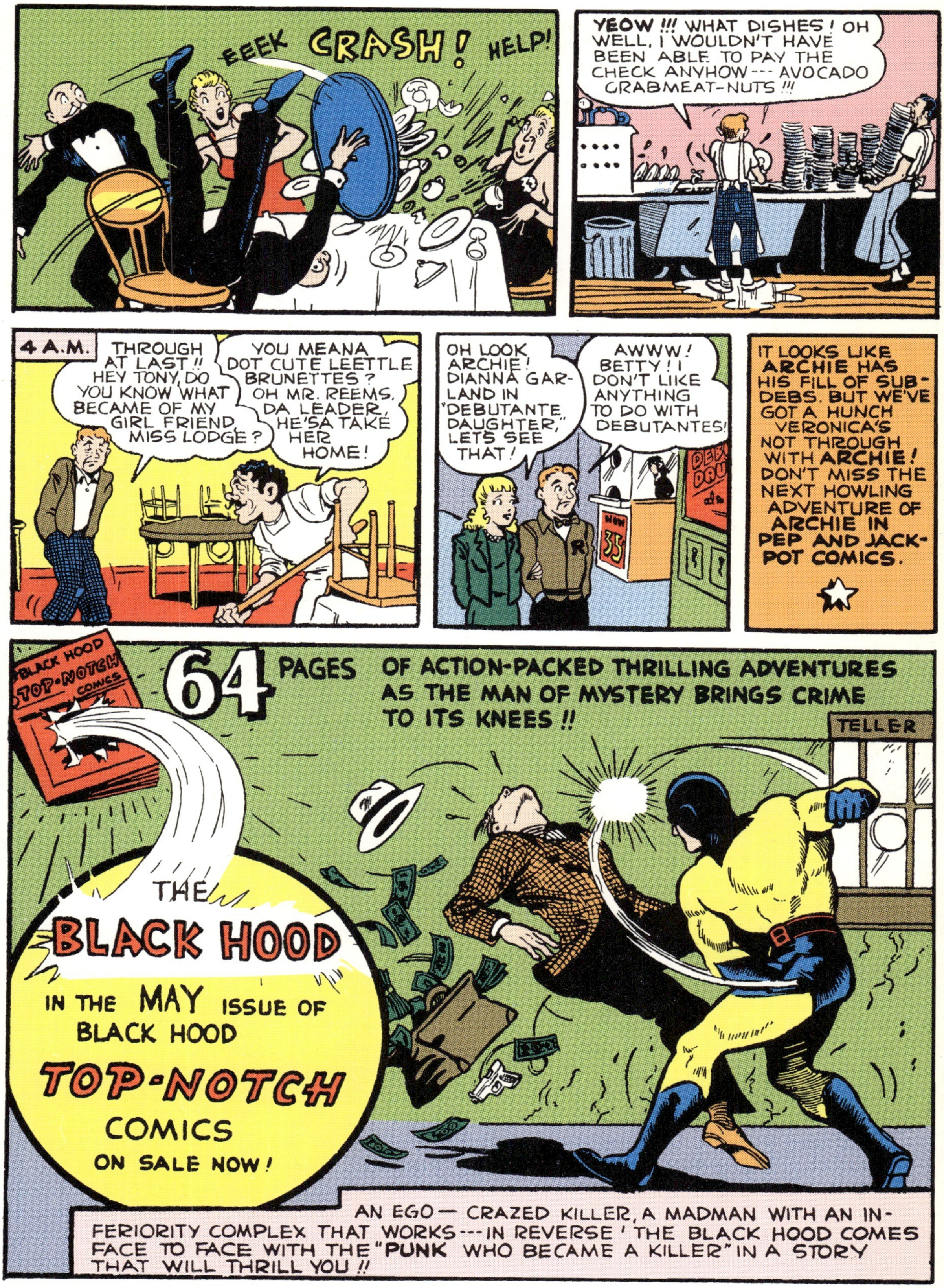
EEEK CRASH! HELP!
YEOW!!! WHAT DISHES! OH WELL, I WOULDN'T HAVE BEEN ABLE TO PAY THE CHECK ANYHOW--- AVOCADO CRABMEAT-NUTS!!!
4 A.M.
THROUGH AT LAST!! HEY TONY, DO YOU KNOW WHAT BECAME OF MY GIRL FRIEND, MISS LODGE?
YOU MEANA DOT CUTE LEETTLE BRUNETTES? OH MR. REEMS, DA LEADER, HE'SA TAKE HER HOME!
OH LOOK ARCHIE! DIANNA GARLAND IN "DEBUTANTE DAUGHTER," LETS SEE THAT!
AWWW! BETTY! I DON'T LIKE ANYTHING TO DO WITH DEBUTANTES!
IT LOOKS LIKE ARCHIE HAS HIS FILL OF SUB-DEBS. BUT WE'VE GOT A HUNCH VERONICA'S NOT THROUGH WITH ARCHIE! DON'T MISS THE NEXT HOWLING ADVENTURE OF ARCHIE IN PEP AND JACKPOT COMICS.
BLACK HOOD TOP-NOTCH COMICS
64 PAGES OF ACTION-PACKED THRILLING ADVENTURES AS THE MAN OF MYSTERY BRINGS CRIME TO ITS KNEES!!
TELLER
THE BLACK HOOD IN THE MAY ISSUE OF BLACK HOOD TOP-NOTCH COMICS ON SALE NOW!
AN EGO— CRAZED KILLER, A MADMAN WITH AN INFERIORITY COMPLEX THAT WORKS---IN REVERSE! THE BLACK HOOD COMES FACE TO FACE WITH THE "PUNK WHO BECAME A KILLER" IN A STORY THAT WILL THRILL YOU!!

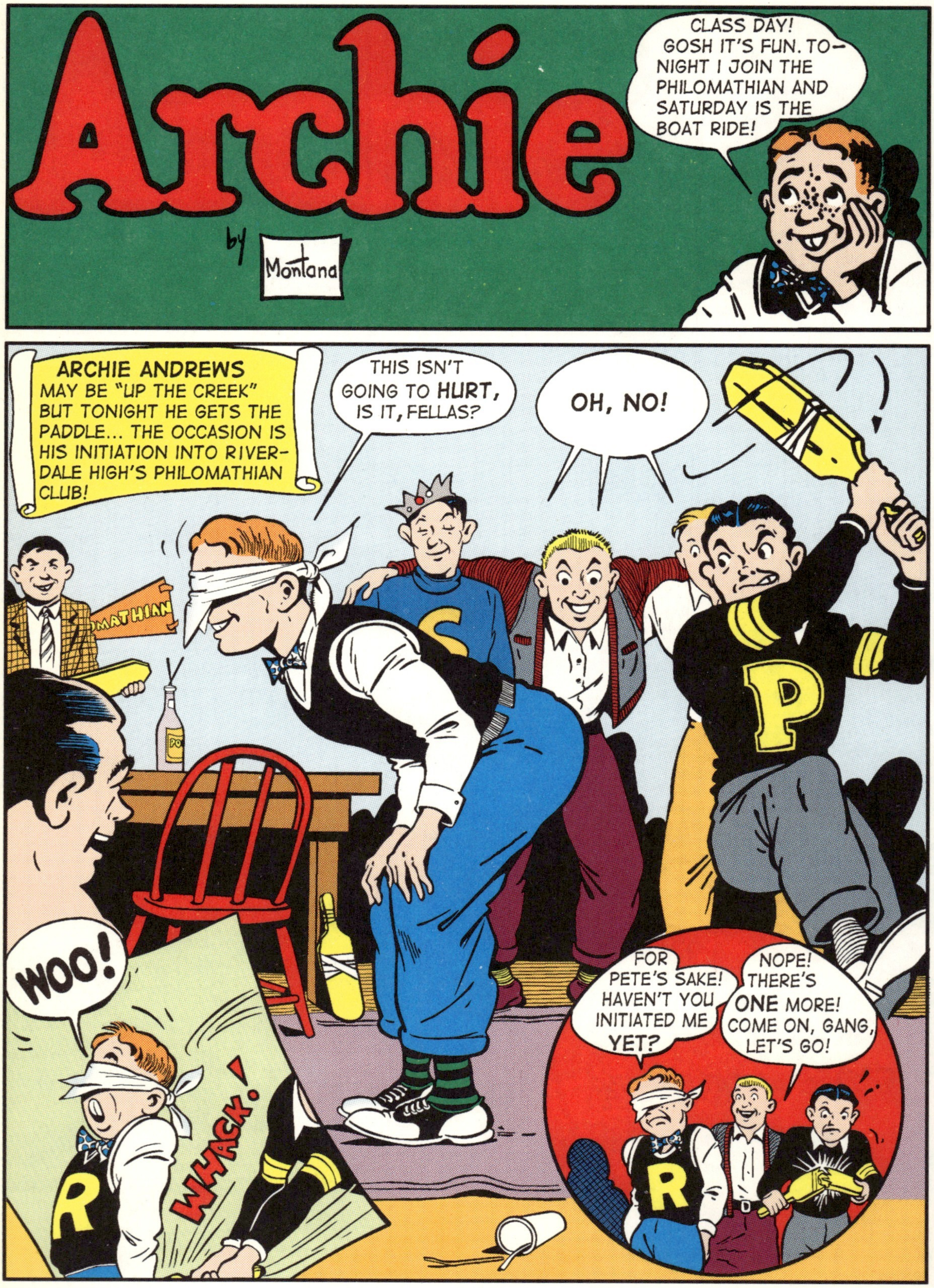
Archie
by
Montana
CLASS DAY! GOSH IT'S FUN. TO-NIGHT I JOIN THE PHILOMATHIAN AND SATURDAY IS THE BOAT RIDE!
ARCHIE ANDREWS MAY BE "UP THE CREEK" BUT TONIGHT HE GETS THE PADDLE... THE OCCASION IS HIS INITIATION INTO RIVER-DALE HIGH'S PHILOMATHIAN CLUB!
THIS ISN'T GOING TO HURT, IS IT, FELLAS?
OH, NO!
MATHIAN
P
WOO!
WHACK!
R
FOR PETE'S SAKE! HAVEN'T YOU INITIATED ME YET?
NOPE! THERE'S ONE MORE! COME ON, GANG, LET'S GO!
R

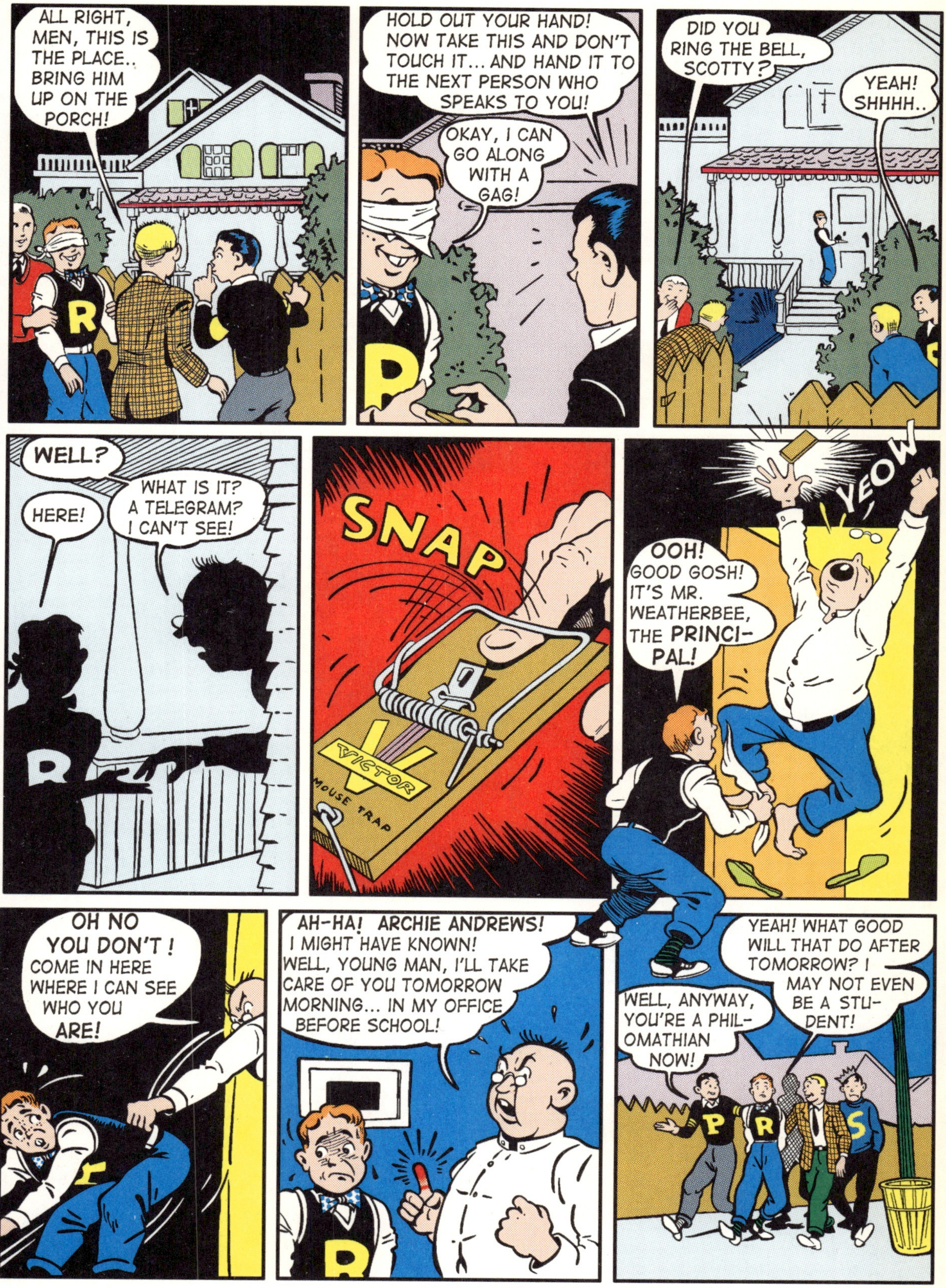
ALL RIGHT, MEN, THIS IS THE PLACE.. BRING HIM UP ON THE PORCH!
HOLD OUT YOUR HAND! NOW TAKE THIS AND DON'T TOUCH IT... AND HAND IT TO THE NEXT PERSON WHO SPEAKS TO YOU!
OKAY, I CAN GO ALONG WITH A GAG!
DID YOU RING THE BELL, SCOTTY?
YEAH! SHHHH..
WELL?
HERE!
WHAT IS IT? A TELEGRAM? I CAN'T SEE!
SNAP
VICTOR
MOUSE TRAP
YEOW
OOH! GOOD GOSH! IT'S MR. WEATHERBEE, THE PRINCI-PAL!
OH NO YOU DON'T! COME IN HERE WHERE I CAN SEE WHO YOU ARE!
AH-HA! ARCHIE ANDREWS! I MIGHT HAVE KNOWN! WELL, YOUNG MAN, I'LL TAKE CARE OF YOU TOMORROW MORNING... IN MY OFFICE BEFORE SCHOOL!
WELL, ANYWAY, YOU'RE A PHIL-OMATHIAN NOW!
YEAH! WHAT GOOD WILL THAT DO AFTER TOMORROW? I MAY NOT EVEN BE A STU-DENT!

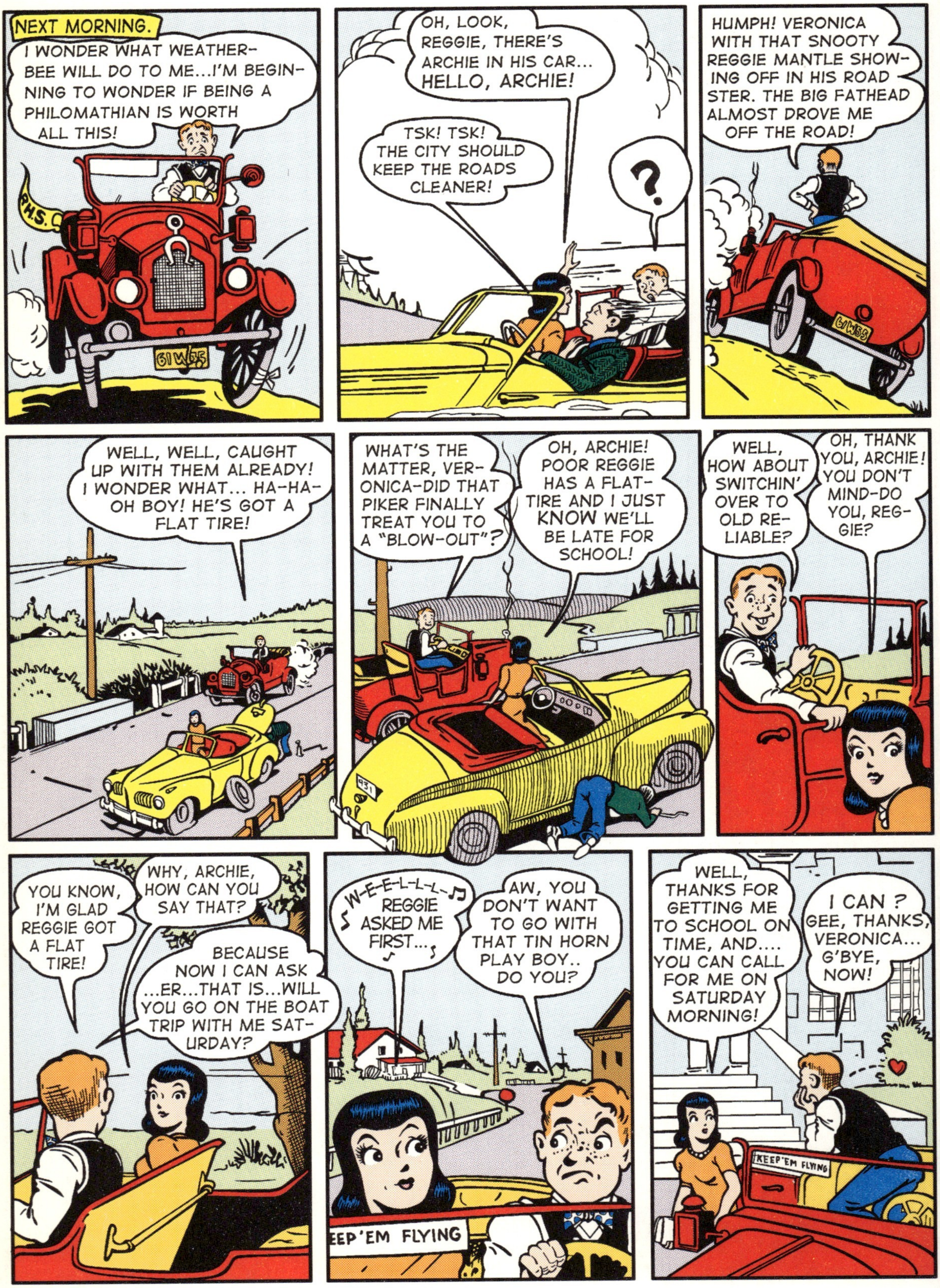
NEXT MORNING.
I WONDER WHAT WEATHERBEE WILL DO TO ME...I'M BEGINNING TO WONDER IF BEING A PHILOMATHIAN IS WORTH ALL THIS!
61 W35
OH, LOOK, REGGIE, THERE'S ARCHIE IN HIS CAR... HELLO, ARCHIE!
TSK! TSK! THE CITY SHOULD KEEP THE ROADS CLEANER!
?
HUMPH! VERONICA WITH THAT SNOOTY REGGIE MANTLE SHOWING OFF IN HIS ROAD STER. THE BIG FATHEAD ALMOST DROVE ME OFF THE ROAD!
WELL, WELL, CAUGHT UP WITH THEM ALREADY! I WONDER WHAT... HA-HA-OH BOY! HE'S GOT A FLAT TIRE!
WHAT'S THE MATTER, VERONICA-DID THAT PIKER FINALLY TREAT YOU TO A "BLOW-OUT"?
OH, ARCHIE! POOR REGGIE HAS A FLAT-TIRE AND I JUST KNOW WE'LL BE LATE FOR SCHOOL!
WELL, HOW ABOUT SWITCHIN' OVER TO OLD RELIABLE?
OH, THANK YOU, ARCHIE! YOU DON'T MIND-DO YOU, REGGIE?
YOU KNOW, I'M GLAD REGGIE GOT A FLAT TIRE!
WHY, ARCHIE, HOW CAN YOU SAY THAT?
BECAUSE NOW I CAN ASK ...ER...THAT IS...WILL YOU GO ON THE BOAT TRIP WITH ME SATURDAY?
W-E-E-L-L-L- REGGIE ASKED ME FIRST...
AW, YOU DON'T WANT TO GO WITH THAT TIN HORN PLAY BOY.. DO YOU?
EEP 'EM FLYING
WELL, THANKS FOR GETTING ME TO SCHOOL ON TIME, AND.... YOU CAN CALL FOR ME ON SATURDAY MORNING!
I CAN ? GEE, THANKS, VERONICA... G'BYE, NOW!
KEEP 'EM FLYING

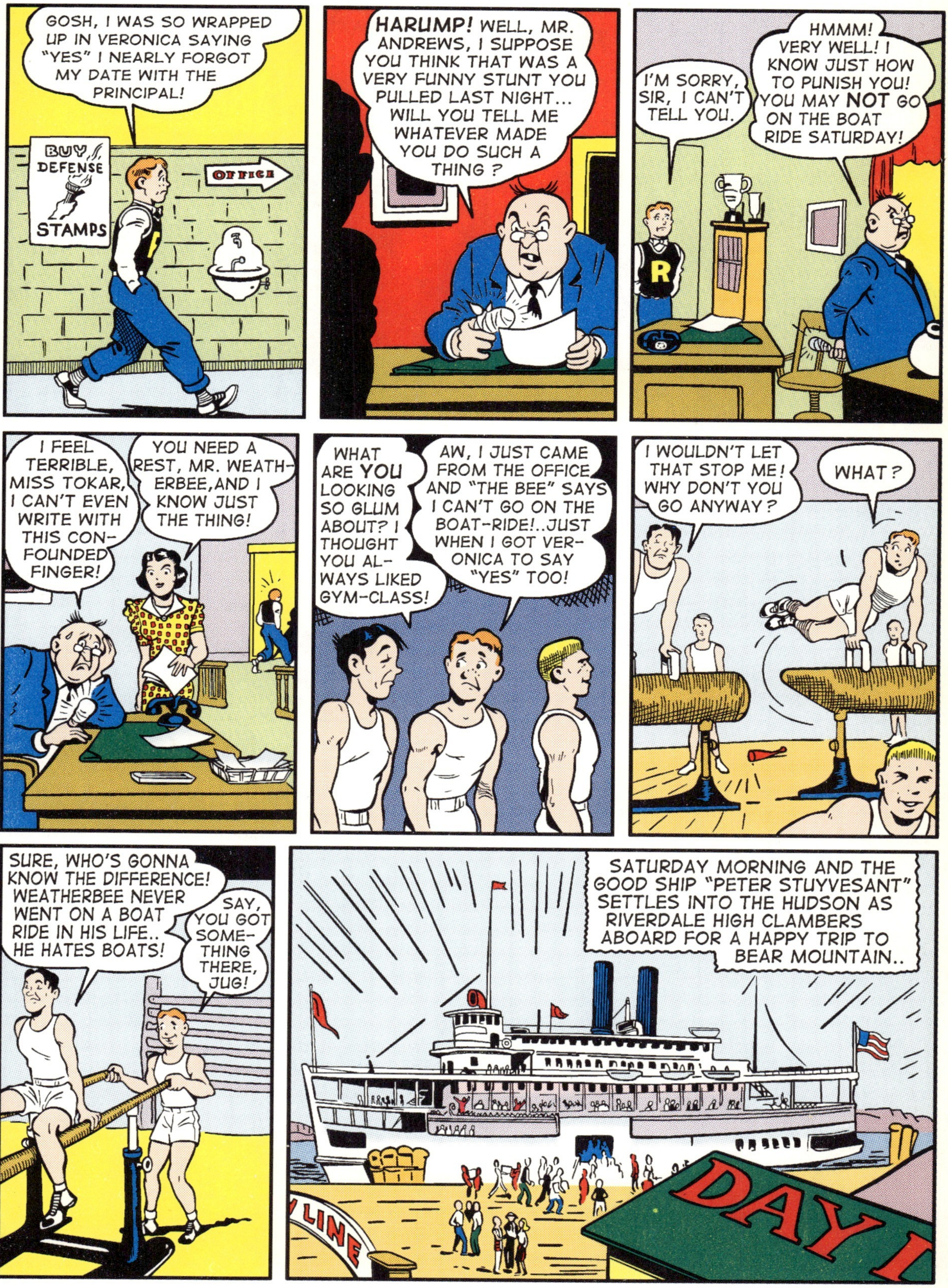

GOSH, I WAS SO WRAPPED UP IN VERONICA SAYING "YES" I NEARLY FORGOT MY DATE WITH THE PRINCIPAL!
BUY DEFENSE STAMPS
OFFICE
HARUMP! WELL, MR. ANDREWS, I SUPPOSE YOU THINK THAT WAS A VERY FUNNY STUNT YOU PULLED LAST NIGHT... WILL YOU TELL ME WHATEVER MADE YOU DO SUCH A THING ?
I'M SORRY, SIR, I CAN'T TELL YOU.
HMMM! VERY WELL! I KNOW JUST HOW TO PUNISH YOU! YOU MAY NOT GO ON THE BOAT RIDE SATURDAY!
I FEEL TERRIBLE, MISS TOKAR, I CAN'T EVEN WRITE WITH THIS CONFOUNDED FINGER!
YOU NEED A REST, MR. WEATHERBEE, AND I KNOW JUST THE THING!
WHAT ARE YOU LOOKING SO GLUM ABOUT? I THOUGHT YOU ALWAYS LIKED GYM-CLASS!
AW, I JUST CAME FROM THE OFFICE AND "THE BEE" SAYS I CAN'T GO ON THE BOAT-RIDE!..JUST WHEN I GOT VERONICA TO SAY "YES" TOO!
I WOULDN'T LET THAT STOP ME! WHY DON'T YOU GO ANYWAY ?
WHAT ?
SURE, WHO'S GONNA KNOW THE DIFFERENCE! WEATHERBEE NEVER WENT ON A BOAT RIDE IN HIS LIFE.. HE HATES BOATS!
SAY, YOU GOT SOMETHING THERE, JUG!
SATURDAY MORNING AND THE GOOD SHIP "PETER STUYVESANT" SETTLES INTO THE HUDSON AS RIVERDALE HIGH CLAMBERS ABOARD FOR A HAPPY TRIP TO BEAR MOUNTAIN..
LINE
DAY L

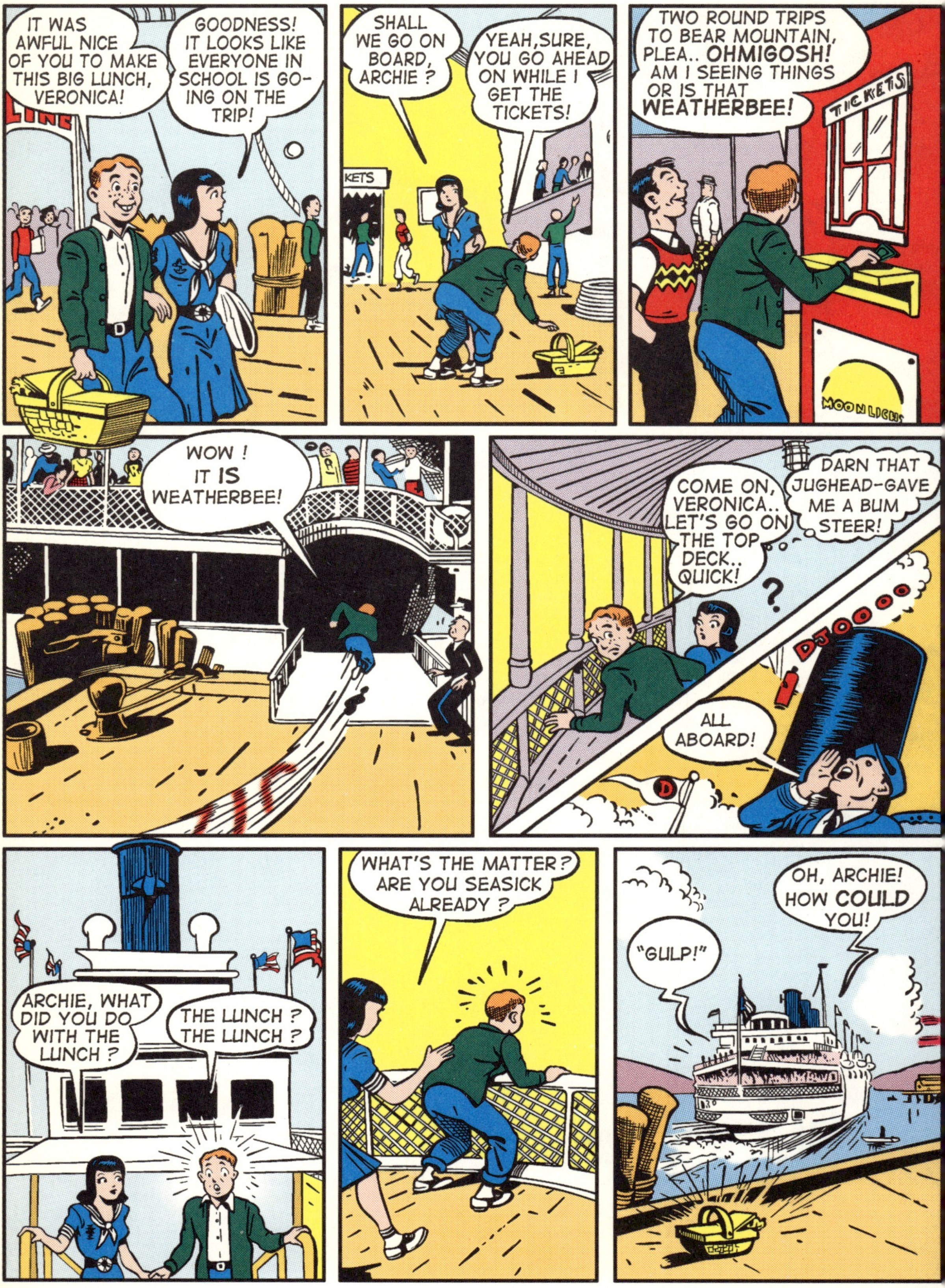

IT WAS AWFUL NICE OF YOU TO MAKE THIS BIG LUNCH, VERONICA!
GOODNESS! IT LOOKS LIKE EVERYONE IN SCHOOL IS GO-ING ON THE TRIP!
SHALL WE GO ON BOARD, ARCHIE ?
YEAH, SURE, YOU GO AHEAD ON WHILE I GET THE TICKETS!
KETS
TWO ROUND TRIPS TO BEAR MOUNTAIN, PLEA.. OHMIGOSH! AM I SEEING THINGS OR IS THAT WEATHERBEE!
TICKETS
MOONLIGHT
WOW ! IT IS WEATHERBEE!
COME ON, VERONICA.. LET'S GO ON THE TOP DECK.. QUICK!
DARN THAT JUGHEAD-GAVE ME A BUM STEER!
?
DJOOOO
ALL ABOARD!
ARCHIE, WHAT DID YOU DO WITH THE LUNCH ?
THE LUNCH ? THE LUNCH ?
WHAT'S THE MATTER? ARE YOU SEASICK ALREADY ?
OH, ARCHIE! HOW COULD YOU!
"GULP!"

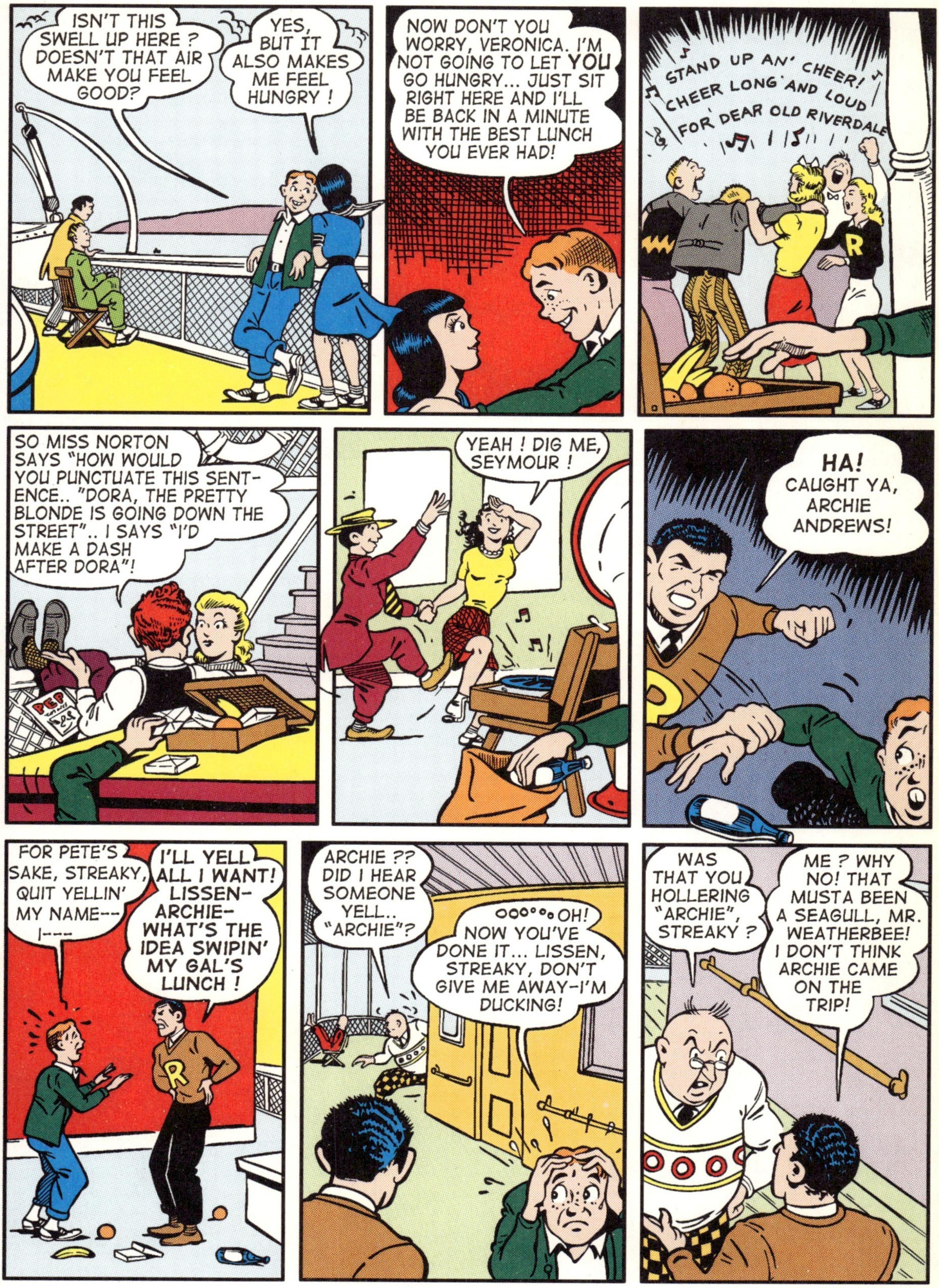
ISN'T THIS SWELL UP HERE ? DOESN'T THAT AIR MAKE YOU FEEL GOOD?
YES, BUT IT ALSO MAKES ME FEEL HUNGRY !
NOW DON'T YOU WORRY, VERONICA. I'M NOT GOING TO LET YOU GO HUNGRY... JUST SIT RIGHT HERE AND I'LL BE BACK IN A MINUTE WITH THE BEST LUNCH YOU EVER HAD!
STAND UP AN' CHEER! CHEER LONG AND LOUD FOR DEAR OLD RIVERDALE
SO MISS NORTON SAYS "HOW WOULD YOU PUNCTUATE THIS SENTENCE.. "DORA, THE PRETTY BLONDE IS GOING DOWN THE STREET".. I SAYS "I'D MAKE A DASH AFTER DORA"!
PEP
YEAH ! DIG ME, SEYMOUR !
HA! CAUGHT YA, ARCHIE ANDREWS!
FOR PETE'S SAKE, STREAKY, QUIT YELLIN' MY NAME-- I----
I'LL YELL ALL I WANT! LISSEN- ARCHIE- WHAT'S THE IDEA SWIPIN' MY GAL'S LUNCH !
ARCHIE ?? DID I HEAR SOMEONE YELL.. "ARCHIE"?
OOO°°O OH! NOW YOU'VE DONE IT... LISSEN, STREAKY, DON'T GIVE ME AWAY-I'M DUCKING!
WAS THAT YOU HOLLERING "ARCHIE", STREAKY ?
ME ? WHY NO! THAT MUSTA BEEN A SEAGULL, MR. WEATHERBEE! I DON'T THINK ARCHIE CAME ON THE TRIP!

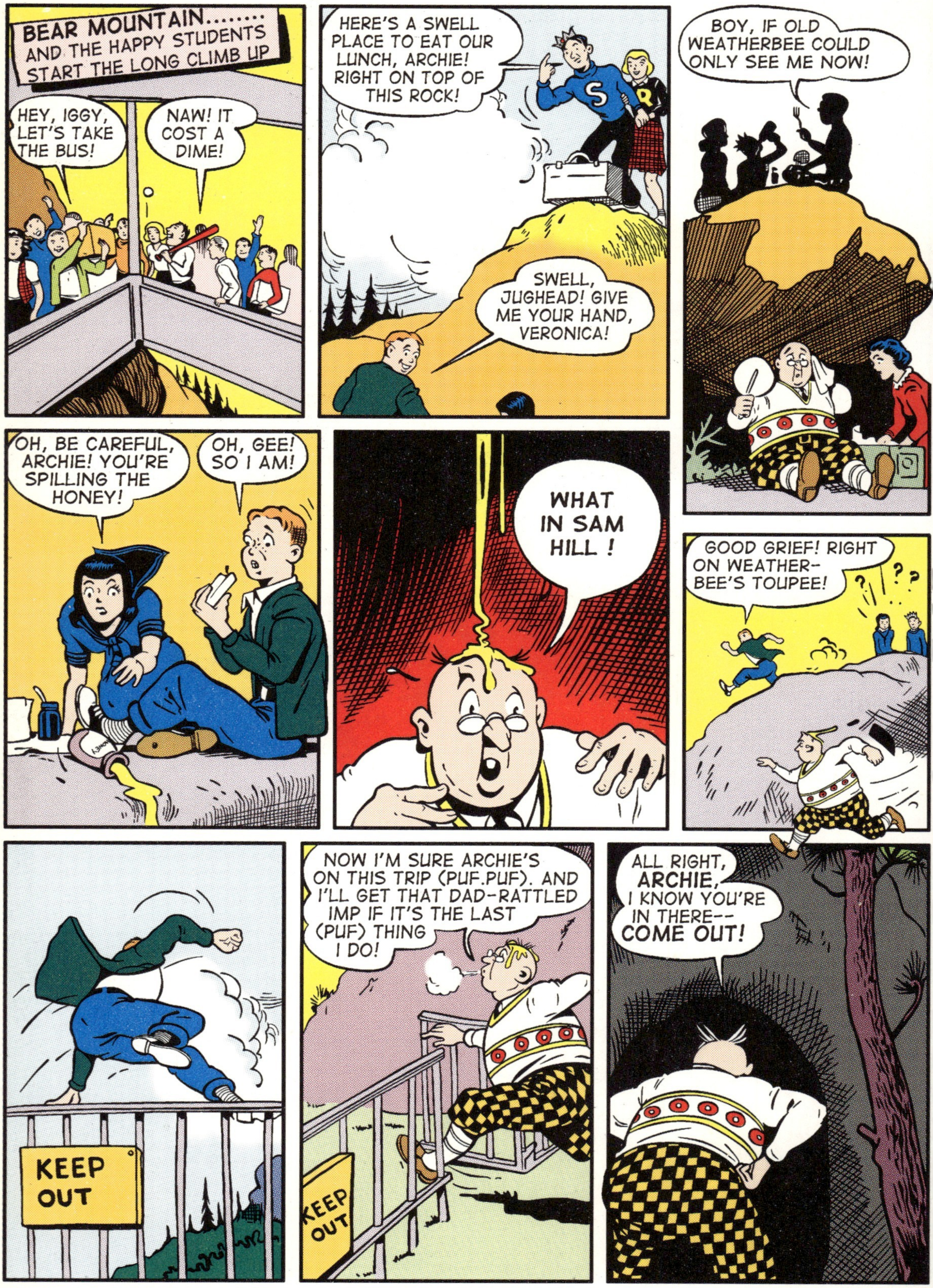
BEAR MOUNTAIN........ AND THE HAPPY STUDENTS START THE LONG CLIMB UP
HEY, IGGY, LET'S TAKE THE BUS!
NAW! IT COST A DIME!
HERE'S A SWELL PLACE TO EAT OUR LUNCH, ARCHIE! RIGHT ON TOP OF THIS ROCK!
SWELL, JUGHEAD! GIVE ME YOUR HAND, VERONICA!
BOY, IF OLD WEATHERBEE COULD ONLY SEE ME NOW!
OH, BE CAREFUL, ARCHIE! YOU'RE SPILLING THE HONEY!
OH, GEE! SO I AM!
WHAT IN SAM HILL !
GOOD GRIEF! RIGHT ON WEATHER-BEE'S TOUPEE!
KEEP OUT
NOW I'M SURE ARCHIE'S ON THIS TRIP (PUF.PUF). AND I'LL GET THAT DAD-RATTLED IMP IF IT'S THE LAST (PUF) THING I DO!
KEEP OUT
ALL RIGHT, ARCHIE, I KNOW YOU'RE IN THERE-- COME OUT!

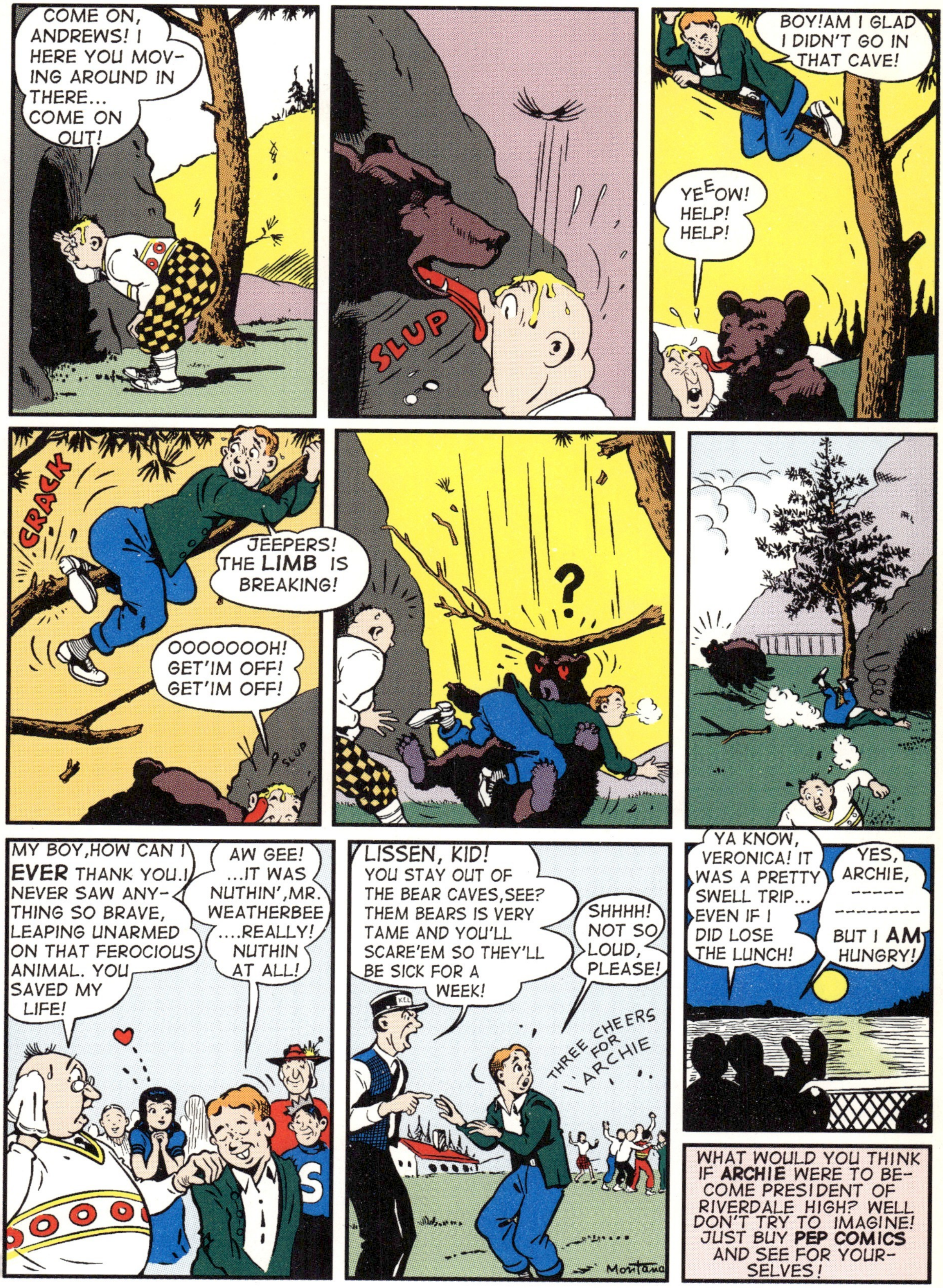
COME ON, ANDREWS! I HERE YOU MOVING AROUND IN THERE... COME ON OUT!
SLUP
BOY! AM I GLAD I DIDN'T GO IN THAT CAVE!
YEEOW! HELP! HELP!
CRACK
JEEPERS! THE LIMB IS BREAKING!
OOOOOOOH! GET'IM OFF! GET'IM OFF!
SLUP
?
MY BOY, HOW CAN I EVER THANK YOU..I NEVER SAW ANYTHING SO BRAVE, LEAPING UNARMED ON THAT FEROCIOUS ANIMAL. YOU SAVED MY LIFE!
AW GEE! ...IT WAS NUTHIN', MR. WEATHERBEE ....REALLY! NUTHIN AT ALL!
LISSEN, KID! YOU STAY OUT OF THE BEAR CAVES, SEE? THEM BEARS IS VERY TAME AND YOU'LL SCARE'EM SO THEY'LL BE SICK FOR A WEEK!
SHHHH! NOT SO LOUD, PLEASE!
THREE CHEERS FOR ARCHIE
Montana
YA KNOW, VERONICA! IT WAS A PRETTY SWELL TRIP... EVEN IF I DID LOSE THE LUNCH!
YES, ARCHIE, ----- --------- BUT I AM HUNGRY!
WHAT WOULD YOU THINK IF ARCHIE WERE TO BECOME PRESIDENT OF RIVERDALE HIGH? WELL DON'T TRY TO IMAGINE! JUST BUY PEP COMICS AND SEE FOR YOURSELVES!

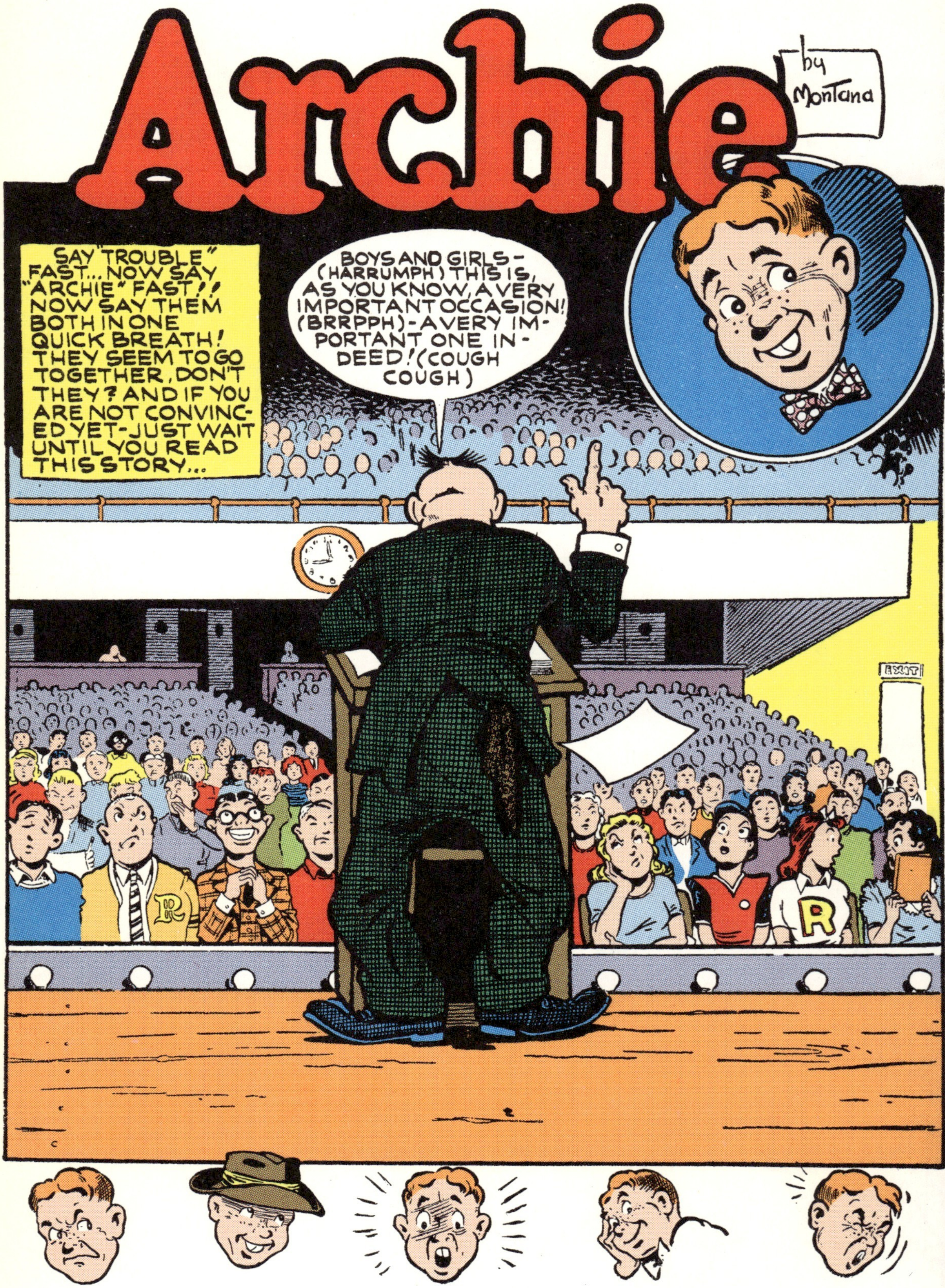
Archie
by Montana
SAY "TROUBLE" FAST... NOW SAY "ARCHIE" FAST!! NOW SAY THEM BOTH IN ONE QUICK BREATH! THEY SEEM TO GO TOGETHER, DON'T THEY? AND IF YOU ARE NOT CONVINCED YET-JUST WAIT UNTIL YOU READ THIS STORY...
BOYS AND GIRLS-(HARRUMPH) THIS IS, AS YOU KNOW, A VERY IMPORTANT OCCASION! (BRRPPH)-A VERY IMPORTANT ONE INDEED! (COUGH COUGH)
EXIT

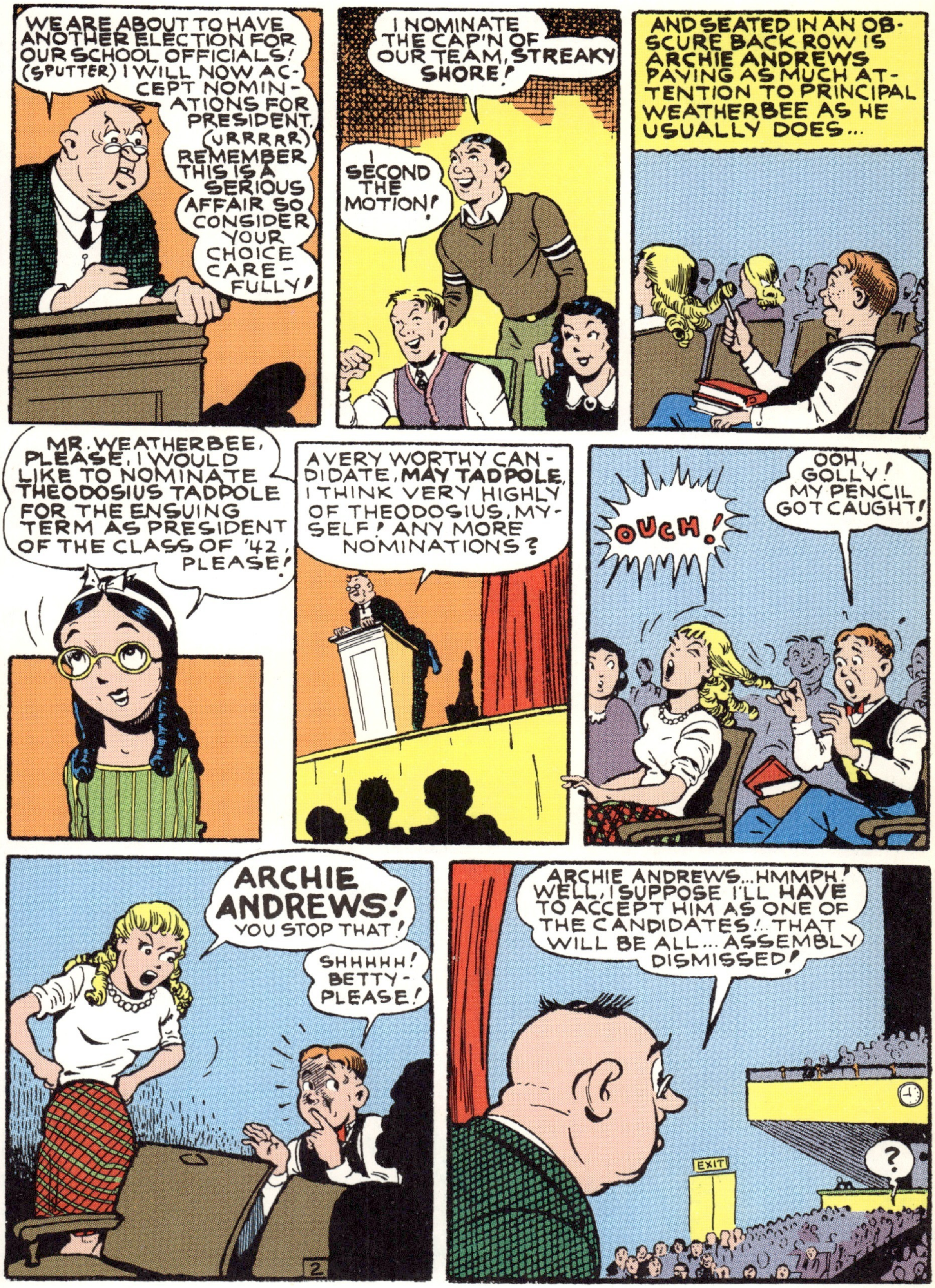

WE ARE ABOUT TO HAVE ANOTHER ELECTION FOR OUR SCHOOL OFFICIALS! (SPUTTER) I WILL NOW ACCEPT NOMINATIONS FOR PRESIDENT. (URRRRR) REMEMBER THIS IS A SERIOUS AFFAIR SO CONSIDER YOUR CHOICE CAREFULLY!
I NOMINATE THE CAP'N OF OUR TEAM, STREAKY SHORE!
I SECOND THE MOTION!
AND SEATED IN AN OBSCURE BACK ROW IS ARCHIE ANDREWS PAYING AS MUCH ATTENTION TO PRINCIPAL WEATHERBEE AS HE USUALLY DOES...
MR. WEATHERBEE, PLEASE, I WOULD LIKE TO NOMINATE THEODOSIUS TADPOLE FOR THE ENSUING TERM AS PRESIDENT OF THE CLASS OF '42, PLEASE!
A VERY WORTHY CANDIDATE, MAY TADPOLE, I THINK VERY HIGHLY OF THEODOSIUS, MYSELF! ANY MORE NOMINATIONS?
OUCH!
OOH, GOLLY! MY PENCIL GOT CAUGHT!
ARCHIE ANDREWS! YOU STOP THAT!
SHHHHH! BETTY-PLEASE!
2
ARCHIE ANDREWS...HMMPH! WELL, I SUPPOSE I'LL HAVE TO ACCEPT HIM AS ONE OF THE CANDIDATES!.. THAT WILL BE ALL... ASSEMBLY DISMISSED!
EXIT
?

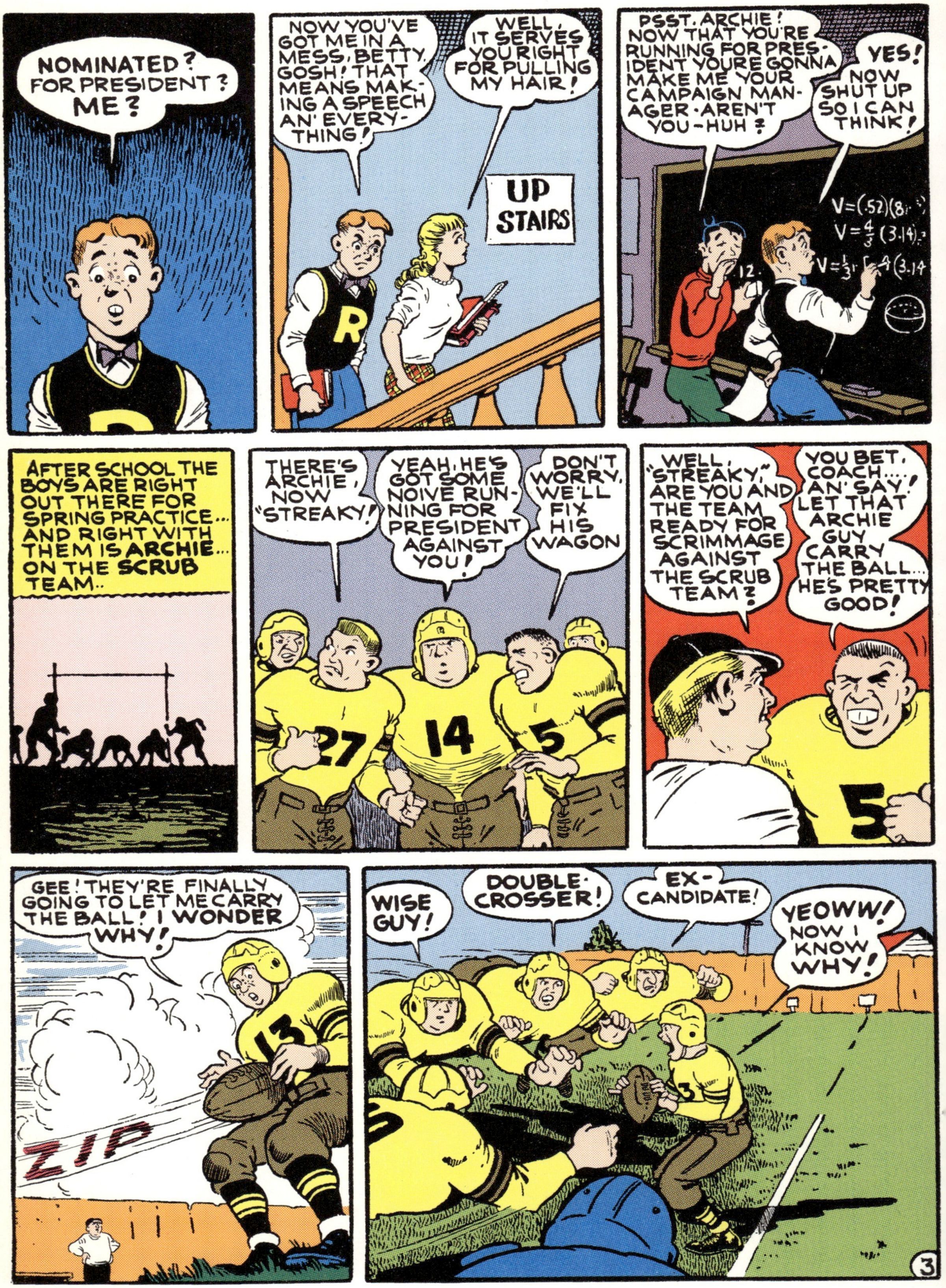
NOMINATED? FOR PRESIDENT? ME?
NOW YOU'VE GOT ME IN A MESS, BETTY. GOSH! THAT MEANS MAKING A SPEECH AN' EVERYTHING!
WELL, IT SERVES YOU RIGHT FOR PULLING MY HAIR!
UP STAIRS
PSST, ARCHIE! NOW THAT YOU'RE RUNNING FOR PRESIDENT YOU'RE GONNA MAKE ME YOUR CAMPAIGN MANAGER - AREN'T YOU - HUH?
YES! NOW SHUT UP SO I CAN THINK!
AFTER SCHOOL THE BOYS ARE RIGHT OUT THERE FOR SPRING PRACTICE... AND RIGHT WITH THEM IS ARCHIE... ON THE SCRUB TEAM..
THERE'S ARCHIE, NOW "STREAKY!"
YEAH, HE'S GOT SOME NOIVE RUNNING FOR PRESIDENT AGAINST YOU!
DON'T WORRY, WE'LL FIX HIS WAGON
WELL, "STREAKY," ARE YOU AND THE TEAM READY FOR SCRIMMAGE AGAINST THE SCRUB TEAM?
YOU BET, COACH.... AN' SAY! LET THAT ARCHIE GUY CARRY THE BALL... HE'S PRETTY GOOD!
GEE! THEY'RE FINALLY GOING TO LET ME CARRY THE BALL! I WONDER WHY!
ZIP
WISE GUY!
DOUBLE-CROSSER!
EX-CANDIDATE!
YEOWW! NOW I KNOW WHY!
3

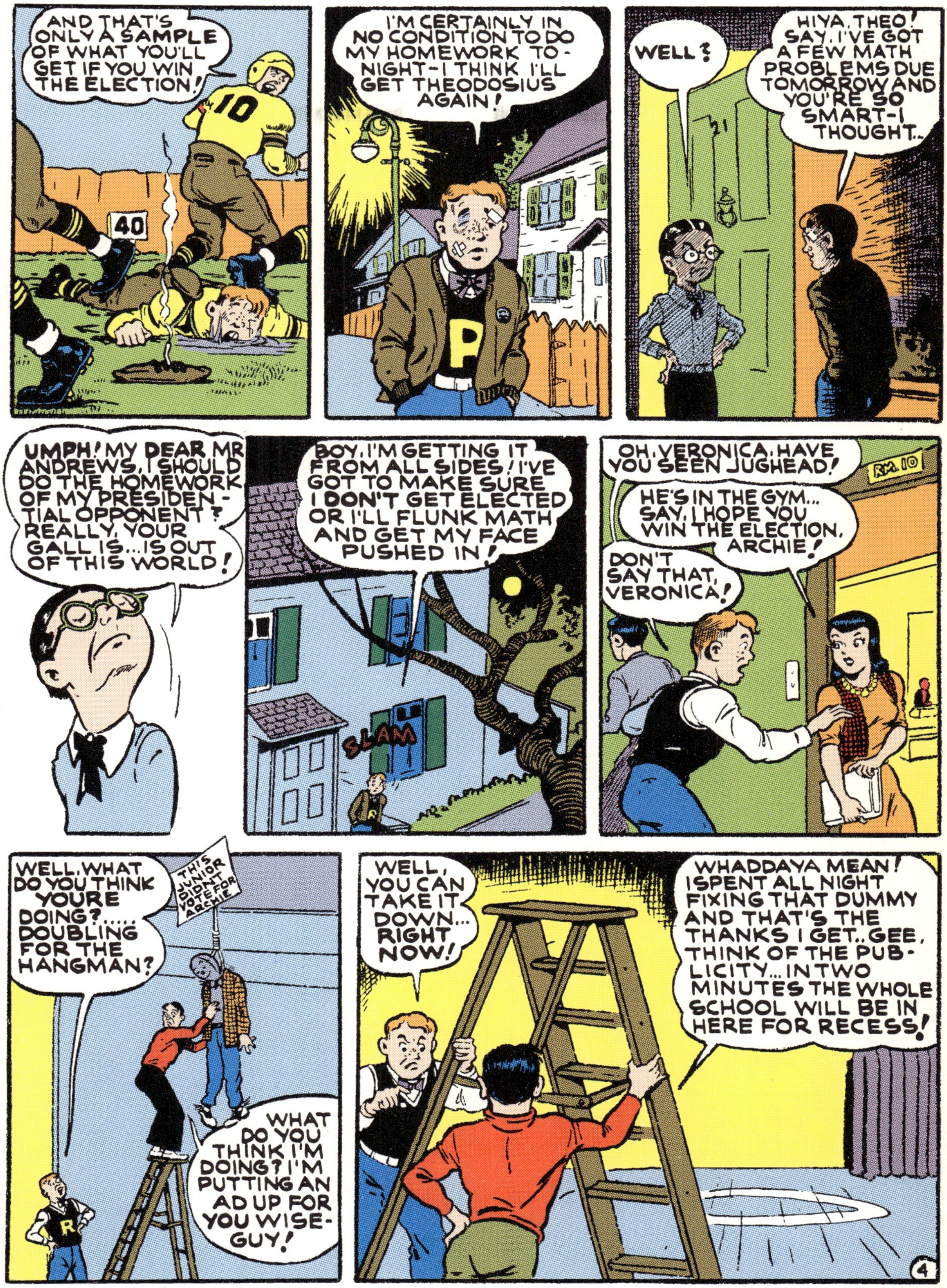
AND THAT'S ONLY A SAMPLE OF WHAT YOU'LL GET IF YOU WIN THE ELECTION!
10
40
I'M CERTAINLY IN NO CONDITION TO DO MY HOMEWORK TO-NIGHT-I THINK I'LL GET THEODOSIUS AGAIN!
P
WELL ?
HIYA, THEO! SAY, I'VE GOT A FEW MATH PROBLEMS DUE TOMORROW AND YOU'RE SO SMART-I THOUGHT..
21
UMPH! MY DEAR MR ANDREWS, I SHOULD DO THE HOMEWORK OF MY PRESIDEN-TIAL OPPONENT? REALLY, YOUR GALL IS...IS OUT OF THIS WORLD!
BOY, I'M GETTING IT FROM ALL SIDES! I'VE GOT TO MAKE SURE I DON'T GET ELECTED OR I'LL FLUNK MATH AND GET MY FACE PUSHED IN!
SLAM
R
OH, VERONICA, HAVE YOU SEEN JUGHEAD!
RM. 10
HE'S IN THE GYM... SAY, I HOPE YOU WIN THE ELECTION, ARCHIE!
DON'T SAY THAT, VERONICA!
WELL, WHAT DO YOU THINK YOURE DOING?..... DOUBLING FOR THE HANGMAN?
THIS JUNIOR DIDN'T VOTE FOR ARCHIE
R
WHAT DO YOU THINK I'M DOING? I'M PUTTING AN AD UP FOR YOU WISE-GUY!
WELL, YOU CAN TAKE IT DOWN... RIGHT NOW!
WHADDAYA MEAN! I SPENT ALL NIGHT FIXING THAT DUMMY AND THAT'S THE THANKS I GET.. GEE, THINK OF THE PUB-LICITY... IN TWO MINUTES THE WHOLE SCHOOL WILL BE IN HERE FOR RECESS!
4

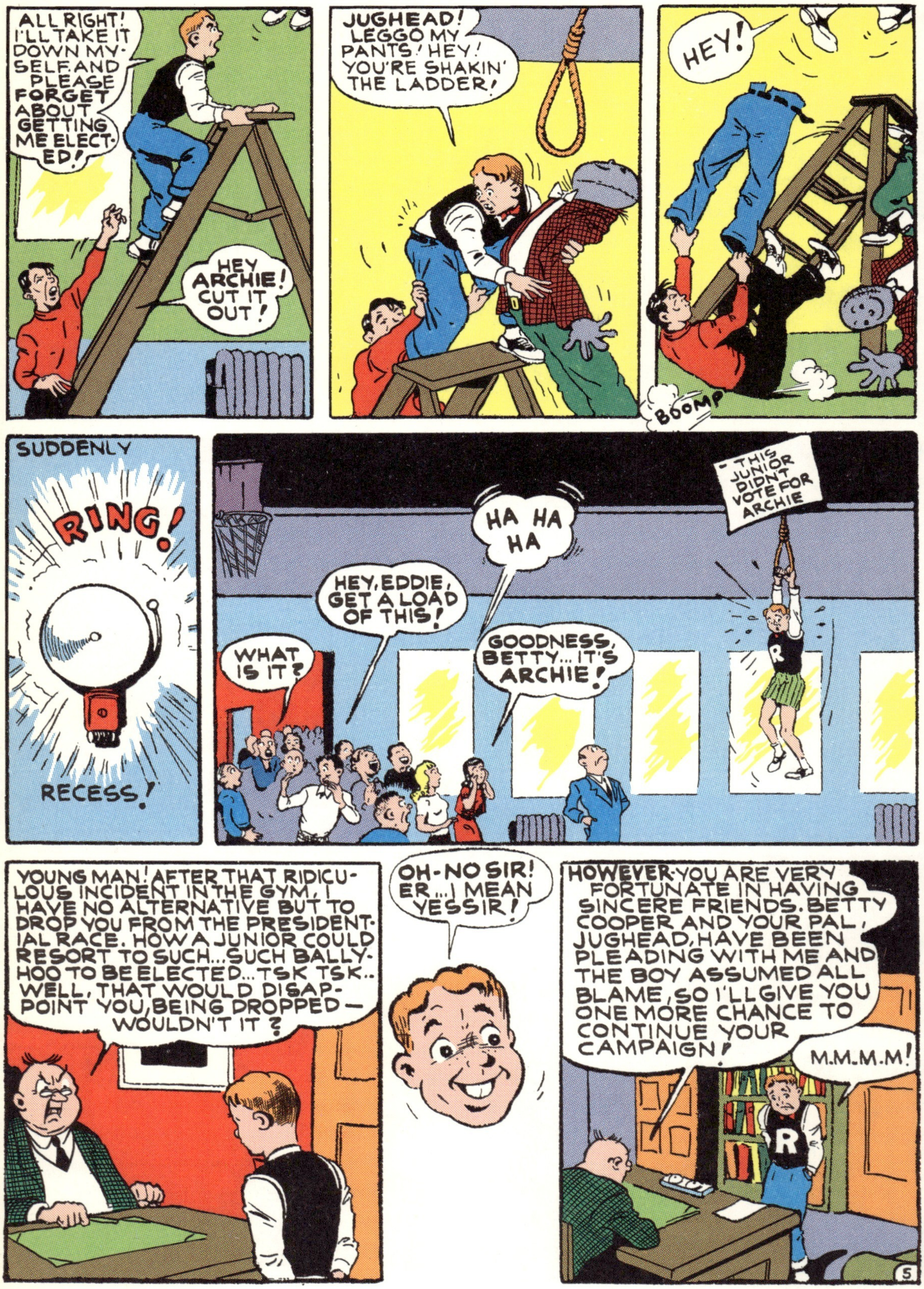
ALL RIGHT! I'LL TAKE IT DOWN MYSELF AND PLEASE FORGET ABOUT GETTING ME ELECTED!
HEY ARCHIE! CUT IT OUT!
JUGHEAD! LEGGO MY PANTS! HEY! YOU'RE SHAKIN' THE LADDER!
HEY!
BOOMP
SUDDENLY
RING!
RECESS!
THIS JUNIOR DIDN'T VOTE FOR ARCHIE
HA HA HA
HEY, EDDIE, GET A LOAD OF THIS!
WHAT IS IT?
GOODNESS, BETTY... IT'S ARCHIE!
YOUNG MAN! AFTER THAT RIDICULOUS INCIDENT IN THE GYM, I HAVE NO ALTERNATIVE BUT TO DROP YOU FROM THE PRESIDENTIAL RACE. HOW A JUNIOR COULD RESORT TO SUCH...SUCH BALLYHOO TO BE ELECTED... TSK TSK.. WELL, THAT WOULD DISAPPOINT YOU, BEING DROPPED — WOULDN'T IT?
OH-NO SIR! ER...I MEAN YESSIR!
HOWEVER-YOU ARE VERY FORTUNATE IN HAVING SINCERE FRIENDS. BETTY COOPER AND YOUR PAL, JUGHEAD, HAVE BEEN PLEADING WITH ME AND THE BOY ASSUMED ALL BLAME, SO I'LL GIVE YOU ONE MORE CHANCE TO CONTINUE YOUR CAMPAIGN!
M.M.M.M!
5

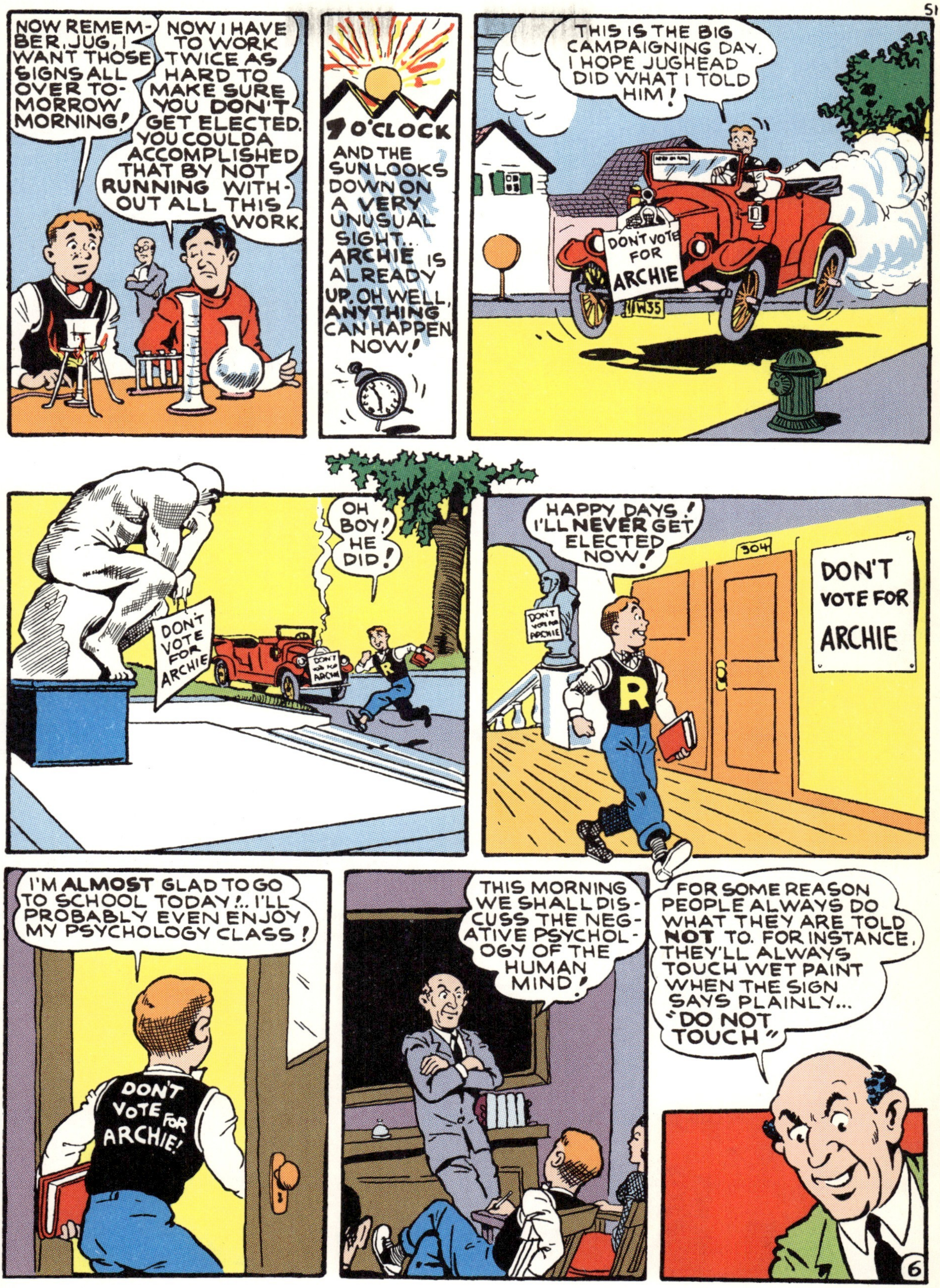
NOW REMEMBER, JUG, I WANT THOSE SIGNS ALL OVER TOMORROW MORNING!
NOW I HAVE TO WORK TWICE AS HARD TO MAKE SURE YOU DON'T GET ELECTED. YOU COULDA ACCOMPLISHED THAT BY NOT RUNNING WITHOUT ALL THIS WORK.
7 O'CLOCK AND THE SUN LOOKS DOWN ON A VERY UNUSUAL SIGHT.. ARCHIE IS ALREADY UP. OH WELL, ANYTHING CAN HAPPEN NOW!
THIS IS THE BIG CAMPAIGNING DAY. I HOPE JUGHEAD DID WHAT I TOLD HIM!
DON'T VOTE FOR ARCHIE
DON'T VOTE FOR ARCHIE
OH BOY! HE DID!
HAPPY DAYS! I'LL NEVER GET ELECTED NOW!
304
DON'T VOTE FOR ARCHIE
I'M ALMOST GLAD TO GO TO SCHOOL TODAY!.. I'LL PROBABLY EVEN ENJOY MY PSYCHOLOGY CLASS!
DON'T VOTE FOR ARCHIE!
THIS MORNING WE SHALL DISCUSS THE NEGATIVE PSYCHOLOGY OF THE HUMAN MIND!
FOR SOME REASON PEOPLE ALWAYS DO WHAT THEY ARE TOLD NOT TO. FOR INSTANCE, THEY'LL ALWAYS TOUCH WET PAINT WHEN THE SIGN SAYS PLAINLY... "DO NOT TOUCH"
6

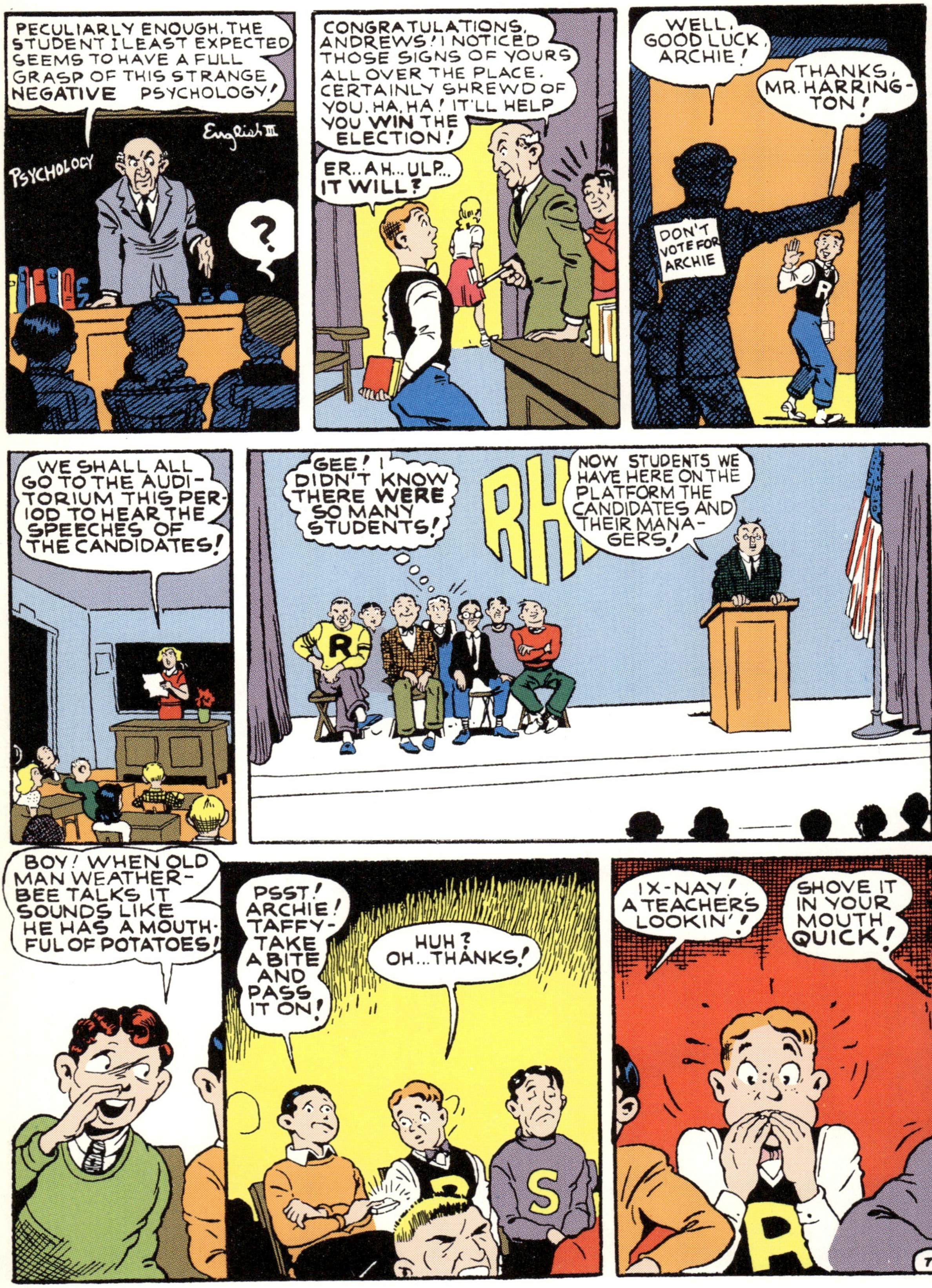
PECULIARLY ENOUGH, THE STUDENT I LEAST EXPECTED SEEMS TO HAVE A FULL GRASP OF THIS STRANGE NEGATIVE PSYCHOLOGY!
English III
PSYCHOLOGY
?
CONGRATULATIONS, ANDREWS! I NOTICED THOSE SIGNS OF YOURS ALL OVER THE PLACE. CERTAINLY SHREWD OF YOU. HA, HA! IT'LL HELP YOU WIN THE ELECTION!
ER.. AH... ULP... IT WILL?
WELL, GOOD LUCK, ARCHIE!
THANKS, MR. HARRINGTON!
DON'T VOTE FOR ARCHIE
WE SHALL ALL GO TO THE AUDITORIUM THIS PERIOD TO HEAR THE SPEECHES OF THE CANDIDATES!
GEE! I DIDN'T KNOW THERE WERE SO MANY STUDENTS!
RH
NOW STUDENTS WE HAVE HERE ON THE PLATFORM THE CANDIDATES AND THEIR MANAGERS!
BOY! WHEN OLD MAN WEATHERBEE TALKS IT SOUNDS LIKE HE HAS A MOUTHFUL OF POTATOES!
PSST! ARCHIE! TAFFY - TAKE A BITE AND PASS IT ON!
HUH? OH... THANKS!
IX-NAY! A TEACHER'S LOOKIN'!
SHOVE IT IN YOUR MOUTH QUICK!
7

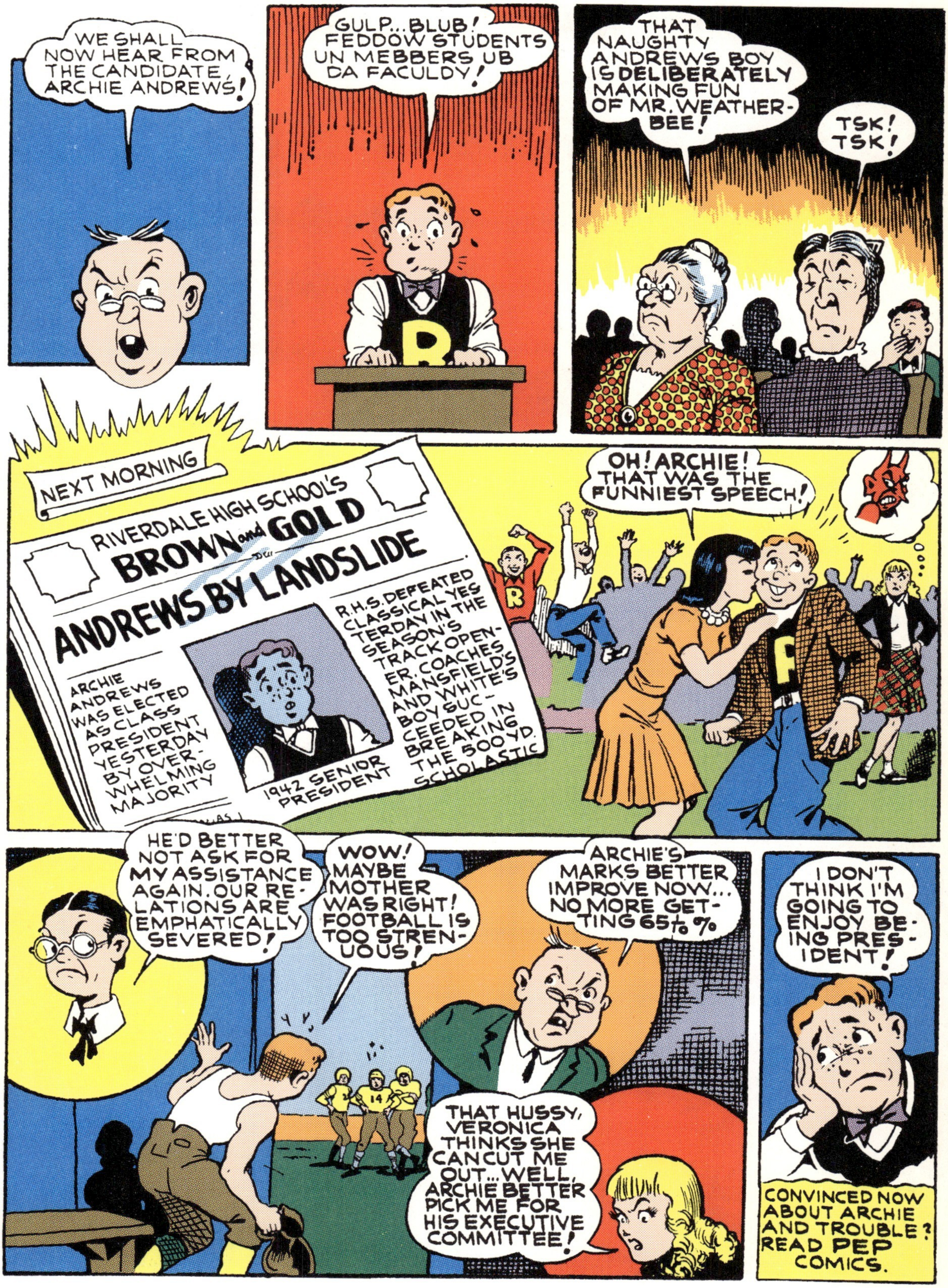
WE SHALL NOW HEAR FROM THE CANDIDATE, ARCHIE ANDREWS!
GULP...BLUB! FEDDOW STUDENTS UN MEBBERS UB DA FACULDY!
THAT NAUGHTY ANDREWS BOY IS DELIBERATELY MAKING FUN OF MR. WEATHER-BEE!
TSK! TSK!
NEXT MORNING
RIVERDALE HIGH SCHOOL'S
BROWN and GOLD
ANDREWS BY LANDSLIDE
ARCHIE ANDREWS WAS ELECTED AS CLASS PRESIDENT YESTERDAY BY OVER-WHELMING MAJORITY
1942 SENIOR PRESIDENT
R.H.S. DEFEATED CLASSICAL YES TERDAY IN THE SEASON'S TRACK OPEN-ER. COACHES MANSFIELD'S AND WHITE'S BOYS SUC-CEEDED IN BREAKING THE 500 YD. SCHOLASTIC
OH! ARCHIE! THAT WAS THE FUNNIEST SPEECH!
HE'D BETTER NOT ASK FOR MY ASSISTANCE AGAIN. OUR RE-LATIONS ARE EMPHATICALLY SEVERED!
WOW! MAYBE MOTHER WAS RIGHT! FOOTBALL IS TOO STREN-UOUS!
ARCHIE'S MARKS BETTER IMPROVE NOW... NO MORE GET-TING 65 1/10 %
THAT HUSSY, VERONICA THINKS SHE CAN CUT ME OUT... WELL, ARCHIE BETTER PICK ME FOR HIS EXECUTIVE COMMITTEE!
I DON'T THINK I'M GOING TO ENJOY BE-ING PRES-IDENT!
CONVINCED NOW ABOUT ARCHIE AND TROUBLE? READ PEP COMICS.

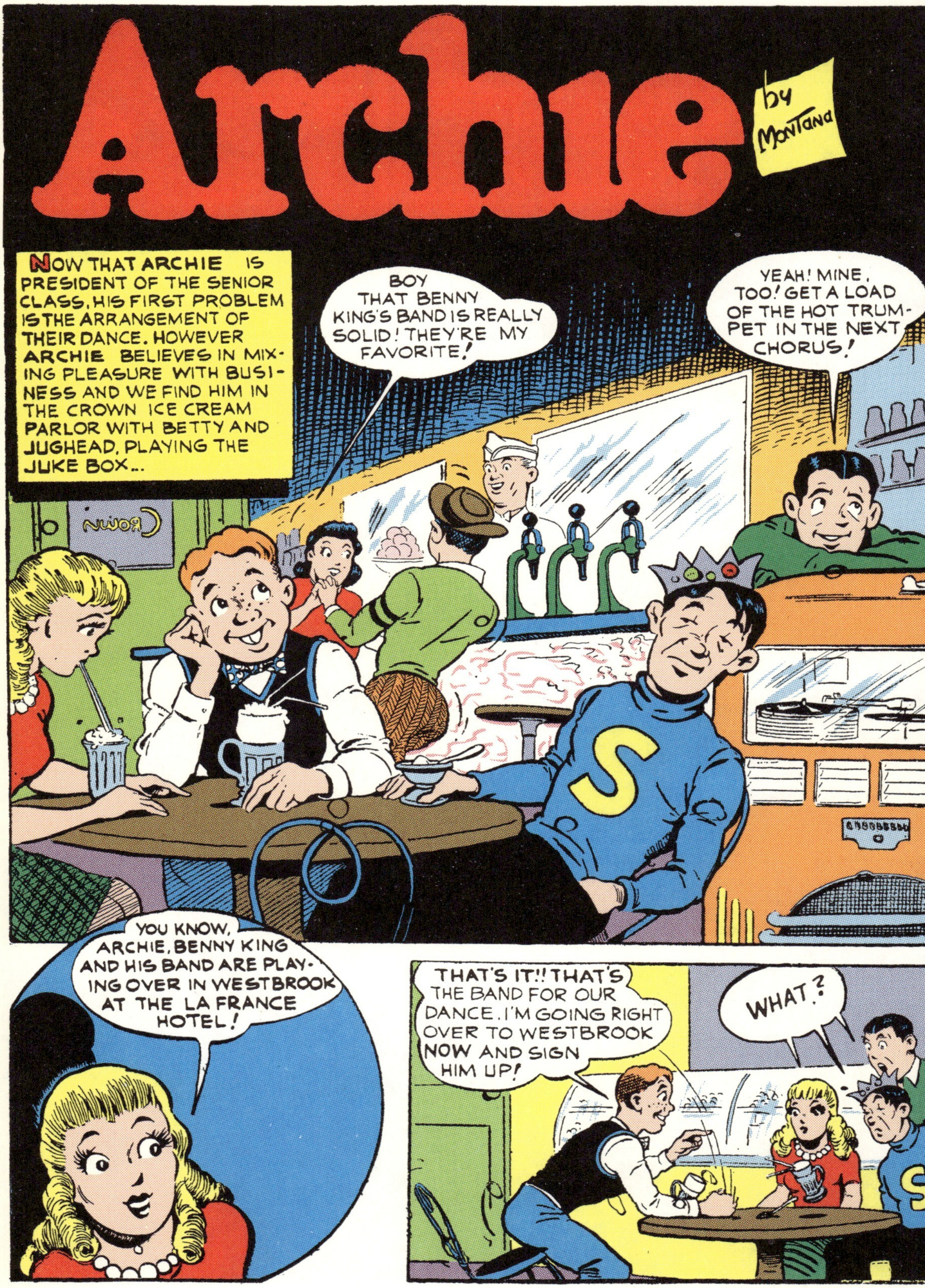
Archie
by Montana
NOW THAT ARCHIE IS PRESIDENT OF THE SENIOR CLASS, HIS FIRST PROBLEM IS THE ARRANGEMENT OF THEIR DANCE. HOWEVER ARCHIE BELIEVES IN MIXING PLEASURE WITH BUSINESS AND WE FIND HIM IN THE CROWN ICE CREAM PARLOR WITH BETTY AND JUGHEAD, PLAYING THE JUKE BOX...
BOY THAT BENNY KING'S BAND IS REALLY SOLID! THEY'RE MY FAVORITE!
YEAH! MINE, TOO! GET A LOAD OF THE HOT TRUMPET IN THE NEXT CHORUS!
YOU KNOW, ARCHIE, BENNY KING AND HIS BAND ARE PLAYING OVER IN WESTBROOK AT THE LA FRANCE HOTEL!
THAT'S IT!! THAT'S THE BAND FOR OUR DANCE. I'M GOING RIGHT OVER TO WESTBROOK NOW AND SIGN HIM UP!
WHAT?

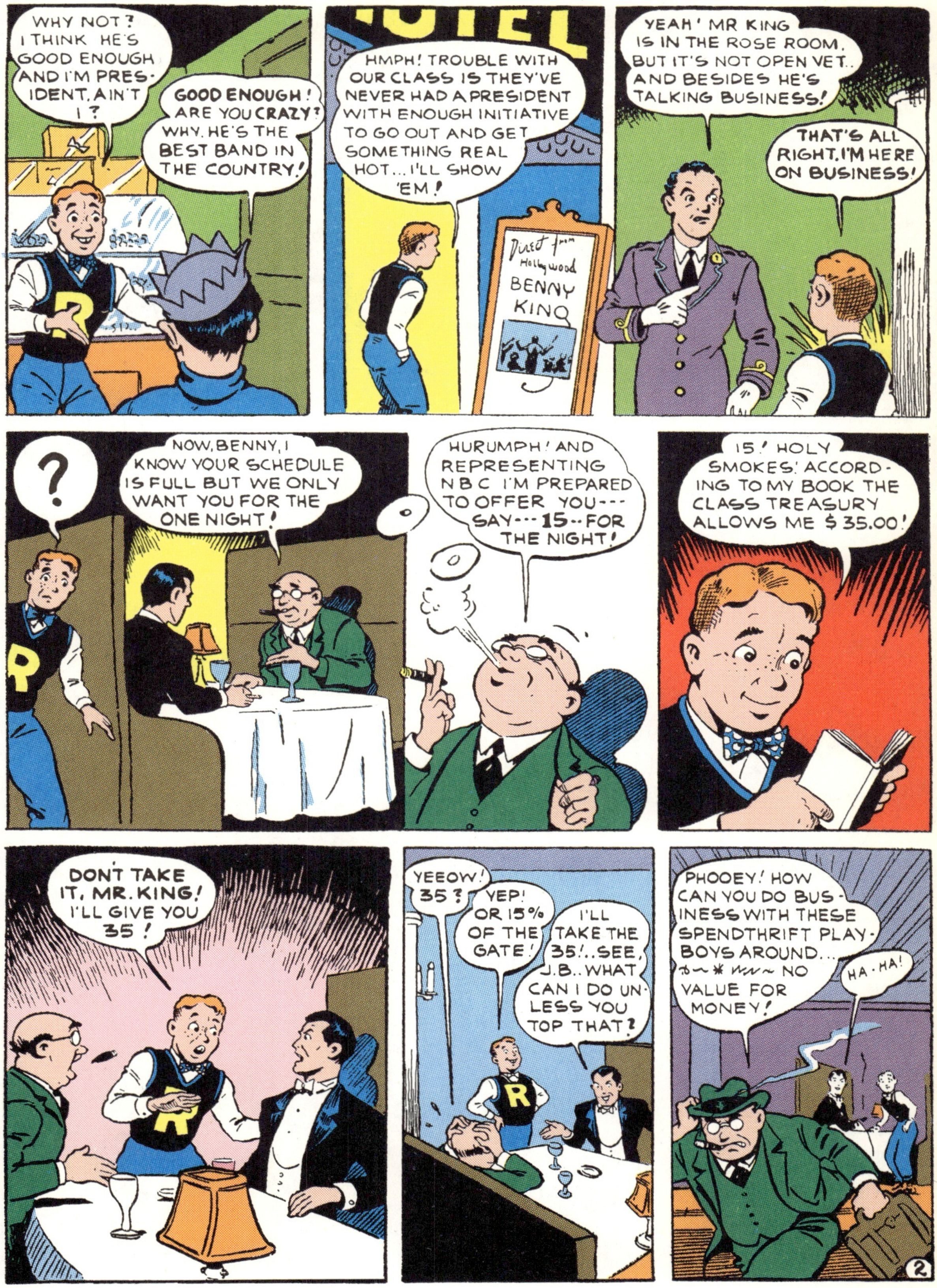

WHY NOT? I THINK HE'S GOOD ENOUGH AND I'M PRES-IDENT, AIN'T I?
GOOD ENOUGH! ARE YOU CRAZY? WHY, HE'S THE BEST BAND IN THE COUNTRY!
HMPH! TROUBLE WITH OUR CLASS IS THEY'VE NEVER HAD A PRESIDENT WITH ENOUGH INITIATIVE TO GO OUT AND GET SOMETHING REAL HOT... I'LL SHOW 'EM!
Direct from Hollywood
BENNY KING
YEAH! MR KING IS IN THE ROSE ROOM, BUT IT'S NOT OPEN YET.. AND BESIDES HE'S TALKING BUSINESS!
THAT'S ALL RIGHT, I'M HERE ON BUSINESS!
?
NOW, BENNY, I KNOW YOUR SCHEDULE IS FULL BUT WE ONLY WANT YOU FOR THE ONE NIGHT!
HURUMPH! AND REPRESENTING N B C I'M PREPARED TO OFFER YOU--- SAY--- 15 -- FOR THE NIGHT!
15! HOLY SMOKES! ACCORD-ING TO MY BOOK THE CLASS TREASURY ALLOWS ME $ 35.00!
DON'T TAKE IT, MR. KING! I'LL GIVE YOU 35!
YEEOW! 35?
YEP! OR 15% OF THE GATE!
I'LL TAKE THE 35!.. SEE, J.B.. WHAT CAN I DO UN-LESS YOU TOP THAT?
PHOOEY! HOW CAN YOU DO BUS-INESS WITH THESE SPENDTHRIFT PLAY-BOYS AROUND... NO VALUE FOR MONEY!
HA-HA!
2

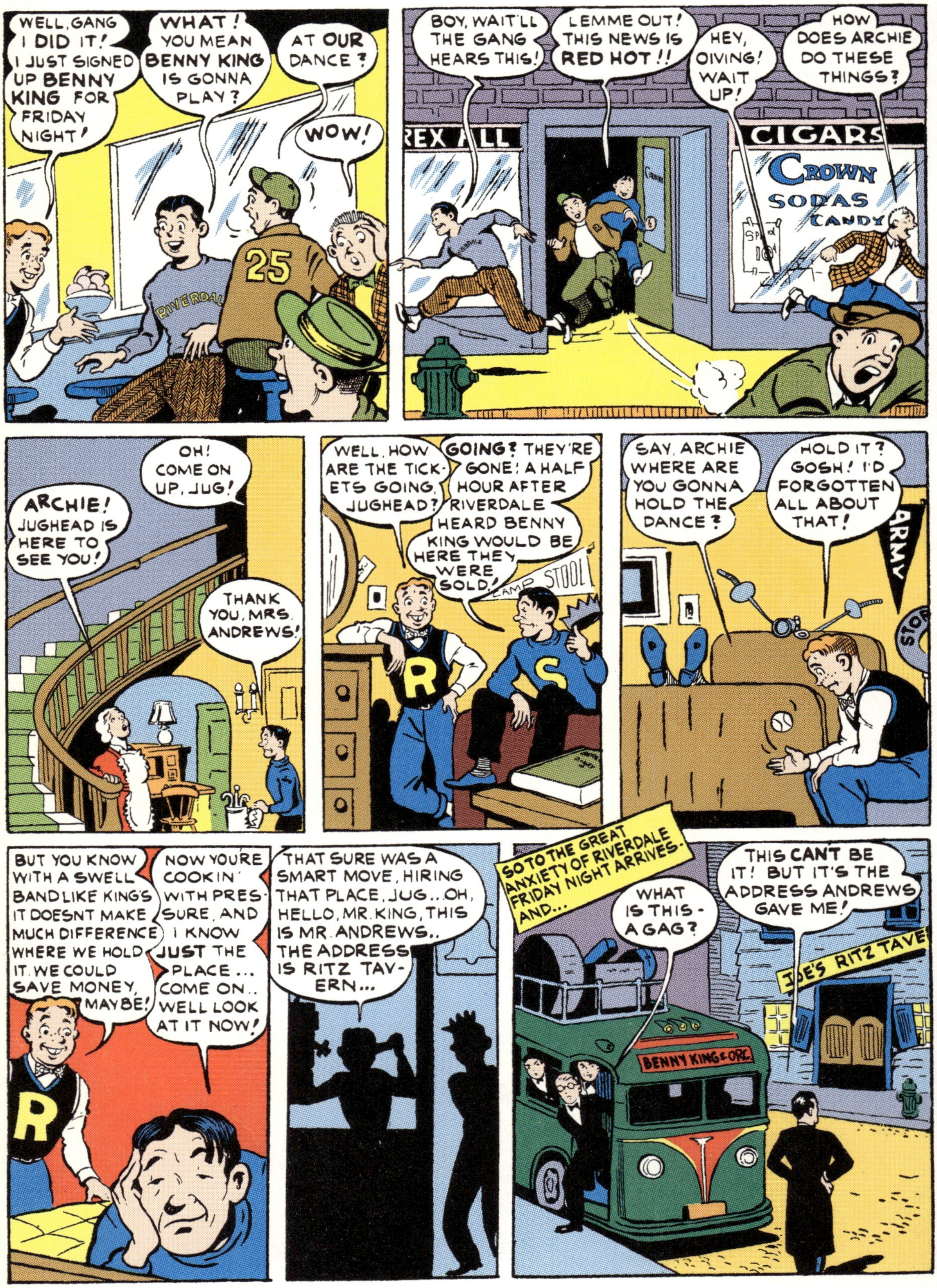
WELL, GANG I DID IT! I JUST SIGNED UP BENNY KING FOR FRIDAY NIGHT!
WHAT! YOU MEAN BENNY KING IS GONNA PLAY?
AT OUR DANCE?
WOW!
BOY, WAIT'LL THE GANG HEARS THIS!
LEMME OUT! THIS NEWS IS RED HOT!!
HEY, OIVING! WAIT UP!
HOW DOES ARCHIE DO THESE THINGS?
REX ALL
CIGARS
CROWN
SODAS
CANDY
OH! COME ON UP, JUG!
ARCHIE! JUGHEAD IS HERE TO SEE YOU!
THANK YOU, MRS. ANDREWS!
WELL, HOW ARE THE TICKETS GOING, JUGHEAD?
GOING? THEY'RE GONE! A HALF HOUR AFTER RIVERDALE HEARD BENNY KING WOULD BE HERE THEY WERE SOLD!
CAMP STOOL
SAY, ARCHIE WHERE ARE YOU GONNA HOLD THE DANCE?
HOLD IT? GOSH! I'D FORGOTTEN ALL ABOUT THAT!
ARMY
BUT YOU KNOW WITH A SWELL BAND LIKE KING'S IT DOESN'T MAKE MUCH DIFFERENCE WHERE WE HOLD IT. WE COULD SAVE MONEY, MAYBE!
NOW YOU'RE COOKIN' WITH PRESSURE, AND I KNOW JUST THE PLACE... COME ON.. WE'LL LOOK AT IT NOW!
THAT SURE WAS A SMART MOVE, HIRING THAT PLACE, JUG.. OH, HELLO, MR. KING, THIS IS MR. ANDREWS.. THE ADDRESS IS RITZ TAVERN...
SO TO THE GREAT ANXIETY OF RIVERDALE FRIDAY NIGHT ARRIVES. AND...
WHAT IS THIS - A GAG?
THIS CAN'T BE IT! BUT IT'S THE ADDRESS ANDREWS GAVE ME!
JOE'S RITZ TAVE
BENNY KING & ORC.

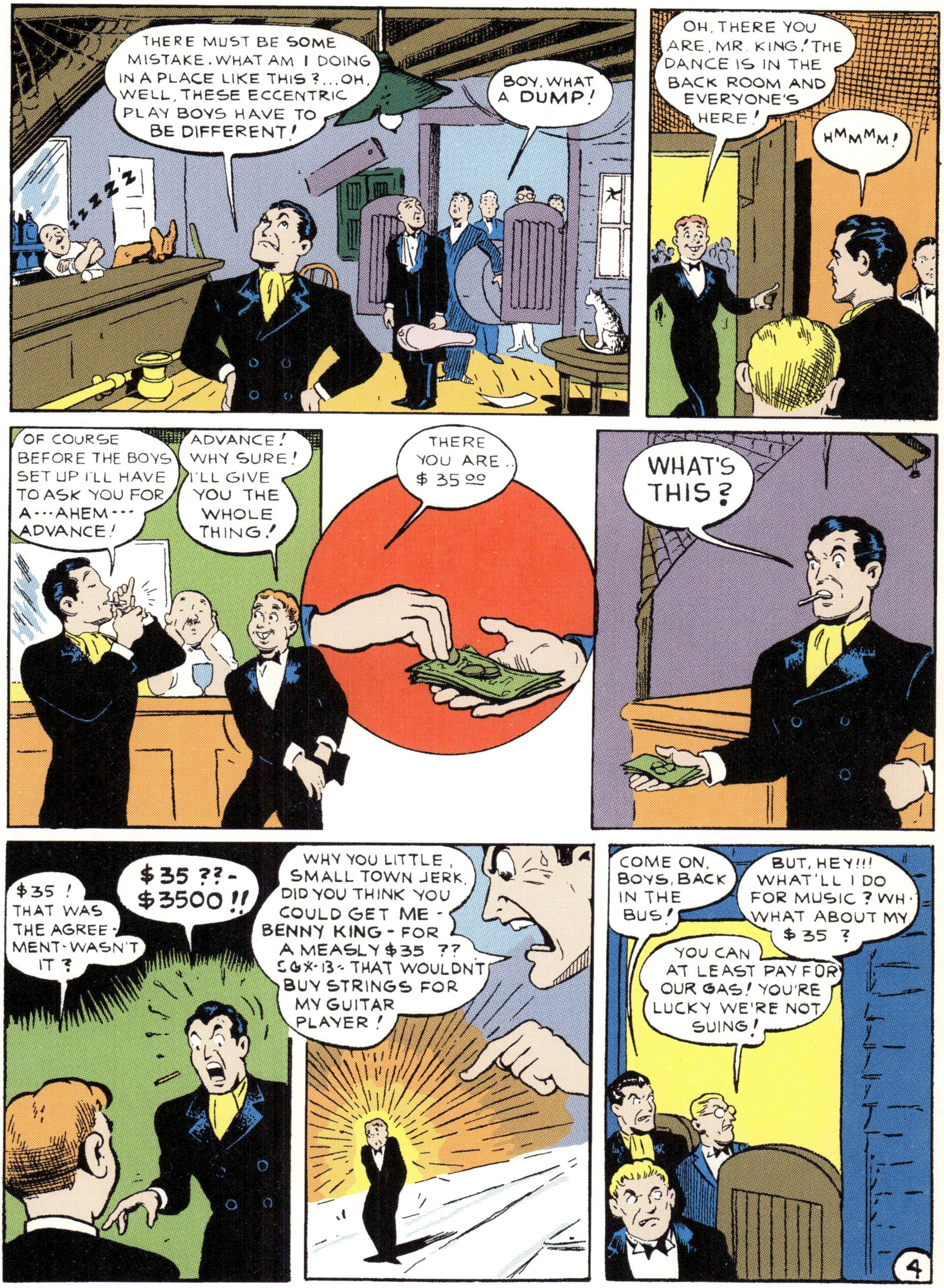
THERE MUST BE SOME MISTAKE. WHAT AM I DOING IN A PLACE LIKE THIS?...OH, WELL, THESE ECCENTRIC PLAY BOYS HAVE TO BE DIFFERENT!
BOY, WHAT A DUMP!
OH, THERE YOU ARE, MR. KING! THE DANCE IS IN THE BACK ROOM AND EVERYONE'S HERE!
HMMMM!
OF COURSE BEFORE THE BOYS SET UP I'LL HAVE TO ASK YOU FOR A···AHEM··· ADVANCE!
ADVANCE! WHY SURE! I'LL GIVE YOU THE WHOLE THING!
THERE YOU ARE.. $35.00
WHAT'S THIS?
$35! THAT WAS THE AGREEMENT-WASN'T IT?
$35??- $3500!!
WHY YOU LITTLE, SMALL TOWN JERK, DID YOU THINK YOU COULD GET ME - BENNY KING - FOR A MEASLY $35?? SGX-13- THAT WOULDN'T BUY STRINGS FOR MY GUITAR PLAYER!
COME ON, BOYS, BACK IN THE BUS!
BUT, HEY!!! WHAT'LL I DO FOR MUSIC? WH- WHAT ABOUT MY $35?
YOU CAN AT LEAST PAY FOR OUR GAS! YOU'RE LUCKY WE'RE NOT SUING!
4

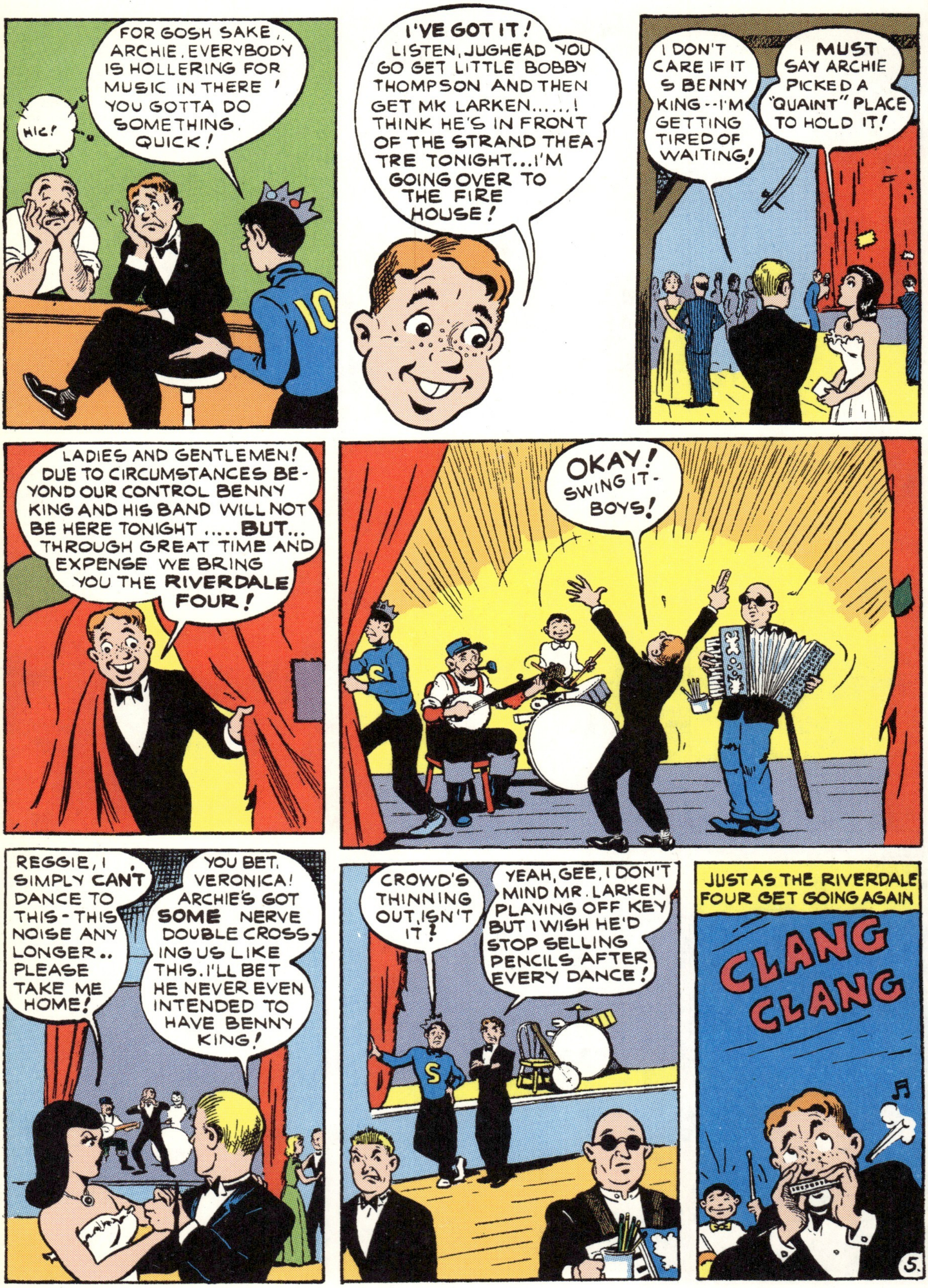
FOR GOSH SAKE, ARCHIE, EVERYBODY IS HOLLERING FOR MUSIC IN THERE! YOU GOTTA DO SOMETHING, QUICK!
HIC!
I'VE GOT IT! LISTEN, JUGHEAD YOU GO GET LITTLE BOBBY THOMPSON AND THEN GET MK LARKEN......! THINK HE'S IN FRONT OF THE STRAND THEATRE TONIGHT...I'M GOING OVER TO THE FIRE HOUSE!
I DON'T CARE IF IT S BENNY KING--I'M GETTING TIRED OF WAITING!
I MUST SAY ARCHIE PICKED A "QUAINT" PLACE TO HOLD IT!
LADIES AND GENTLEMEN! DUE TO CIRCUMSTANCES BEYOND OUR CONTROL BENNY KING AND HIS BAND WILL NOT BE HERE TONIGHT .....BUT... THROUGH GREAT TIME AND EXPENSE WE BRING YOU THE RIVERDALE FOUR!
OKAY! SWING IT BOYS!
REGGIE, I SIMPLY CAN'T DANCE TO THIS-THIS NOISE ANY LONGER.. PLEASE TAKE ME HOME!
YOU BET, VERONICA! ARCHIE'S GOT SOME NERVE DOUBLE CROSSING US LIKE THIS. I'LL BET HE NEVER EVEN INTENDED TO HAVE BENNY KING!
CROWD'S THINNING OUT, ISN'T IT?
YEAH, GEE, I DON'T MIND MR. LARKEN PLAYING OFF KEY BUT I WISH HE'D STOP SELLING PENCILS AFTER EVERY DANCE!
JUST AS THE RIVERDALE FOUR GET GOING AGAIN
CLANG CLANG
5.

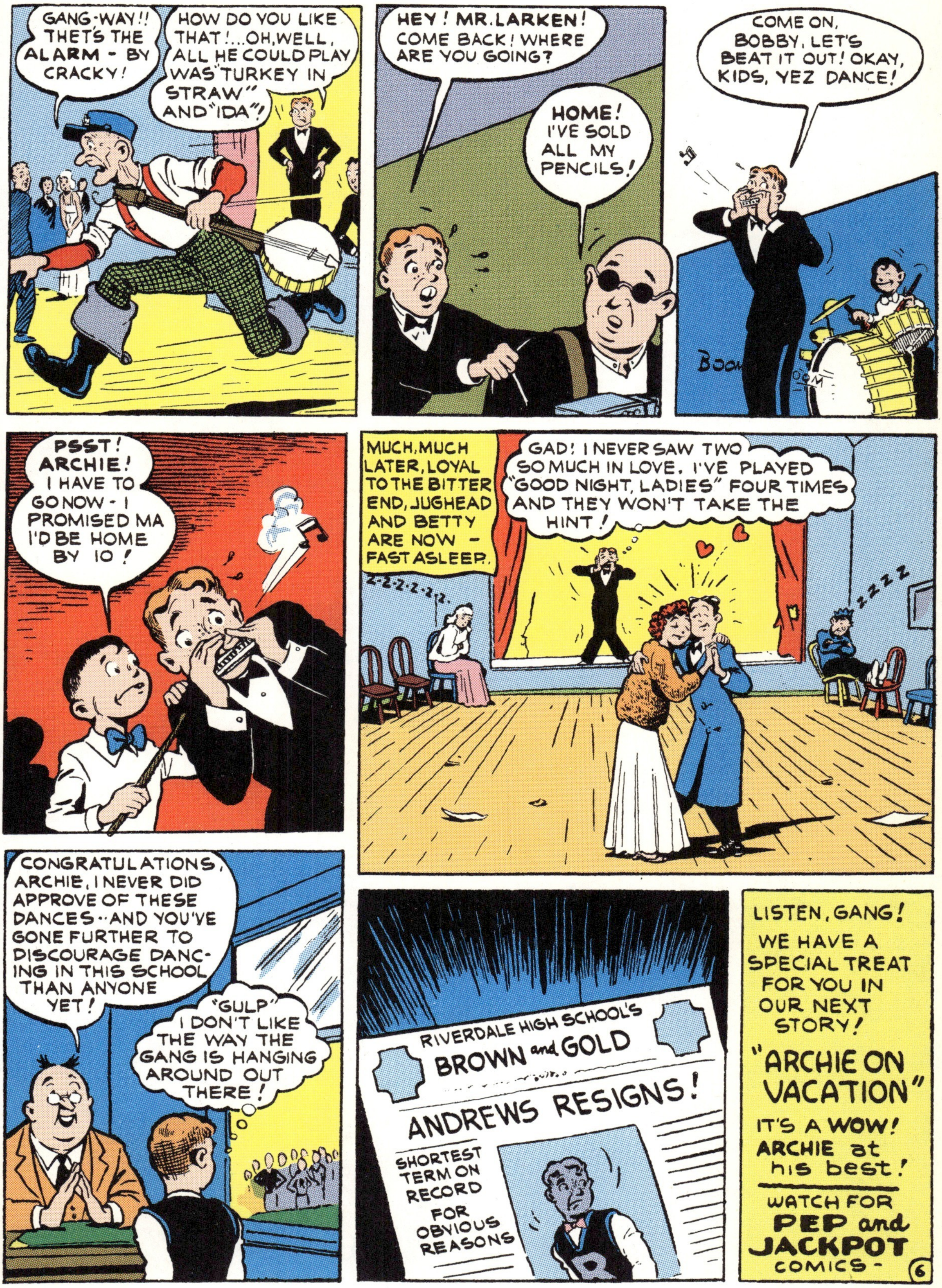
GANG-WAY!! THET'S THE ALARM - BY CRACKY!
HOW DO YOU LIKE THAT!...OH,WELL, ALL HE COULD PLAY WAS "TURKEY IN STRAW" AND "IDA"!
HEY! MR.LARKEN! COME BACK! WHERE ARE YOU GOING?
HOME! I'VE SOLD ALL MY PENCILS!
COME ON, BOBBY, LET'S BEAT IT OUT! OKAY, KIDS, YEZ DANCE!
PSST! ARCHIE! I HAVE TO GO NOW - I PROMISED MA I'D BE HOME BY 10!
MUCH, MUCH LATER, LOYAL TO THE BITTER END, JUGHEAD AND BETTY ARE NOW - FAST ASLEEP.
GAD! I NEVER SAW TWO SO MUCH IN LOVE. I'VE PLAYED "GOOD NIGHT, LADIES" FOUR TIMES AND THEY WON'T TAKE THE HINT!
Z-Z-Z-Z-Z-Z.
Z Z Z Z
CONGRATULATIONS, ARCHIE, I NEVER DID APPROVE OF THESE DANCES--AND YOU'VE GONE FURTHER TO DISCOURAGE DANCING IN THIS SCHOOL THAN ANYONE YET!
"GULP" I DON'T LIKE THE WAY THE GANG IS HANGING AROUND OUT THERE!
RIVERDALE HIGH SCHOOL'S
BROWN and GOLD
ANDREWS RESIGNS!
SHORTEST TERM ON RECORD FOR OBVIOUS REASONS
LISTEN, GANG! WE HAVE A SPECIAL TREAT FOR YOU IN OUR NEXT STORY!
"ARCHIE ON VACATION"
IT'S A WOW! ARCHIE at his best!
WATCH FOR PEP and JACKPOT COMICS -
6

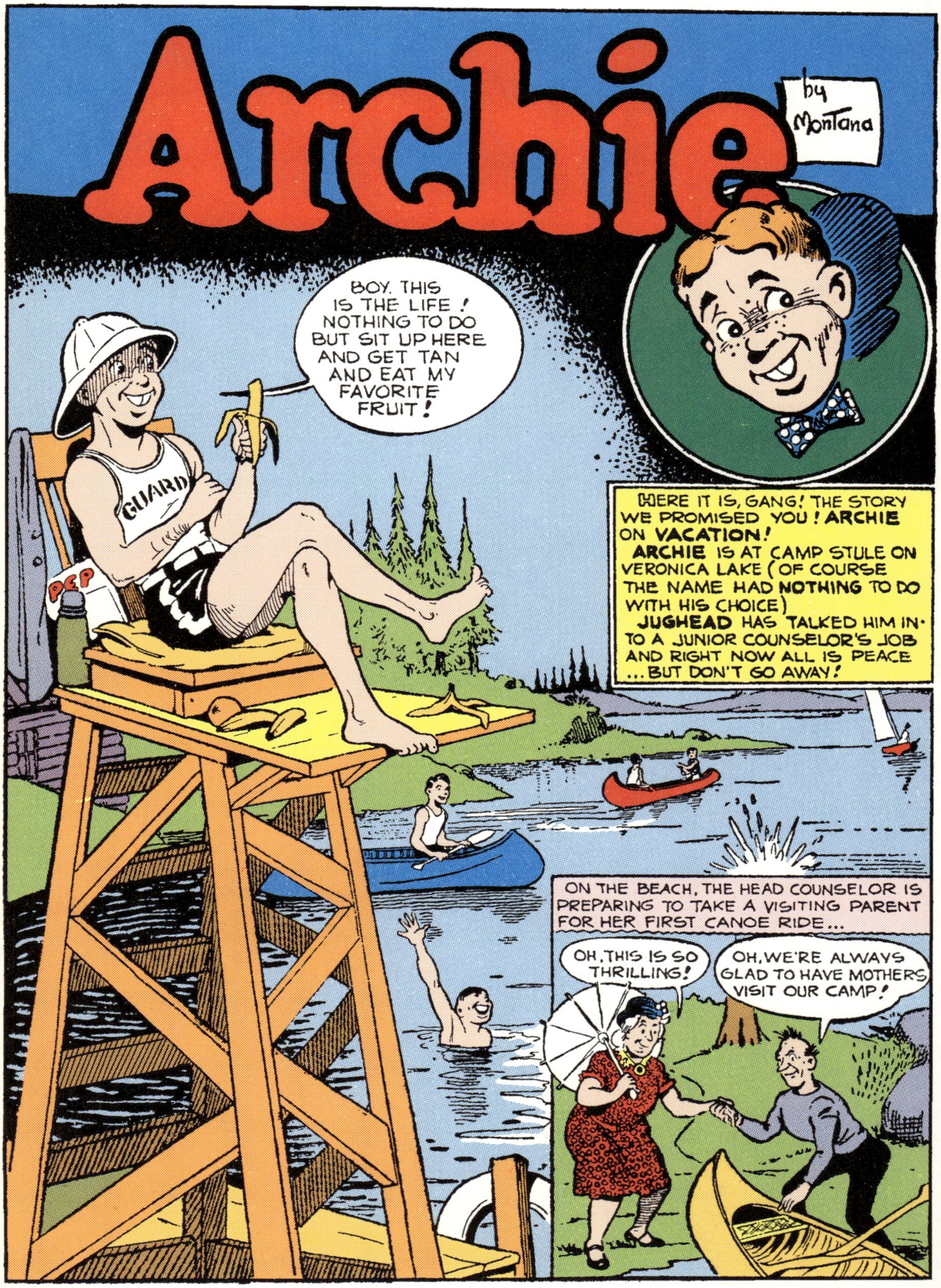

Archie
by Montana
BOY. THIS IS THE LIFE! NOTHING TO DO BUT SIT UP HERE AND GET TAN AND EAT MY FAVORITE FRUIT!
GUARD
PEP
HERE IT IS, GANG! THE STORY WE PROMISED YOU! ARCHIE ON VACATION! ARCHIE IS AT CAMP STULE ON VERONICA LAKE (OF COURSE THE NAME HAD NOTHING TO DO WITH HIS CHOICE) JUGHEAD HAS TALKED HIM INTO A JUNIOR COUNSELOR'S JOB AND RIGHT NOW ALL IS PEACE ...BUT DON'T GO AWAY!
ON THE BEACH, THE HEAD COUNSELOR IS PREPARING TO TAKE A VISITING PARENT FOR HER FIRST CANOE RIDE...
OH, THIS IS SO THRILLING!
OH, WE'RE ALWAYS GLAD TO HAVE MOTHERS VISIT OUR CAMP!

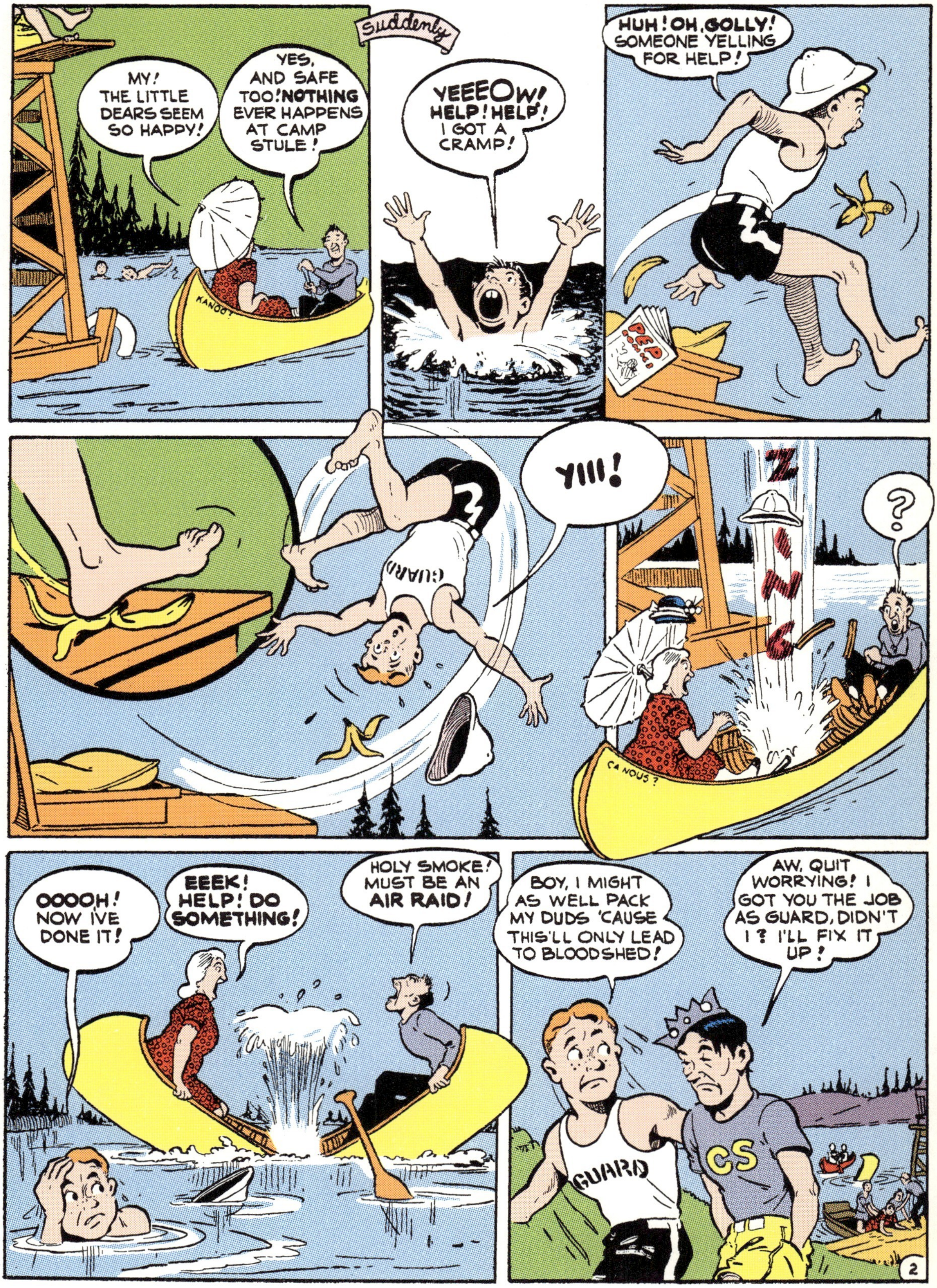
MY! THE LITTLE DEARS SEEM SO HAPPY!
YES, AND SAFE TOO! NOTHING EVER HAPPENS AT CAMP STULE!
KANOO?
Suddenly
YEEEOW! HELP! HELP! I GOT A CRAMP!
HUH! OH, GOLLY! SOMEONE YELLING FOR HELP!
PEP
YIII!
GUARD
ZING
?
CA NOUS?
OOOOH! NOW I'VE DONE IT!
EEEK! HELP! DO SOMETHING!
HOLY SMOKE! MUST BE AN AIR RAID!
BOY, I MIGHT AS WELL PACK MY DUDS 'CAUSE THIS'LL ONLY LEAD TO BLOODSHED!
AW, QUIT WORRYING! I GOT YOU THE JOB AS GUARD, DIDN'T I? I'LL FIX IT UP!
GUARD
CS
2

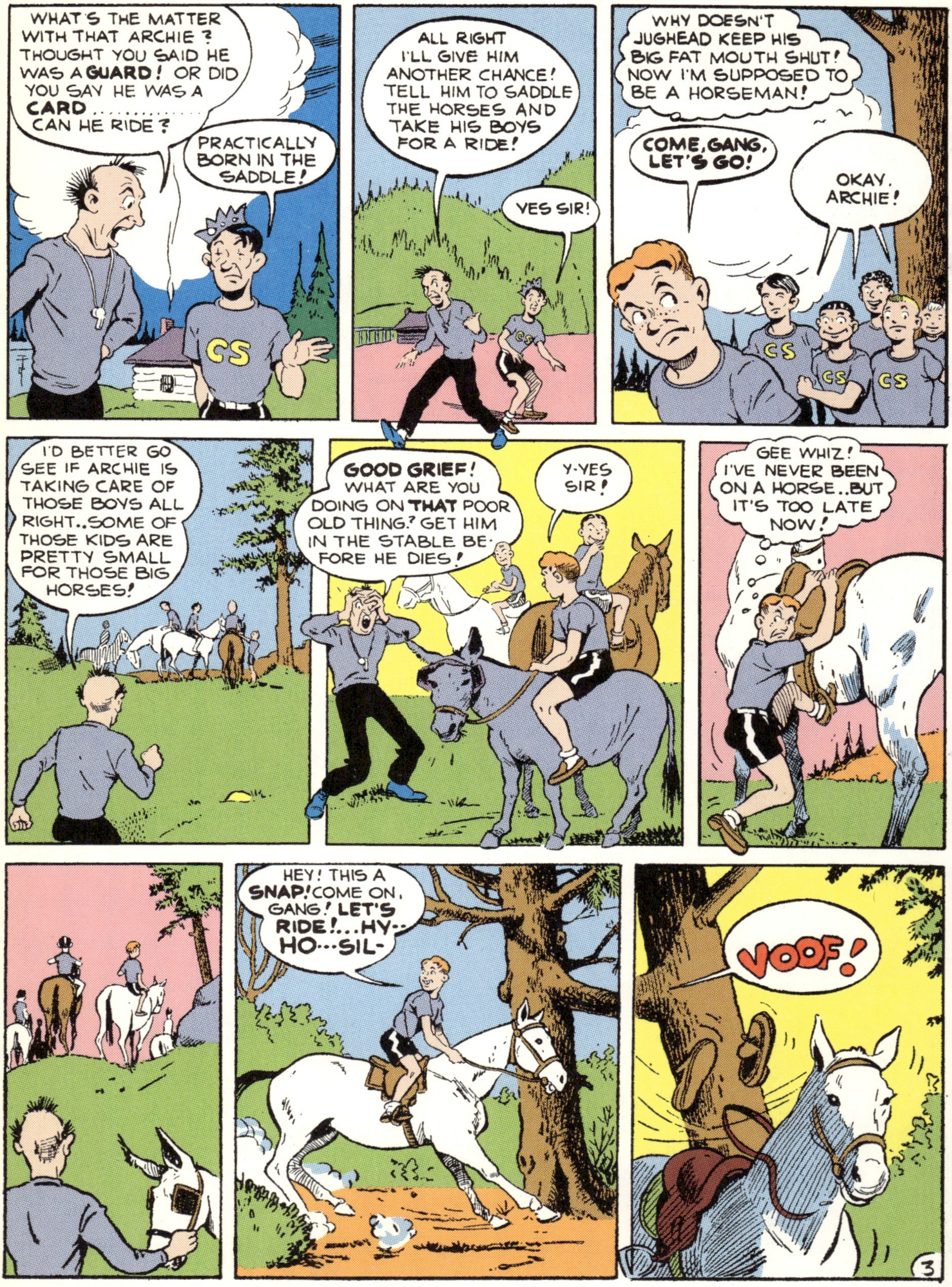
WHAT'S THE MATTER WITH THAT ARCHIE ? THOUGHT YOU SAID HE WAS A GUARD ! OR DID YOU SAY HE WAS A CARD .... CAN HE RIDE ?
PRACTICALLY BORN IN THE SADDLE !
CS
ALL RIGHT I'LL GIVE HIM ANOTHER CHANCE ! TELL HIM TO SADDLE THE HORSES AND TAKE HIS BOYS FOR A RIDE !
YES SIR !
WHY DOESN'T JUGHEAD KEEP HIS BIG FAT MOUTH SHUT ! NOW I'M SUPPOSED TO BE A HORSEMAN !
COME, GANG, LET'S GO !
OKAY, ARCHIE !
I'D BETTER GO SEE IF ARCHIE IS TAKING CARE OF THOSE BOYS ALL RIGHT..SOME OF THOSE KIDS ARE PRETTY SMALL FOR THOSE BIG HORSES !
GOOD GRIEF ! WHAT ARE YOU DOING ON THAT POOR OLD THING ? GET HIM IN THE STABLE BEFORE HE DIES !
Y-YES SIR !
GEE WHIZ ! I'VE NEVER BEEN ON A HORSE..BUT IT'S TOO LATE NOW !
HEY ! THIS A SNAP ! COME ON, GANG ! LET'S RIDE !...HY-HO...SIL-
VOOF !
3

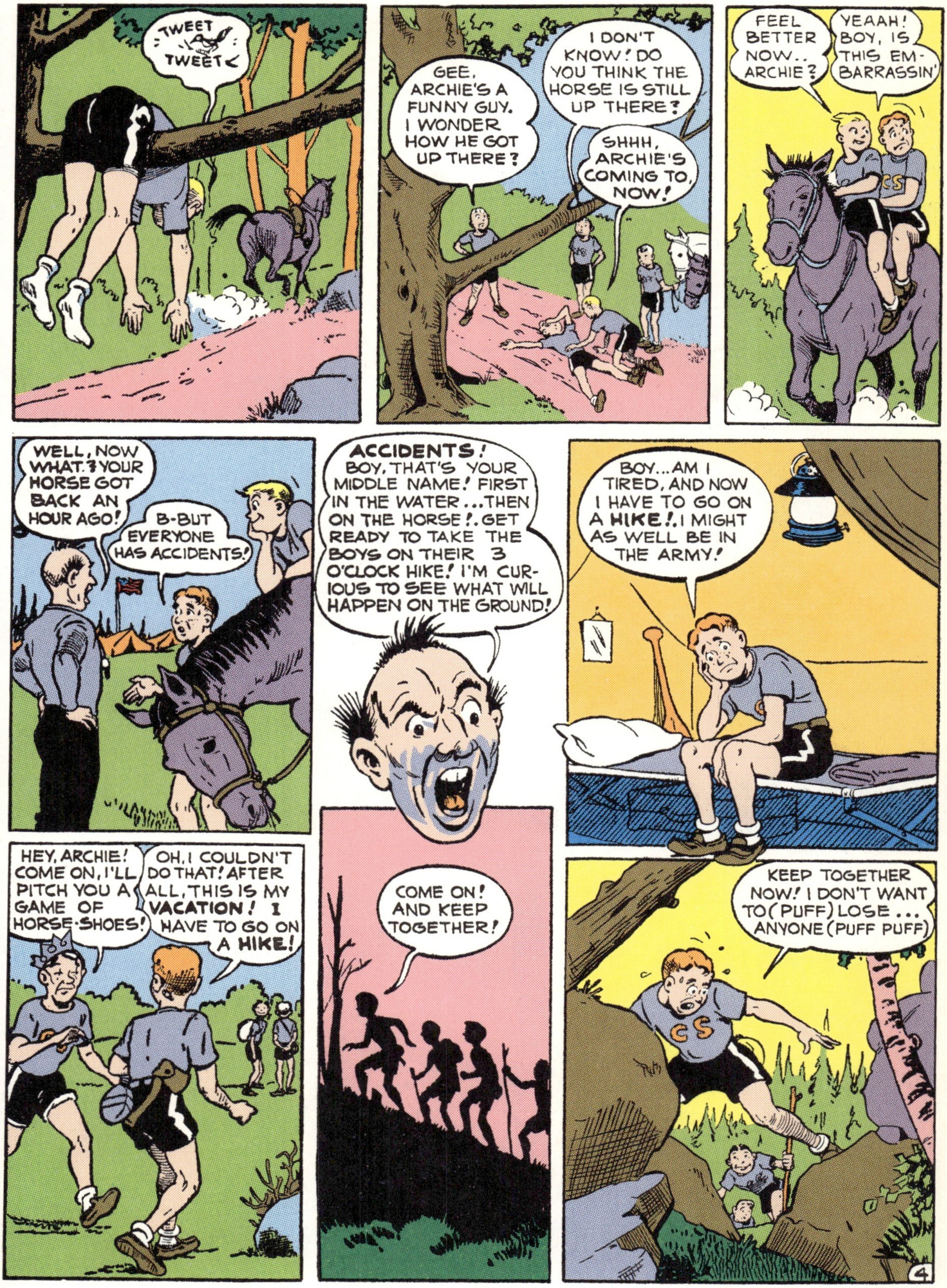

TWEET TWEET
GEE, ARCHIE'S A FUNNY GUY. I WONDER HOW HE GOT UP THERE?
I DON'T KNOW! DO YOU THINK THE HORSE IS STILL UP THERE?
SHHH, ARCHIE'S COMING TO, NOW!
FEEL BETTER NOW.. ARCHIE?
YEAAH! BOY, IS THIS EM-BARRASSIN'
WELL, NOW WHAT.? YOUR HORSE GOT BACK AN HOUR AGO!
B-BUT EVERYONE HAS ACCIDENTS!
ACCIDENTS! BOY, THAT'S YOUR MIDDLE NAME! FIRST IN THE WATER...THEN ON THE HORSE!. GET READY TO TAKE THE BOYS ON THEIR 3 O'CLOCK HIKE! I'M CURIOUS TO SEE WHAT WILL HAPPEN ON THE GROUND!
BOY...AM I TIRED, AND NOW I HAVE TO GO ON A HIKE!. I MIGHT AS WELL BE IN THE ARMY!
HEY, ARCHIE! COME ON, I'LL PITCH YOU A GAME OF HORSE-SHOES!
OH, I COULDN'T DO THAT! AFTER ALL, THIS IS MY VACATION! I HAVE TO GO ON A HIKE!
COME ON! AND KEEP TOGETHER!
KEEP TOGETHER NOW! I DON'T WANT TO (PUFF) LOSE... ANYONE (PUFF PUFF)
4

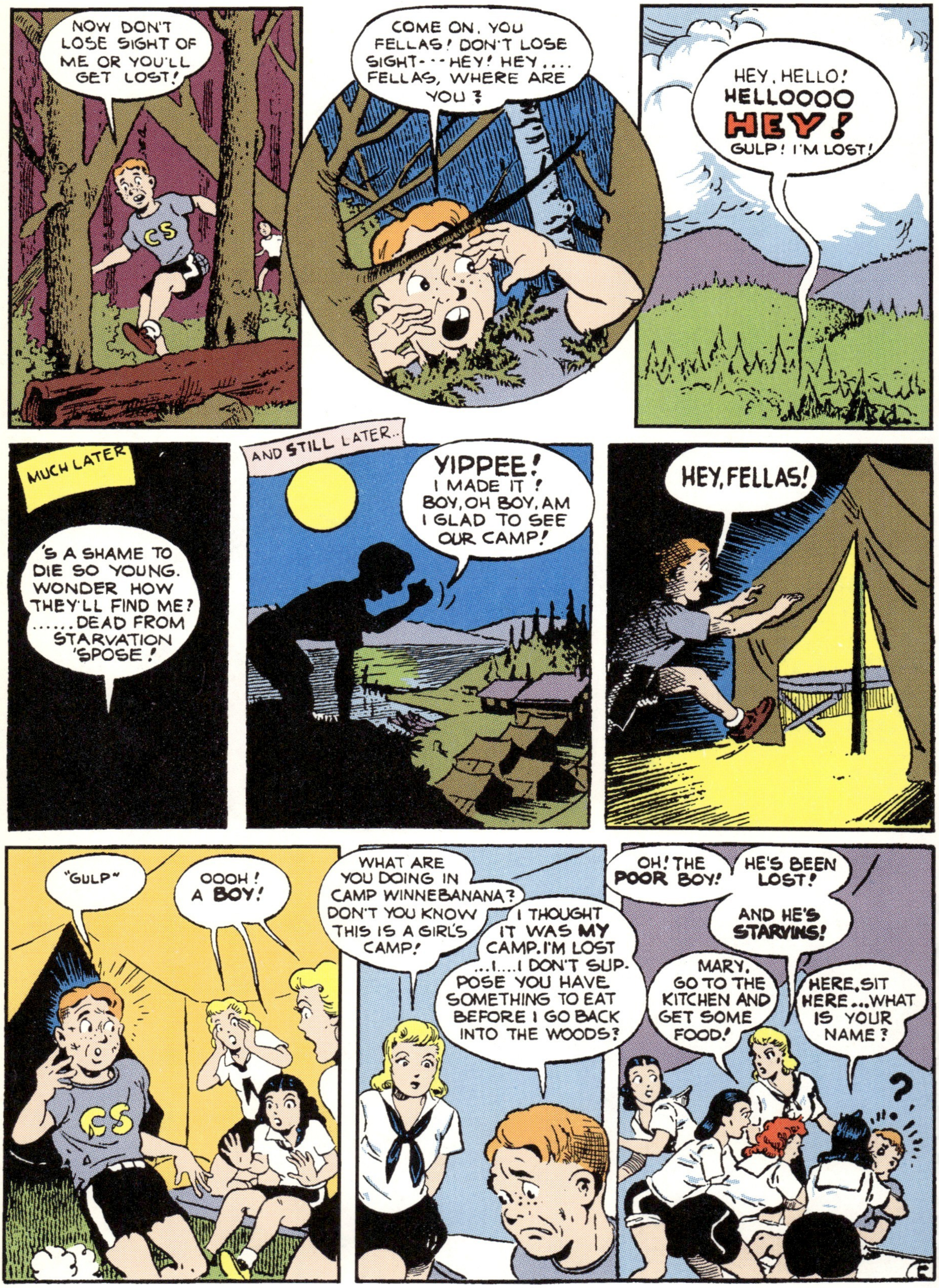
NOW DON'T LOSE SIGHT OF ME OR YOU'LL GET LOST!
COME ON, YOU FELLAS! DON'T LOSE SIGHT--- HEY! HEY.... FELLAS, WHERE ARE YOU?
HEY, HELLO! HELLOOOO HEY! GULP! I'M LOST!
MUCH LATER
'S A SHAME TO DIE SO YOUNG. WONDER HOW THEY'LL FIND ME? ......DEAD FROM STARVATION 'SPOSE!
AND STILL LATER..
YIPPEE! I MADE IT! BOY, OH BOY, AM I GLAD TO SEE OUR CAMP!
HEY, FELLAS!
"GULP"
OOOH! A BOY!
WHAT ARE YOU DOING IN CAMP WINNEBANANA? DON'T YOU KNOW THIS IS A GIRL'S CAMP!
I THOUGHT IT WAS MY CAMP. I'M LOST ...I....I DON'T SUP-POSE YOU HAVE SOMETHING TO EAT BEFORE I GO BACK INTO THE WOODS?
OH! THE POOR BOY!
HE'S BEEN LOST!
AND HE'S STARVING!
MARY, GO TO THE KITCHEN AND GET SOME FOOD!
HERE, SIT HERE...WHAT IS YOUR NAME?
?

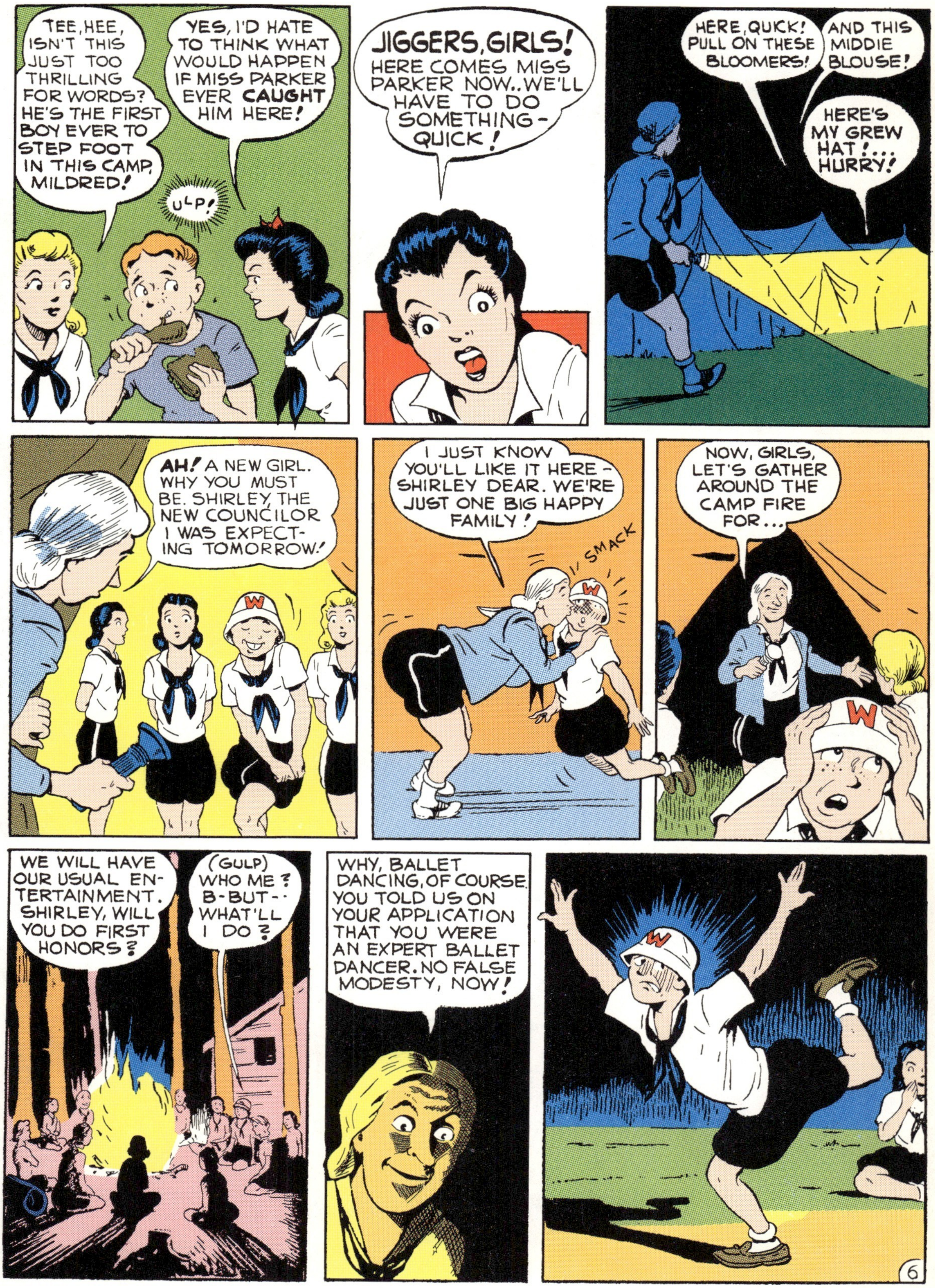
TEE, HEE, ISN'T THIS JUST TOO THRILLING FOR WORDS? HE'S THE FIRST BOY EVER TO STEP FOOT IN THIS CAMP, MILDRED!
YES, I'D HATE TO THINK WHAT WOULD HAPPEN IF MISS PARKER EVER CAUGHT HIM HERE!
ULP!
JIGGERS, GIRLS! HERE COMES MISS PARKER NOW.. WE'LL HAVE TO DO SOMETHING - QUICK!
HERE, QUICK! PULL ON THESE BLOOMERS!
AND THIS MIDDIE BLOUSE!
HERE'S MY GREW HAT!... HURRY!
AH! A NEW GIRL. WHY YOU MUST BE. SHIRLEY, THE NEW COUNCILOR I WAS EXPECTING TOMORROW!
I JUST KNOW YOU'LL LIKE IT HERE - SHIRLEY DEAR. WE'RE JUST ONE BIG HAPPY FAMILY!
SMACK
NOW, GIRLS, LET'S GATHER AROUND THE CAMP FIRE FOR...
WE WILL HAVE OUR USUAL ENTERTAINMENT. SHIRLEY, WILL YOU DO FIRST HONORS?
(GULP) WHO ME? B-BUT-- WHAT'LL I DO?
WHY, BALLET DANCING, OF COURSE. YOU TOLD US ON YOUR APPLICATION THAT YOU WERE AN EXPERT BALLET DANCER. NO FALSE MODESTY, NOW!
6

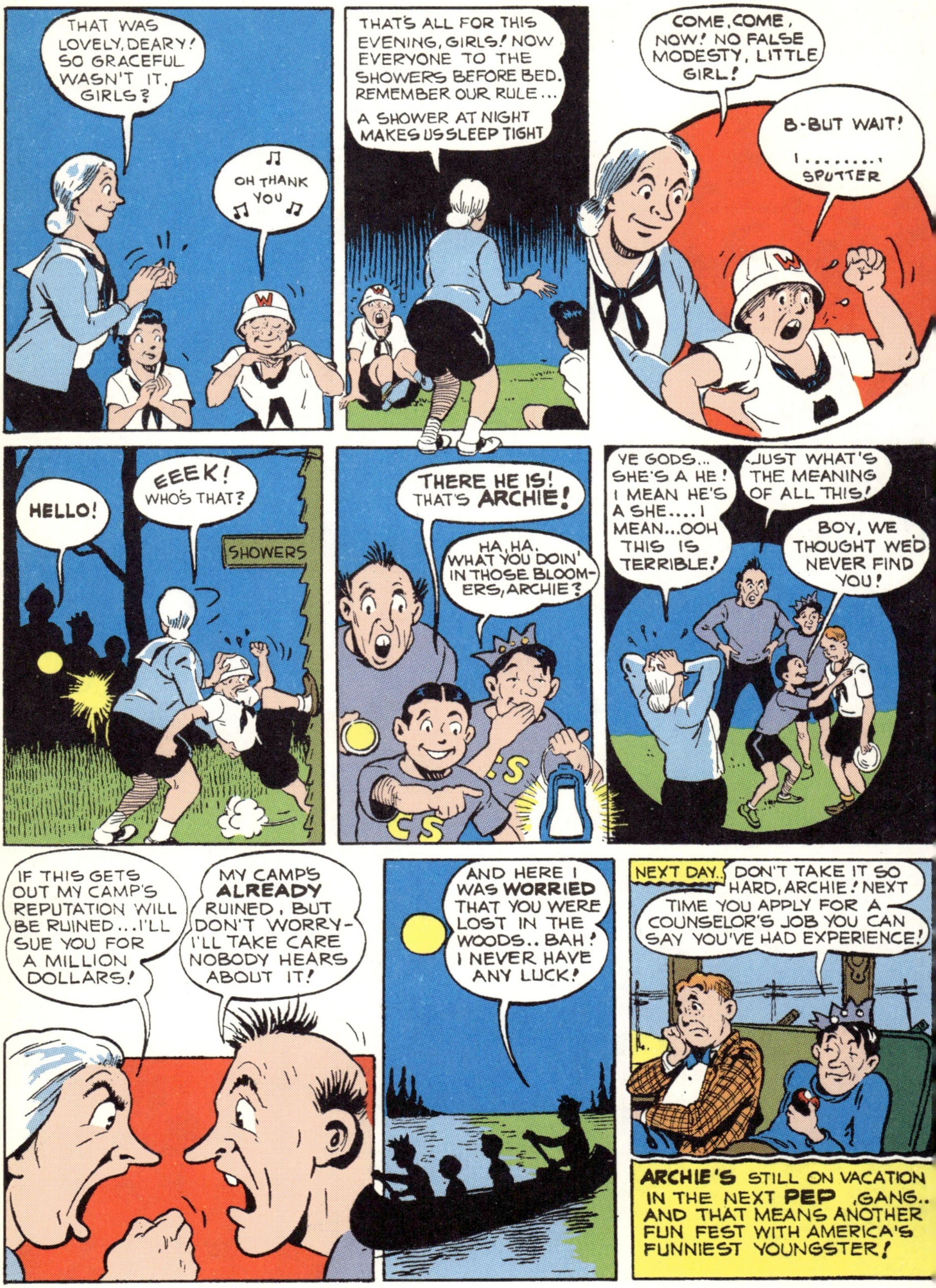
THAT WAS LOVELY, DEARY! SO GRACEFUL WASN'T IT, GIRLS?
OH THANK YOU
THAT'S ALL FOR THIS EVENING, GIRLS! NOW EVERYONE TO THE SHOWERS BEFORE BED. REMEMBER OUR RULE...
A SHOWER AT NIGHT MAKES US SLEEP TIGHT
COME, COME, NOW! NO FALSE MODESTY, LITTLE GIRL!
B-BUT WAIT!
SPUTTER
HELLO!
EEEK! WHO'S THAT?
SHOWERS
THERE HE IS! THAT'S ARCHIE!
HA, HA, WHAT YOU DOIN' IN THOSE BLOOMERS, ARCHIE?
YE GODS... SHE'S A HE! I MEAN HE'S A SHE.... I MEAN...OOH THIS IS TERRIBLE!
JUST WHAT'S THE MEANING OF ALL THIS!
BOY, WE THOUGHT WE'D NEVER FIND YOU!
IF THIS GETS OUT MY CAMP'S REPUTATION WILL BE RUINED...I'LL SUE YOU FOR A MILLION DOLLARS!
MY CAMP'S ALREADY RUINED, BUT DON'T WORRY- I'LL TAKE CARE NOBODY HEARS ABOUT IT!
AND HERE I WAS WORRIED THAT YOU WERE LOST IN THE WOODS.. BAH! I NEVER HAVE ANY LUCK!
NEXT DAY..
DON'T TAKE IT SO HARD, ARCHIE! NEXT TIME YOU APPLY FOR A COUNSELOR'S JOB YOU CAN SAY YOU'VE HAD EXPERIENCE!
ARCHIE'S STILL ON VACATION IN THE NEXT PEP, GANG.. AND THAT MEANS ANOTHER FUN FEST WITH AMERICA'S FUNNIEST YOUNGSTER!

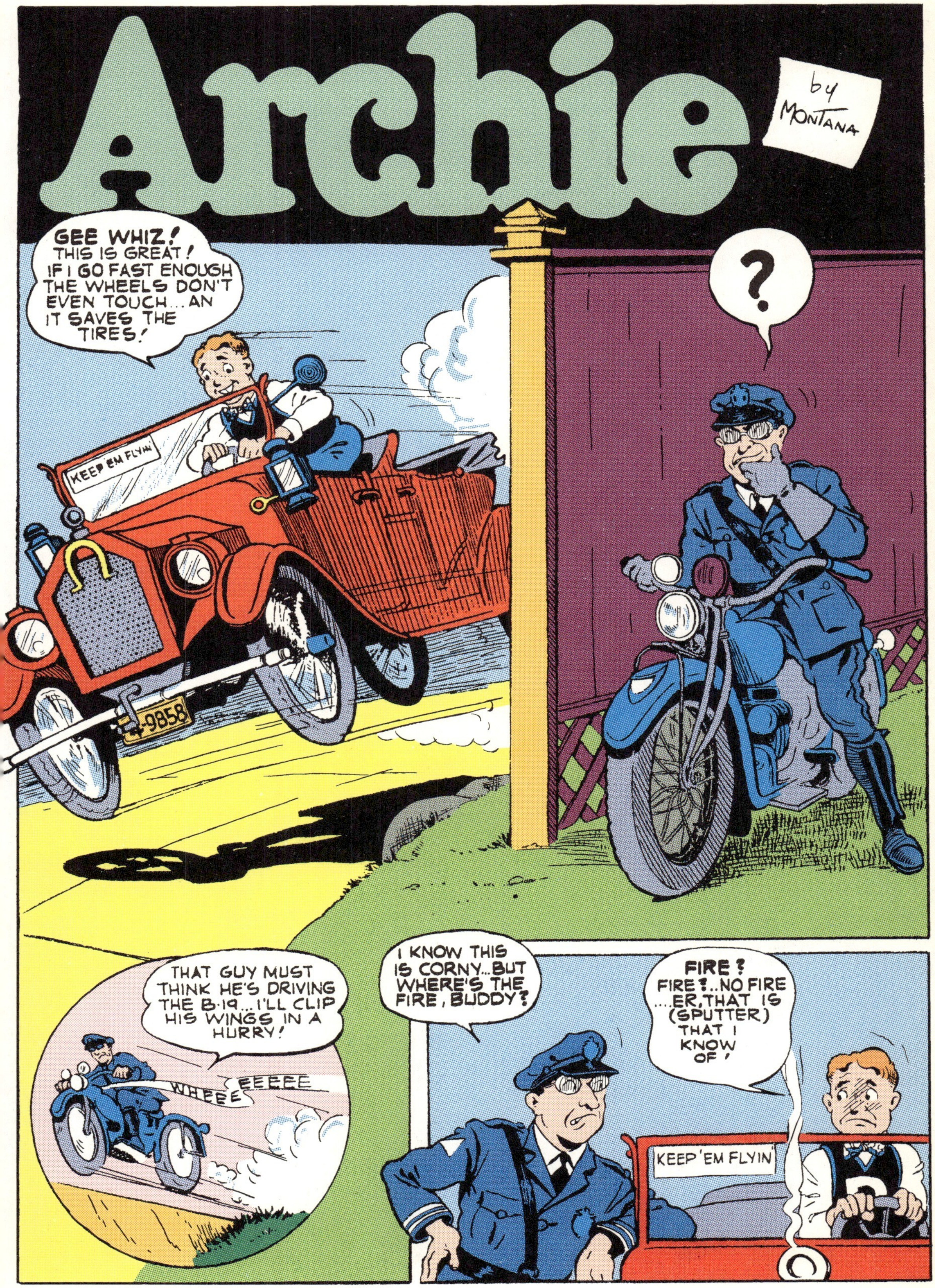
Archie
by MONTANA
GEE WHIZ! THIS IS GREAT! IF I GO FAST ENOUGH THE WHEELS DON'T EVEN TOUCH... AN IT SAVES THE TIRES!
KEEP 'EM FLYIN'
?
THAT GUY MUST THINK HE'S DRIVING THE B-19... I'LL CLIP HIS WINGS IN A HURRY!
WHEEEEEEEEE
I KNOW THIS IS CORNY...BUT WHERE'S THE FIRE, BUDDY?
FIRE? FIRE?..NO FIRE ....ER, THAT IS (SPUTTER) THAT I KNOW OF!
KEEP 'EM FLYIN'

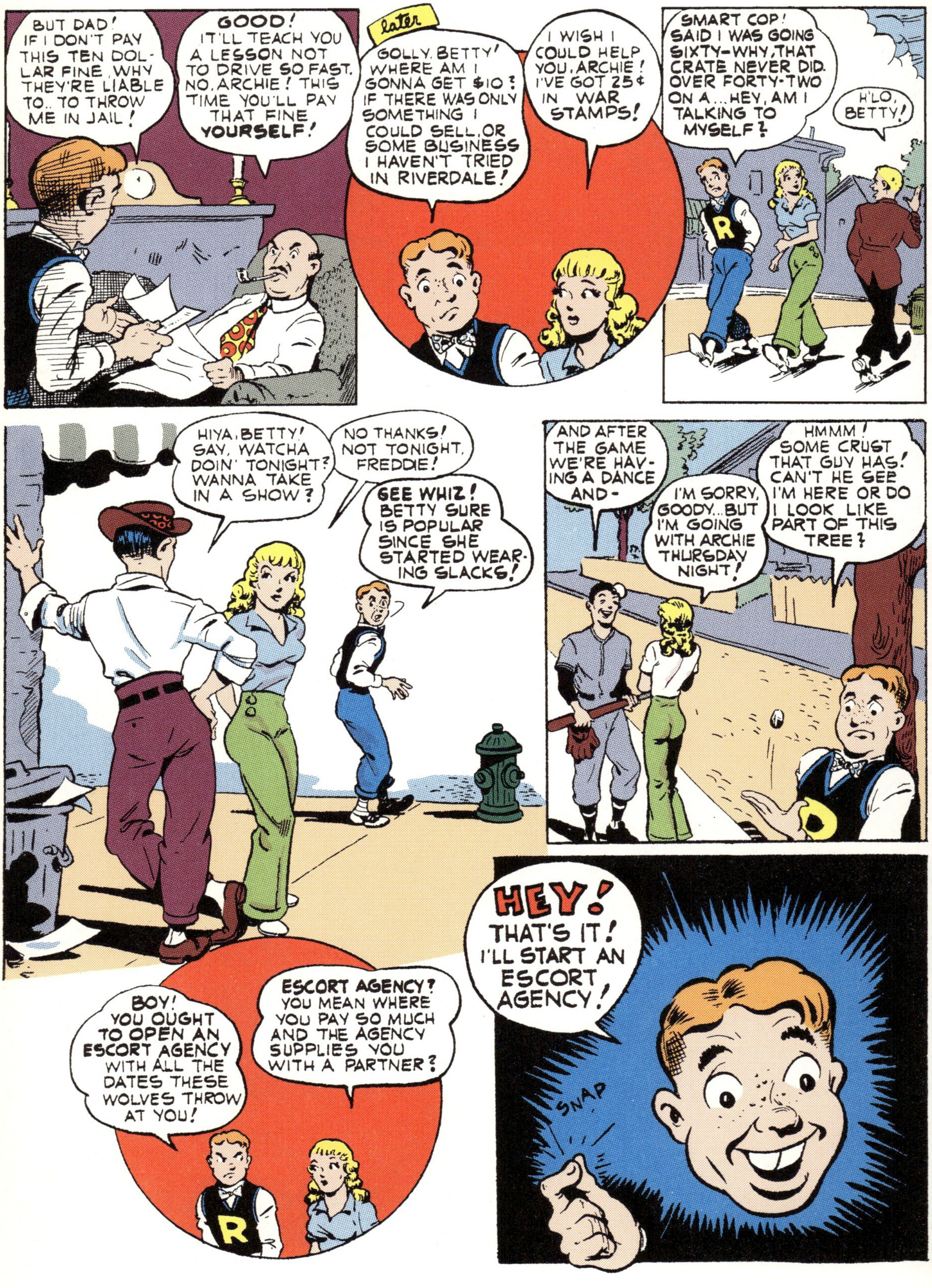
BUT DAD! IF I DON'T PAY THIS TEN DOLLAR FINE, WHY THEY'RE LIABLE TO.. TO THROW ME IN JAIL!
GOOD! IT'LL TEACH YOU A LESSON NOT TO DRIVE SO FAST. NO, ARCHIE! THIS TIME YOU'LL PAY THAT FINE YOURSELF!
later
GOLLY, BETTY! WHERE AM I GONNA GET $10? IF THERE WAS ONLY SOMETHING I COULD SELL, OR SOME BUSINESS I HAVEN'T TRIED IN RIVERDALE!
I WISH I COULD HELP YOU, ARCHIE! I'VE GOT 25¢ IN WAR STAMPS!
SMART COP! SAID I WAS GOING SIXTY-WHY, THAT CRATE NEVER DID OVER FORTY-TWO ON A... HEY, AM I TALKING TO MYSELF?
H'LO, BETTY!
HIYA, BETTY! SAY, WATCHA DOIN' TONIGHT? WANNA TAKE IN A SHOW?
NO THANKS! NOT TONIGHT, FREDDIE!
GEE WHIZ! BETTY SURE IS POPULAR SINCE SHE STARTED WEARING SLACKS!
AND AFTER THE GAME WE'RE HAVING A DANCE AND-
I'M SORRY, GOODY...BUT I'M GOING WITH ARCHIE THURSDAY NIGHT!
HMMM! SOME CRUST THAT GUY HAS! CAN'T HE SEE I'M HERE OR DO I LOOK LIKE PART OF THIS TREE?
BOY! YOU OUGHT TO OPEN AN ESCORT AGENCY WITH ALL THE DATES THESE WOLVES THROW AT YOU!
ESCORT AGENCY? YOU MEAN WHERE YOU PAY SO MUCH AND THE AGENCY SUPPLIES YOU WITH A PARTNER?
HEY! THAT'S IT! I'LL START AN ESCORT AGENCY!
SNAP

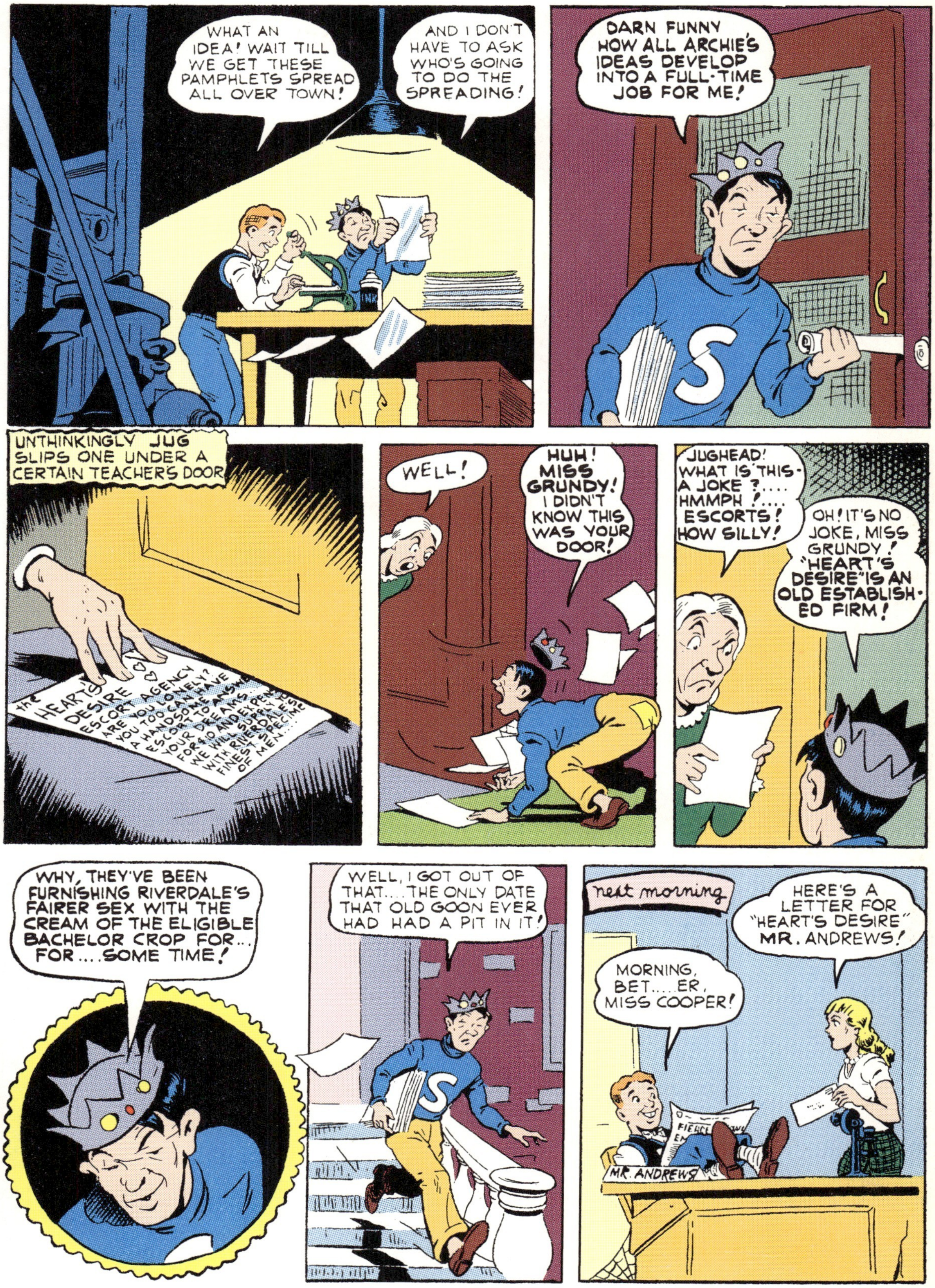

WHAT AN IDEA! WAIT TILL WE GET THESE PAMPHLETS SPREAD ALL OVER TOWN!
AND I DON'T HAVE TO ASK WHO'S GOING TO DO THE SPREADING!
DARN FUNNY HOW ALL ARCHIE'S IDEAS DEVELOP INTO A FULL-TIME JOB FOR ME!
UNTHINKINGLY JUG SLIPS ONE UNDER A CERTAIN TEACHER'S DOOR
the HEART'S DESIRE
ESCORT AGENCY
ARE YOU LONELY?
YOU TOO CAN HAVE
A HANDSOME
ESCORT TO
YOUR DREAMS
WE WILL
WITH RIVERDALE'S
OF MEN...
WELL!
HUH! MISS GRUNDY! I DIDN'T KNOW THIS WAS YOUR DOOR!
JUGHEAD! WHAT IS THIS-A JOKE?.... HMMPH?.... ESCORTS! HOW SILLY!
OH! IT'S NO JOKE, MISS GRUNDY! "HEART'S DESIRE" IS AN OLD ESTABLISHED FIRM!
WHY, THEY'VE BEEN FURNISHING RIVERDALE'S FAIRER SEX WITH THE CREAM OF THE ELIGIBLE BACHELOR CROP FOR... FOR.... SOME TIME!
WELL, I GOT OUT OF THAT.... THE ONLY DATE THAT OLD GOON EVER HAD HAD A PIT IN IT!
next morning
MORNING, BET.... ER, MISS COOPER!
HERE'S A LETTER FOR "HEART'S DESIRE" MR. ANDREWS!
MR. ANDREWS

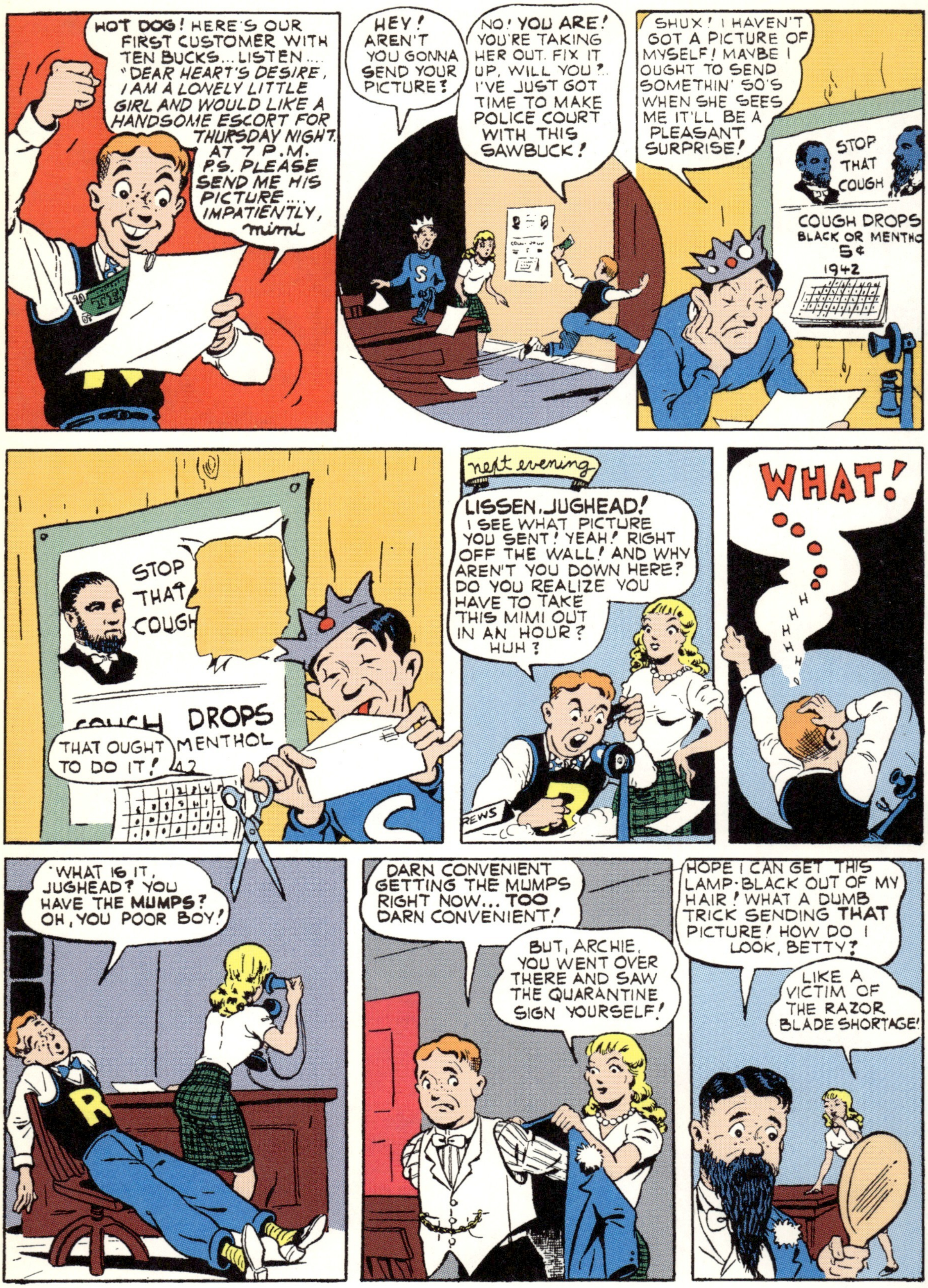

HOT DOG! HERE'S OUR FIRST CUSTOMER WITH TEN BUCKS... LISTEN.... "DEAR HEART'S DESIRE, I AM A LONELY LITTLE GIRL AND WOULD LIKE A HANDSOME ESCORT FOR THURSDAY NIGHT AT 7 P.M. P.S. PLEASE SEND ME HIS PICTURE.... IMPATIENTLY, mimi
HEY! AREN'T YOU GONNA SEND YOUR PICTURE?
NO! YOU ARE! YOU'RE TAKING HER OUT. FIX IT UP, WILL YOU? I'VE JUST GOT TIME TO MAKE POLICE COURT WITH THIS SAWBUCK!
SHUX! I HAVEN'T GOT A PICTURE OF MYSELF! MAYBE I OUGHT TO SEND SOMETHIN' SO'S WHEN SHE SEES ME IT'LL BE A PLEASANT SURPRISE!
STOP THAT COUGH
COUGH DROPS
BLACK OR MENTHO
5¢
1942
STOP THAT COUGH
DROPS
MENTHOL
THAT OUGHT TO DO IT!
next evening
LISSEN, JUGHEAD! I SEE WHAT PICTURE YOU SENT! YEAH! RIGHT OFF THE WALL! AND WHY AREN'T YOU DOWN HERE? DO YOU REALIZE YOU HAVE TO TAKE THIS MIMI OUT IN AN HOUR? HUH?
WHAT!
HHHHH
WHAT IS IT, JUGHEAD? YOU HAVE THE MUMPS? OH, YOU POOR BOY!
DARN CONVENIENT GETTING THE MUMPS RIGHT NOW... TOO DARN CONVENIENT!
BUT, ARCHIE, YOU WENT OVER THERE AND SAW THE QUARANTINE SIGN YOURSELF!
HOPE I CAN GET THIS LAMP-BLACK OUT OF MY HAIR! WHAT A DUMB TRICK SENDING THAT PICTURE! HOW DO I LOOK, BETTY?
LIKE A VICTIM OF THE RAZOR BLADE SHORTAGE!

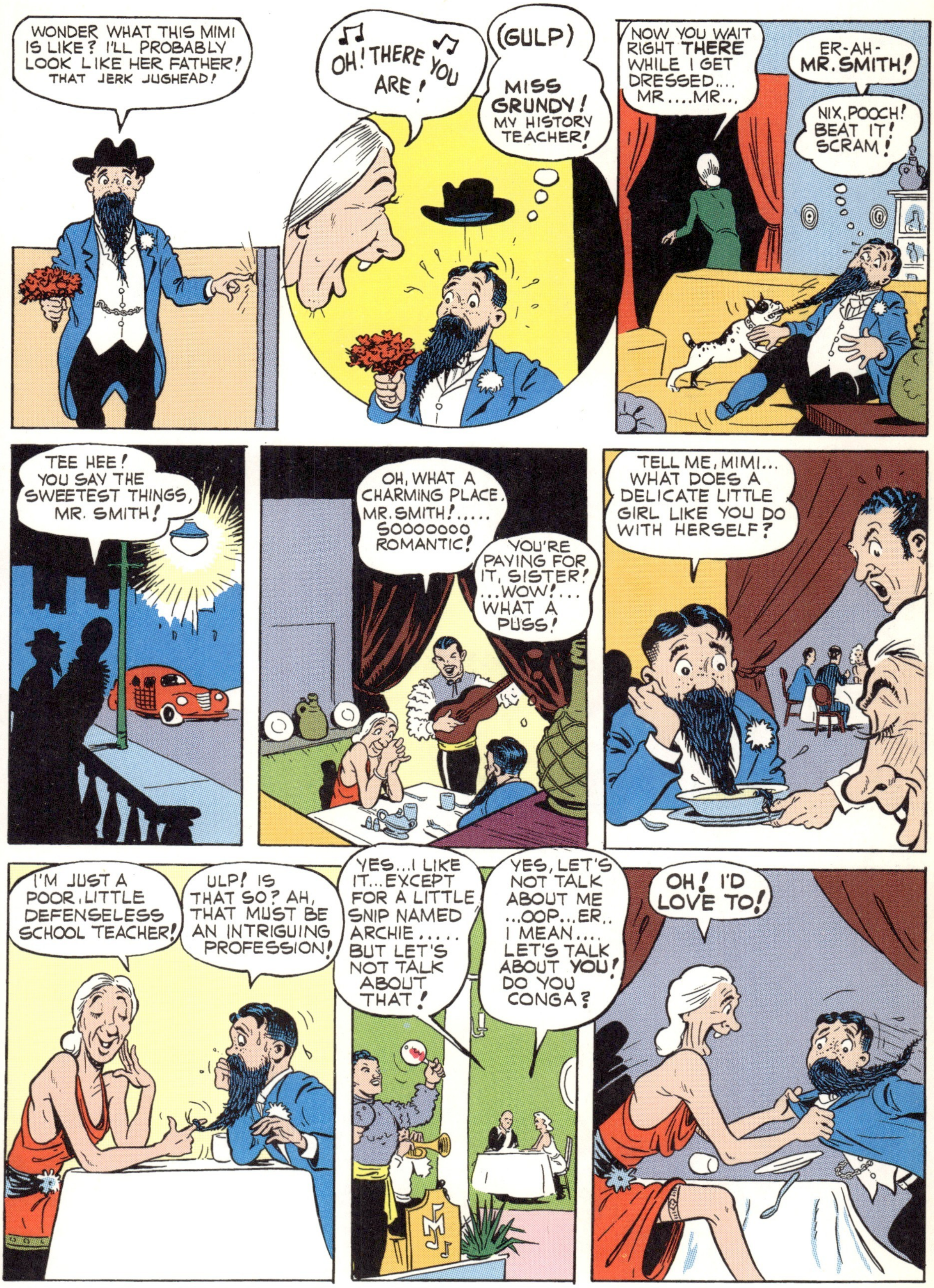
WONDER WHAT THIS MIMI IS LIKE? I'LL PROBABLY LOOK LIKE HER FATHER! THAT JERK JUGHEAD!
OH! THERE YOU ARE!
(GULP)
MISS GRUNDY! MY HISTORY TEACHER!
NOW YOU WAIT RIGHT THERE WHILE I GET DRESSED.... MR....MR...
ER-AH- MR. SMITH!
NIX, POOCH! BEAT IT! SCRAM!
TEE HEE! YOU SAY THE SWEETEST THINGS, MR. SMITH!
OH, WHAT A CHARMING PLACE, MR. SMITH!..... SOOOOOOO ROMANTIC!
YOU'RE PAYING FOR IT, SISTER! ...WOW!... WHAT A PUSS!
TELL ME, MIMI... WHAT DOES A DELICATE LITTLE GIRL LIKE YOU DO WITH HERSELF?
I'M JUST A POOR, LITTLE DEFENSELESS SCHOOL TEACHER!
ULP! IS THAT SO? AH, THAT MUST BE AN INTRIGUING PROFESSION!
YES...I LIKE IT...EXCEPT FOR A LITTLE SNIP NAMED ARCHIE..... BUT LET'S NOT TALK ABOUT THAT!
YES, LET'S NOT TALK ABOUT ME ...OOP...ER.. I MEAN.... LET'S TALK ABOUT YOU! DO YOU CONGA?
OH! I'D LOVE TO!

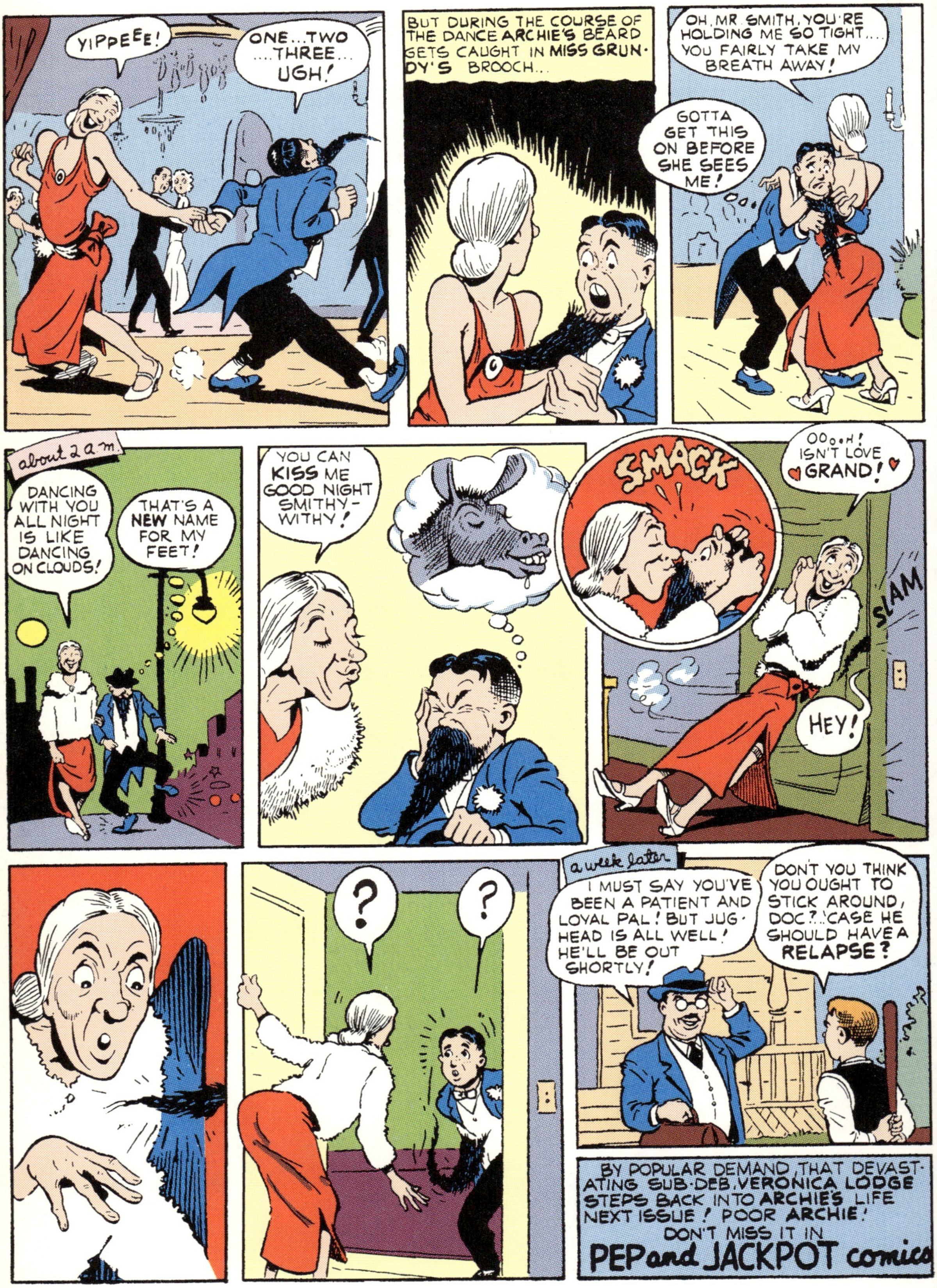
YIPPEEE!
ONE...TWO ....THREE... UGH!
BUT DURING THE COURSE OF THE DANCE ARCHIE'S BEARD GETS CAUGHT IN MISS GRUNDY'S BROOCH...
OH, MR. SMITH, YOU'RE HOLDING ME SO TIGHT.... YOU FAIRLY TAKE MY BREATH AWAY!
GOTTA GET THIS ON BEFORE SHE SEES ME!
about 2 a.m.
DANCING WITH YOU ALL NIGHT IS LIKE DANCING ON CLOUDS!
THAT'S A NEW NAME FOR MY FEET!
YOU CAN KISS ME GOOD NIGHT SMITHY-WITHY!
SMACK
OOOOH! ISN'T LOVE GRAND!
SLAM
HEY!
?
?
a week later
I MUST SAY YOU'VE BEEN A PATIENT AND LOYAL PAL! BUT JUG-HEAD IS ALL WELL! HE'LL BE OUT SHORTLY!
DON'T YOU THINK YOU OUGHT TO STICK AROUND, DOC?..'CASE HE SHOULD HAVE A RELAPSE?
BY POPULAR DEMAND THAT DEVASTATING SUB-DEB, VERONICA LODGE STEPS BACK INTO ARCHIE'S LIFE NEXT ISSUE! POOR ARCHIE!
DON'T MISS IT IN
PEP and JACKPOT comics

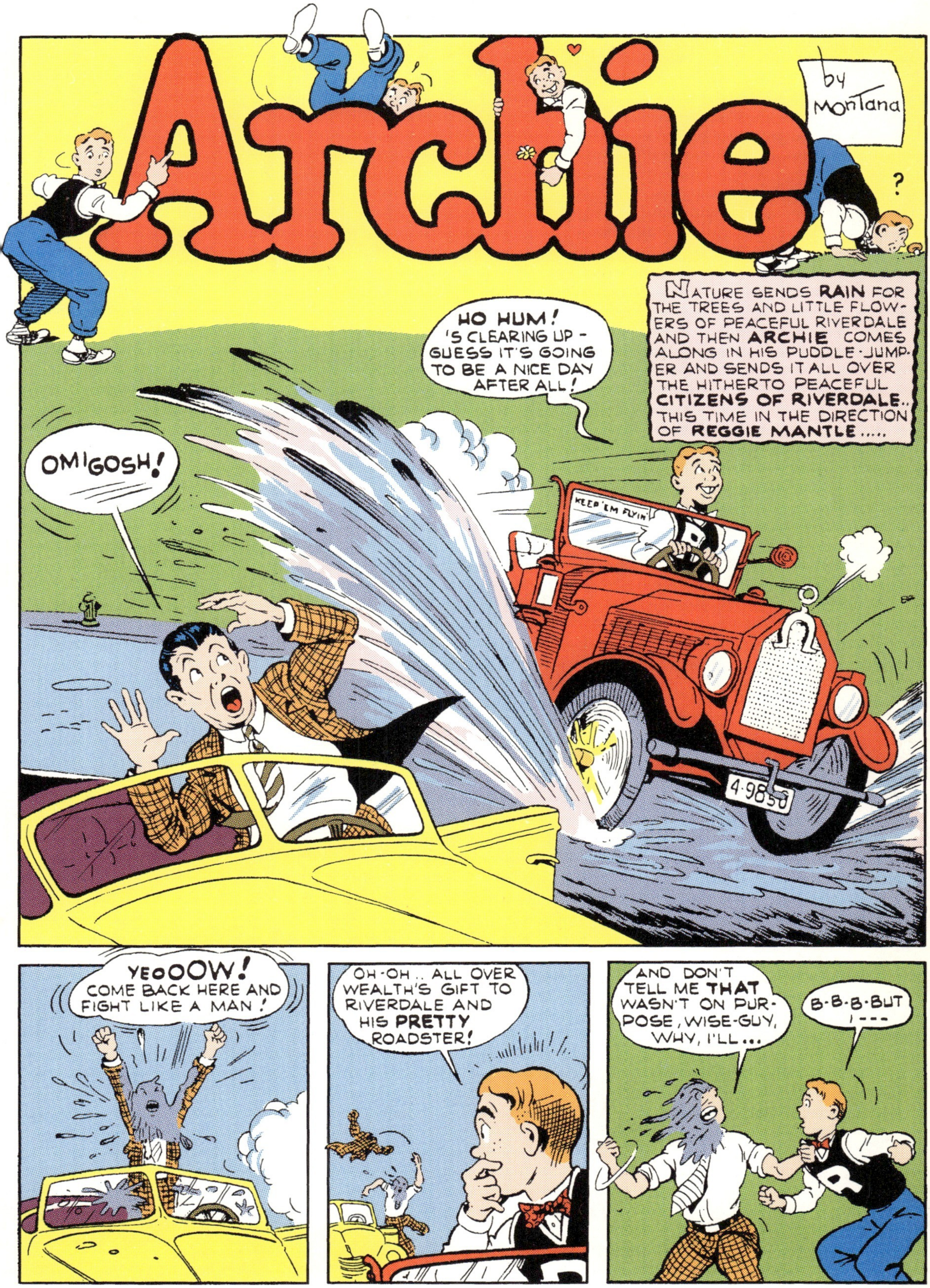
Archie
by Montana
?
NATURE SENDS RAIN FOR THE TREES AND LITTLE FLOWERS OF PEACEFUL RIVERDALE AND THEN ARCHIE COMES ALONG IN HIS PUDDLE-JUMPER AND SENDS IT ALL OVER THE HITHERTO PEACEFUL CITIZENS OF RIVERDALE.. THIS TIME IN THE DIRECTION OF REGGIE MANTLE.....
HO HUM! 'S CLEARING UP - GUESS IT'S GOING TO BE A NICE DAY AFTER ALL!
OMIGOSH!
KEEP 'EM FLYIN'
4-985J
YEOOOW! COME BACK HERE AND FIGHT LIKE A MAN!
OH-OH .. ALL OVER WEALTH'S GIFT TO RIVERDALE AND HIS PRETTY ROADSTER!
AND DON'T TELL ME THAT WASN'T ON PURPOSE, WISE-GUY, WHY, I'LL...
B-B-B-BUT I---

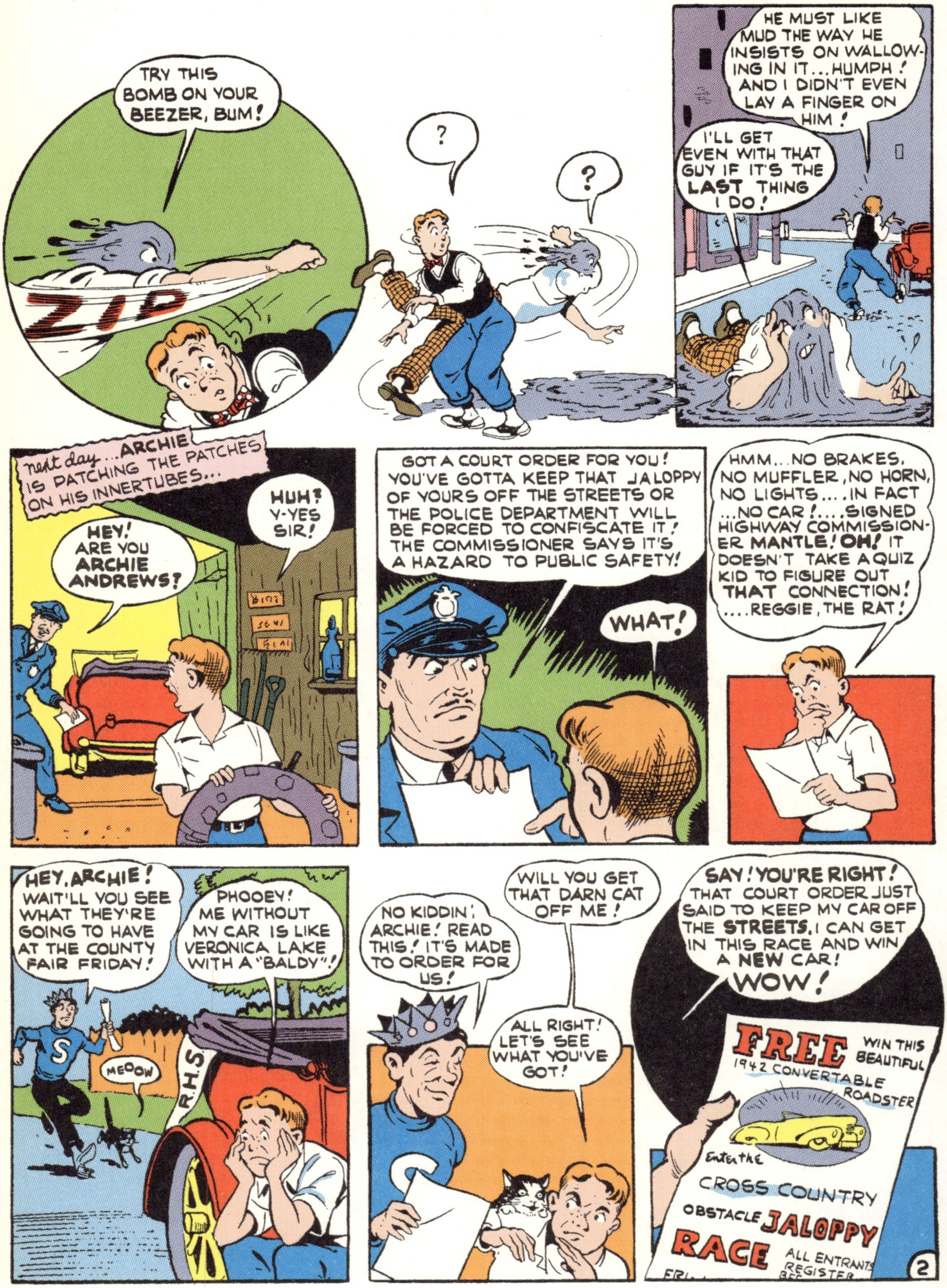

TRY THIS BOMB ON YOUR BEEZER, BUM!
ZIP
?
?
HE MUST LIKE MUD THE WAY HE INSISTS ON WALLOWING IN IT... HUMPH! AND I DIDN'T EVEN LAY A FINGER ON HIM!
I'LL GET EVEN WITH THAT GUY IF IT'S THE LAST THING I DO!
next day... ARCHIE IS PATCHING THE PATCHES ON HIS INNERTUBES...
HEY! ARE YOU ARCHIE ANDREWS?
HUH? Y-YES SIR!
GOT A COURT ORDER FOR YOU! YOU'VE GOTTA KEEP THAT JALOPPY OF YOURS OFF THE STREETS OR THE POLICE DEPARTMENT WILL BE FORCED TO CONFISCATE IT! THE COMMISSIONER SAYS IT'S A HAZARD TO PUBLIC SAFETY!
WHAT!
HMM... NO BRAKES, NO MUFFLER, NO HORN, NO LIGHTS.... IN FACT ...NO CAR!.... SIGNED HIGHWAY COMMISSIONER MANTLE! OH! IT DOESN'T TAKE A QUIZ KID TO FIGURE OUT THAT CONNECTION! ....REGGIE, THE RAT!
HEY, ARCHIE! WAIT'LL YOU SEE WHAT THEY'RE GOING TO HAVE AT THE COUNTY FAIR FRIDAY!
PHOOEY! ME WITHOUT MY CAR IS LIKE VERONICA LAKE WITH A "BALDY"!
MEOOW
R.H.S.
NO KIDDIN', ARCHIE! READ THIS! IT'S MADE TO ORDER FOR US!
WILL YOU GET THAT DARN CAT OFF ME!
ALL RIGHT! LET'S SEE WHAT YOU'VE GOT!
SAY! YOU'RE RIGHT! THAT COURT ORDER JUST SAID TO KEEP MY CAR OFF THE STREETS, I CAN GET IN THIS RACE AND WIN A NEW CAR! WOW!
FREE WIN THIS BEAUTIFUL 1942 CONVERTABLE ROADSTER
Enter the CROSS COUNTRY OBSTACLE JALOPPY RACE
ALL ENTRANTS REGISTER
2

NEXT MORNING AT SCHOOL

ARE YOU REALLY GOING IN THE JALOPPY RACE, ARCHIE?

ISN'T IT EXCITING!

AREN'T YOU AFRAID OF THE DANGER, ARCHIE?

I HOPE YOU WIN, ARCHIE! IT'S AN AWFULLY NICE ROADSTER!

CAN YOU BEAT IT! THAT WOULD-BE BARNEY OLDFIELD GOES IN A RACE AND THOSE DIZZY DAMES FALL ALL OVER HIM... WELL, TWO CAN PLAY AT THIS GAME!

YEAH, THAT'S IT - I WANT THAT MOTOR TAKEN OUT AND PUT IN THE OLDEST JALOPPY YOU HAVE!

IT WOULD LOOK BETTER IN A TANK!

JALOPPY CROSS COUNTRY RACE

Entrance

FRIDAY, DAY OF THE RACE

HA! HA! HA! GET A LOAD OF THAT SEWING MACHINE REGGIE'S GOING TO RACE - I'LL BET HE CAN'T EVEN START IT!

GO AHEAD! LAUGH, SUCKER!

KEEP 'EM AWAY

2

HEH HEH!

R-R-ROARRRRRRRRRR

HEY! WAIT A MINUTE, BUD! THAT MOTOR SOUNDS FAMILIAR!

BANG

THEY'RE OFF!

ARCHIE, QUICK! GET BACK IN HERE — THE RACE HAS STARTED!

3

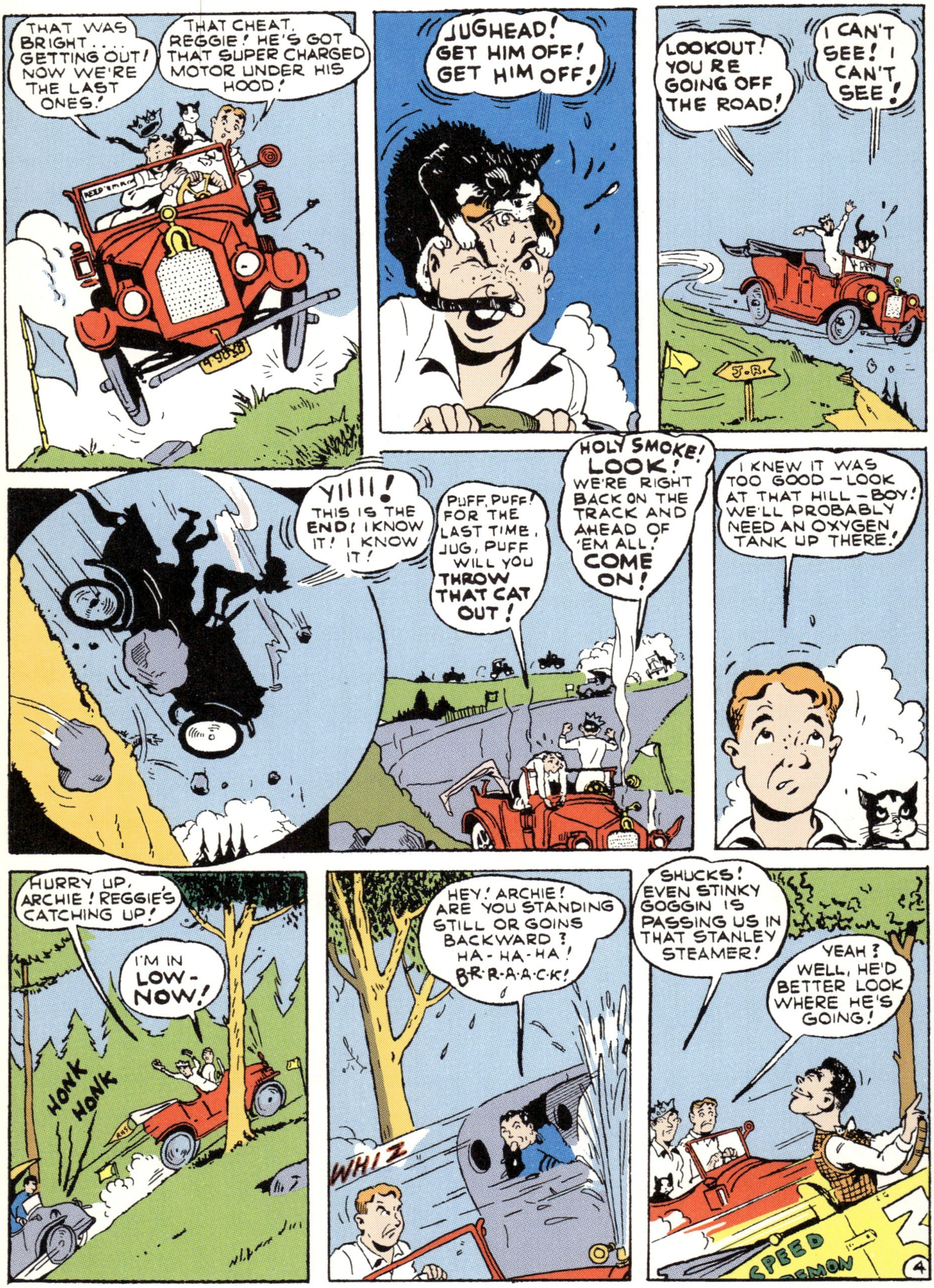
THAT WAS BRIGHT.... GETTING OUT! NOW WE'RE THE LAST ONES!
THAT CHEAT, REGGIE! HE'S GOT THAT SUPER CHARGED MOTOR UNDER HIS HOOD!
JUGHEAD! GET HIM OFF! GET HIM OFF!
LOOKOUT! YOU RE GOING OFF THE ROAD!
I CAN'T SEE! I CAN'T SEE!
YIIII! THIS IS THE END! I KNOW IT! I KNOW IT!
PUFF, PUFF! FOR THE LAST TIME, JUG, PUFF WILL YOU THROW THAT CAT OUT!
HOLY SMOKE! LOOK! WE'RE RIGHT BACK ON THE TRACK AND AHEAD OF 'EM ALL! COME ON!
I KNEW IT WAS TOO GOOD — LOOK AT THAT HILL — BOY! WE'LL PROBABLY NEED AN OXYGEN TANK UP THERE!
HURRY UP, ARCHIE! REGGIE'S CATCHING UP!
I'M IN LOW-NOW!
HONK HONK
HEY! ARCHIE! ARE YOU STANDING STILL OR GOING BACKWARD? HA-HA-HA! B-R-R-A-A-C-K!
WHIZ
SHUCKS! EVEN STINKY GOGGIN IS PASSING US IN THAT STANLEY STEAMER!
YEAH? WELL, HE'D BETTER LOOK WHERE HE'S GOING!
SPEED DEMON
4

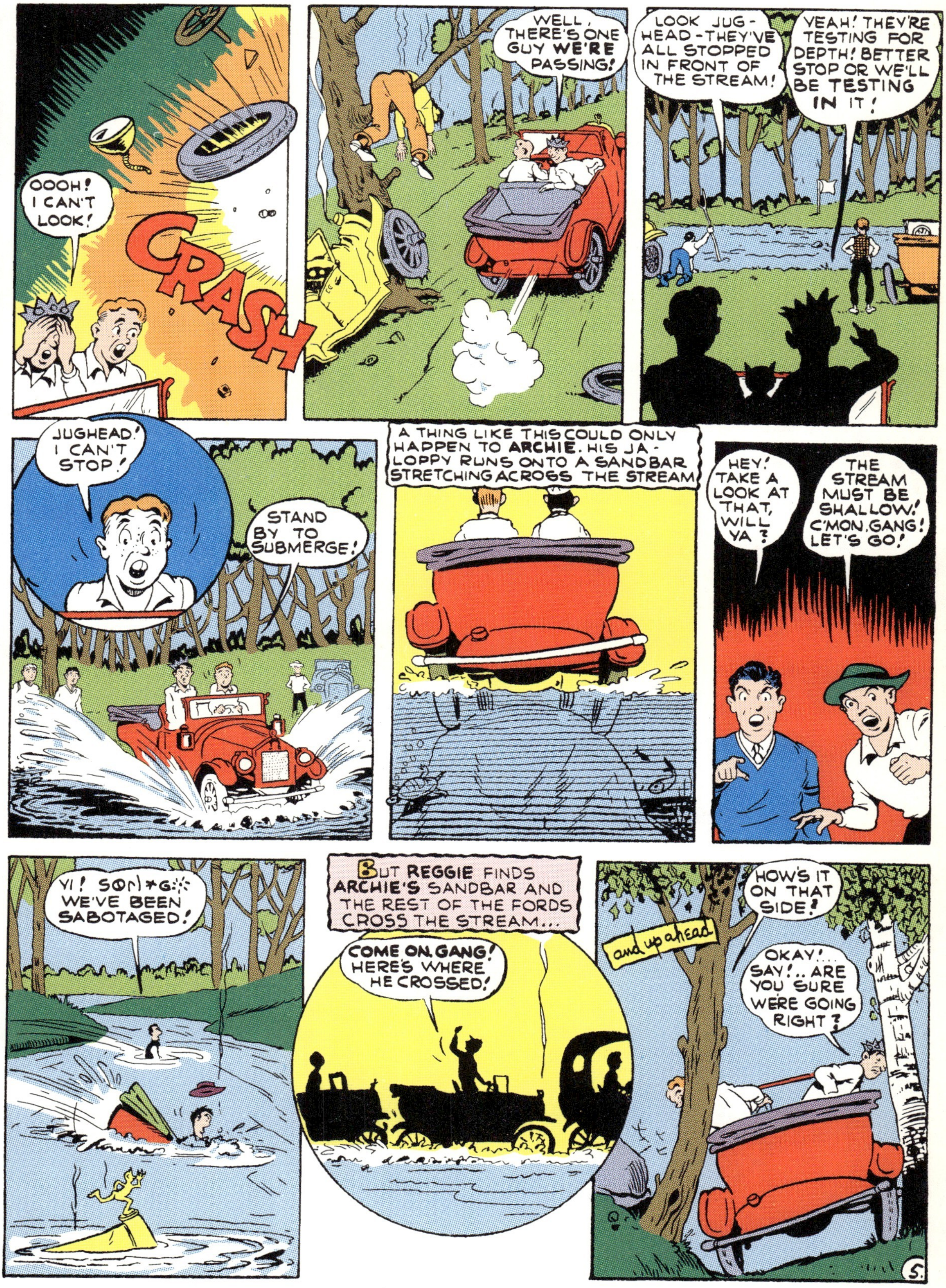
OOOH! I CAN'T LOOK!
CRASH
WELL, THERE'S ONE GUY WE'RE PASSING!
LOOK JUG-HEAD-THEY'VE ALL STOPPED IN FRONT OF THE STREAM!
YEAH! THEY'RE TESTING FOR DEPTH! BETTER STOP OR WE'LL BE TESTING IN IT!
JUGHEAD! I CAN'T STOP!
STAND BY TO SUBMERGE!
A THING LIKE THIS COULD ONLY HAPPEN TO ARCHIE. HIS JA-LOPPY RUNS ONTO A SANDBAR STRETCHING ACROSS THE STREAM
HEY! TAKE A LOOK AT THAT, WILL YA?
THE STREAM MUST BE SHALLOW! C'MON, GANG! LET'S GO!
YI! WE'VE BEEN SABOTAGED!
BUT REGGIE FINDS ARCHIE'S SANDBAR AND THE REST OF THE FORDS CROSS THE STREAM...
COME ON, GANG! HERE'S WHERE HE CROSSED!
and up ahead
HOW'S IT ON THAT SIDE?
OKAY!... SAY!.. ARE YOU SURE WE'RE GOING RIGHT?
5.

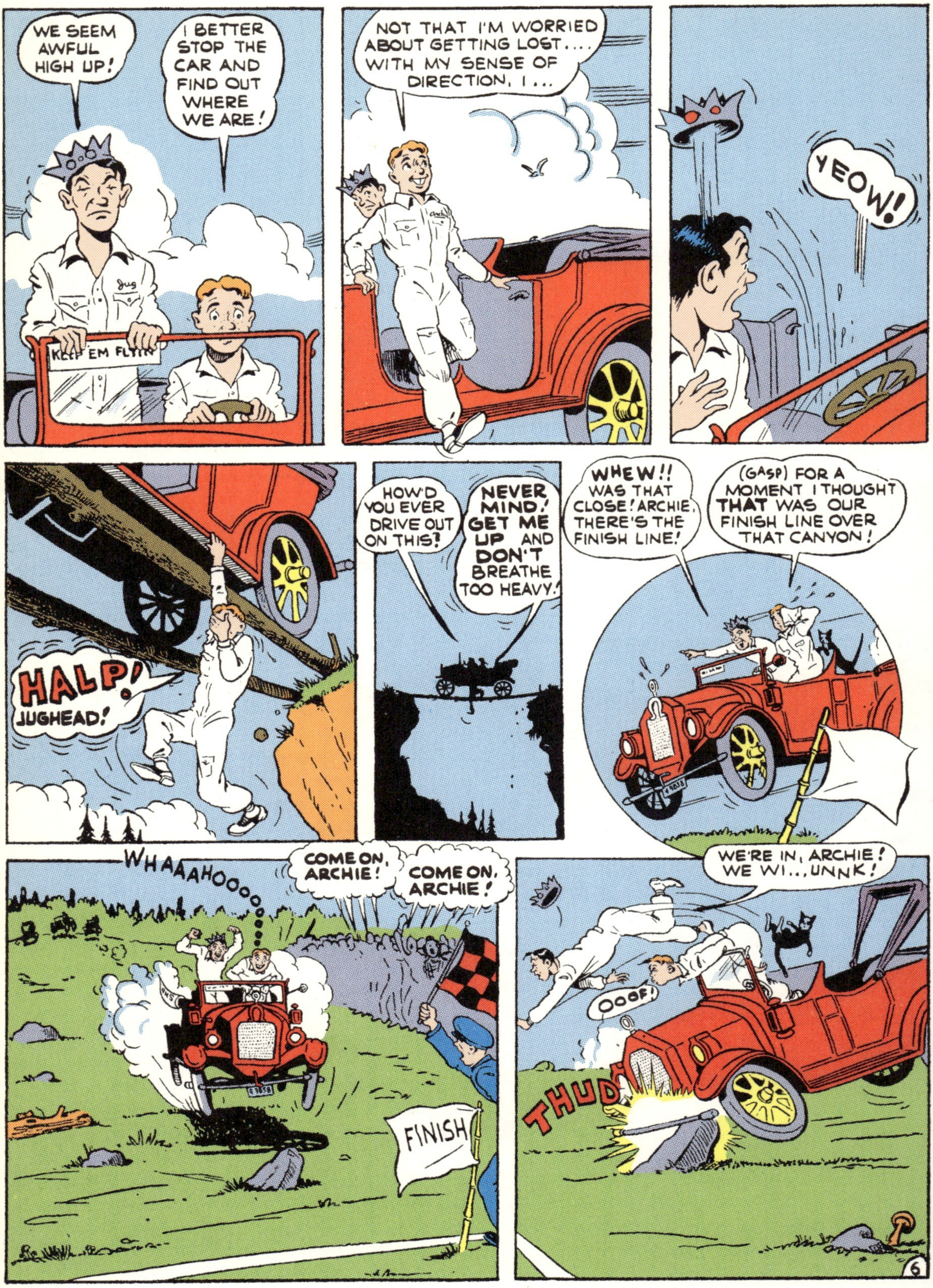
WE SEEM AWFUL HIGH UP!
I BETTER STOP THE CAR AND FIND OUT WHERE WE ARE!
NOT THAT I'M WORRIED ABOUT GETTING LOST.... WITH MY SENSE OF DIRECTION, I...
YEOW!
HALP! JUGHEAD!
HOW'D YOU EVER DRIVE OUT ON THIS?
NEVER MIND! GET ME UP AND DON'T BREATHE TOO HEAVY!
WHEW!! WAS THAT CLOSE! ARCHIE, THERE'S THE FINISH LINE!
(GASP) FOR A MOMENT I THOUGHT THAT WAS OUR FINISH LINE OVER THAT CANYON!
WHAAAAHOOOOOOO
COME ON, ARCHIE!
COME ON, ARCHIE!
FINISH
WE'RE IN, ARCHIE! WE WI... UNNK!
OOOF!
THUD
6

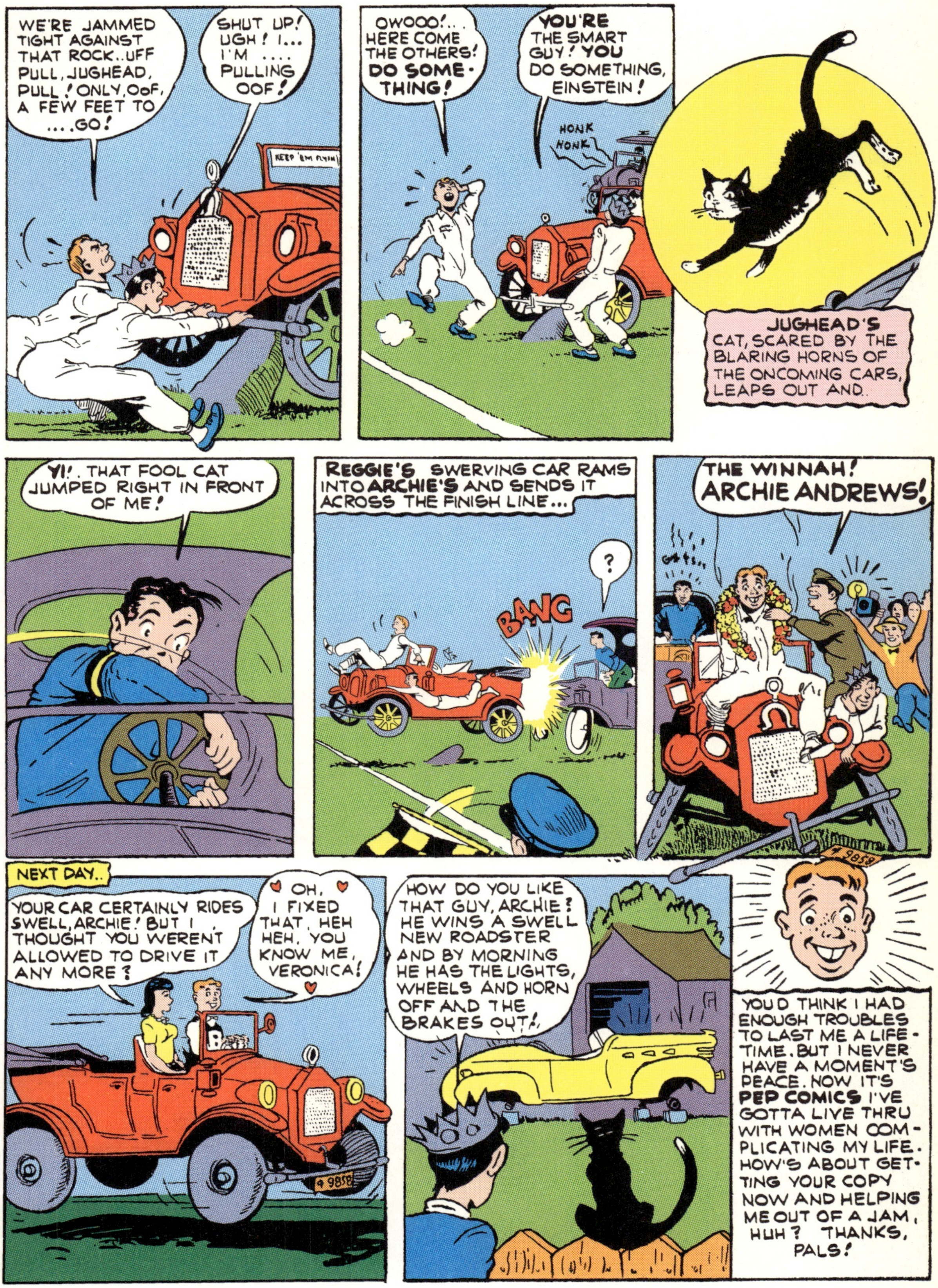
WE'RE JAMMED TIGHT AGAINST THAT ROCK..UFF PULL, JUGHEAD, PULL! ONLY, OOF, A FEW FEET TO ....GO!
SHUT UP! UGH! I... I'M .... PULLING OOF!
KEEP 'EM FLYIN
OWOOO!.. HERE COME THE OTHERS! DO SOME-THING!
YOU'RE THE SMART GUY! YOU DO SOMETHING, EINSTEIN!
HONK HONK
JUGHEAD'S CAT, SCARED BY THE BLARING HORNS OF THE ONCOMING CARS, LEAPS OUT AND..
YI!. THAT FOOL CAT JUMPED RIGHT IN FRONT OF ME!
REGGIE'S SWERVING CAR RAMS INTO ARCHIE'S AND SENDS IT ACROSS THE FINISH LINE...
?
BANG
THE WINNAH! ARCHIE ANDREWS!
NEXT DAY..
YOUR CAR CERTAINLY RIDES SWELL, ARCHIE! BUT I THOUGHT YOU WERENT ALLOWED TO DRIVE IT ANY MORE?
OH, I FIXED THAT, HEH HEH, YOU KNOW ME, VERONICA!
HOW DO YOU LIKE THAT GUY, ARCHIE? HE WINS A SWELL NEW ROADSTER AND BY MORNING HE HAS THE LIGHTS, WHEELS AND HORN OFF AND THE BRAKES OUT!
YOU'D THINK I HAD ENOUGH TROUBLES TO LAST ME A LIFE-TIME. BUT I NEVER HAVE A MOMENT'S PEACE. NOW IT'S PEP COMICS I'VE GOTTA LIVE THRU WITH WOMEN COM-PLICATING MY LIFE. HOW'S ABOUT GET-TING YOUR COPY NOW AND HELPING ME OUT OF A JAM, HUH? THANKS, PALS!

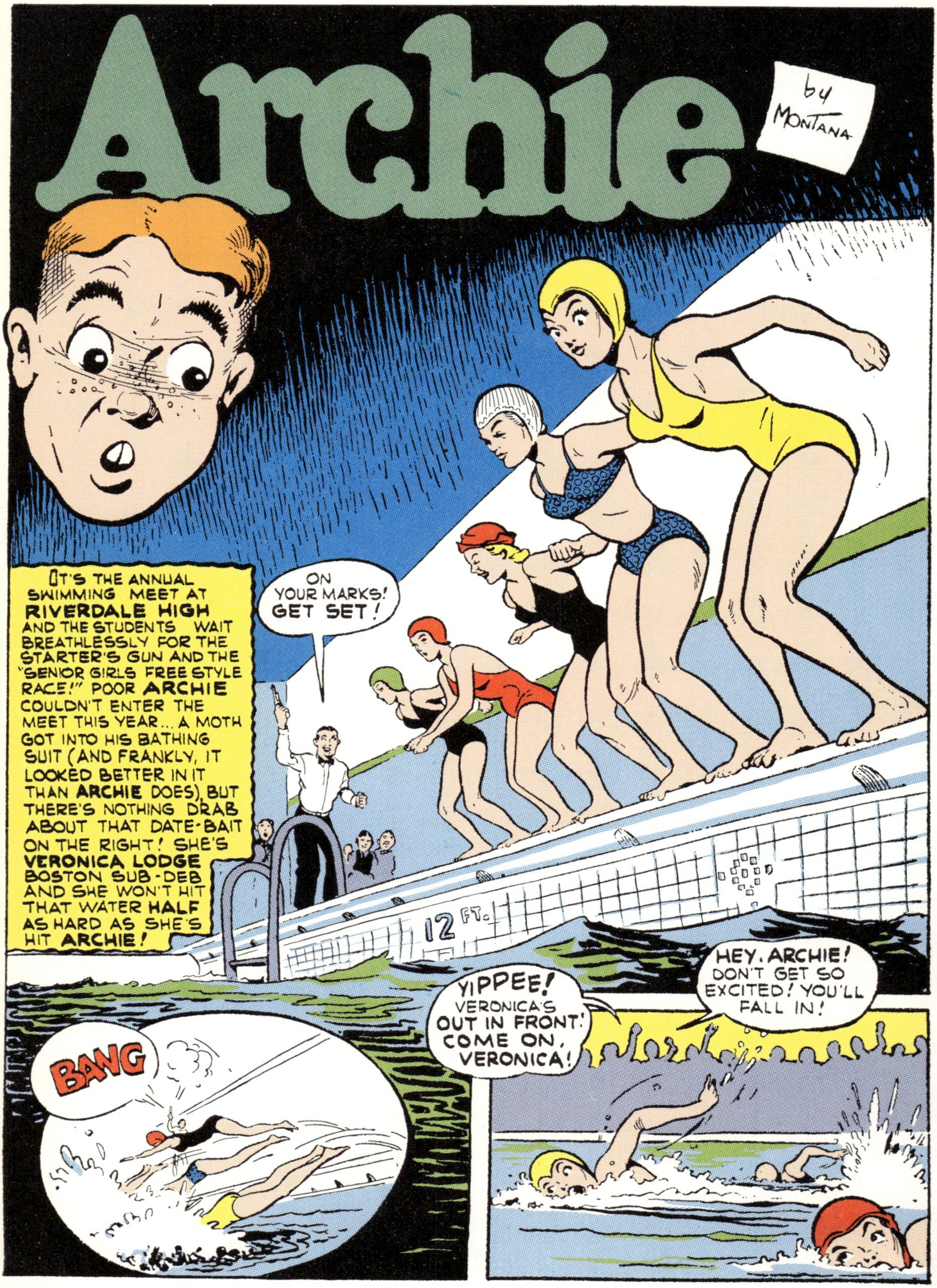

Archie
by MONTANA
IT'S THE ANNUAL SWIMMING MEET AT RIVERDALE HIGH AND THE STUDENTS WAIT BREATHLESSLY FOR THE STARTER'S GUN AND THE "SENIOR GIRLS FREE STYLE RACE!" POOR ARCHIE COULDN'T ENTER THE MEET THIS YEAR... A MOTH GOT INTO HIS BATHING SUIT (AND FRANKLY, IT LOOKED BETTER IN IT THAN ARCHIE DOES), BUT THERE'S NOTHING DRAB ABOUT THAT DATE-BAIT ON THE RIGHT! SHE'S VERONICA LODGE BOSTON SUB-DEB AND SHE WON'T HIT THAT WATER HALF AS HARD AS SHE'S HIT ARCHIE!
ON YOUR MARKS! GET SET!
12 FT.
BANG
YIPPEE! VERONICA'S OUT IN FRONT! COME ON, VERONICA!
HEY, ARCHIE! DON'T GET SO EXCITED! YOU'LL FALL IN!

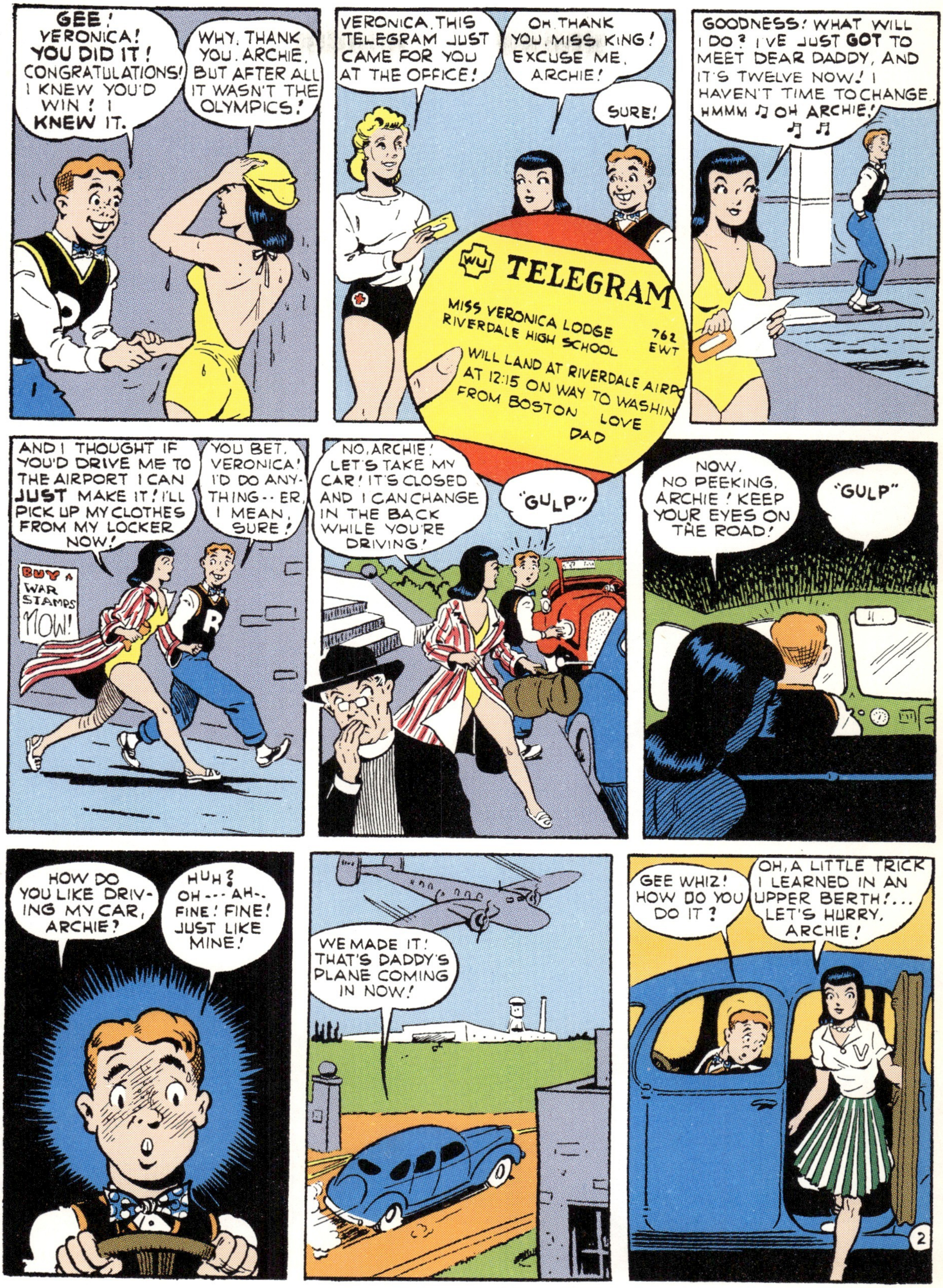
GEE! VERONICA! YOU DID IT! CONGRATULATIONS! I KNEW YOU'D WIN! I KNEW IT.
WHY, THANK YOU, ARCHIE. BUT AFTER ALL IT WASN'T THE OLYMPICS!
VERONICA, THIS TELEGRAM JUST CAME FOR YOU AT THE OFFICE!
OH, THANK YOU, MISS KING! EXCUSE ME, ARCHIE!
SURE!
TELEGRAM
MISS VERONICA LODGE
RIVERDALE HIGH SCHOOL
762 EWT
WILL LAND AT RIVERDALE AIRP
AT 12:15 ON WAY TO WASHIN
FROM BOSTON LOVE
DAD
GOODNESS! WHAT WILL I DO? I'VE JUST GOT TO MEET DEAR DADDY, AND IT'S TWELVE NOW! I HAVEN'T TIME TO CHANGE. HMMM ♫ OH ARCHIE! ♫ ♫
AND I THOUGHT IF YOU'D DRIVE ME TO THE AIRPORT I CAN JUST MAKE IT! I'LL PICK UP MY CLOTHES FROM MY LOCKER NOW!
YOU BET, VERONICA! I'D DO ANYTHING-- ER, I MEAN, SURE!
BUY WAR STAMPS NOW!
NO, ARCHIE! LET'S TAKE MY CAR! IT'S CLOSED AND I CAN CHANGE IN THE BACK WHILE YOU'RE DRIVING!
"GULP"
NOW, NO PEEKING, ARCHIE! KEEP YOUR EYES ON THE ROAD!
"GULP"
HOW DO YOU LIKE DRIVING MY CAR, ARCHIE?
HUH? OH--- AH-- FINE! FINE! JUST LIKE MINE!
WE MADE IT! THAT'S DADDY'S PLANE COMING IN NOW!
GEE WHIZ! HOW DO YOU DO IT?
OH, A LITTLE TRICK I LEARNED IN AN UPPER BERTH!... LET'S HURRY, ARCHIE!
2

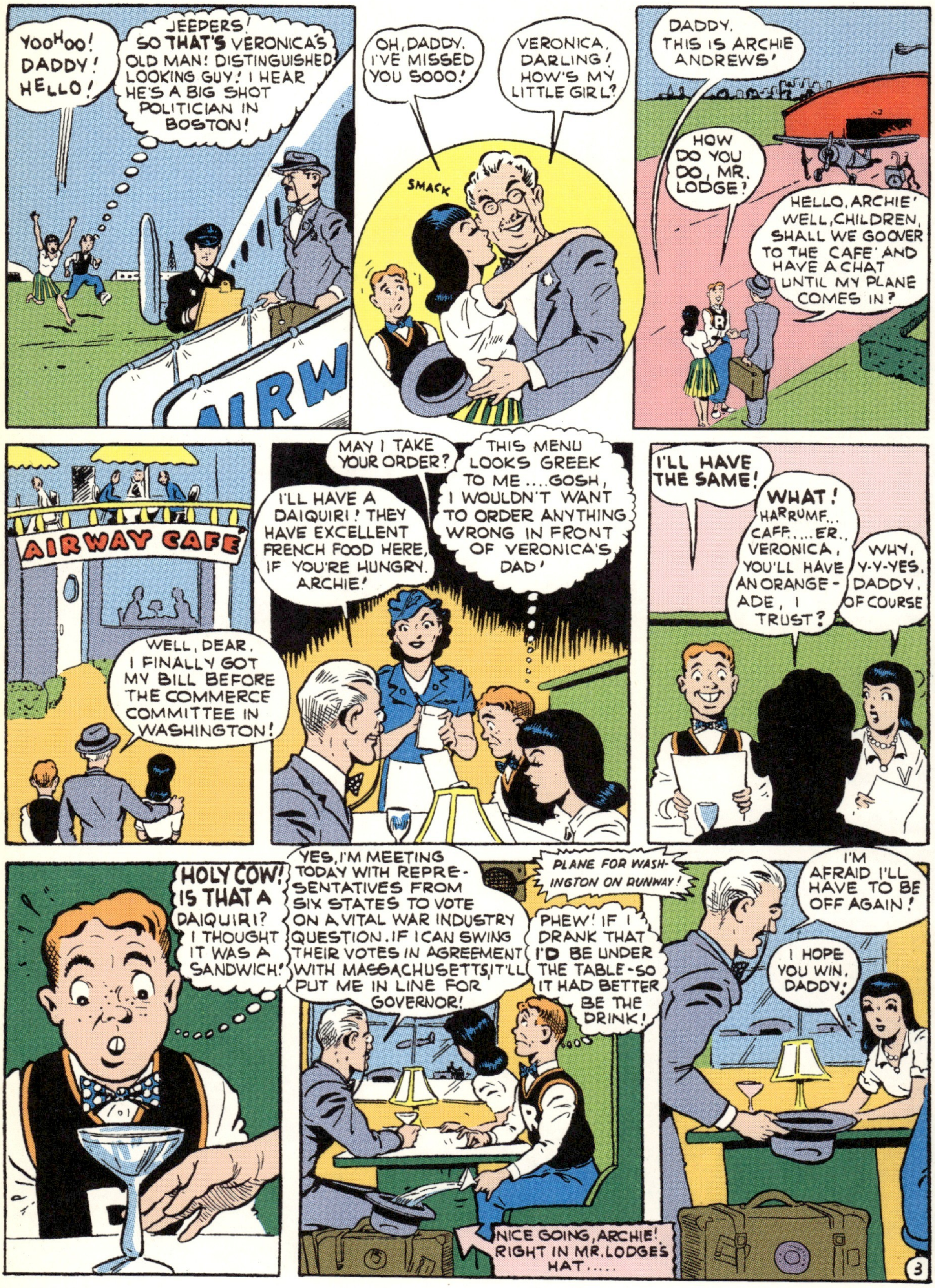
YOOHOO! DADDY! HELLO!
JEEPERS! SO THAT'S VERONICA'S OLD MAN! DISTINGUISHED LOOKING GUY! I HEAR HE'S A BIG SHOT POLITICIAN IN BOSTON!
AIRW
OH, DADDY, I'VE MISSED YOU SOOO!
VERONICA, DARLING! HOW'S MY LITTLE GIRL?
SMACK
DADDY, THIS IS ARCHIE ANDREWS!
HOW DO YOU DO, MR. LODGE!
HELLO, ARCHIE! WELL, CHILDREN, SHALL WE GO OVER TO THE CAFE AND HAVE A CHAT UNTIL MY PLANE COMES IN?
AIRWAY CAFE
WELL, DEAR, I FINALLY GOT MY BILL BEFORE THE COMMERCE COMMITTEE IN WASHINGTON!
MAY I TAKE YOUR ORDER?
I'LL HAVE A DAIQUIRI! THEY HAVE EXCELLENT FRENCH FOOD HERE, IF YOU'RE HUNGRY, ARCHIE!
THIS MENU LOOKS GREEK TO ME....GOSH, I WOULDN'T WANT TO ORDER ANYTHING WRONG IN FRONT OF VERONICA'S DAD!
I'LL HAVE THE SAME!
WHAT! HARRUMF... CAFF.....ER.. VERONICA, YOU'LL HAVE AN ORANGE-ADE, I TRUST?
WHY, Y-Y-YES, DADDY, OF COURSE
HOLY COW! IS THAT A DAIQUIRI? I THOUGHT IT WAS A SANDWICH!
YES, I'M MEETING TODAY WITH REPRESENTATIVES FROM SIX STATES TO VOTE ON A VITAL WAR INDUSTRY QUESTION. IF I CAN SWING THEIR VOTES IN AGREEMENT WITH MASSACHUSETTS, IT'LL PUT ME IN LINE FOR GOVERNOR!
PLANE FOR WASHINGTON ON RUNWAY!
PHEW! IF I DRANK THAT I'D BE UNDER THE TABLE-SO IT HAD BETTER BE THE DRINK!
NICE GOING, ARCHIE! RIGHT IN MR. LODGES HAT....
I'M AFRAID I'LL HAVE TO BE OFF AGAIN!
I HOPE YOU WIN, DADDY!
3

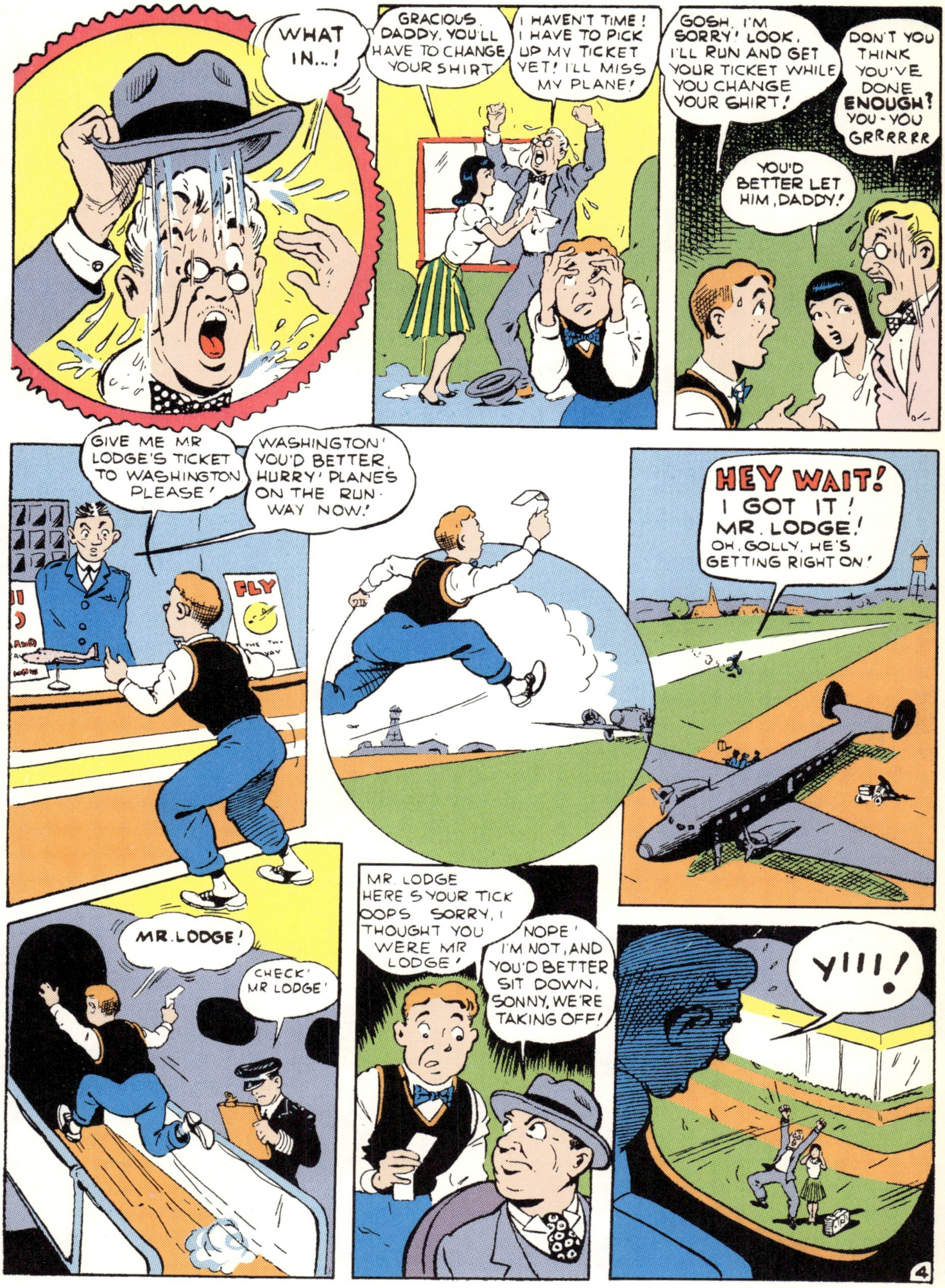
WHAT IN...!
GRACIOUS. DADDY, YOU'LL HAVE TO CHANGE YOUR SHIRT.
I HAVEN'T TIME! I HAVE TO PICK UP MY TICKET YET! I'LL MISS MY PLANE!
GOSH, I'M SORRY! LOOK, I'LL RUN AND GET YOUR TICKET WHILE YOU CHANGE YOUR SHIRT!
DON'T YOU THINK YOU'VE DONE ENOUGH? YOU-YOU GRRRRRR
YOU'D BETTER LET HIM, DADDY!
GIVE ME MR LODGE'S TICKET TO WASHINGTON, PLEASE!
WASHINGTON! YOU'D BETTER HURRY! PLANE'S ON THE RUN-WAY NOW!
FLY
HEY WAIT! I GOT IT! MR. LODGE! OH, GOLLY, HE'S GETTING RIGHT ON!
MR. LODGE!
CHECK! MR LODGE!
MR. LODGE HERE S YOUR TICK OOPS SORRY, I THOUGHT YOU WERE MR LODGE!
NOPE! I'M NOT, AND YOU'D BETTER SIT DOWN, SONNY, WE'RE TAKING OFF!
YIII!
4

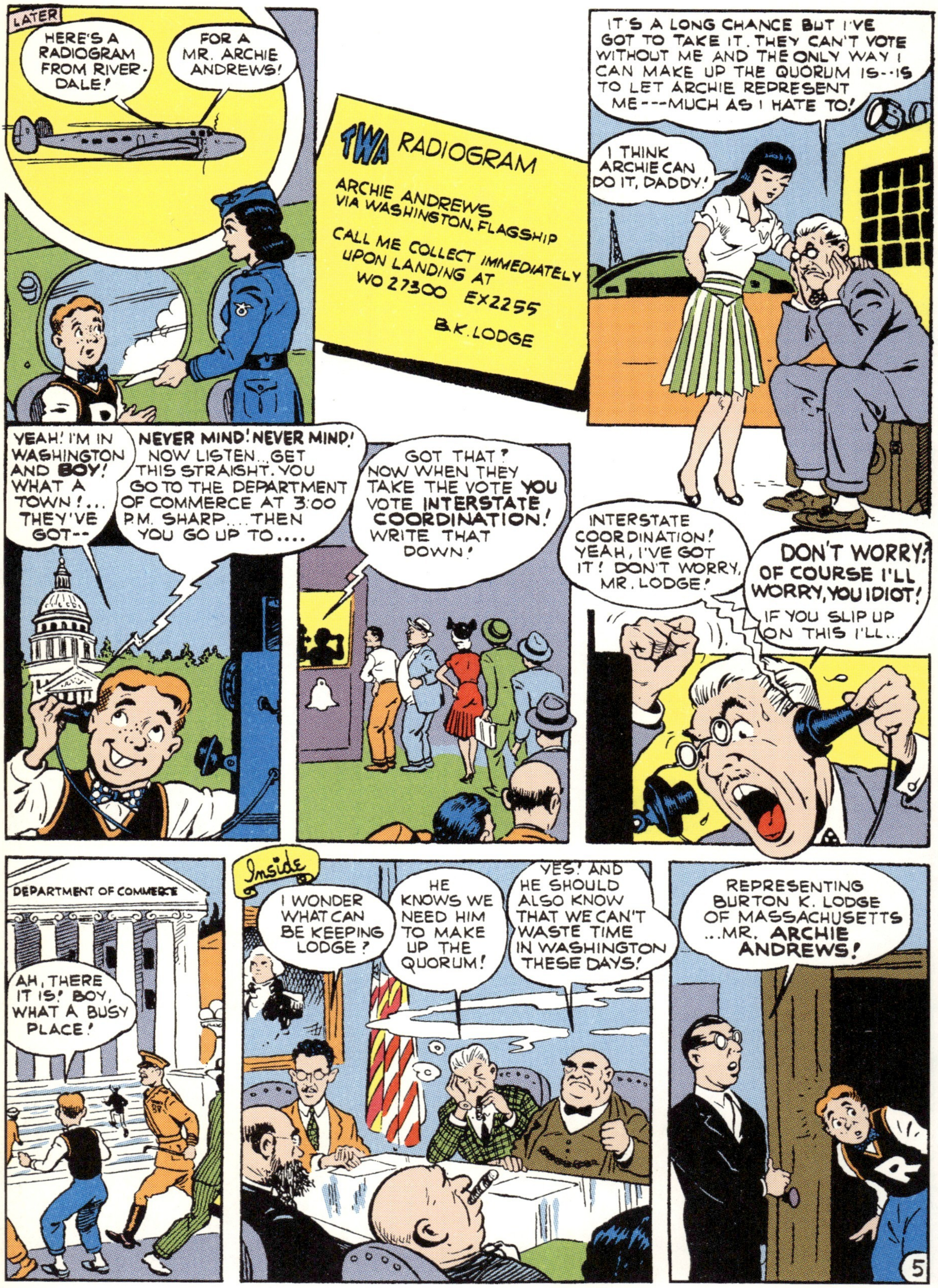
LATER
HERE'S A RADIOGRAM FROM RIVER-DALE!
FOR A MR. ARCHIE ANDREWS!
TWA RADIOGRAM
ARCHIE ANDREWS VIA WASHINGTON, FLAGSHIP
CALL ME COLLECT IMMEDIATELY UPON LANDING AT WO 27300 EX2255
B.K. LODGE
IT'S A LONG CHANCE BUT I'VE GOT TO TAKE IT. THEY CAN'T VOTE WITHOUT ME AND THE ONLY WAY I CAN MAKE UP THE QUORUM IS--IS TO LET ARCHIE REPRESENT ME---MUCH AS I HATE TO!
I THINK ARCHIE CAN DO IT, DADDY!
YEAH! I'M IN WASHINGTON AND BOY! WHAT A TOWN!... THEY'VE GOT--
NEVER MIND! NEVER MIND! NOW LISTEN... GET THIS STRAIGHT. YOU GO TO THE DEPARTMENT OF COMMERCE AT 3:00 P.M. SHARP.... THEN YOU GO UP TO....
GOT THAT? NOW WHEN THEY TAKE THE VOTE YOU VOTE INTERSTATE COORDINATION! WRITE THAT DOWN!
INTERSTATE COORDINATION! YEAH, I'VE GOT IT! DON'T WORRY, MR. LODGE!
DON'T WORRY? OF COURSE I'LL WORRY, YOU IDIOT! IF YOU SLIP UP ON THIS I'LL...
DEPARTMENT OF COMMERCE
AH, THERE IT IS! BOY, WHAT A BUSY PLACE!
Inside
I WONDER WHAT CAN BE KEEPING LODGE?
HE KNOWS WE NEED HIM TO MAKE UP THE QUORUM!
YES! AND HE SHOULD ALSO KNOW THAT WE CAN'T WASTE TIME IN WASHINGTON THESE DAYS!
REPRESENTING BURTON K. LODGE OF MASSACHUSETTS ...MR. ARCHIE ANDREWS!
5

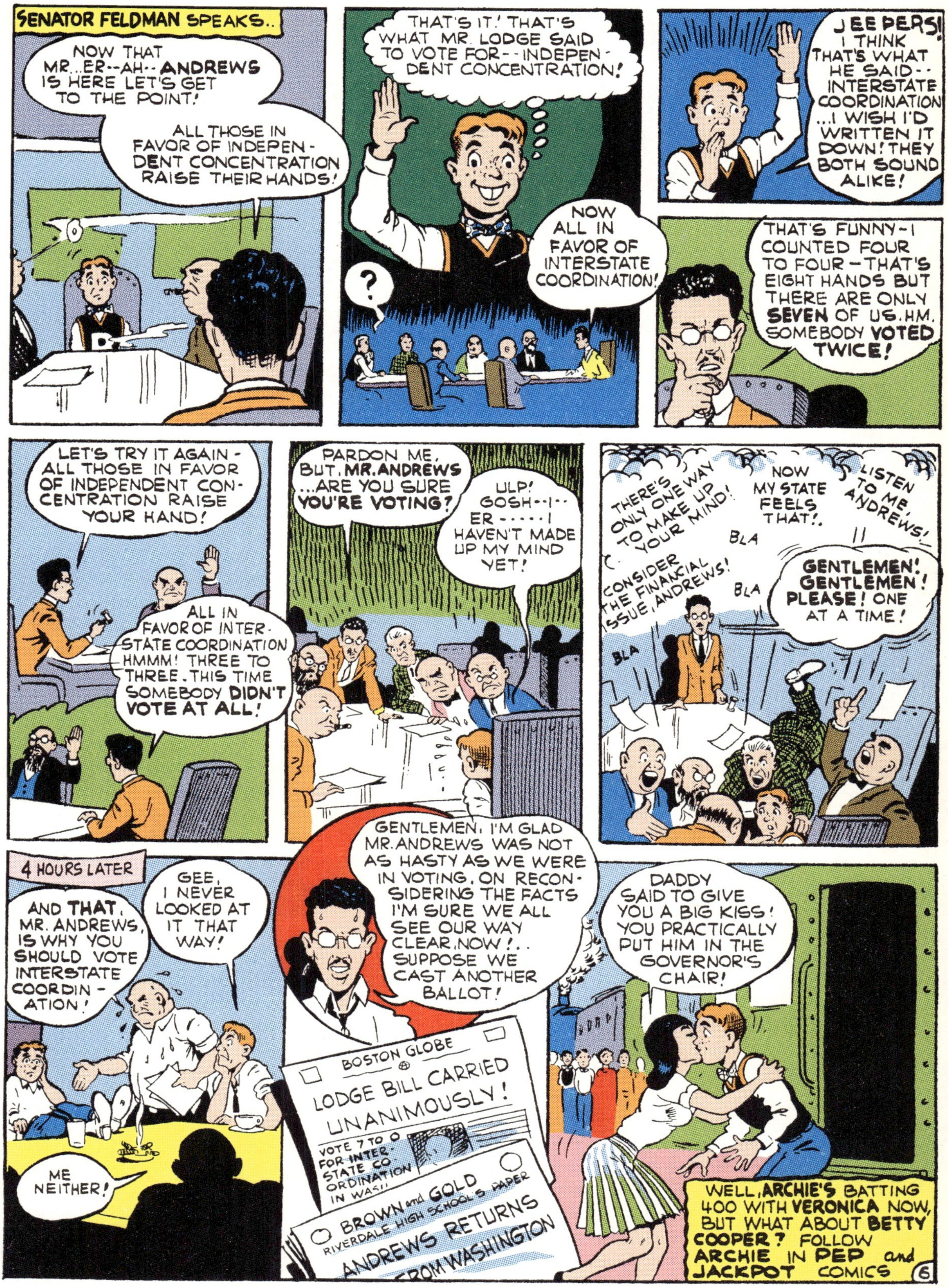
SENATOR FELDMAN SPEAKS..
NOW THAT MR..ER--AH--ANDREWS IS HERE LET'S GET TO THE POINT!
ALL THOSE IN FAVOR OF INDEPENDENT CONCENTRATION RAISE THEIR HANDS!
THAT'S IT! THAT'S WHAT MR. LODGE SAID TO VOTE FOR--INDEPENDENT CONCENTRATION!
?
NOW ALL IN FAVOR OF INTERSTATE COORDINATION!
JEEPERS! I THINK THAT'S WHAT HE SAID--INTERSTATE COORDINATION ...I WISH I'D WRITTEN IT DOWN! THEY BOTH SOUND ALIKE!
THAT'S FUNNY-I COUNTED FOUR TO FOUR-THAT'S EIGHT HANDS BUT THERE ARE ONLY SEVEN OF US.HM. SOMEBODY VOTED TWICE!
LET'S TRY IT AGAIN-ALL THOSE IN FAVOR OF INDEPENDENT CONCENTRATION RAISE YOUR HAND!
ALL IN FAVOR OF INTERSTATE COORDINATION HMMM! THREE TO THREE. THIS TIME SOMEBODY DIDN'T VOTE AT ALL!
PARDON ME, BUT, MR. ANDREWS ...ARE YOU SURE YOU'RE VOTING?
ULP! GOSH--I--ER-----I HAVEN'T MADE UP MY MIND YET!
THERE'S ONLY ONE WAY TO MAKE UP YOUR MIND!
NOW MY STATE FEELS THAT!.
LISTEN TO ME, ANDREWS!
CONSIDER THE FINANCIAL ISSUE, ANDREWS!
BLA
BLA
BLA
GENTLEMEN! GENTLEMEN! PLEASE! ONE AT A TIME!
4 HOURS LATER
AND THAT, MR. ANDREWS, IS WHY YOU SHOULD VOTE INTERSTATE COORDINATION!
GEE, I NEVER LOOKED AT IT THAT WAY!
ME NEITHER!
GENTLEMEN, I'M GLAD MR. ANDREWS WAS NOT AS HASTY AS WE WERE IN VOTING. ON RECONSIDERING THE FACTS I'M SURE WE ALL SEE OUR WAY CLEAR NOW!.. SUPPOSE WE CAST ANOTHER BALLOT!
BOSTON GLOBE
LODGE BILL CARRIED UNANIMOUSLY!
VOTE 7 TO 0 FOR INTER-STATE CO-ORDINATION IN WASH
BROWN and GOLD
RIVERDALE HIGH SCHOOL'S PAPER
ANDREWS RETURNS FROM WASHINGTON
DADDY SAID TO GIVE YOU A BIG KISS! YOU PRACTICALLY PUT HIM IN THE GOVERNOR'S CHAIR!
WELL, ARCHIE'S BATTING 400 WITH VERONICA NOW, BUT WHAT ABOUT BETTY COOPER? FOLLOW ARCHIE IN PEP and JACKPOT COMICS
6

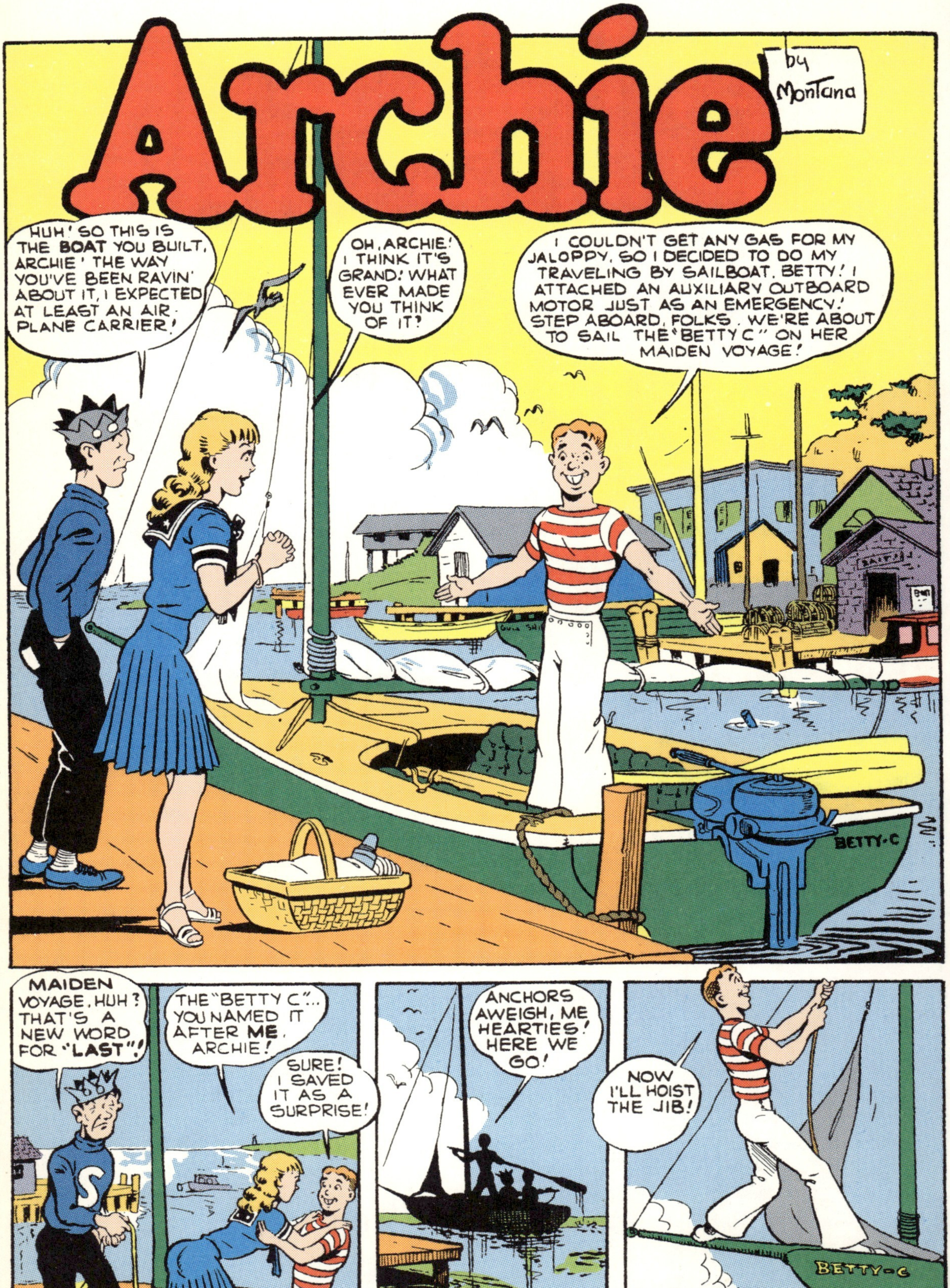
Archie
by Montana
HUH! SO THIS IS THE BOAT YOU BUILT, ARCHIE! THE WAY YOU'VE BEEN RAVIN' ABOUT IT, I EXPECTED AT LEAST AN AIR-PLANE CARRIER!
OH, ARCHIE! I THINK IT'S GRAND! WHAT EVER MADE YOU THINK OF IT?
I COULDN'T GET ANY GAS FOR MY JALOPPY, SO I DECIDED TO DO MY TRAVELING BY SAILBOAT, BETTY! I ATTACHED AN AUXILIARY OUTBOARD MOTOR JUST AS AN EMERGENCY! STEP ABOARD, FOLKS. WE'RE ABOUT TO SAIL THE "BETTY C" ON HER MAIDEN VOYAGE!
BETTY-C
MAIDEN VOYAGE, HUH? THAT'S A NEW WORD FOR "LAST"!
THE "BETTY C"... YOU NAMED IT AFTER ME, ARCHIE!
SURE! I SAVED IT AS A SURPRISE!
ANCHORS AWEIGH, ME HEARTIES! HERE WE GO!
NOW I'LL HOIST THE JIB!
BETTY-C

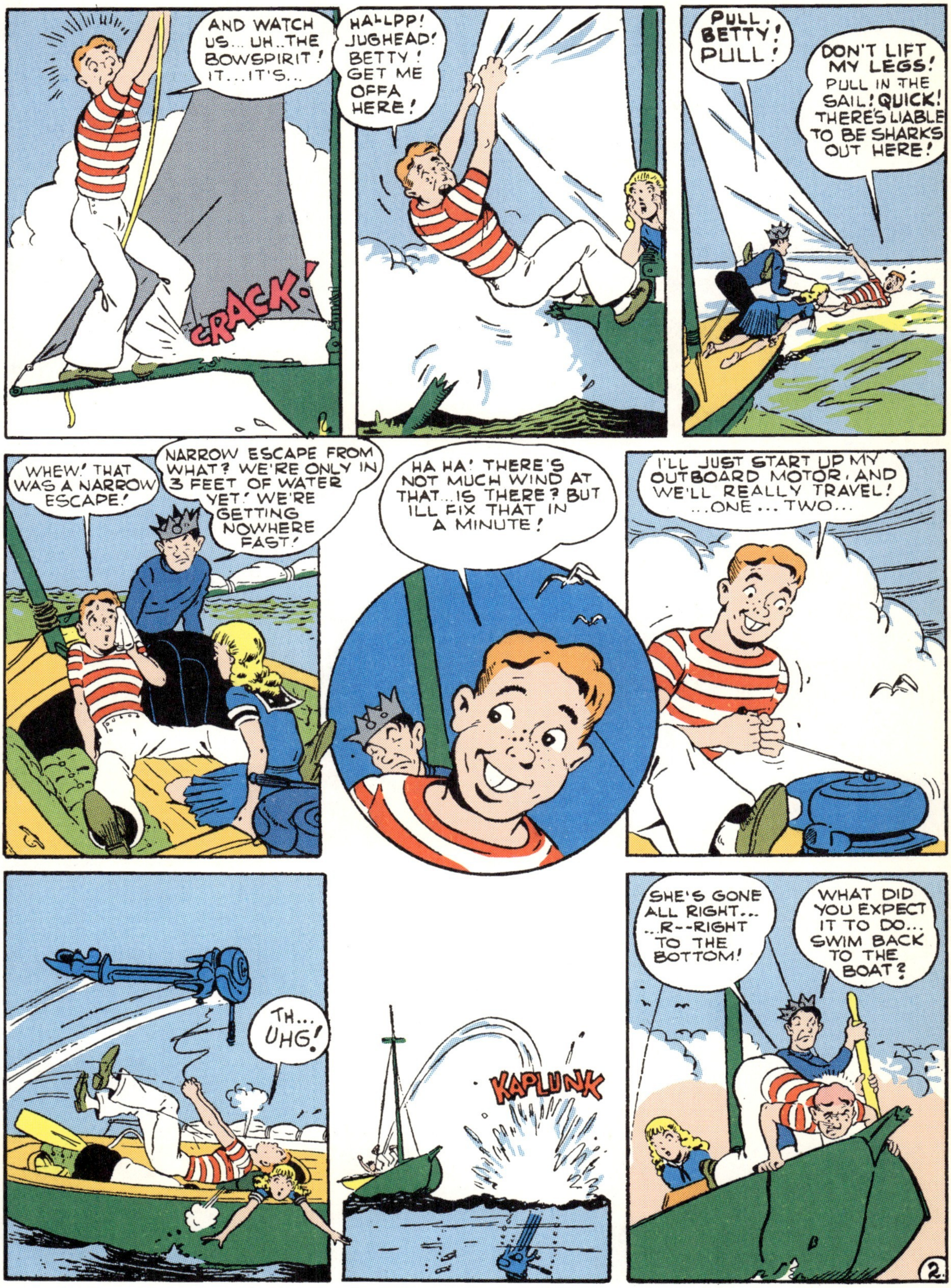
AND WATCH US... UH.. THE BOWSPIRIT! IT... IT'S...
CRACK!
HALLPP! JUGHEAD! BETTY! GET ME OFFA HERE!
PULL, BETTY! PULL!
DON'T LIFT MY LEGS! PULL IN THE SAIL! QUICK! THERE'S LIABLE TO BE SHARKS OUT HERE!
WHEW! THAT WAS A NARROW ESCAPE!
NARROW ESCAPE FROM WHAT? WE'RE ONLY IN 3 FEET OF WATER YET! WE'RE GETTING NOWHERE FAST!
HA HA! THERE'S NOT MUCH WIND AT THAT... IS THERE? BUT I'LL FIX THAT IN A MINUTE!
I'LL JUST START UP MY OUTBOARD MOTOR, AND WE'LL REALLY TRAVEL! ...ONE... TWO...
TH... UHG!
KAPLUNK
SHE'S GONE ALL RIGHT... ...R--RIGHT TO THE BOTTOM!
WHAT DID YOU EXPECT IT TO DO... SWIM BACK TO THE BOAT?
2.

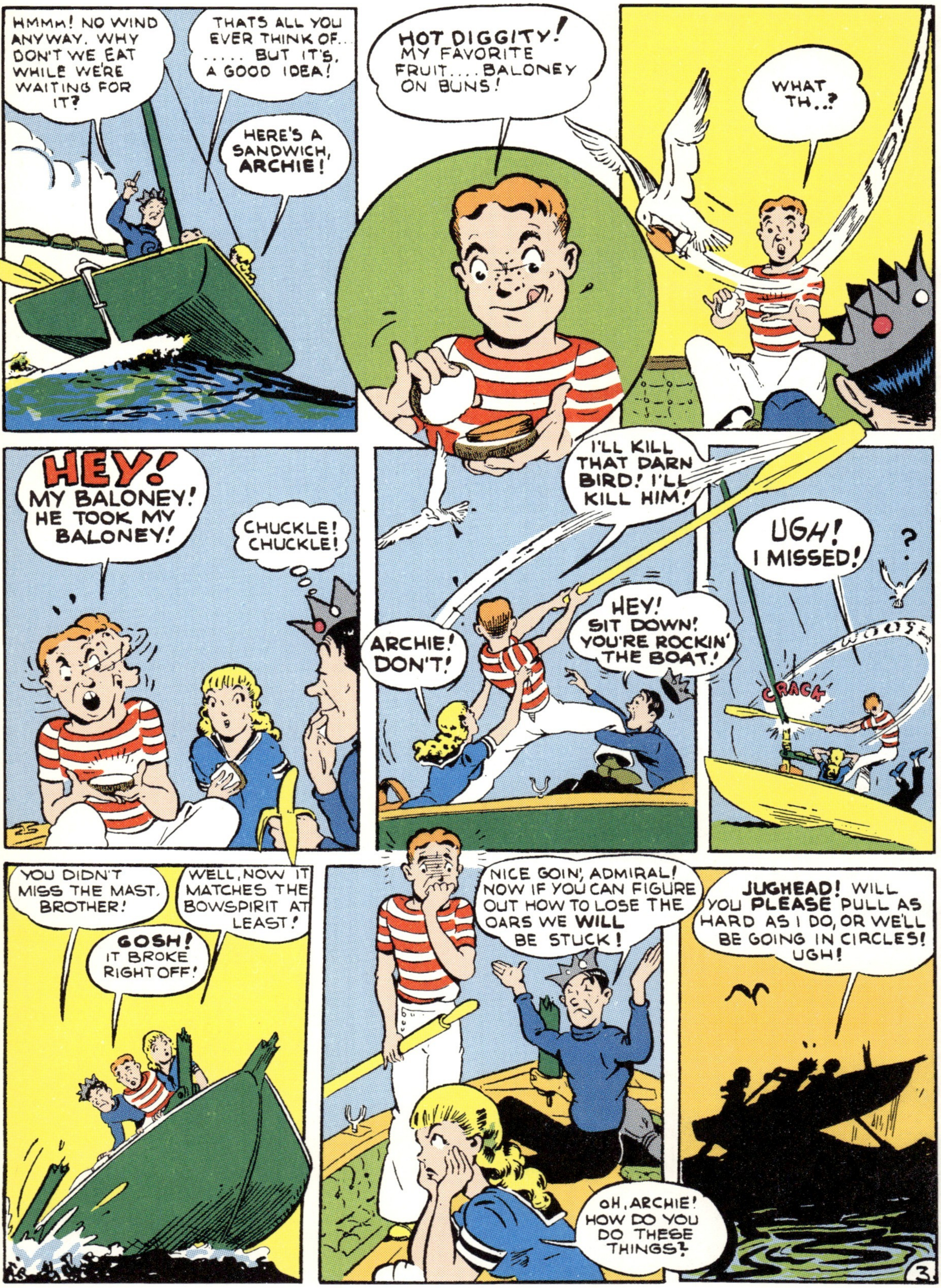
HMMM! NO WIND ANYWAY. WHY DON'T WE EAT WHILE WE'RE WAITING FOR IT?
THATS ALL YOU EVER THINK OF.. ..... BUT IT'S, A GOOD IDEA!
HERE'S A SANDWICH, ARCHIE!
HOT DIGGITY! MY FAVORITE FRUIT.... BALONEY ON BUNS!
WHAT TH..?
HEY! MY BALONEY! HE TOOK MY BALONEY!
CHUCKLE! CHUCKLE!
I'LL KILL THAT DARN BIRD! I'LL KILL HIM!
ARCHIE! DON'T!
HEY! SIT DOWN! YOU'RE ROCKIN' THE BOAT!
UGH! I MISSED!
?
CRACK
YOU DIDN'T MISS THE MAST, BROTHER!
WELL, NOW IT MATCHES THE BOWSPIRIT AT LEAST!
GOSH! IT BROKE RIGHT OFF!
NICE GOIN', ADMIRAL! NOW IF YOU CAN FIGURE OUT HOW TO LOSE THE OARS WE WILL BE STUCK!
OH, ARCHIE! HOW DO YOU DO THESE THINGS?
JUGHEAD! WILL YOU PLEASE PULL AS HARD AS I DO, OR WE'LL BE GOING IN CIRCLES! UGH!
3

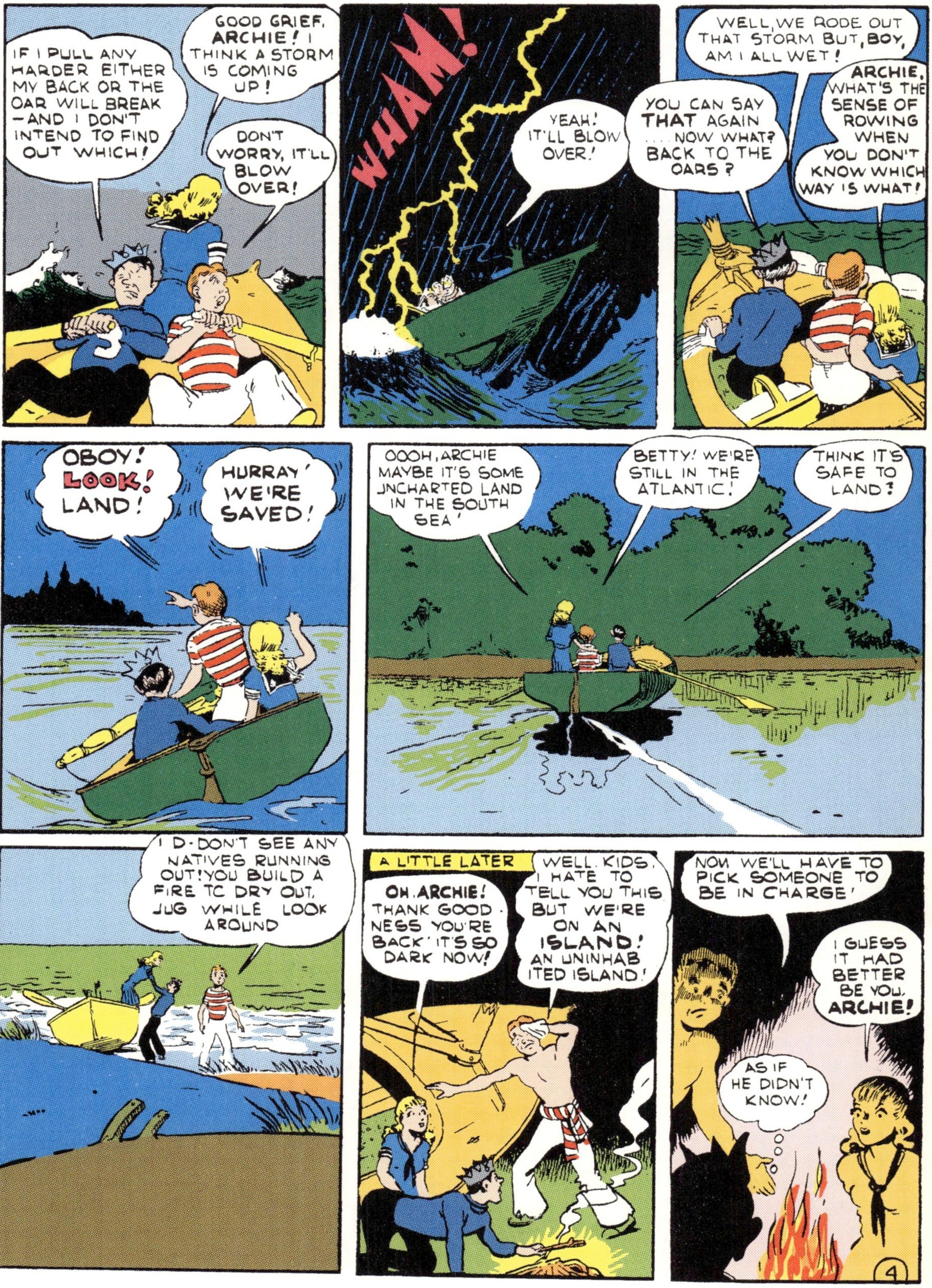

IF I PULL ANY HARDER EITHER MY BACK OR THE OAR WILL BREAK —AND I DON'T INTEND TO FIND OUT WHICH!
GOOD GRIEF, ARCHIE! I THINK A STORM IS COMING UP!
DON'T WORRY, IT'LL BLOW OVER!
WHAM!
YEAH! IT'LL BLOW OVER!
WELL, WE RODE OUT THAT STORM BUT, BOY, AM I ALL WET!
YOU CAN SAY THAT AGAIN ....NOW WHAT? BACK TO THE OARS?
ARCHIE, WHAT'S THE SENSE OF ROWING WHEN YOU DON'T KNOW WHICH WAY IS WHAT!
OBOY! LOOK! LAND!
HURRAY! WE'RE SAVED!
OOOH, ARCHIE MAYBE IT'S SOME UNCHARTED LAND IN THE SOUTH SEA!
BETTY! WE'RE STILL IN THE ATLANTIC!
THINK IT'S SAFE TO LAND?
I D-DON'T SEE ANY NATIVES RUNNING OUT! YOU BUILD A FIRE TO DRY OUT, JUG WHILE LOOK AROUND
A LITTLE LATER
OH, ARCHIE! THANK GOODNESS YOU'RE BACK! IT'S SO DARK NOW!
WELL, KIDS, I HATE TO TELL YOU THIS BUT WE'RE ON AN ISLAND! AN UNINHABITED ISLAND!
NOW WE'LL HAVE TO PICK SOMEONE TO BE IN CHARGE!
I GUESS IT HAD BETTER BE YOU, ARCHIE!
AS IF HE DIDN'T KNOW!
4

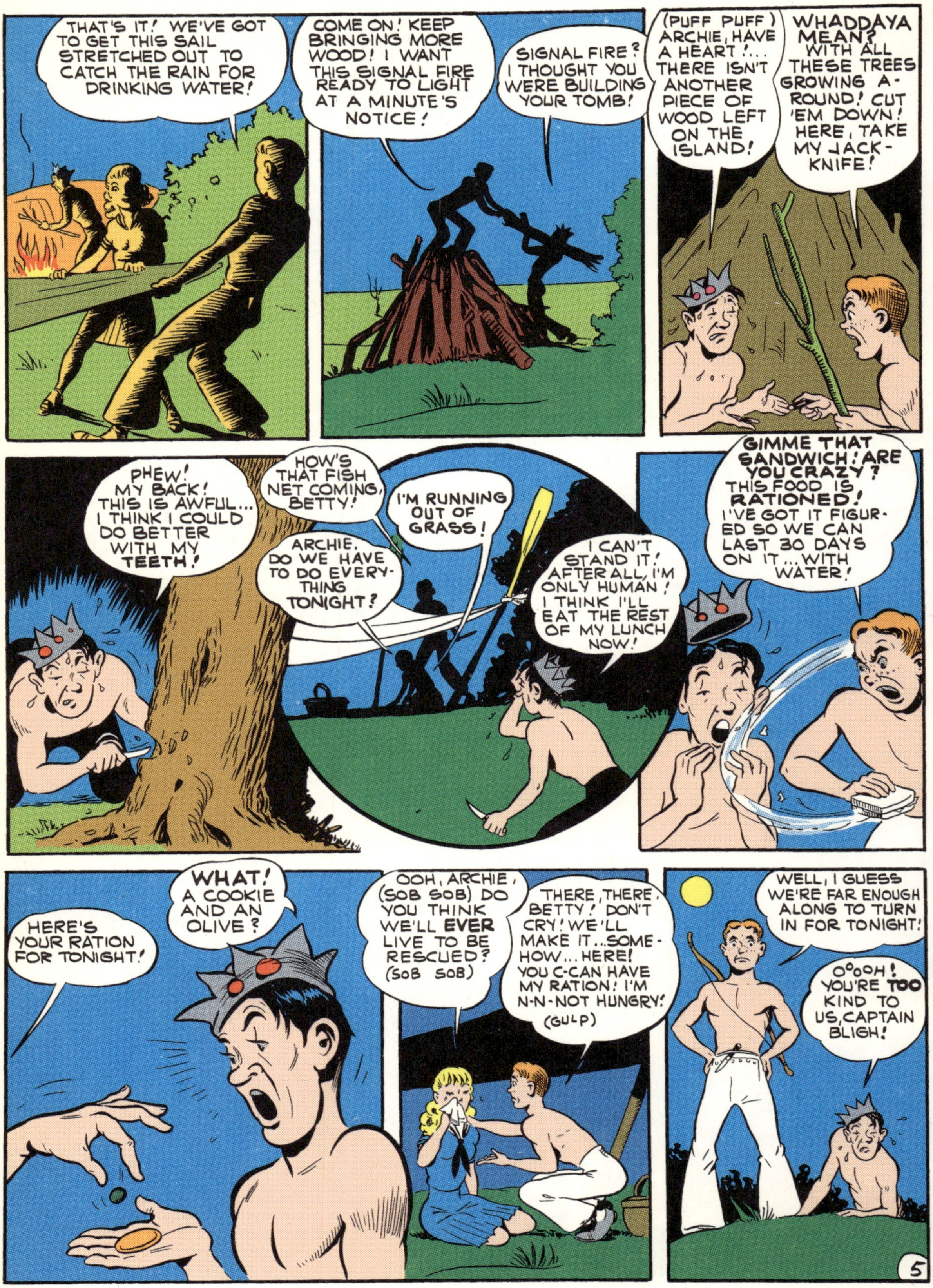
THAT'S IT! WE'VE GOT TO GET THIS SAIL STRETCHED OUT TO CATCH THE RAIN FOR DRINKING WATER!
COME ON! KEEP BRINGING MORE WOOD! I WANT THIS SIGNAL FIRE READY TO LIGHT AT A MINUTE'S NOTICE!
SIGNAL FIRE? I THOUGHT YOU WERE BUILDING YOUR TOMB!
(PUFF PUFF) ARCHIE, HAVE A HEART!... THERE ISN'T ANOTHER PIECE OF WOOD LEFT ON THE ISLAND!
WHADDAYA MEAN? WITH ALL THESE TREES GROWING A-ROUND! CUT 'EM DOWN! HERE, TAKE MY JACK-KNIFE!
PHEW! MY BACK! THIS IS AWFUL... I THINK I COULD DO BETTER WITH MY TEETH!
HOW'S THAT FISH NET COMING, BETTY?
I'M RUNNING OUT OF GRASS!
ARCHIE, DO WE HAVE TO DO EVERY-THING TONIGHT?
I CAN'T STAND IT! AFTER ALL, I'M ONLY HUMAN! I THINK I'LL EAT THE REST OF MY LUNCH NOW!
GIMME THAT SANDWICH! ARE YOU CRAZY? THIS FOOD IS RATIONED! I'VE GOT IT FIGUR-ED SO WE CAN LAST 30 DAYS ON IT... WITH WATER!
HERE'S YOUR RATION FOR TONIGHT!
WHAT! A COOKIE AND AN OLIVE?
OOH, ARCHIE, (SOB SOB) DO YOU THINK WE'LL EVER LIVE TO BE RESCUED? (SOB SOB)
THERE, THERE, BETTY! DON'T CRY! WE'LL MAKE IT... SOME-HOW... HERE! YOU C-CAN HAVE MY RATION! I'M N-N-NOT HUNGRY! (GULP)
WELL, I GUESS WE'RE FAR ENOUGH ALONG TO TURN IN FOR TONIGHT!
OOOOH! YOU'RE TOO KIND TO US, CAPTAIN BLIGH!
5

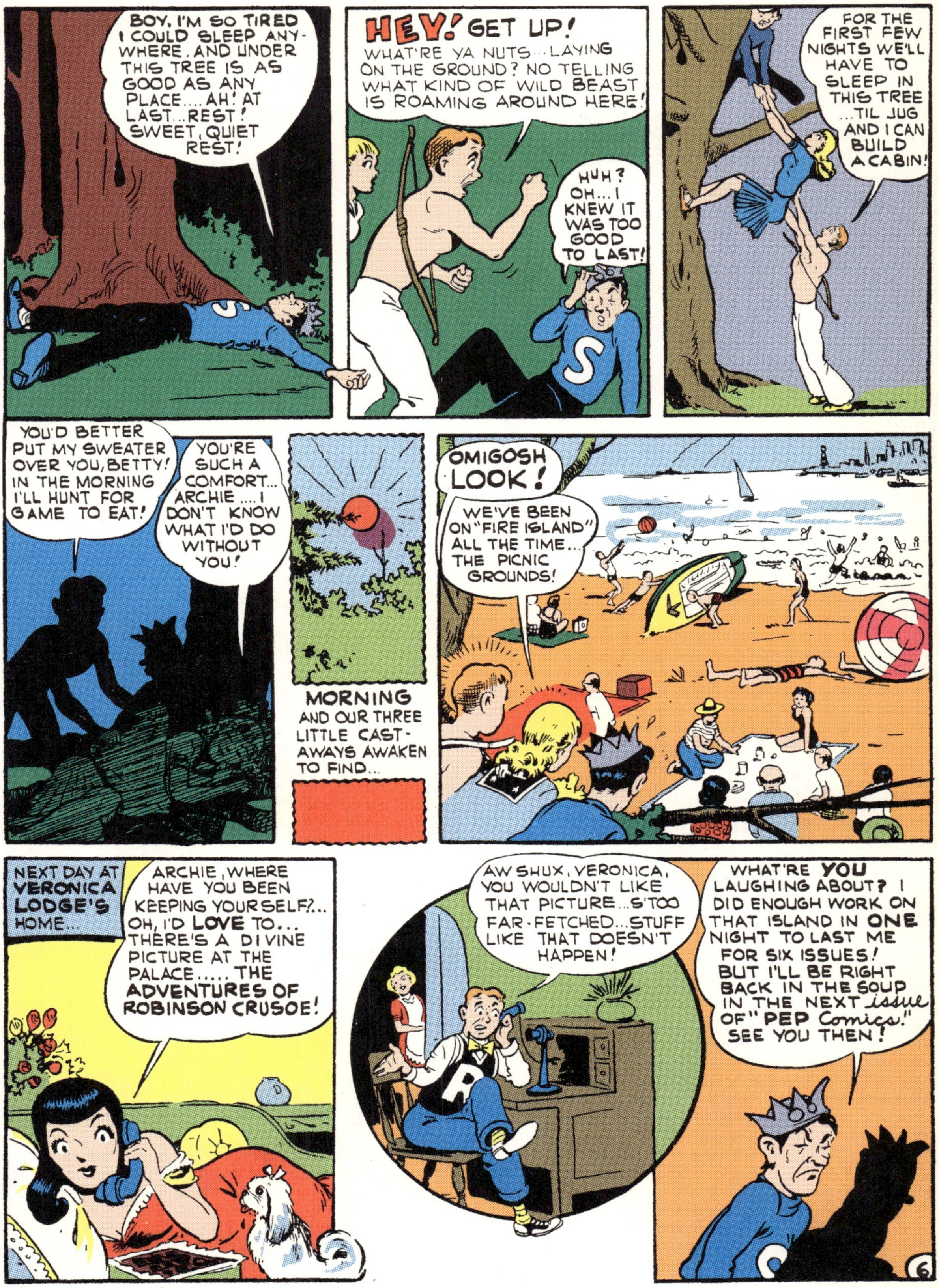
BOY, I'M SO TIRED I COULD SLEEP ANYWHERE, AND UNDER THIS TREE IS AS GOOD AS ANY PLACE.... AH! AT LAST...REST! SWEET, QUIET REST!
HEY! GET UP! WHAT'RE YA NUTS...LAYING ON THE GROUND? NO TELLING WHAT KIND OF WILD BEAST IS ROAMING AROUND HERE!
HUH? OH... I KNEW IT WAS TOO GOOD TO LAST!
FOR THE FIRST FEW NIGHTS WE'LL HAVE TO SLEEP IN THIS TREE ...TIL JUG AND I CAN BUILD A CABIN!
YOU'D BETTER PUT MY SWEATER OVER YOU, BETTY! IN THE MORNING I'LL HUNT FOR GAME TO EAT!
YOU'RE SUCH A COMFORT... ARCHIE.... I DON'T KNOW WHAT I'D DO WITHOUT YOU!
MORNING AND OUR THREE LITTLE CASTAWAYS AWAKEN TO FIND...
OMIGOSH LOOK!
WE'VE BEEN ON "FIRE ISLAND" ALL THE TIME... THE PICNIC GROUNDS!
NEXT DAY AT VERONICA LODGE'S HOME...
ARCHIE, WHERE HAVE YOU BEEN KEEPING YOURSELF?... OH, I'D LOVE TO... THERE'S A DIVINE PICTURE AT THE PALACE..... THE ADVENTURES OF ROBINSON CRUSOE!
AW SHUX, VERONICA, YOU WOULDN'T LIKE THAT PICTURE...S'TOO FAR-FETCHED...STUFF LIKE THAT DOESN'T HAPPEN!
WHAT'RE YOU LAUGHING ABOUT? I DID ENOUGH WORK ON THAT ISLAND IN ONE NIGHT TO LAST ME FOR SIX ISSUES! BUT I'LL BE RIGHT BACK IN THE SOUP IN THE NEXT issue OF "PEP Comics!" SEE YOU THEN!
6

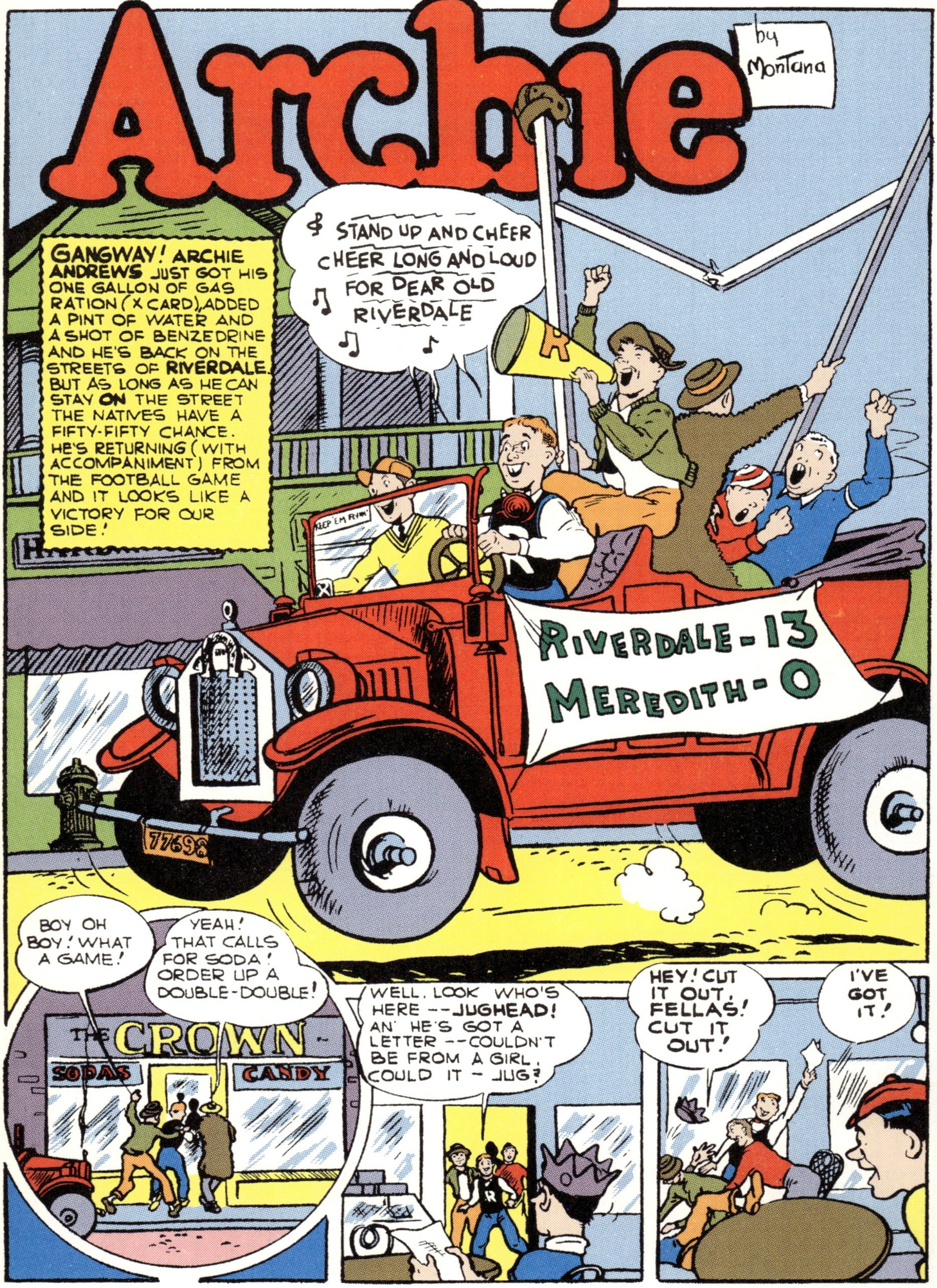
Archie
by Montana
GANGWAY! ARCHIE ANDREWS JUST GOT HIS ONE GALLON OF GAS RATION (X CARD), ADDED A PINT OF WATER AND A SHOT OF BENZEDRINE AND HE'S BACK ON THE STREETS OF RIVERDALE. BUT AS LONG AS HE CAN STAY ON THE STREET THE NATIVES HAVE A FIFTY-FIFTY CHANCE. HE'S RETURNING (WITH ACCOMPANIMENT) FROM THE FOOTBALL GAME AND IT LOOKS LIKE A VICTORY FOR OUR SIDE!
STAND UP AND CHEER CHEER LONG AND LOUD FOR DEAR OLD RIVERDALE
KEEP 'EM ROLLIN'
RIVERDALE - 13 MEREDITH - 0
77698
BOY OH BOY! WHAT A GAME!
YEAH! THAT CALLS FOR SODA! ORDER UP A DOUBLE-DOUBLE!
THE CROWN
SODAS
CANDY
WELL, LOOK WHO'S HERE --JUGHEAD! AN' HE'S GOT A LETTER --COULDN'T BE FROM A GIRL, COULD IT - JUG?
HEY! CUT IT OUT, FELLAS! CUT IT OUT!
I'VE GOT IT!

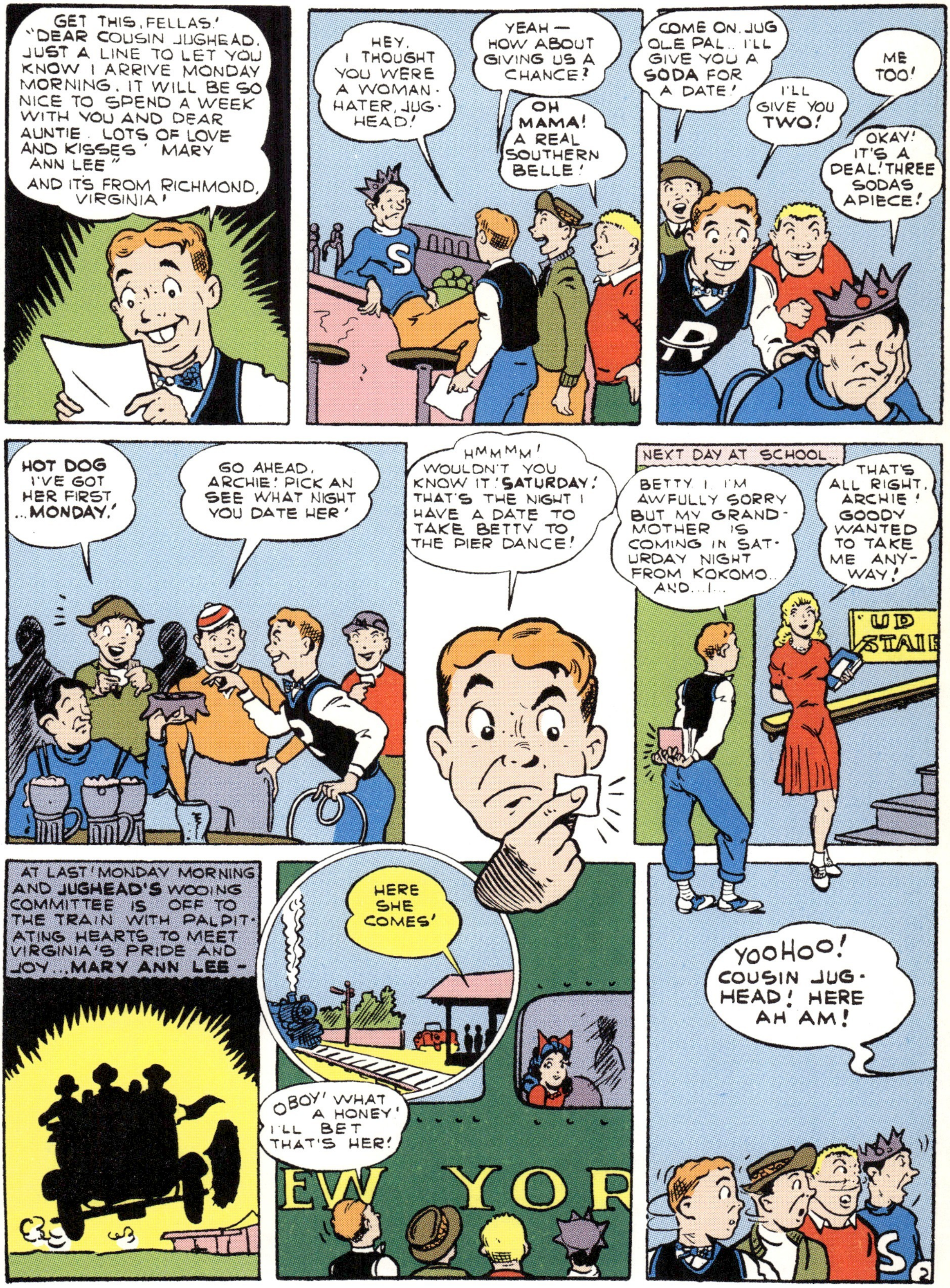
GET THIS, FELLAS! "DEAR COUSIN JUGHEAD. JUST A LINE TO LET YOU KNOW I ARRIVE MONDAY MORNING. IT WILL BE SO NICE TO SPEND A WEEK WITH YOU AND DEAR AUNTIE. LOTS OF LOVE AND KISSES. MARY ANN LEE" AND IT'S FROM RICHMOND, VIRGINIA!
HEY, I THOUGHT YOU WERE A WOMAN-HATER, JUG-HEAD!
YEAH — HOW ABOUT GIVING US A CHANCE?
OH MAMA! A REAL SOUTHERN BELLE!
COME ON, JUG OLE PAL.. I'LL GIVE YOU A SODA FOR A DATE!
I'LL GIVE YOU TWO!
ME TOO!
OKAY! IT'S A DEAL! THREE SODAS APIECE!
HOT DOG I'VE GOT HER FIRST ...MONDAY!
GO AHEAD, ARCHIE! PICK AN SEE WHAT NIGHT YOU DATE HER!
HMMMM! WOULDN'T YOU KNOW IT! SATURDAY! THAT'S THE NIGHT I HAVE A DATE TO TAKE BETTY TO THE PIER DANCE!
NEXT DAY AT SCHOOL...
BETTY I.. I'M AWFULLY SORRY BUT MY GRAND-MOTHER IS COMING IN SAT-URDAY NIGHT FROM KOKOMO.. AND...I...
THAT'S ALL RIGHT, ARCHIE! GOODY WANTED TO TAKE ME ANY-WAY!
UP STAIR
AT LAST! MONDAY MORNING AND JUGHEAD'S WOOING COMMITTEE IS OFF TO THE TRAIN WITH PALPIT-ATING HEARTS TO MEET VIRGINIA'S PRIDE AND JOY...MARY ANN LEE -
HERE SHE COMES!
OBOY! WHAT A HONEY! I'LL BET THAT'S HER!
EW YOR
YOOHOO! COUSIN JUG-HEAD! HERE AH AM!
2

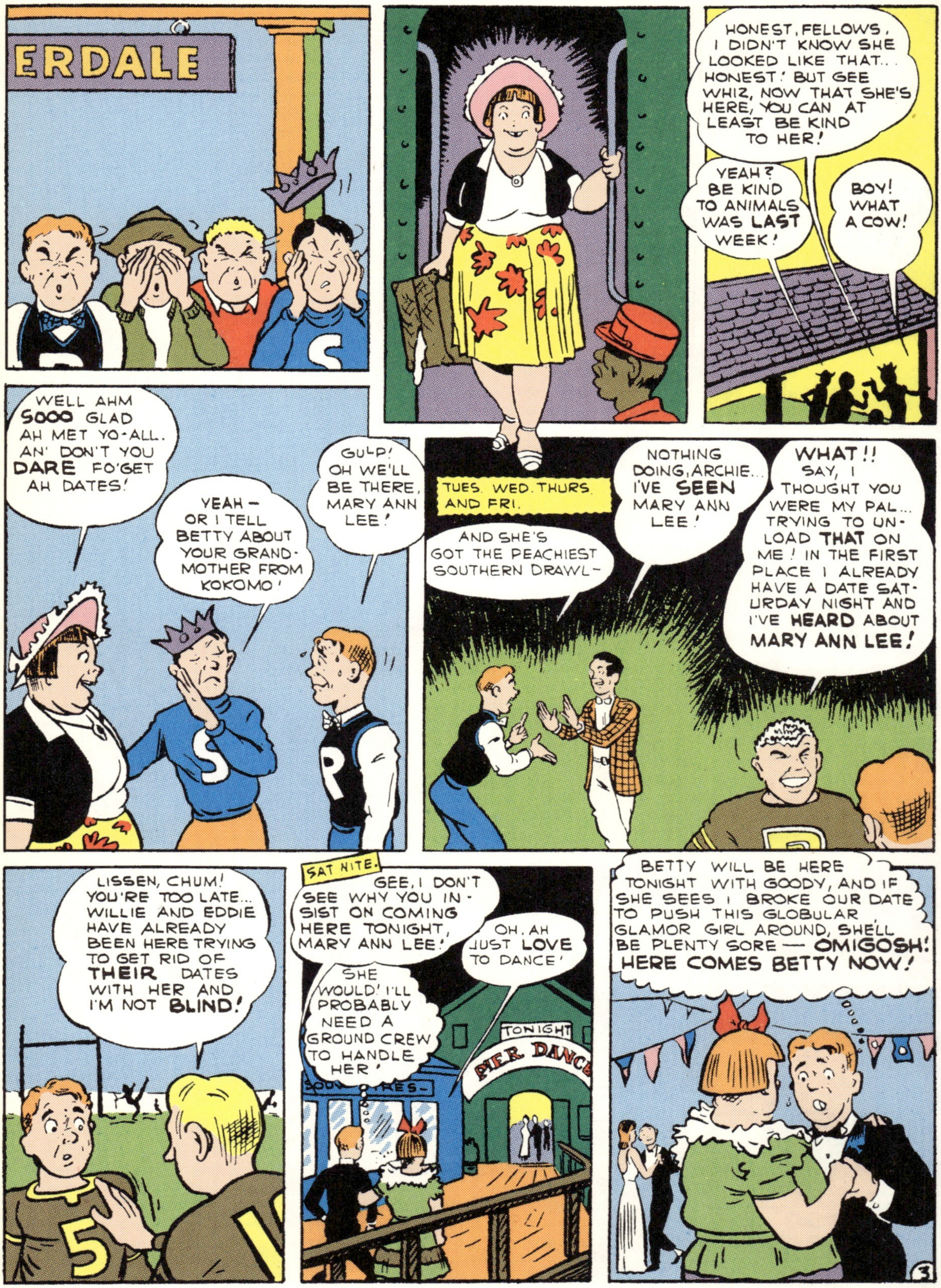
ERDALE
HONEST, FELLOWS, I DIDN'T KNOW SHE LOOKED LIKE THAT.. HONEST! BUT GEE WHIZ, NOW THAT SHE'S HERE, YOU CAN AT LEAST BE KIND TO HER!
YEAH? BE KIND TO ANIMALS WAS LAST WEEK!
BOY! WHAT A COW!
WELL AHM SOOO GLAD AH MET YO-ALL. AN' DON'T YOU DARE FO'GET AH DATES!
YEAH — OR I TELL BETTY ABOUT YOUR GRAND-MOTHER FROM KOKOMO!
GULP! OH WE'LL BE THERE, MARY ANN LEE!
TUES. WED. THURS. AND FRI.
AND SHE'S GOT THE PEACHIEST SOUTHERN DRAWL—
NOTHING DOING, ARCHIE... I'VE SEEN MARY ANN LEE!
WHAT!! SAY, I THOUGHT YOU WERE MY PAL... TRYING TO UN-LOAD THAT ON ME! IN THE FIRST PLACE I ALREADY HAVE A DATE SAT-URDAY NIGHT AND I'VE HEARD ABOUT MARY ANN LEE!
LISSEN, CHUM! YOU'RE TOO LATE... WILLIE AND EDDIE HAVE ALREADY BEEN HERE TRYING TO GET RID OF THEIR DATES WITH HER AND I'M NOT BLIND!
SAT NITE.
GEE, I DON'T SEE WHY YOU IN-SIST ON COMING HERE TONIGHT, MARY ANN LEE!
OH, AH JUST LOVE TO DANCE!
SHE WOULD! I'LL PROBABLY NEED A GROUND CREW TO HANDLE HER!
TONIGHT
PIER DANCE
BETTY WILL BE HERE TONIGHT WITH GOODY, AND IF SHE SEES I BROKE OUR DATE TO PUSH THIS GLOBULAR GLAMOR GIRL AROUND, SHE'LL BE PLENTY SORE — OMIGOSH! HERE COMES BETTY NOW!
3

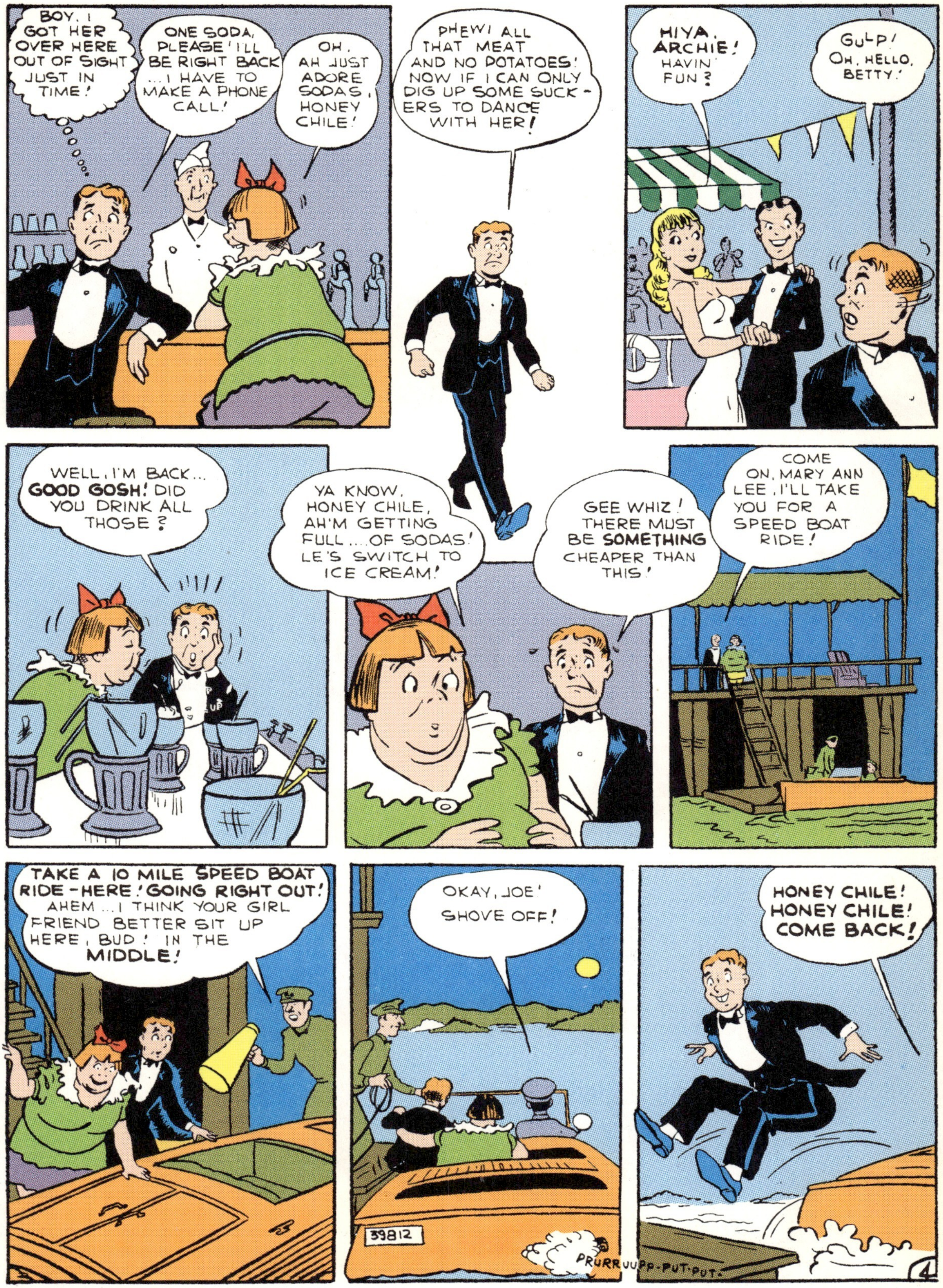
BOY, I GOT HER OVER HERE OUT OF SIGHT JUST IN TIME!
ONE SODA, PLEASE! I'LL BE RIGHT BACK ...I HAVE TO MAKE A PHONE CALL!
OH, AH JUST ADORE SODAS, HONEY CHILE!
PHEW! ALL THAT MEAT AND NO POTATOES! NOW IF I CAN ONLY DIG UP SOME SUCK-ERS TO DANCE WITH HER!
HIYA, ARCHIE! HAVIN' FUN?
GULP! OH, HELLO, BETTY!
WELL, I'M BACK... GOOD GOSH! DID YOU DRINK ALL THOSE?
YA KNOW, HONEY CHILE, AH'M GETTING FULL....OF SODAS! LE'S SWITCH TO ICE CREAM!
GEE WHIZ! THERE MUST BE SOMETHING CHEAPER THAN THIS!
COME ON, MARY ANN LEE, I'LL TAKE YOU FOR A SPEED BOAT RIDE!
TAKE A 10 MILE SPEED BOAT RIDE - HERE! GOING RIGHT OUT! AHEM ... I THINK YOUR GIRL FRIEND BETTER SIT UP HERE, BUD! IN THE MIDDLE!
OKAY, JOE! SHOVE OFF!
39812
PRURRUUPP-PUT-PUT-
HONEY CHILE! HONEY CHILE! COME BACK!
4

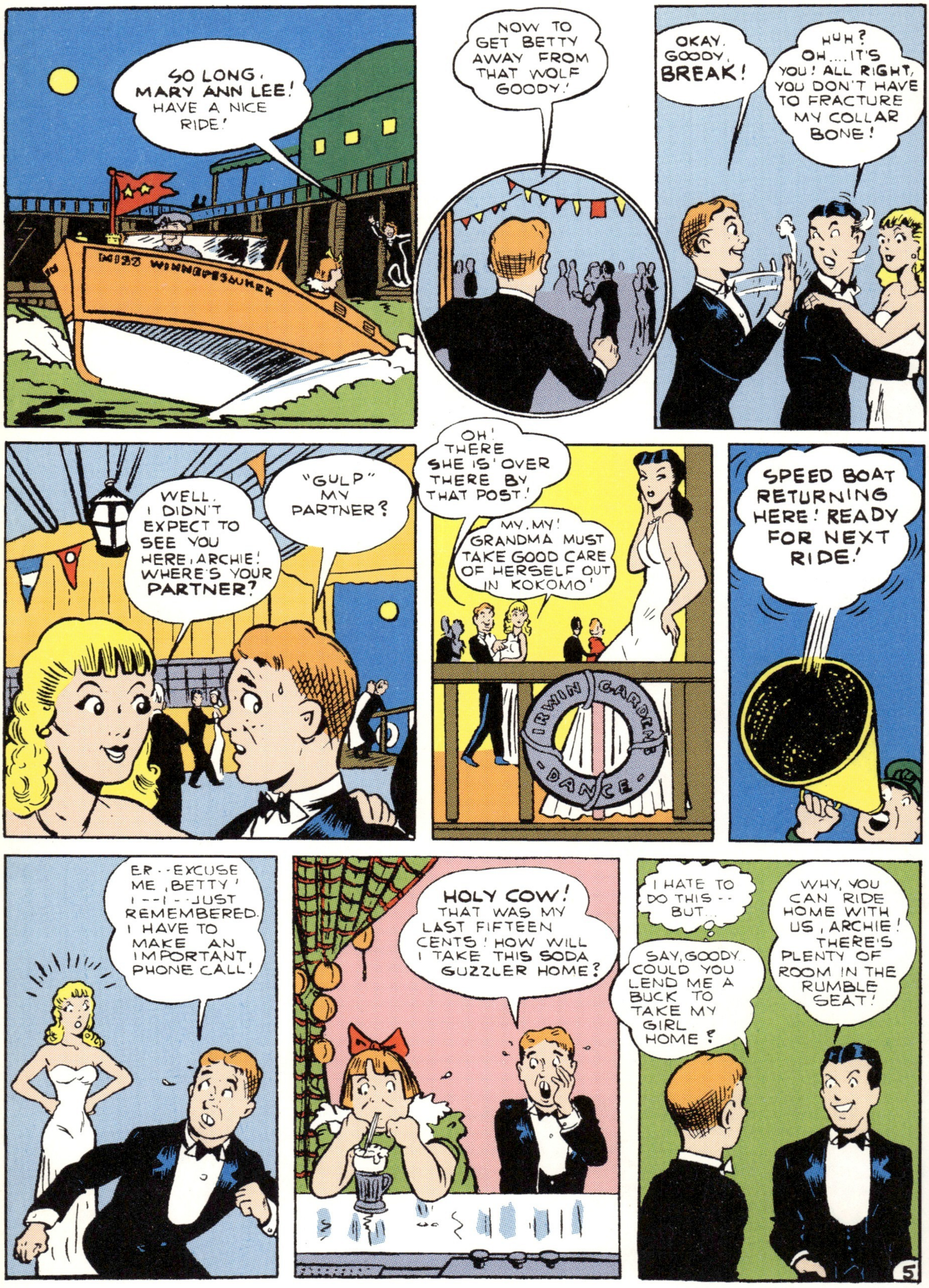
SO LONG, MARY ANN LEE! HAVE A NICE RIDE!
MISS WINNEPESAUKEE
NOW TO GET BETTY AWAY FROM THAT WOLF GOODY!
OKAY, GOODY, BREAK!
HUH? OH....IT'S YOU! ALL RIGHT, YOU DON'T HAVE TO FRACTURE MY COLLAR BONE!
WELL, I DIDN'T EXPECT TO SEE YOU HERE, ARCHIE! WHERE'S YOUR PARTNER?
"GULP" MY PARTNER?
OH! THERE SHE IS OVER THERE BY THAT POST!
MY, MY! GRANDMA MUST TAKE GOOD CARE OF HERSELF OUT IN KOKOMO!
IRWIN GARDENS DANCE
SPEED BOAT RETURNING HERE! READY FOR NEXT RIDE!
ER--EXCUSE ME, BETTY! I--I--JUST REMEMBERED. I HAVE TO MAKE AN IMPORTANT PHONE CALL!
HOLY COW! THAT WAS MY LAST FIFTEEN CENTS! HOW WILL I TAKE THIS SODA GUZZLER HOME?
I HATE TO DO THIS-- BUT..
SAY, GOODY, COULD YOU LEND ME A BUCK TO TAKE MY GIRL HOME?
WHY, YOU CAN RIDE HOME WITH US, ARCHIE! THERE'S PLENTY OF ROOM IN THE RUMBLE SEAT!
5

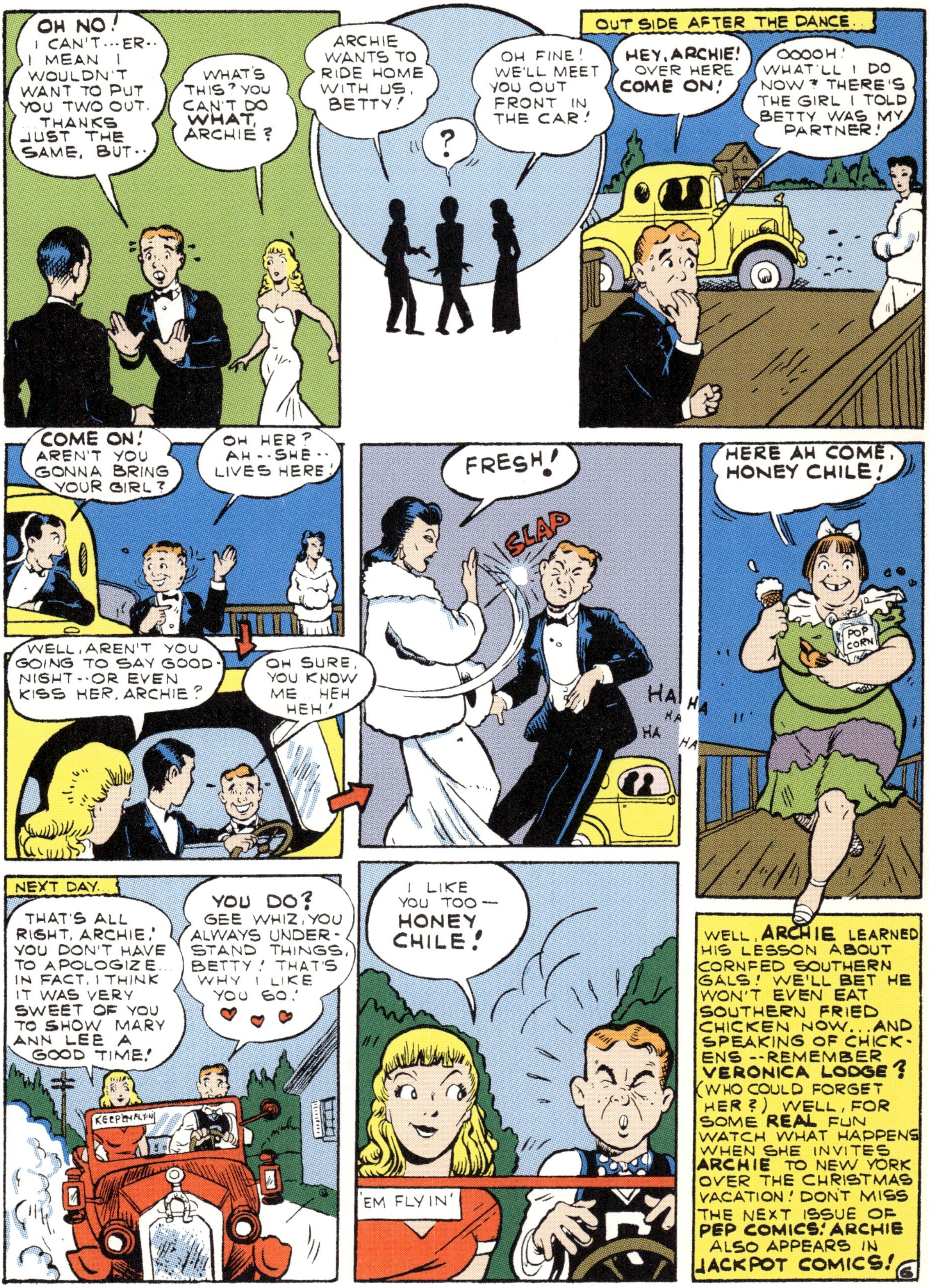
OH NO! I CAN'T---ER-- I MEAN I WOULDN'T WANT TO PUT YOU TWO OUT. ...THANKS JUST THE SAME, BUT--
WHAT'S THIS? YOU CAN'T DO WHAT, ARCHIE?
ARCHIE WANTS TO RIDE HOME WITH US, BETTY!
?
OH FINE! WE'LL MEET YOU OUT FRONT IN THE CAR!
OUT SIDE AFTER THE DANCE..
HEY, ARCHIE! OVER HERE COME ON!
OOOOH! WHAT'LL I DO NOW? THERE'S THE GIRL I TOLD BETTY WAS MY PARTNER!
COME ON! AREN'T YOU GONNA BRING YOUR GIRL?
OH HER? AH--SHE-- LIVES HERE!
WELL, AREN'T YOU GOING TO SAY GOOD-NIGHT--OR EVEN KISS HER, ARCHIE?
OH SURE, YOU KNOW ME..HEH HEH!
FRESH!
SLAP
HA HA HA HA
HERE AH COME, HONEY CHILE!
POP CORN
NEXT DAY...
THAT'S ALL RIGHT, ARCHIE! YOU DON'T HAVE TO APOLOGIZE... IN FACT, I THINK IT WAS VERY SWEET OF YOU TO SHOW MARY ANN LEE A GOOD TIME!
YOU DO? GEE WHIZ, YOU ALWAYS UNDER-STAND THINGS, BETTY! THAT'S WHY I LIKE YOU SO!
KEEP 'EM FLYIN'
I LIKE YOU TOO— HONEY CHILE!
'EM FLYIN'
WELL, ARCHIE LEARNED HIS LESSON ABOUT CORNFED SOUTHERN GALS! WE'LL BET HE WON'T EVEN EAT SOUTHERN FRIED CHICKEN NOW... AND SPEAKING OF CHICK-ENS --REMEMBER VERONICA LODGE? (WHO COULD FORGET HER?) WELL, FOR SOME REAL FUN WATCH WHAT HAPPENS WHEN SHE INVITES ARCHIE TO NEW YORK OVER THE CHRISTMAS VACATION! DON'T MISS THE NEXT ISSUE OF PEP COMICS! ARCHIE ALSO APPEARS IN JACKPOT COMICS!
6

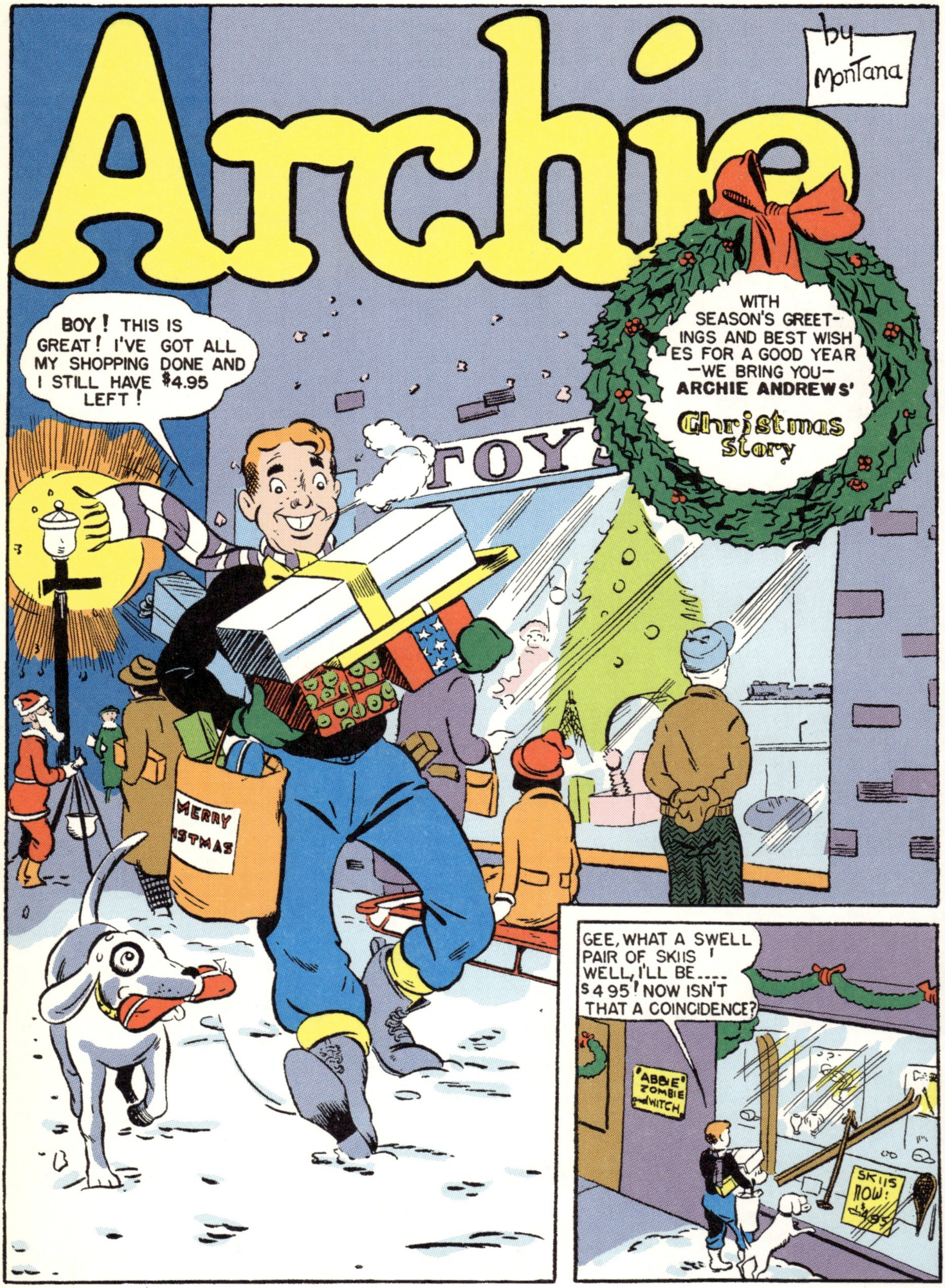
Archie
by MonTana
BOY! THIS IS GREAT! I'VE GOT ALL MY SHOPPING DONE AND I STILL HAVE $4.95 LEFT!
WITH SEASON'S GREETINGS AND BEST WISHES FOR A GOOD YEAR —WE BRING YOU— ARCHIE ANDREWS' Christmas Story
TOYS
MERRY CHRISTMAS
GEE, WHAT A SWELL PAIR OF SKIIS! WELL, I'LL BE.... $4.95! NOW ISN'T THAT A COINCIDENCE?
"ABBIE" ZOMBIE and WITCH
SKIIS NOW! $4.95

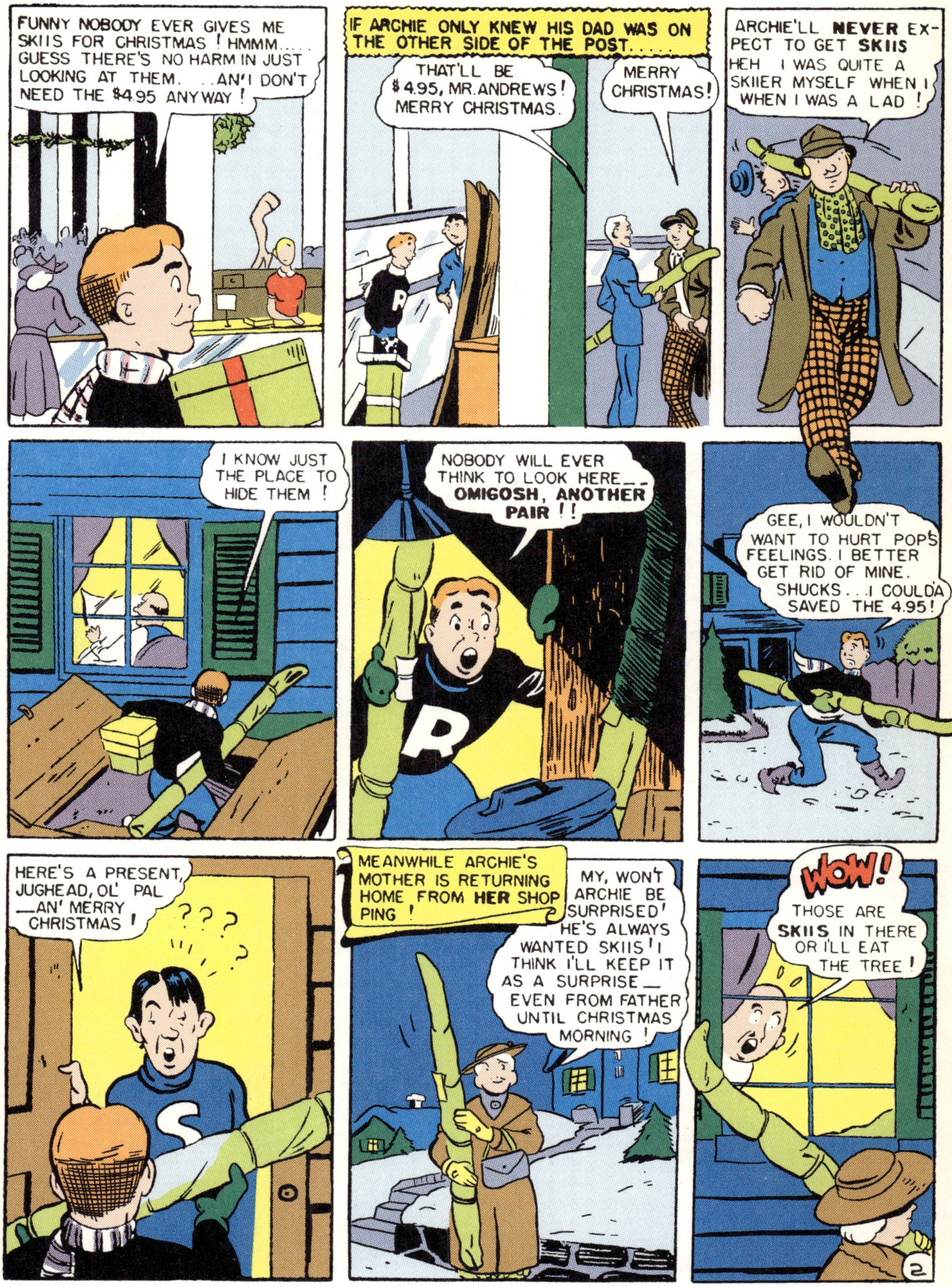

FUNNY NOBODY EVER GIVES ME SKIIS FOR CHRISTMAS ! HMMM..... GUESS THERE'S NO HARM IN JUST LOOKING AT THEM. ...AN' I DON'T NEED THE $4.95 ANYWAY !
IF ARCHIE ONLY KNEW HIS DAD WAS ON THE OTHER SIDE OF THE POST.....
THAT'LL BE $4.95, MR. ANDREWS ! MERRY CHRISTMAS.
MERRY CHRISTMAS !
ARCHIE'LL NEVER EXPECT TO GET SKIIS HEH I WAS QUITE A SKIIER MYSELF WHEN I WHEN I WAS A LAD !
I KNOW JUST THE PLACE TO HIDE THEM !
NOBODY WILL EVER THINK TO LOOK HERE__ OMIGOSH, ANOTHER PAIR !!
GEE, I WOULDN'T WANT TO HURT POP'S FEELINGS. I BETTER GET RID OF MINE. SHUCKS . . . I COULDA SAVED THE 4.95 !
HERE'S A PRESENT, JUGHEAD, OL' PAL __AN' MERRY CHRISTMAS !
? ? ? ?
MEANWHILE ARCHIE'S MOTHER IS RETURNING HOME FROM HER SHOPPING !
MY, WON'T ARCHIE BE SURPRISED ! HE'S ALWAYS WANTED SKIIS ! I THINK I'LL KEEP IT AS A SURPRISE __ EVEN FROM FATHER UNTIL CHRISTMAS MORNING !
WOW !
THOSE ARE SKIIS IN THERE OR I'LL EAT THE TREE !
2

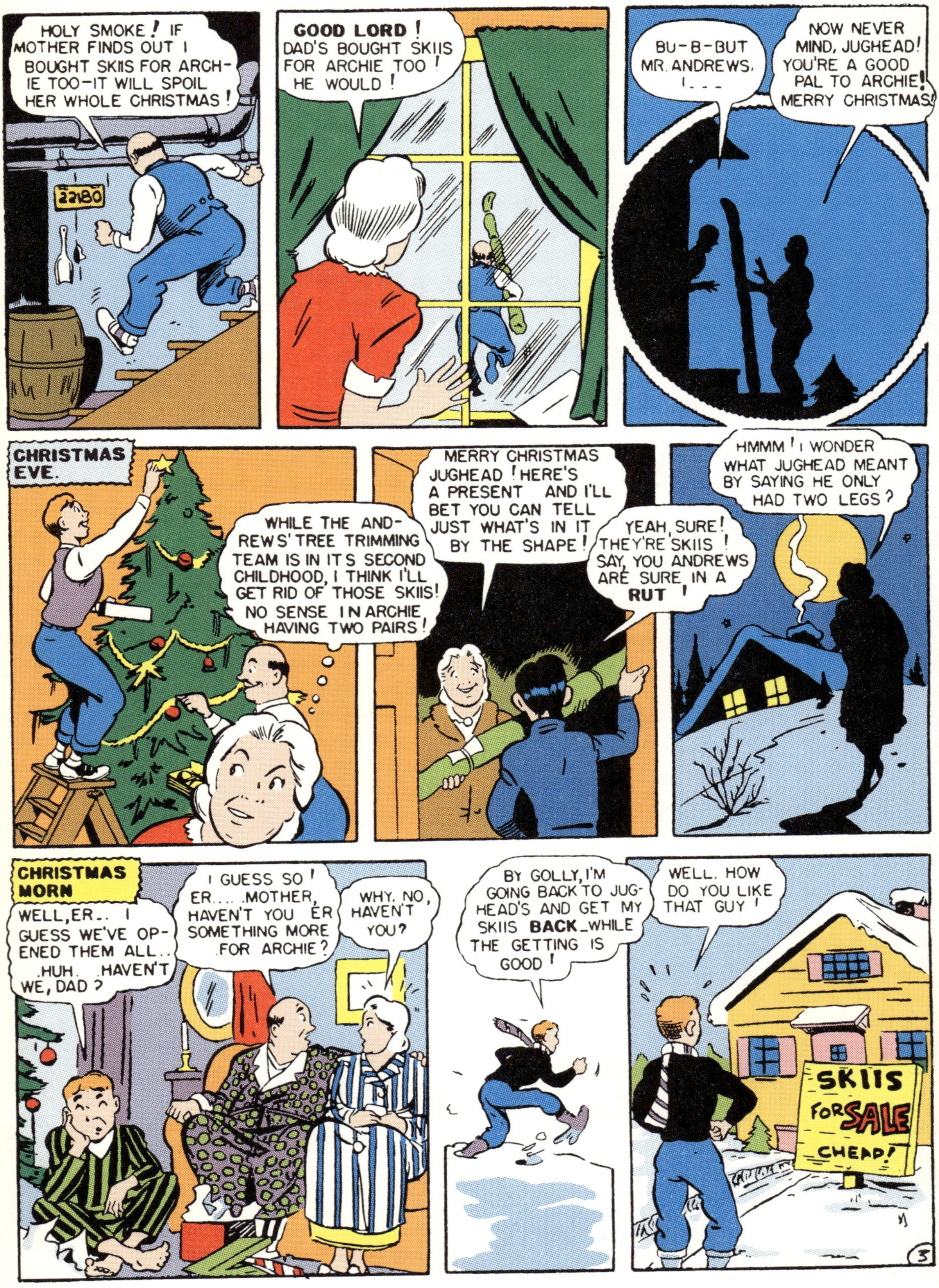
HOLY SMOKE! IF MOTHER FINDS OUT I BOUGHT SKIIS FOR ARCHIE TOO—IT WILL SPOIL HER WHOLE CHRISTMAS!
2280
GOOD LORD! DAD'S BOUGHT SKIIS FOR ARCHIE TOO! HE WOULD!
BU-B-BUT MR. ANDREWS, I- - -
NOW NEVER MIND, JUGHEAD! YOU'RE A GOOD PAL TO ARCHIE! MERRY CHRISTMAS!
CHRISTMAS EVE.
WHILE THE ANDREWS' TREE TRIMMING TEAM IS IN ITS SECOND CHILDHOOD, I THINK I'LL GET RID OF THOSE SKIIS! NO SENSE IN ARCHIE HAVING TWO PAIRS!
MERRY CHRISTMAS JUGHEAD! HERE'S A PRESENT AND I'LL BET YOU CAN TELL JUST WHAT'S IN IT BY THE SHAPE!
YEAH, SURE! THEY'RE SKIIS! SAY, YOU ANDREWS ARE SURE IN A RUT!
HMMM! I WONDER WHAT JUGHEAD MEANT BY SAYING HE ONLY HAD TWO LEGS?
CHRISTMAS MORN
WELL, ER.. I GUESS WE'VE OPENED THEM ALL.. HUH.. HAVEN'T WE, DAD?
I GUESS SO! ER.... MOTHER, HAVEN'T YOU ER SOMETHING MORE FOR ARCHIE?
WHY, NO, HAVEN'T YOU?
BY GOLLY, I'M GOING BACK TO JUGHEAD'S AND GET MY SKIIS BACK—WHILE THE GETTING IS GOOD!
WELL, HOW DO YOU LIKE THAT GUY!
SKIIS FOR SALE CHEAP!
3

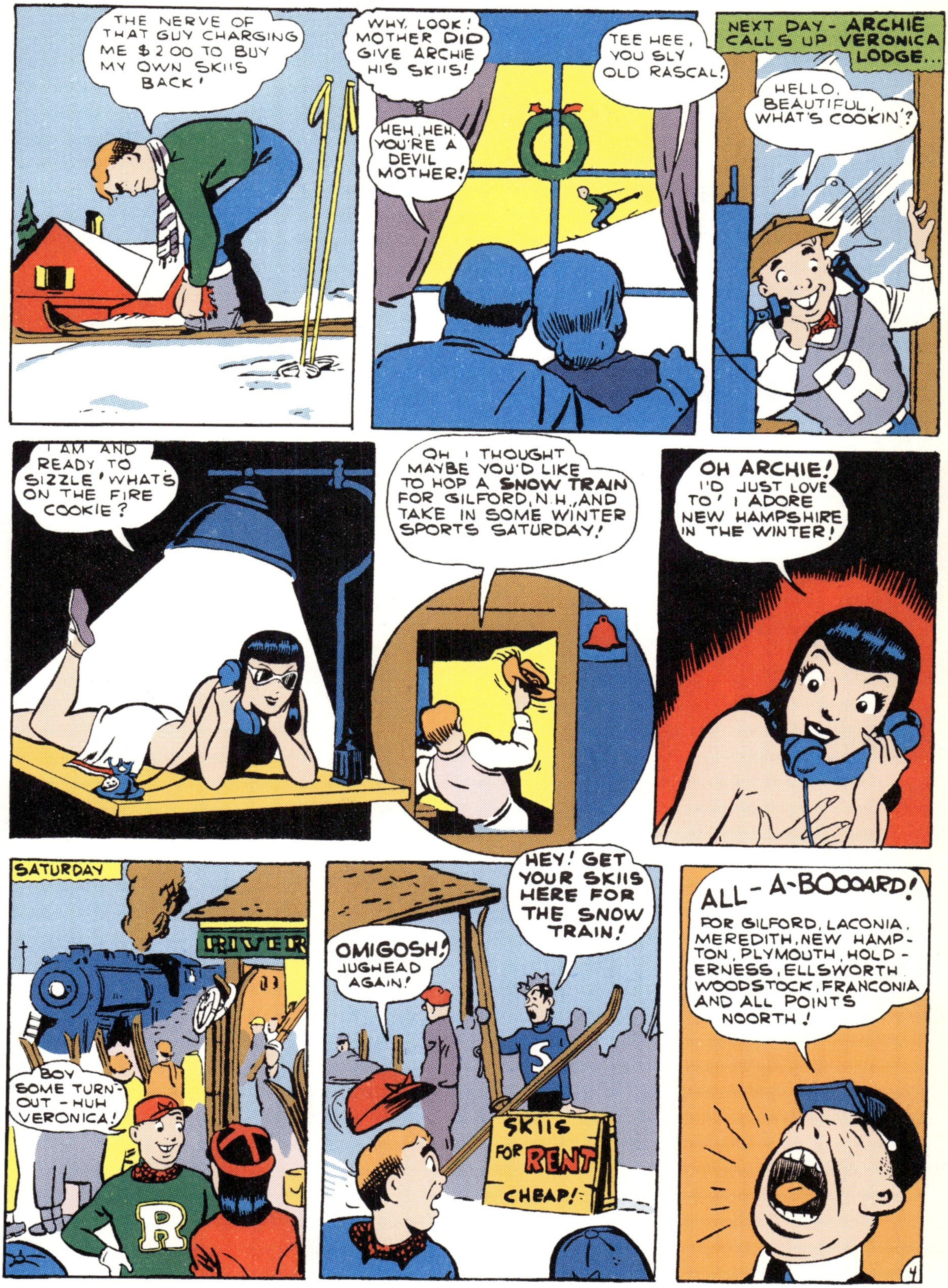
THE NERVE OF THAT GUY CHARGING ME $2.00 TO BUY MY OWN SKIIS BACK!
WHY, LOOK! MOTHER DID GIVE ARCHIE HIS SKIIS!
TEE HEE, YOU SLY OLD RASCAL!
HEH, HEH, YOU'RE A DEVIL MOTHER!
NEXT DAY - ARCHIE CALLS UP VERONICA LODGE...
HELLO, BEAUTIFUL, WHAT'S COOKIN'?
I AM AND READY TO SIZZLE! WHAT'S ON THE FIRE COOKIE?
OH I THOUGHT MAYBE YOU'D LIKE TO HOP A SNOW TRAIN FOR GILFORD, N.H., AND TAKE IN SOME WINTER SPORTS SATURDAY!
OH ARCHIE! I'D JUST LOVE TO! I ADORE NEW HAMPSHIRE IN THE WINTER!
SATURDAY
RIVER
BOY SOME TURN-OUT - HUH VERONICA!
OMIGOSH! JUGHEAD AGAIN!
HEY! GET YOUR SKIIS HERE FOR THE SNOW TRAIN!
SKIIS FOR RENT CHEAP!
ALL - A-BOOOARD!
FOR GILFORD, LACONIA, MEREDITH, NEW HAMPTON, PLYMOUTH, HOLDERNESS, ELLSWORTH WOODSTOCK, FRANCONIA AND ALL POINTS NOORTH!
4

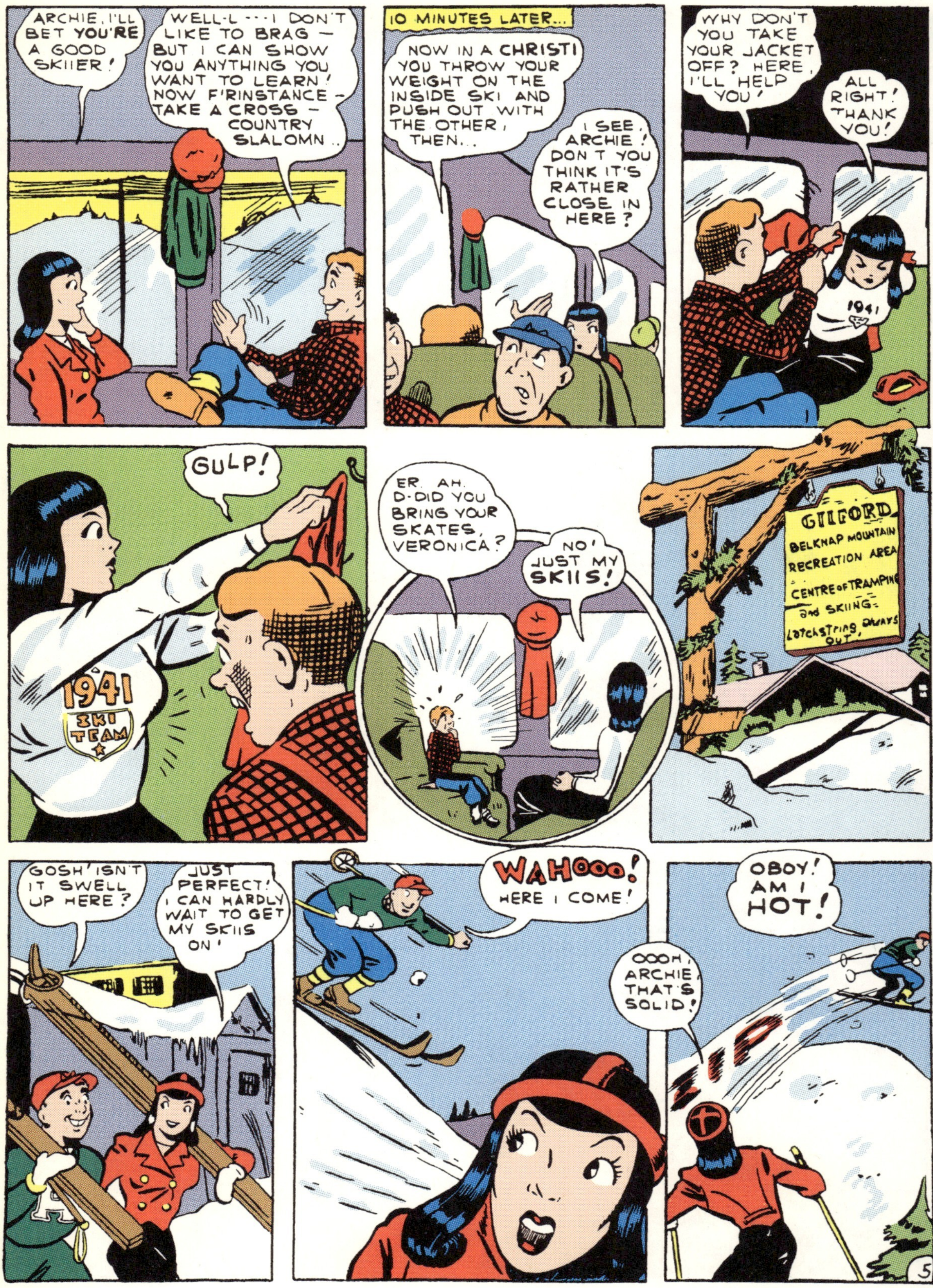
ARCHIE, I'LL BET YOU'RE A GOOD SKIIER!
WELL-L --- I DON'T LIKE TO BRAG — BUT I CAN SHOW YOU ANYTHING YOU WANT TO LEARN! NOW F'RINSTANCE — TAKE A CROSS — COUNTRY SLALOMN..
10 MINUTES LATER...
NOW IN A CHRISTI YOU THROW YOUR WEIGHT ON THE INSIDE SKI AND PUSH OUT WITH THE OTHER, THEN...
I SEE, ARCHIE! DON'T YOU THINK IT'S RATHER CLOSE IN HERE?
WHY DON'T YOU TAKE YOUR JACKET OFF? HERE, I'LL HELP YOU!
ALL RIGHT! THANK YOU!
1941
GULP!
1941 SKI TEAM
ER, AH, D-DID YOU BRING YOUR SKATES, VERONICA?
NO! JUST MY SKIIS!
GILFORD
BELKNAP MOUNTAIN RECREATION AREA
CENTRE OF TRAMPING and SKIING
Latchstring always out
GOSH! ISN'T IT SWELL UP HERE?
JUST PERFECT! I CAN HARDLY WAIT TO GET MY SKIIS ON!
WAHOOO! HERE I COME!
OOOH, ARCHIE, THAT'S SOLID!
OBOY! AM I HOT!
ZIP
5

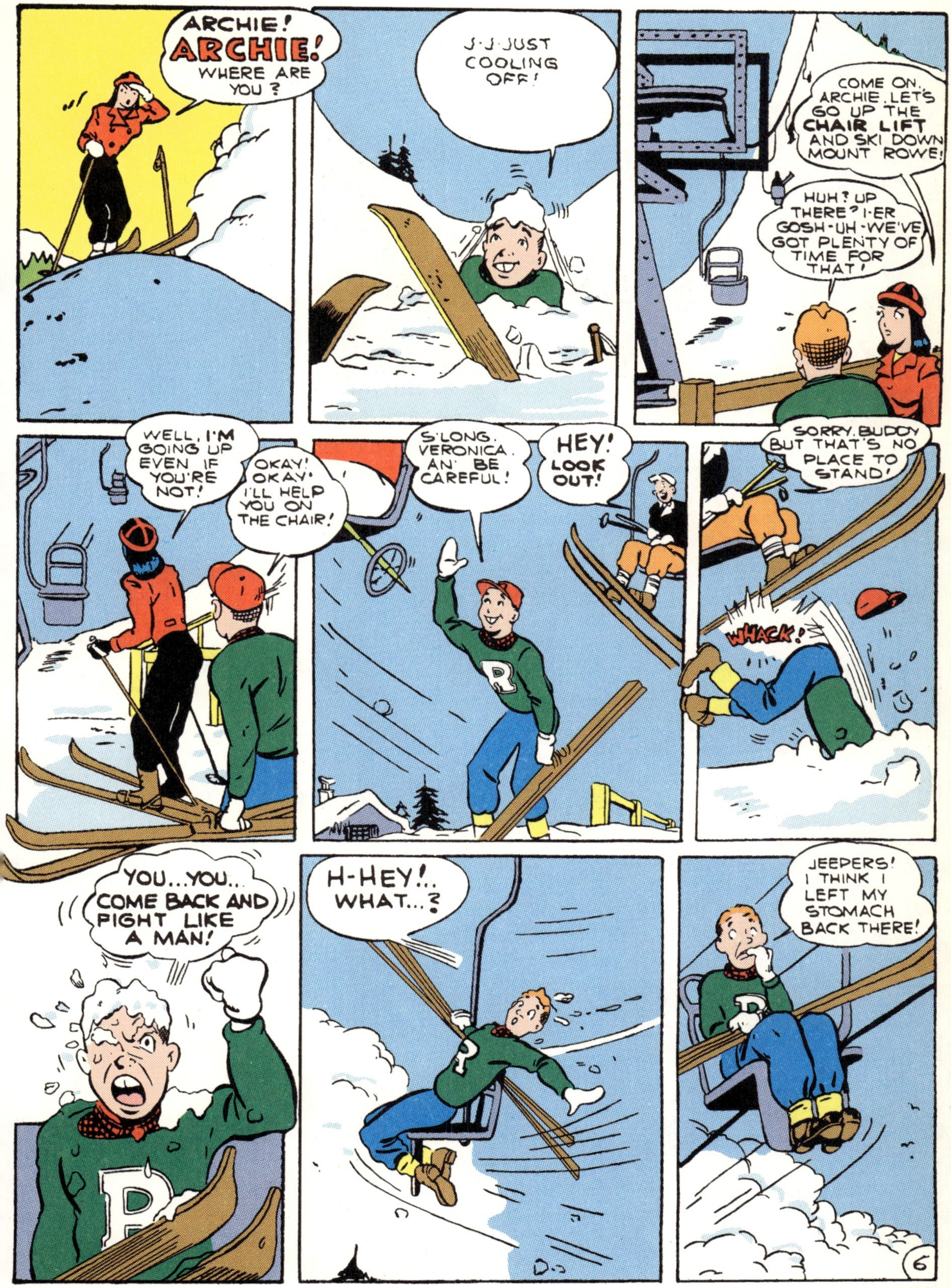
ARCHIE! ARCHIE! WHERE ARE YOU ?
J-J-JUST COOLING OFF!
COME ON, ARCHIE, LET'S GO UP THE CHAIR LIFT AND SKI DOWN MOUNT ROWE!
HUH? UP THERE? I-ER GOSH-UH-WE'VE GOT PLENTY OF TIME FOR THAT!
WELL, I'M GOING UP EVEN IF YOU'RE NOT!
OKAY! OKAY! I'LL HELP YOU ON THE CHAIR!
S'LONG, VERONICA, AN' BE CAREFUL!
HEY! LOOK OUT!
SORRY, BUDDY BUT THAT'S NO PLACE TO STAND!
WHACK!
YOU...YOU... COME BACK AND FIGHT LIKE A MAN!
H-HEY!.. WHAT...?
JEEPERS! I THINK I LEFT MY STOMACH BACK THERE!
6

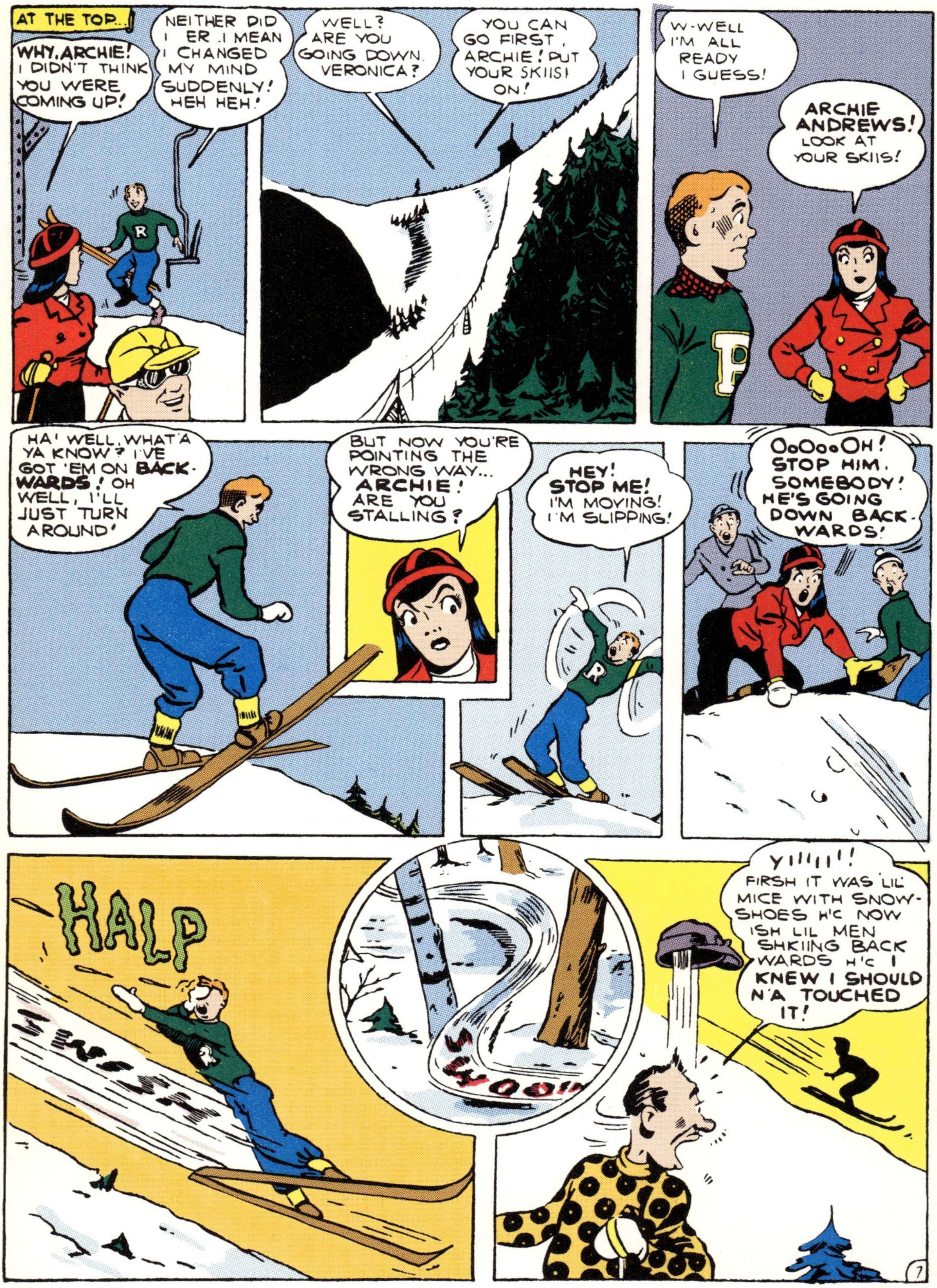
AT THE TOP...
WHY, ARCHIE! I DIDN'T THINK YOU WERE COMING UP!
NEITHER DID I ER..I MEAN I CHANGED MY MIND SUDDENLY! HEH HEH!
WELL? ARE YOU GOING DOWN, VERONICA?
YOU CAN GO FIRST, ARCHIE! PUT YOUR SKIIS! ON!
W-WELL I'M ALL READY I GUESS!
ARCHIE ANDREWS! LOOK AT YOUR SKIIS!
HA! WELL, WHAT'A YA KNOW? I'VE GOT 'EM ON BACKWARDS! OH WELL, I'LL JUST TURN AROUND!
BUT NOW YOU'RE POINTING THE WRONG WAY... ARCHIE! ARE YOU STALLING?
HEY! STOP ME! I'M MOVING! I'M SLIPPING!
OoOooOH! STOP HIM, SOMEBODY! HE'S GOING DOWN BACKWARDS!
HALP
YI!!!!!
FIRSH IT WAS LIL MICE WITH SNOWSHOES H'C NOW ISH LIL MEN SHKIING BACK WARDS H'C I KNEW I SHOULD N'A TOUCHED IT!
7

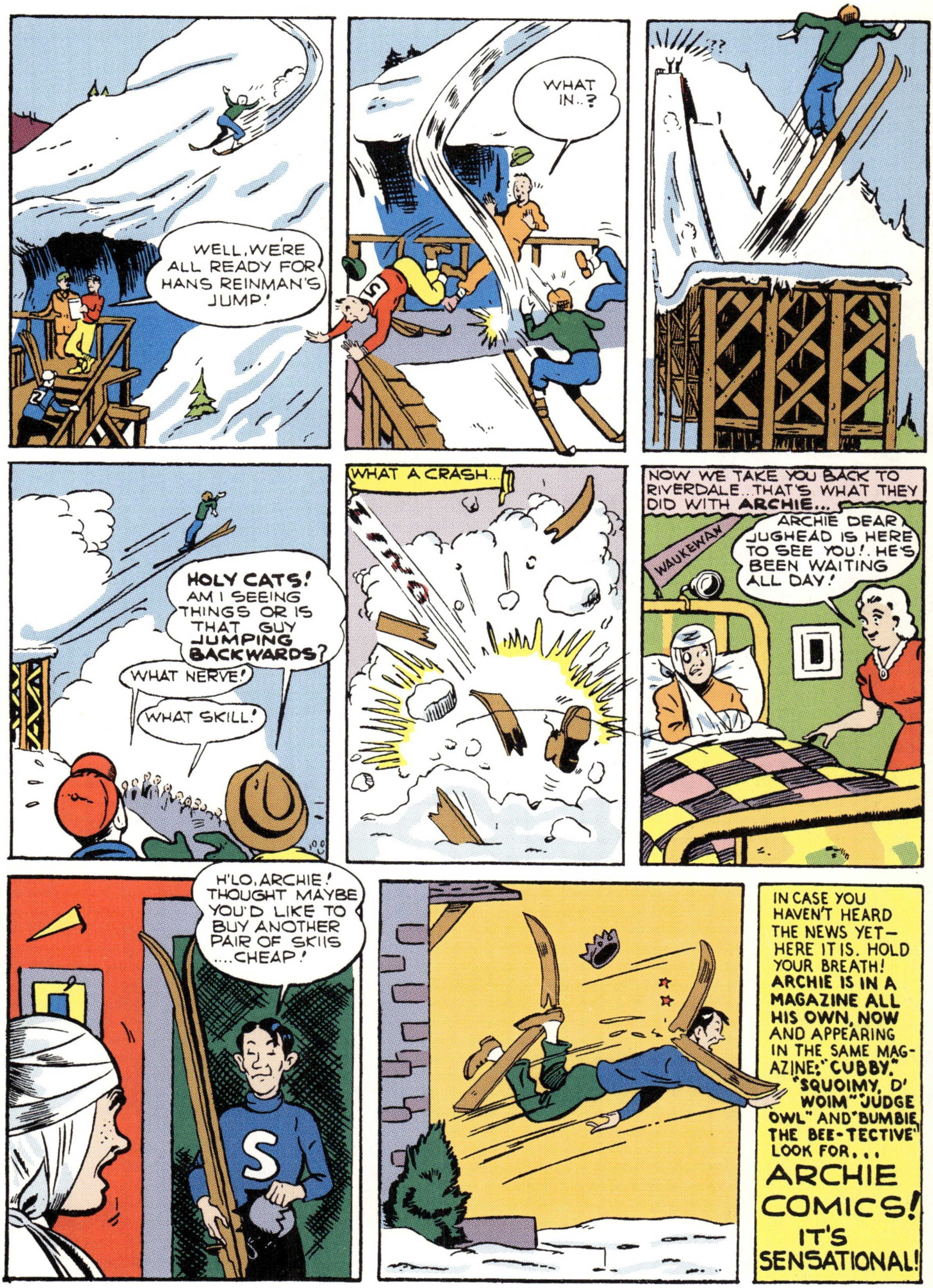

WELL, WE'RE ALL READY FOR HANS REINMAN'S JUMP!
WHAT IN..?
??
HOLY CATS! AM I SEEING THINGS OR IS THAT GUY JUMPING BACKWARDS?
WHAT NERVE!
WHAT SKILL!
WHAT A CRASH...
NOW WE TAKE YOU BACK TO RIVERDALE.. THAT'S WHAT THEY DID WITH ARCHIE...
ARCHIE DEAR, JUGHEAD IS HERE TO SEE YOU!. HE'S BEEN WAITING ALL DAY!
WAUKEWAN
H'LO, ARCHIE! THOUGHT MAYBE YOU'D LIKE TO BUY ANOTHER PAIR OF SKIIS ....CHEAP!
IN CASE YOU HAVEN'T HEARD THE NEWS YET- HERE IT IS. HOLD YOUR BREATH! ARCHIE IS IN A MAGAZINE ALL HIS OWN, NOW AND APPEARING IN THE SAME MAGAZINE: "CUBBY," "SQUOIMY, D' WOIM" "JUDGE OWL" AND "BUMBIE THE BEE-TECTIVE" LOOK FOR. . .
ARCHIE COMICS!
IT'S SENSATIONAL!

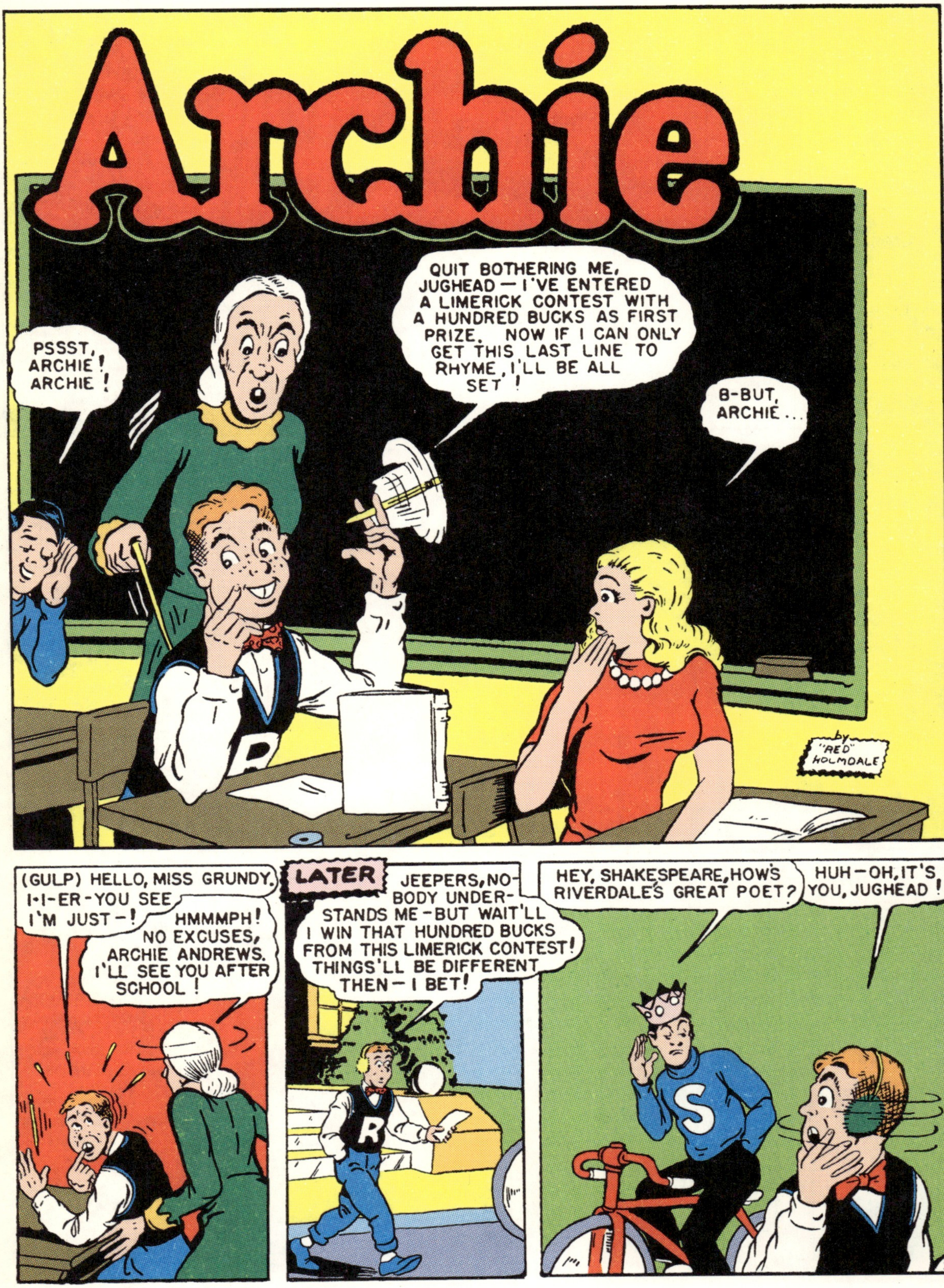
Archie
PSSST, ARCHIE! ARCHIE!
QUIT BOTHERING ME, JUGHEAD — I'VE ENTERED A LIMERICK CONTEST WITH A HUNDRED BUCKS AS FIRST PRIZE. NOW IF I CAN ONLY GET THIS LAST LINE TO RHYME, I'LL BE ALL SET!
B-BUT, ARCHIE...
by "RED" HOLMDALE
(GULP) HELLO, MISS GRUNDY. I-I-ER-YOU SEE I'M JUST—!
HMMMPH! NO EXCUSES, ARCHIE ANDREWS. I'LL SEE YOU AFTER SCHOOL!
LATER
JEEPERS, NOBODY UNDERSTANDS ME—BUT WAIT'LL I WIN THAT HUNDRED BUCKS FROM THIS LIMERICK CONTEST! THINGS'LL BE DIFFERENT THEN—I BET!
HEY, SHAKESPEARE, HOW'S RIVERDALE'S GREAT POET?
HUH—OH, IT'S YOU, JUGHEAD!
1

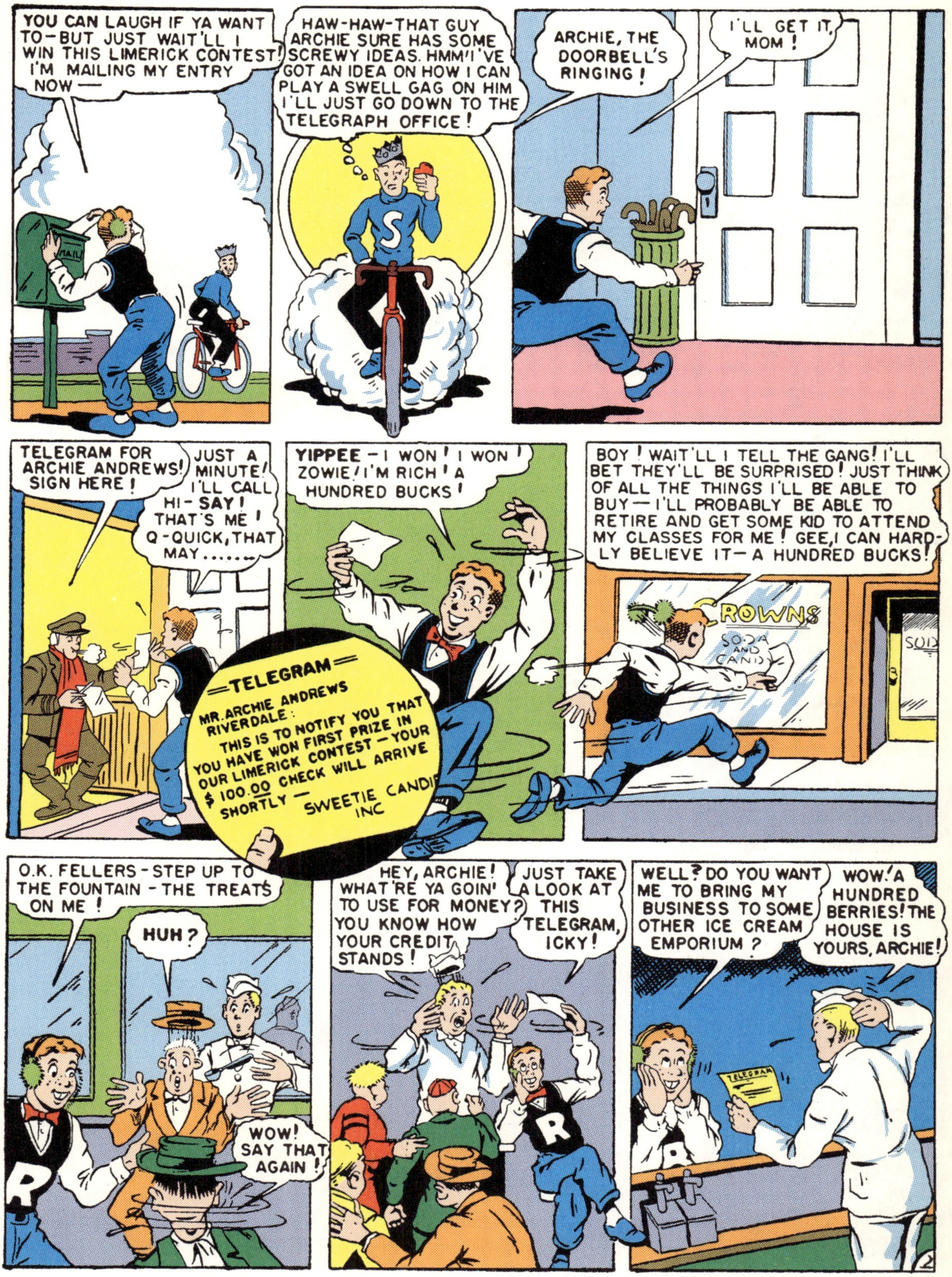
YOU CAN LAUGH IF YA WANT TO—BUT JUST WAIT'LL I WIN THIS LIMERICK CONTEST! I'M MAILING MY ENTRY NOW—
MAIL
HAW-HAW-THAT GUY ARCHIE SURE HAS SOME SCREWY IDEAS. HMM! I'VE GOT AN IDEA ON HOW I CAN PLAY A SWELL GAG ON HIM I'LL JUST GO DOWN TO THE TELEGRAPH OFFICE!
ARCHIE, THE DOORBELL'S RINGING!
I'LL GET IT, MOM!
TELEGRAM FOR ARCHIE ANDREWS! SIGN HERE!
JUST A MINUTE! I'LL CALL HI-SAY! THAT'S ME! Q-QUICK, THAT MAY.......
TELEGRAM
MR. ARCHIE ANDREWS RIVERDALE: THIS IS TO NOTIFY YOU THAT YOU HAVE WON FIRST PRIZE IN OUR LIMERICK CONTEST—YOUR $100.00 CHECK WILL ARRIVE SHORTLY— SWEETIE CANDI INC
YIPPEE—I WON! I WON! ZOWIE! I'M RICH! A HUNDRED BUCKS!
BOY! WAIT'LL I TELL THE GANG! I'LL BET THEY'LL BE SURPRISED! JUST THINK OF ALL THE THINGS I'LL BE ABLE TO BUY—I'LL PROBABLY BE ABLE TO RETIRE AND GET SOME KID TO ATTEND MY CLASSES FOR ME! GEE, I CAN HARDLY BELIEVE IT—A HUNDRED BUCKS!
CROWNS
O.K. FELLERS-STEP UP TO THE FOUNTAIN-THE TREATS ON ME!
HUH?
WOW! SAY THAT AGAIN!
HEY, ARCHIE! WHAT'RE YA GOIN' TO USE FOR MONEY? YOU KNOW HOW YOUR CREDIT STANDS!
JUST TAKE A LOOK AT THIS TELEGRAM, ICKY!
WELL? DO YOU WANT ME TO BRING MY BUSINESS TO SOME OTHER ICE CREAM EMPORIUM?
WOW! A HUNDRED BERRIES! THE HOUSE IS YOURS, ARCHIE!

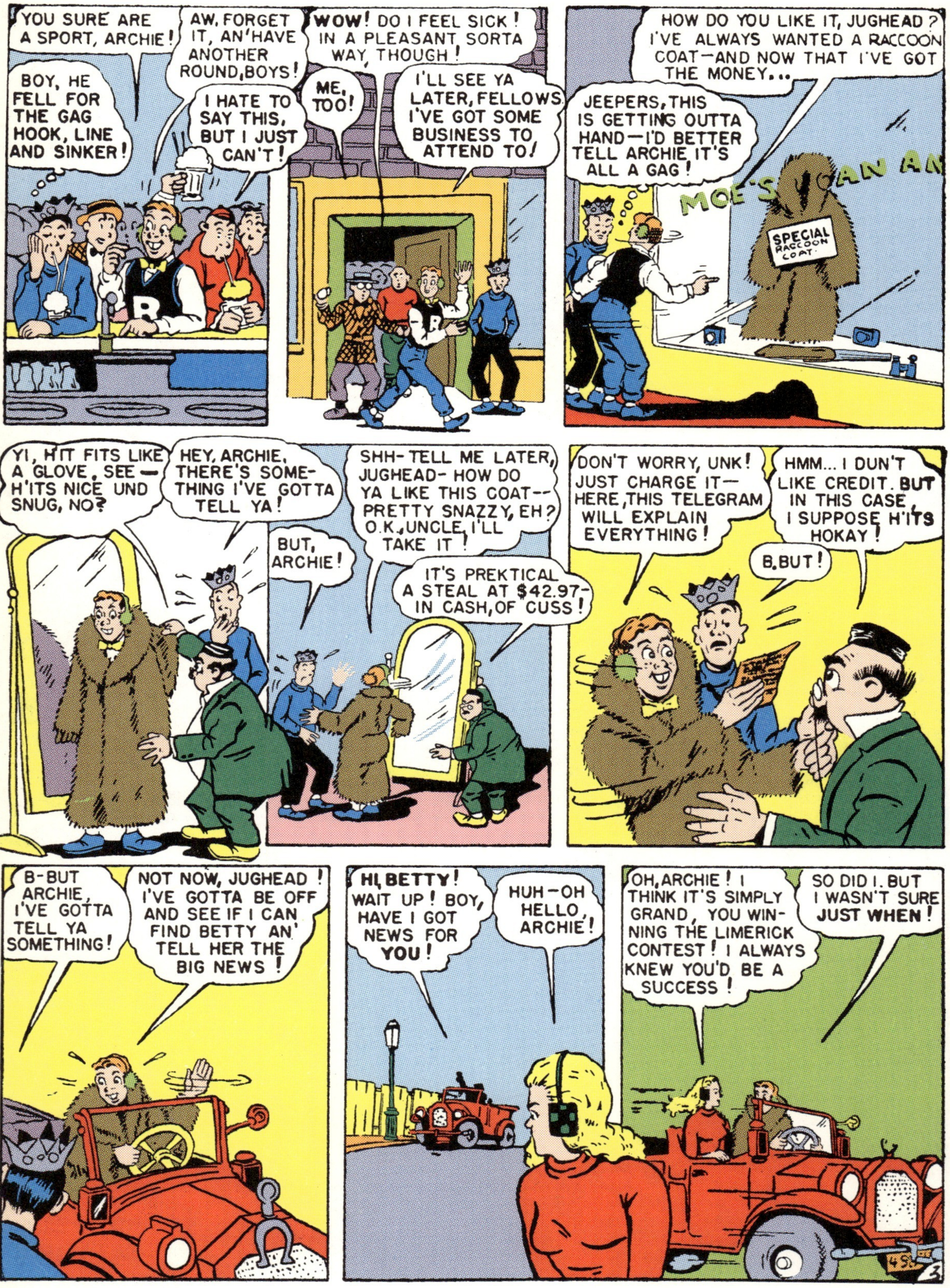
YOU SURE ARE A SPORT, ARCHIE!
BOY, HE FELL FOR THE GAG HOOK, LINE AND SINKER!
AW, FORGET IT, AN' HAVE ANOTHER ROUND, BOYS!
I HATE TO SAY THIS, BUT I JUST CAN'T!
WOW! DO I FEEL SICK! IN A PLEASANT SORTA WAY, THOUGH!
ME, TOO!
I'LL SEE YA LATER, FELLOWS. I'VE GOT SOME BUSINESS TO ATTEND TO!
HOW DO YOU LIKE IT, JUGHEAD? I'VE ALWAYS WANTED A RACCOON COAT—AND NOW THAT I'VE GOT THE MONEY...
JEEPERS, THIS IS GETTING OUTTA HAND—I'D BETTER TELL ARCHIE IT'S ALL A GAG!
MOE'S ...AN AN
SPECIAL RACCOON COAT
YI, H'IT FITS LIKE A GLOVE, SEE—H'ITS NICE UND SNUG, NO?
HEY, ARCHIE, THERE'S SOMETHING I'VE GOTTA TELL YA!
BUT, ARCHIE!
SHH- TELL ME LATER, JUGHEAD- HOW DO YA LIKE THIS COAT-- PRETTY SNAZZY, EH? O.K., UNCLE, I'LL TAKE IT!
IT'S PREKTICAL A STEAL AT $42.97- IN CASH, OF CUSS!
DON'T WORRY, UNK! JUST CHARGE IT— HERE, THIS TELEGRAM WILL EXPLAIN EVERYTHING!
HMM... I DUN'T LIKE CREDIT. BUT IN THIS CASE, I SUPPOSE H'ITS HOKAY!
B.BUT!
B-BUT ARCHIE, I'VE GOTTA TELL YA SOMETHING!
NOT NOW, JUGHEAD! I'VE GOTTA BE OFF AND SEE IF I CAN FIND BETTY AN' TELL HER THE BIG NEWS!
HI, BETTY! WAIT UP! BOY, HAVE I GOT NEWS FOR YOU!
HUH—OH HELLO, ARCHIE!
OH, ARCHIE! I THINK IT'S SIMPLY GRAND, YOU WINNING THE LIMERICK CONTEST! I ALWAYS KNEW YOU'D BE A SUCCESS!
SO DID I. BUT I WASN'T SURE JUST WHEN!
3

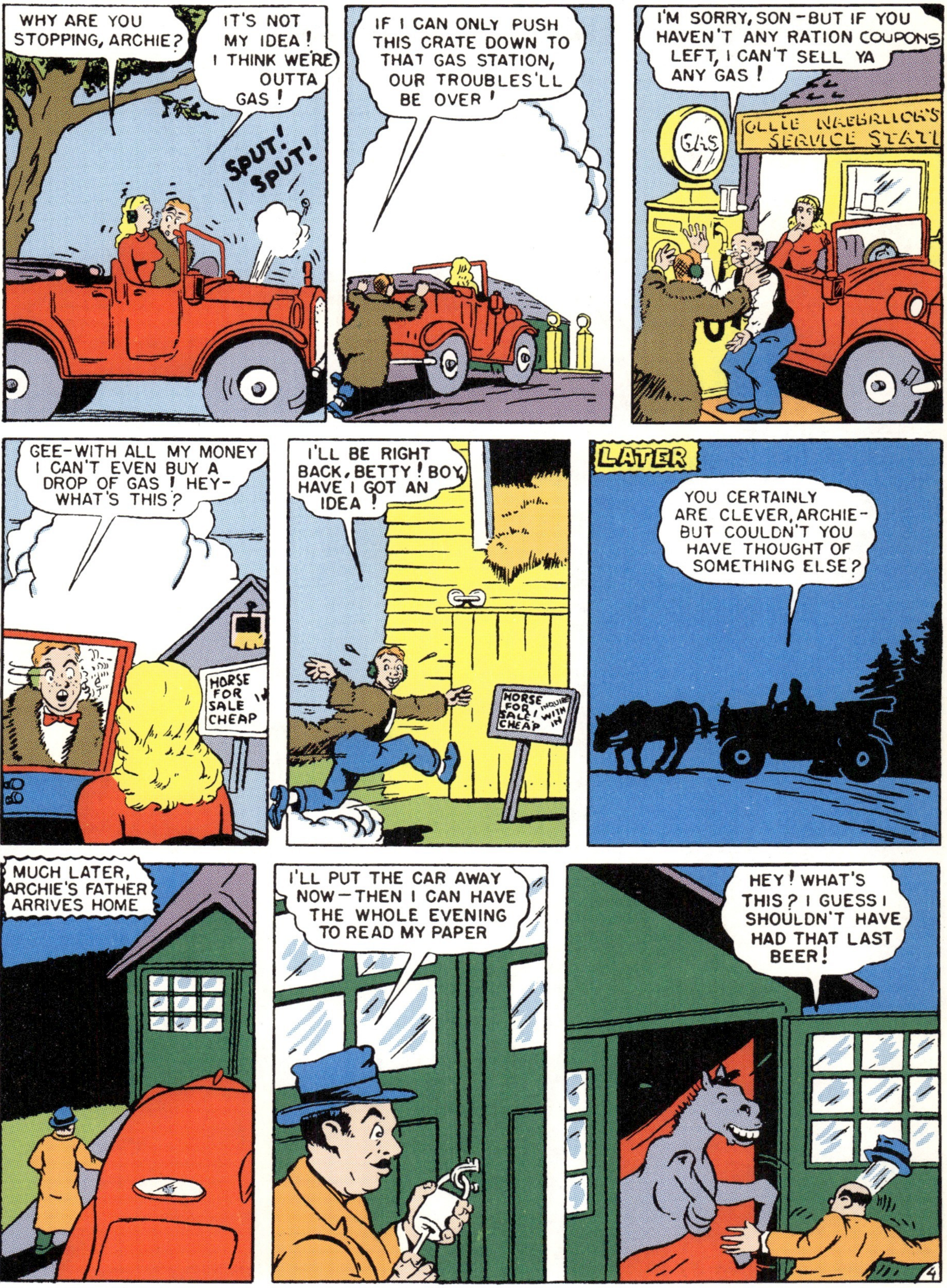
WHY ARE YOU STOPPING, ARCHIE?
IT'S NOT MY IDEA! I THINK WE'RE OUTTA GAS!
SPUT! SPUT!
IF I CAN ONLY PUSH THIS CRATE DOWN TO THAT GAS STATION, OUR TROUBLES'LL BE OVER!
I'M SORRY, SON-BUT IF YOU HAVEN'T ANY RATION COUPONS LEFT, I CAN'T SELL YA ANY GAS!
GAS
GEE-WITH ALL MY MONEY I CAN'T EVEN BUY A DROP OF GAS! HEY-WHAT'S THIS?
HORSE FOR SALE CHEAP
I'LL BE RIGHT BACK, BETTY! BOY, HAVE I GOT AN IDEA!
HORSE FOR SALE! CHEAP INQUIRE WITHIN
LATER
YOU CERTAINLY ARE CLEVER, ARCHIE-BUT COULDN'T YOU HAVE THOUGHT OF SOMETHING ELSE?
MUCH LATER, ARCHIE'S FATHER ARRIVES HOME
I'LL PUT THE CAR AWAY NOW-THEN I CAN HAVE THE WHOLE EVENING TO READ MY PAPER
HEY! WHAT'S THIS? I GUESS I SHOULDN'T HAVE HAD THAT LAST BEER!
4

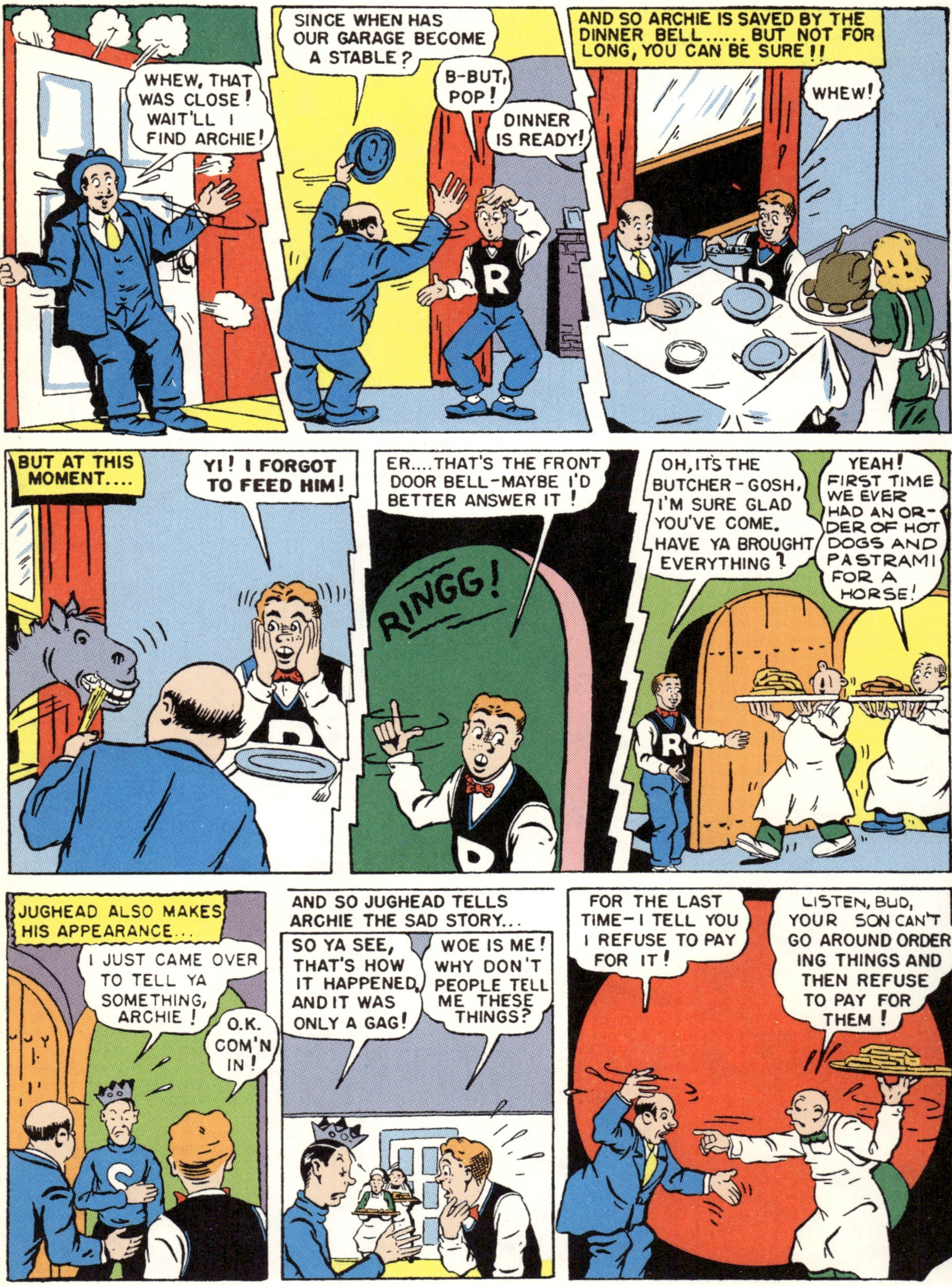
WHEW, THAT WAS CLOSE! WAIT'LL I FIND ARCHIE!
SINCE WHEN HAS OUR GARAGE BECOME A STABLE?
B-BUT, POP!
DINNER IS READY!
AND SO ARCHIE IS SAVED BY THE DINNER BELL...... BUT NOT FOR LONG, YOU CAN BE SURE!!
WHEW!
BUT AT THIS MOMENT....
YI! I FORGOT TO FEED HIM!
ER....THAT'S THE FRONT DOOR BELL-MAYBE I'D BETTER ANSWER IT!
RINGG!
OH, IT'S THE BUTCHER-GOSH, I'M SURE GLAD YOU'VE COME. HAVE YA BROUGHT EVERYTHING?
YEAH! FIRST TIME WE EVER HAD AN ORDER OF HOT DOGS AND PASTRAMI FOR A HORSE!
JUGHEAD ALSO MAKES HIS APPEARANCE...
I JUST CAME OVER TO TELL YA SOMETHING, ARCHIE!
O.K. COM'N IN!
AND SO JUGHEAD TELLS ARCHIE THE SAD STORY...
SO YA SEE, THAT'S HOW IT HAPPENED, AND IT WAS ONLY A GAG!
WOE IS ME! WHY DON'T PEOPLE TELL ME THESE THINGS?
FOR THE LAST TIME-I TELL YOU I REFUSE TO PAY FOR IT!
LISTEN, BUD, YOUR SON CAN'T GO AROUND ORDERING THINGS AND THEN REFUSE TO PAY FOR THEM!

AND AS IF ARCHIE DIDN'T HAVE ENOUGH TROUBLE:

HOW ABOUT PAYING FOR THAT HORSE YA BOUGHT?

NEVER MIND THE HORSE — JUST SETTLE FOR THAT RACCOON COAT!

GEE — YOU'VE GOT COMPANY ARCHIE!

WE WANT OUR MONEY!

I CAN'T HEAR A WORD YOU'RE SAYING!

JEEZ, HERE'S ANOTHER GUY!

MUST BE SOME KIND OF A CONVENTION GOING ON HERE — HEY! SPECIAL DELIVERY FOR ARCHIE ANDREWS!

THAT'S ME!

TWEET! TWEET!!

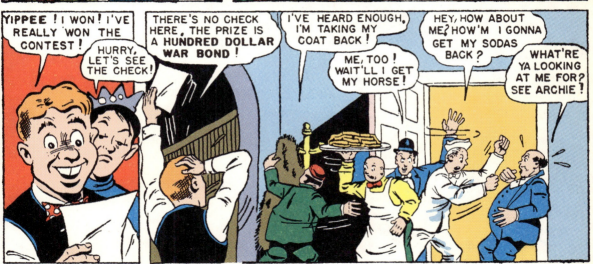

YIPPEE! I WON! I'VE REALLY WON THE CONTEST!

HURRY, LET'S SEE THE CHECK!

THERE'S NO CHECK HERE, THE PRIZE IS A HUNDRED DOLLAR WAR BOND!

I'VE HEARD ENOUGH, I'M TAKING MY COAT BACK!

ME, TOO! WAIT'LL I GET MY HORSE!

HEY, HOW ABOUT ME? HOW'M I GONNA GET MY SODAS BACK?

WHAT'RE YA LOOKING AT ME FOR? SEE ARCHIE!

NOW THAT YOUR DEBTS ARE SETTLED WITH THOSE OTHER GUYS — YOU CAN COME WITH ME AND SQUARE OFF THAT SODA BILL!

B-BUT, I DON'T SEE HOW, DO YOU?

HOW CAN YA DRINK THAT STUFF, JUGHEAD? WHEN I GET FINISHED WORKING MY BILL OFF — I HOPE I NEVER SEE ICE CREAM AGAIN!

The END

HEY, GANG! HAVE YA HEARD OF THE SPECIAL TREAT WE'RE GONNA HAVE FOR YOU SOON? IT'S A BRAND NEW COMIC MAGAZINE, AND IT'S NAMED AFTER ME! SO WATCH FOR IT AT YOUR NEWS DEALERS! THANKS, PALS!

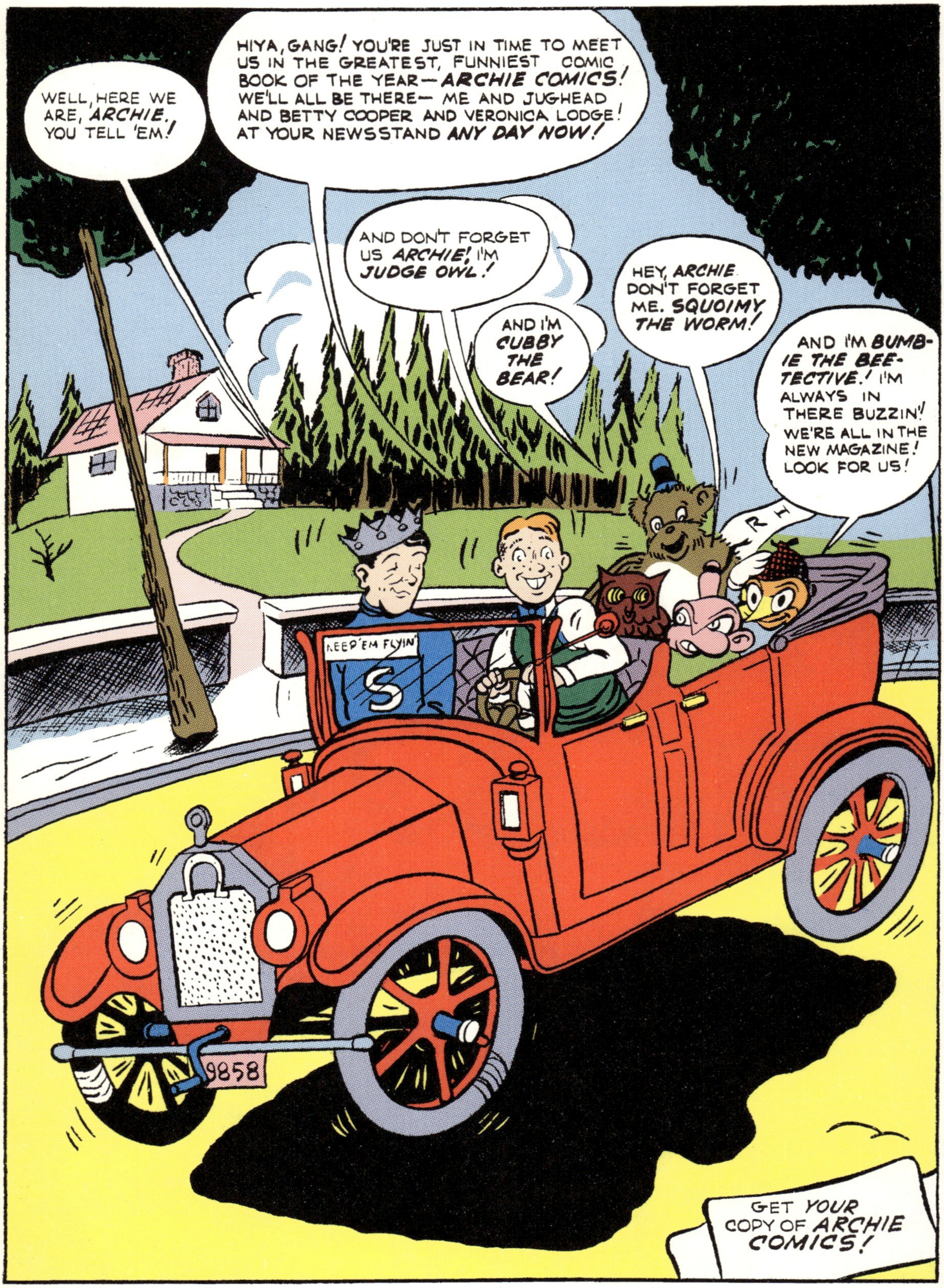
WELL, HERE WE ARE, ARCHIE. YOU TELL 'EM!
HIYA, GANG! YOU'RE JUST IN TIME TO MEET US IN THE GREATEST, FUNNIEST COMIC BOOK OF THE YEAR—ARCHIE COMICS! WE'LL ALL BE THERE— ME AND JUGHEAD AND BETTY COOPER AND VERONICA LODGE! AT YOUR NEWSSTAND ANY DAY NOW!
AND DON'T FORGET US ARCHIE! I'M JUDGE OWL!
AND I'M CUBBY THE BEAR!
HEY, ARCHIE DON'T FORGET ME. SQUOIMY THE WORM!
AND I'M BUMBIE THE BEE-TECTIVE! I'M ALWAYS IN THERE BUZZIN'! WE'RE ALL IN THE NEW MAGAZINE! LOOK FOR US!
KEEP 'EM FLYIN
S
9858
GET YOUR COPY OF ARCHIE COMICS!

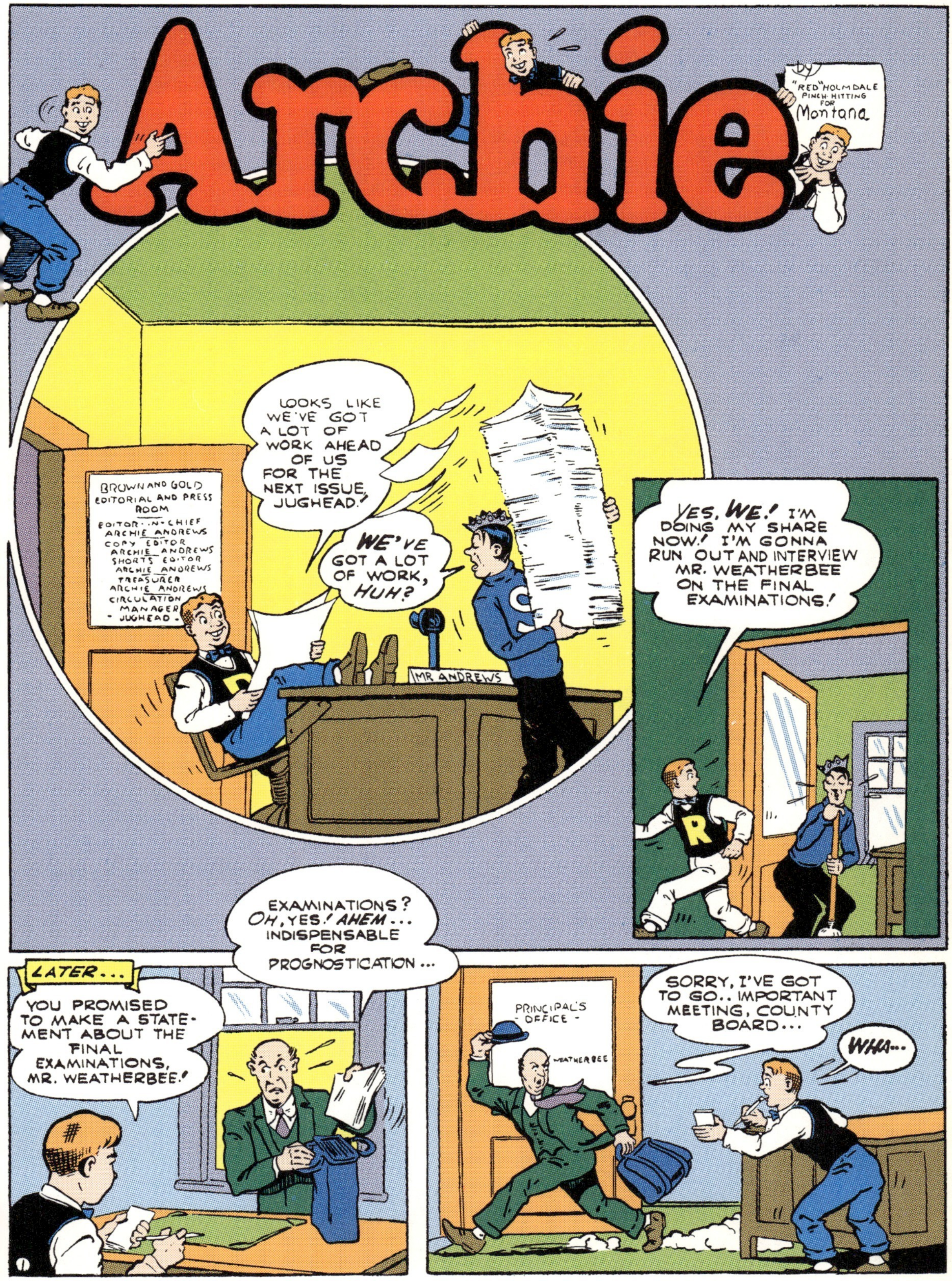
Archie
"RED" HOLMDALE PINCH-HITTING FOR Montana
BROWN AND GOLD EDITORIAL AND PRESS ROOM
EDITOR-IN-CHIEF ARCHIE ANDREWS
COPY EDITOR ARCHIE ANDREWS
SHORTS EDITOR ARCHIE ANDREWS
TREASURER ARCHIE ANDREWS
CIRCULATION MANAGER - JUGHEAD -
LOOKS LIKE WE'VE GOT A LOT OF WORK AHEAD OF US FOR THE NEXT ISSUE, JUGHEAD!
WE'VE GOT A LOT OF WORK, HUH?
MR. ANDREWS
YES, WE! I'M DOING MY SHARE NOW! I'M GONNA RUN OUT AND INTERVIEW MR. WEATHERBEE ON THE FINAL EXAMINATIONS!
LATER...
YOU PROMISED TO MAKE A STATEMENT ABOUT THE FINAL EXAMINATIONS, MR. WEATHERBEE!
EXAMINATIONS? OH, YES! AHEM... INDISPENSABLE FOR PROGNOSTICATION...
PRINCIPAL'S OFFICE
WEATHERBEE
SORRY, I'VE GOT TO GO.. IMPORTANT MEETING, COUNTY BOARD...
WHA...

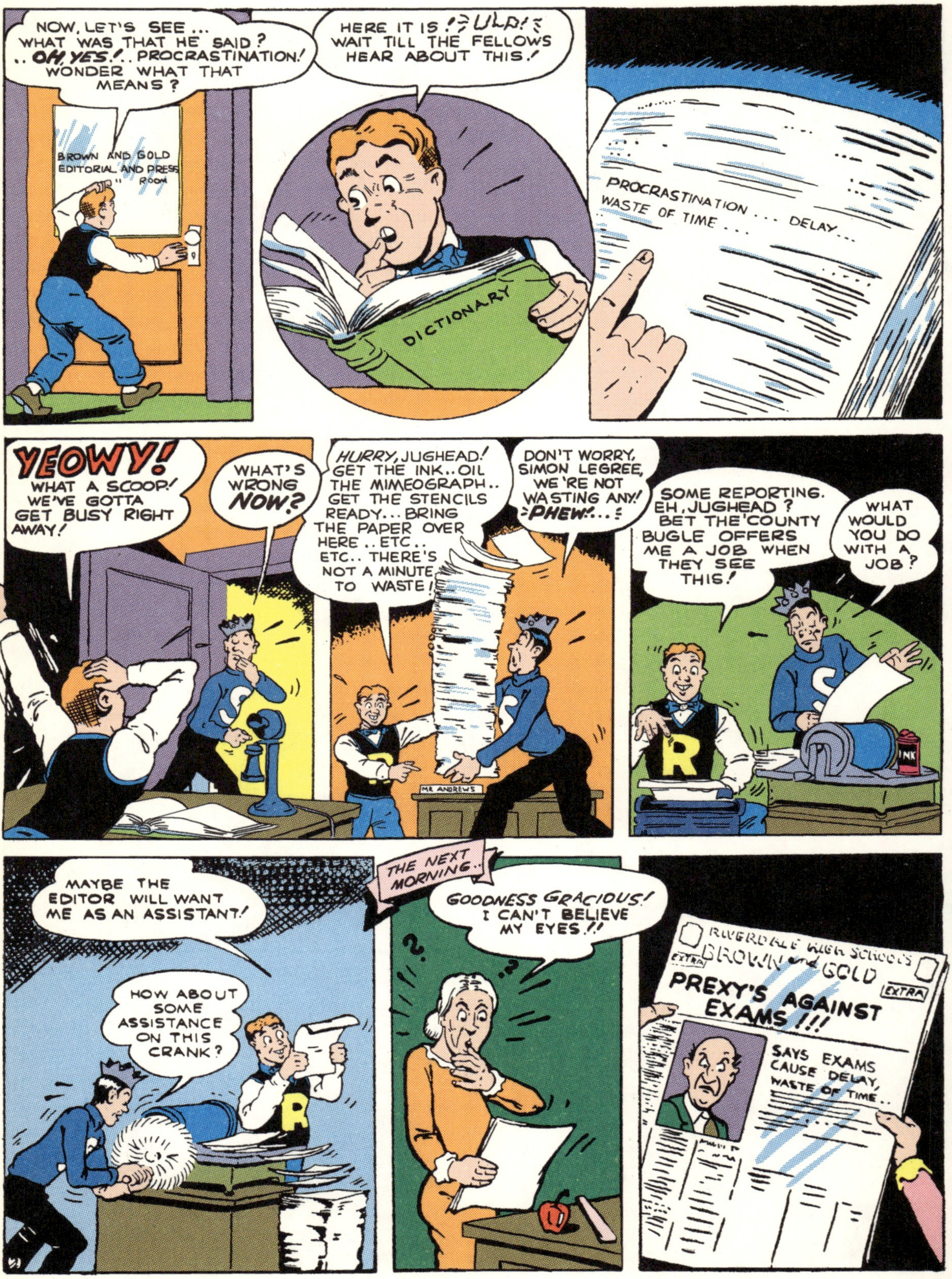
NOW, LET'S SEE... WHAT WAS THAT HE SAID? ..OH, YES!.. PROCRASTINATION! WONDER WHAT THAT MEANS?
BROWN AND GOLD EDITORIAL AND PRESS ROOM
HERE IT IS! ULP! WAIT TILL THE FELLOWS HEAR ABOUT THIS!
DICTIONARY
PROCRASTINATION... DELAY... WASTE OF TIME...
YEOWY! WHAT A SCOOP! WE'VE GOTTA GET BUSY RIGHT AWAY!
WHAT'S WRONG NOW?
HURRY, JUGHEAD! GET THE INK..OIL THE MIMEOGRAPH.. GET THE STENCILS READY... BRING THE PAPER OVER HERE..ETC.. ETC.. THERE'S NOT A MINUTE TO WASTE!
DON'T WORRY, SIMON LEGREE, WE'RE NOT WASTING ANY! PHEW!..
MR ANDREWS
SOME REPORTING, EH, JUGHEAD? BET THE COUNTY BUGLE OFFERS ME A JOB WHEN THEY SEE THIS!
WHAT WOULD YOU DO WITH A JOB?
INK
MAYBE THE EDITOR WILL WANT ME AS AN ASSISTANT!
HOW ABOUT SOME ASSISTANCE ON THIS CRANK?
THE NEXT MORNING..
GOODNESS GRACIOUS! I CAN'T BELIEVE MY EYES!!
RIVERDALE HIGH SCHOOL'S BROWN and GOLD
EXTRA
EXTRA
PREXY'S AGAINST EXAMS!!!
SAYS EXAMS CAUSE DELAY, WASTE OF TIME..

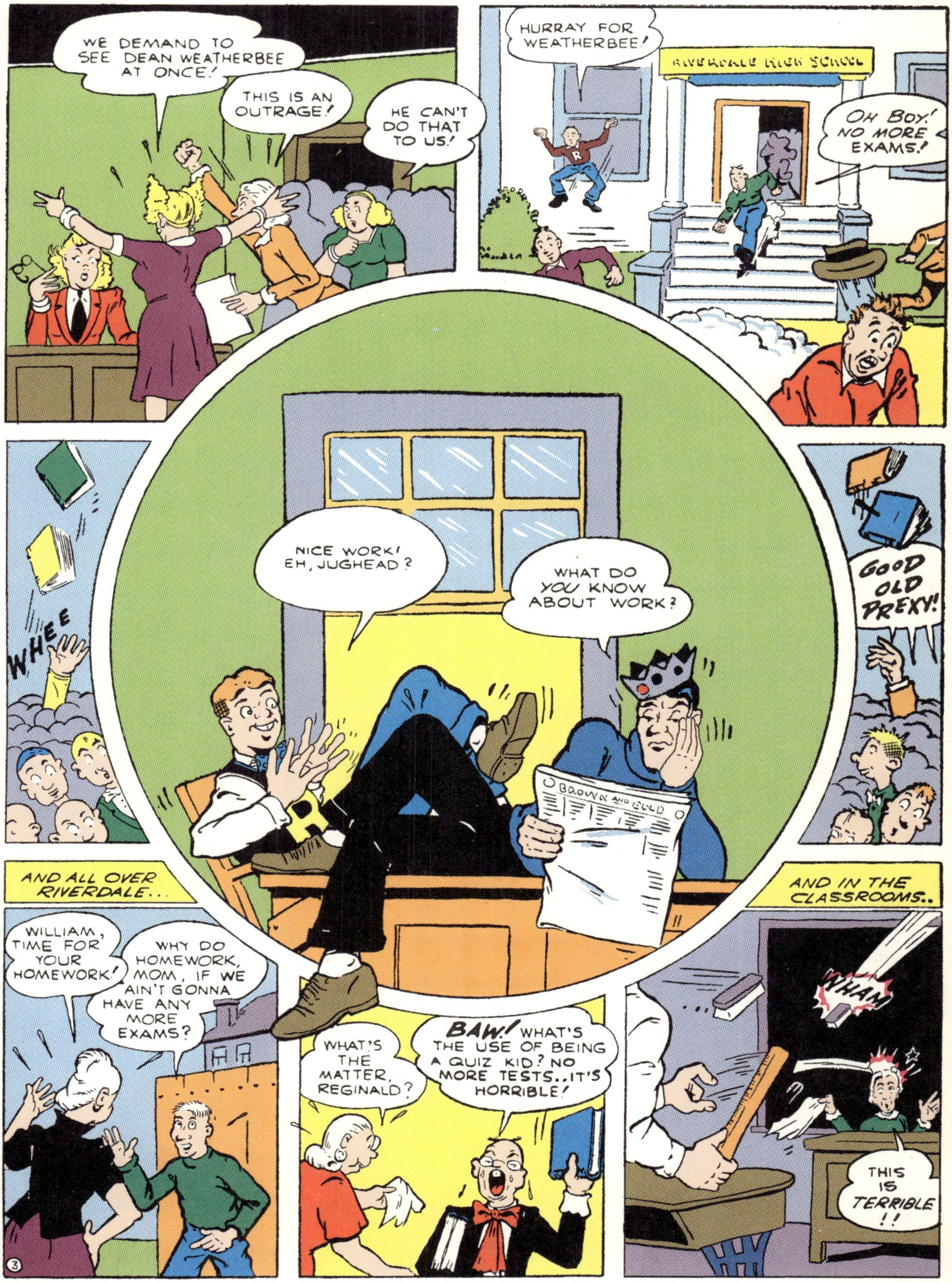

WE DEMAND TO SEE DEAN WEATHERBEE AT ONCE!
THIS IS AN OUTRAGE!
HE CAN'T DO THAT TO US!
HURRAY FOR WEATHERBEE!
RIVERDALE HIGH SCHOOL
OH BOY! NO MORE EXAMS!
WHEE
NICE WORK! EH, JUGHEAD?
WHAT DO YOU KNOW ABOUT WORK?
BROWN AND GOLD
GOOD OLD PREXY!
AND ALL OVER RIVERDALE...
WILLIAM, TIME FOR YOUR HOMEWORK!
WHY DO HOMEWORK, MOM, IF WE AIN'T GONNA HAVE ANY MORE EXAMS?
WHAT'S THE MATTER, REGINALD?
BAW! WHAT'S THE USE OF BEING A QUIZ KID? NO MORE TESTS..IT'S HORRIBLE!
AND IN THE CLASSROOMS..
WHAM
THIS IS TERRIBLE!!
3

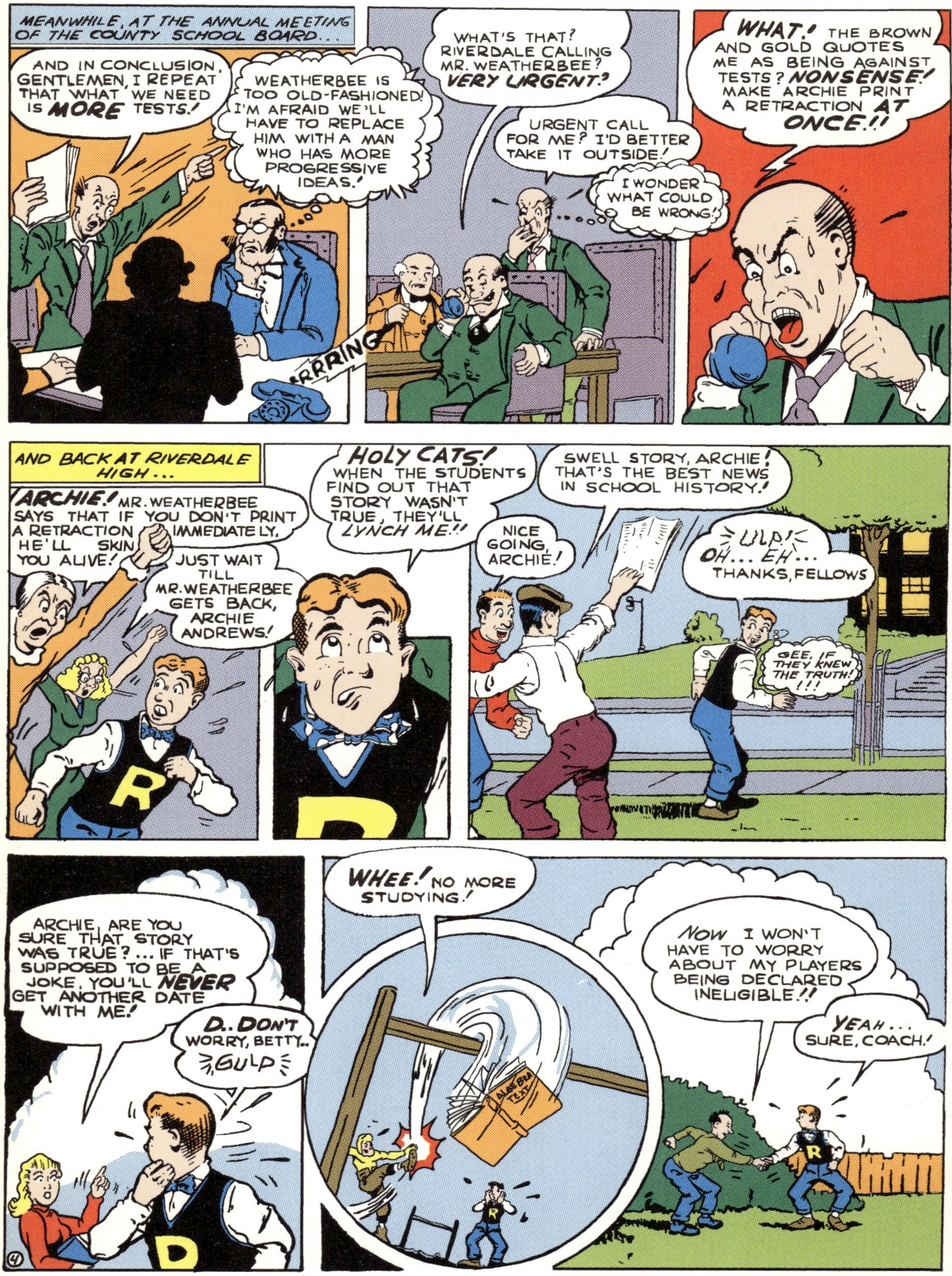
MEANWHILE, AT THE ANNUAL MEETING OF THE COUNTY SCHOOL BOARD...
AND IN CONCLUSION, GENTLEMEN, I REPEAT THAT WHAT WE NEED IS MORE TESTS!
WEATHERBEE IS TOO OLD-FASHIONED! I'M AFRAID WE'LL HAVE TO REPLACE HIM WITH A MAN WHO HAS MORE PROGRESSIVE IDEAS!
RRRING
WHAT'S THAT? RIVERDALE CALLING MR. WEATHERBEE? VERY URGENT?
URGENT CALL FOR ME? I'D BETTER TAKE IT OUTSIDE!
I WONDER WHAT COULD BE WRONG!
WHAT! THE BROWN AND GOLD QUOTES ME AS BEING AGAINST TESTS? NONSENSE! MAKE ARCHIE PRINT A RETRACTION AT ONCE!!
AND BACK AT RIVERDALE HIGH...
ARCHIE! MR. WEATHERBEE SAYS THAT IF YOU DON'T PRINT A RETRACTION IMMEDIATELY, HE'LL SKIN YOU ALIVE!
JUST WAIT TILL MR. WEATHERBEE GETS BACK, ARCHIE ANDREWS!
HOLY CATS! WHEN THE STUDENTS FIND OUT THAT STORY WASN'T TRUE, THEY'LL LYNCH ME!!
SWELL STORY, ARCHIE! THAT'S THE BEST NEWS IN SCHOOL HISTORY!
NICE GOING, ARCHIE!
ULP! OH... EH... THANKS, FELLOWS
GEE, IF THEY KNEW THE TRUTH! !!!
ARCHIE, ARE YOU SURE THAT STORY WAS TRUE?... IF THAT'S SUPPOSED TO BE A JOKE, YOU'LL NEVER GET ANOTHER DATE WITH ME!
D.. DON'T WORRY, BETTY.. GULP
WHEE! NO MORE STUDYING!
ALGEBRA TEXT
NOW I WON'T HAVE TO WORRY ABOUT MY PLAYERS BEING DECLARED INELIGIBLE!!
YEAH... SURE, COACH!
4

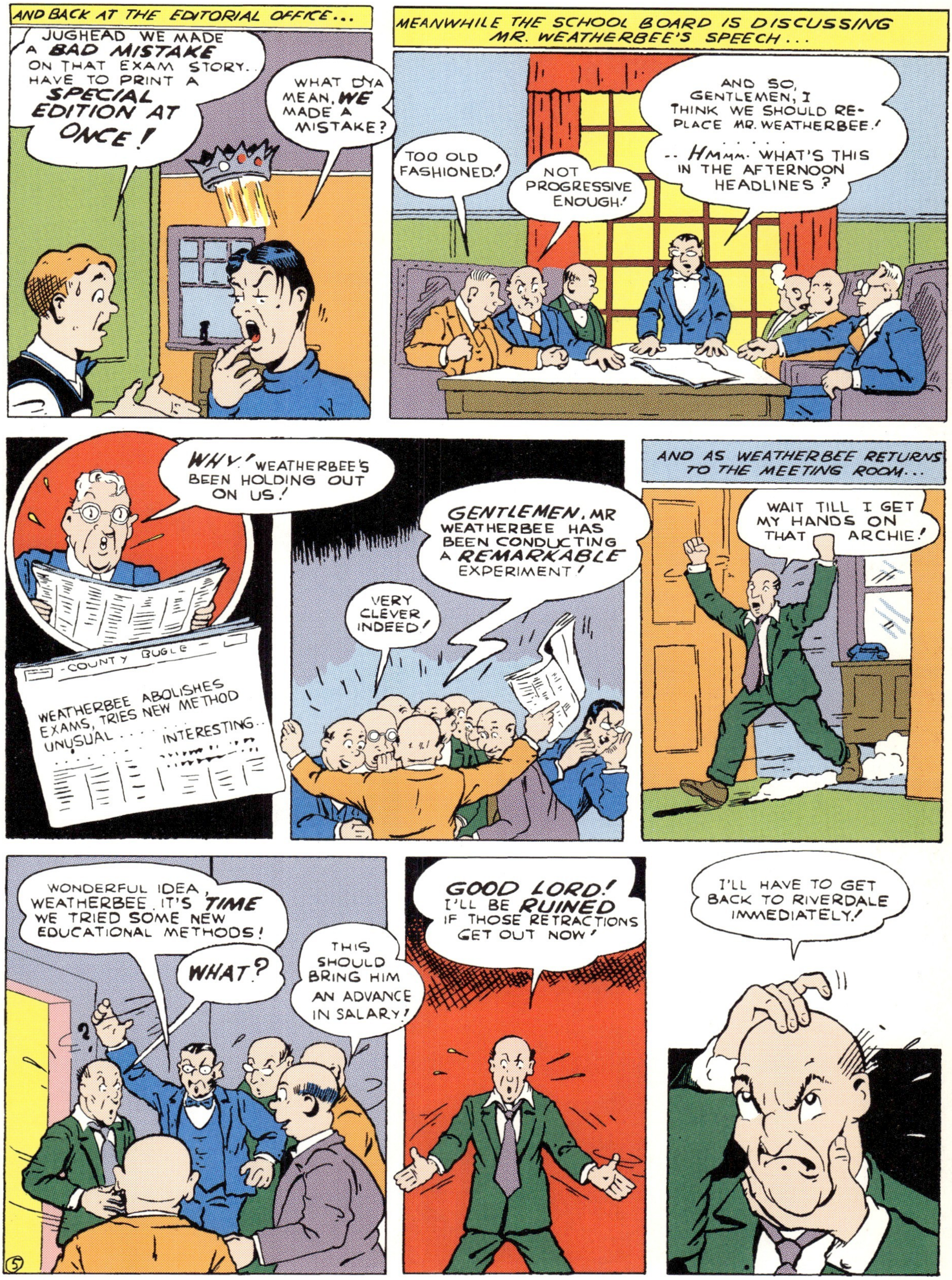
AND BACK AT THE EDITORIAL OFFICE...
JUGHEAD WE MADE A BAD MISTAKE ON THAT EXAM STORY.. HAVE TO PRINT A SPECIAL EDITION AT ONCE!
WHAT D'YA MEAN, WE MADE A MISTAKE?
MEANWHILE THE SCHOOL BOARD IS DISCUSSING MR. WEATHERBEE'S SPEECH...
TOO OLD FASHIONED!
NOT PROGRESSIVE ENOUGH!
AND SO, GENTLEMEN, I THINK WE SHOULD RE-PLACE MR. WEATHERBEE! ..... -- HMMM. WHAT'S THIS IN THE AFTERNOON HEADLINES?
WHY! WEATHERBEE'S BEEN HOLDING OUT ON US!
COUNTY BUGLE
WEATHERBEE ABOLISHES EXAMS, TRIES NEW METHOD
UNUSUAL ... INTERESTING..
GENTLEMEN, MR WEATHERBEE HAS BEEN CONDUCTING A REMARKABLE EXPERIMENT!
VERY CLEVER INDEED!
AND AS WEATHERBEE RETURNS TO THE MEETING ROOM...
WAIT TILL I GET MY HANDS ON THAT ARCHIE!
WONDERFUL IDEA, WEATHERBEE. IT'S TIME WE TRIED SOME NEW EDUCATIONAL METHODS!
WHAT?
THIS SHOULD BRING HIM AN ADVANCE IN SALARY!
5
GOOD LORD! I'LL BE RUINED IF THOSE RETRACTIONS GET OUT NOW!
I'LL HAVE TO GET BACK TO RIVERDALE IMMEDIATELY!

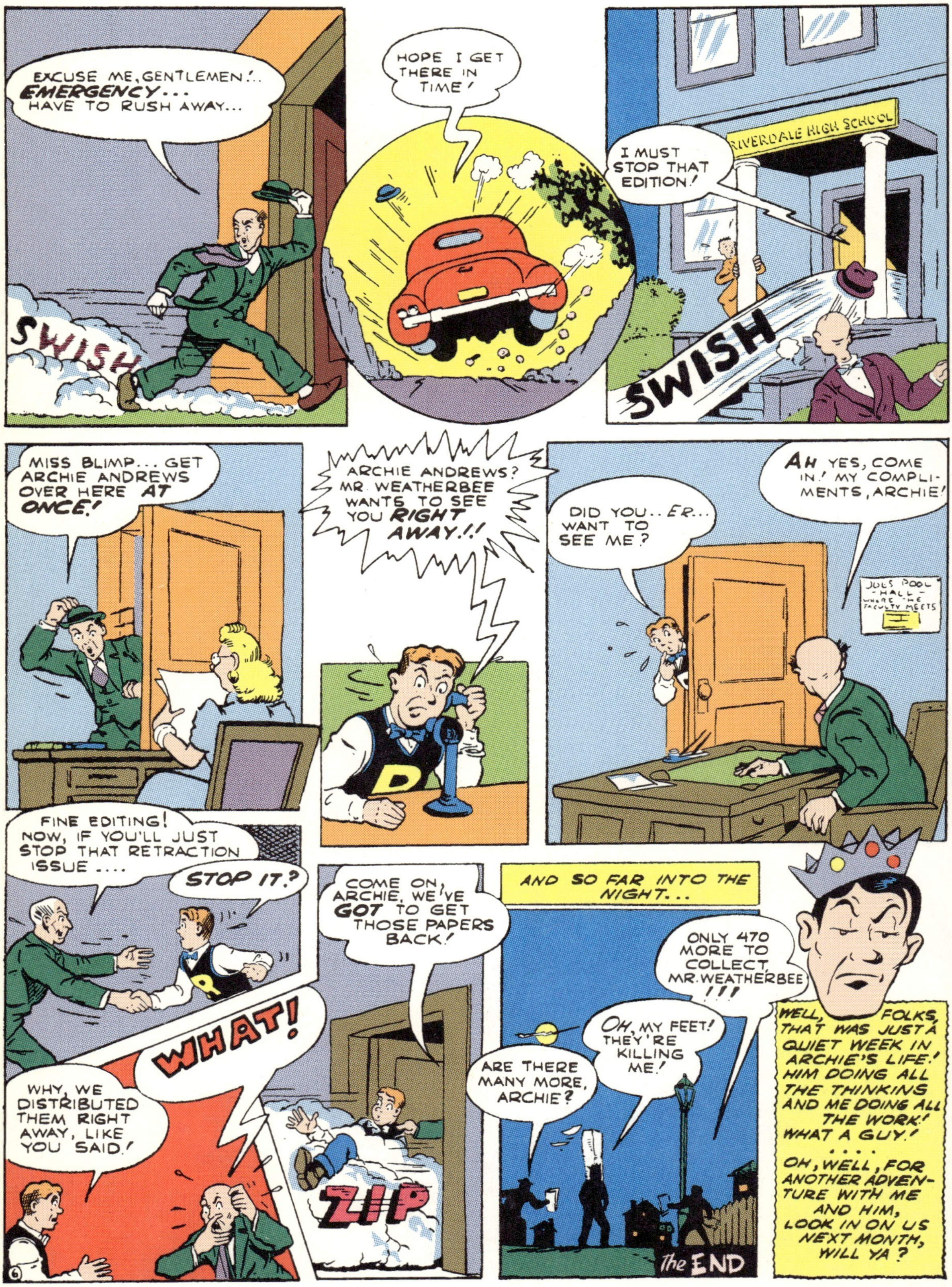
EXCUSE ME, GENTLEMEN!.. EMERGENCY... HAVE TO RUSH AWAY...
SWISH
HOPE I GET THERE IN TIME!
RIVERDALE HIGH SCHOOL
I MUST STOP THAT EDITION!
SWISH
MISS BLIMP... GET ARCHIE ANDREWS OVER HERE AT ONCE!
ARCHIE ANDREWS? MR. WEATHERBEE WANTS TO SEE YOU RIGHT AWAY.!!
DID YOU.. ER... WANT TO SEE ME?
AH YES, COME IN! MY COMPLIMENTS, ARCHIE!
JOE'S POOL -HALL- WHERE THE FACULTY MEETS
FINE EDITING! NOW, IF YOU'LL JUST STOP THAT RETRACTION ISSUE....
STOP IT?
WHAT!
WHY, WE DISTRIBUTED THEM RIGHT AWAY, LIKE YOU SAID!
COME ON, ARCHIE, WE'VE GOT TO GET THOSE PAPERS BACK!
ZIP
AND SO FAR INTO THE NIGHT...
ONLY 470 MORE TO COLLECT, MR. WEATHERBEE!!!
OH, MY FEET! THEY'RE KILLING ME!
ARE THERE MANY MORE, ARCHIE?
The END
WELL, FOLKS, THAT WAS JUST A QUIET WEEK IN ARCHIE'S LIFE! HIM DOING ALL THE THINKING AND ME DOING ALL THE WORK! WHAT A GUY! .... OH, WELL, FOR ANOTHER ADVENTURE WITH ME AND HIM, LOOK IN ON US NEXT MONTH, WILL YA?

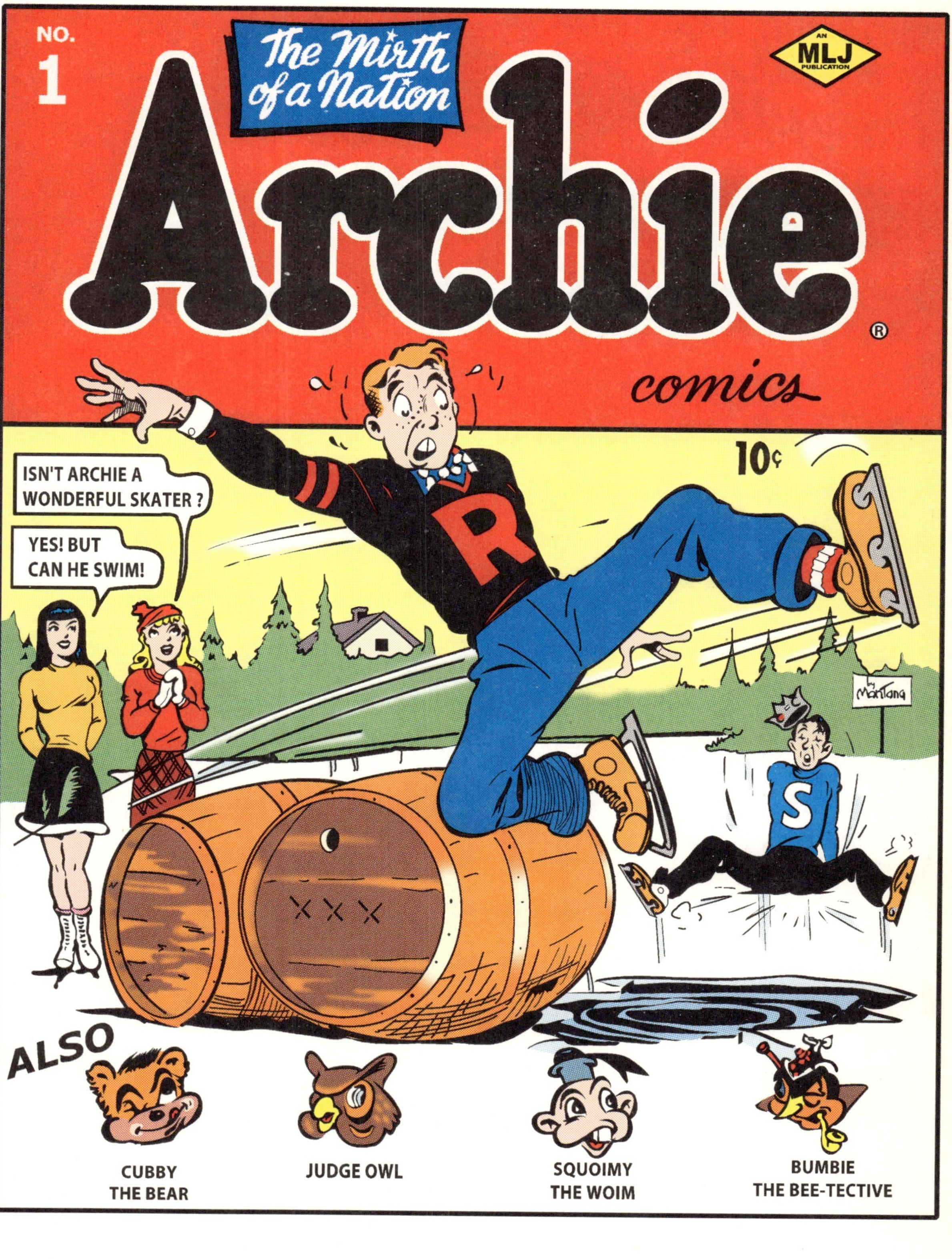
NO. 1
The Mirth of a Nation
AN MLJ PUBLICATION
Archie
comics
10¢
ISN'T ARCHIE A WONDERFUL SKATER ?
YES! BUT CAN HE SWIM!
R
S
ALSO
CUBBY THE BEAR
JUDGE OWL
SQUOIMY THE WOIM
BUMBIE THE BEE-TECTIVE

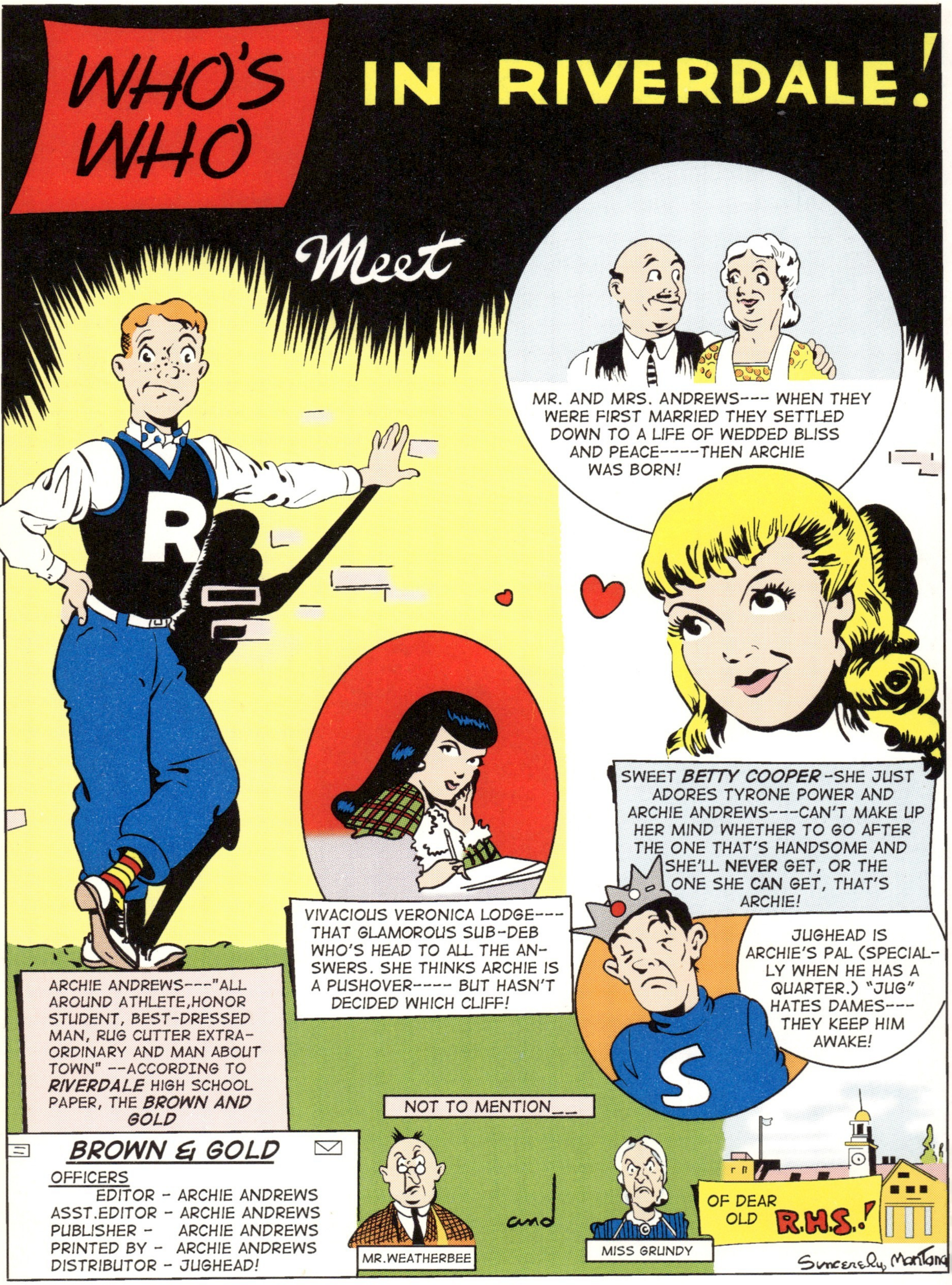
WHO'S WHO IN RIVERDALE!
Meet
MR. AND MRS. ANDREWS--- WHEN THEY WERE FIRST MARRIED THEY SETTLED DOWN TO A LIFE OF WEDDED BLISS AND PEACE----THEN ARCHIE WAS BORN!
SWEET BETTY COOPER -SHE JUST ADORES TYRONE POWER AND ARCHIE ANDREWS---CAN'T MAKE UP HER MIND WHETHER TO GO AFTER THE ONE THAT'S HANDSOME AND SHE'LL NEVER GET, OR THE ONE SHE CAN GET, THAT'S ARCHIE!
VIVACIOUS VERONICA LODGE---THAT GLAMOROUS SUB-DEB WHO'S HEAD TO ALL THE AN-SWERS. SHE THINKS ARCHIE IS A PUSHOVER---- BUT HASN'T DECIDED WHICH CLIFF!
JUGHEAD IS ARCHIE'S PAL (SPECIAL-LY WHEN HE HAS A QUARTER.) "JUG" HATES DAMES--- THEY KEEP HIM AWAKE!
ARCHIE ANDREWS---"ALL AROUND ATHLETE,HONOR STUDENT, BEST-DRESSED MAN, RUG CUTTER EXTRA-ORDINARY AND MAN ABOUT TOWN" --ACCORDING TO RIVERDALE HIGH SCHOOL PAPER, THE BROWN AND GOLD
BROWN & GOLD
OFFICERS
EDITOR - ARCHIE ANDREWS
ASST.EDITOR - ARCHIE ANDREWS
PUBLISHER - ARCHIE ANDREWS
PRINTED BY - ARCHIE ANDREWS
DISTRIBUTOR - JUGHEAD!
NOT TO MENTION__
MR.WEATHERBEE
and
MISS GRUNDY
OF DEAR OLD R.H.S.!
Sincerely, Montana

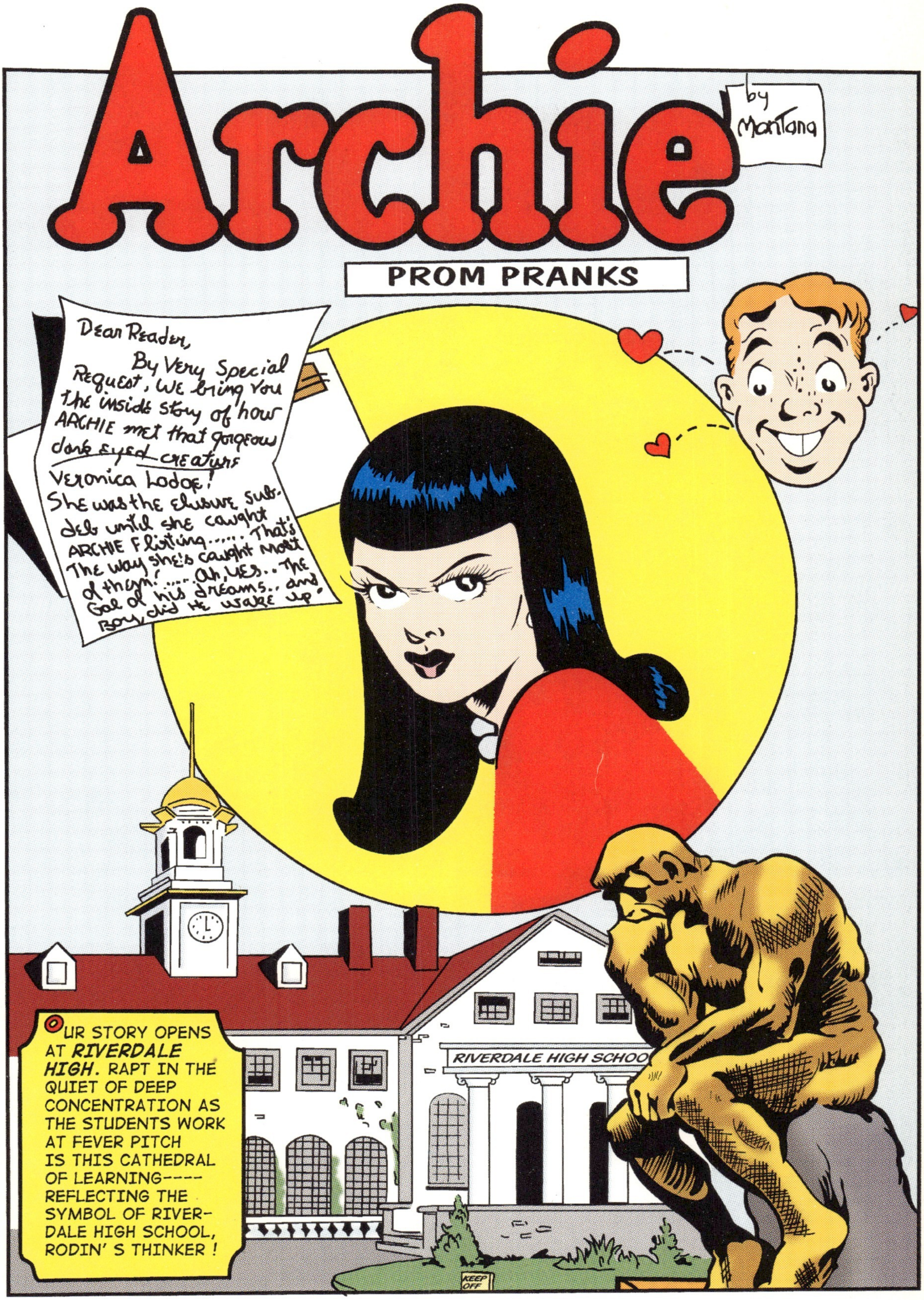
Archie
by Montana
PROM PRANKS
Dear Reader,
By Very Special Request, we bring you the inside story of how ARCHIE met that gorgeous dark eyed creature Veronica Lodge!
She was the elusive sub-deb until she caught ARCHIE flirting...... That's the way she's caught most of them! .....Ah, yes.. the gal of his dreams.. and boy, did he wake up!
OUR STORY OPENS AT RIVERDALE HIGH. RAPT IN THE QUIET OF DEEP CONCENTRATION AS THE STUDENTS WORK AT FEVER PITCH IS THIS CATHEDRAL OF LEARNING---- REFLECTING THE SYMBOL OF RIVERDALE HIGH SCHOOL, RODIN' S THINKER !
RIVERDALE HIGH SCHOO
KEEP OFF

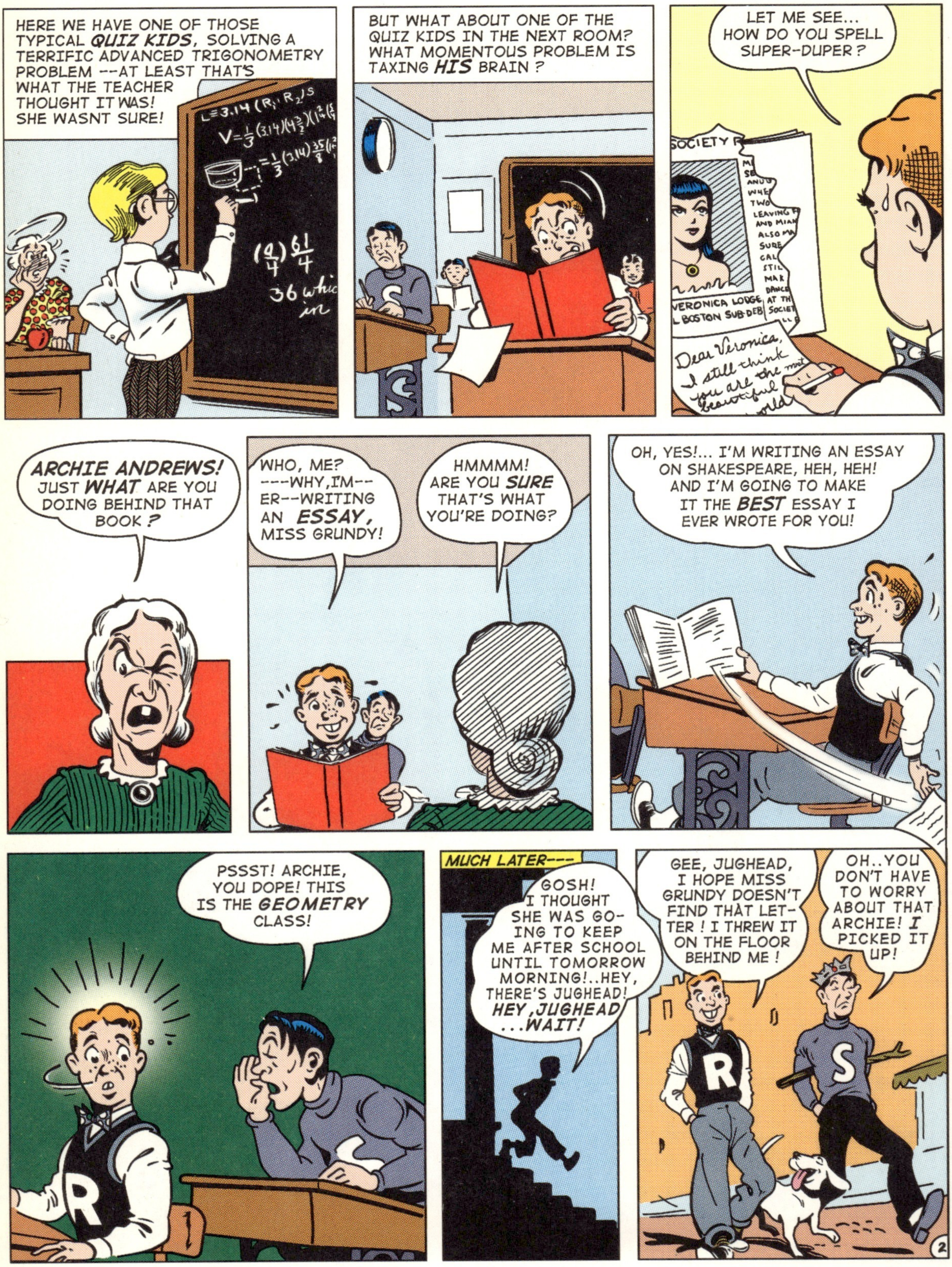
HERE WE HAVE ONE OF THOSE TYPICAL QUIZ KIDS, SOLVING A TERRIFIC ADVANCED TRIGONOMETRY PROBLEM --AT LEAST THAT'S WHAT THE TEACHER THOUGHT IT WAS! SHE WASNT SURE!
BUT WHAT ABOUT ONE OF THE QUIZ KIDS IN THE NEXT ROOM? WHAT MOMENTOUS PROBLEM IS TAXING HIS BRAIN ?
LET ME SEE... HOW DO YOU SPELL SUPER-DUPER ?
VERONICA LODGE
Dear Veronica, I still think you are the most beautiful
ARCHIE ANDREWS! JUST WHAT ARE YOU DOING BEHIND THAT BOOK ?
WHO, ME? ---WHY, I'M-- ER--WRITING AN ESSAY, MISS GRUNDY!
HMMMM! ARE YOU SURE THAT'S WHAT YOU'RE DOING?
OH, YES!... I'M WRITING AN ESSAY ON SHAKESPEARE, HEH, HEH! AND I'M GOING TO MAKE IT THE BEST ESSAY I EVER WROTE FOR YOU!
PSSST! ARCHIE, YOU DOPE! THIS IS THE GEOMETRY CLASS!
MUCH LATER---
GOSH! I THOUGHT SHE WAS GO-ING TO KEEP ME AFTER SCHOOL UNTIL TOMORROW MORNING!..HEY, THERE'S JUGHEAD! HEY, JUGHEAD ...WAIT!
GEE, JUGHEAD, I HOPE MISS GRUNDY DOESN'T FIND THAT LET-TER! I THREW IT ON THE FLOOR BEHIND ME!
OH..YOU DON'T HAVE TO WORRY ABOUT THAT ARCHIE! I PICKED IT UP!
2

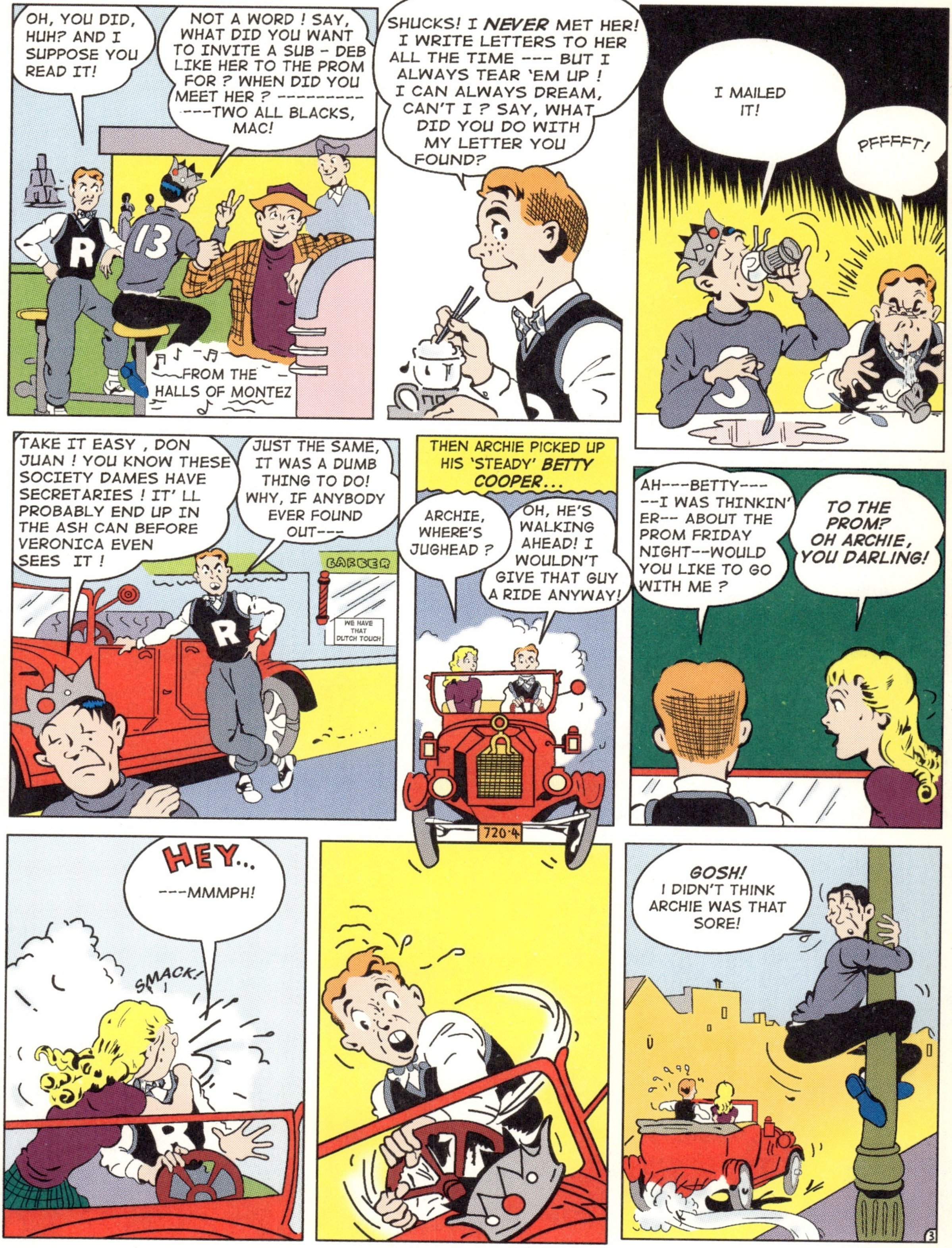
OH, YOU DID, HUH? AND I SUPPOSE YOU READ IT!
NOT A WORD ! SAY, WHAT DID YOU WANT TO INVITE A SUB - DEB LIKE HER TO THE PROM FOR ? WHEN DID YOU MEET HER ? ---------- ----TWO ALL BLACKS, MAC!
FROM THE HALLS OF MONTEZ
SHUCKS! I NEVER MET HER! I WRITE LETTERS TO HER ALL THE TIME --- BUT I ALWAYS TEAR 'EM UP ! I CAN ALWAYS DREAM, CAN'T I ? SAY, WHAT DID YOU DO WITH MY LETTER YOU FOUND?
I MAILED IT!
PFFFFT!
TAKE IT EASY , DON JUAN ! YOU KNOW THESE SOCIETY DAMES HAVE SECRETARIES ! IT' LL PROBABLY END UP IN THE ASH CAN BEFORE VERONICA EVEN SEES IT !
JUST THE SAME, IT WAS A DUMB THING TO DO! WHY, IF ANYBODY EVER FOUND OUT---
BARBER
WE HAVE THAT DUTCH TOUCH
THEN ARCHIE PICKED UP HIS 'STEADY' BETTY COOPER...
ARCHIE, WHERE'S JUGHEAD ?
OH, HE'S WALKING AHEAD! I WOULDN'T GIVE THAT GUY A RIDE ANYWAY!
720-4
AH---BETTY--- --I WAS THINKIN' ER-- ABOUT THE PROM FRIDAY NIGHT--WOULD YOU LIKE TO GO WITH ME ?
TO THE PROM? OH ARCHIE, YOU DARLING!
HEY... ---MMMPH!
SMACK!
GOSH! I DIDN'T THINK ARCHIE WAS THAT SORE!
3

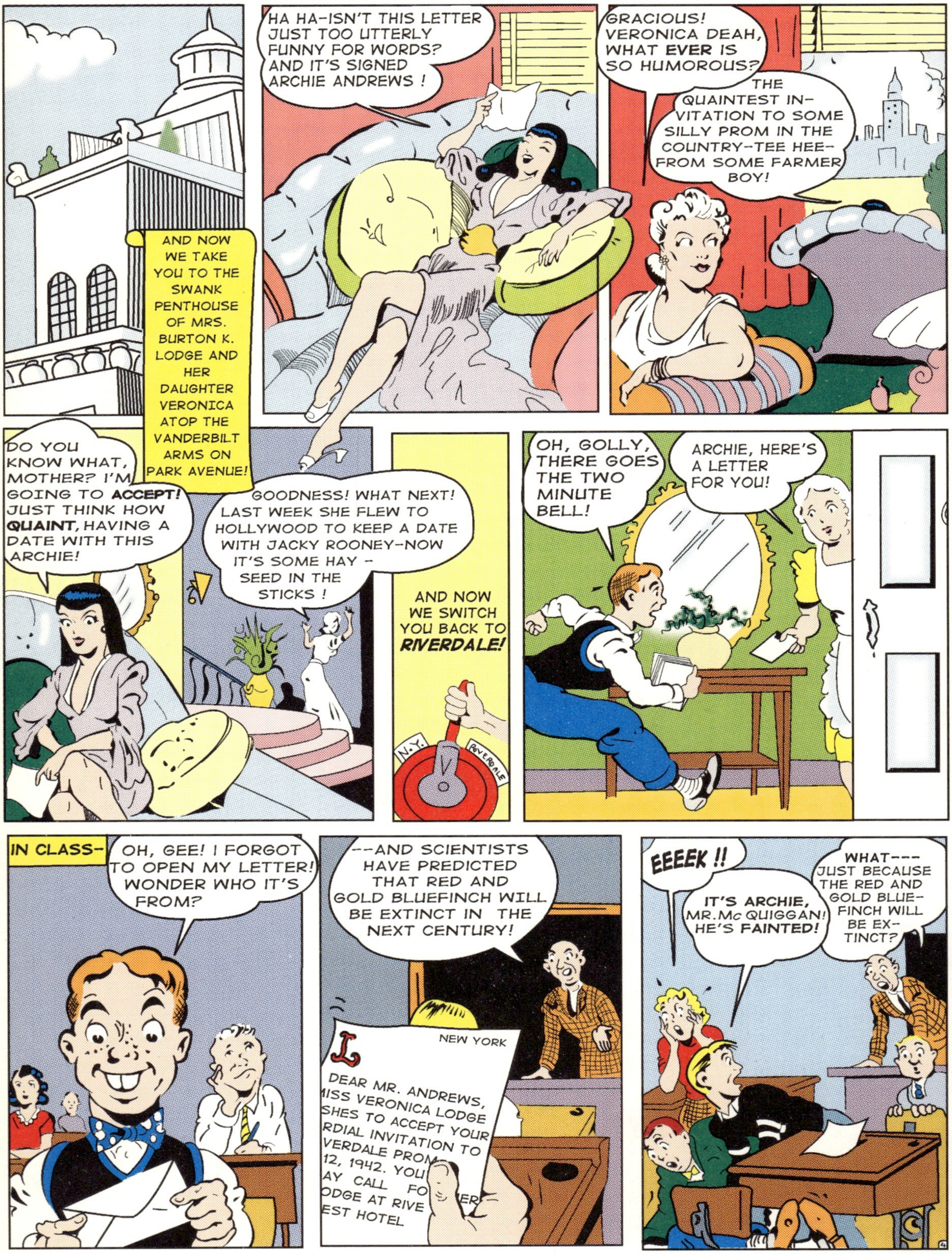
AND NOW WE TAKE YOU TO THE SWANK PENTHOUSE OF MRS. BURTON K. LODGE AND HER DAUGHTER VERONICA ATOP THE VANDERBILT ARMS ON PARK AVENUE!
HA HA-ISN'T THIS LETTER JUST TOO UTTERLY FUNNY FOR WORDS? AND IT'S SIGNED ARCHIE ANDREWS !
GRACIOUS! VERONICA DEAH, WHAT EVER IS SO HUMOROUS?
THE QUAINTEST IN-VITATION TO SOME SILLY PROM IN THE COUNTRY--TEE HEE--FROM SOME FARMER BOY!
DO YOU KNOW WHAT, MOTHER? I'M GOING TO ACCEPT! JUST THINK HOW QUAINT, HAVING A DATE WITH THIS ARCHIE!
GOODNESS! WHAT NEXT! LAST WEEK SHE FLEW TO HOLLYWOOD TO KEEP A DATE WITH JACKY ROONEY--NOW IT'S SOME HAY - SEED IN THE STICKS !
AND NOW WE SWITCH YOU BACK TO RIVERDALE!
N.Y.
RIVERDALE
OH, GOLLY, THERE GOES THE TWO MINUTE BELL!
ARCHIE, HERE'S A LETTER FOR YOU!
IN CLASS--
OH, GEE! I FORGOT TO OPEN MY LETTER! WONDER WHO IT'S FROM?
--AND SCIENTISTS HAVE PREDICTED THAT RED AND GOLD BLUEFINCH WILL BE EXTINCT IN THE NEXT CENTURY!
L
NEW YORK
DEAR MR. ANDREWS,
ISS VERONICA LODGE
SHES TO ACCEPT YOUR
RDIAL INVITATION TO
VERDALE PROM
12, 1942. YOU
AY CALL FO ER
ODGE AT RIVE
EST HOTEL
EEEEK !!
IT'S ARCHIE, MR. Mc QUIGGAN! HE'S FAINTED!
WHAT--- JUST BECAUSE THE RED AND GOLD BLUE-FINCH WILL BE EX-TINCT?

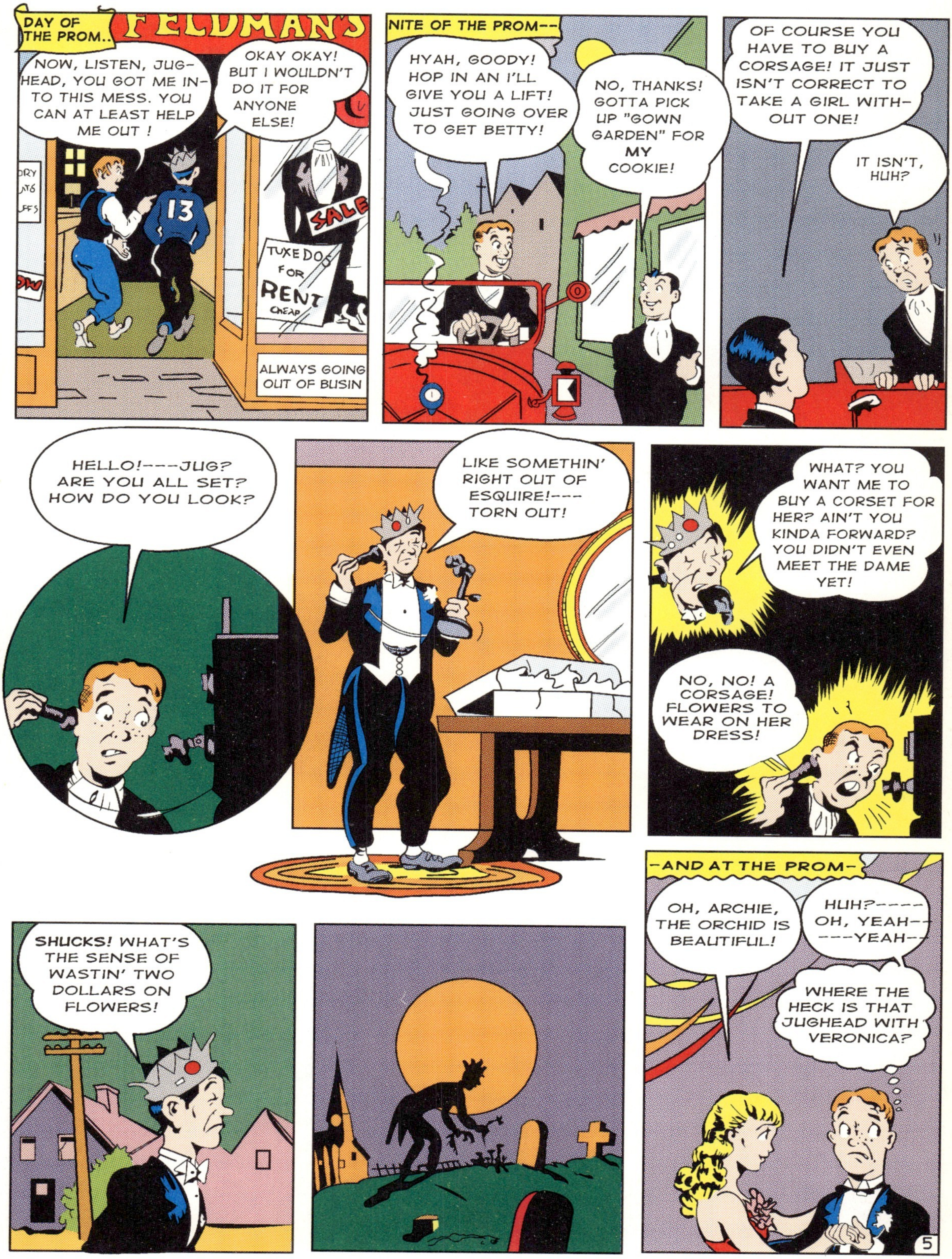
DAY OF THE PROM..
FELDMAN'S
NOW, LISTEN, JUGHEAD, YOU GOT ME INTO THIS MESS. YOU CAN AT LEAST HELP ME OUT !
OKAY OKAY! BUT I WOULDN'T DO IT FOR ANYONE ELSE!
13
SALE
TUXEDOS FOR RENT CHEAP
ALWAYS GOING OUT OF BUSIN
NITE OF THE PROM--
HYAH, GOODY! HOP IN AN I'LL GIVE YOU A LIFT! JUST GOING OVER TO GET BETTY!
NO, THANKS! GOTTA PICK UP "GOWN GARDEN" FOR MY COOKIE!
OF COURSE YOU HAVE TO BUY A CORSAGE! IT JUST ISN'T CORRECT TO TAKE A GIRL WITHOUT ONE!
IT ISN'T, HUH?
HELLO!---JUG? ARE YOU ALL SET? HOW DO YOU LOOK?
LIKE SOMETHIN' RIGHT OUT OF ESQUIRE!--- TORN OUT!
WHAT? YOU WANT ME TO BUY A CORSET FOR HER? AIN'T YOU KINDA FORWARD? YOU DIDN'T EVEN MEET THE DAME YET!
NO, NO! A CORSAGE! FLOWERS TO WEAR ON HER DRESS!
SHUCKS! WHAT'S THE SENSE OF WASTIN' TWO DOLLARS ON FLOWERS!
-AND AT THE PROM-
OH, ARCHIE, THE ORCHID IS BEAUTIFUL!
HUH?---- OH, YEAH-- ---YEAH--
WHERE THE HECK IS THAT JUGHEAD WITH VERONICA?
5

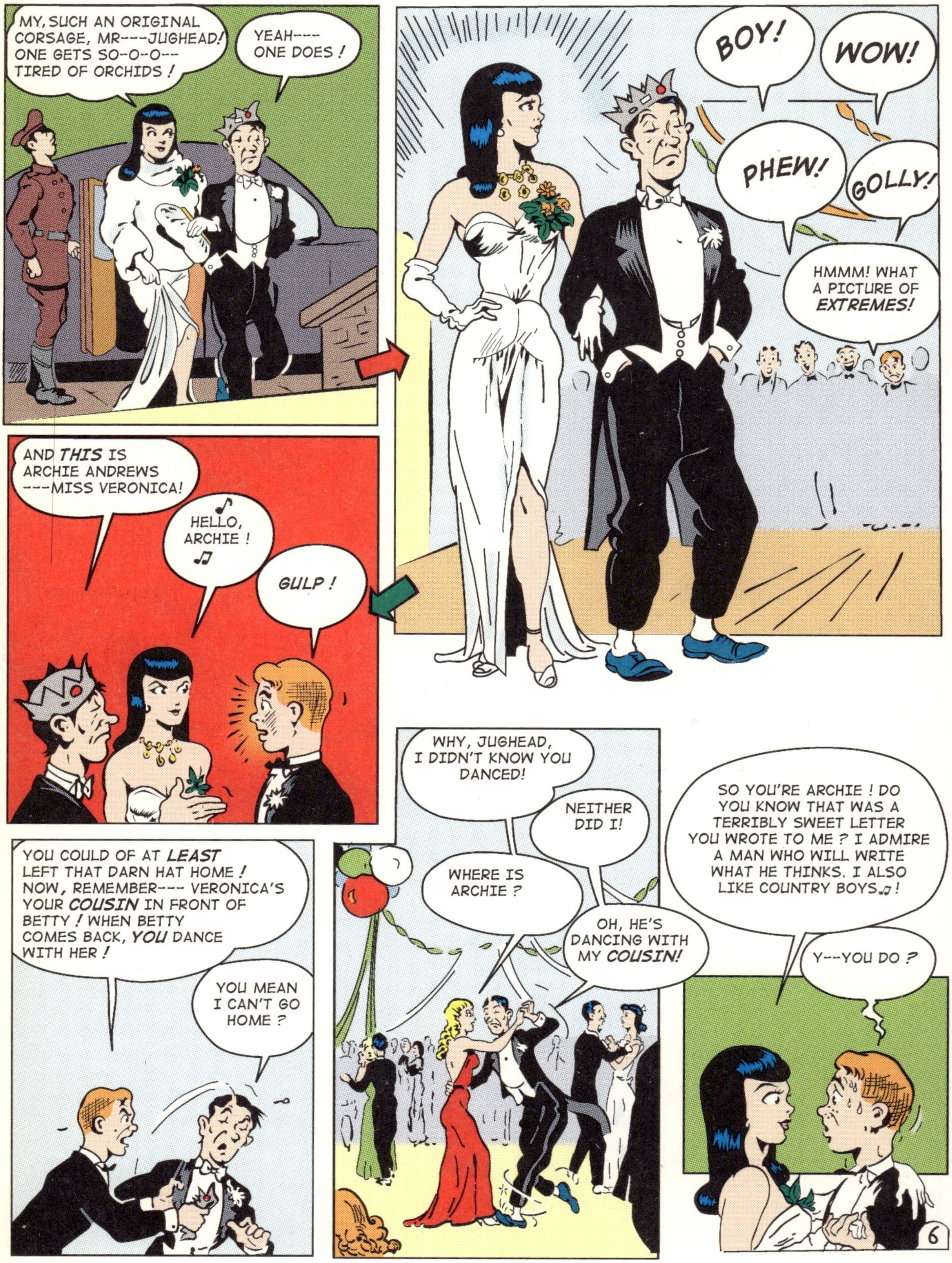
MY, SUCH AN ORIGINAL CORSAGE, MR---JUGHEAD! ONE GETS SO-O-O-- TIRED OF ORCHIDS !
YEAH---- ONE DOES !
BOY!
WOW!
PHEW!
GOLLY!
HMMM! WHAT A PICTURE OF EXTREMES!
AND THIS IS ARCHIE ANDREWS ---MISS VERONICA!
HELLO, ARCHIE !
GULP !
YOU COULD OF AT LEAST LEFT THAT DARN HAT HOME ! NOW, REMEMBER--- VERONICA'S YOUR COUSIN IN FRONT OF BETTY ! WHEN BETTY COMES BACK, YOU DANCE WITH HER !
YOU MEAN I CAN'T GO HOME ?
WHY, JUGHEAD, I DIDN'T KNOW YOU DANCED!
NEITHER DID I!
WHERE IS ARCHIE ?
OH, HE'S DANCING WITH MY COUSIN!
SO YOU'RE ARCHIE ! DO YOU KNOW THAT WAS A TERRIBLY SWEET LETTER YOU WROTE TO ME ? I ADMIRE A MAN WHO WILL WRITE WHAT HE THINKS. I ALSO LIKE COUNTRY BOYS♫!
Y--YOU DO ?
6

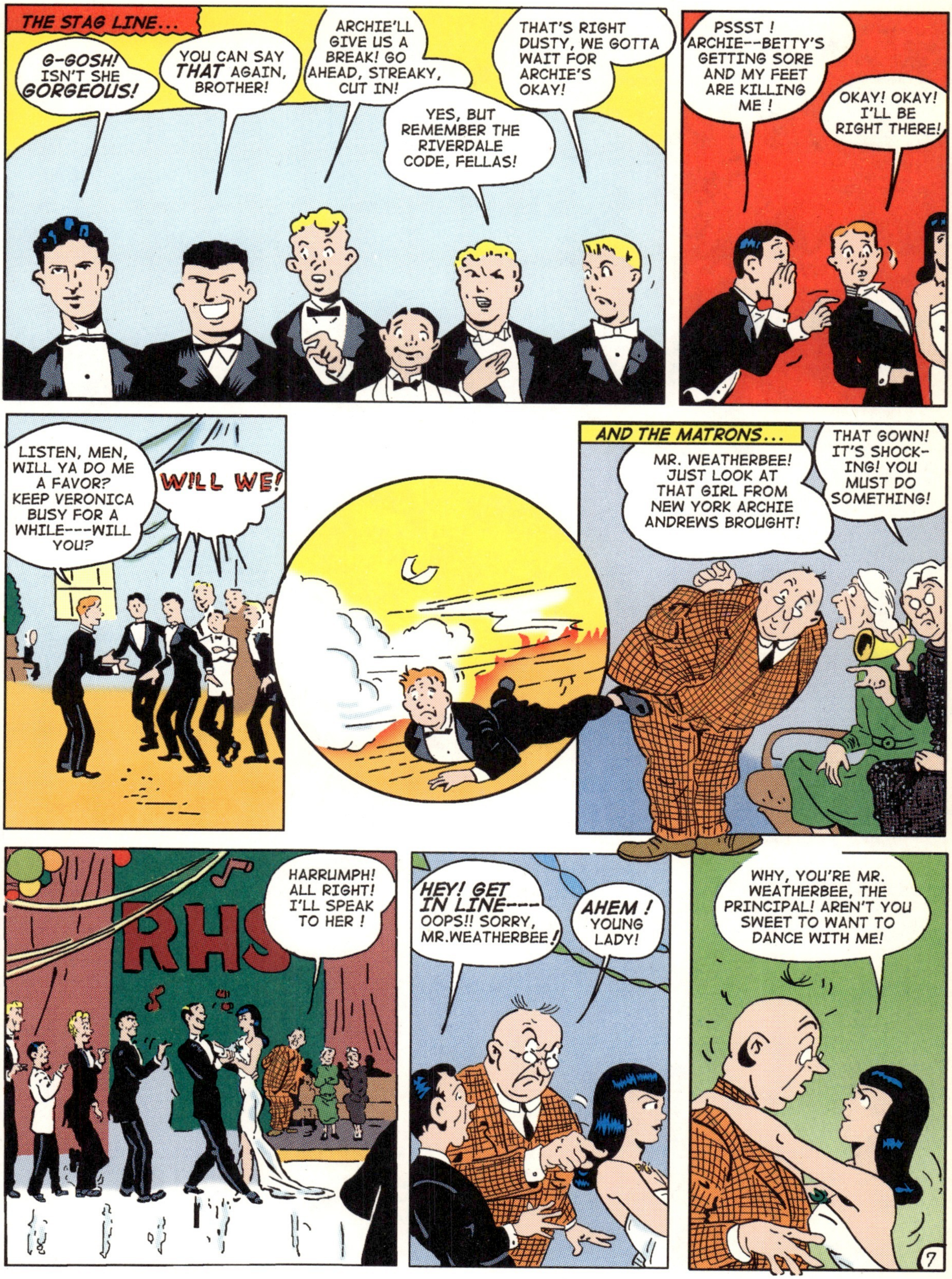
THE STAG LINE...
G-GOSH! ISN'T SHE GORGEOUS!
YOU CAN SAY THAT AGAIN, BROTHER!
ARCHIE'LL GIVE US A BREAK! GO AHEAD, STREAKY, CUT IN!
YES, BUT REMEMBER THE RIVERDALE CODE, FELLAS!
THAT'S RIGHT DUSTY, WE GOTTA WAIT FOR ARCHIE'S OKAY!
PSSST ! ARCHIE--BETTY'S GETTING SORE AND MY FEET ARE KILLING ME !
OKAY! OKAY! I'LL BE RIGHT THERE!
LISTEN, MEN, WILL YA DO ME A FAVOR? KEEP VERONICA BUSY FOR A WHILE---WILL YOU?
WILL WE!
AND THE MATRONS...
MR. WEATHERBEE! JUST LOOK AT THAT GIRL FROM NEW YORK ARCHIE ANDREWS BROUGHT!
THAT GOWN! IT'S SHOCKING! YOU MUST DO SOMETHING!
HARRUMPH! ALL RIGHT! I'LL SPEAK TO HER !
RHS
HEY! GET IN LINE---- OOPS!! SORRY, MR.WEATHERBEE!
AHEM ! YOUNG LADY!
WHY, YOU'RE MR. WEATHERBEE, THE PRINCIPAL! AREN'T YOU SWEET TO WANT TO DANCE WITH ME!
7

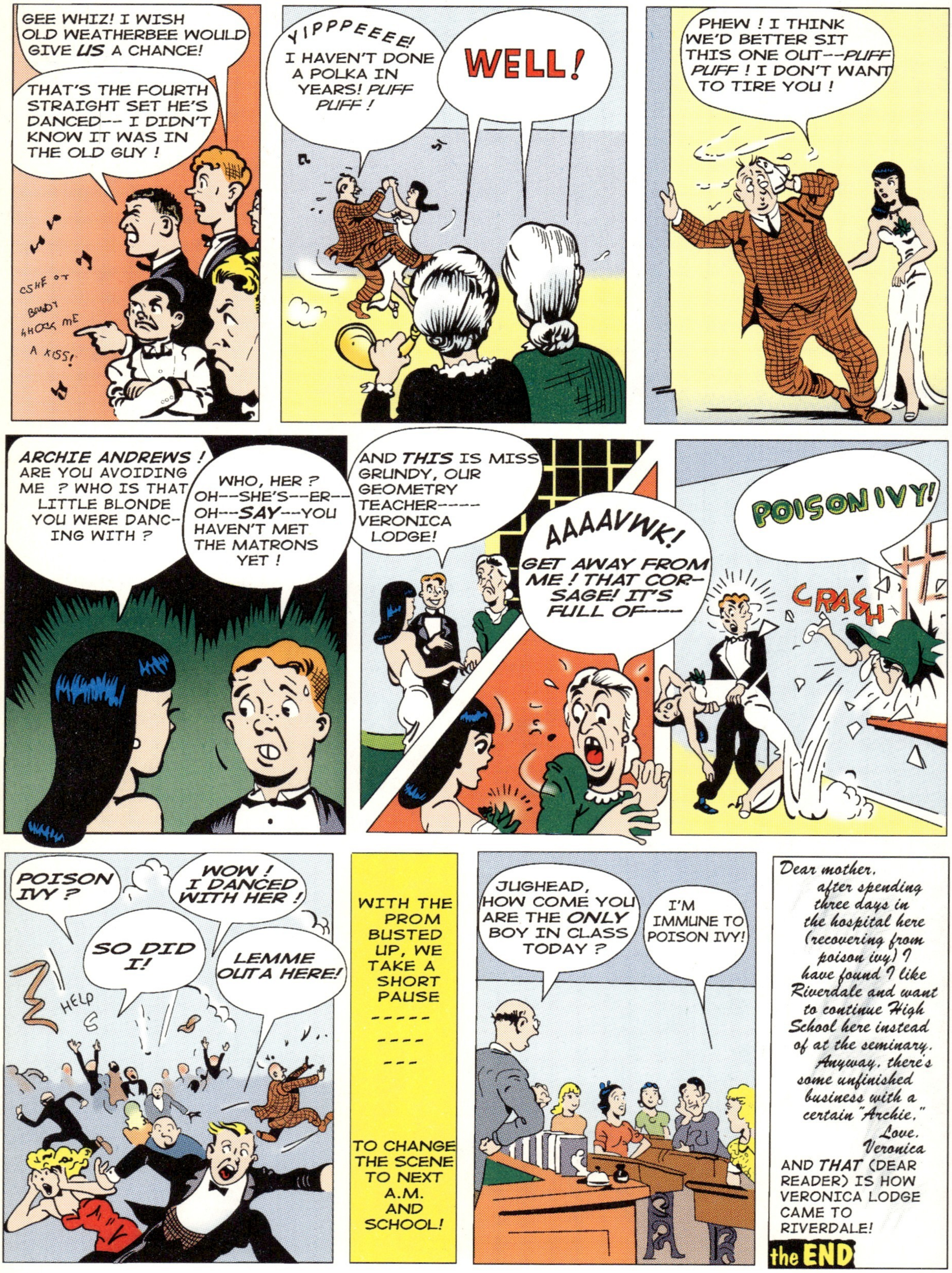
GEE WHIZ! I WISH OLD WEATHERBEE WOULD GIVE US A CHANCE!
THAT'S THE FOURTH STRAIGHT SET HE'S DANCED-- I DIDN'T KNOW IT WAS IN THE OLD GUY!
YIPPPEEEE! I HAVEN'T DONE A POLKA IN YEARS! PUFF PUFF!
WELL!
PHEW! I THINK WE'D BETTER SIT THIS ONE OUT--PUFF PUFF! I DON'T WANT TO TIRE YOU!
ARCHIE ANDREWS! ARE YOU AVOIDING ME ? WHO IS THAT LITTLE BLONDE YOU WERE DANC-ING WITH ?
WHO, HER ? OH--SHE'S--ER--OH--SAY--YOU HAVEN'T MET THE MATRONS YET !
AND THIS IS MISS GRUNDY, OUR GEOMETRY TEACHER----VERONICA LODGE!
AAAAVWK!
GET AWAY FROM ME ! THAT COR-SAGE! IT'S FULL OF----
POISON IVY!
CRASH
POISON IVY ?
WOW! I DANCED WITH HER!
SO DID I!
LEMME OUTA HERE!
HELP
WITH THE PROM BUSTED UP, WE TAKE A SHORT PAUSE ----- ---- --- TO CHANGE THE SCENE TO NEXT A.M. AND SCHOOL!
JUGHEAD, HOW COME YOU ARE THE ONLY BOY IN CLASS TODAY ?
I'M IMMUNE TO POISON IVY!
Dear mother, after spending three days in the hospital here (recovering from poison ivy) I have found I like Riverdale and want to continue High School here instead of at the seminary. Anyway, there's some unfinished business with a certain "Archie." Love, Veronica
AND THAT (DEAR READER) IS HOW VERONICA LODGE CAME TO RIVERDALE!
the END

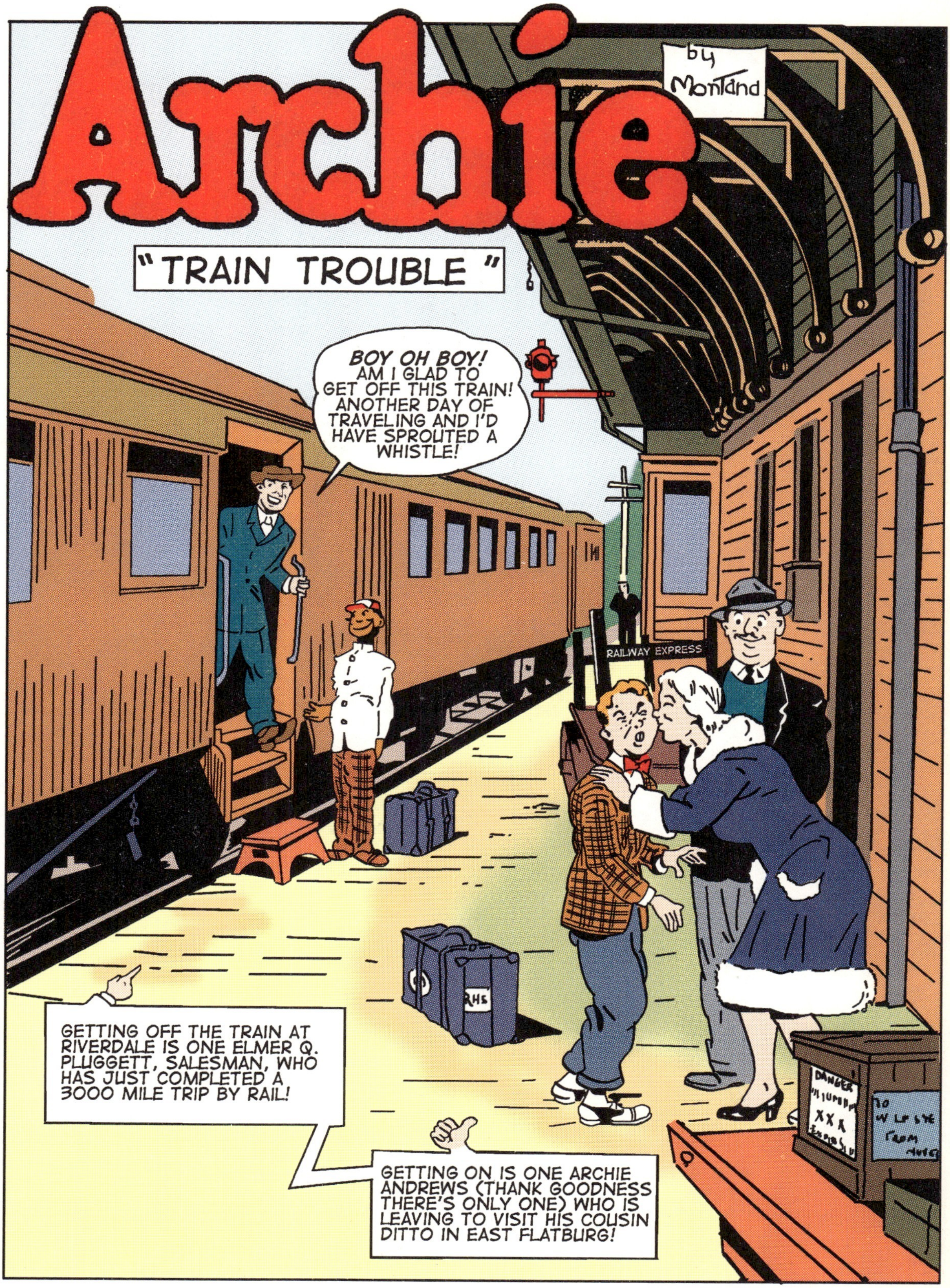
Archie
by Montand
"TRAIN TROUBLE"
BOY OH BOY! AM I GLAD TO GET OFF THIS TRAIN! ANOTHER DAY OF TRAVELING AND I'D HAVE SPROUTED A WHISTLE!
RAILWAY EXPRESS
GETTING OFF THE TRAIN AT RIVERDALE IS ONE ELMER Q. PLUGGETT, SALESMAN, WHO HAS JUST COMPLETED A 3000 MILE TRIP BY RAIL!
GETTING ON IS ONE ARCHIE ANDREWS (THANK GOODNESS THERE'S ONLY ONE) WHO IS LEAVING TO VISIT HIS COUSIN DITTO IN EAST FLATBURG!

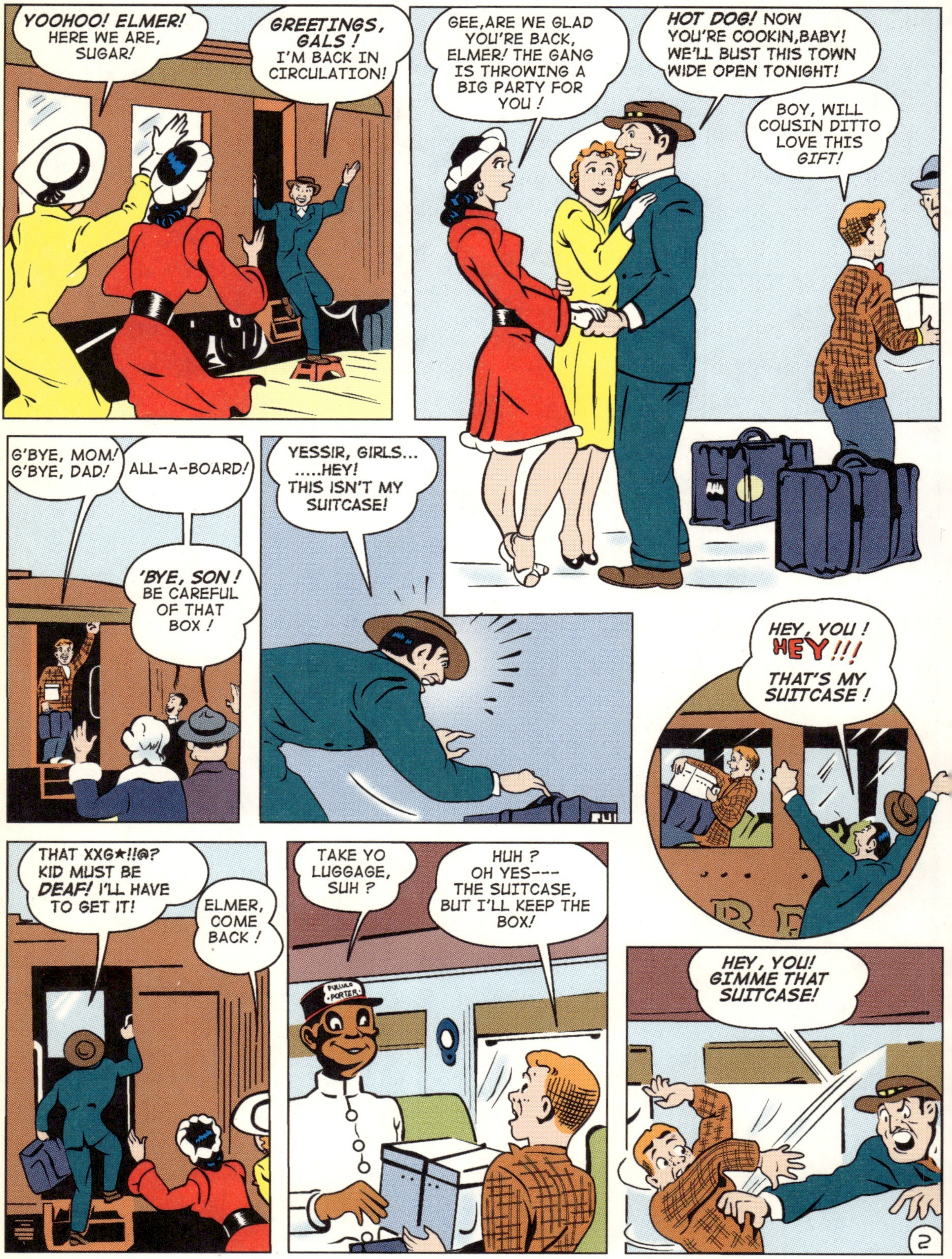

YOOHOO! ELMER! HERE WE ARE, SUGAR!
GREETINGS, GALS! I'M BACK IN CIRCULATION!
GEE, ARE WE GLAD YOU'RE BACK, ELMER! THE GANG IS THROWING A BIG PARTY FOR YOU!
HOT DOG! NOW YOU'RE COOKIN, BABY! WE'LL BUST THIS TOWN WIDE OPEN TONIGHT!
BOY, WILL COUSIN DITTO LOVE THIS GIFT!
G'BYE, MOM! G'BYE, DAD!
ALL-A-BOARD!
'BYE, SON! BE CAREFUL OF THAT BOX!
YESSIR, GIRLS... .....HEY! THIS ISN'T MY SUITCASE!
HEY, YOU! HEY!!! THAT'S MY SUITCASE!
THAT XXG★!!@? KID MUST BE DEAF! I'LL HAVE TO GET IT!
ELMER, COME BACK!
TAKE YO LUGGAGE, SUH?
HUH? OH YES--- THE SUITCASE, BUT I'LL KEEP THE BOX!
PULLMAN PORTER
HEY, YOU! GIMME THAT SUITCASE!
2

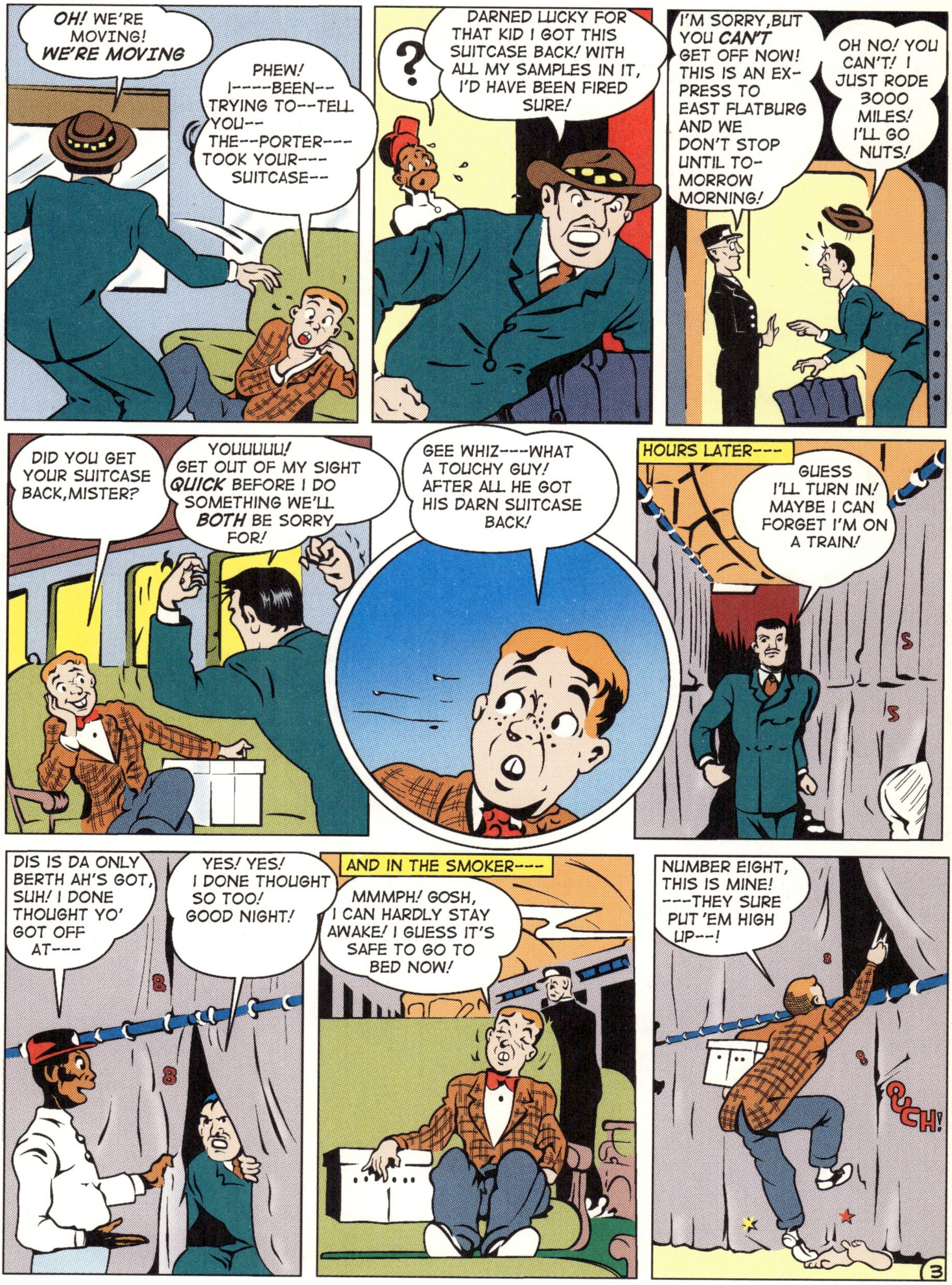

OH! WE'RE MOVING! WE'RE MOVING
PHEW! I----BEEN-- TRYING TO--TELL YOU-- THE--PORTER--- TOOK YOUR--- SUITCASE--
?
DARNED LUCKY FOR THAT KID I GOT THIS SUITCASE BACK! WITH ALL MY SAMPLES IN IT, I'D HAVE BEEN FIRED SURE!
I'M SORRY, BUT YOU CAN'T GET OFF NOW! THIS IS AN EX- PRESS TO EAST FLATBURG AND WE DON'T STOP UNTIL TO- MORROW MORNING!
OH NO! YOU CAN'T! I JUST RODE 3000 MILES! I'LL GO NUTS!
DID YOU GET YOUR SUITCASE BACK, MISTER?
YOUUUUU! GET OUT OF MY SIGHT QUICK BEFORE I DO SOMETHING WE'LL BOTH BE SORRY FOR!
GEE WHIZ---WHAT A TOUCHY GUY! AFTER ALL HE GOT HIS DARN SUITCASE BACK!
HOURS LATER---
GUESS I'LL TURN IN! MAYBE I CAN FORGET I'M ON A TRAIN!
DIS IS DA ONLY BERTH AH'S GOT, SUH! I DONE THOUGHT YO' GOT OFF AT---
YES! YES! I DONE THOUGHT SO TOO! GOOD NIGHT!
AND IN THE SMOKER---
MMMPH! GOSH, I CAN HARDLY STAY AWAKE! I GUESS IT'S SAFE TO GO TO BED NOW!
NUMBER EIGHT, THIS IS MINE! ---THEY SURE PUT 'EM HIGH UP--!
OUCH!
3

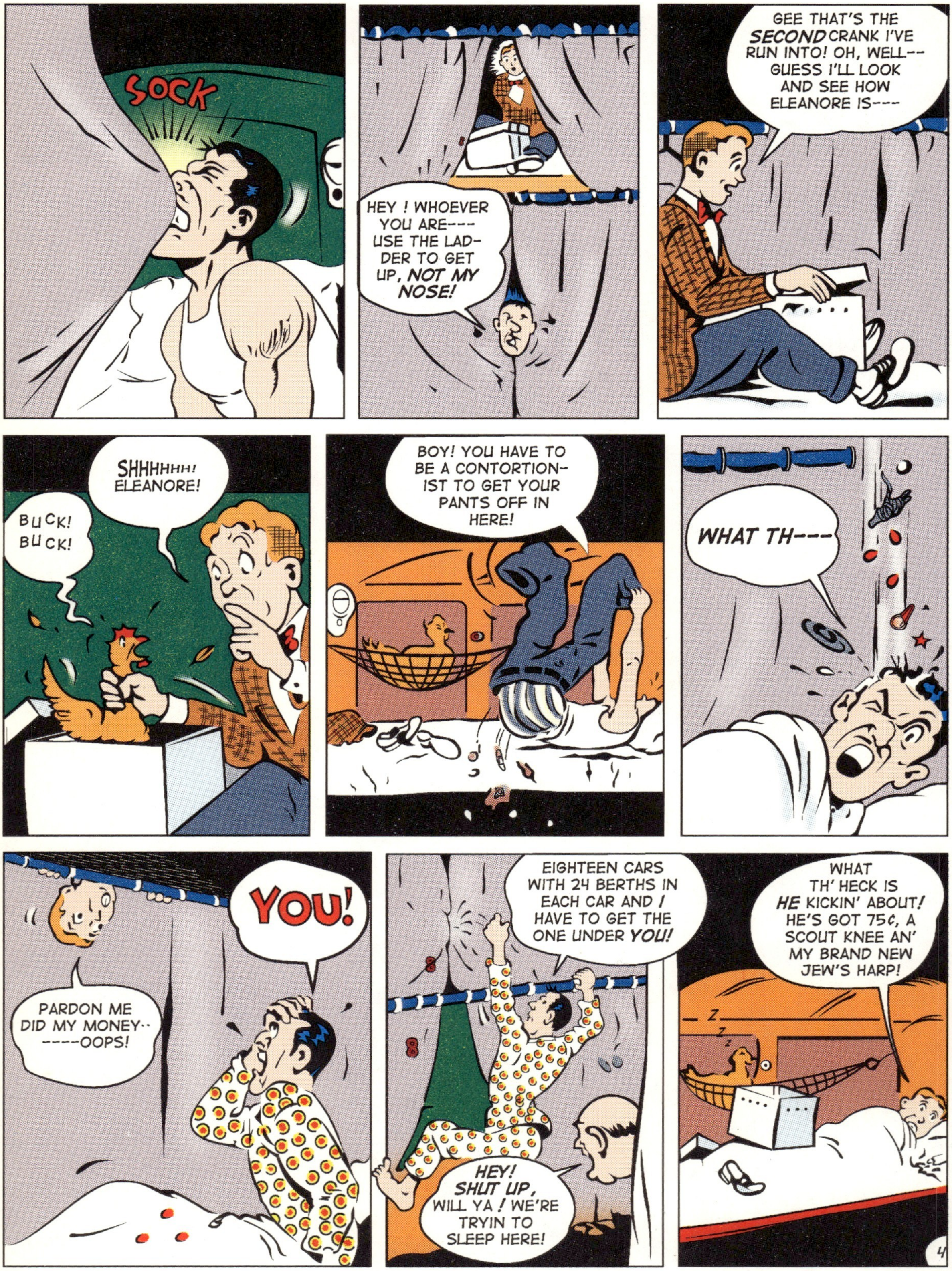
SOCK
HEY ! WHOEVER YOU ARE--- USE THE LADDER TO GET UP, NOT MY NOSE!
GEE THAT'S THE SECOND CRANK I'VE RUN INTO! OH, WELL-- GUESS I'LL LOOK AND SEE HOW ELEANORE IS---
SHHHHHH! ELEANORE!
BUCK! BUCK!
BOY! YOU HAVE TO BE A CONTORTIONIST TO GET YOUR PANTS OFF IN HERE!
WHAT TH---
YOU!
PARDON ME DID MY MONEY-- -----OOPS!
EIGHTEEN CARS WITH 24 BERTHS IN EACH CAR AND I HAVE TO GET THE ONE UNDER YOU!
HEY! SHUT UP, WILL YA ! WE'RE TRYIN TO SLEEP HERE!
WHAT TH' HECK IS HE KICKIN' ABOUT! HE'S GOT 75¢, A SCOUT KNEE AN' MY BRAND NEW JEW'S HARP!
Z Z Z
4

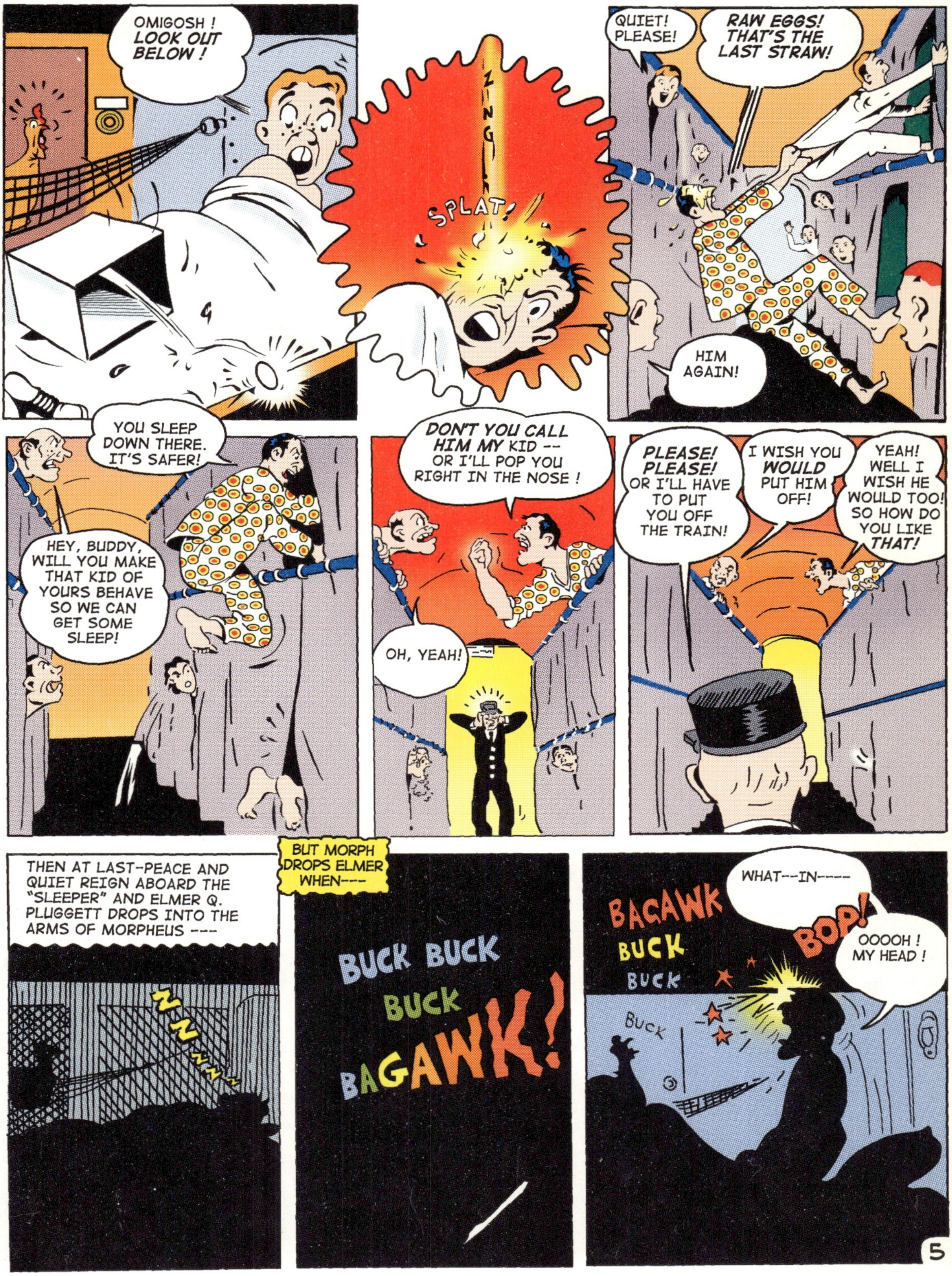
OMIGOSH ! LOOK OUT BELOW !
ZING
SPLAT!
QUIET! PLEASE!
RAW EGGS! THAT'S THE LAST STRAW!
HIM AGAIN!
YOU SLEEP DOWN THERE. IT'S SAFER!
HEY, BUDDY, WILL YOU MAKE THAT KID OF YOURS BEHAVE SO WE CAN GET SOME SLEEP!
DON'T YOU CALL HIM MY KID -- OR I'LL POP YOU RIGHT IN THE NOSE !
OH, YEAH!
PLEASE! PLEASE! OR I'LL HAVE TO PUT YOU OFF THE TRAIN!
I WISH YOU WOULD PUT HIM OFF!
YEAH! WELL I WISH HE WOULD TOO! SO HOW DO YOU LIKE THAT!
THEN AT LAST-PEACE AND QUIET REIGN ABOARD THE "SLEEPER" AND ELMER Q. PLUGGETT DROPS INTO THE ARMS OF MORPHEUS ---
ZZZZZ
BUT MORPH DROPS ELMER WHEN---
BUCK BUCK
BUCK
BAGAWK!
BAGAWK
BUCK
BUCK
BUCK
WHAT--IN----
BOP!
OOOOH ! MY HEAD !
5

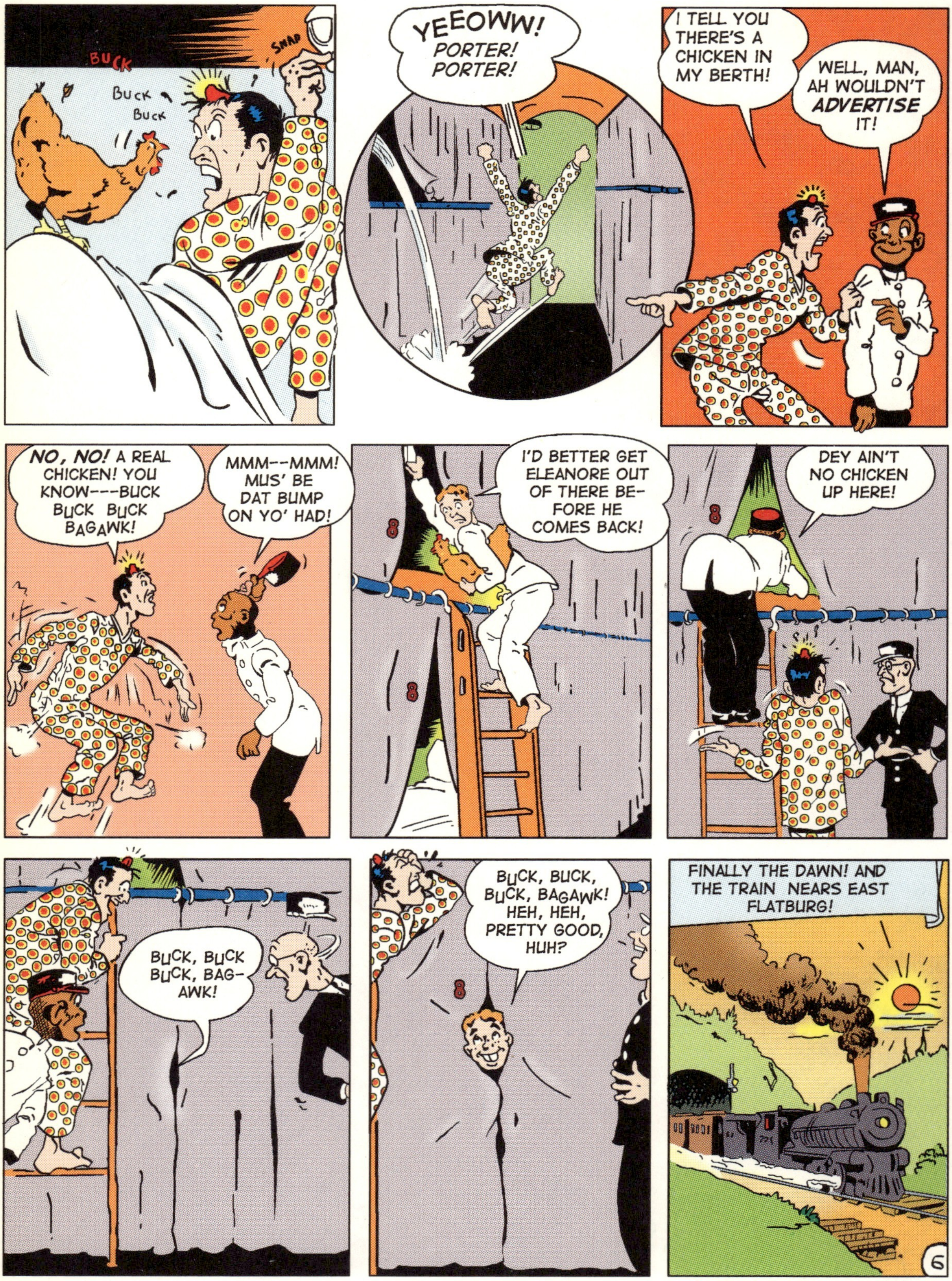
BUCK
SMAP
BUCK
BUCK
YEEOWW! PORTER! PORTER!
I TELL YOU THERE'S A CHICKEN IN MY BERTH!
WELL, MAN, AH WOULDN'T ADVERTISE IT!
NO, NO! A REAL CHICKEN! YOU KNOW---BUCK BUCK BUCK BAGAWK!
MMM--MMM! MUS' BE DAT BUMP ON YO' HAD!
I'D BETTER GET ELEANORE OUT OF THERE BE-FORE HE COMES BACK!
DEY AIN'T NO CHICKEN UP HERE!
BUCK, BUCK BUCK, BAG-AWK!
BUCK, BUCK, BUCK, BAGAWK! HEH, HEH, PRETTY GOOD, HUH?
FINALLY THE DAWN! AND THE TRAIN NEARS EAST FLATBURG!
6

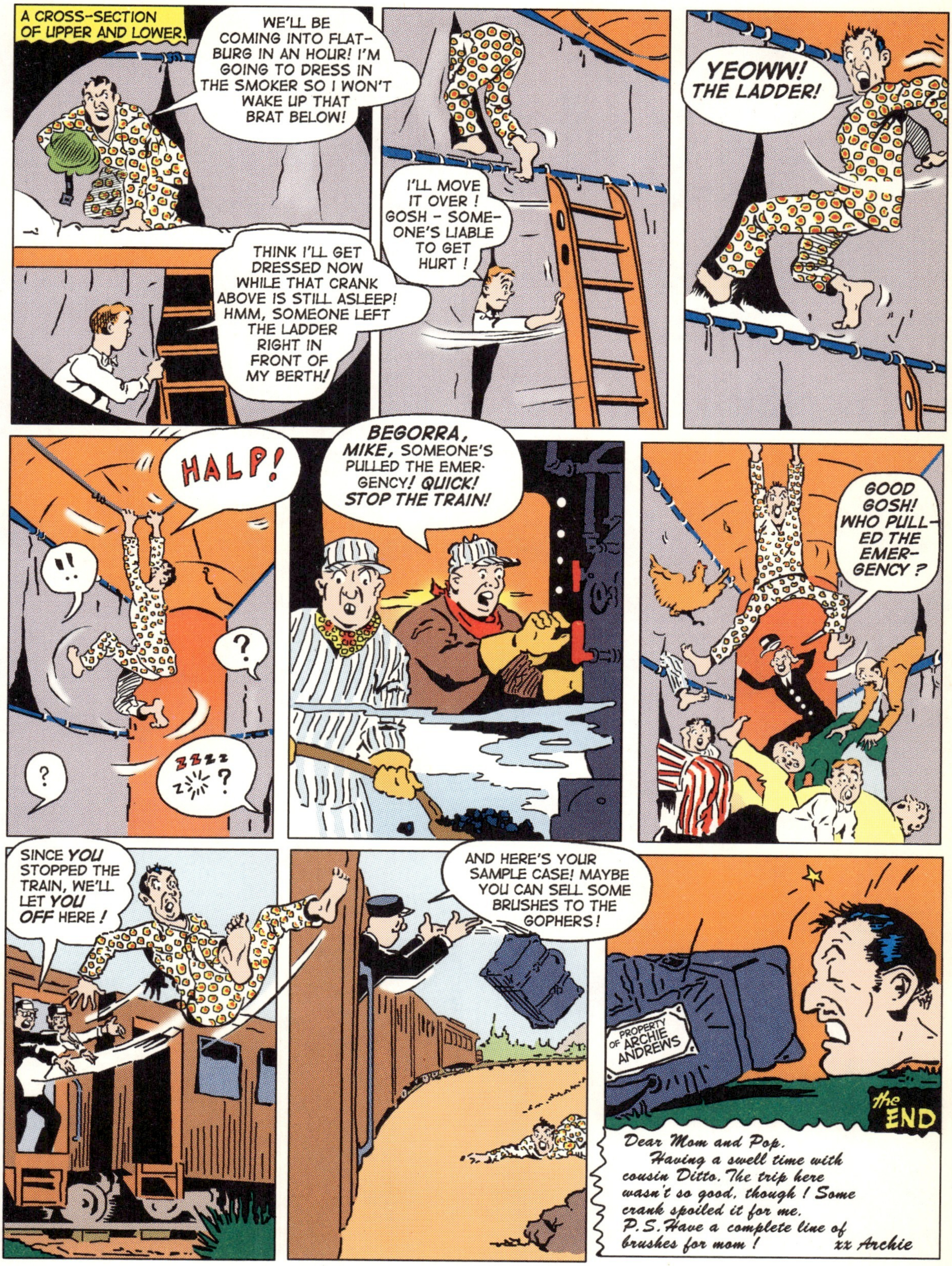
A CROSS-SECTION OF UPPER AND LOWER.
WE'LL BE COMING INTO FLAT-BURG IN AN HOUR! I'M GOING TO DRESS IN THE SMOKER SO I WON'T WAKE UP THAT BRAT BELOW!
THINK I'LL GET DRESSED NOW WHILE THAT CRANK ABOVE IS STILL ASLEEP! HMM, SOMEONE LEFT THE LADDER RIGHT IN FRONT OF MY BERTH!
I'LL MOVE IT OVER ! GOSH - SOME-ONE'S LIABLE TO GET HURT !
YEOWW! THE LADDER!
HALP!
!!
?
?
ZZZZ ?
BEGORRA, MIKE, SOMEONE'S PULLED THE EMER-GENCY! QUICK! STOP THE TRAIN!
GOOD GOSH! WHO PULL-ED THE EMER-GENCY ?
SINCE YOU STOPPED THE TRAIN, WE'LL LET YOU OFF HERE !
AND HERE'S YOUR SAMPLE CASE! MAYBE YOU CAN SELL SOME BRUSHES TO THE GOPHERS!
PROPERTY OF ARCHIE ANDREWS
the END
Dear Mom and Pop.
Having a swell time with cousin Ditto. The trip here wasn't so good, though ! Some crank spoiled it for me.
P.S. Have a complete line of brushes for mom ! xx Archie

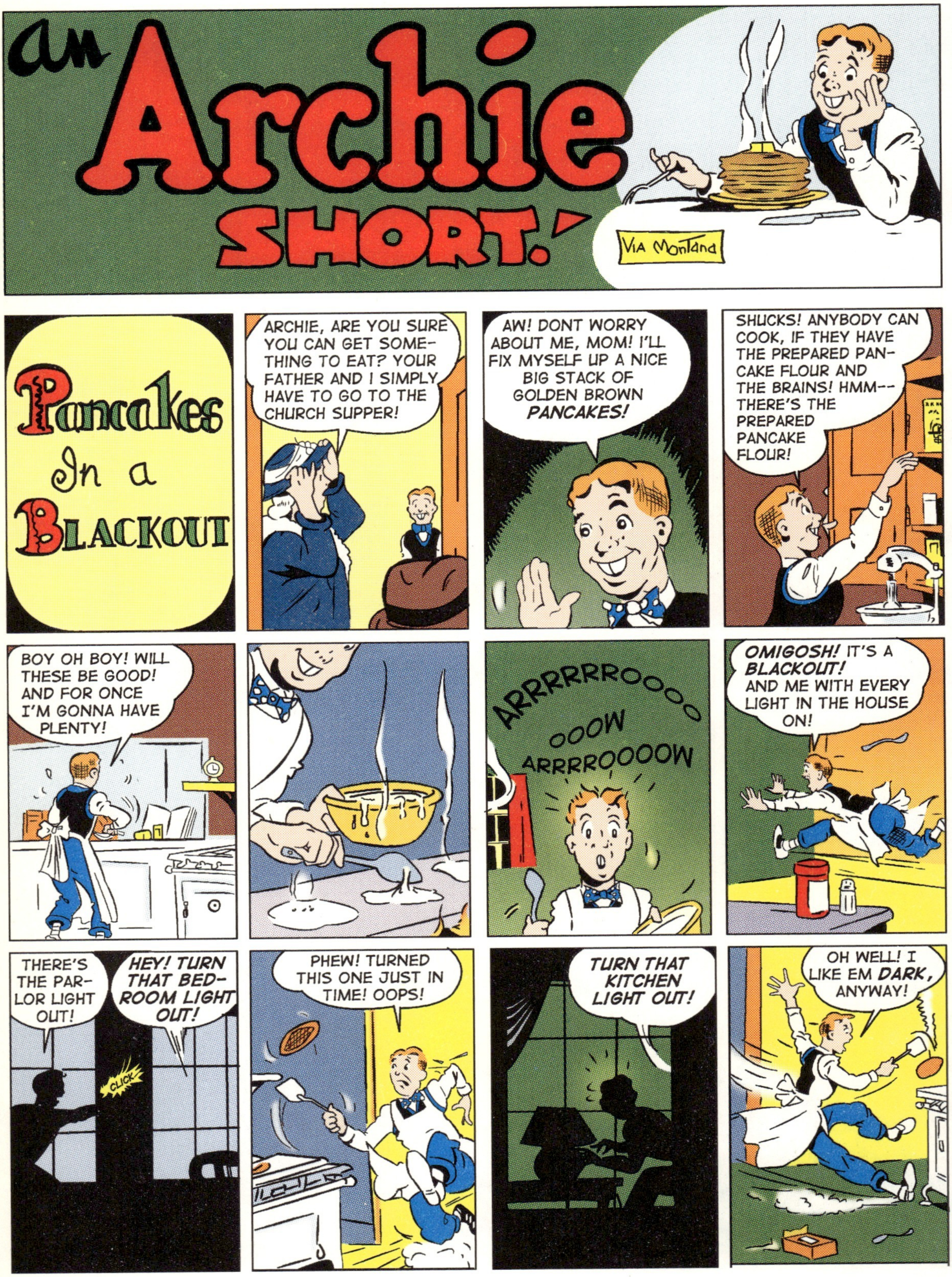
An Archie SHORT!
VIA MONTANA
Pancakes In a Blackout
ARCHIE, ARE YOU SURE YOU CAN GET SOME-THING TO EAT? YOUR FATHER AND I SIMPLY HAVE TO GO TO THE CHURCH SUPPER!
AW! DONT WORRY ABOUT ME, MOM! I'LL FIX MYSELF UP A NICE BIG STACK OF GOLDEN BROWN PANCAKES!
SHUCKS! ANYBODY CAN COOK, IF THEY HAVE THE PREPARED PAN-CAKE FLOUR AND THE BRAINS! HMM-- THERE'S THE PREPARED PANCAKE FLOUR!
BOY OH BOY! WILL THESE BE GOOD! AND FOR ONCE I'M GONNA HAVE PLENTY!
ARRRRRROOOO OOOW ARRRROOOOW
OMIGOSH! IT'S A BLACKOUT! AND ME WITH EVERY LIGHT IN THE HOUSE ON!
THERE'S THE PAR-LOR LIGHT OUT!
HEY! TURN THAT BED-ROOM LIGHT OUT!
CLICK
PHEW! TURNED THIS ONE JUST IN TIME! OOPS!
TURN THAT KITCHEN LIGHT OUT!
OH WELL! I LIKE EM DARK, ANYWAY!

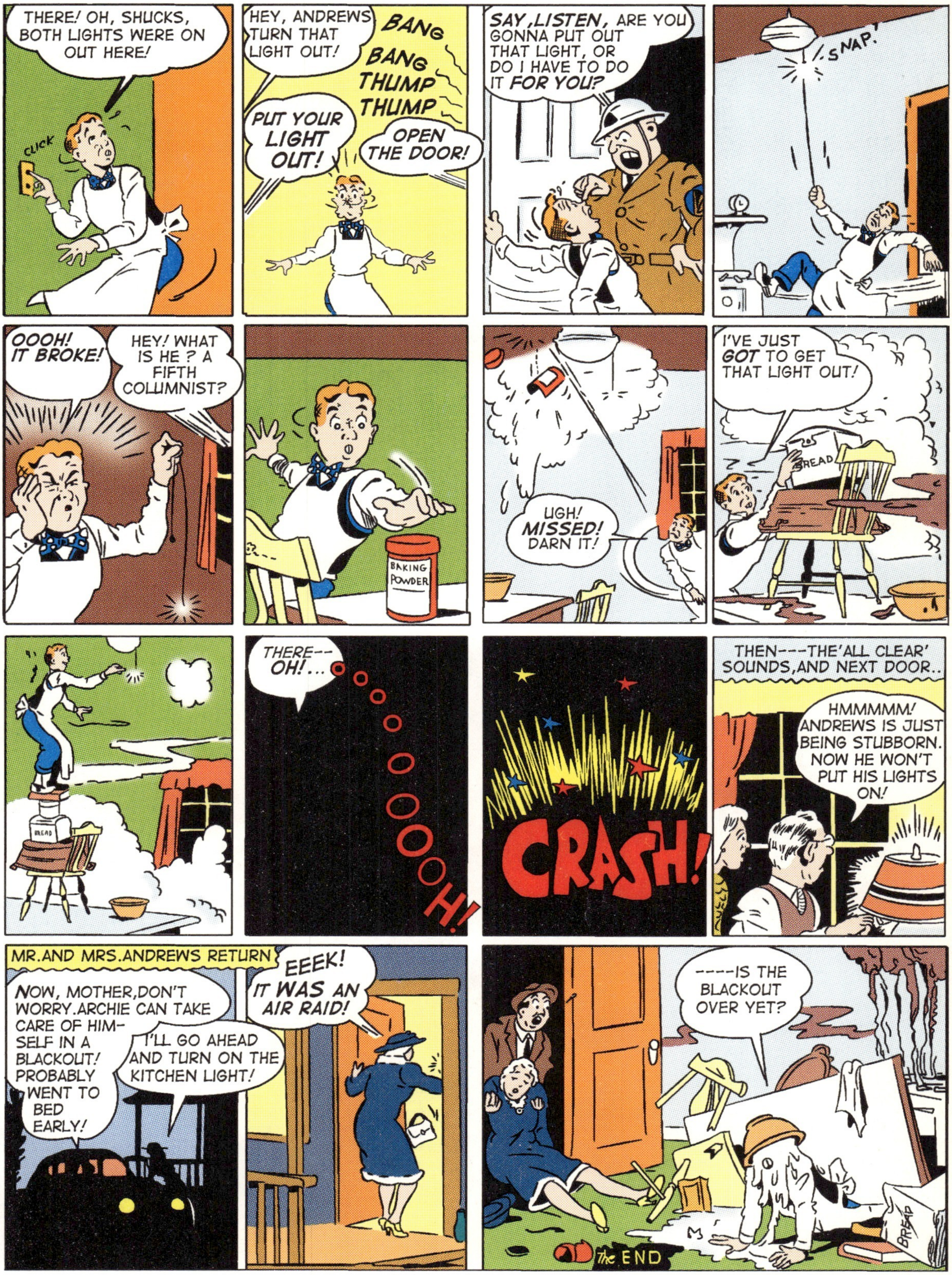
THERE! OH, SHUCKS, BOTH LIGHTS WERE ON OUT HERE!
CLICK
HEY, ANDREWS TURN THAT LIGHT OUT!
BANG BANG THUMP THUMP
PUT YOUR LIGHT OUT!
OPEN THE DOOR!
SAY, LISTEN, ARE YOU GONNA PUT OUT THAT LIGHT, OR DO I HAVE TO DO IT FOR YOU?
SNAP!
OOOH! IT BROKE!
HEY! WHAT IS HE ? A FIFTH COLUMNIST?
BAKING POWDER
UGH! MISSED! DARN IT!
I'VE JUST GOT TO GET THAT LIGHT OUT!
BREAD
BREAD
THERE-- OH!...OOOOOOOOH!
CRASH!
THEN---THE 'ALL CLEAR' SOUNDS, AND NEXT DOOR..
HMMMMM! ANDREWS IS JUST BEING STUBBORN. NOW HE WON'T PUT HIS LIGHTS ON!
MR. AND MRS. ANDREWS RETURN
NOW, MOTHER, DON'T WORRY. ARCHIE CAN TAKE CARE OF HIM-SELF IN A BLACKOUT! PROBABLY WENT TO BED EARLY!
I'LL GO AHEAD AND TURN ON THE KITCHEN LIGHT!
EEEK! IT WAS AN AIR RAID!
----IS THE BLACKOUT OVER YET?
BREAD
the END

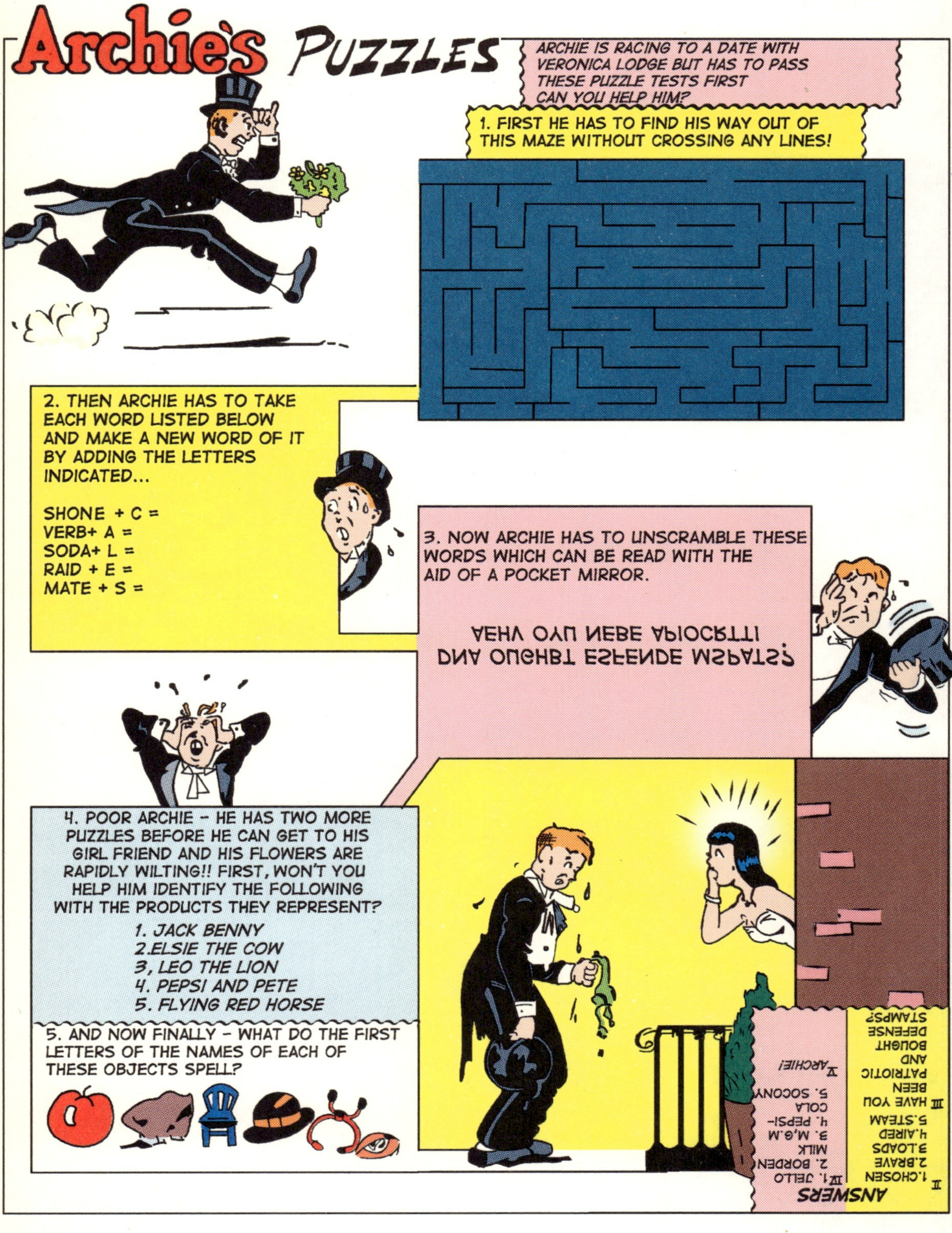

Archie's PUZZLES
ARCHIE IS RACING TO A DATE WITH VERONICA LODGE BUT HAS TO PASS THESE PUZZLE TESTS FIRST CAN YOU HELP HIM?
1. FIRST HE HAS TO FIND HIS WAY OUT OF THIS MAZE WITHOUT CROSSING ANY LINES!
2. THEN ARCHIE HAS TO TAKE EACH WORD LISTED BELOW AND MAKE A NEW WORD OF IT BY ADDING THE LETTERS INDICATED...
SHONE + C =
VERB+ A =
SODA+ L =
RAID + E =
MATE + S =
3. NOW ARCHIE HAS TO UNSCRAMBLE THESE WORDS WHICH CAN BE READ WITH THE AID OF A POCKET MIRROR.
VEHA OYU NEBE APIOCRTTI
DNA OUGHBT ESFENDE MSPATS?
4. POOR ARCHIE - HE HAS TWO MORE PUZZLES BEFORE HE CAN GET TO HIS GIRL FRIEND AND HIS FLOWERS ARE RAPIDLY WILTING!! FIRST, WON'T YOU HELP HIM IDENTIFY THE FOLLOWING WITH THE PRODUCTS THEY REPRESENT?
1. JACK BENNY
2.ELSIE THE COW
3, LEO THE LION
4. PEPSI AND PETE
5. FLYING RED HORSE
5. AND NOW FINALLY - WHAT DO THE FIRST LETTERS OF THE NAMES OF EACH OF THESE OBJECTS SPELL?
ANSWERS
II 1.CHOSEN 2.BRAVE 3.LOADS 4.AIRED 5.STEAM
III HAVE YOU BEEN PATRIOTIC AND BOUGHT DEFENSE STAMPS?
IV 1. JELLO 2. BORDEN MILK 3. M.G.M 4. PEPSI-COLA 5. SOCONY
V ARCHIE!

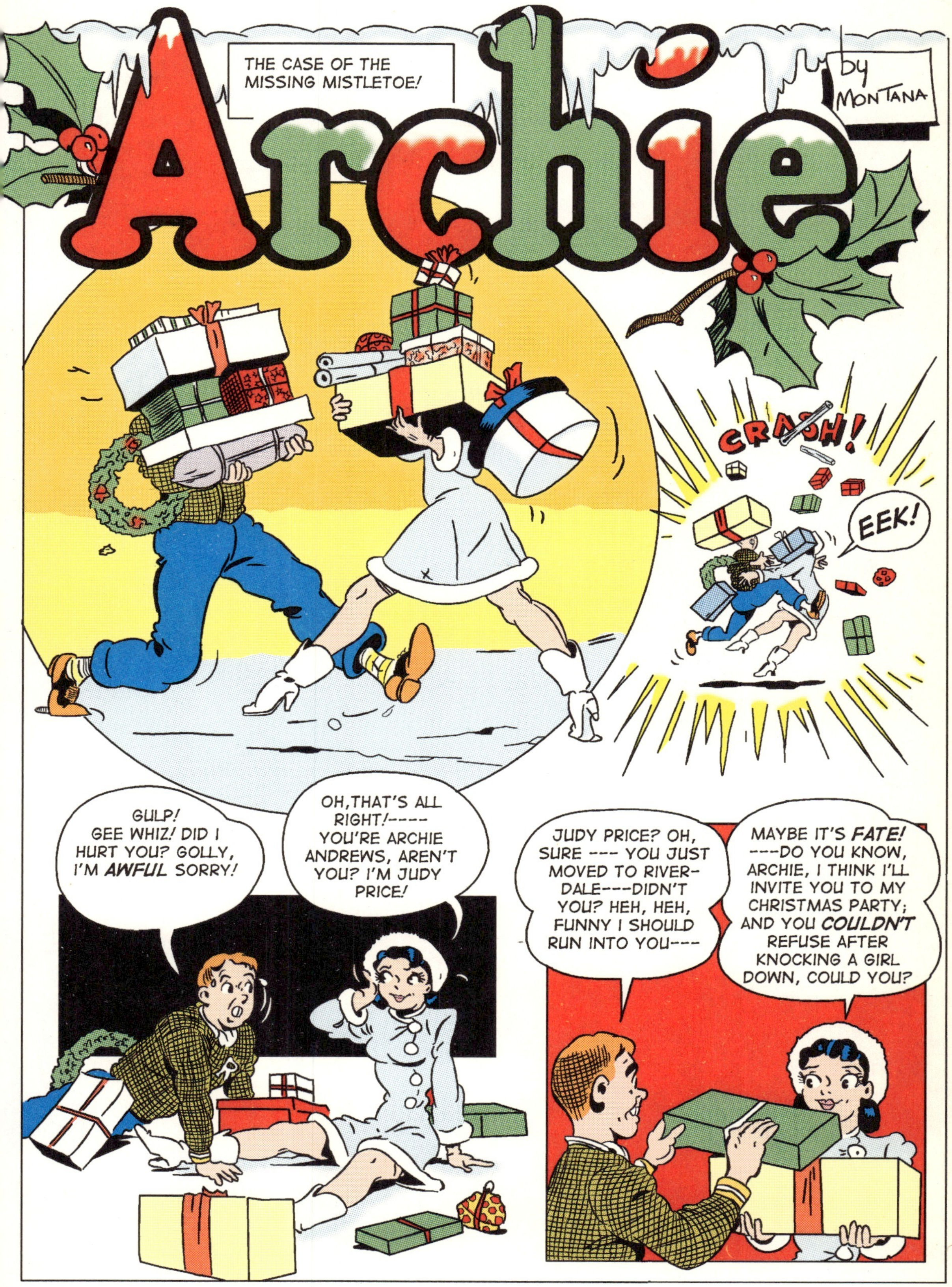
Archie
THE CASE OF THE MISSING MISTLETOE!
by MONTANA
CRASH!
EEK!
GULP! GEE WHIZ! DID I HURT YOU? GOLLY, I'M AWFUL SORRY!
OH, THAT'S ALL RIGHT!----- YOU'RE ARCHIE ANDREWS, AREN'T YOU? I'M JUDY PRICE!
JUDY PRICE? OH, SURE --- YOU JUST MOVED TO RIVER-DALE---DIDN'T YOU? HEH, HEH, FUNNY I SHOULD RUN INTO YOU---
MAYBE IT'S FATE! ---DO YOU KNOW, ARCHIE, I THINK I'LL INVITE YOU TO MY CHRISTMAS PARTY; AND YOU COULDN'T REFUSE AFTER KNOCKING A GIRL DOWN, COULD YOU?

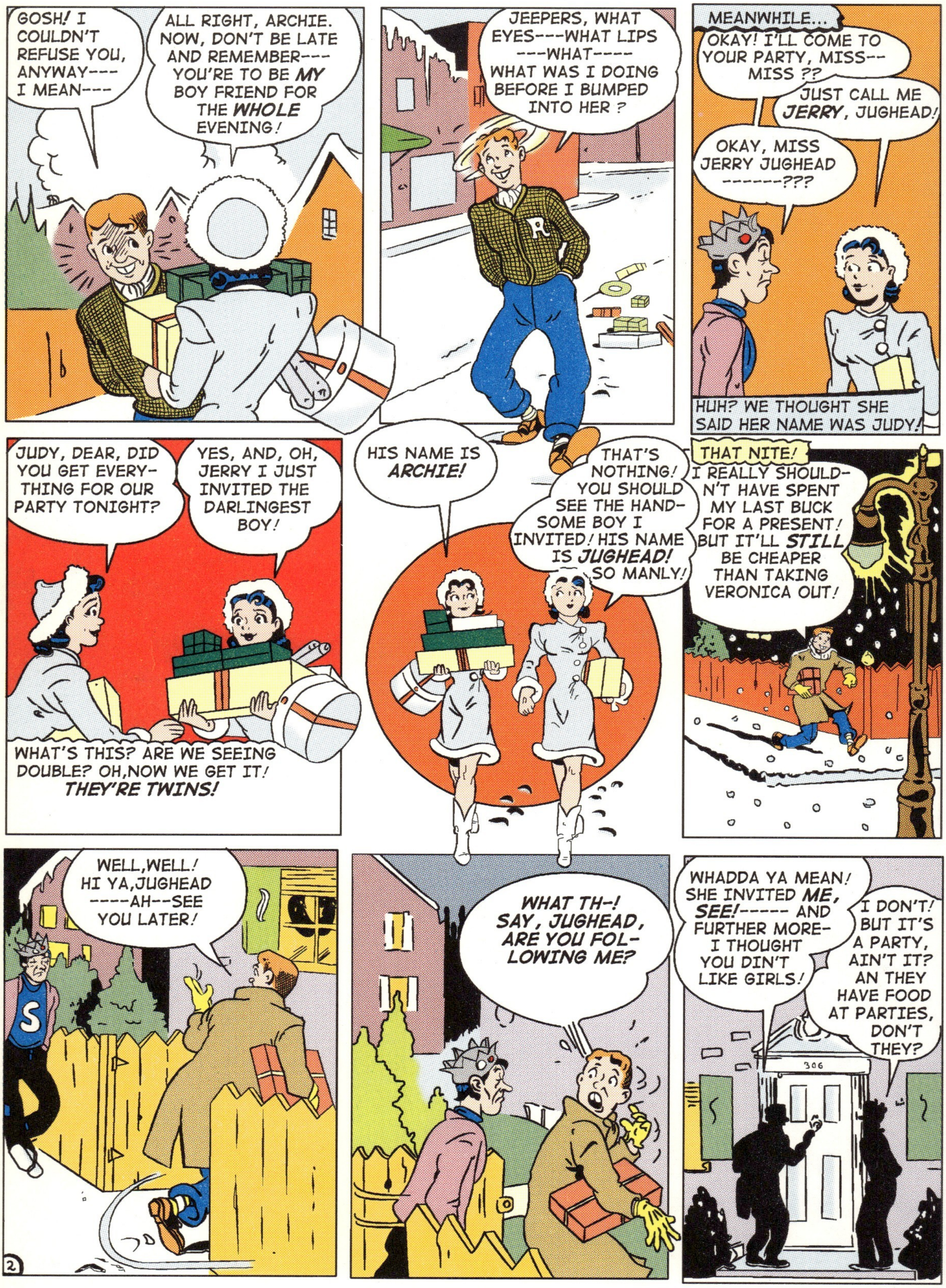
GOSH! I COULDN'T REFUSE YOU, ANYWAY--- I MEAN---
ALL RIGHT, ARCHIE. NOW, DON'T BE LATE AND REMEMBER--- YOU'RE TO BE MY BOY FRIEND FOR THE WHOLE EVENING!
JEEPERS, WHAT EYES---WHAT LIPS ---WHAT---- WHAT WAS I DOING BEFORE I BUMPED INTO HER ?
MEANWHILE...
OKAY! I'LL COME TO YOUR PARTY, MISS-- MISS ??
JUST CALL ME JERRY, JUGHEAD!
OKAY, MISS JERRY JUGHEAD ------???
HUH? WE THOUGHT SHE SAID HER NAME WAS JUDY!
JUDY, DEAR, DID YOU GET EVERY-THING FOR OUR PARTY TONIGHT?
YES, AND, OH, JERRY I JUST INVITED THE DARLINGEST BOY!
WHAT'S THIS? ARE WE SEEING DOUBLE? OH, NOW WE GET IT! THEY'RE TWINS!
HIS NAME IS ARCHIE!
THAT'S NOTHING! YOU SHOULD SEE THE HAND-SOME BOY I INVITED! HIS NAME IS JUGHEAD! SO MANLY!
THAT NITE!
I REALLY SHOULD-N'T HAVE SPENT MY LAST BUCK FOR A PRESENT! BUT IT'LL STILL BE CHEAPER THAN TAKING VERONICA OUT!
WELL, WELL! HI YA, JUGHEAD ----AH--SEE YOU LATER!
2
WHAT TH-! SAY, JUGHEAD, ARE YOU FOL-LOWING ME?
WHADDA YA MEAN! SHE INVITED ME, SEE!----- AND FURTHER MORE- I THOUGHT YOU DIN'T LIKE GIRLS!
I DON'T! BUT IT'S A PARTY, AIN'T IT? AN THEY HAVE FOOD AT PARTIES, DON'T THEY?
306

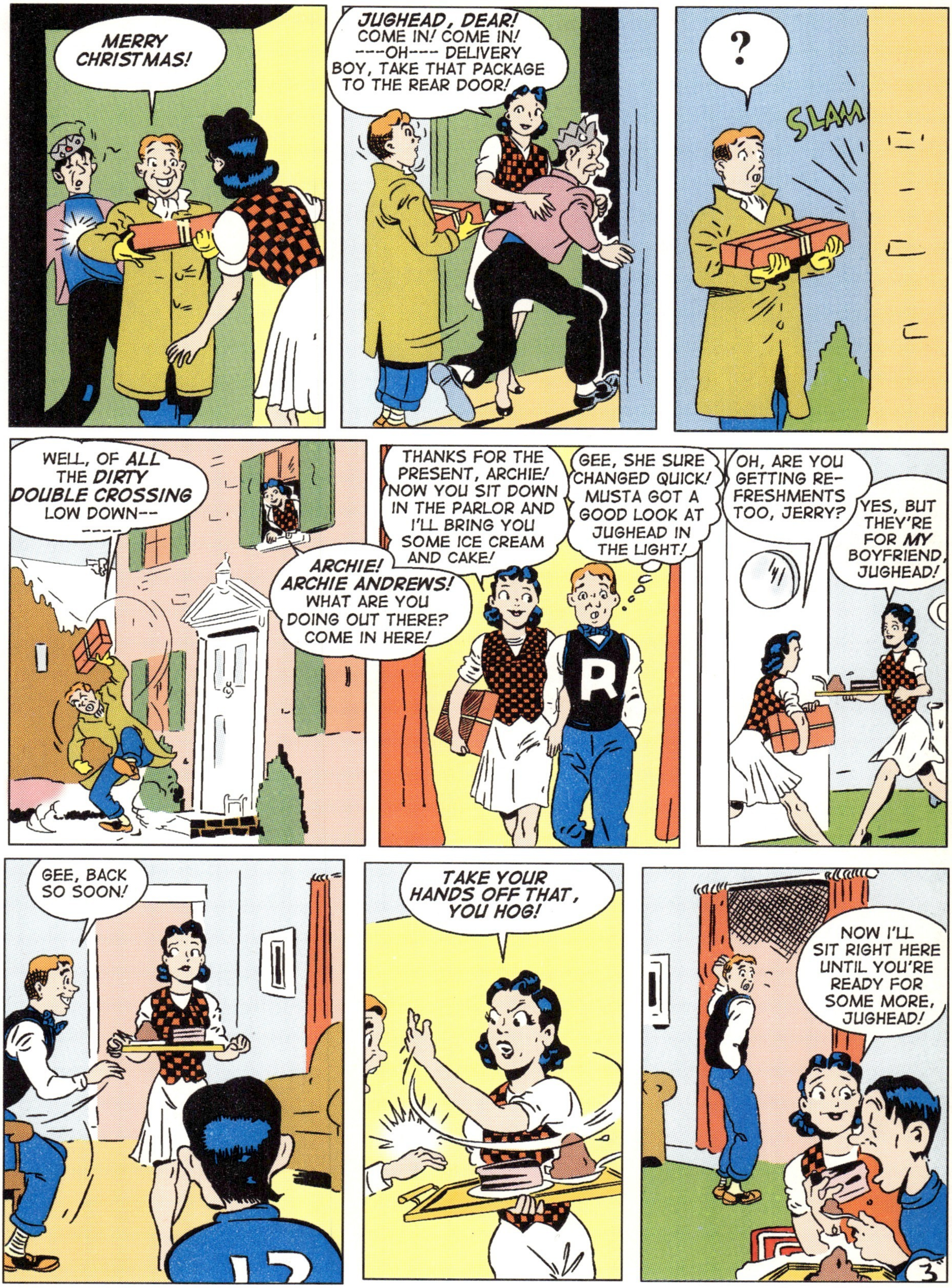
MERRY CHRISTMAS!
JUGHEAD, DEAR! COME IN! COME IN! ----OH---- DELIVERY BOY, TAKE THAT PACKAGE TO THE REAR DOOR!
?
SLAM
WELL, OF ALL THE DIRTY DOUBLE CROSSING LOW DOWN-- -----
ARCHIE! ARCHIE ANDREWS! WHAT ARE YOU DOING OUT THERE? COME IN HERE!
THANKS FOR THE PRESENT, ARCHIE! NOW YOU SIT DOWN IN THE PARLOR AND I'LL BRING YOU SOME ICE CREAM AND CAKE!
GEE, SHE SURE CHANGED QUICK! MUSTA GOT A GOOD LOOK AT JUGHEAD IN THE LIGHT!
OH, ARE YOU GETTING RE-FRESHMENTS TOO, JERRY?
YES, BUT THEY'RE FOR MY BOYFRIEND, JUGHEAD!
GEE, BACK SO SOON!
TAKE YOUR HANDS OFF THAT, YOU HOG!
NOW I'LL SIT RIGHT HERE UNTIL YOU'RE READY FOR SOME MORE, JUGHEAD!
3

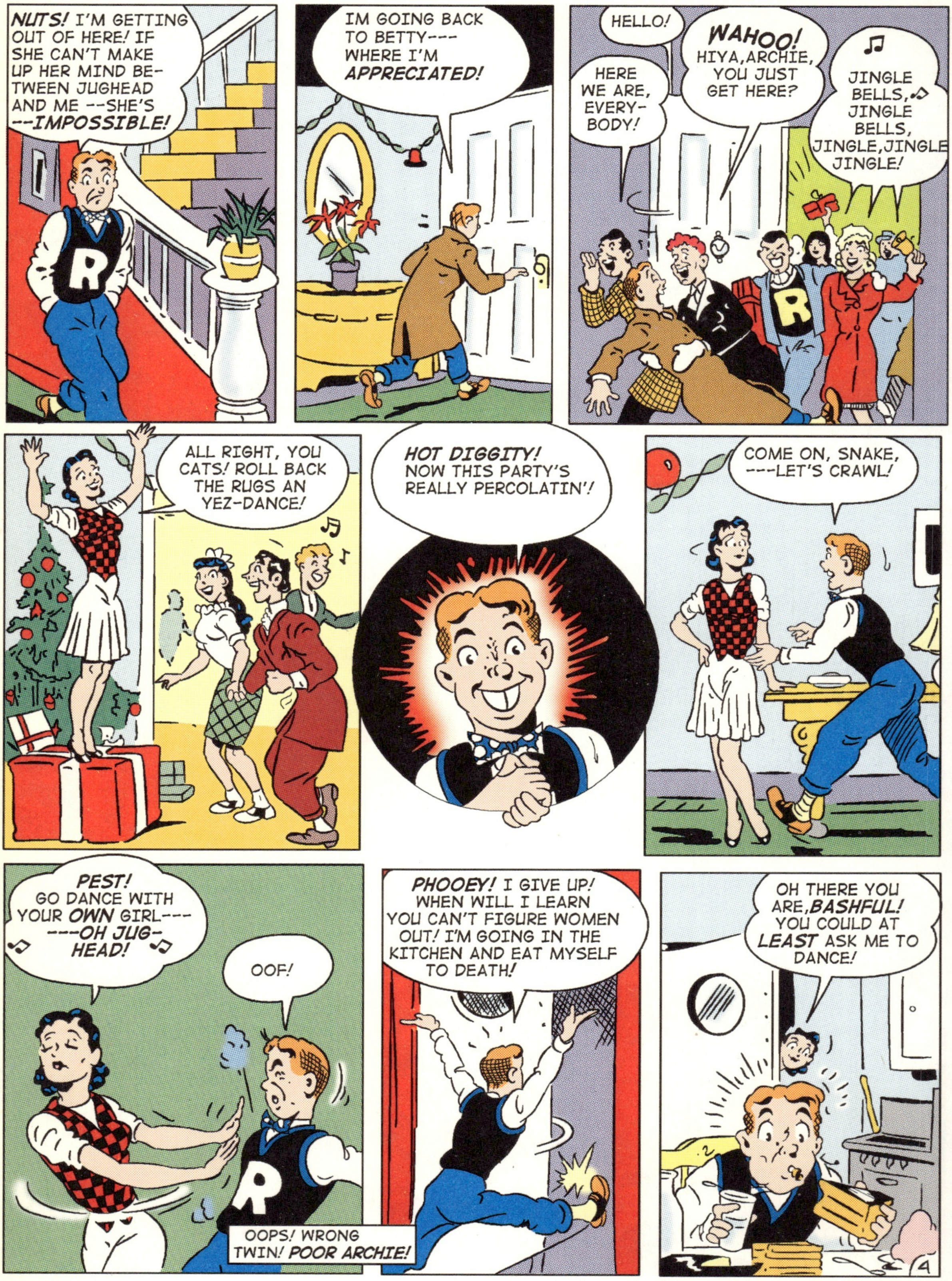

NUTS! I'M GETTING OUT OF HERE! IF SHE CAN'T MAKE UP HER MIND BE-TWEEN JUGHEAD AND ME --SHE'S ---IMPOSSIBLE!
IM GOING BACK TO BETTY--- WHERE I'M APPRECIATED!
HELLO!
HERE WE ARE, EVERY-BODY!
WAHOO! HIYA, ARCHIE, YOU JUST GET HERE?
JINGLE BELLS, JINGLE BELLS, JINGLE, JINGLE JINGLE!
ALL RIGHT, YOU CATS! ROLL BACK THE RUGS AN YEZ-DANCE!
HOT DIGGITY! NOW THIS PARTY'S REALLY PERCOLATIN'!
COME ON, SNAKE, ---LET'S CRAWL!
PEST! GO DANCE WITH YOUR OWN GIRL--- ---OH JUG-HEAD!
OOF!
OOPS! WRONG TWIN! POOR ARCHIE!
PHOOEY! I GIVE UP! WHEN WILL I LEARN YOU CAN'T FIGURE WOMEN OUT! I'M GOING IN THE KITCHEN AND EAT MYSELF TO DEATH!
OH THERE YOU ARE, BASHFUL! YOU COULD AT LEAST ASK ME TO DANCE!
4

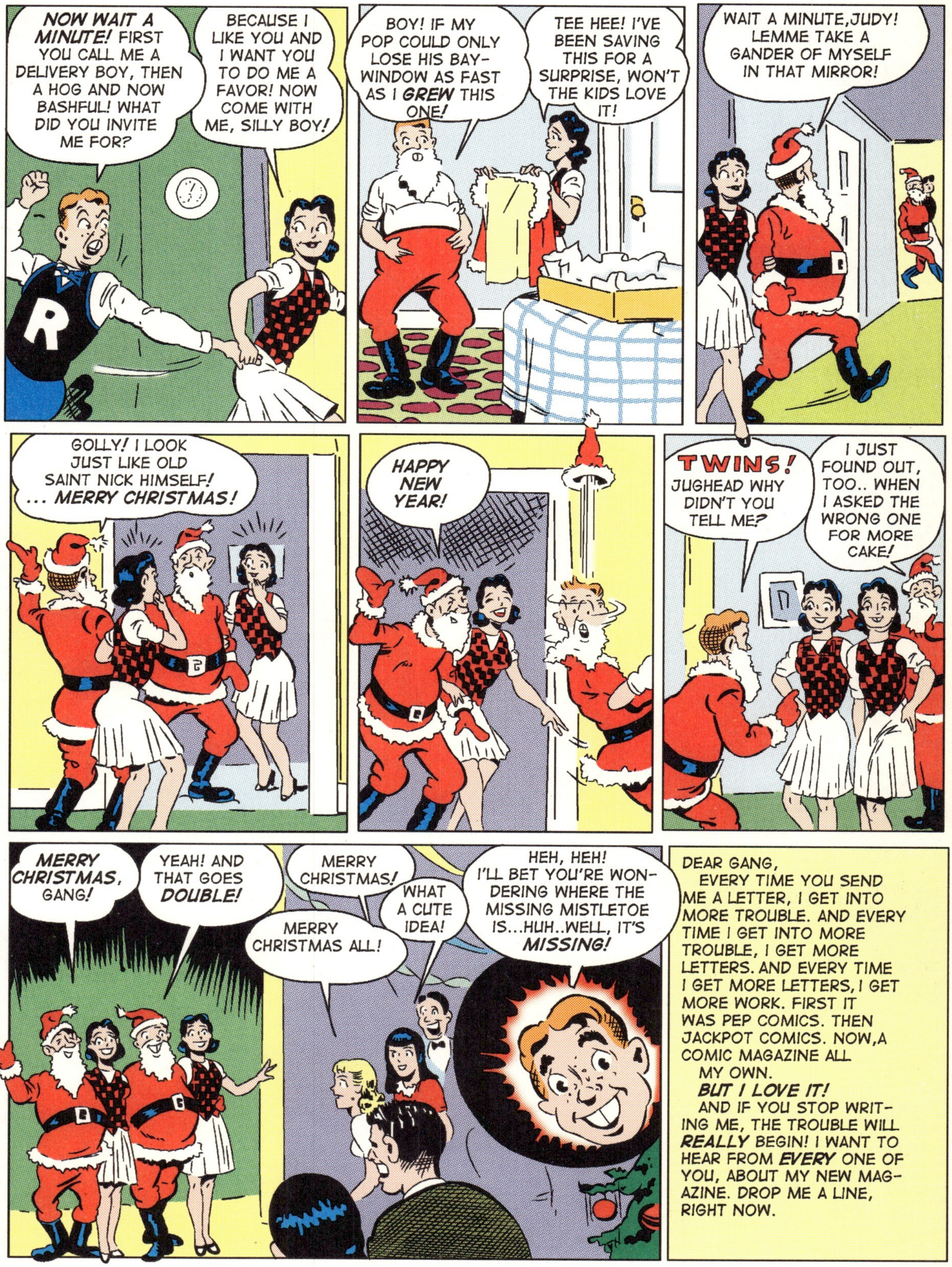
NOW WAIT A MINUTE! FIRST YOU CALL ME A DELIVERY BOY, THEN A HOG AND NOW BASHFUL! WHAT DID YOU INVITE ME FOR?
BECAUSE I LIKE YOU AND I WANT YOU TO DO ME A FAVOR! NOW COME WITH ME, SILLY BOY!
BOY! IF MY POP COULD ONLY LOSE HIS BAY-WINDOW AS FAST AS I GREW THIS ONE!
TEE HEE! I'VE BEEN SAVING THIS FOR A SURPRISE, WON'T THE KIDS LOVE IT!
WAIT A MINUTE, JUDY! LEMME TAKE A GANDER OF MYSELF IN THAT MIRROR!
GOLLY! I LOOK JUST LIKE OLD SAINT NICK HIMSELF! ... MERRY CHRISTMAS!
HAPPY NEW YEAR!
TWINS! JUGHEAD WHY DIDN'T YOU TELL ME?
I JUST FOUND OUT, TOO.. WHEN I ASKED THE WRONG ONE FOR MORE CAKE!
MERRY CHRISTMAS, GANG!
YEAH! AND THAT GOES DOUBLE!
MERRY CHRISTMAS!
WHAT A CUTE IDEA!
MERRY CHRISTMAS ALL!
HEH, HEH! I'LL BET YOU'RE WON-DERING WHERE THE MISSING MISTLETOE IS...HUH..WELL, IT'S MISSING!
DEAR GANG,
EVERY TIME YOU SEND ME A LETTER, I GET INTO MORE TROUBLE. AND EVERY TIME I GET INTO MORE TROUBLE, I GET MORE LETTERS. AND EVERY TIME I GET MORE LETTERS, I GET MORE WORK. FIRST IT WAS PEP COMICS. THEN JACKPOT COMICS. NOW, A COMIC MAGAZINE ALL MY OWN.
BUT I LOVE IT!
AND IF YOU STOP WRIT-ING ME, THE TROUBLE WILL REALLY BEGIN! I WANT TO HEAR FROM EVERY ONE OF YOU, ABOUT MY NEW MAG-AZINE. DROP ME A LINE, RIGHT NOW.

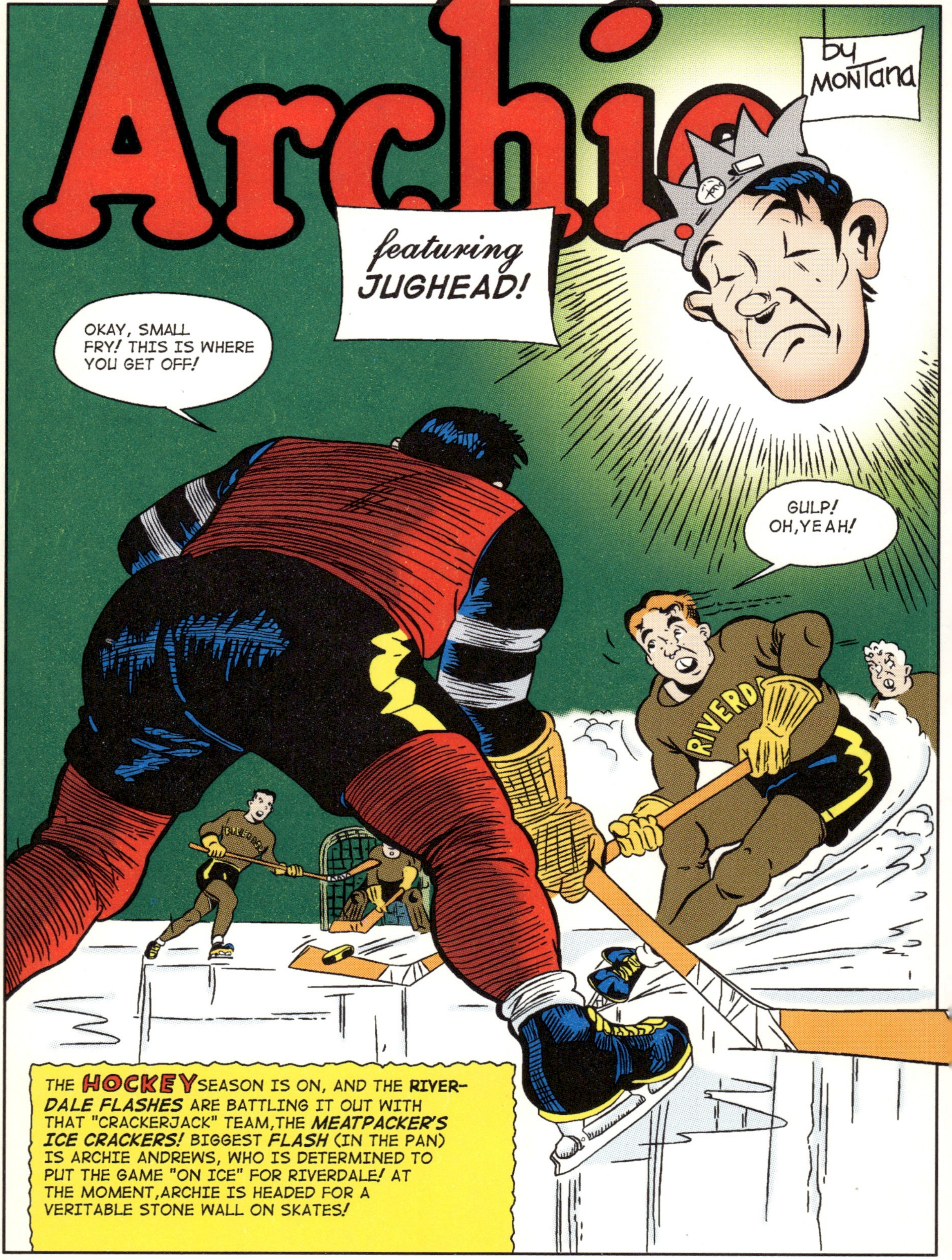
Archie
by MONTANA
featuring JUGHEAD!
OKAY, SMALL FRY! THIS IS WHERE YOU GET OFF!
GULP! OH,YEAH!
RIVERDA
THE HOCKEY SEASON IS ON, AND THE RIVER-DALE FLASHES ARE BATTLING IT OUT WITH THAT "CRACKERJACK" TEAM, THE MEATPACKER'S ICE CRACKERS! BIGGEST FLASH (IN THE PAN) IS ARCHIE ANDREWS, WHO IS DETERMINED TO PUT THE GAME "ON ICE" FOR RIVERDALE! AT THE MOMENT, ARCHIE IS HEADED FOR A VERITABLE STONE WALL ON SKATES!

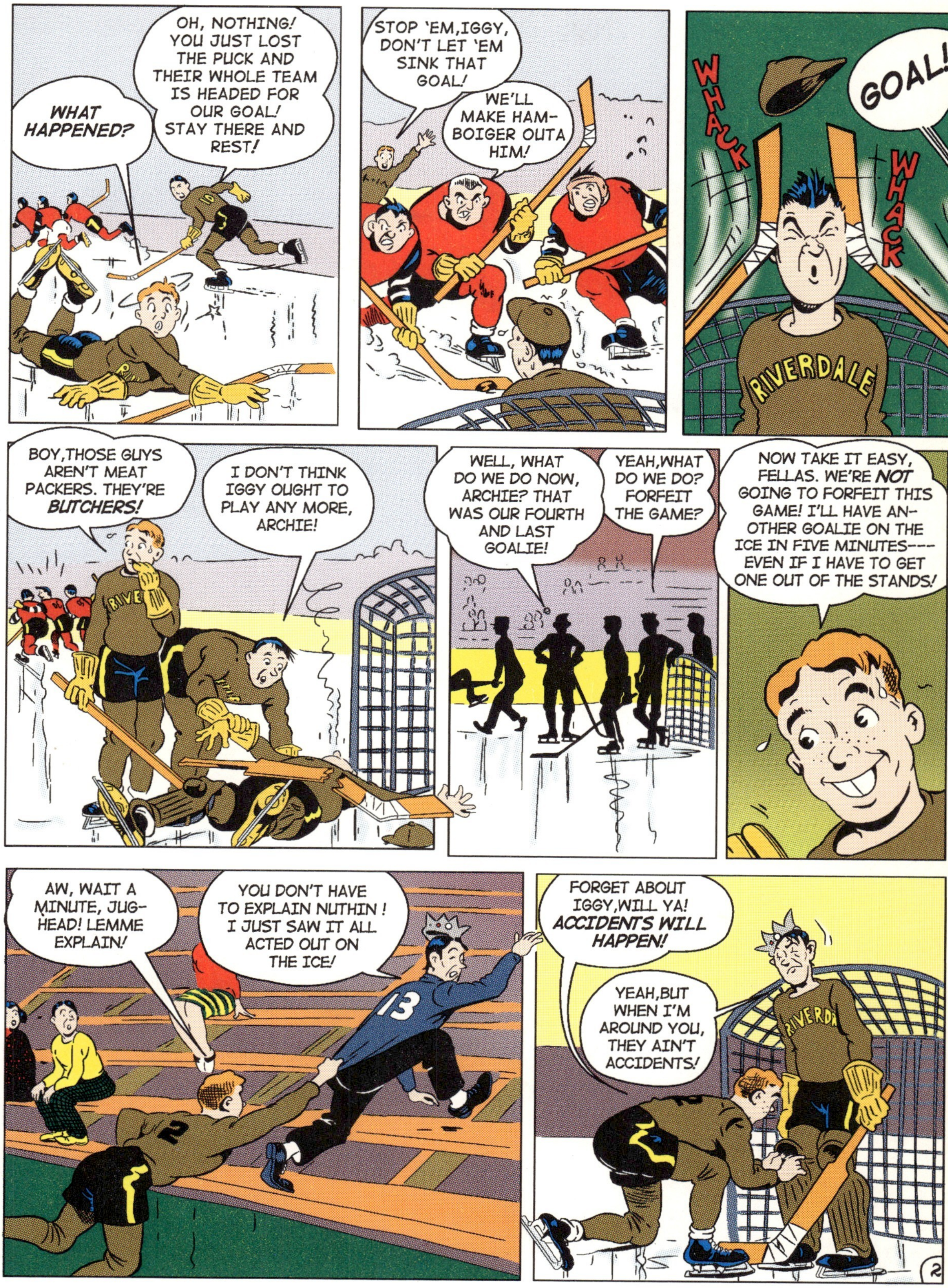
WHAT HAPPENED?
OH, NOTHING! YOU JUST LOST THE PUCK AND THEIR WHOLE TEAM IS HEADED FOR OUR GOAL! STAY THERE AND REST!
STOP 'EM, IGGY, DON'T LET 'EM SINK THAT GOAL!
WE'LL MAKE HAM-BOIGER OUTA HIM!
WHACK
WHACK
GOAL!
RIVERDALE
BOY, THOSE GUYS AREN'T MEAT PACKERS. THEY'RE BUTCHERS!
I DON'T THINK IGGY OUGHT TO PLAY ANY MORE, ARCHIE!
WELL, WHAT DO WE DO NOW, ARCHIE? THAT WAS OUR FOURTH AND LAST GOALIE!
YEAH, WHAT DO WE DO? FORFEIT THE GAME?
NOW TAKE IT EASY, FELLAS. WE'RE NOT GOING TO FORFEIT THIS GAME! I'LL HAVE AN-OTHER GOALIE ON THE ICE IN FIVE MINUTES--- EVEN IF I HAVE TO GET ONE OUT OF THE STANDS!
AW, WAIT A MINUTE, JUG-HEAD! LEMME EXPLAIN!
YOU DON'T HAVE TO EXPLAIN NUTHIN! I JUST SAW IT ALL ACTED OUT ON THE ICE!
FORGET ABOUT IGGY, WILL YA! ACCIDENTS WILL HAPPEN!
YEAH, BUT WHEN I'M AROUND YOU, THEY AIN'T ACCIDENTS!
2

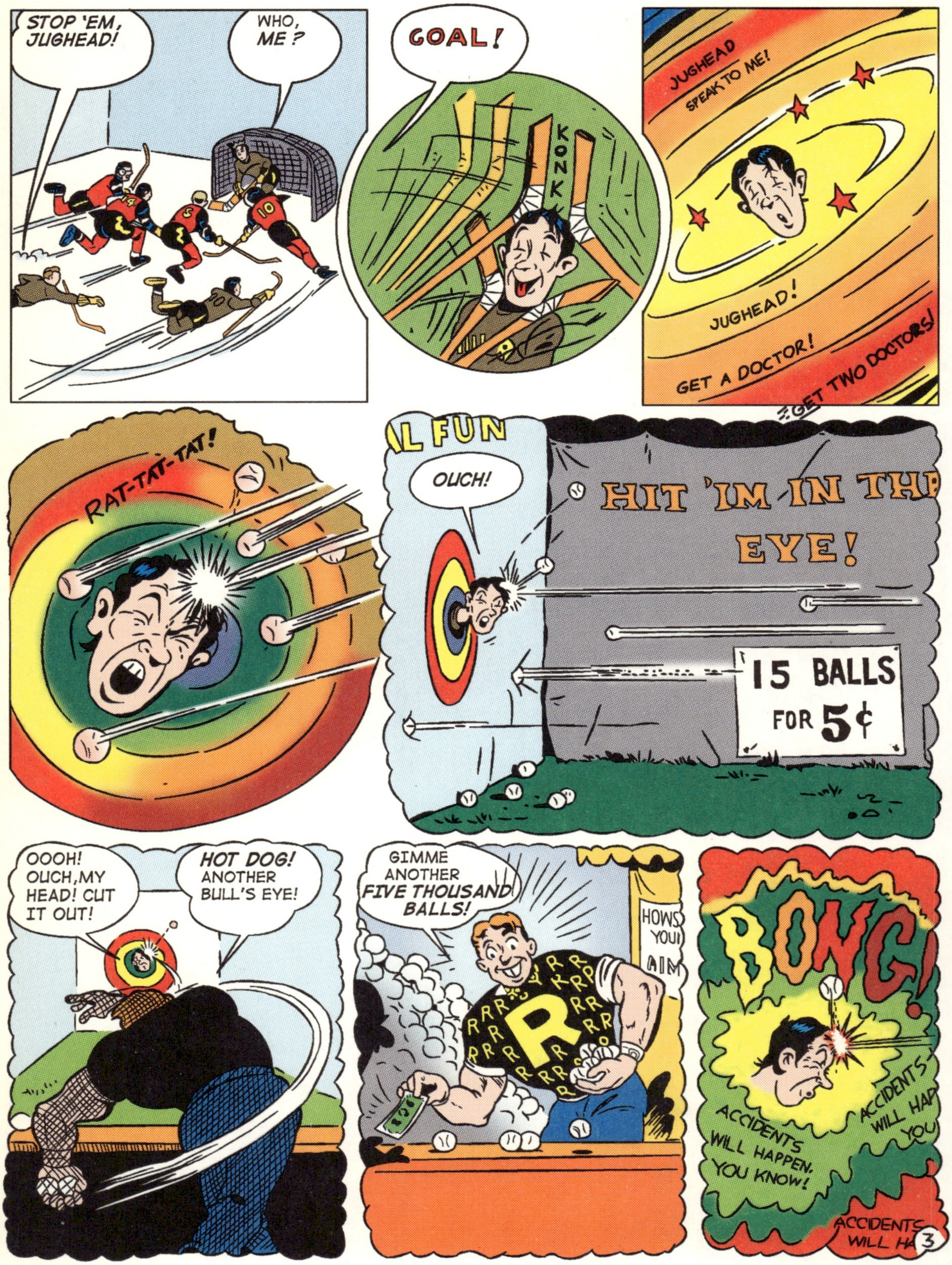
STOP 'EM, JUGHEAD!
WHO, ME ?
GOAL!
KONK
JUGHEAD
SPEAK TO ME!
JUGHEAD!
GET A DOCTOR!
GET TWO DOCTORS!
RAT-TAT-TAT!
OUCH!
EYE!
15 BALLS FOR 5¢
OOOH! OUCH,MY HEAD! CUT IT OUT!
HOT DOG! ANOTHER BULL'S EYE!
GIMME ANOTHER FIVE THOUSAND BALLS!
BONG!
ACCIDENTS WILL HAPPEN, YOU KNOW!
3

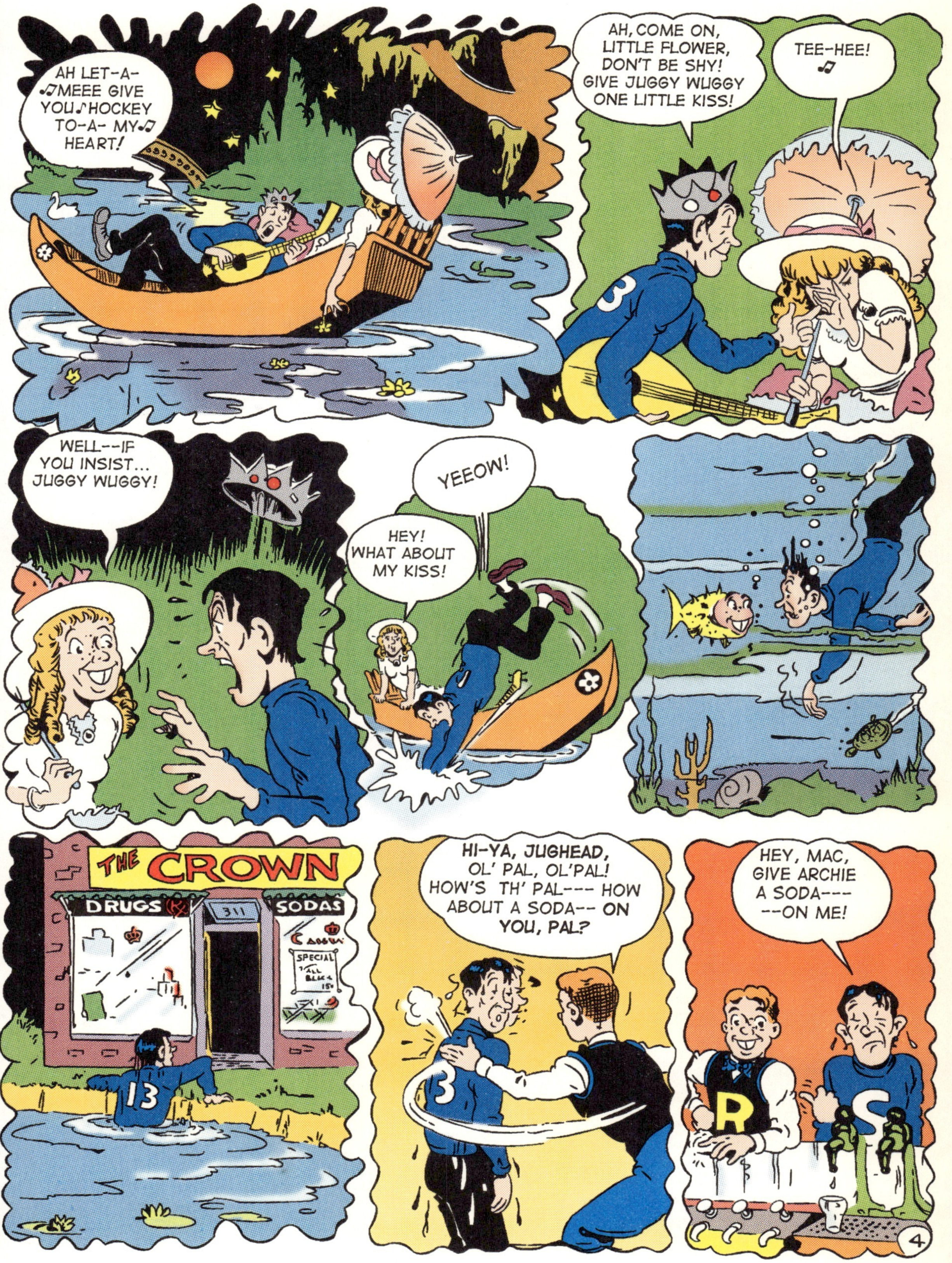
AH LET-A-♫MEEE GIVE YOU♪HOCKEY TO-A- MY♫ HEART!
AH, COME ON, LITTLE FLOWER, DON'T BE SHY! GIVE JUGGY WUGGY ONE LITTLE KISS!
TEE-HEE! ♫
WELL--IF YOU INSIST... JUGGY WUGGY!
YEEOW!
HEY! WHAT ABOUT MY KISS!
THE CROWN
DRUGS
311
SODAS
SPECIAL
HI-YA, JUGHEAD, OL' PAL, OL'PAL! HOW'S TH' PAL--- HOW ABOUT A SODA-- ON YOU, PAL?
HEY, MAC, GIVE ARCHIE A SODA--- --ON ME!
4

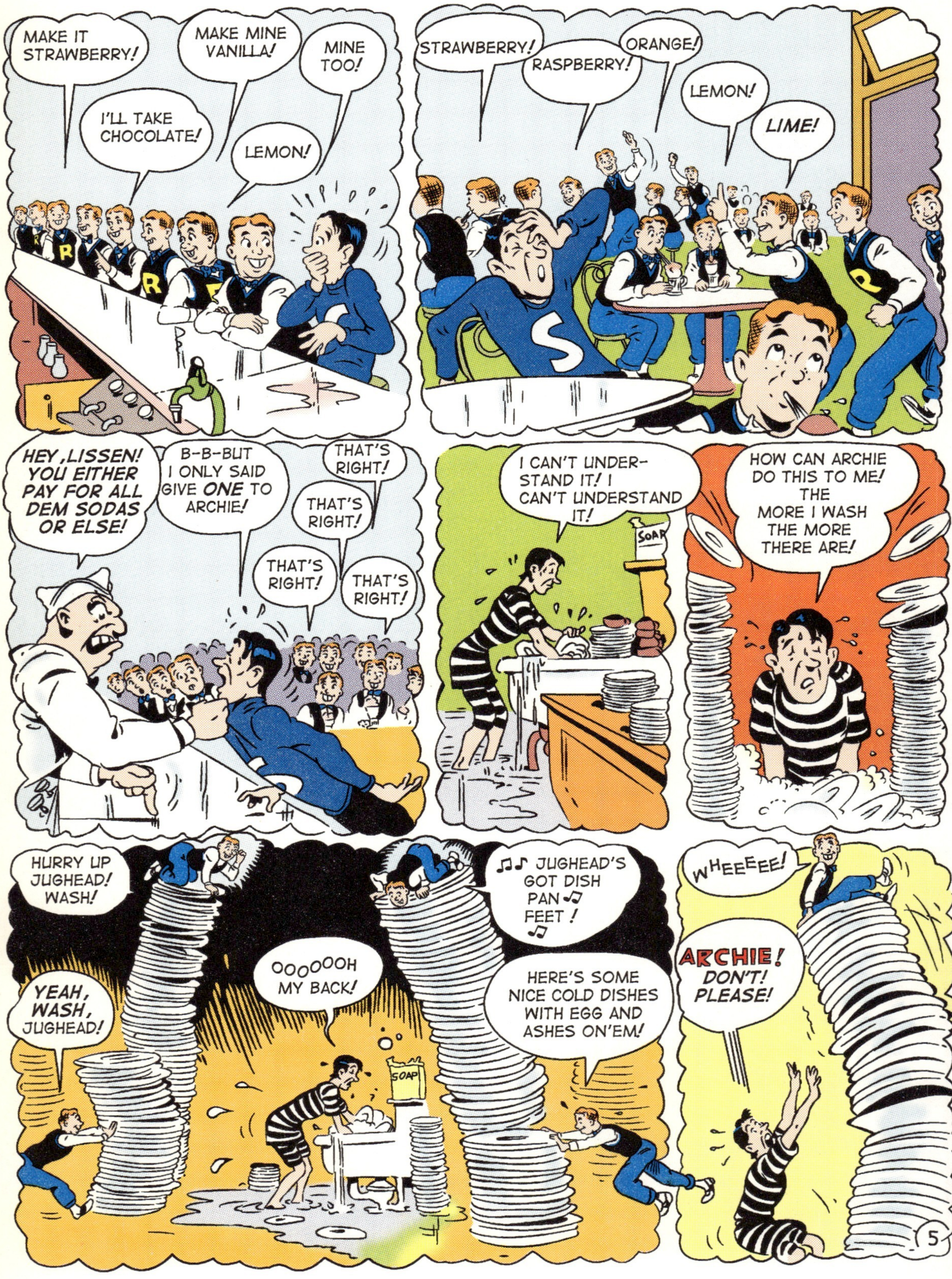
MAKE IT STRAWBERRY!
MAKE MINE VANILLA!
MINE TOO!
I'LL TAKE CHOCOLATE!
LEMON!
STRAWBERRY!
RASPBERRY!
ORANGE!
LEMON!
LIME!
HEY, LISSEN! YOU EITHER PAY FOR ALL DEM SODAS OR ELSE!
B-B-BUT I ONLY SAID GIVE ONE TO ARCHIE!
THAT'S RIGHT!
THAT'S RIGHT!
THAT'S RIGHT!
THAT'S RIGHT!
I CAN'T UNDER-STAND IT! I CAN'T UNDERSTAND IT!
SOAP
HOW CAN ARCHIE DO THIS TO ME! THE MORE I WASH THE MORE THERE ARE!
HURRY UP JUGHEAD! WASH!
♫♪ JUGHEAD'S GOT DISH PAN ♫ FEET! ♫
OOOOOOH MY BACK!
YEAH, WASH, JUGHEAD!
HERE'S SOME NICE COLD DISHES WITH EGG AND ASHES ON'EM!
SOAP
WHEEEEEE!
ARCHIE! DON'T! PLEASE!
5

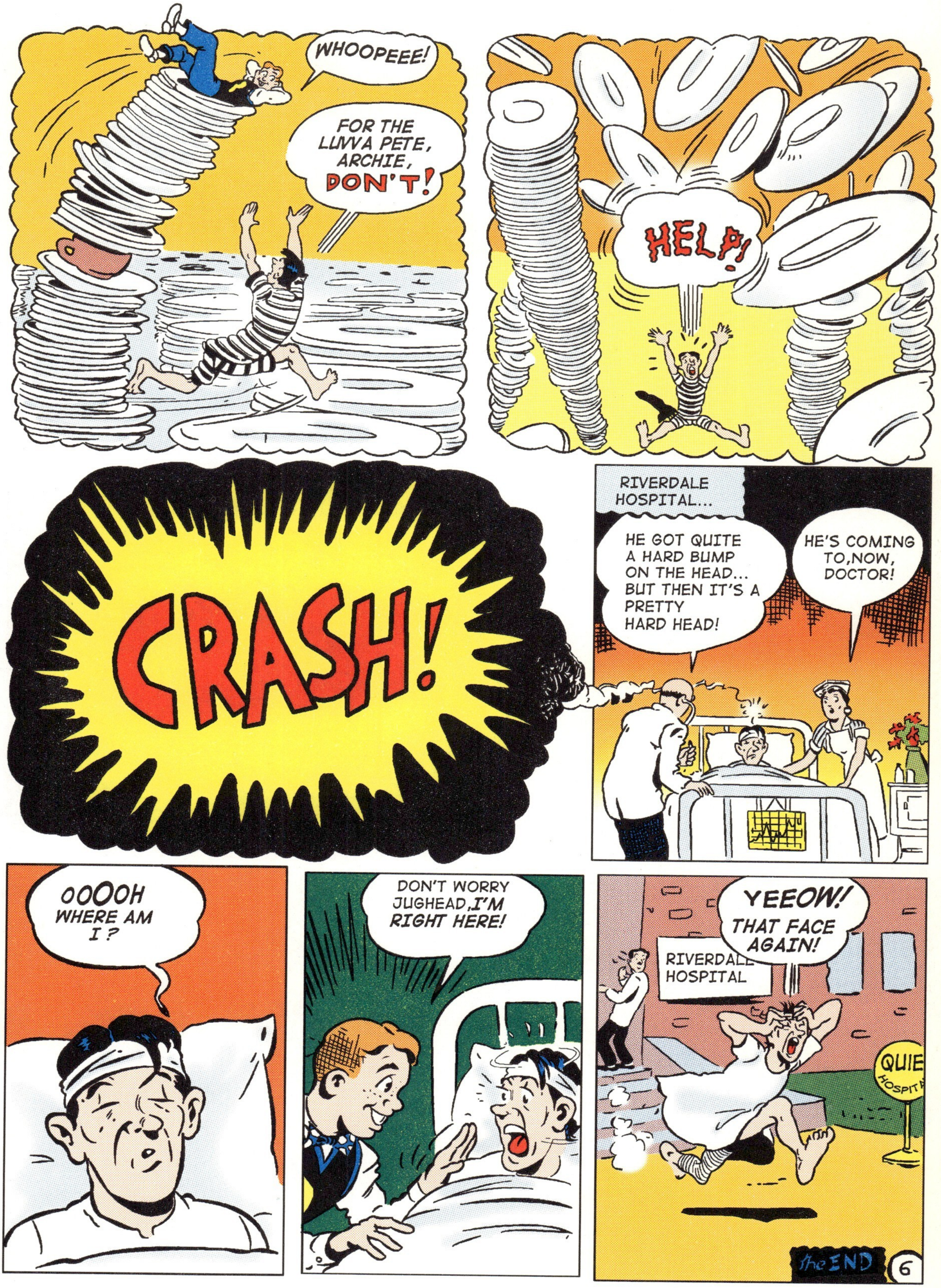
WHOOPEEE!
FOR THE LUVVA PETE, ARCHIE, DON'T!
HELP!
CRASH!
RIVERDALE HOSPITAL...
HE GOT QUITE A HARD BUMP ON THE HEAD... BUT THEN IT'S A PRETTY HARD HEAD!
HE'S COMING TO,NOW, DOCTOR!
OOOOH WHERE AM I?
DON'T WORRY JUGHEAD,I'M RIGHT HERE!
YEEOW! THAT FACE AGAIN!
RIVERDALE HOSPITAL
the END
6

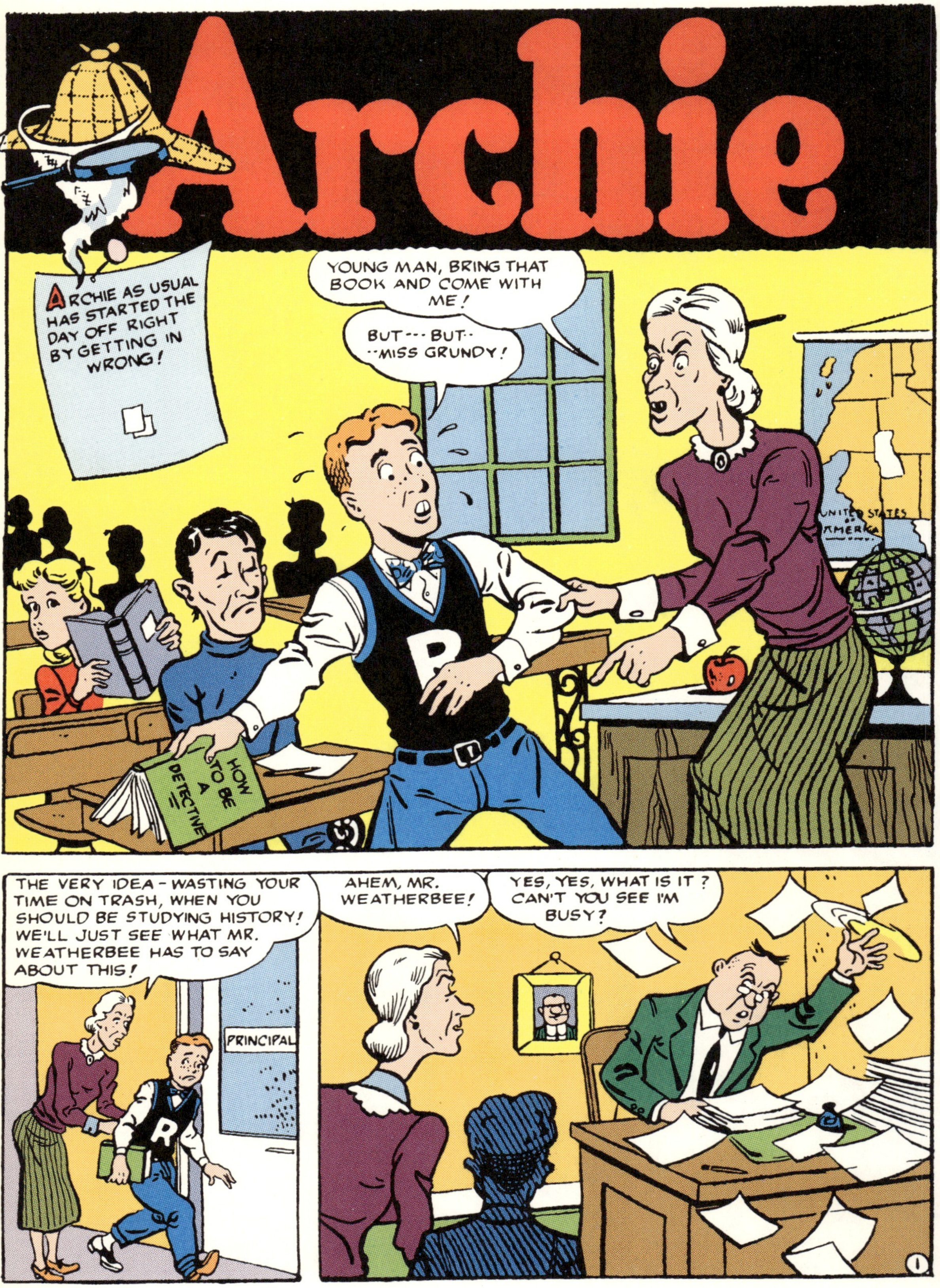
Archie
ARCHIE AS USUAL HAS STARTED THE DAY OFF RIGHT BY GETTING IN WRONG!
YOUNG MAN, BRING THAT BOOK AND COME WITH ME!
BUT--- BUT- --MISS GRUNDY!
UNITED STATES AMERICA
HOW TO BE A DETECTIVE
THE VERY IDEA - WASTING YOUR TIME ON TRASH, WHEN YOU SHOULD BE STUDYING HISTORY! WE'LL JUST SEE WHAT MR. WEATHERBEE HAS TO SAY ABOUT THIS!
PRINCIPAL
AHEM, MR. WEATHERBEE!
YES, YES, WHAT IS IT? CAN'T YOU SEE I'M BUSY?
1

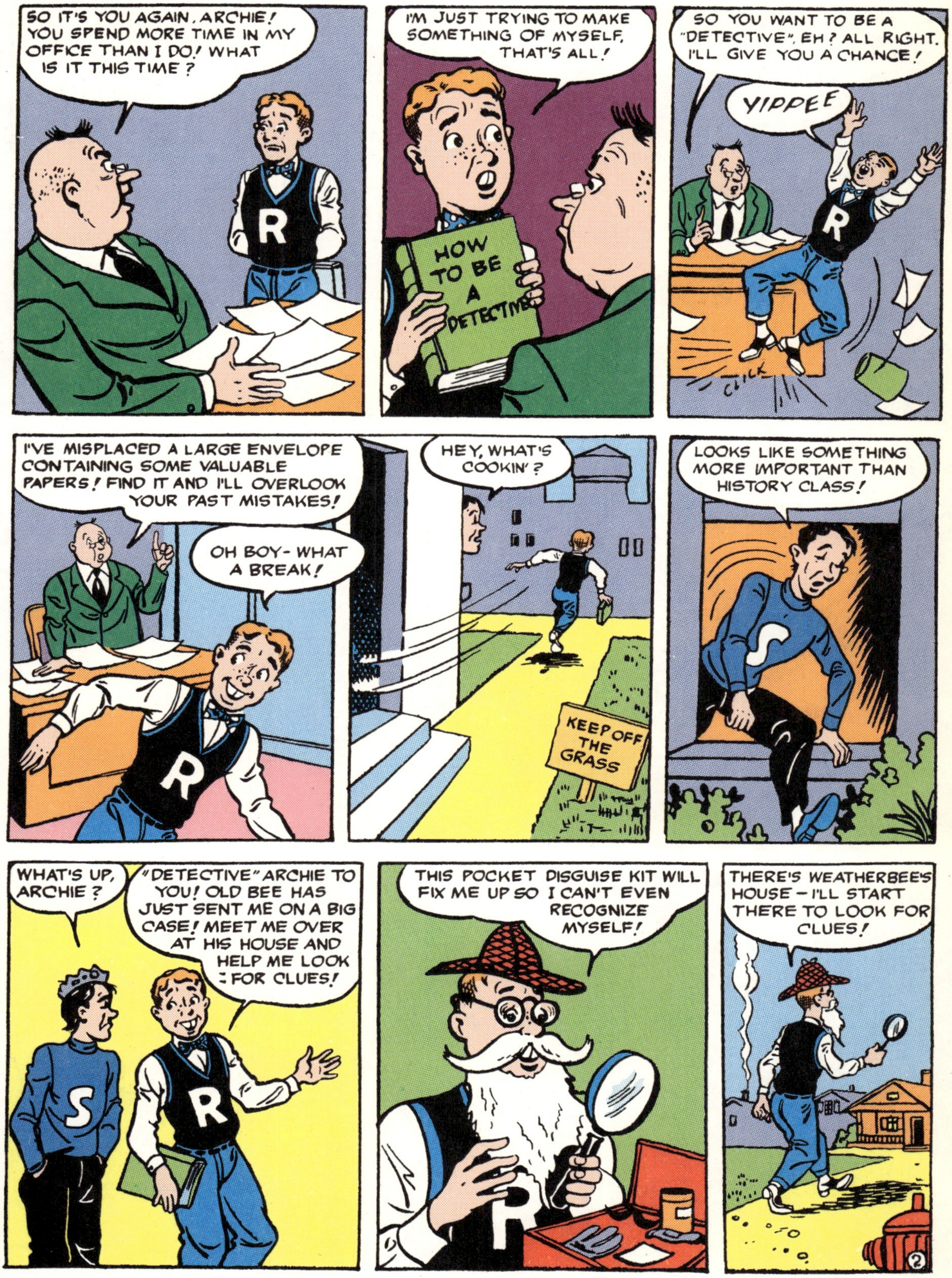
SO IT'S YOU AGAIN, ARCHIE! YOU SPEND MORE TIME IN MY OFFICE THAN I DO! WHAT IS IT THIS TIME?
I'M JUST TRYING TO MAKE SOMETHING OF MYSELF, THAT'S ALL!
HOW TO BE A DETECTIVE
SO YOU WANT TO BE A "DETECTIVE", EH? ALL RIGHT. I'LL GIVE YOU A CHANCE!
YIPPEE
CLICK
I'VE MISPLACED A LARGE ENVELOPE CONTAINING SOME VALUABLE PAPERS! FIND IT AND I'LL OVERLOOK YOUR PAST MISTAKES!
OH BOY- WHAT A BREAK!
HEY, WHAT'S COOKIN'?
KEEP OFF THE GRASS
LOOKS LIKE SOMETHING MORE IMPORTANT THAN HISTORY CLASS!
WHAT'S UP, ARCHIE?
"DETECTIVE" ARCHIE TO YOU! OLD BEE HAS JUST SENT ME ON A BIG CASE! MEET ME OVER AT HIS HOUSE AND HELP ME LOOK FOR CLUES!
THIS POCKET DISGUISE KIT WILL FIX ME UP SO I CAN'T EVEN RECOGNIZE MYSELF!
THERE'S WEATHERBEE'S HOUSE – I'LL START THERE TO LOOK FOR CLUES!
2

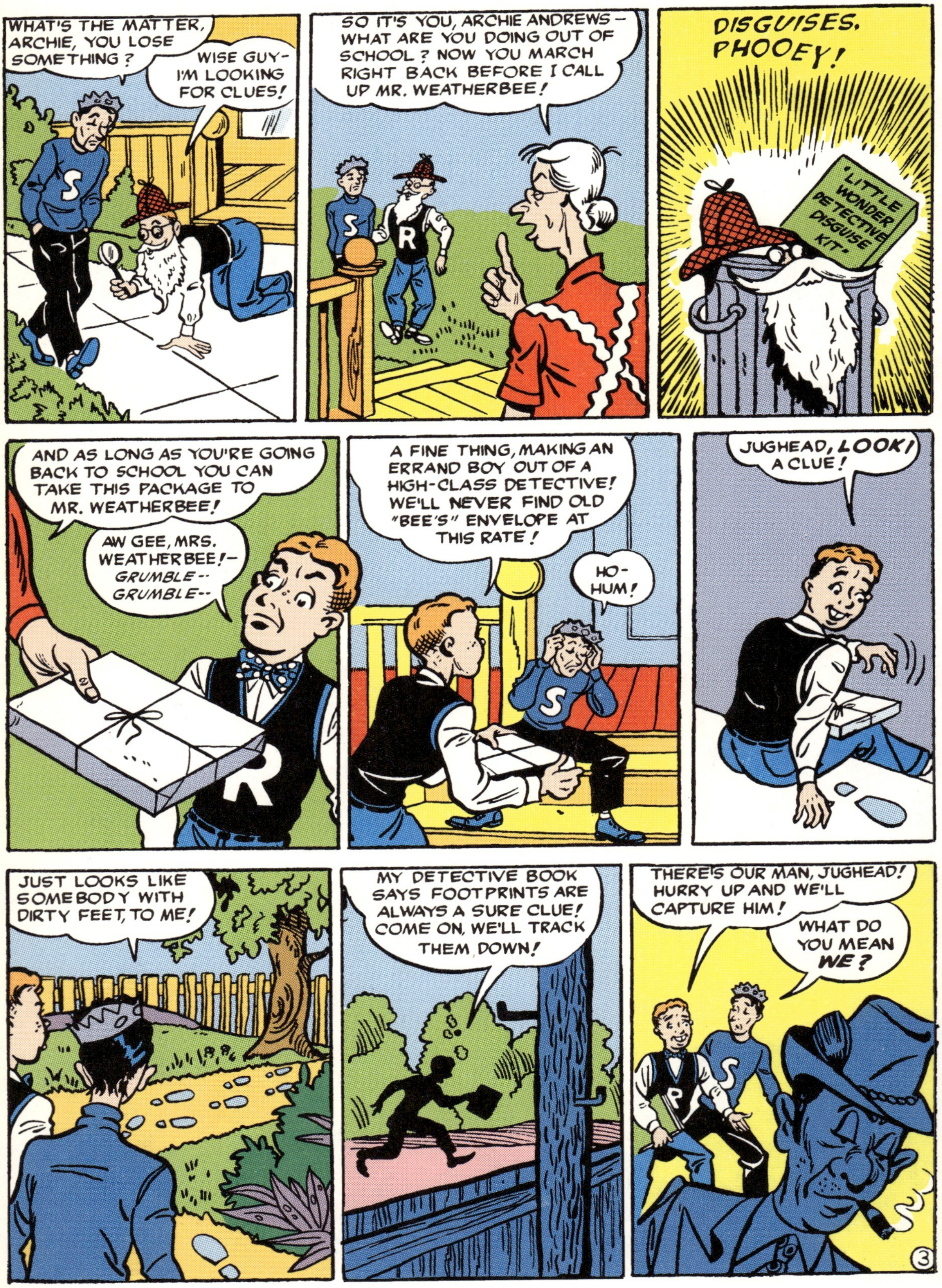
WHAT'S THE MATTER, ARCHIE, YOU LOSE SOMETHING?
WISE GUY- I'M LOOKING FOR CLUES!
SO IT'S YOU, ARCHIE ANDREWS - WHAT ARE YOU DOING OUT OF SCHOOL? NOW YOU MARCH RIGHT BACK BEFORE I CALL UP MR. WEATHERBEE!
DISGUISES. PHOOEY!
"LITTLE WONDER DETECTIVE DISGUISE KIT"
AND AS LONG AS YOU'RE GOING BACK TO SCHOOL YOU CAN TAKE THIS PACKAGE TO MR. WEATHERBEE!
AW GEE, MRS. WEATHERBEE!- GRUMBLE-- GRUMBLE--
A FINE THING, MAKING AN ERRAND BOY OUT OF A HIGH-CLASS DETECTIVE! WE'LL NEVER FIND OLD "BEE'S" ENVELOPE AT THIS RATE!
HO-HUM!
JUGHEAD, LOOK! A CLUE!
JUST LOOKS LIKE SOMEBODY WITH DIRTY FEET, TO ME!
MY DETECTIVE BOOK SAYS FOOTPRINTS ARE ALWAYS A SURE CLUE! COME ON, WE'LL TRACK THEM DOWN!
THERE'S OUR MAN, JUGHEAD! HURRY UP AND WE'LL CAPTURE HIM!
WHAT DO YOU MEAN WE?
3

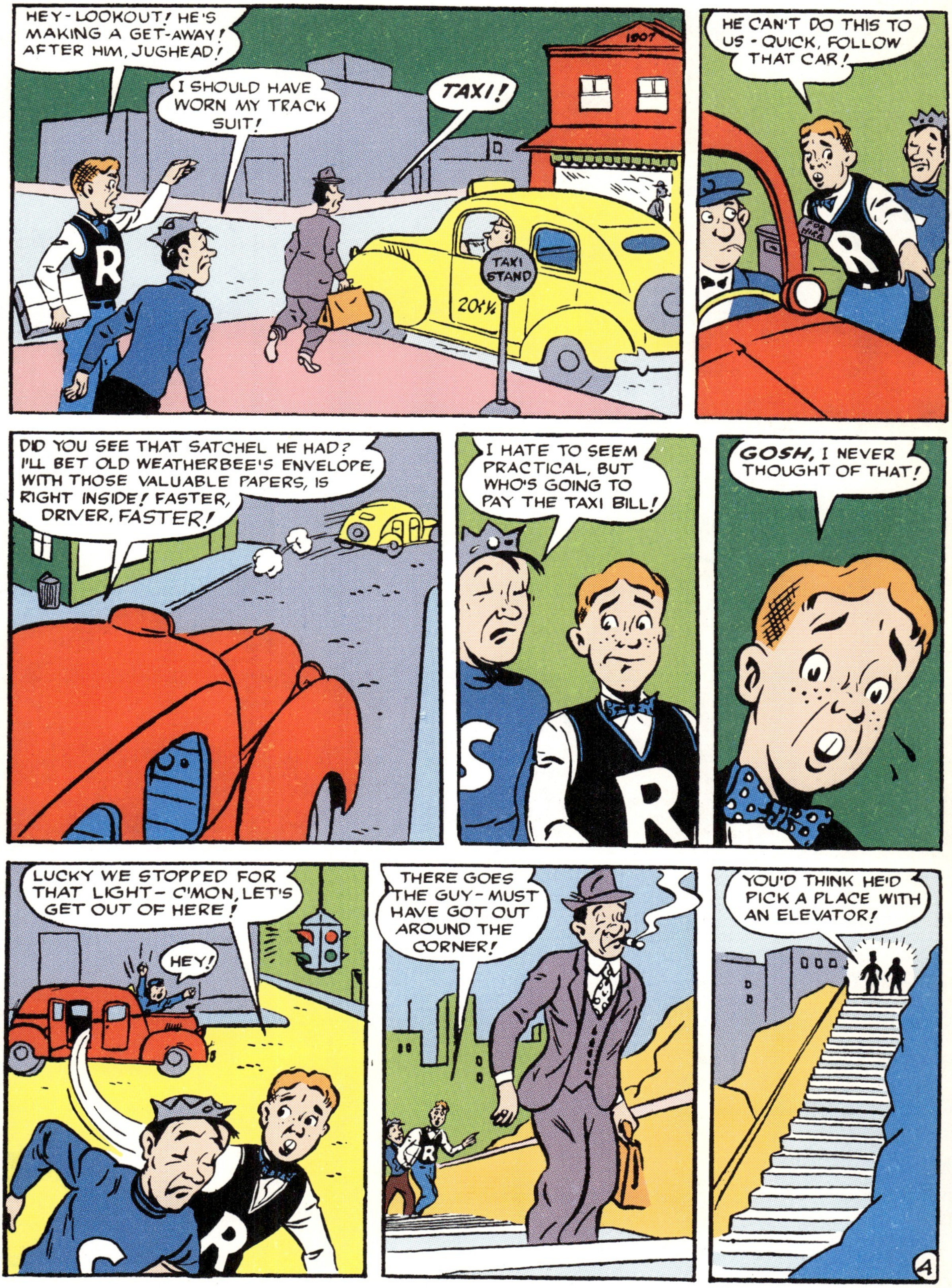

HEY-LOOKOUT! HE'S MAKING A GET-AWAY! AFTER HIM, JUGHEAD!
I SHOULD HAVE WORN MY TRACK SUIT!
TAXI!
1907
TAXI STAND
HE CAN'T DO THIS TO US - QUICK, FOLLOW THAT CAR!
DID YOU SEE THAT SATCHEL HE HAD? I'LL BET OLD WEATHERBEE'S ENVELOPE, WITH THOSE VALUABLE PAPERS, IS RIGHT INSIDE! FASTER, DRIVER, FASTER!
I HATE TO SEEM PRACTICAL, BUT WHO'S GOING TO PAY THE TAXI BILL!
GOSH, I NEVER THOUGHT OF THAT!
LUCKY WE STOPPED FOR THAT LIGHT- C'MON, LET'S GET OUT OF HERE!
HEY!
THERE GOES THE GUY- MUST HAVE GOT OUT AROUND THE CORNER!
YOU'D THINK HE'D PICK A PLACE WITH AN ELEVATOR!
4

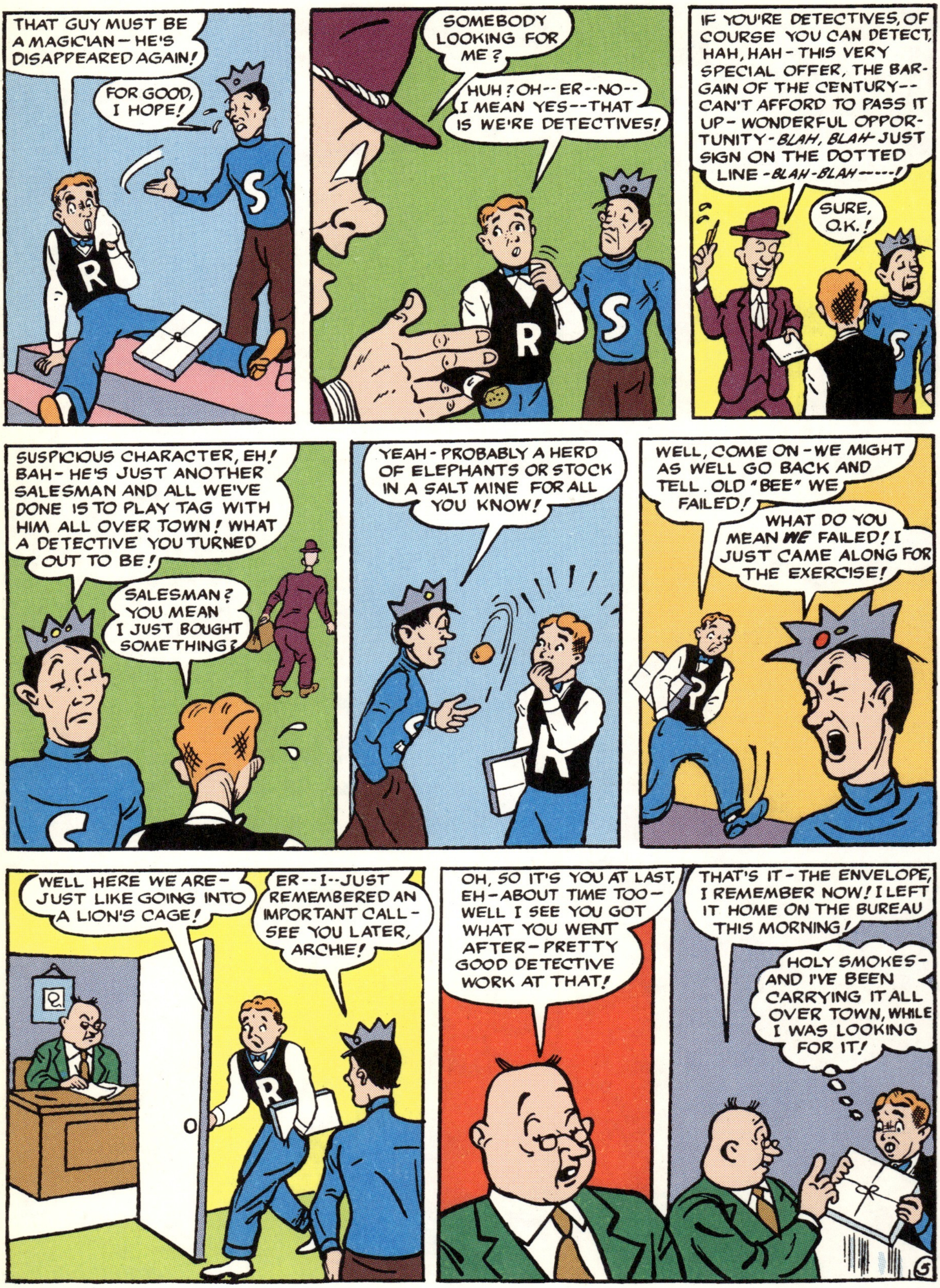
THAT GUY MUST BE A MAGICIAN - HE'S DISAPPEARED AGAIN!
FOR GOOD, I HOPE!
SOMEBODY LOOKING FOR ME?
HUH? OH-- ER --NO-- I MEAN YES--THAT IS WE'RE DETECTIVES!
IF YOU'RE DETECTIVES, OF COURSE YOU CAN DETECT, HAH, HAH - THIS VERY SPECIAL OFFER, THE BARGAIN OF THE CENTURY-- CAN'T AFFORD TO PASS IT UP - WONDERFUL OPPORTUNITY - BLAH, BLAH - JUST SIGN ON THE DOTTED LINE - BLAH-BLAH-----!
SURE, O.K.!
SUSPICIOUS CHARACTER, EH! BAH - HE'S JUST ANOTHER SALESMAN AND ALL WE'VE DONE IS TO PLAY TAG WITH HIM ALL OVER TOWN! WHAT A DETECTIVE YOU TURNED OUT TO BE!
SALESMAN? YOU MEAN I JUST BOUGHT SOMETHING?
YEAH - PROBABLY A HERD OF ELEPHANTS OR STOCK IN A SALT MINE FOR ALL YOU KNOW!
WELL, COME ON - WE MIGHT AS WELL GO BACK AND TELL OLD "BEE" WE FAILED!
WHAT DO YOU MEAN WE FAILED! I JUST CAME ALONG FOR THE EXERCISE!
WELL HERE WE ARE - JUST LIKE GOING INTO A LION'S CAGE!
ER--I--JUST REMEMBERED AN IMPORTANT CALL - SEE YOU LATER, ARCHIE!
OH, SO IT'S YOU AT LAST, EH - ABOUT TIME TOO - WELL I SEE YOU GOT WHAT YOU WENT AFTER - PRETTY GOOD DETECTIVE WORK AT THAT!
THAT'S IT - THE ENVELOPE, I REMEMBER NOW! I LEFT IT HOME ON THE BUREAU THIS MORNING!
HOLY SMOKES - AND I'VE BEEN CARRYING IT ALL OVER TOWN, WHILE I WAS LOOKING FOR IT!
5

ARCHIE, YOU'VE DONE A GOOD JOB AND I'LL SEE THAT YOU ARE PROPERLY REWARDED!
JUST A MOMENT UNTIL I OPEN THIS ENVELOPE WITH THE RESULTS OF YESTERDAY'S EXAMINATION PAPERS!
EXAMINATION PAPERS?
AHA - JUST AS I SUSPECTED - ARCHIE ANDREWS "F"! YOUNG MAN - JUST FOR THAT YOU WON'T BE ALLOWED TO ATTEND THE ANNUAL PROM!
GOSH, WHAT WILL VERONICA SAY WHEN I TELL HER I CAN'T TAKE HER TO THE PROM! AND WHAT WILL POP SAY WHEN I GET HOME LATE FOR SUPPER!
BONG BONG BONG BONG BONG BONG
I'D BETTER SNEAK IN QUIET-LIKE AND--- OH-OH!
ARCHIE!
WHAT'S THE MEANING OF THIS BILL FOR TWENTY YEARS SUBSCRIPTION TO "WHOOSIS MAGAZINE"?
HOLY SMOKE - I FORGOT ALL ABOUT THAT SALESMAN!
RING
SAVED BY THE BELL!
YOU SIT DOWN AND REST, POP, I'LL ANSWER THE BELL!
SO YOU THOUGHT YOU COULD SKIP OUT ON A CAB BILL, EH! LUCKY I FOUND THIS PEN WITH YOUR NAME ON IT!
FARE 24.55
NEXT DAY---
NO PROM - TAXI BILLS - MAGAZINE BILLS - AND POP SAYS I HAVE TO STUDY EVERY NIGHT UNTIL I GET "A" IN ALL MY CLASSES!
BOY - LOOKS LIKE YOU'RE IN FOR THE DURATION!
6

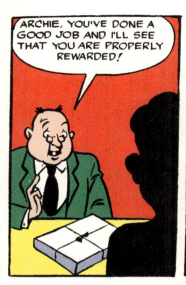

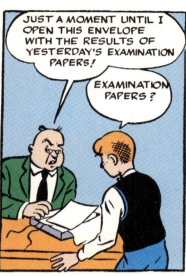

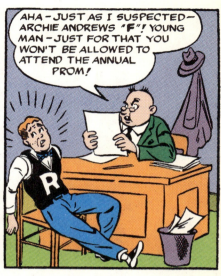

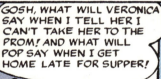

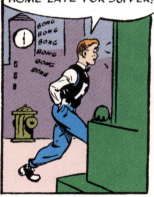

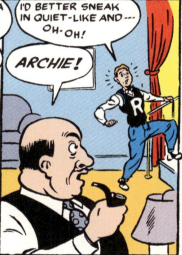

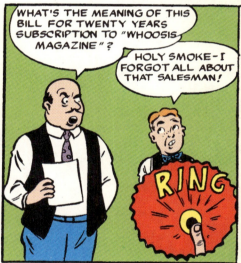

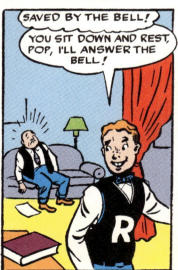

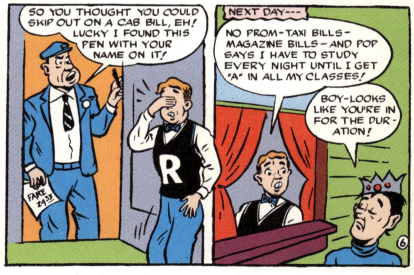

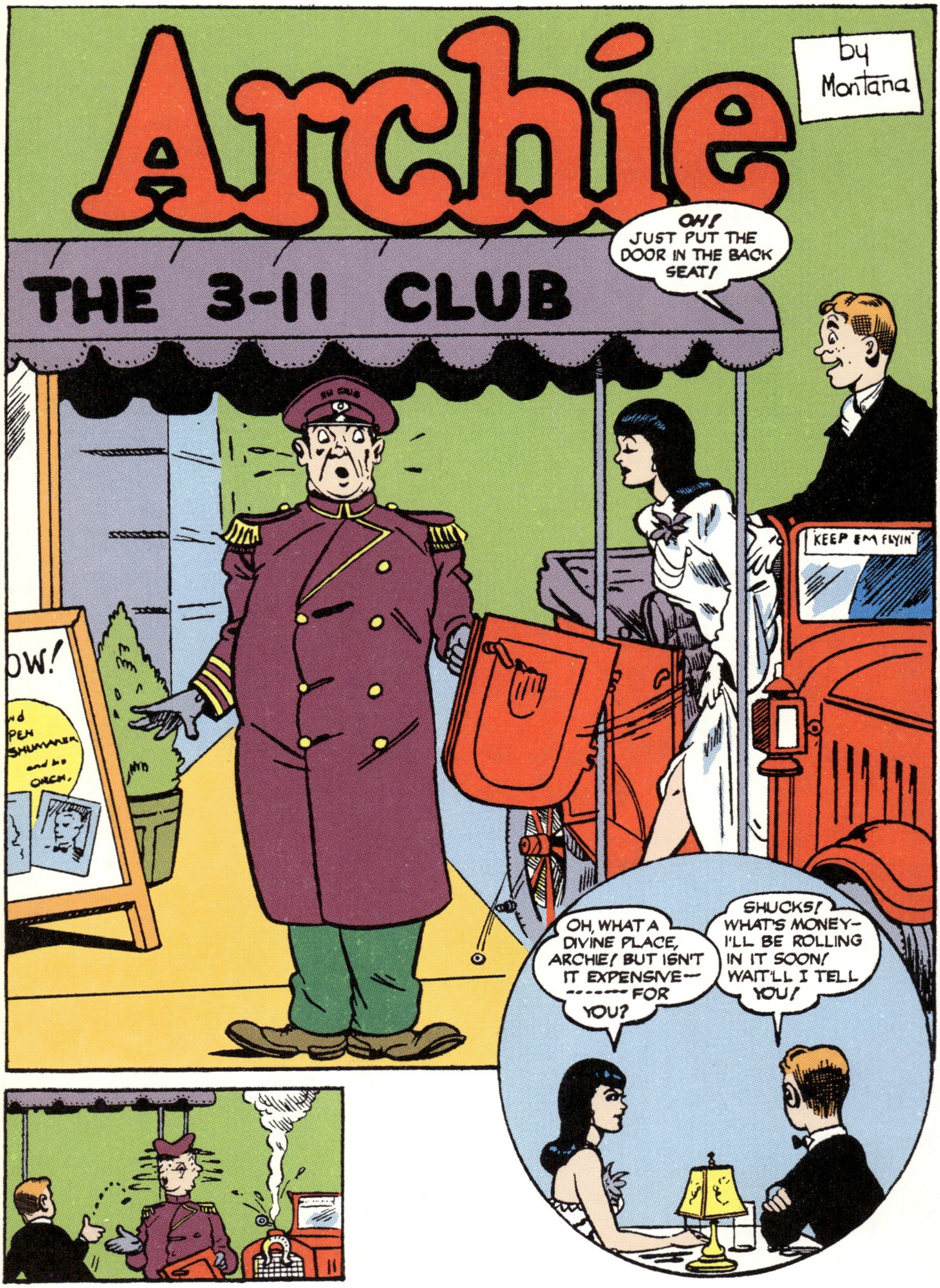
Archie
by Montana
THE 3-11 CLUB
OH! JUST PUT THE DOOR IN THE BACK SEAT!
KEEP EM FLYIN
OH, WHAT A DIVINE PLACE, ARCHIE! BUT ISN'T IT EXPENSIVE-- ------ FOR YOU?
SHUCKS! WHAT'S MONEY- I'LL BE ROLLING IN IT SOON! WAIT'LL I TELL YOU!

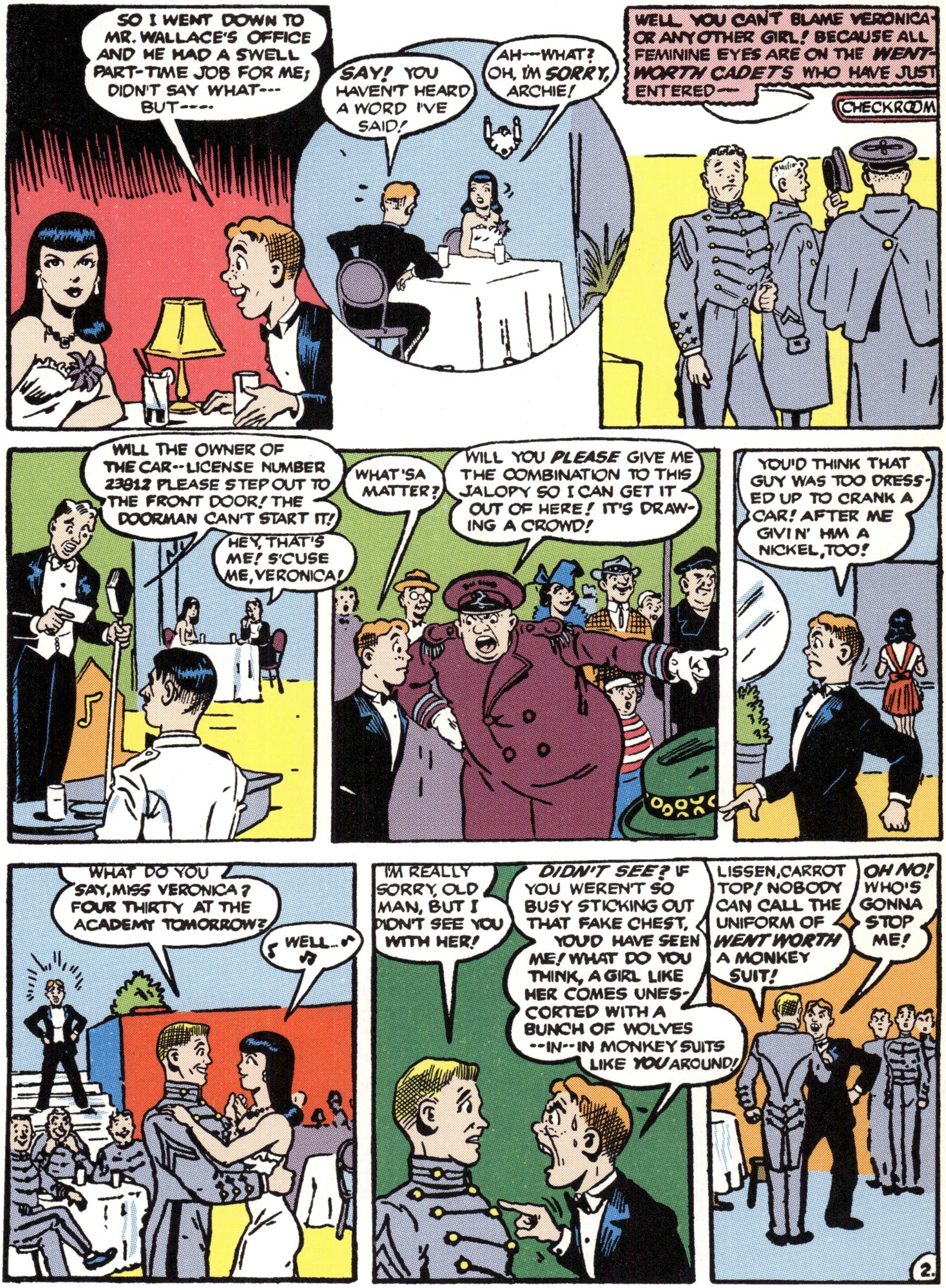
SO I WENT DOWN TO MR. WALLACE'S OFFICE AND HE HAD A SWELL PART-TIME JOB FOR ME; DIDN'T SAY WHAT--- BUT----
SAY! YOU HAVEN'T HEARD A WORD I'VE SAID!
AH---WHAT? OH, I'M SORRY, ARCHIE!
WELL, YOU CAN'T BLAME VERONICA OR ANY OTHER GIRL! BECAUSE ALL FEMININE EYES ARE ON THE WENTWORTH CADETS WHO HAVE JUST ENTERED—
CHECKROOM
WILL THE OWNER OF THE CAR--LICENSE NUMBER 23812 PLEASE STEP OUT TO THE FRONT DOOR! THE DOORMAN CAN'T START IT!
HEY, THAT'S ME! S'CUSE ME, VERONICA!
WHAT'SA MATTER?
WILL YOU PLEASE GIVE ME THE COMBINATION TO THIS JALOPY SO I CAN GET IT OUT OF HERE! IT'S DRAWING A CROWD!
YOU'D THINK THAT GUY WAS TOO DRESSED UP TO CRANK A CAR! AFTER ME GIVIN' HIM A NICKEL, TOO!
WHAT DO YOU SAY, MISS VERONICA? FOUR THIRTY AT THE ACADEMY TOMORROW?
WELL...
I'M REALLY SORRY, OLD MAN, BUT I DIDN'T SEE YOU WITH HER!
DIDN'T SEE? IF YOU WEREN'T SO BUSY STICKING OUT THAT FAKE CHEST, YOU'D HAVE SEEN ME! WHAT DO YOU THINK, A GIRL LIKE HER COMES UNESCORTED WITH A BUNCH OF WOLVES --IN--IN MONKEY SUITS LIKE YOU AROUND!
LISSEN, CARROT TOP! NOBODY CAN CALL THE UNIFORM OF WENTWORTH A MONKEY SUIT!
OH NO! WHO'S GONNA STOP ME!
2.

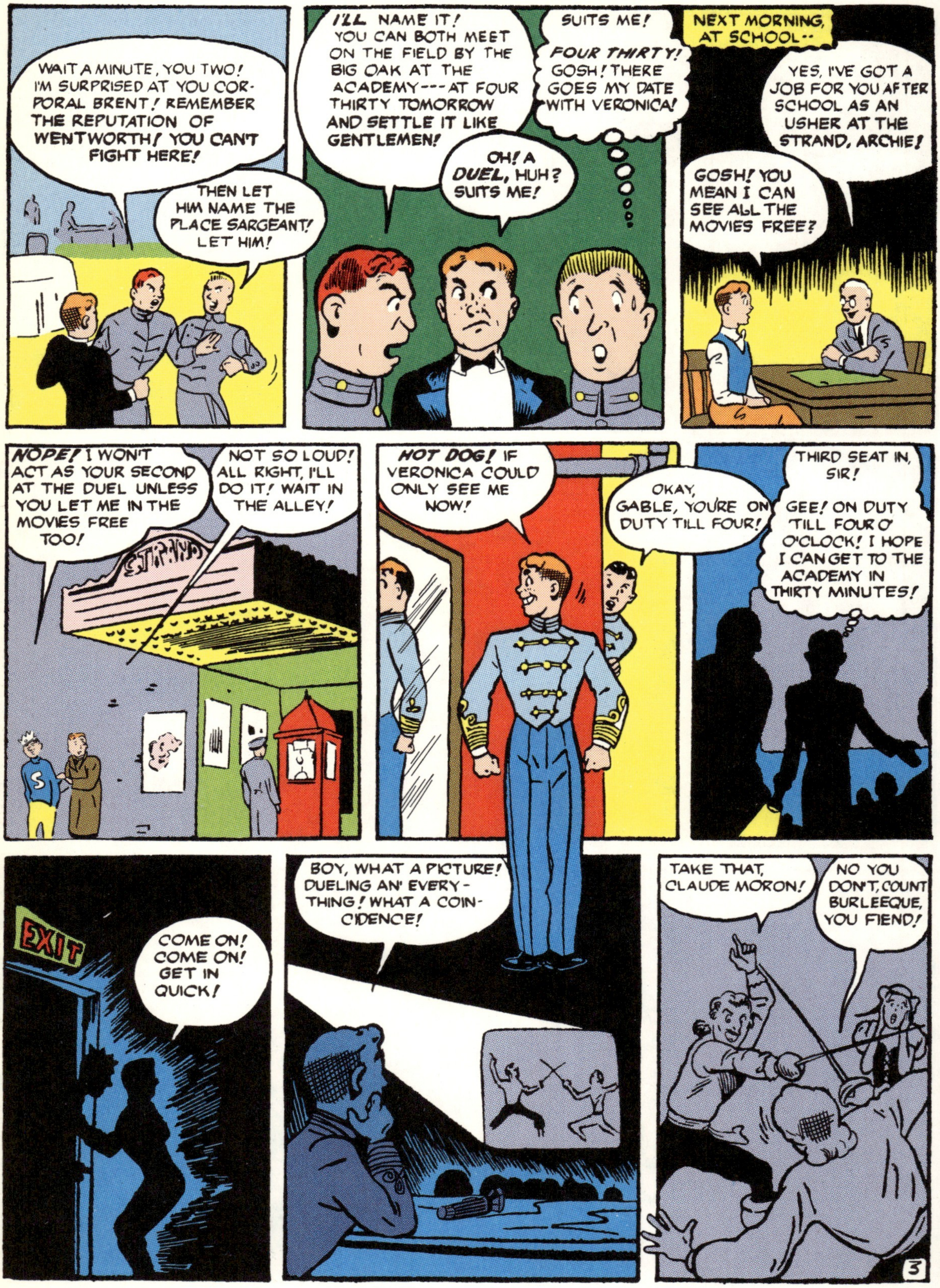
WAIT A MINUTE, YOU TWO! I'M SURPRISED AT YOU CORPORAL BRENT! REMEMBER THE REPUTATION OF WENTWORTH! YOU CAN'T FIGHT HERE!
THEN LET HIM NAME THE PLACE SARGEANT! LET HIM!
I'LL NAME IT! YOU CAN BOTH MEET ON THE FIELD BY THE BIG OAK AT THE ACADEMY---AT FOUR THIRTY TOMORROW AND SETTLE IT LIKE GENTLEMEN!
OH! A DUEL, HUH? SUITS ME!
SUITS ME!
FOUR THIRTY! GOSH! THERE GOES MY DATE WITH VERONICA!
NEXT MORNING, AT SCHOOL--
YES, I'VE GOT A JOB FOR YOU AFTER SCHOOL AS AN USHER AT THE STRAND, ARCHIE!
GOSH! YOU MEAN I CAN SEE ALL THE MOVIES FREE?
NOPE! I WON'T ACT AS YOUR SECOND AT THE DUEL UNLESS YOU LET ME IN THE MOVIES FREE TOO!
NOT SO LOUD! ALL RIGHT, I'LL DO IT! WAIT IN THE ALLEY!
HOT DOG! IF VERONICA COULD ONLY SEE ME NOW!
OKAY, GABLE, YOU'RE ON DUTY TILL FOUR!
THIRD SEAT IN, SIR!
GEE! ON DUTY 'TILL FOUR O' O'CLOCK! I HOPE I CAN GET TO THE ACADEMY IN THIRTY MINUTES!
EXIT
COME ON! COME ON! GET IN QUICK!
BOY, WHAT A PICTURE! DUELING AN' EVERYTHING! WHAT A COINCIDENCE!
TAKE THAT, CLAUDE MORON!
NO YOU DON'T, COUNT BURLEEQUE, YOU FIEND!
3

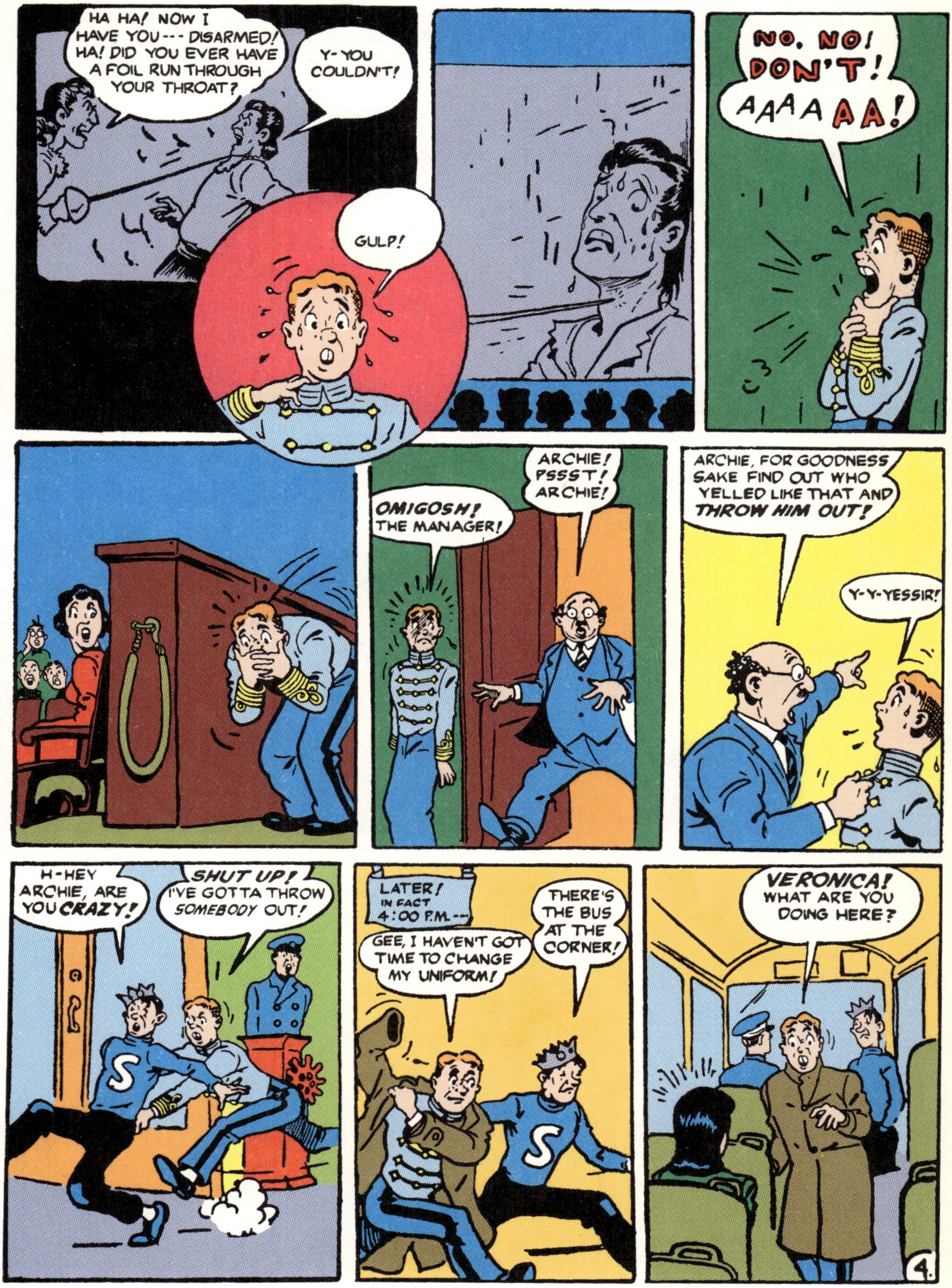
HA HA! NOW I HAVE YOU--- DISARMED! HA! DID YOU EVER HAVE A FOIL RUN THROUGH YOUR THROAT?
Y-YOU COULDN'T!
GULP!
NO, NO! DON'T! AAAAAA!
OMIGOSH! THE MANAGER!
ARCHIE! PSSST! ARCHIE!
ARCHIE, FOR GOODNESS SAKE FIND OUT WHO YELLED LIKE THAT AND THROW HIM OUT!
Y-Y-YESSIR!
H-HEY ARCHIE, ARE YOU CRAZY!
SHUT UP! I'VE GOTTA THROW SOMEBODY OUT!
LATER! IN FACT 4:00 P.M.--
GEE, I HAVEN'T GOT TIME TO CHANGE MY UNIFORM!
THERE'S THE BUS AT THE CORNER!
VERONICA! WHAT ARE YOU DOING HERE?
4.

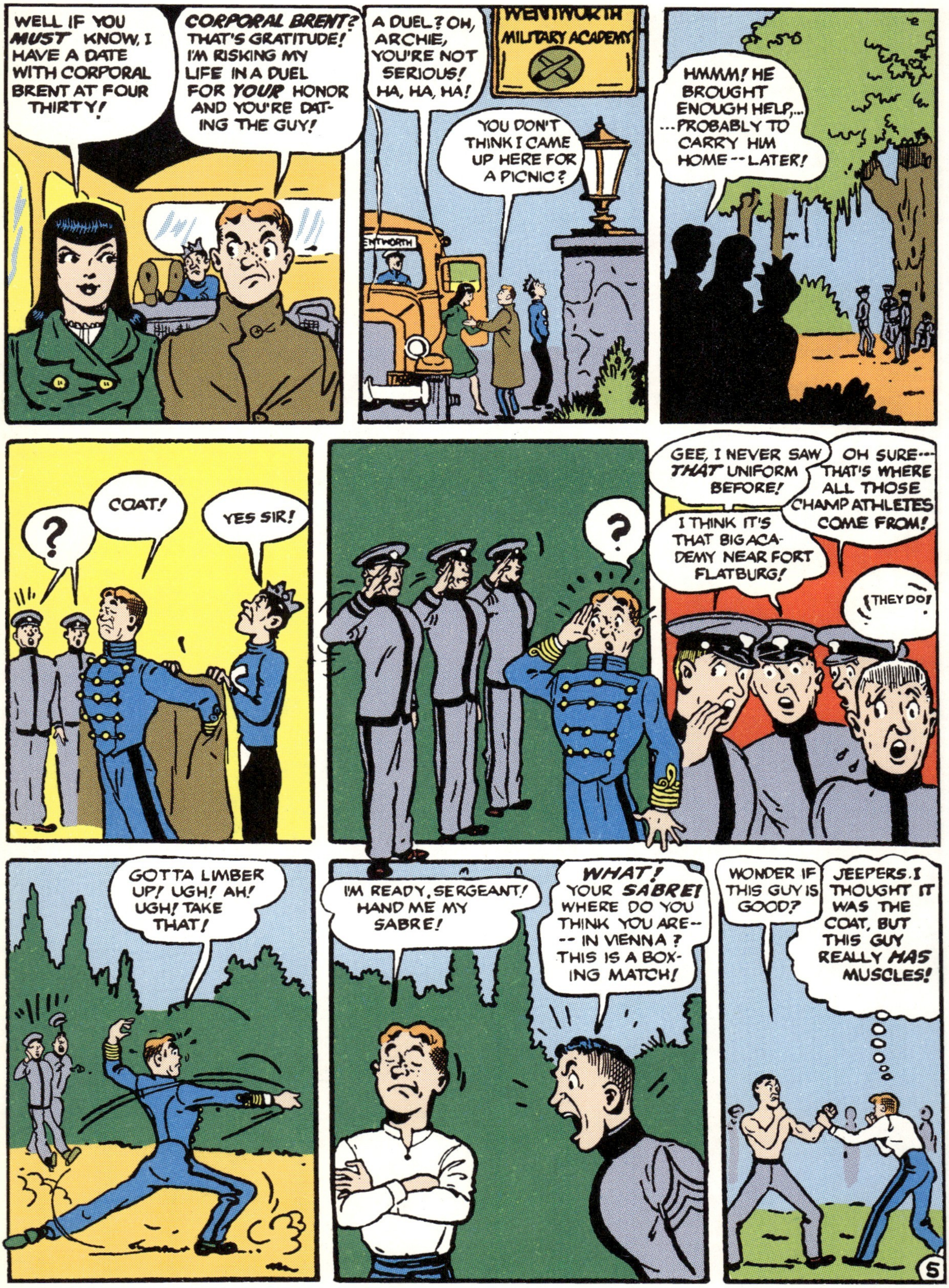
WELL IF YOU MUST KNOW, I HAVE A DATE WITH CORPORAL BRENT AT FOUR THIRTY!
CORPORAL BRENT? THAT'S GRATITUDE! I'M RISKING MY LIFE IN A DUEL FOR YOUR HONOR AND YOU'RE DATING THE GUY!
A DUEL? OH, ARCHIE, YOU'RE NOT SERIOUS! HA, HA, HA!
WENTWORTH MILITARY ACADEMY
YOU DON'T THINK I CAME UP HERE FOR A PICNIC?
HMMM! HE BROUGHT ENOUGH HELP... ...PROBABLY TO CARRY HIM HOME -- LATER!
?
COAT!
YES SIR!
?
GEE, I NEVER SAW THAT UNIFORM BEFORE!
OH SURE-- THAT'S WHERE ALL THOSE CHAMP ATHLETES COME FROM!
I THINK IT'S THAT BIG ACADEMY NEAR FORT FLATBURG!
THEY DO!
GOTTA LIMBER UP! UGH! AH! UGH! TAKE THAT!
I'M READY, SERGEANT! HAND ME MY SABRE!
WHAT! YOUR SABRE! WHERE DO YOU THINK YOU ARE-- -- IN VIENNA? THIS IS A BOXING MATCH!
WONDER IF THIS GUY IS GOOD?
JEEPERS, I THOUGHT IT WAS THE COAT, BUT THIS GUY REALLY HAS MUSCLES!
5

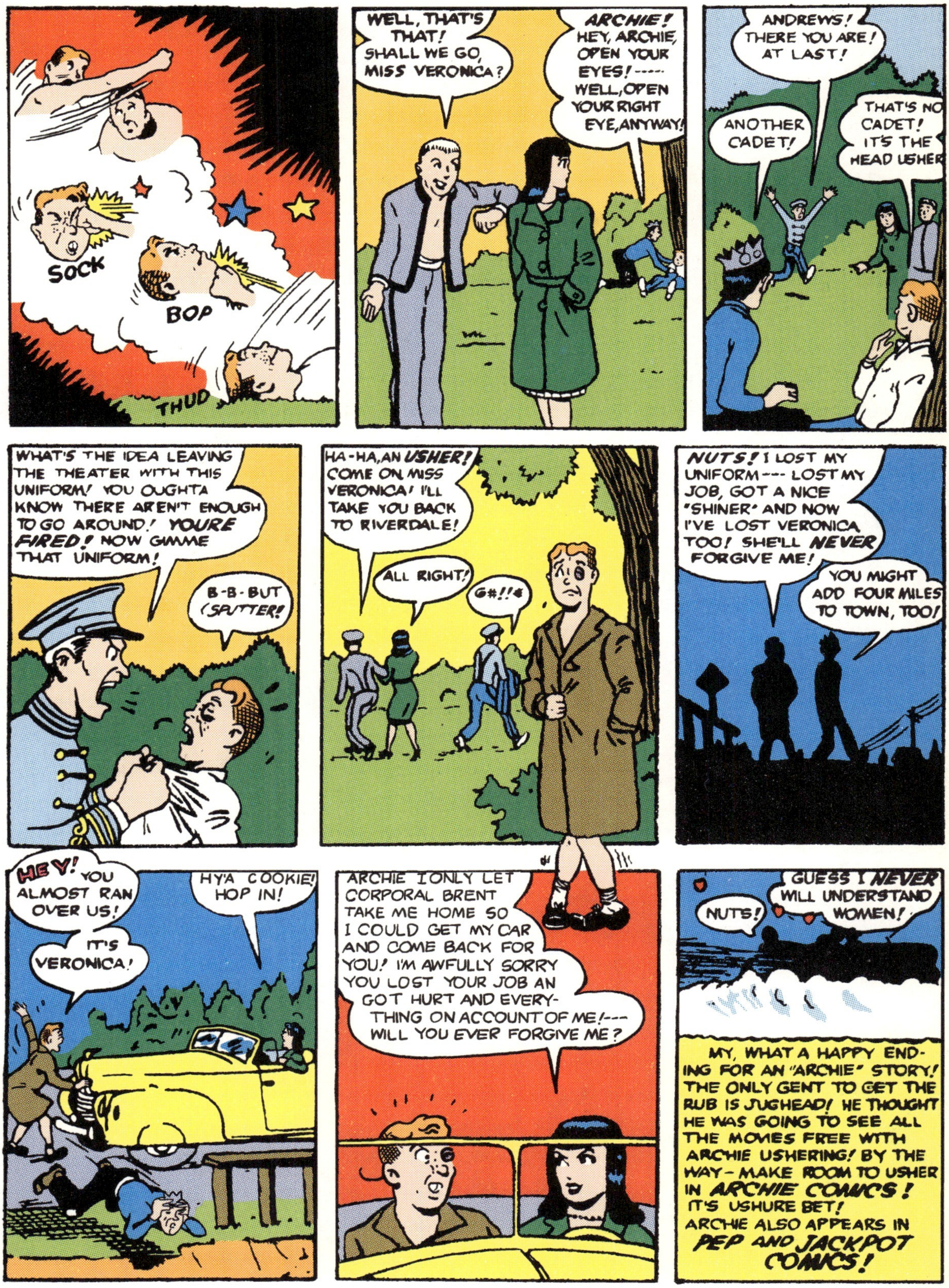
SOCK
BOP
THUD
WELL, THAT'S THAT! SHALL WE GO, MISS VERONICA?
ARCHIE! HEY, ARCHIE, OPEN YOUR EYES!---- WELL, OPEN YOUR RIGHT EYE, ANYWAY!
ANDREWS! THERE YOU ARE! AT LAST!
ANOTHER CADET!
THAT'S NO CADET! IT'S THE HEAD USHER
WHAT'S THE IDEA LEAVING THE THEATER WITH THIS UNIFORM! YOU OUGHTA KNOW THERE AREN'T ENOUGH TO GO AROUND! YOURE FIRED! NOW GIMME THAT UNIFORM!
B-B-BUT (SPUTTER!
HA-HA, AN USHER! COME ON MISS VERONICA! I'LL TAKE YOU BACK TO RIVERDALE!
ALL RIGHT!
G#!!¢
NUTS! I LOST MY UNIFORM--- LOST MY JOB, GOT A NICE "SHINER" AND NOW I'VE LOST VERONICA TOO! SHE'LL NEVER FORGIVE ME!
YOU MIGHT ADD FOUR MILES TO TOWN, TOO!
HEY! YOU ALMOST RAN OVER US!
IT'S VERONICA!
HY'A COOKIE! HOP IN!
ARCHIE I ONLY LET CORPORAL BRENT TAKE ME HOME SO I COULD GET MY CAR AND COME BACK FOR YOU! I'M AWFULLY SORRY YOU LOST YOUR JOB AN GOT HURT AND EVERYTHING ON ACCOUNT OF ME!--- WILL YOU EVER FORGIVE ME?
NUTS!
GUESS I NEVER WILL UNDERSTAND WOMEN!
MY, WHAT A HAPPY ENDING FOR AN "ARCHIE" STORY! THE ONLY GENT TO GET THE RUB IS JUGHEAD! HE THOUGHT HE WAS GOING TO SEE ALL THE MOVIES FREE WITH ARCHIE USHERING! BY THE WAY- MAKE ROOM TO USHER IN ARCHIE COMICS! IT'S USHURE BET! ARCHIE ALSO APPEARS IN PEP AND JACKPOT COMICS!

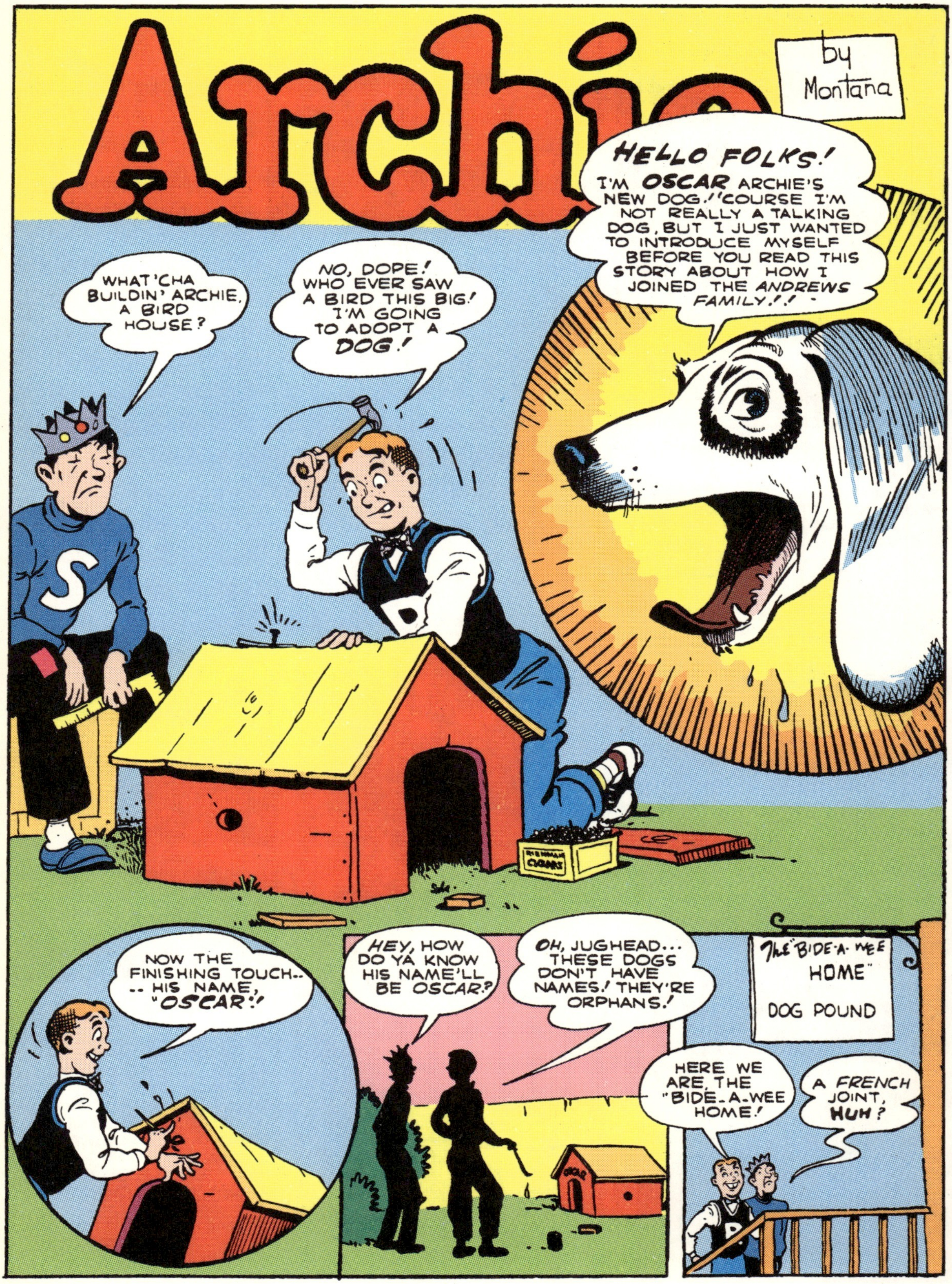
Archie
by Montana
HELLO FOLKS! I'M OSCAR ARCHIE'S NEW DOG! 'COURSE I'M NOT REALLY A TALKING DOG, BUT I JUST WANTED TO INTRODUCE MYSELF BEFORE YOU READ THIS STORY ABOUT HOW I JOINED THE ANDREWS FAMILY!!
WHAT'CHA BUILDIN' ARCHIE, A BIRD HOUSE?
NO, DOPE! WHO EVER SAW A BIRD THIS BIG! I'M GOING TO ADOPT A DOG!
NOW THE FINISHING TOUCH-- HIS NAME, "OSCAR"!
HEY, HOW DO YA KNOW HIS NAME'LL BE OSCAR?
OH, JUGHEAD... THESE DOGS DON'T HAVE NAMES! THEY'RE ORPHANS!
The "BIDE-A-WEE HOME" DOG POUND
HERE WE ARE, THE "BIDE-A-WEE HOME!"
A FRENCH JOINT, HUH?

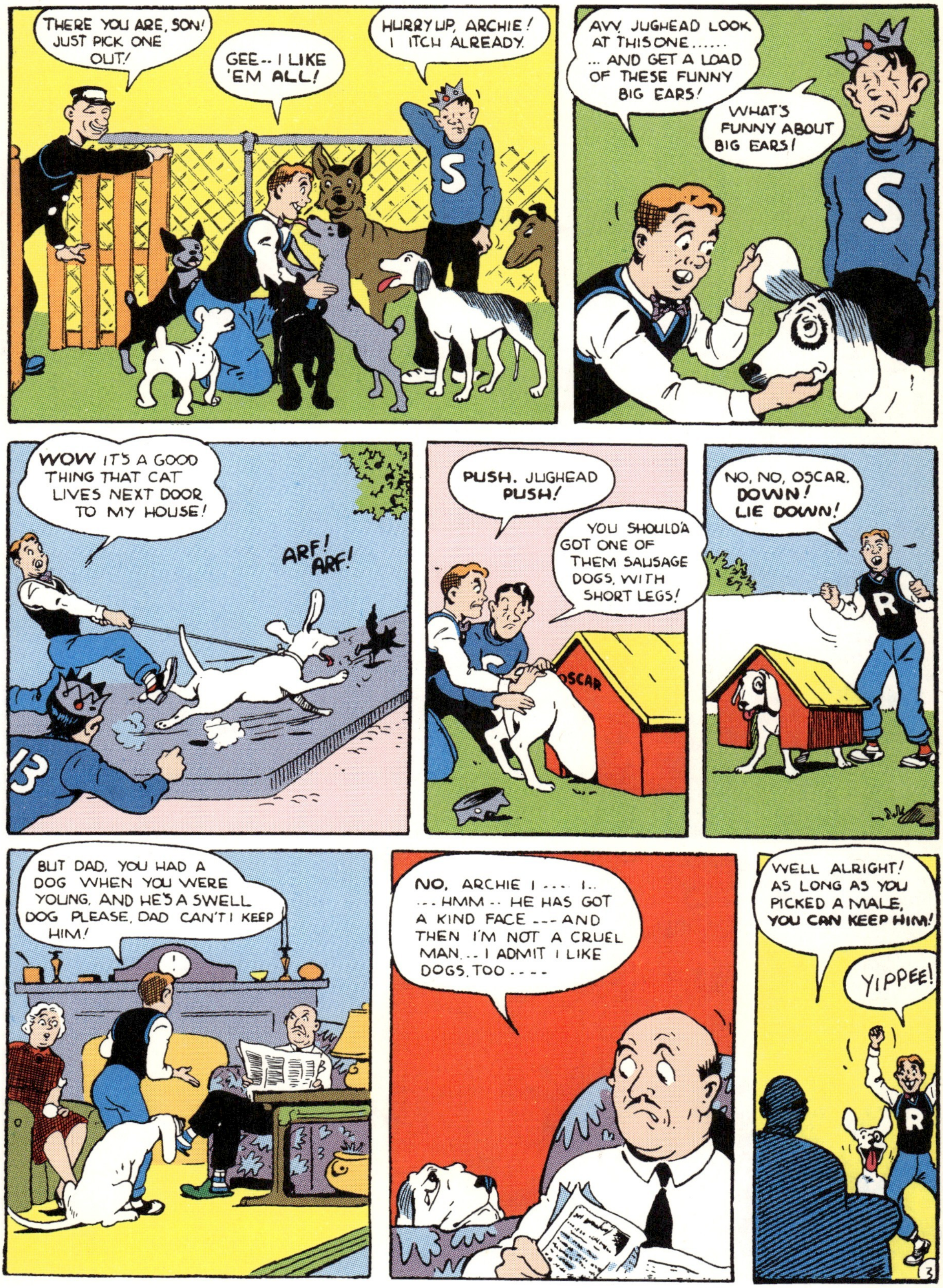
THERE YOU ARE, SON! JUST PICK ONE OUT!
GEE-- I LIKE 'EM ALL!
HURRY UP, ARCHIE! I ITCH ALREADY.
AW, JUGHEAD LOOK AT THIS ONE...... ... AND GET A LOAD OF THESE FUNNY BIG EARS!
WHAT'S FUNNY ABOUT BIG EARS!
WOW IT'S A GOOD THING THAT CAT LIVES NEXT DOOR TO MY HOUSE!
ARF! ARF!
13
PUSH. JUGHEAD PUSH!
YOU SHOULD'A GOT ONE OF THEM SAUSAGE DOGS, WITH SHORT LEGS!
OSCAR
NO, NO, OSCAR. DOWN! LIE DOWN!
BUT DAD, YOU HAD A DOG WHEN YOU WERE YOUNG, AND HE'S A SWELL DOG PLEASE, DAD CAN'T I KEEP HIM!
NO, ARCHIE I --- I.. --- HMM -- HE HAS GOT A KIND FACE --- AND THEN I'M NOT A CRUEL MAN... I ADMIT I LIKE DOGS, TOO ----
WELL ALRIGHT! AS LONG AS YOU PICKED A MALE, YOU CAN KEEP HIM!
YIPPEE!
3

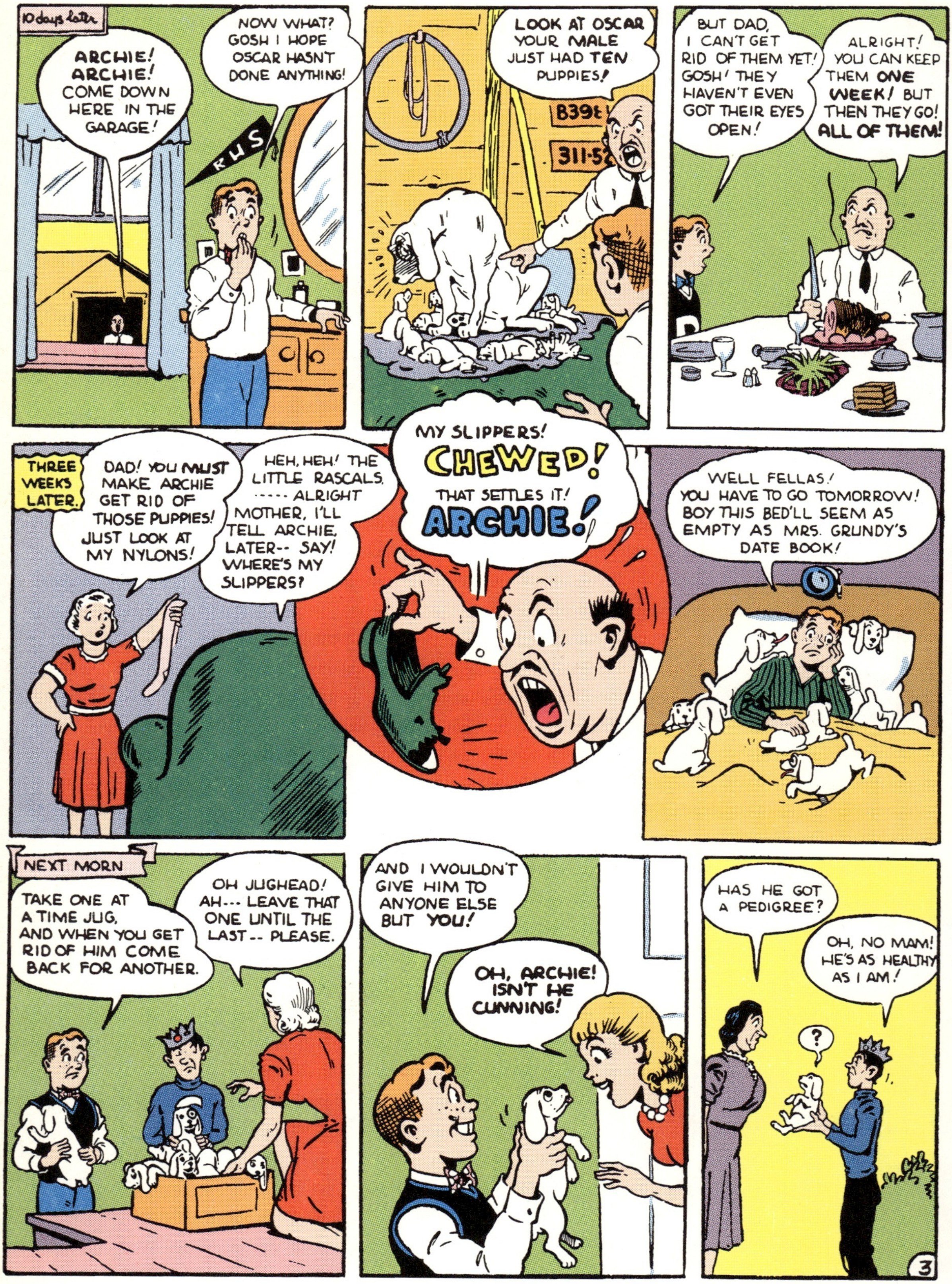
10 days later
ARCHIE! ARCHIE! COME DOWN HERE IN THE GARAGE!
NOW WHAT? GOSH I HOPE OSCAR HASN'T DONE ANYTHING!
R H S
LOOK AT OSCAR YOUR MALE JUST HAD TEN PUPPIES!
BUT DAD, I CAN'T GET RID OF THEM YET! GOSH! THEY HAVEN'T EVEN GOT THEIR EYES OPEN!
ALRIGHT! YOU CAN KEEP THEM ONE WEEK! BUT THEN THEY GO! ALL OF THEM!
THREE WEEKS LATER.
DAD! YOU MUST MAKE ARCHIE GET RID OF THOSE PUPPIES! JUST LOOK AT MY NYLONS!
HEH, HEH! THE LITTLE RASCALS. ----- ALRIGHT MOTHER, I'LL TELL ARCHIE, LATER-- SAY! WHERE'S MY SLIPPERS?
MY SLIPPERS! CHEWED! THAT SETTLES IT! ARCHIE!
WELL FELLAS! YOU HAVE TO GO TOMORROW! BOY THIS BED'LL SEEM AS EMPTY AS MRS. GRUNDY'S DATE BOOK!
NEXT MORN
TAKE ONE AT A TIME JUG, AND WHEN YOU GET RID OF HIM COME BACK FOR ANOTHER.
OH JUGHEAD! AH--- LEAVE THAT ONE UNTIL THE LAST -- PLEASE.
AND I WOULDN'T GIVE HIM TO ANYONE ELSE BUT YOU!
OH, ARCHIE! ISN'T HE CUNNING!
HAS HE GOT A PEDIGREE?
OH, NO MAM! HE'S AS HEALTHY AS I AM!
?
3

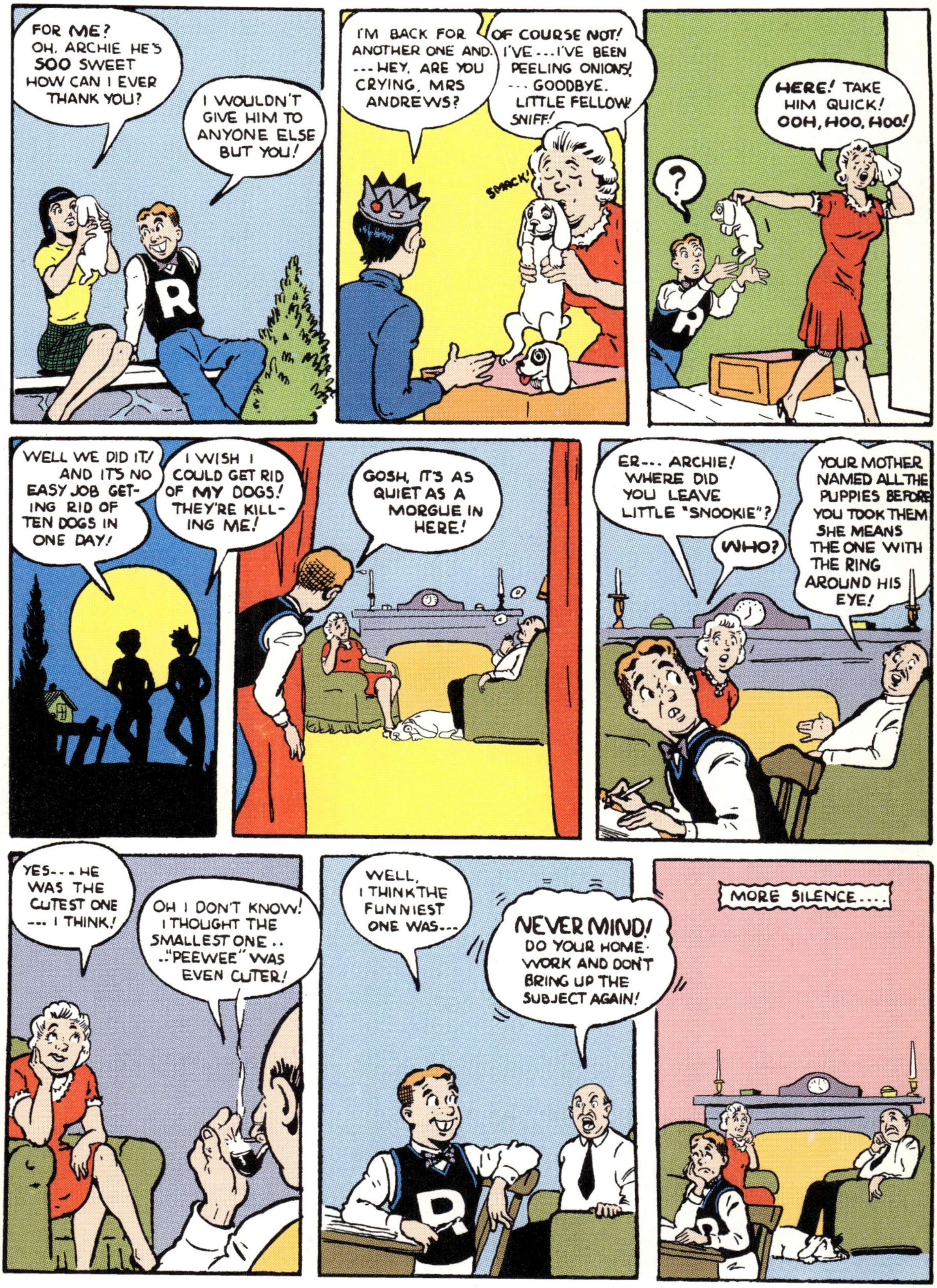
FOR ME? OH, ARCHIE HE'S SOO SWEET HOW CAN I EVER THANK YOU?
I WOULDN'T GIVE HIM TO ANYONE ELSE BUT YOU!
I'M BACK FOR ANOTHER ONE AND. --- HEY, ARE YOU CRYING, MRS ANDREWS?
OF COURSE NOT! I'VE --- I'VE BEEN PEELING ONIONS! --- GOODBYE. LITTLE FELLOW! SNIFF!
SMACK!
HERE! TAKE HIM QUICK! OOH, HOO, HOO!
?
WELL WE DID IT! AND IT'S NO EASY JOB GETTING RID OF TEN DOGS IN ONE DAY!
I WISH I COULD GET RID OF MY DOGS! THEY'RE KILLING ME!
GOSH, IT'S AS QUIET AS A MORGUE IN HERE!
ER--- ARCHIE! WHERE DID YOU LEAVE LITTLE "SNOOKIE"?
WHO?
YOUR MOTHER NAMED ALL THE PUPPIES BEFORE YOU TOOK THEM SHE MEANS THE ONE WITH THE RING AROUND HIS EYE!
YES--- HE WAS THE CUTEST ONE --- I THINK!
OH I DON'T KNOW! I THOUGHT THE SMALLEST ONE .. .."PEEWEE" WAS EVEN CUTER!
WELL, I THINK THE FUNNIEST ONE WAS---
NEVER MIND! DO YOUR HOMEWORK AND DON'T BRING UP THE SUBJECT AGAIN!
MORE SILENCE....

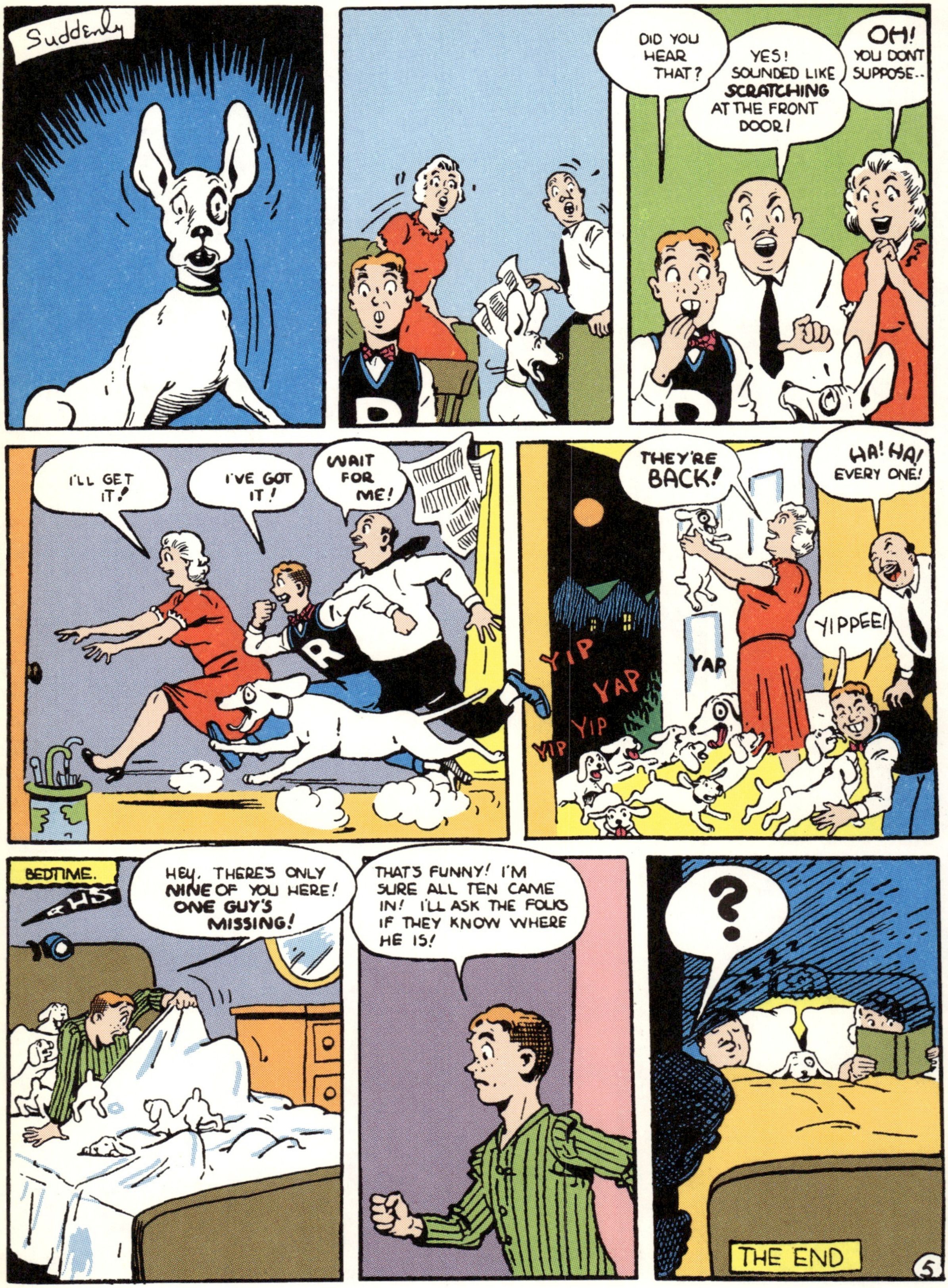

Suddenly
DID YOU HEAR THAT?
YES! SOUNDED LIKE SCRATCHING AT THE FRONT DOOR!
OH! YOU DONT SUPPOSE..
I'LL GET IT!
I'VE GOT IT!
WAIT FOR ME!
THEY'RE BACK!
HA! HA! EVERY ONE!
YIP YAP YIP YIP
YAP
YIPPEE!
BEDTIME.
HEY, THERE'S ONLY NINE OF YOU HERE! ONE GUY'S MISSING!
THAT'S FUNNY! I'M SURE ALL TEN CAME IN! I'LL ASK THE FOLKS IF THEY KNOW WHERE HE IS!
?
THE END
5

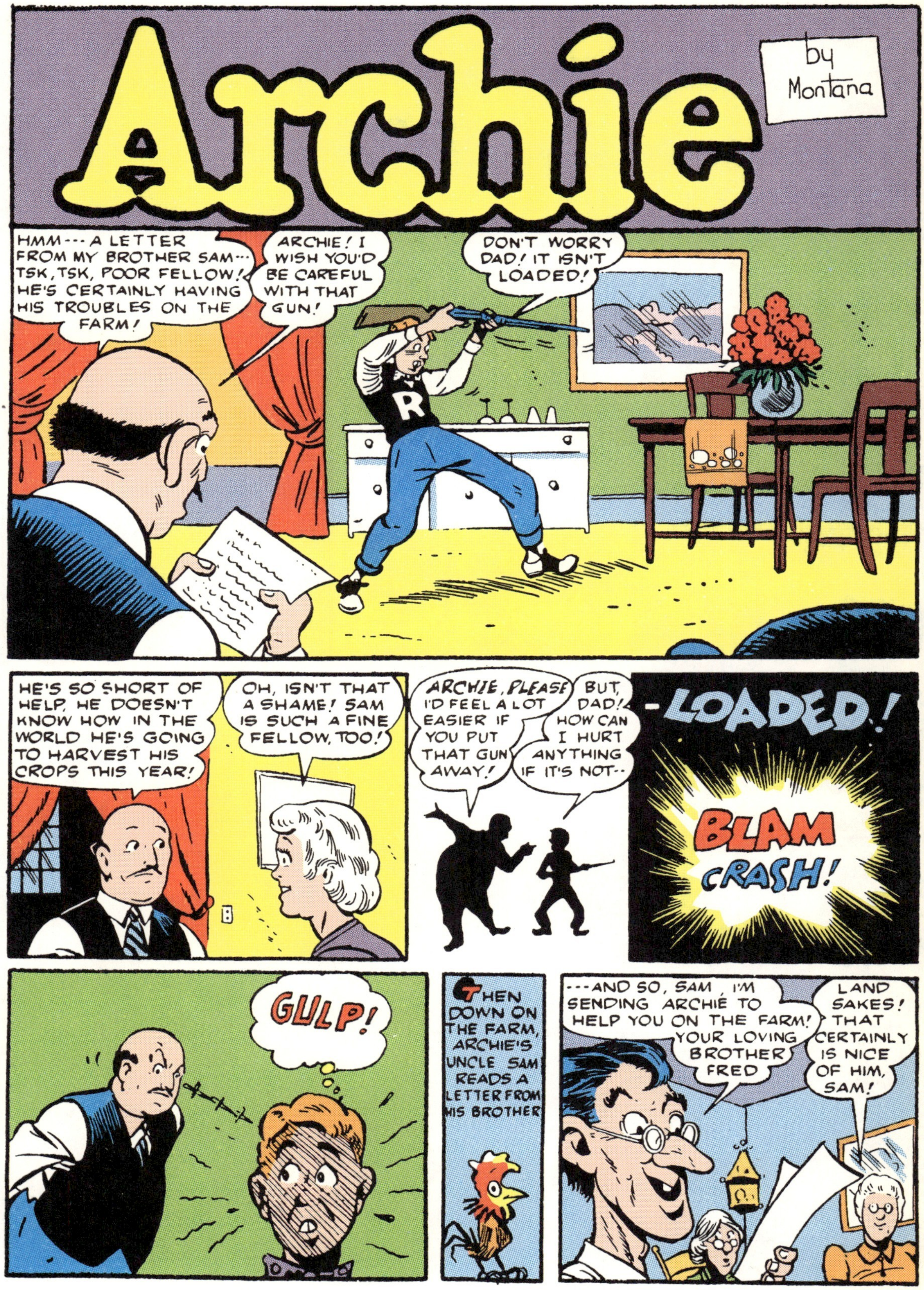
Archie
by Montana
HMM--- A LETTER FROM MY BROTHER SAM--- TSK, TSK, POOR FELLOW! HE'S CERTAINLY HAVING HIS TROUBLES ON THE FARM!
ARCHIE! I WISH YOU'D BE CAREFUL WITH THAT GUN!
DON'T WORRY DAD! IT ISN'T LOADED!
HE'S SO SHORT OF HELP, HE DOESN'T KNOW HOW IN THE WORLD HE'S GOING TO HARVEST HIS CROPS THIS YEAR!
OH, ISN'T THAT A SHAME! SAM IS SUCH A FINE FELLOW, TOO!
ARCHIE, PLEASE I'D FEEL A LOT EASIER IF YOU PUT THAT GUN AWAY!
BUT, DAD! HOW CAN I HURT ANYTHING IF IT'S NOT--
-LOADED!
BLAM
CRASH!
GULP!
THEN DOWN ON THE FARM, ARCHIE'S UNCLE SAM READS A LETTER FROM HIS BROTHER
---AND SO, SAM, I'M SENDING ARCHIE TO HELP YOU ON THE FARM! YOUR LOVING BROTHER FRED
LAND SAKES! THAT CERTAINLY IS NICE OF HIM, SAM!

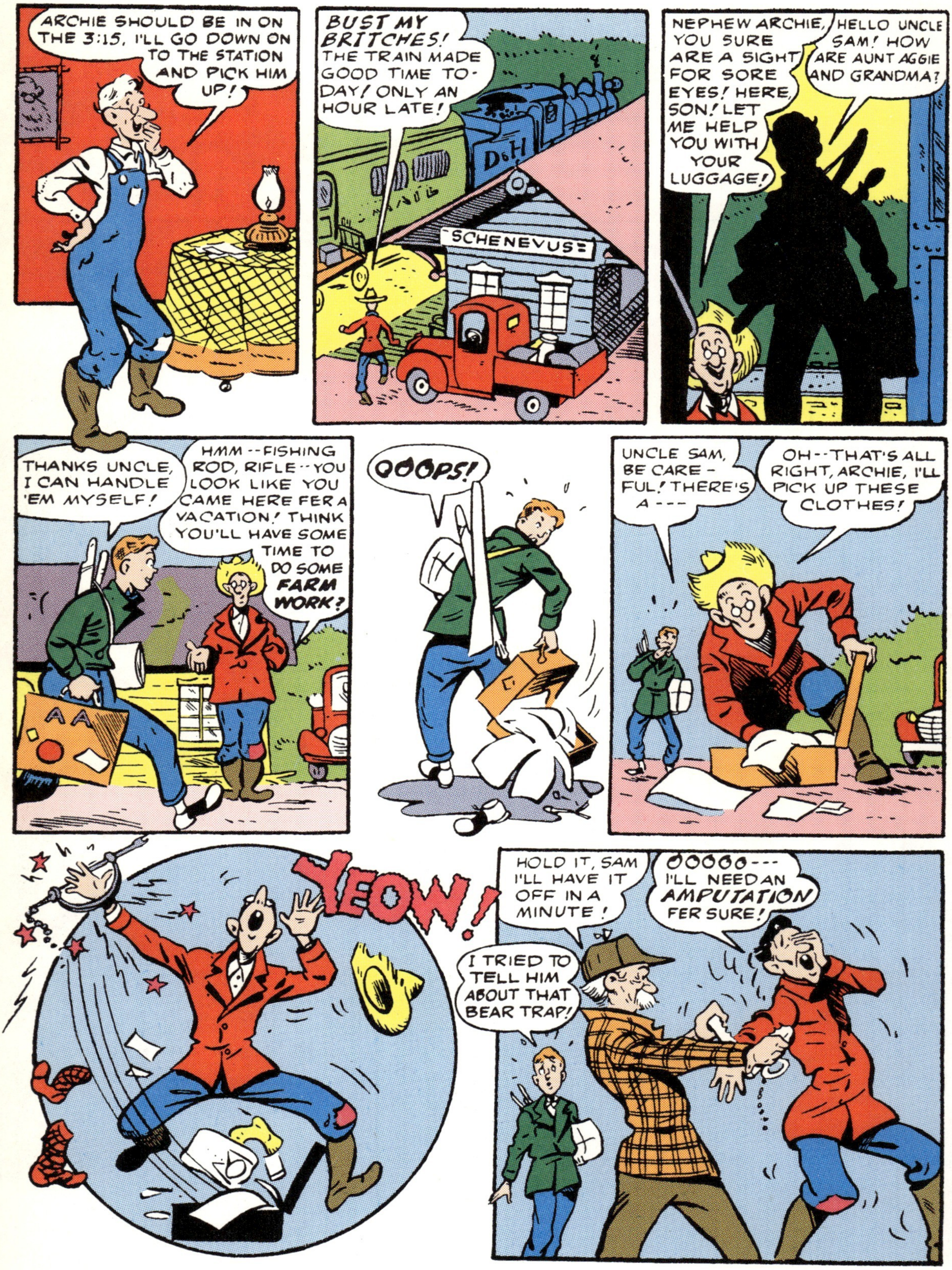
ARCHIE SHOULD BE IN ON THE 3:15. I'LL GO DOWN ON TO THE STATION AND PICK HIM UP!
BUST MY BRITCHES! THE TRAIN MADE GOOD TIME TO-DAY! ONLY AN HOUR LATE!
SCHENEVUS
D&H
NEPHEW ARCHIE, YOU SURE ARE A SIGHT FOR SORE EYES! HERE, SON! LET ME HELP YOU WITH YOUR LUGGAGE!
HELLO UNCLE SAM! HOW ARE AUNT AGGIE AND GRANDMA?
THANKS UNCLE, I CAN HANDLE 'EM MYSELF!
HMM--FISHING ROD, RIFLE--YOU LOOK LIKE YOU CAME HERE FER A VACATION! THINK YOU'LL HAVE SOME TIME TO DO SOME FARM WORK?
AA
OOOPS!
UNCLE SAM, BE CARE-FUL! THERE'S A---
OH--THAT'S ALL RIGHT, ARCHIE, I'LL PICK UP THESE CLOTHES!
YEOW!
HOLD IT, SAM I'LL HAVE IT OFF IN A MINUTE!
OOOOO--- I'LL NEED AN AMPUTATION FER SURE!
I TRIED TO TELL HIM ABOUT THAT BEAR TRAP!

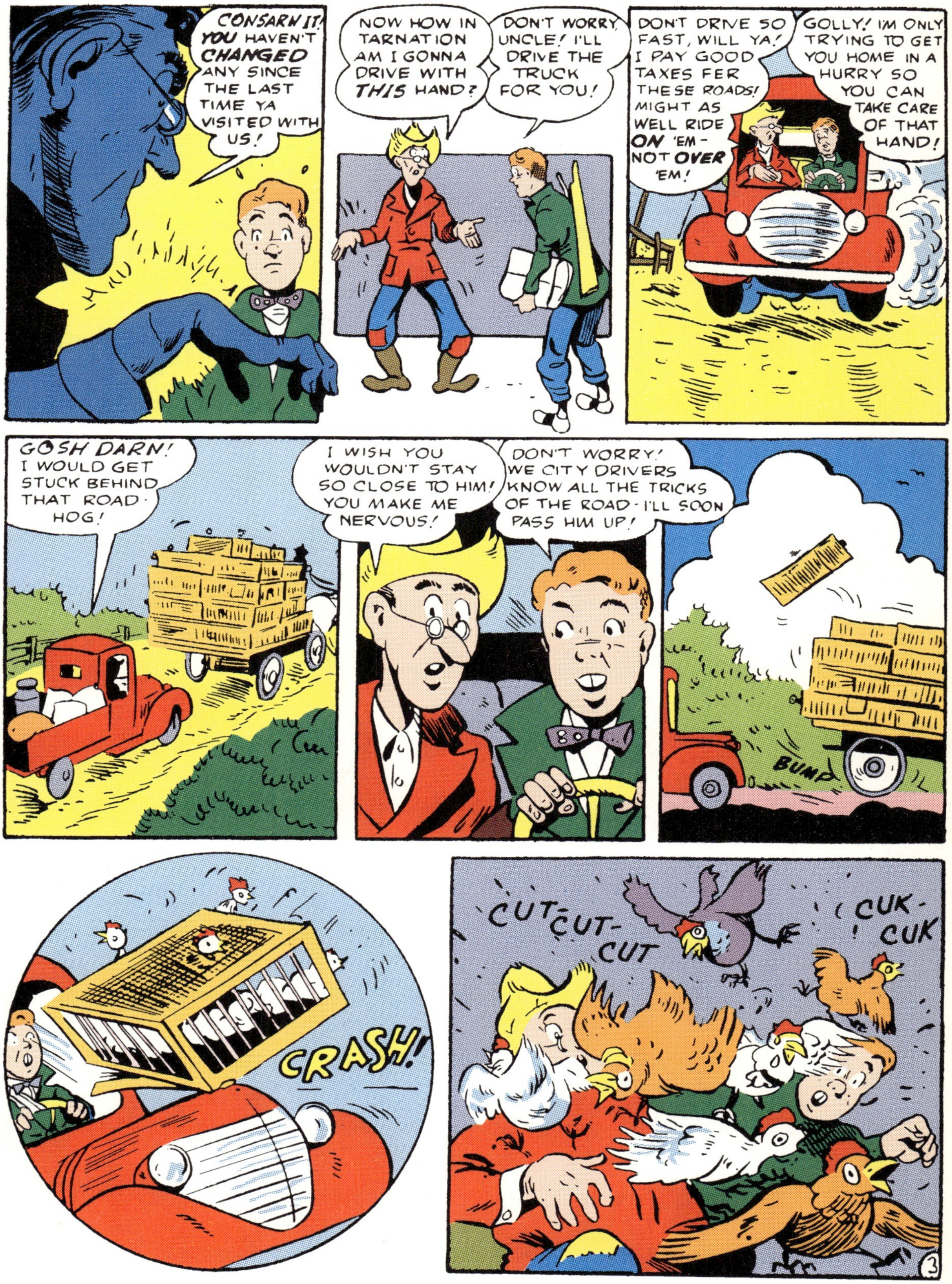
CONSARN IT! YOU HAVEN'T CHANGED ANY SINCE THE LAST TIME YA VISITED WITH US!
NOW HOW IN TARNATION AM I GONNA DRIVE WITH THIS HAND?
DON'T WORRY, UNCLE! I'LL DRIVE THE TRUCK FOR YOU!
DON'T DRIVE SO FAST, WILL YA! I PAY GOOD TAXES FER THESE ROADS! MIGHT AS WELL RIDE ON 'EM - NOT OVER 'EM!
GOLLY! I'M ONLY TRYING TO GET YOU HOME IN A HURRY SO YOU CAN TAKE CARE OF THAT HAND!
GOSH DARN! I WOULD GET STUCK BEHIND THAT ROAD-HOG!
I WISH YOU WOULDN'T STAY SO CLOSE TO HIM! YOU MAKE ME NERVOUS!
DON'T WORRY! WE CITY DRIVERS KNOW ALL THE TRICKS OF THE ROAD - I'LL SOON PASS HIM UP!
BUMP
CRASH!
CUT-CUT-CUT
CUK-CUK
3

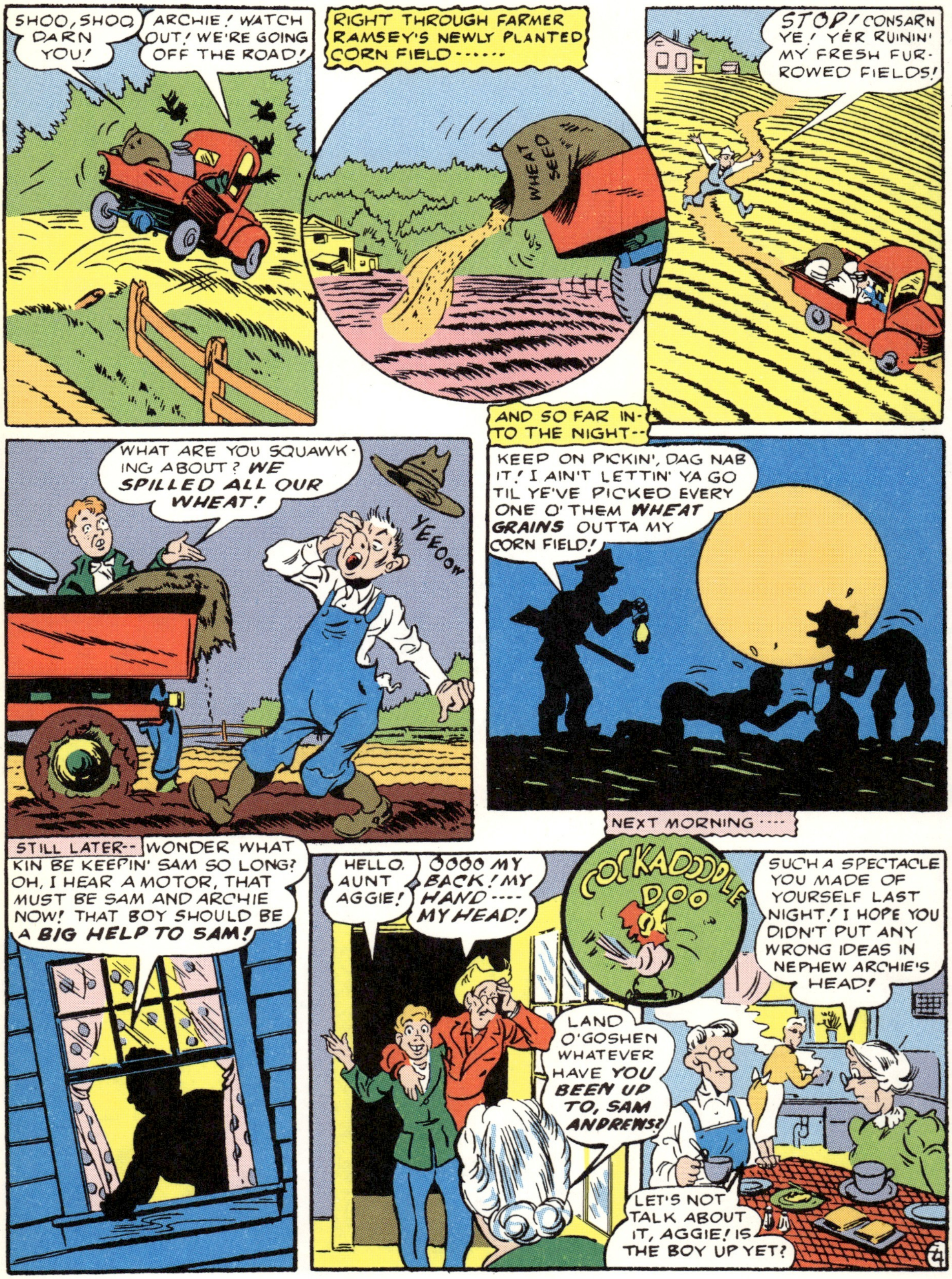

SHOO, SHOO, DARN YOU!
ARCHIE! WATCH OUT! WE'RE GOING OFF THE ROAD!
RIGHT THROUGH FARMER RAMSEY'S NEWLY PLANTED CORN FIELD------
WHEAT SEED
STOP! CONSARN YE! YER RUININ' MY FRESH FUR-ROWED FIELDS!
WHAT ARE YOU SQUAWKING ABOUT? WE SPILLED ALL OUR WHEAT!
YEEOOW
AND SO FAR INTO THE NIGHT--
KEEP ON PICKIN', DAG NAB IT! I AIN'T LETTIN' YA GO TIL YE'VE PICKED EVERY ONE O' THEM WHEAT GRAINS OUTTA MY CORN FIELD!
STILL LATER--
WONDER WHAT KIN BE KEEPIN' SAM SO LONG? OH, I HEAR A MOTOR, THAT MUST BE SAM AND ARCHIE NOW! THAT BOY SHOULD BE A BIG HELP TO SAM!
HELLO, AUNT AGGIE!
OOOO MY BACK! MY HAND---- MY HEAD!
LAND O'GOSHEN WHATEVER HAVE YOU BEEN UP TO, SAM ANDREWS?
NEXT MORNING----
COCKADOODLE DOO
SUCH A SPECTACLE YOU MADE OF YOURSELF LAST NIGHT! I HOPE YOU DIDN'T PUT ANY WRONG IDEAS IN NEPHEW ARCHIE'S HEAD!
LET'S NOT TALK ABOUT IT, AGGIE! IS THE BOY UP YET?
4

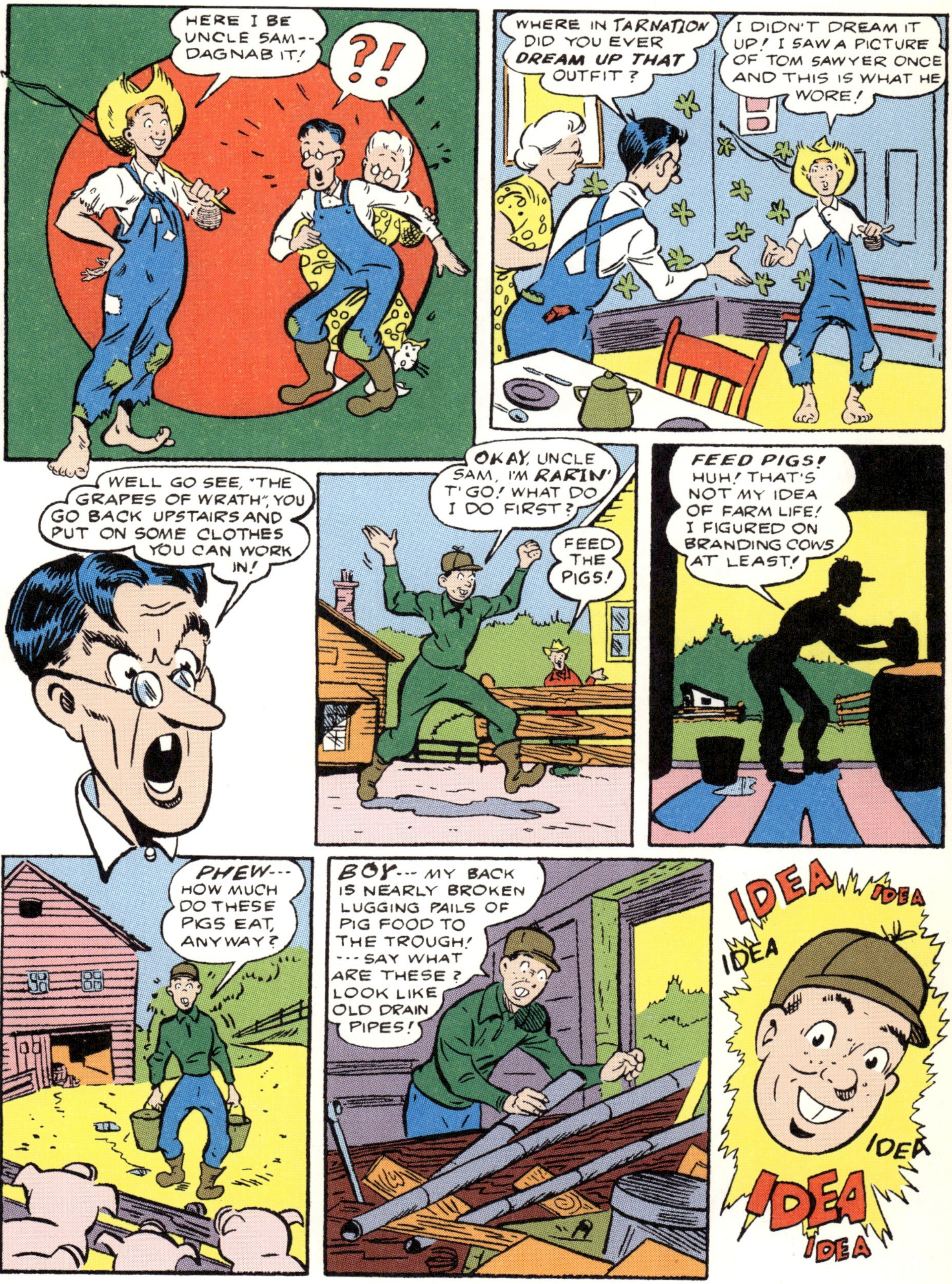

HERE I BE UNCLE SAM-- DAGNAB IT!
?!
WHERE IN TARNATION DID YOU EVER DREAM UP THAT OUTFIT?
I DIDN'T DREAM IT UP! I SAW A PICTURE OF TOM SAWYER ONCE AND THIS IS WHAT HE WORE!
WELL GO SEE, "THE GRAPES OF WRATH", YOU GO BACK UPSTAIRS AND PUT ON SOME CLOTHES YOU CAN WORK IN!
OKAY, UNCLE SAM, I'M RARIN' T'GO! WHAT DO I DO FIRST?
FEED THE PIGS!
FEED PIGS! HUH! THAT'S NOT MY IDEA OF FARM LIFE! I FIGURED ON BRANDING COWS AT LEAST!
PHEW--- HOW MUCH DO THESE PIGS EAT, ANYWAY?
BOY--- MY BACK IS NEARLY BROKEN LUGGING PAILS OF PIG FOOD TO THE TROUGH! --- SAY WHAT ARE THESE? LOOK LIKE OLD DRAIN PIPES!
IDEA
IDEA
IDEA
IDEA
IDEA
IDEA

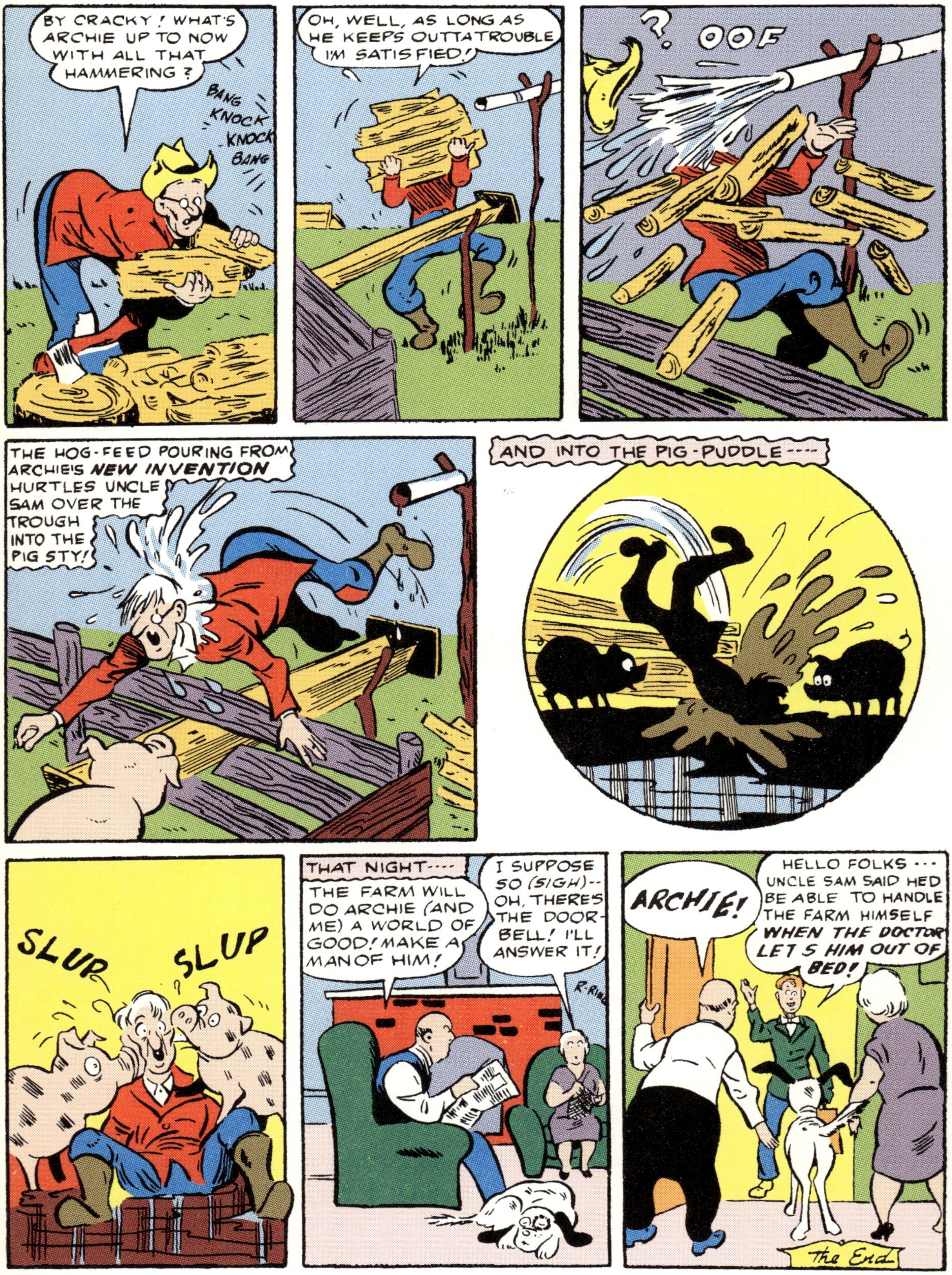
BY CRACKY! WHAT'S ARCHIE UP TO NOW WITH ALL THAT HAMMERING?
BANG KNOCK KNOCK BANG
OH, WELL, AS LONG AS HE KEEPS OUTTATROUBLE I'M SATISFIED!
? OOF
THE HOG-FEED POURING FROM ARCHIE'S NEW INVENTION HURTLES UNCLE SAM OVER THE TROUGH INTO THE PIG STY!
AND INTO THE PIG-PUDDLE----
SLUP SLUP
THAT NIGHT----
THE FARM WILL DO ARCHIE (AND ME) A WORLD OF GOOD! MAKE A MAN OF HIM!
I SUPPOSE SO (SIGH)-- OH, THERE'S THE DOOR-BELL! I'LL ANSWER IT!
ARCHIE!
HELLO FOLKS--- UNCLE SAM SAID HE'D BE ABLE TO HANDLE THE FARM HIMSELF WHEN THE DOCTOR LETS HIM OUT OF BED!
The End

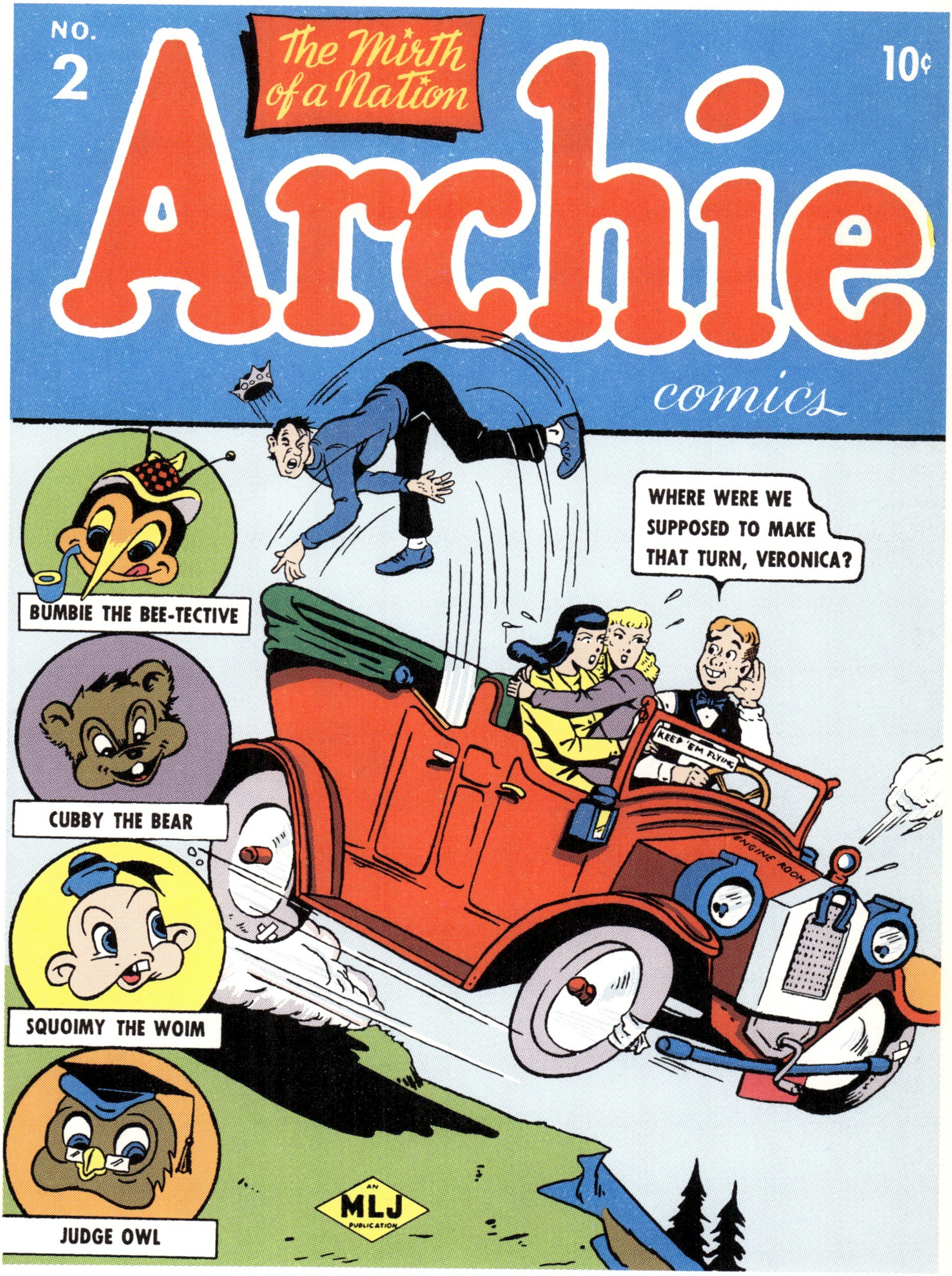
NO. 2
The Mirth of a Nation
Archie
10¢
comics
WHERE WERE WE SUPPOSED TO MAKE THAT TURN, VERONICA?
KEEP 'EM FLYING
ENGINE ROOM
BUMBIE THE BEE-TECTIVE
CUBBY THE BEAR
SQUOIMY THE WOIM
JUDGE OWL
AN MLJ PUBLICATION

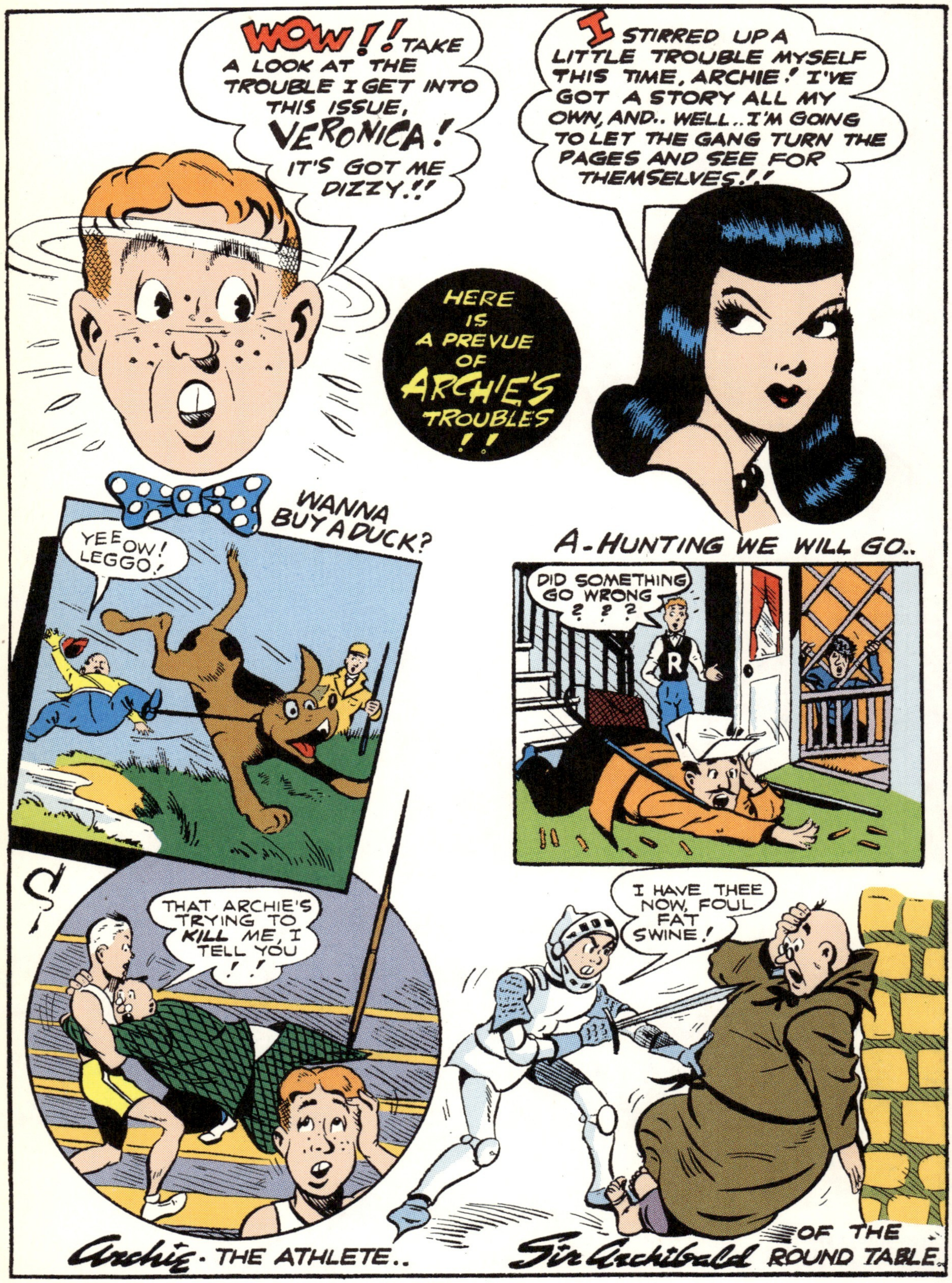
WOW!! TAKE A LOOK AT THE TROUBLE I GET INTO THIS ISSUE, VERONICA! IT'S GOT ME DIZZY!!
I STIRRED UP A LITTLE TROUBLE MYSELF THIS TIME, ARCHIE! I'VE GOT A STORY ALL MY OWN, AND.. WELL..I'M GOING TO LET THE GANG TURN THE PAGES AND SEE FOR THEMSELVES!!
HERE IS A PREVUE OF ARCHIE'S TROUBLES!!
WANNA BUY A DUCK?
YEEOW! LEGGO!
A-HUNTING WE WILL GO..
DID SOMETHING GO WRONG ???
THAT ARCHIE'S TRYING TO KILL ME, I TELL YOU!!
I HAVE THEE NOW, FOUL FAT SWINE!
Archie - THE ATHLETE..
Sir Archibald OF THE ROUND TABLE.

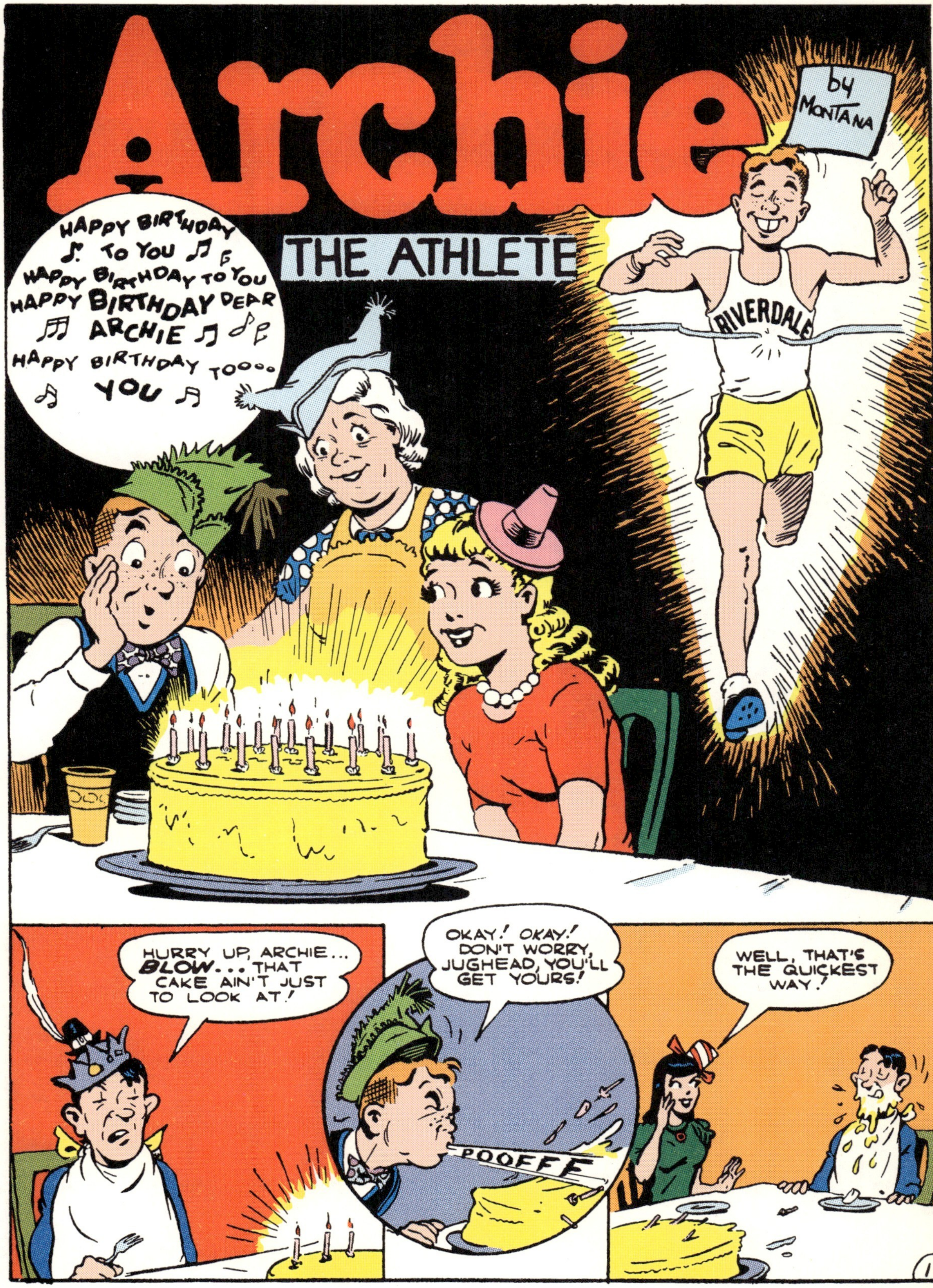
Archie
by MONTANA
THE ATHLETE
RIVERDALE
HAPPY BIRTHDAY TO YOU HAPPY BIRTHDAY TO YOU HAPPY BIRTHDAY DEAR ARCHIE HAPPY BIRTHDAY TOOOO YOU
HURRY UP, ARCHIE... BLOW... THAT CAKE AIN'T JUST TO LOOK AT!
OKAY! OKAY! DON'T WORRY, JUGHEAD, YOU'LL GET YOURS!
POOFFF
WELL, THAT'S THE QUICKEST WAY!
1

AHEM! AS AN EXPERIENCED BIG GAME HUNTER, ALL AROUND MARKSMAN AND...

OH, COME ON, DAD, DON'T MAKE A SPEECH! GIVE IT TO HIM!

OH BOY! JUST WHAT I WANTED! A 22 BOLT ACTION RIFLE!

YOU GET SO. YOU'RE A CRACK POT..ER.. I MEAN A SHOT LIKE ME, AND I'LL TAKE YOU HUNTING WITH ME THIS FALL!

HEY, ARCHIE! COME ON OR YOU'LL BE LATE FOR SCHOOL!

WHATCH THIS SHOT, JUGHEAD!

WELL FOR GOODNESS SAKES! " RIFLE TEAM, REPORTS TODAY AT RANGE IN BASEMENT! WITH OUR NEWEST MEMBER OF THE FACULTY, MR. GLEENBORE!"

TRACK TEAM REPORT TODAY AT STADIUM FOR TRY-OUTS

COACH CHARLIE WHITE WILL H L? TRY-OUTS AND PRACTICE TODAY AT THE RIVERDALE STADIUM IMMEDIATELY AFTER SCHOOL. BRING YOUR OWN TRACK SUIT THERE WILL BE TRYOUS SHOT PUT HIGH JUMP BROAD JUMP JAVELIN T... POLE V... HAM... .00 RELA...

RIFLE TEAM

... WEATHERBEE PRINC.

BETTY LOOK! ISN'T THAT, ARCHIE READING THE TRACK NOTICE?

HOT DOG! THAT'S MADE TO ORDER FOR ME! I'M GONNA SIGN UP FOR THE TEAM, RIGHT NOW!

SAY, WHERE'S THE NEW TEACHER, THIS MR. GLEENBORE ??

HE HAS A CLASS THIS PERIOD..BUT YOU JUST SIGN UP THERE, AND YOU'LL MEET HIM AFTER SCHOOL!

FOR THE RIFLE TE

2

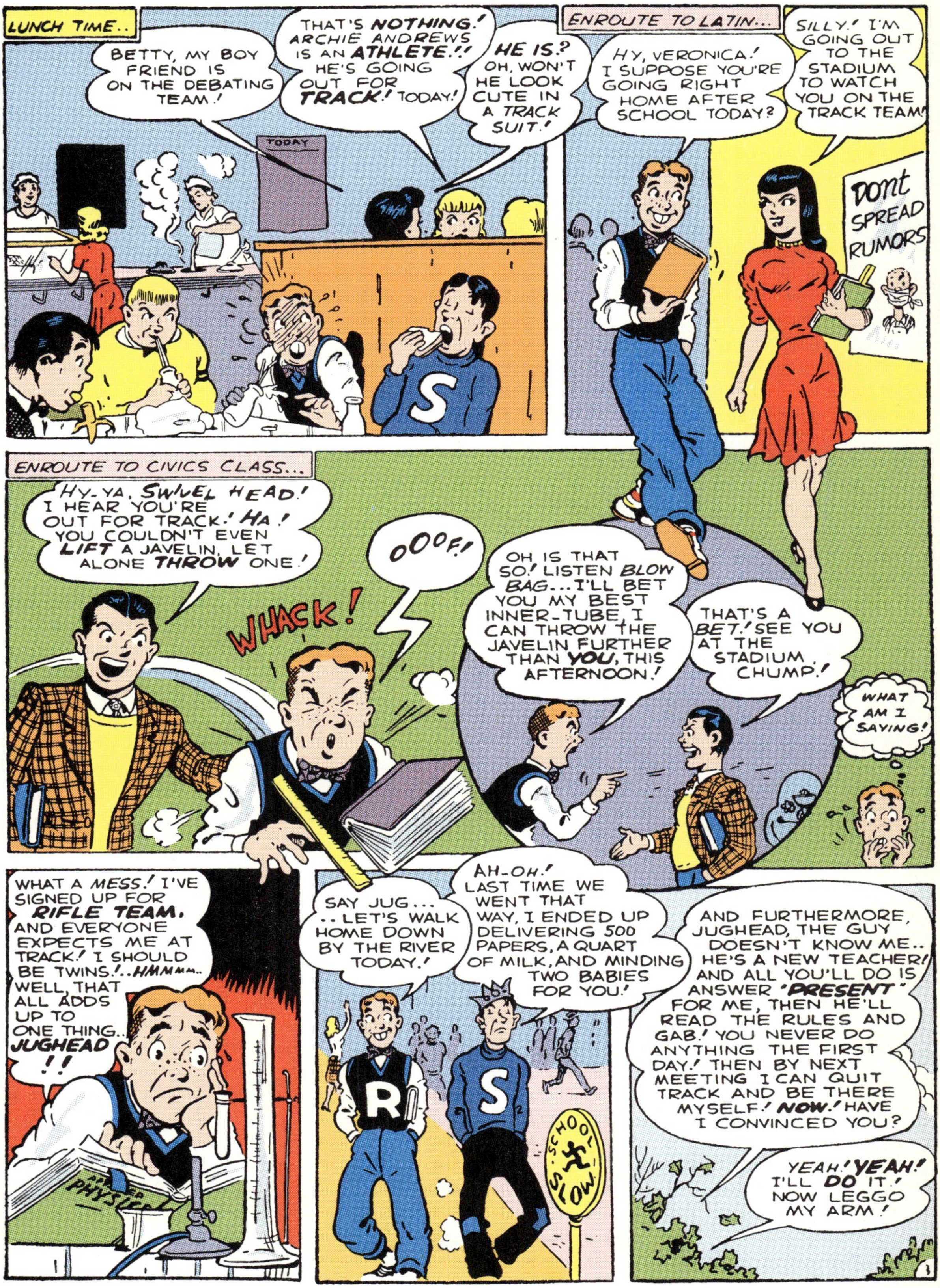
LUNCH TIME..
BETTY, MY BOY FRIEND IS ON THE DEBATING TEAM!
THAT'S NOTHING! ARCHIE ANDREWS IS AN ATHLETE!! HE'S GOING OUT FOR TRACK! TODAY!
HE IS? OH, WON'T HE LOOK CUTE IN A TRACK SUIT!
TODAY
ENROUTE TO LATIN...
HY, VERONICA! I SUPPOSE YOU'RE GOING RIGHT HOME AFTER SCHOOL TODAY?
SILLY! I'M GOING OUT TO THE STADIUM TO WATCH YOU ON THE TRACK TEAM!
DONT SPREAD RUMORS
ENROUTE TO CIVICS CLASS...
HY-YA, SWIVEL HEAD! I HEAR YOU'RE OUT FOR TRACK! HA! YOU COULDN'T EVEN LIFT A JAVELIN, LET ALONE THROW ONE!
WHACK!
OOOF!
OH IS THAT SO! LISTEN BLOW BAG... I'LL BET YOU MY BEST INNER-TUBE, I CAN THROW THE JAVELIN FURTHER THAN YOU, THIS AFTERNOON!
THAT'S A BET! SEE YOU AT THE STADIUM, CHUMP!
WHAT AM I SAYING!
WHAT A MESS! I'VE SIGNED UP FOR RIFLE TEAM, AND EVERYONE EXPECTS ME AT TRACK! I SHOULD BE TWINS!..HMMMM.. WELL, THAT ALL ADDS UP TO ONE THING.. JUGHEAD!!
PHYSICS
SAY JUG... ..LET'S WALK HOME DOWN BY THE RIVER TODAY!
AH-OH! LAST TIME WE WENT THAT WAY, I ENDED UP DELIVERING 500 PAPERS, A QUART OF MILK, AND MINDING TWO BABIES FOR YOU!
R
S
SCHOOL SLOW
AND FURTHERMORE, JUGHEAD, THE GUY DOESN'T KNOW ME.. HE'S A NEW TEACHER! AND ALL YOU'LL DO IS ANSWER "PRESENT" FOR ME, THEN HE'LL READ THE RULES AND GAB! YOU NEVER DO ANYTHING THE FIRST DAY! THEN BY NEXT MEETING I CAN QUIT TRACK AND BE THERE MYSELF! NOW! HAVE I CONVINCED YOU?
YEAH! YEAH! I'LL DO IT! NOW LEGGO MY ARM!

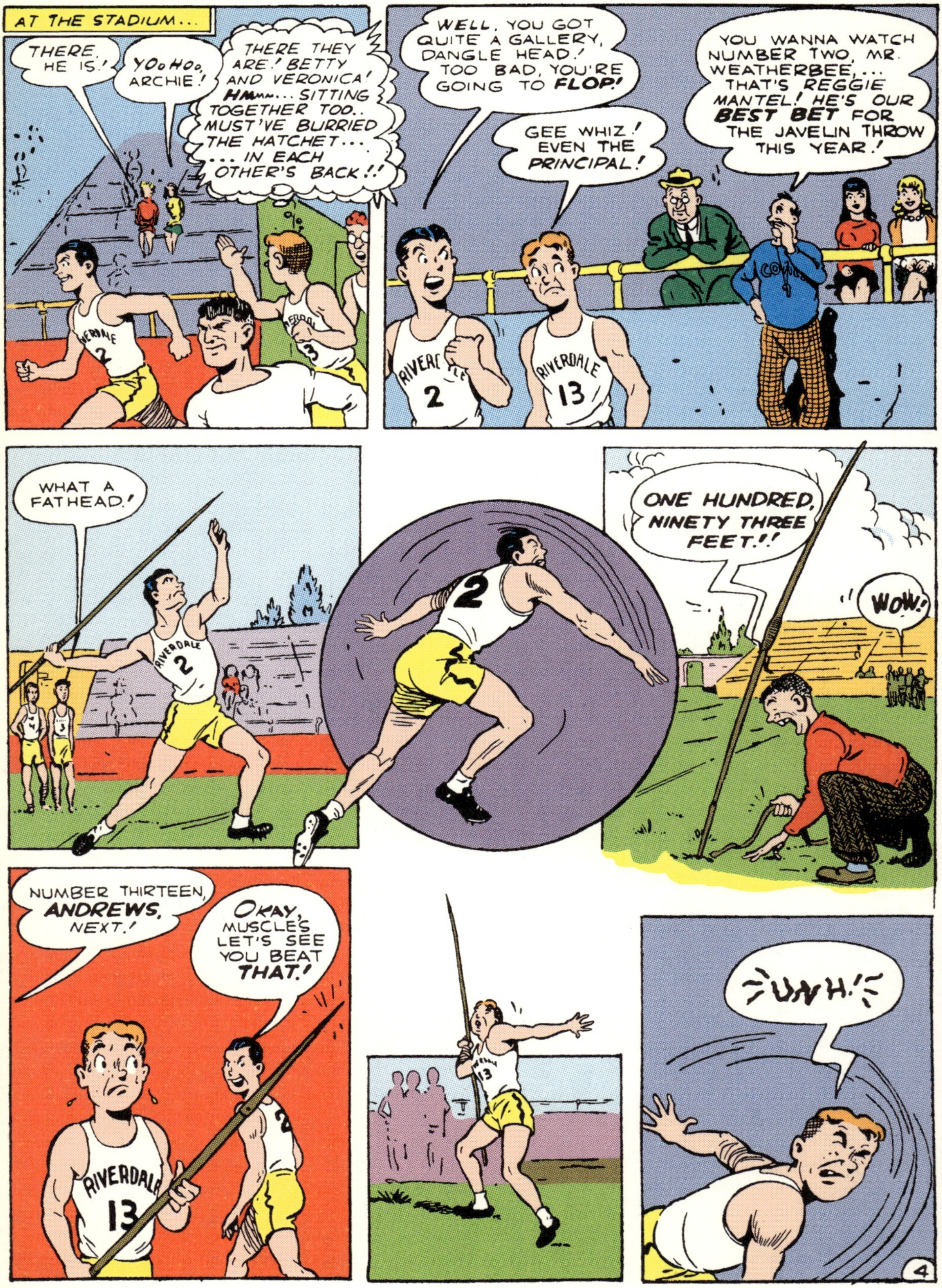
AT THE STADIUM...
THERE. HE IS.!
YOoHOo, ARCHIE!
THERE THEY ARE.! BETTY AND VERONICA! HMMM... SITTING TOGETHER TOO.. MUST'VE BURRIED THE HATCHET.... ...IN EACH OTHER'S BACK!!
WELL, YOU GOT QUITE A GALLERY, DANGLE HEAD.! TOO BAD, YOU'RE GOING TO FLOP!
GEE WHIZ! EVEN THE PRINCIPAL!
YOU WANNA WATCH NUMBER TWO, MR. WEATHERBEE,... THAT'S REGGIE MANTEL! HE'S OUR BEST BET FOR THE JAVELIN THROW THIS YEAR.!
WHAT A FATHEAD.!
ONE HUNDRED, NINETY THREE FEET.!!
WOW!
NUMBER THIRTEEN, ANDREWS, NEXT.!
OKAY, MUSCLES LET'S SEE YOU BEAT THAT.!
UNH!
4

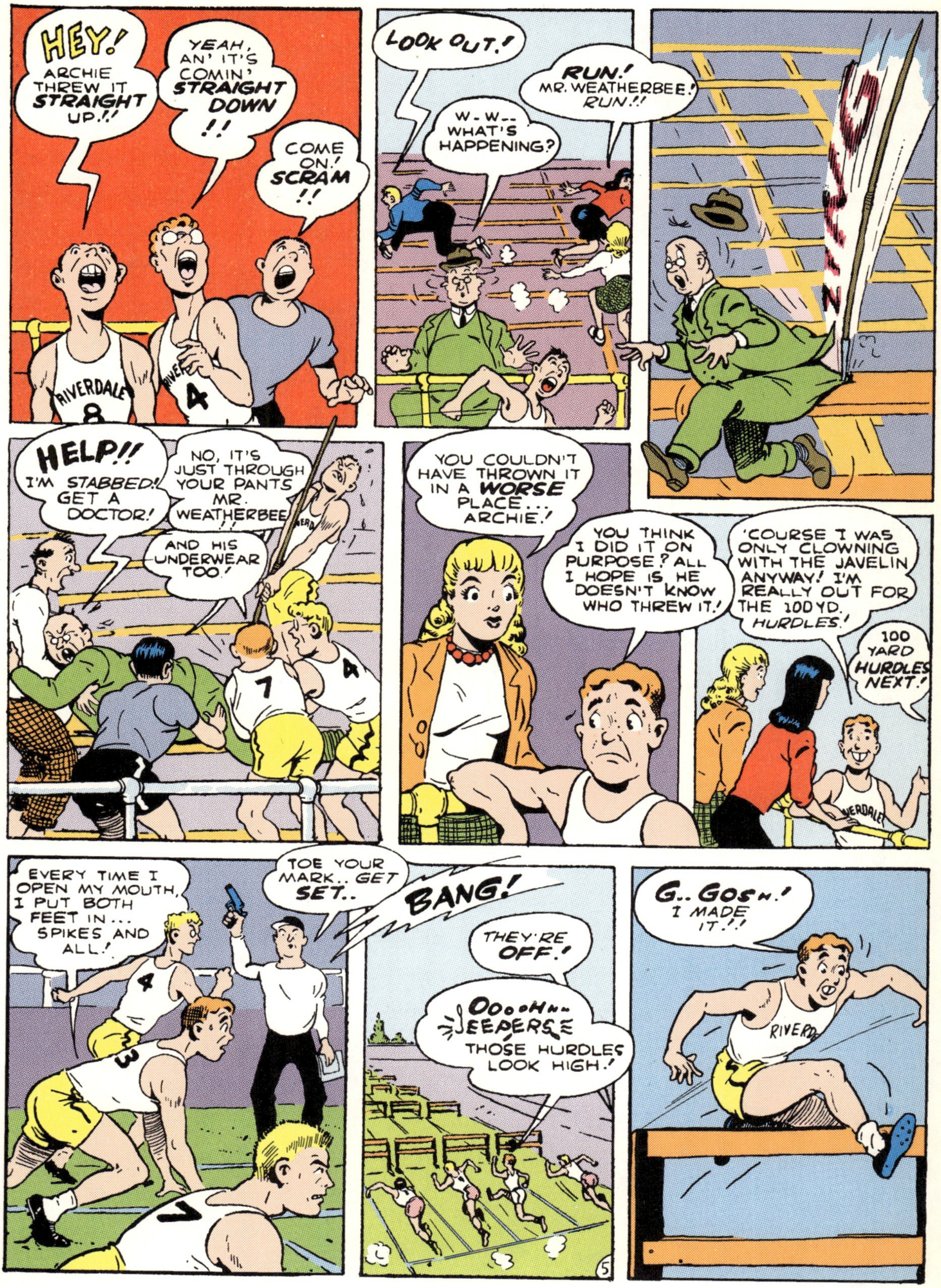

HEY! ARCHIE THREW IT STRAIGHT UP!!
YEAH, AN' IT'S COMIN' STRAIGHT DOWN !!
COME ON! SCRAM !!
LOOK OUT!
RUN! MR. WEATHERBEE! RUN!!
W-W-- WHAT'S HAPPENING?
ZING
HELP!! I'M STABBED! GET A DOCTOR!
NO, IT'S JUST THROUGH YOUR PANTS MR. WEATHERBEE!!
AND HIS UNDERWEAR TOO!
YOU COULDN'T HAVE THROWN IT IN A WORSE PLACE... ARCHIE!
YOU THINK I DID IT ON PURPOSE? ALL I HOPE IS HE DOESN'T KNOW WHO THREW IT!
'COURSE I WAS ONLY CLOWNING WITH THE JAVELIN ANYWAY! I'M REALLY OUT FOR THE 100 YD. HURDLES!
100 YARD HURDLES NEXT!
EVERY TIME I OPEN MY MOUTH, I PUT BOTH FEET IN... SPIKES AND ALL!
TOE YOUR MARK.. GET SET..
BANG!
THEY'RE OFF!
OOOOHH-- JEEPERS THOSE HURDLES LOOK HIGH!
G..GOSH! I MADE IT!!

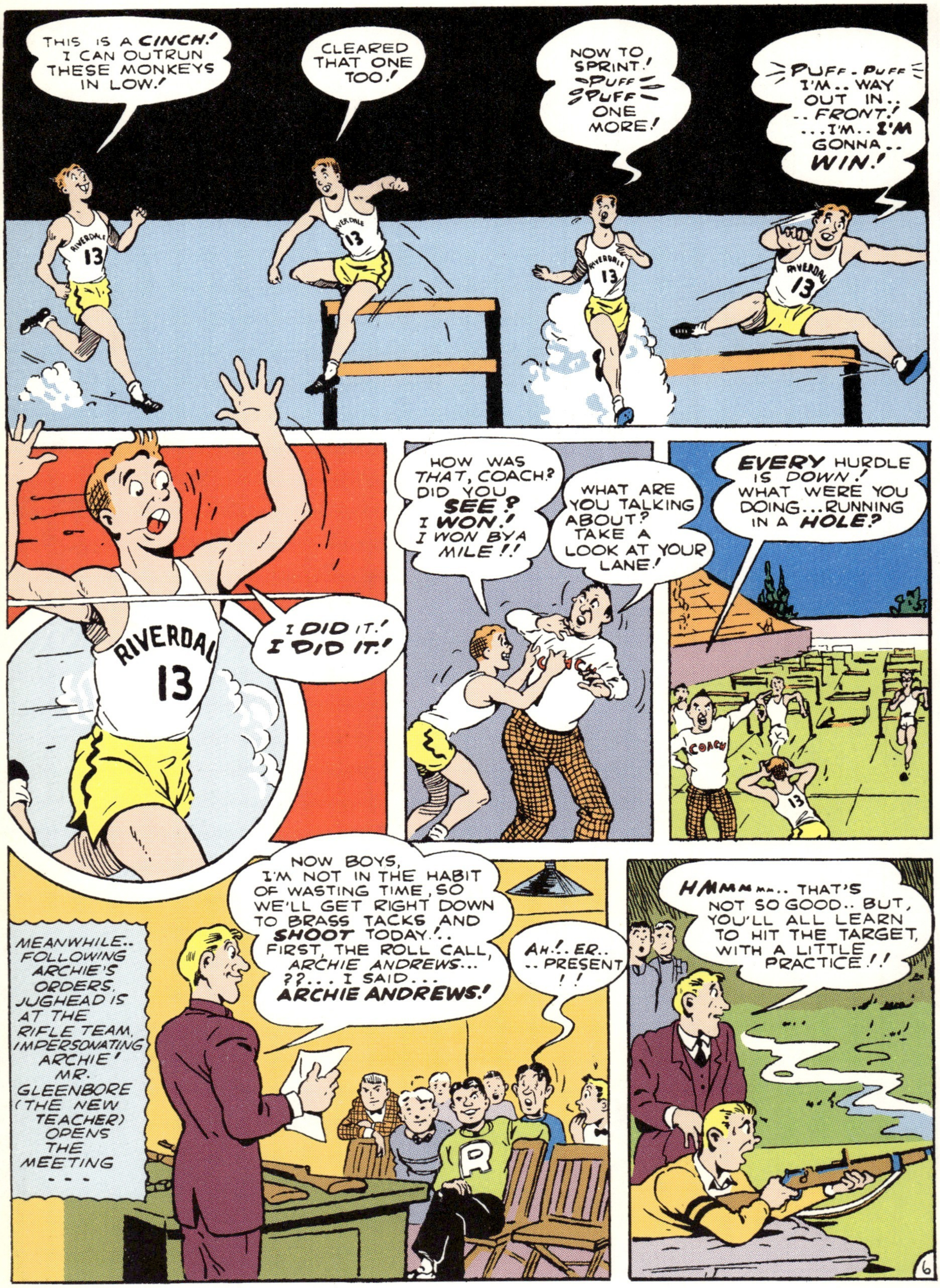

THIS IS A CINCH! I CAN OUTRUN THESE MONKEYS IN LOW!
CLEARED THAT ONE TOO!
NOW TO SPRINT! PUFF PUFF ONE MORE!
PUFF - PUFF I'M.. WAY OUT IN.. ..FRONT! ...I'M.. I'M GONNA.. WIN!
RIVERDALE 13
I DID IT! I DID IT!
HOW WAS THAT, COACH? DID YOU SEE? I WON! I WON BYA MILE!!
WHAT ARE YOU TALKING ABOUT? TAKE A LOOK AT YOUR LANE!
COACH
EVERY HURDLE IS DOWN! WHAT WERE YOU DOING...RUNNING IN A HOLE?
MEANWHILE.. FOLLOWING ARCHIE'S ORDERS, JUGHEAD IS AT THE RIFLE TEAM, IMPERSONATING ARCHIE! MR. GLEENBORE (THE NEW TEACHER) OPENS THE MEETING - - -
NOW BOYS, I'M NOT IN THE HABIT OF WASTING TIME, SO WE'LL GET RIGHT DOWN TO BRASS TACKS AND SHOOT TODAY!.. FIRST, THE ROLL CALL, ARCHIE ANDREWS... ??... I SAID... ARCHIE ANDREWS!
AH!.. ER.. ..PRESENT !!
HMMM... THAT'S NOT SO GOOD.. BUT, YOU'LL ALL LEARN TO HIT THE TARGET, WITH A LITTLE PRACTICE!!
6

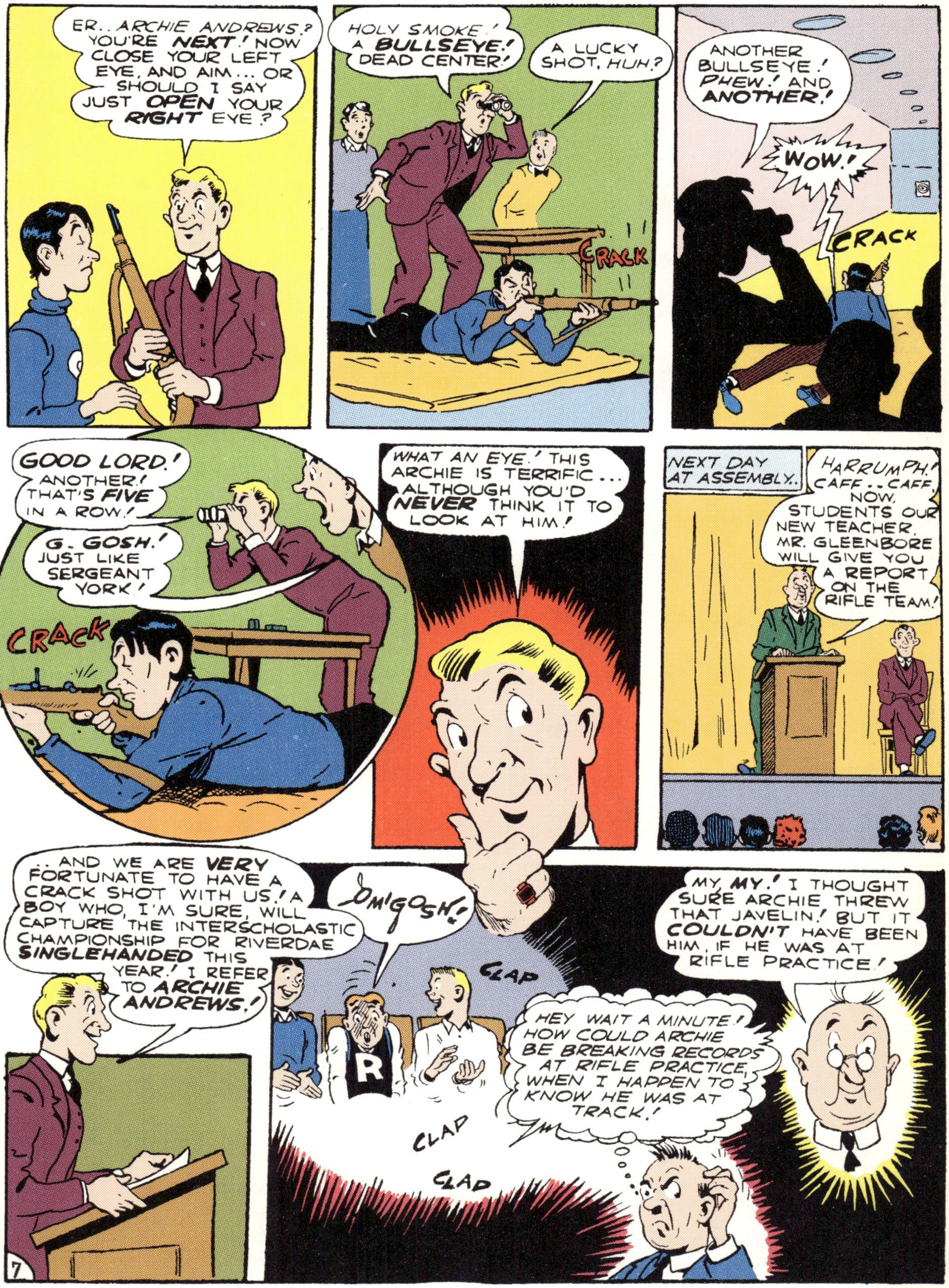
ER.. ARCHIE ANDREWS? YOU'RE NEXT! NOW CLOSE YOUR LEFT EYE, AND AIM... OR SHOULD I SAY JUST OPEN YOUR RIGHT EYE?
HOLY SMOKE! A BULLSEYE! DEAD CENTER!
A LUCKY SHOT, HUH?
CRACK
ANOTHER BULLSEYE! PHEW! AND ANOTHER!
WOW!
CRACK
GOOD LORD! ANOTHER! THAT'S FIVE IN A ROW!
G. GOSH! JUST LIKE SERGEANT YORK!
CRACK
WHAT AN EYE! THIS ARCHIE IS TERRIFIC... ALTHOUGH YOU'D NEVER THINK IT TO LOOK AT HIM!
NEXT DAY AT ASSEMBLY.
HARRUMPH! CAFF.. CAFF, NOW, STUDENTS OUR NEW TEACHER, MR. GLEENBORE WILL GIVE YOU A REPORT ON THE RIFLE TEAM!
.. AND WE ARE VERY FORTUNATE TO HAVE A CRACK SHOT WITH US! A BOY WHO, I'M SURE, WILL CAPTURE THE INTERSCHOLASTIC CHAMPIONSHIP FOR RIVERDAE SINGLEHANDED THIS YEAR! I REFER TO ARCHIE ANDREWS!
OMIGOSH!
CLAP
MY, MY! I THOUGHT SURE ARCHIE THREW THAT JAVELIN! BUT IT COULDN'T HAVE BEEN HIM, IF HE WAS AT RIFLE PRACTICE!
HEY WAIT A MINUTE! HOW COULD ARCHIE BE BREAKING RECORDS AT RIFLE PRACTICE, WHEN I HAPPEN TO KNOW HE WAS AT TRACK!
CLAP
CLAP
7

OUTSIDE ASSEMBLY..

I ASK YOU JUST TO SAY *"PRESENT,"* FOR ME...BUT *NO!* YOU HAVE TO BE A SHARP SHOOTER, A REGULAR COWBOY!

CAN I HELP IT IF MY UNCLE *"BAB"* WAS A BOONE?

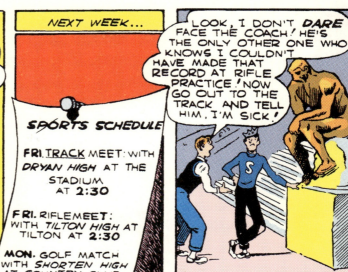

NEXT WEEK...

SPORTS SCHEDULE

FRI. TRACK MEET: WITH *DRYAN HIGH* AT THE STADIUM AT 2:30

FRI. RIFLE MEET: WITH *TILTON HIGH* AT TILTON AT 2:30

MON. GOLF MATCH WITH *SHORTEN HIGH* AT COUNTRY CLUB..

LOOK, I DON'T *DARE* FACE THE COACH! HE'S THE ONLY OTHER ONE WHO KNOWS I COULDN'T HAVE MADE THAT RECORD AT RIFLE PRACTICE! NOW GO OUT TO THE TRACK AND TELL HIM, I'M SICK!

GEE, I CAN'T EVEN GO TO THE RIFLE MEET, 'CAUSE, MR. GLEENBORE THINKS JUGHEAD IS ME!

OH THERE, HE IS!

ARCHIE! WE'VE BEEN LOOKING FOR YOU! COME ON, GET IN! DO YOU WANT TO BE LATE!

B..BUT MR. WEATHERBEE!

MR. GLEENBORE IS ILL, SO *I'M* TAKING THE BOYS TO THE RIFLE MEET! HEH, HEH, WE COULDN'T GO WITHOUT OUR *STAR SHOOTER*, COULD WE ARCHIE?

MEANWHILE..

HE'S SICK? WHAT DOES HE THINK HE IS.. A PRIMADONNA? I'VE ENTERED HIM IN *FOUR* EVENTS! WHAT'S WRONG WITH HIM?

WHO? *OH!* ARCHIE? DANDRUFF!!

B- BUT, COACH I DON'T KNOW NOTHIN' ABOUT TRACK!

I *DON'T* CARE! JUST SO THAT YOU'RE IN THERE! ELSE I HAVE TO FORFEIT THE WHOLE EVENT! ANYWAY WITH THAT HAT AND NUMBER YOU'LL LOOK JUST LIKE ARCHIE FROM THE STANDS!

AND AT THE RIFLE MEET.

HEH, HEH! YOU'D BETTER PUT UP YOUR BEST MAN NOW, BECAUSE WE'RE PUTTING UP OUR *STAR*, ARCHIE ANDREWS!

YEAH! WELL HE'D *BETTER* BE GOOD! TILTON IS 2 POINTS AHEAD OF YOUR SCHOOL NOW!

8

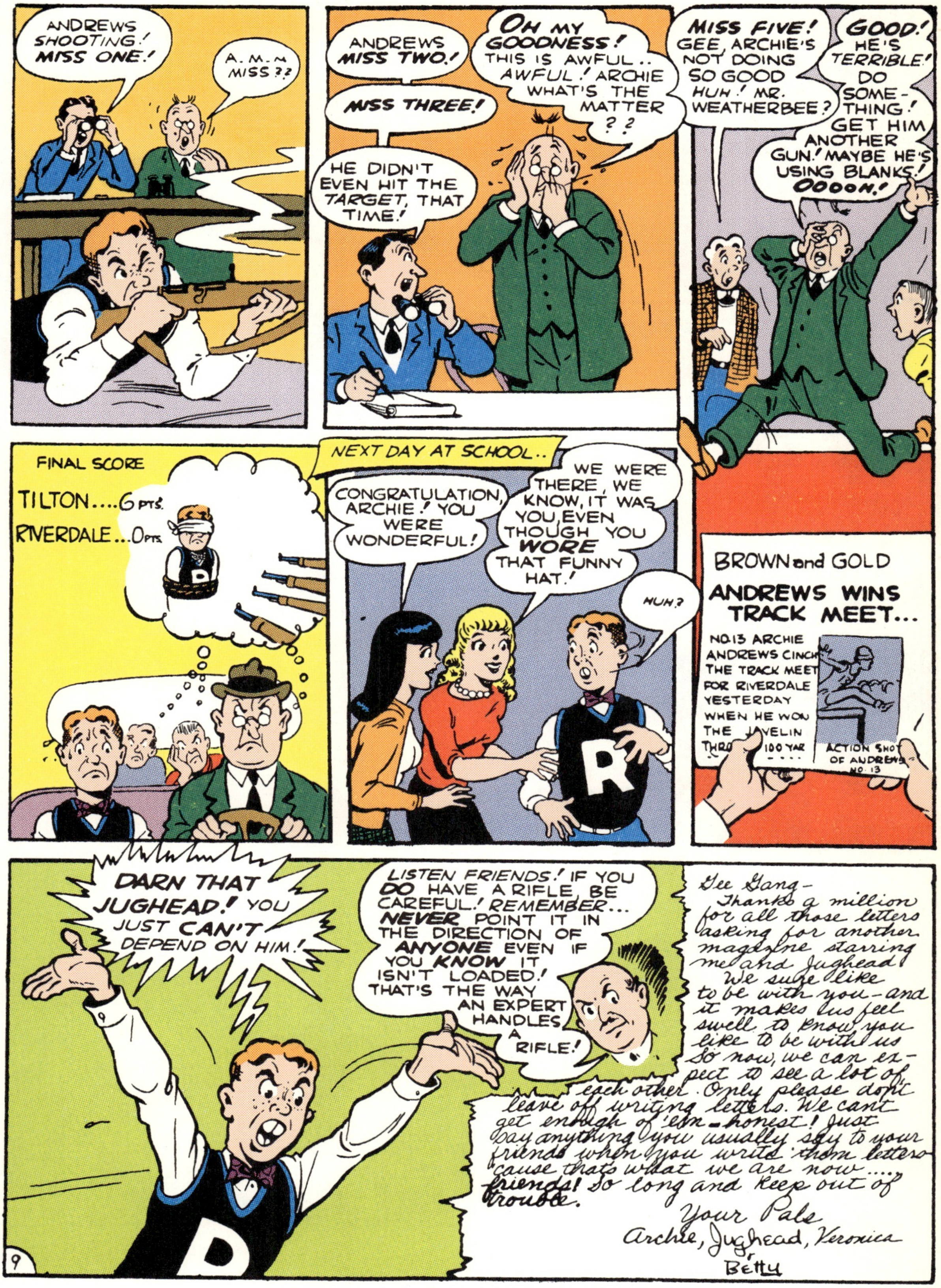

ANDREWS SHOOTING! MISS ONE!
A. M. M MISS ??
ANDREWS MISS TWO!
OH MY GOODNESS! THIS IS AWFUL.. AWFUL! ARCHIE WHAT'S THE MATTER ??
MISS THREE!
HE DIDN'T EVEN HIT THE TARGET, THAT TIME!
MISS FIVE! GEE, ARCHIE'S NOT DOING SO GOOD HUH! MR. WEATHERBEE?
GOOD! HE'S TERRIBLE! DO SOME-THING! GET HIM ANOTHER GUN! MAYBE HE'S USING BLANKS! OOOOH!
FINAL SCORE
TILTON....6 PTS.
RIVERDALE...0 PTS.
NEXT DAY AT SCHOOL..
CONGRATULATION, ARCHIE! YOU WERE WONDERFUL!
WE WERE THERE, WE KNOW, IT WAS YOU, EVEN THOUGH YOU WORE THAT FUNNY HAT!
HUH?
BROWN and GOLD
ANDREWS WINS TRACK MEET...
NO.13 ARCHIE ANDREWS CINCH THE TRACK MEET FOR RIVERDALE YESTERDAY WHEN HE WON THE JAVELIN
ACTION SHOT OF ANDREWS NO. 13
DARN THAT JUGHEAD! YOU JUST CAN'T DEPEND ON HIM!
LISTEN FRIENDS! IF YOU DO HAVE A RIFLE BE CAREFUL! REMEMBER... NEVER POINT IT IN THE DIRECTION OF ANYONE EVEN IF YOU KNOW IT ISN'T LOADED! THAT'S THE WAY AN EXPERT HANDLES A RIFLE!
Gee Gang - Thanks a million for all those letters asking for another magazine starring me and Jughead! We sure like to be with you - and it makes us feel swell to know you like to be with us So now, we can expect to see a lot of each other. Only please don't leave off writing letters. We cant get enough of 'em - honest! Just say anything you usually say to your friends when you write them letters 'cause thats what we are now.... friends! So long and keep out of trouble.
Your Pals
Archie, Jughead, Veronica, Betty
9

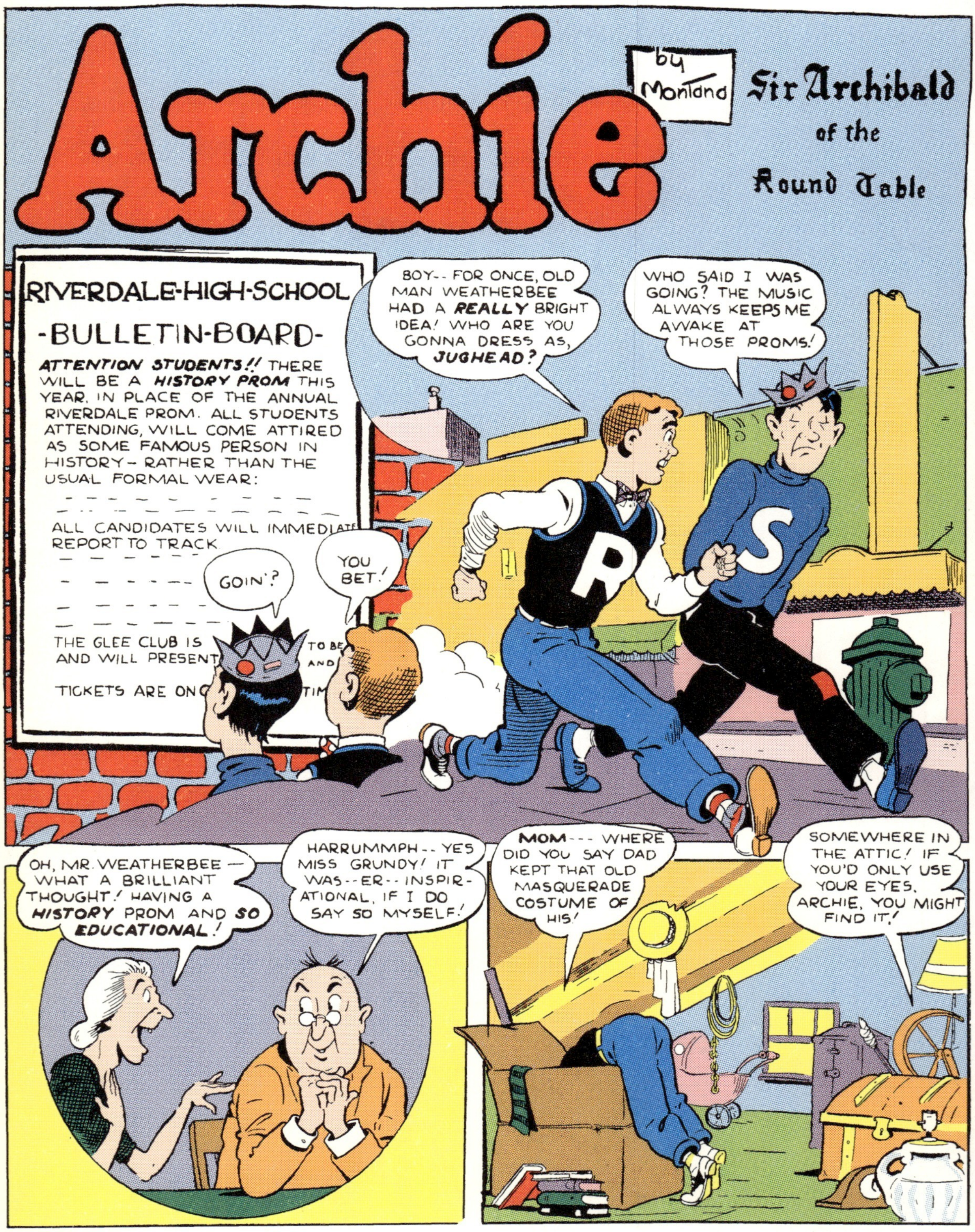

Archie
by Montana
Sir Archibald of the Round Table
RIVERDALE-HIGH-SCHOOL
-BULLETIN-BOARD-
ATTENTION STUDENTS!! THERE WILL BE A HISTORY PROM THIS YEAR, IN PLACE OF THE ANNUAL RIVERDALE PROM. ALL STUDENTS ATTENDING, WILL COME ATTIRED AS SOME FAMOUS PERSON IN HISTORY-- RATHER THAN THE USUAL FORMAL WEAR:
ALL CANDIDATES WILL IMMEDIATE REPORT TO TRACK
THE GLEE CLUB IS AND WILL PRESENT
TO BE AND
TICKETS ARE ON TIM
GOIN'?
YOU BET!
BOY-- FOR ONCE, OLD MAN WEATHERBEE HAD A REALLY BRIGHT IDEA! WHO ARE YOU GONNA DRESS AS, JUGHEAD?
WHO SAID I WAS GOING? THE MUSIC ALWAYS KEEPS ME AWAKE AT THOSE PROMS!
OH, MR. WEATHERBEE— WHAT A BRILLIANT THOUGHT! HAVING A HISTORY PROM AND SO EDUCATIONAL!
HARRUMMPH-- YES MISS GRUNDY! IT WAS--ER-- INSPIRATIONAL, IF I DO SAY SO MYSELF!
MOM--- WHERE DID YOU SAY DAD KEPT THAT OLD MASQUERADE COSTUME OF HIS!
SOMEWHERE IN THE ATTIC! IF YOU'D ONLY USE YOUR EYES, ARCHIE, YOU MIGHT FIND IT!

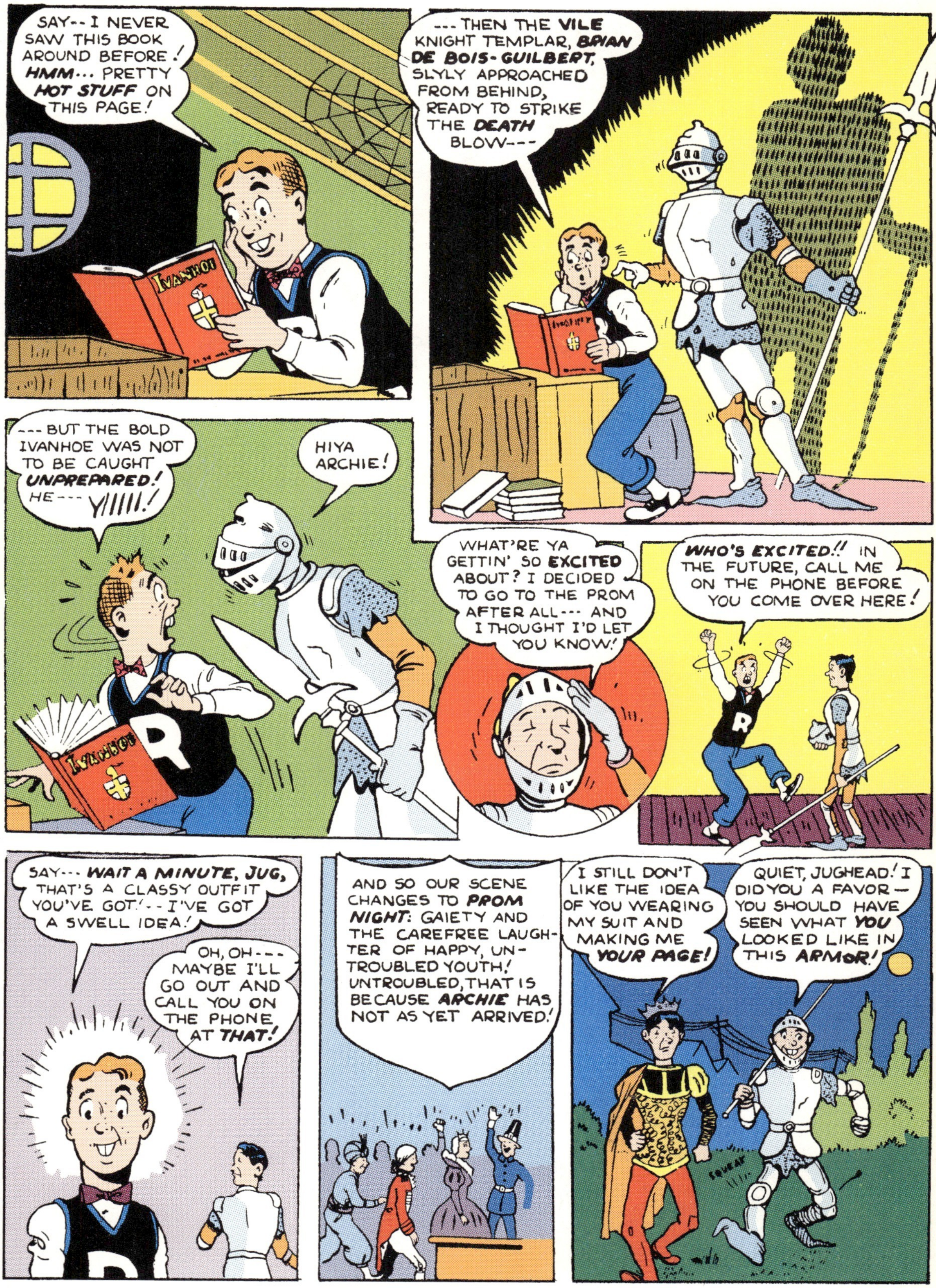
SAY-- I NEVER SAW THIS BOOK AROUND BEFORE! HMM... PRETTY HOT STUFF ON THIS PAGE!
---THEN THE VILE KNIGHT TEMPLAR, BRIAN DE BOIS-GUILBERT, SLYLY APPROACHED FROM BEHIND, READY TO STRIKE THE DEATH BLOW---
---BUT THE BOLD IVANHOE WAS NOT TO BE CAUGHT UNPREPARED! HE--- YIIIII!
HIYA ARCHIE!
WHAT'RE YA GETTIN' SO EXCITED ABOUT? I DECIDED TO GO TO THE PROM AFTER ALL--- AND I THOUGHT I'D LET YOU KNOW!
WHO'S EXCITED!! IN THE FUTURE, CALL ME ON THE PHONE BEFORE YOU COME OVER HERE!
SAY--- WAIT A MINUTE, JUG, THAT'S A CLASSY OUTFIT YOU'VE GOT!--I'VE GOT A SWELL IDEA!
OH, OH--- MAYBE I'LL GO OUT AND CALL YOU ON THE PHONE AT THAT!
AND SO OUR SCENE CHANGES TO PROM NIGHT: GAIETY AND THE CAREFREE LAUGHTER OF HAPPY, UNTROUBLED YOUTH! UNTROUBLED, THAT IS BECAUSE ARCHIE HAS NOT AS YET ARRIVED!
I STILL DON'T LIKE THE IDEA OF YOU WEARING MY SUIT AND MAKING ME YOUR PAGE!
QUIET, JUGHEAD! I DID YOU A FAVOR — YOU SHOULD HAVE SEEN WHAT YOU LOOKED LIKE IN THIS ARMOR!
SQUEAK

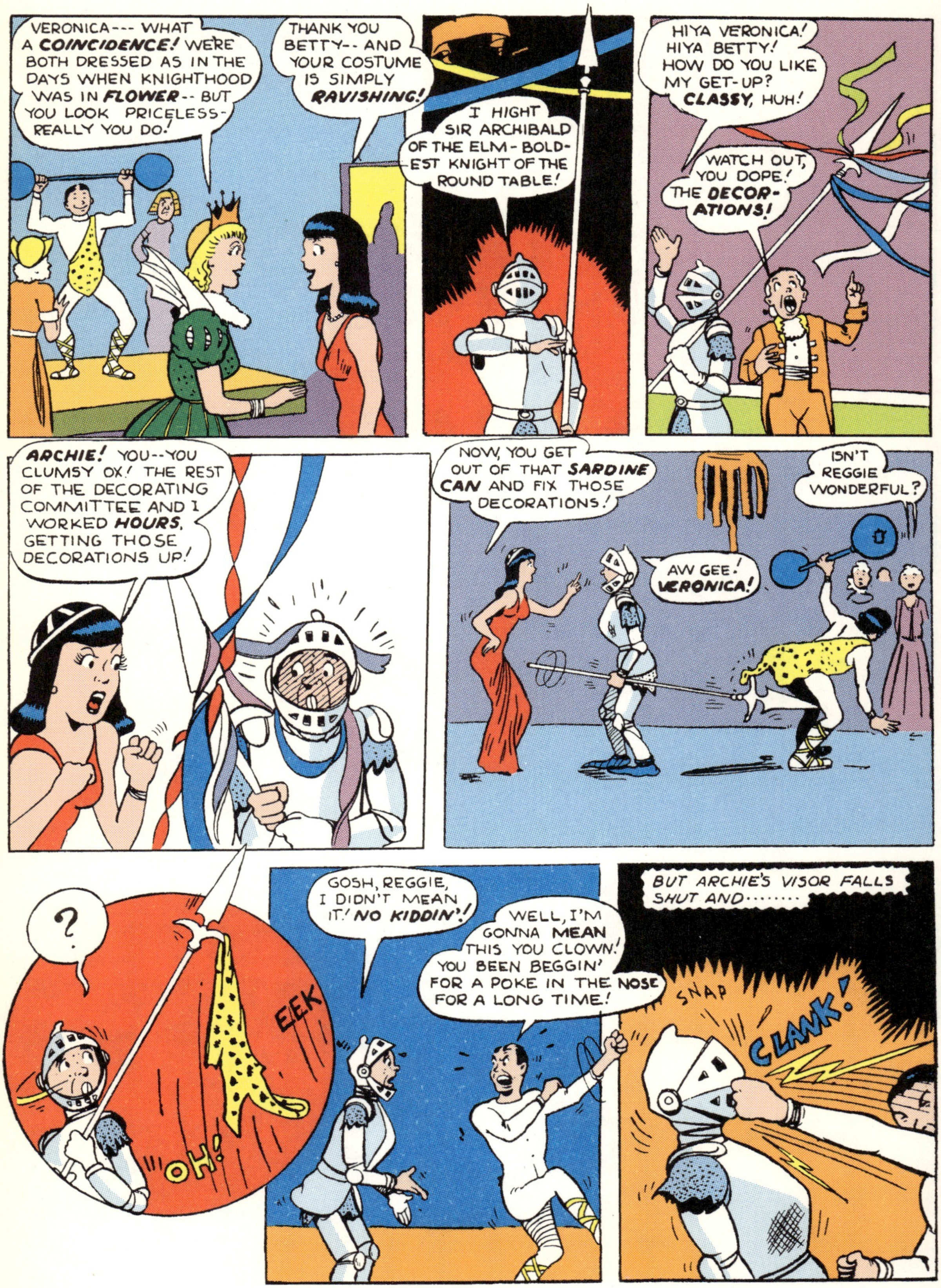
VERONICA--- WHAT A COINCIDENCE! WE'RE BOTH DRESSED AS IN THE DAYS WHEN KNIGHTHOOD WAS IN FLOWER-- BUT YOU LOOK PRICELESS-REALLY YOU DO!
THANK YOU BETTY-- AND YOUR COSTUME IS SIMPLY RAVISHING!
I HIGHT SIR ARCHIBALD OF THE ELM-BOLDEST KNIGHT OF THE ROUND TABLE!
HIYA VERONICA! HIYA BETTY! HOW DO YOU LIKE MY GET-UP? CLASSY, HUH!
WATCH OUT, YOU DOPE! THE DECORATIONS!
ARCHIE! YOU--YOU CLUMSY OX! THE REST OF THE DECORATING COMMITTEE AND I WORKED HOURS, GETTING THOSE DECORATIONS UP!
NOW, YOU GET OUT OF THAT SARDINE CAN AND FIX THOSE DECORATIONS!
AW GEE! VERONICA!
ISN'T REGGIE WONDERFUL?
?
EEK
OH!
GOSH, REGGIE, I DIDN'T MEAN IT! NO KIDDIN'!
WELL, I'M GONNA MEAN THIS YOU CLOWN! YOU BEEN BEGGIN' FOR A POKE IN THE NOSE FOR A LONG TIME!
BUT ARCHIE'S VISOR FALLS SHUT AND........
SNAP
CLANK!

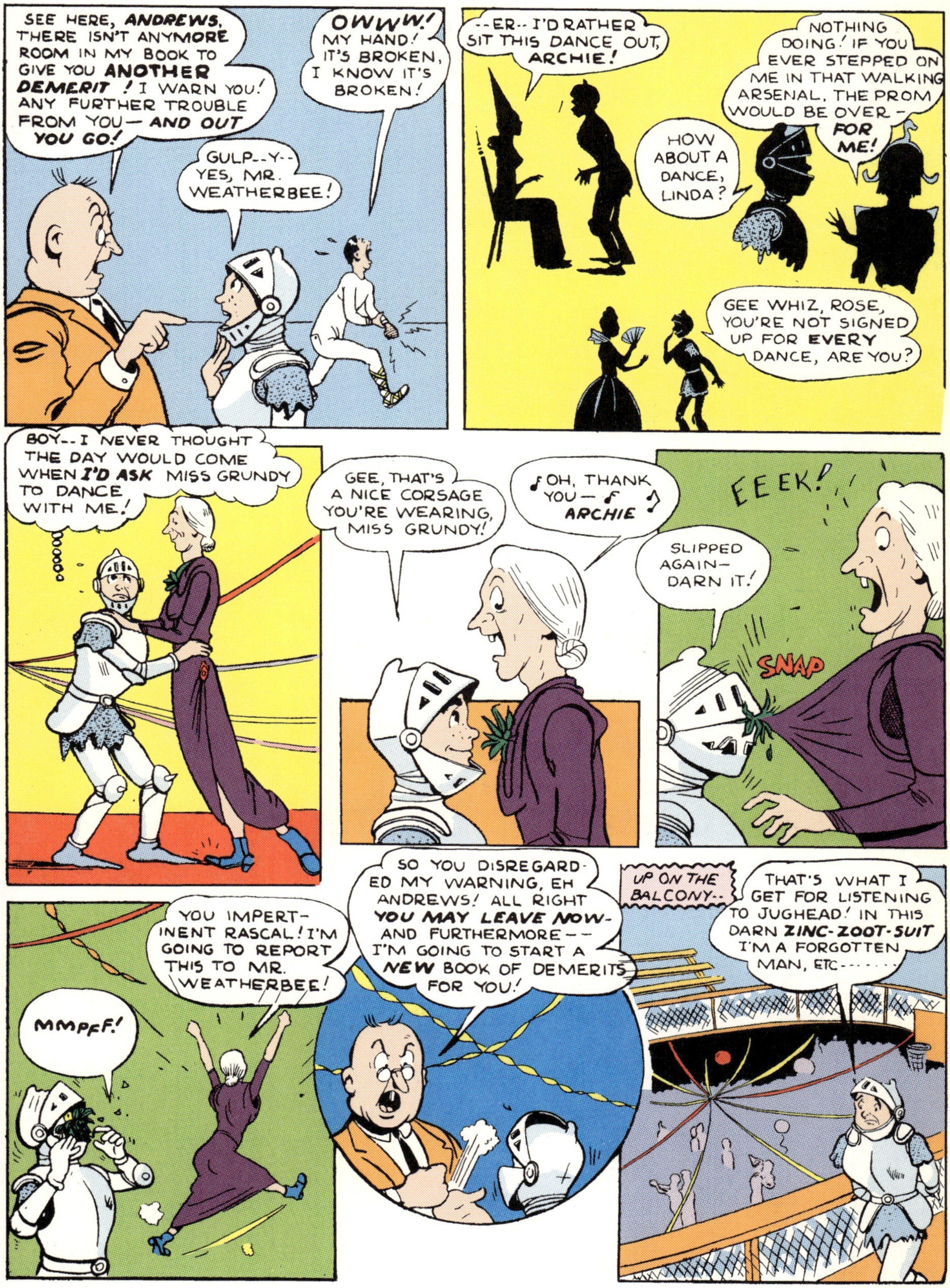
SEE HERE, ANDREWS, THERE ISN'T ANYMORE ROOM IN MY BOOK TO GIVE YOU ANOTHER DEMERIT! I WARN YOU! ANY FURTHER TROUBLE FROM YOU— AND OUT YOU GO!
OWWW! MY HAND! IT'S BROKEN, I KNOW IT'S BROKEN!
GULP--Y-- YES, MR. WEATHERBEE!
--ER-- I'D RATHER SIT THIS DANCE OUT, ARCHIE!
NOTHING DOING! IF YOU EVER STEPPED ON ME IN THAT WALKING ARSENAL, THE PROM WOULD BE OVER— FOR ME!
HOW ABOUT A DANCE, LINDA?
GEE WHIZ, ROSE, YOU'RE NOT SIGNED UP FOR EVERY DANCE, ARE YOU?
BOY-- I NEVER THOUGHT THE DAY WOULD COME WHEN I'D ASK MISS GRUNDY TO DANCE WITH ME!
GEE, THAT'S A NICE CORSAGE YOU'RE WEARING, MISS GRUNDY!
OH, THANK YOU— ARCHIE
EEEK!
SLIPPED AGAIN— DARN IT!
SNAP
YOU IMPERTINENT RASCAL! I'M GOING TO REPORT THIS TO MR. WEATHERBEE!
MMPFF!
SO YOU DISREGARDED MY WARNING, EH ANDREWS! ALL RIGHT YOU MAY LEAVE NOW— AND FURTHERMORE-- I'M GOING TO START A NEW BOOK OF DEMERITS FOR YOU!
UP ON THE BALCONY--
THAT'S WHAT I GET FOR LISTENING TO JUGHEAD! IN THIS DARN ZINC-ZOOT-SUIT I'M A FORGOTTEN MAN, ETC-------

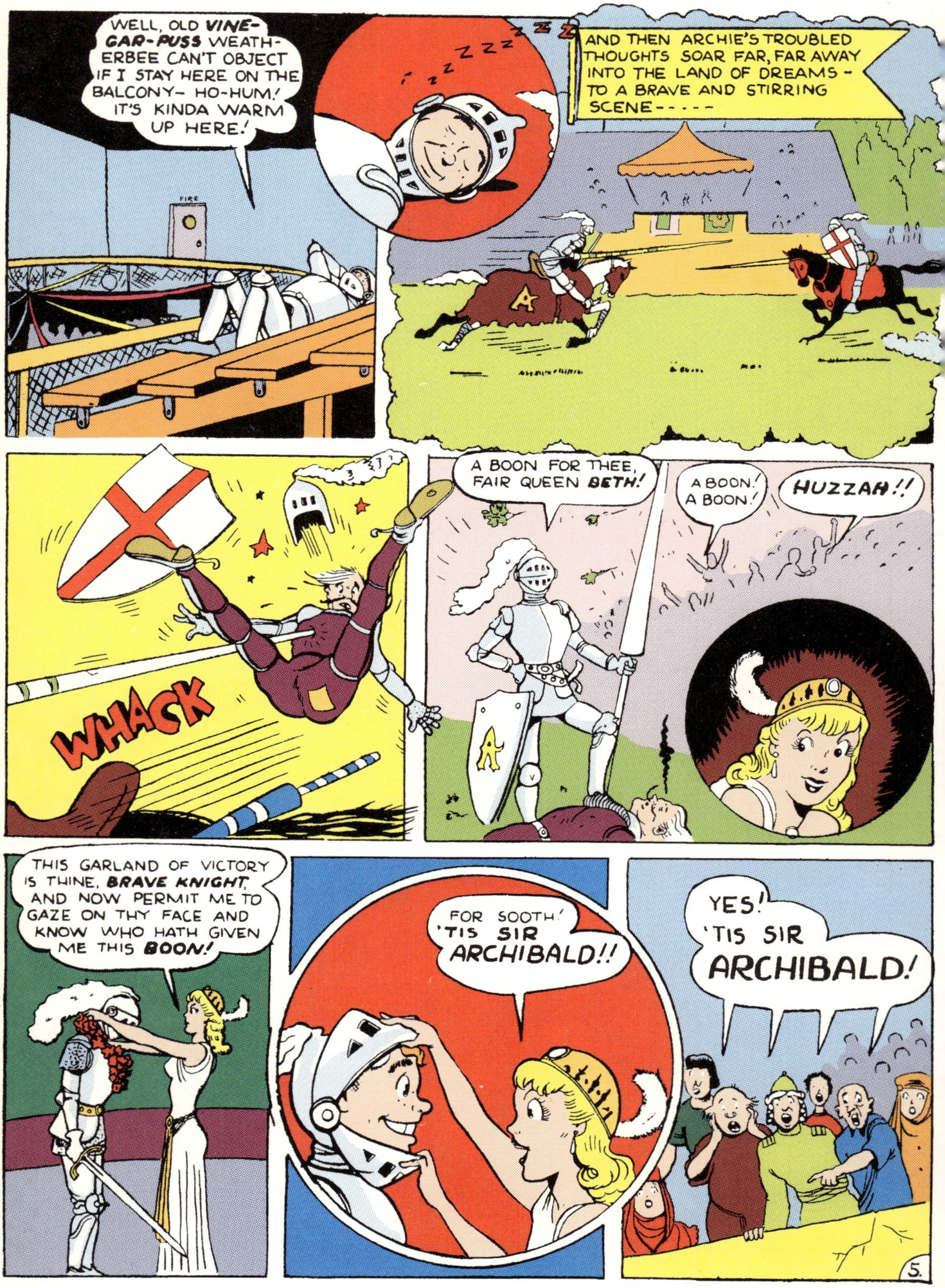
WELL, OLD VINE-GAR-PUSS WEATH-ERBEE CAN'T OBJECT IF I STAY HERE ON THE BALCONY– HO-HUM! IT'S KINDA WARM UP HERE!
Z Z Z Z Z Z Z Z
AND THEN ARCHIE'S TROUBLED THOUGHTS SOAR FAR, FAR AWAY INTO THE LAND OF DREAMS – TO A BRAVE AND STIRRING SCENE - - - - -
WHACK
A BOON FOR THEE, FAIR QUEEN BETH!
A BOON! A BOON!
HUZZAH!!
THIS GARLAND OF VICTORY IS THINE, BRAVE KNIGHT, AND NOW PERMIT ME TO GAZE ON THY FACE AND KNOW WHO HATH GIVEN ME THIS BOON!
FOR SOOTH! 'TIS SIR ARCHIBALD!!
YES! 'TIS SIR ARCHIBALD!
5.

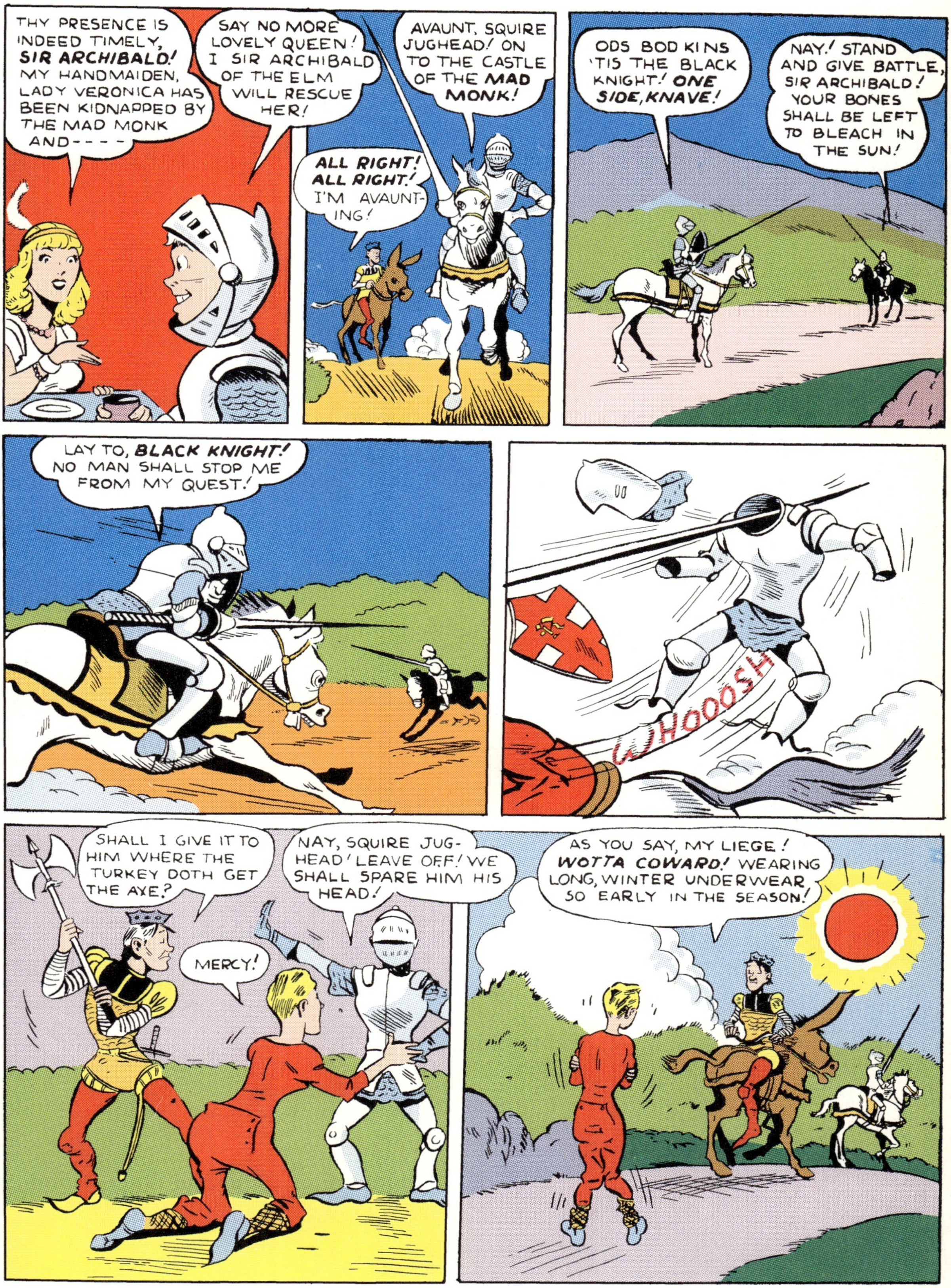

THY PRESENCE IS INDEED TIMELY, SIR ARCHIBALD! MY HANDMAIDEN, LADY VERONICA HAS BEEN KIDNAPPED BY THE MAD MONK AND----
SAY NO MORE LOVELY QUEEN! I SIR ARCHIBALD OF THE ELM WILL RESCUE HER!
AVAUNT, SQUIRE JUGHEAD! ON TO THE CASTLE OF THE MAD MONK!
ALL RIGHT! ALL RIGHT! I'M AVAUNTING!
ODS BOD KINS 'TIS THE BLACK KNIGHT! ONE SIDE, KNAVE!
NAY! STAND AND GIVE BATTLE, SIR ARCHIBALD! YOUR BONES SHALL BE LEFT TO BLEACH IN THE SUN!
LAY TO, BLACK KNIGHT! NO MAN SHALL STOP ME FROM MY QUEST!
WHOOOSH
SHALL I GIVE IT TO HIM WHERE THE TURKEY DOTH GET THE AXE?
NAY, SQUIRE JUGHEAD! LEAVE OFF! WE SHALL SPARE HIM HIS HEAD!
MERCY!
AS YOU SAY, MY LIEGE! WOTTA COWARD! WEARING LONG, WINTER UNDERWEAR SO EARLY IN THE SEASON!

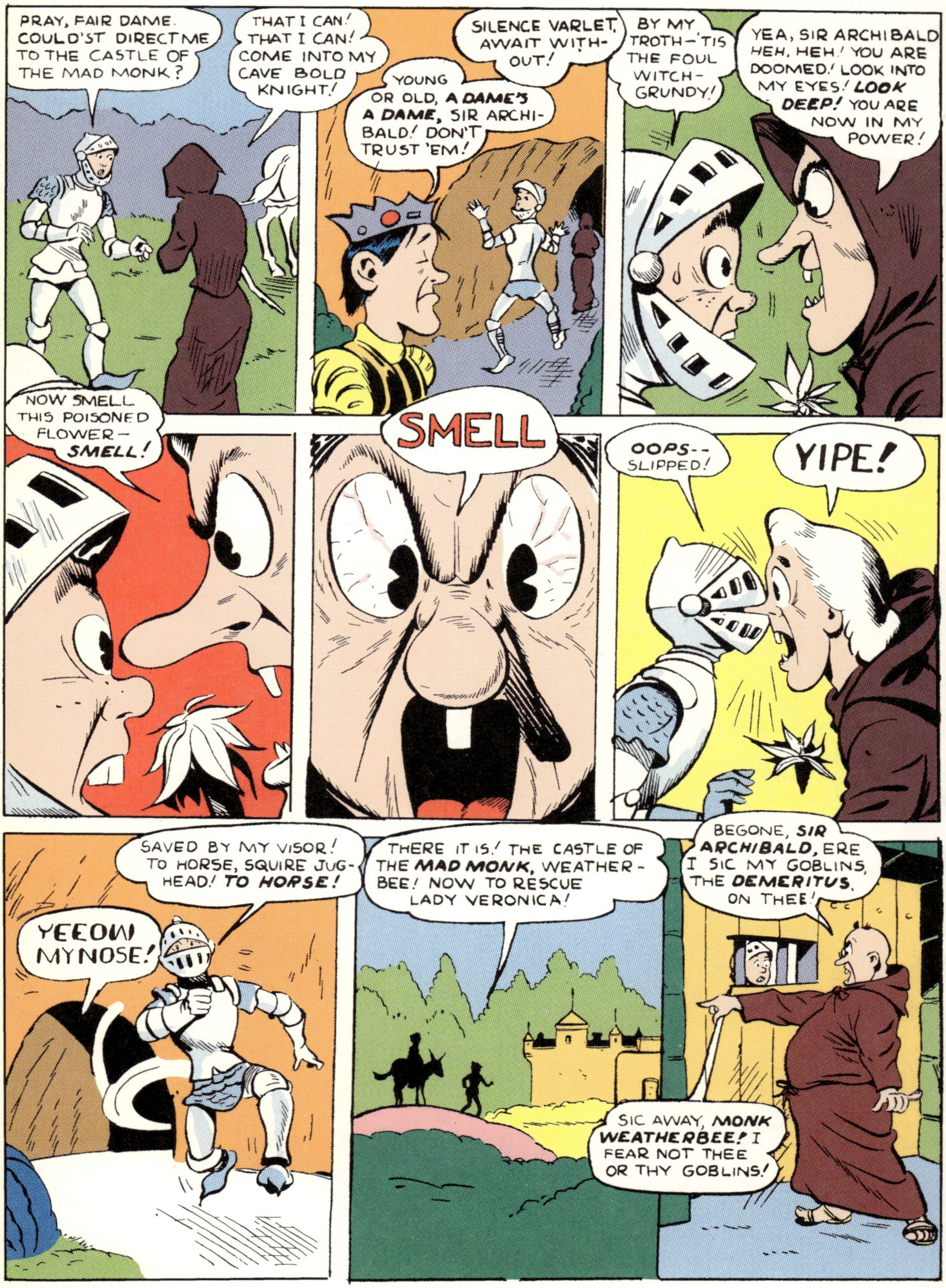
PRAY, FAIR DAME. COULD'ST DIRECT ME TO THE CASTLE OF THE MAD MONK?
THAT I CAN! THAT I CAN! COME INTO MY CAVE BOLD KNIGHT!
SILENCE VARLET, AWAIT WITH-OUT!
YOUNG OR OLD, A DAME'S A DAME, SIR ARCHI-BALD! DON'T TRUST 'EM!
BY MY TROTH—'TIS THE FOUL WITCH-GRUNDY!
YEA, SIR ARCHIBALD HEH, HEH! YOU ARE DOOMED! LOOK INTO MY EYES! LOOK DEEP! YOU ARE NOW IN MY POWER!
NOW SMELL THIS POISONED FLOWER—SMELL!
SMELL
OOPS-- SLIPPED!
YIPE!
YEEOW MY NOSE!
SAVED BY MY VISOR! TO HORSE, SQUIRE JUG-HEAD! TO HORSE!
THERE IT IS! THE CASTLE OF THE MAD MONK, WEATHER-BEE! NOW TO RESCUE LADY VERONICA!
BEGONE, SIR ARCHIBALD, ERE I SIC MY GOBLINS, THE DEMERITUS, ON THEE!
SIC AWAY, MONK WEATHERBEE! I FEAR NOT THEE OR THY GOBLINS!

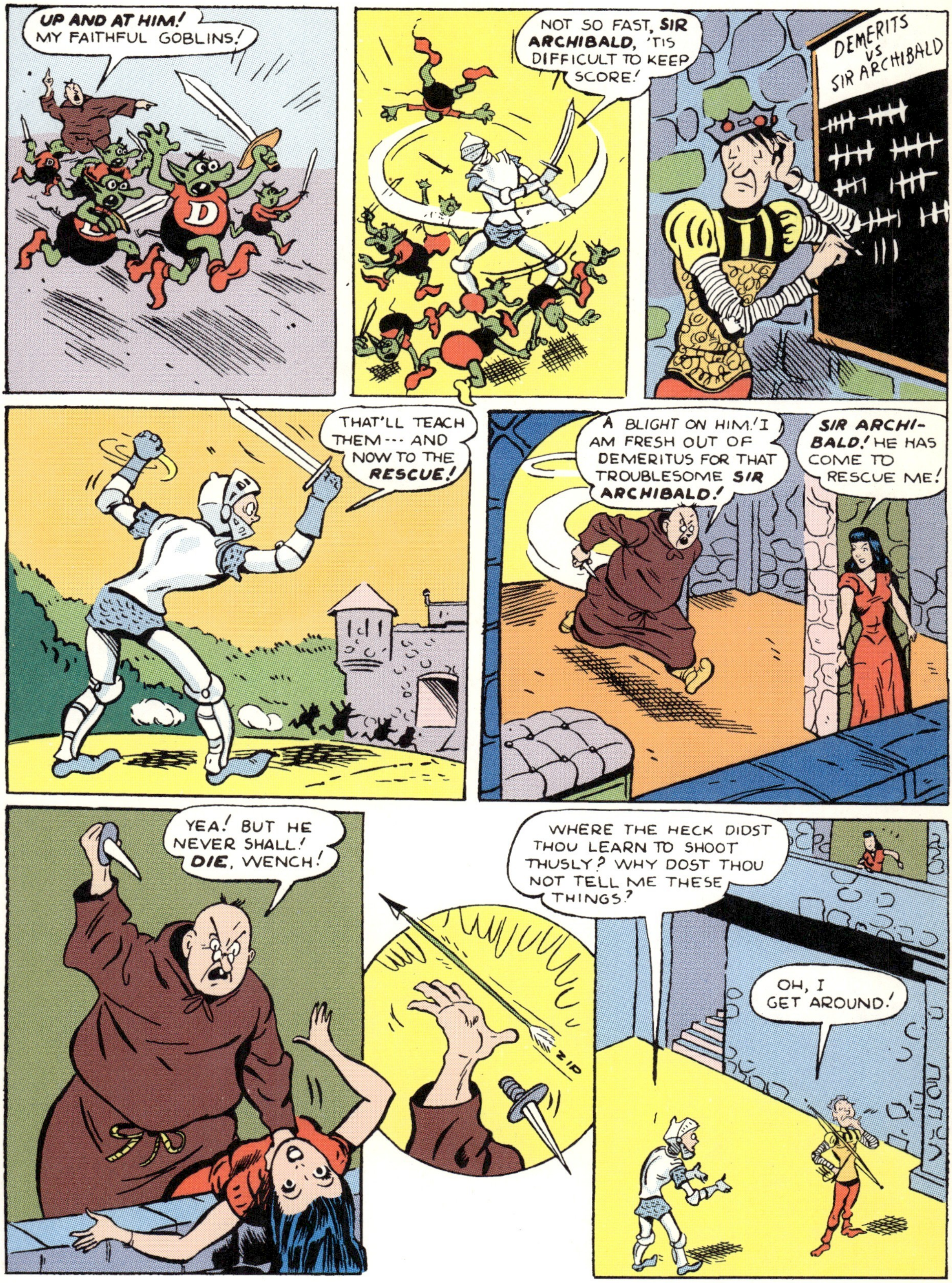
UP AND AT HIM! MY FAITHFUL GOBLINS!
NOT SO FAST, SIR ARCHIBALD, 'TIS DIFFICULT TO KEEP SCORE!
DEMERITS VS SIR ARCHIBALD
THAT'LL TEACH THEM --- AND NOW TO THE RESCUE!
A BLIGHT ON HIM! I AM FRESH OUT OF DEMERITUS FOR THAT TROUBLESOME SIR ARCHIBALD!
SIR ARCHIBALD! HE HAS COME TO RESCUE ME!
YEA! BUT HE NEVER SHALL! DIE, WENCH!
ZIP
WHERE THE HECK DIDST THOU LEARN TO SHOOT THUSLY? WHY DOST THOU NOT TELL ME THESE THINGS?
OH, I GET AROUND!

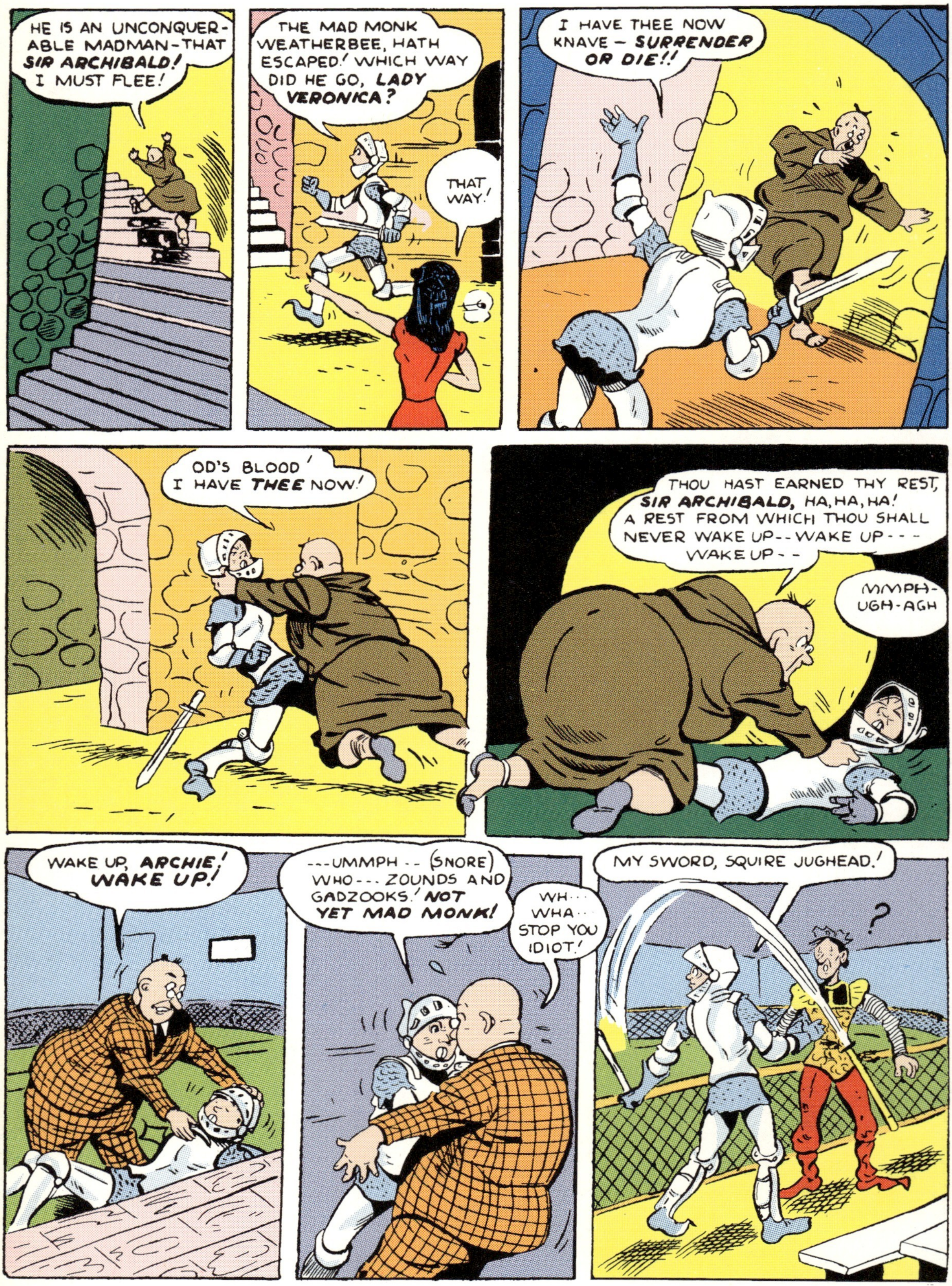
HE IS AN UNCONQUERABLE MADMAN-THAT SIR ARCHIBALD! I MUST FLEE!
THE MAD MONK WEATHERBEE, HATH ESCAPED! WHICH WAY DID HE GO, LADY VERONICA?
THAT WAY!
I HAVE THEE NOW KNAVE — SURRENDER OR DIE!!
OD'S BLOOD! I HAVE THEE NOW!
THOU HAST EARNED THY REST, SIR ARCHIBALD, HA, HA, HA! A REST FROM WHICH THOU SHALL NEVER WAKE UP-- WAKE UP--- WAKE UP--
MMPH-UGH-AGH
WAKE UP, ARCHIE! WAKE UP!
---UMMPH-- (SNORE) WHO--- ZOUNDS AND GADZOOKS! NOT YET MAD MONK!
WH... WHA... STOP YOU IDIOT!
MY SWORD, SQUIRE JUGHEAD!
?

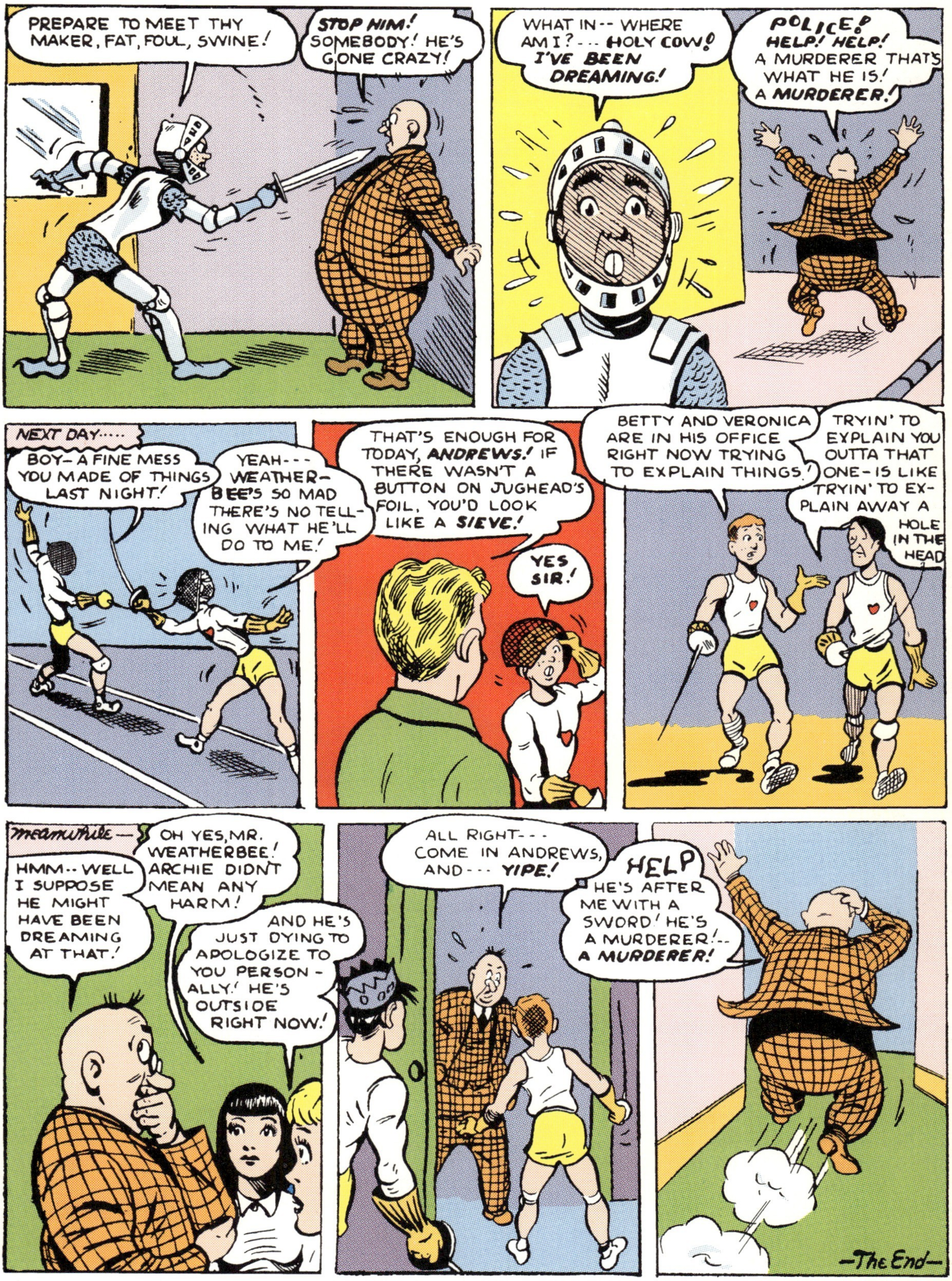
PREPARE TO MEET THY MAKER, FAT, FOUL, SWINE!
STOP HIM! SOMEBODY! HE'S GONE CRAZY!
WHAT IN -- WHERE AM I? --- HOLY COW! I'VE BEEN DREAMING!
POLICE! HELP! HELP! A MURDERER THAT'S WHAT HE IS! A MURDERER!
NEXT DAY.....
BOY- A FINE MESS YOU MADE OF THINGS LAST NIGHT!
YEAH--- WEATHER-BEE'S SO MAD THERE'S NO TELL-ING WHAT HE'LL DO TO ME!
THAT'S ENOUGH FOR TODAY, ANDREWS! IF THERE WASN'T A BUTTON ON JUGHEAD'S FOIL, YOU'D LOOK LIKE A SIEVE!
YES SIR!
BETTY AND VERONICA ARE IN HIS OFFICE RIGHT NOW TRYING TO EXPLAIN THINGS!
TRYIN' TO EXPLAIN YOU OUTTA THAT ONE- IS LIKE TRYIN' TO EX-PLAIN AWAY A HOLE IN THE HEAD
meanwhile —
HMM-- WELL I SUPPOSE HE MIGHT HAVE BEEN DREAMING AT THAT!
OH YES, MR. WEATHERBEE! ARCHIE DIDN'T MEAN ANY HARM!
AND HE'S JUST DYING TO APOLOGIZE TO YOU PERSON-ALLY! HE'S OUTSIDE RIGHT NOW!
ALL RIGHT--- COME IN ANDREWS, AND--- YIPE!
HELP HE'S AFTER ME WITH A SWORD! HE'S A MURDERER!-- A MURDERER!
-The End-

ARCHIE'S SECRET WEAPON

AN ARCHIE STORY

by Kobold Keep

AT LEAST ONCE in his young life, every boy is bitten by the invention bug. Then his parents suffer. If he's bitten when he's married then his wife suffers.

It was Archie's parents and the whole town of Riverdale that were destined to suffer and suffer and suffer.

The cellar of the Andrews' home was almost in pitch blackness as Jughead staggered down the cellar stairs.

"Archie!" he cried, "your mother said you were down cellar."

A ghostly voice floated out of the darkness.

"Come on down, Jughead, but be careful of the wires?"

"What wires?"

"The ones at the bottom of the stairs, you dope!"

Jughead never listened to advice, so it was no surprise to Archie when he stumbled over the wires.

Crash! Spffffst! Brffxxsstt!

"Wow!" screamed Jughead, "there's a snake around me leg and it's spittin' somethin' awful!"

The cellar lights went on.

"Sit down, Jughead," said Archie calmly. He bent down and unravelled a length of thin copper wire from around Jughead's ankles. Jughead sniffed as he noticed a curl of smoke rising from the cuffs of his pants.

"Hey! You're burnin' my pants!" he cried from his position on the floor where he'd fallen.

"Well? I told you to look out for the wire!"

"What you doin'?" asked Jughead curiously, getting up and walking to a workbench in a corner of the cellar.

"Look out, don't touch it," cried Archie. "It's my secret weapon."

But Jughead had already put out an exploring hand and closed the fingers on a shiny copper switch.

"Yeow!" He jumped three feet into the air.

"See?" remarked Archie. He sat down at the bench and began working at the strange machine.

"What's it do?" asked Jughead, sucking on his burned fingers.

"It's an electromagneticsupervelocity sodium chloride projector."

"Oh. Yeah, but what does it *do?*"

Archie made some connections, wearing rubber gloves.

"Well, since you can't understand English, I'll translate it. It's a magnetic machine gun that fires salt bullets."

Jughead stared, openmouthed.

"Why?"

"Well, for one thing it's operated by electricity and not gunpowder. *There's* a saving on expense. Then, the bullets don't kill."

"Oh, no?"

"No, they just get under the skin and start the enemy scratching."

Jughead pointed to the miles of wire, tubing and metal braces.

"How you goin' to get this thing on a battlefield?"

"We'll worry about that later. Why if this thing works I'll be a millionaire and a hero. They're liable to erect a statue to me."

"Local boy makes good. Enemy scratches self to death," replied Jughead sourly.

"Look, Jughead, you don't have to kill a man to get him out of the way. Just get him busy enough so that he can't shoot *you!*"

"Where's the muzzle of this here machine?"

Archie pointed to a series of linked iron loops snaking up and out in all directions.

"This experimental model is designed to discourage attacks on forts and houses. Why it's even good for a burglar trap. I got thirty magnetic muzzles set all over the house from the ground floor. Any thief who gets within a hundred feet of the house—just watch him scratch."

"How do you know he's a thief?" asked Jughead scratching his own head.

"Don't do that! It makes me itchy just to look at you! Anyway, if anyone tries to break into the house all I've got to do is press this button here," Archie pointed to a shiny switch-button, "and he'll spend the next two years pickin' the salt out of himself."

"Where'd you get the bullets?"

"Carved 'em out of rocksalt. I twist a piece of iron wire around each of them and then feed 'em into the gun. The magnets pull the wire ahead and the bullet along with it. It speeds up as it goes along."

"Does your father and mother know anything about this here invention?"

Archie swallowed hard.

"No, they think I'm fixin' my old electric trains for the Ladies' Aid Charity."

"Well, why don't you?"

"Jughead, *millions* are involved in this invention. Besides when I'm rich, I'll buy the poor orphans lots of *new* trains."

"When you goin' to try out the gun?"

Archie looked puzzled.

"I don't know yet. That's what's holdin' up the test. I'm sorta scared to fire it off. There's about five hundred bullets in it now."

"Well you'll never get a million bucks if you don't

even know if the thing works."

Archie looked around the cellar stealthily.

"Well," he said, gulping, "we could try a short run around midnight when there wouldn't be anybody in the street."

"You *know* you got to go to bed at 11:00 o'clock."

Archie groaned, took off his rubber gloves and sat down on a rickety old chair.

"There's a gold mine and a ton of medals down here and I don't dare even see if it works!"

Jughead dropped on an old broken down couch. He put his hands under his head and began singing:

"Archie's sad and am I glad!
But I know what will please him,
A bottle of juice to make him a moose
An' Veronica Lodge to squeeze him!"

Suddenly, through the thin floorboards sounded the heavy voice of Mr. Andrews, Archie's father. He seemed highly excited.

"Here they come," he screamed at the top of his voice, "they're coming down the street!"

"Why, there's almost two hundred of them!" shrieked Archie's mother.

Archie and Jughead sat up with a jerk.

"Two hundred what?" asked Jughead, sleepily.

"Nazis, that's what!" cried Archie excitedly. "It's a parachute attack."

He hurled himself on his electromagneticsupervelocity-sodiumchlorideprojector and turned on the current.

Whizz! Whizzz whizzz whizzz! Whoooooschhhhhh!

Archie's thirty barrels began firing.

Then from outside the house there broke through the open cellar window a horrible series of yells. It sounded like a billion devils, all very uncomfortable. And it went on and on and on and on.

Archie was about to stick his head out of the window when his father shot down the cellar stairs like a bolt of lightning.

"Ye gods, Archie! What's going on down here? Mass murder? Look out the window."

Jughead got there first. And what he and Archie saw was a sight so terrible they remembered it for years.

Staggering down the street were the members of the Riverdale Chowder and Marching Society dressed in their sparkling uniforms. Half of them were scratching themselves furiously while the other half ripped off their uniforms and tried to get at the bullets.

Archie's secret weapon was a *great success!*

Two days later Mr. Andrews marched Archie down to the Riverdale Metal Scrap Collection and contributed the wire and piping to the pile.

The electromagneticsupervelocitysodiumchlorideprojector would get to Berlin—but not in the way Archie intended!

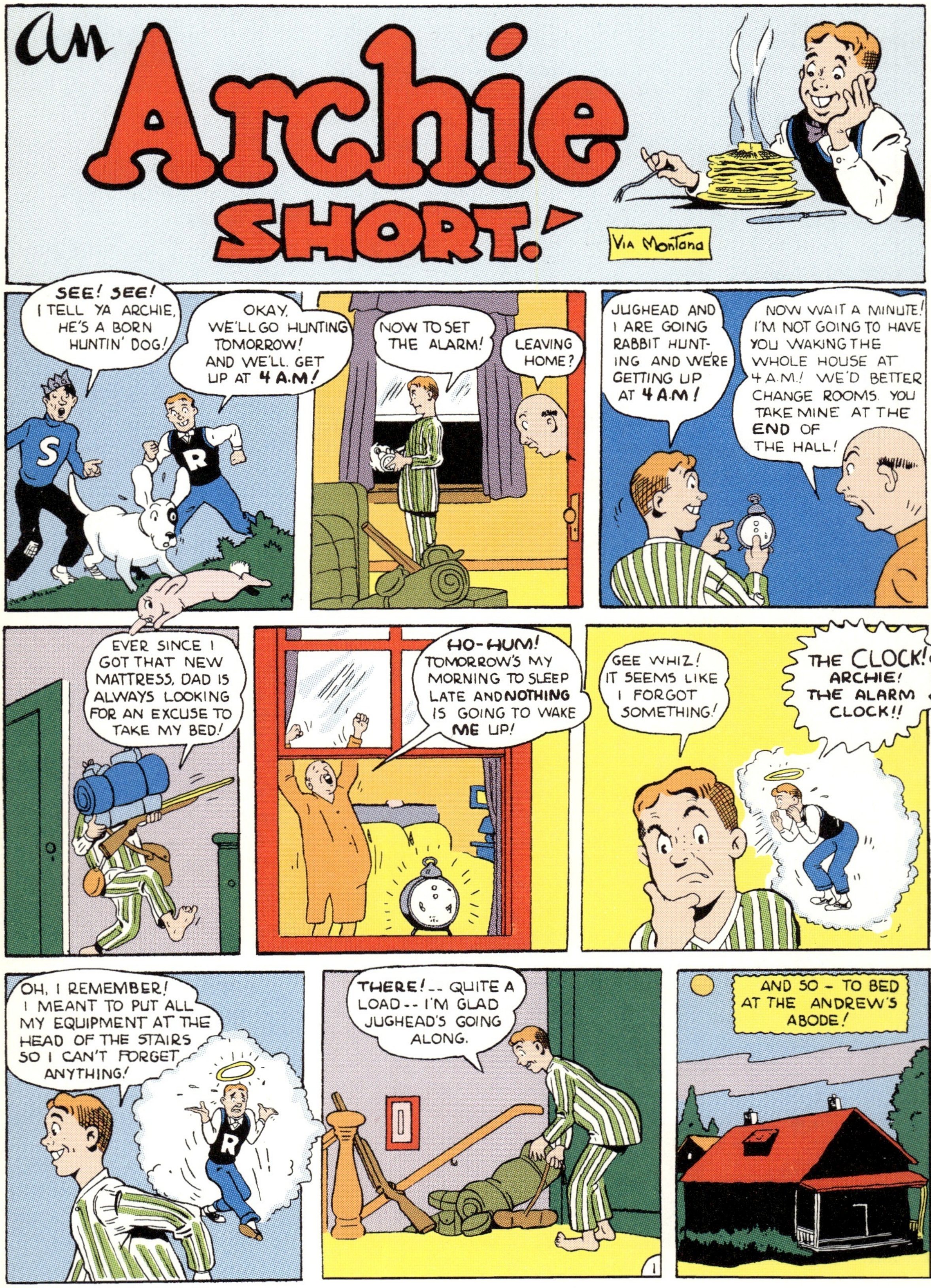
An Archie SHORT!
VIA MONTANA
SEE! SEE! I TELL YA ARCHIE, HE'S A BORN HUNTIN' DOG!
OKAY, WE'LL GO HUNTING TOMORROW! AND WE'LL GET UP AT 4 A.M!
NOW TO SET THE ALARM!
LEAVING HOME?
JUGHEAD AND I ARE GOING RABBIT HUNTING AND WE'RE GETTING UP AT 4 A.M!
NOW WAIT A MINUTE! I'M NOT GOING TO HAVE YOU WAKING THE WHOLE HOUSE AT 4 A.M.! WE'D BETTER CHANGE ROOMS. YOU TAKE MINE AT THE END OF THE HALL!
EVER SINCE I GOT THAT NEW MATTRESS, DAD IS ALWAYS LOOKING FOR AN EXCUSE TO TAKE MY BED!
HO-HUM! TOMORROW'S MY MORNING TO SLEEP LATE AND NOTHING IS GOING TO WAKE ME UP!
GEE WHIZ! IT SEEMS LIKE I FORGOT SOMETHING!
THE CLOCK! ARCHIE! THE ALARM CLOCK!!
OH, I REMEMBER! I MEANT TO PUT ALL MY EQUIPMENT AT THE HEAD OF THE STAIRS SO I CAN'T FORGET ANYTHING!
THERE!-- QUITE A LOAD-- I'M GLAD JUGHEAD'S GOING ALONG.
1
AND SO - TO BED AT THE ANDREW'S ABODE!

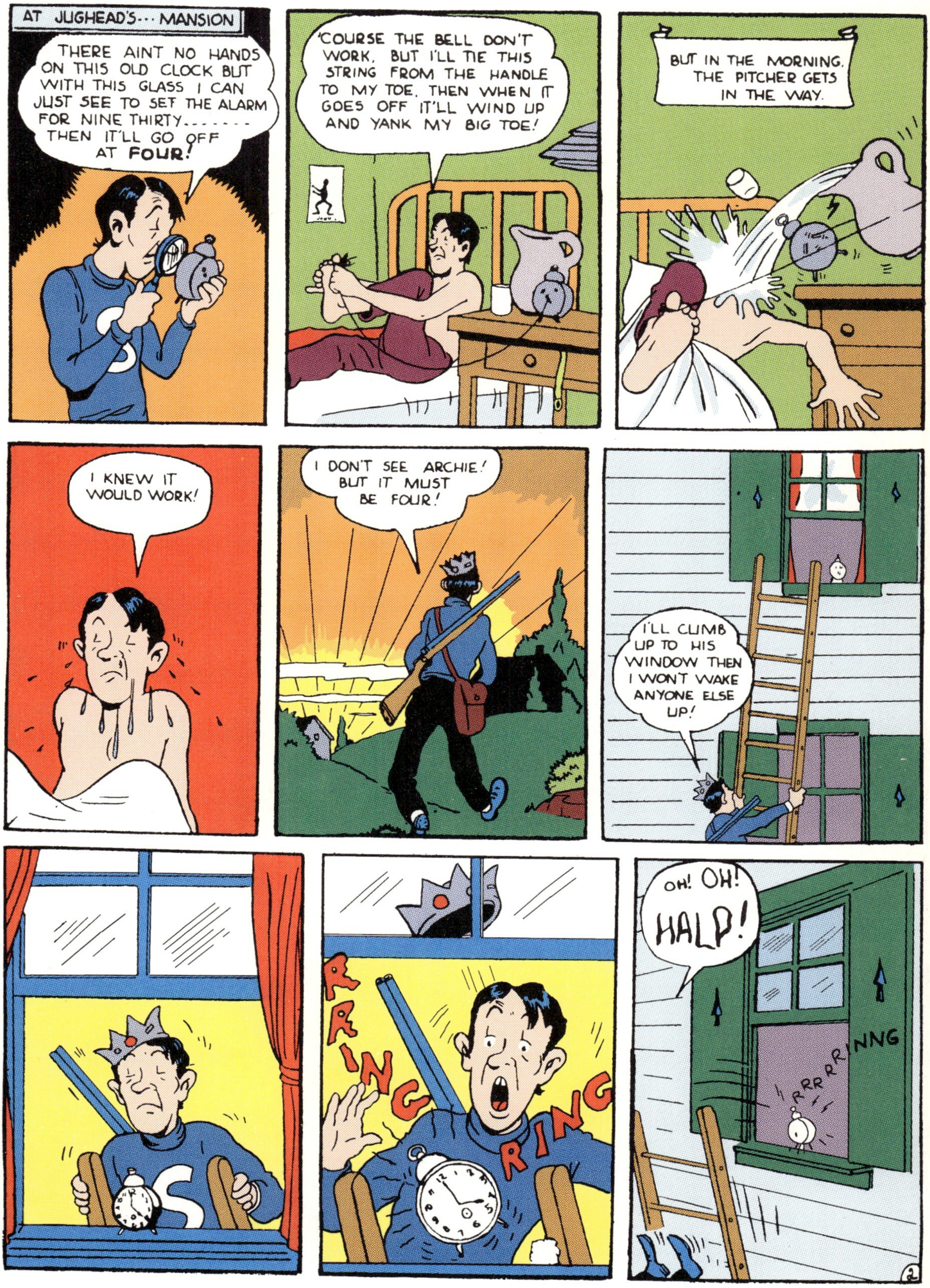
AT JUGHEAD'S... MANSION
THERE AINT NO HANDS ON THIS OLD CLOCK BUT WITH THIS GLASS I CAN JUST SEE TO SET THE ALARM FOR NINE THIRTY....... THEN IT'LL GO OFF AT FOUR!
'COURSE THE BELL DON'T WORK, BUT I'LL TIE THIS STRING FROM THE HANDLE TO MY TOE, THEN WHEN IT GOES OFF IT'LL WIND UP AND YANK MY BIG TOE!
BUT IN THE MORNING, THE PITCHER GETS IN THE WAY.
I KNEW IT WOULD WORK!
I DON'T SEE ARCHIE! BUT IT MUST BE FOUR!
I'LL CLIMB UP TO HIS WINDOW THEN I WON'T WAKE ANYONE ELSE UP!
RRING
RING
OH! OH! HALP!
RRRRINNG
2

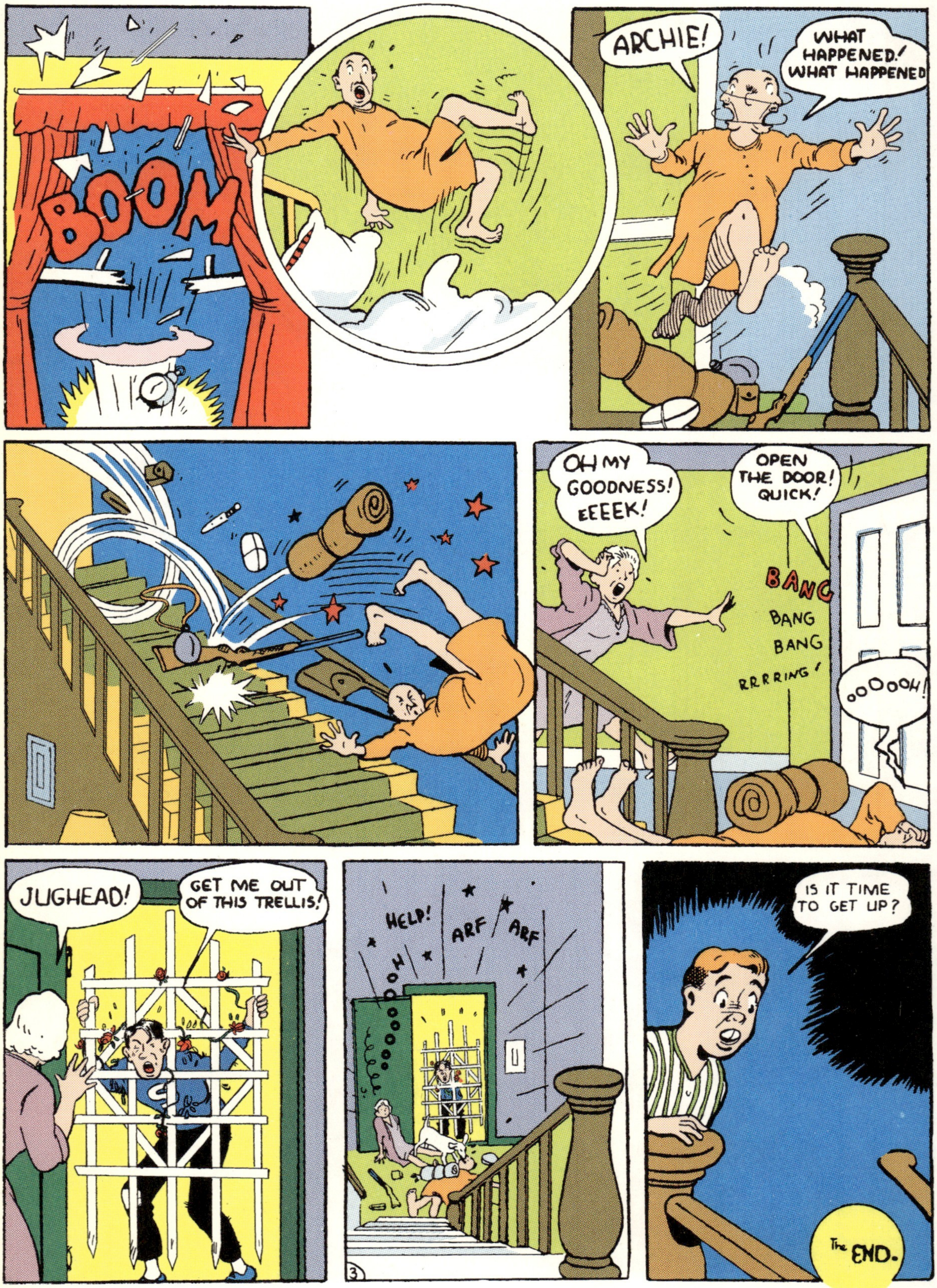
BOOM
ARCHIE!
WHAT HAPPENED! WHAT HAPPENED
OH MY GOODNESS! EEEEK!
OPEN THE DOOR! QUICK!
BANG
BANG
BANG
RRRRING!
OOOOOH!
JUGHEAD!
GET ME OUT OF THIS TRELLIS!
HELP!
ARF
ARF
OOOOOH
IS IT TIME TO GET UP?
The END.

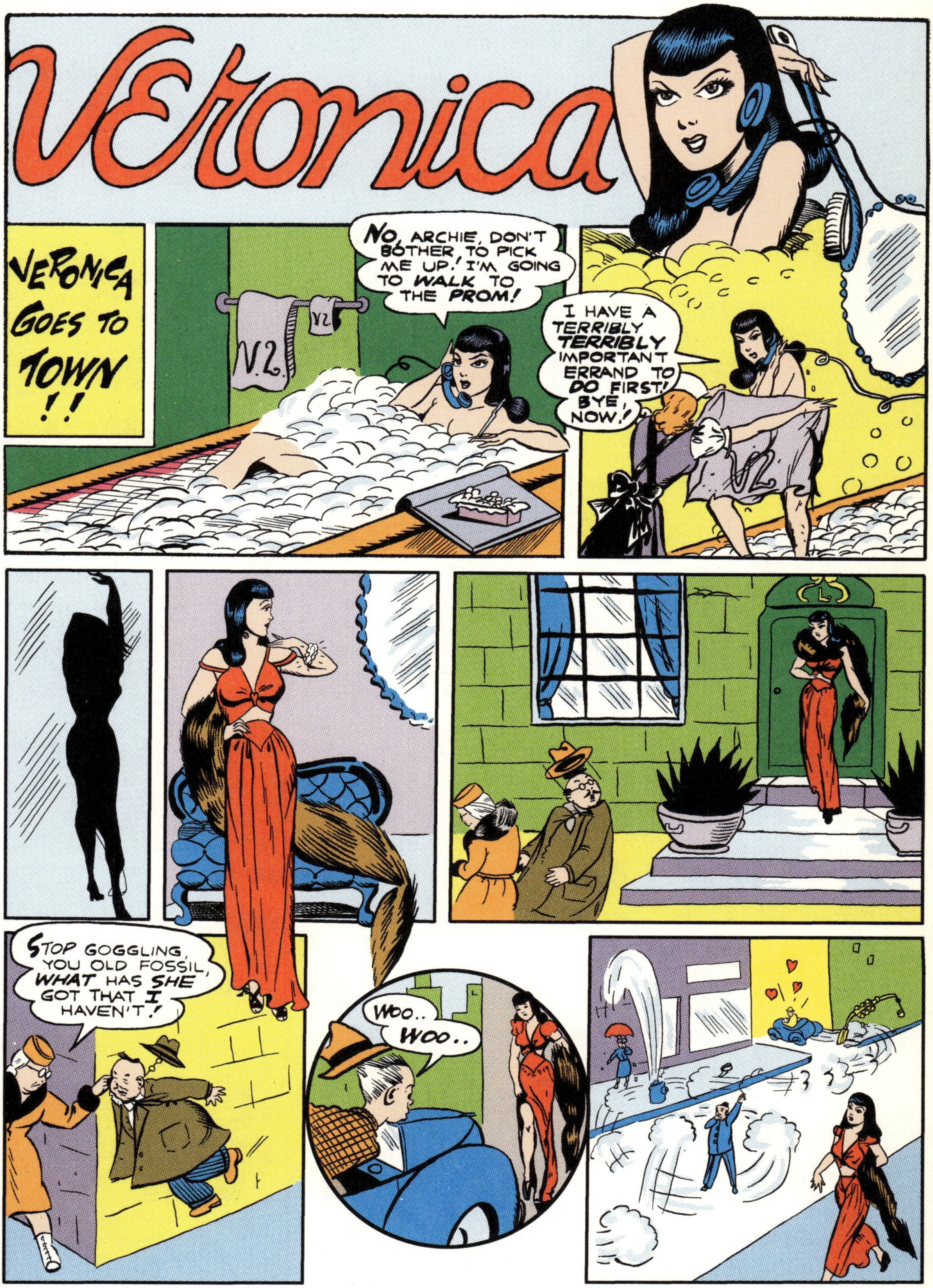
Veronica
VERONICA GOES TO TOWN!!
NO, ARCHIE, DON'T BOTHER, TO PICK ME UP! I'M GOING TO WALK TO THE PROM!
V.2.
I HAVE A TERRIBLY TERRIBLY IMPORTANT ERRAND TO DO FIRST! BYE, NOW!
STOP GOGGLING, YOU OLD FOSSIL, WHAT HAS SHE GOT THAT I HAVEN'T!
WOO.. WOO..

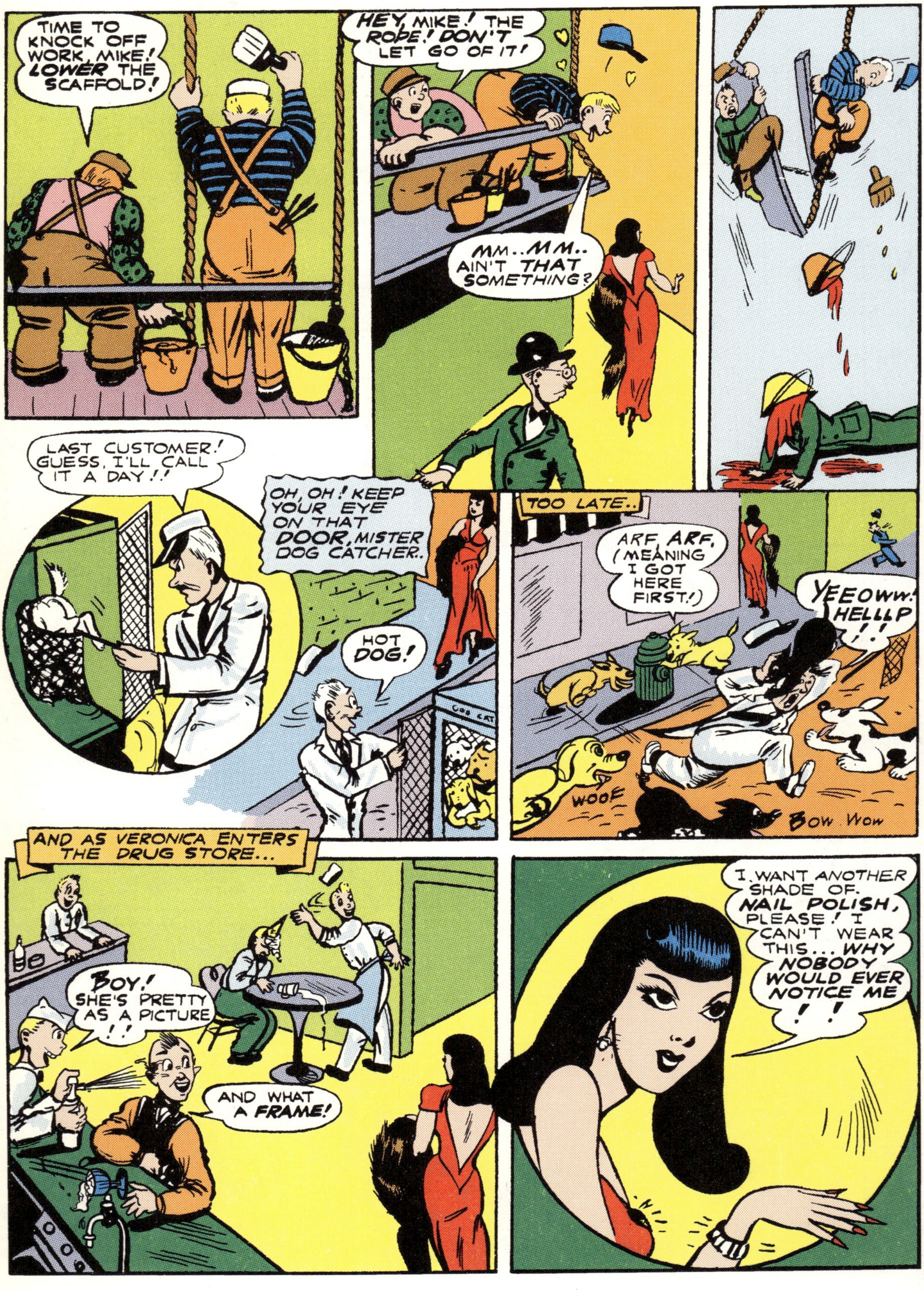
TIME TO KNOCK OFF WORK, MIKE! LOWER THE SCAFFOLD!
HEY, MIKE! THE ROPE! DON'T LET GO OF IT!
MM..MM.. AIN'T THAT SOMETHING?
LAST CUSTOMER! GUESS, I'LL CALL IT A DAY!!
OH, OH! KEEP YOUR EYE ON THAT DOOR, MISTER DOG CATCHER..
HOT DOG!
TOO LATE..
ARF ARF, (MEANING I GOT HERE FIRST!)
YEEOWW! HELLLP!!
WOOF
BOW WOW
AND AS VERONICA ENTERS THE DRUG STORE...
BOY! SHE'S PRETTY AS A PICTURE!!
AND WHAT A FRAME!
I WANT ANOTHER SHADE OF NAIL POLISH, PLEASE! I CAN'T WEAR THIS... WHY NOBODY WOULD EVER NOTICE ME!!

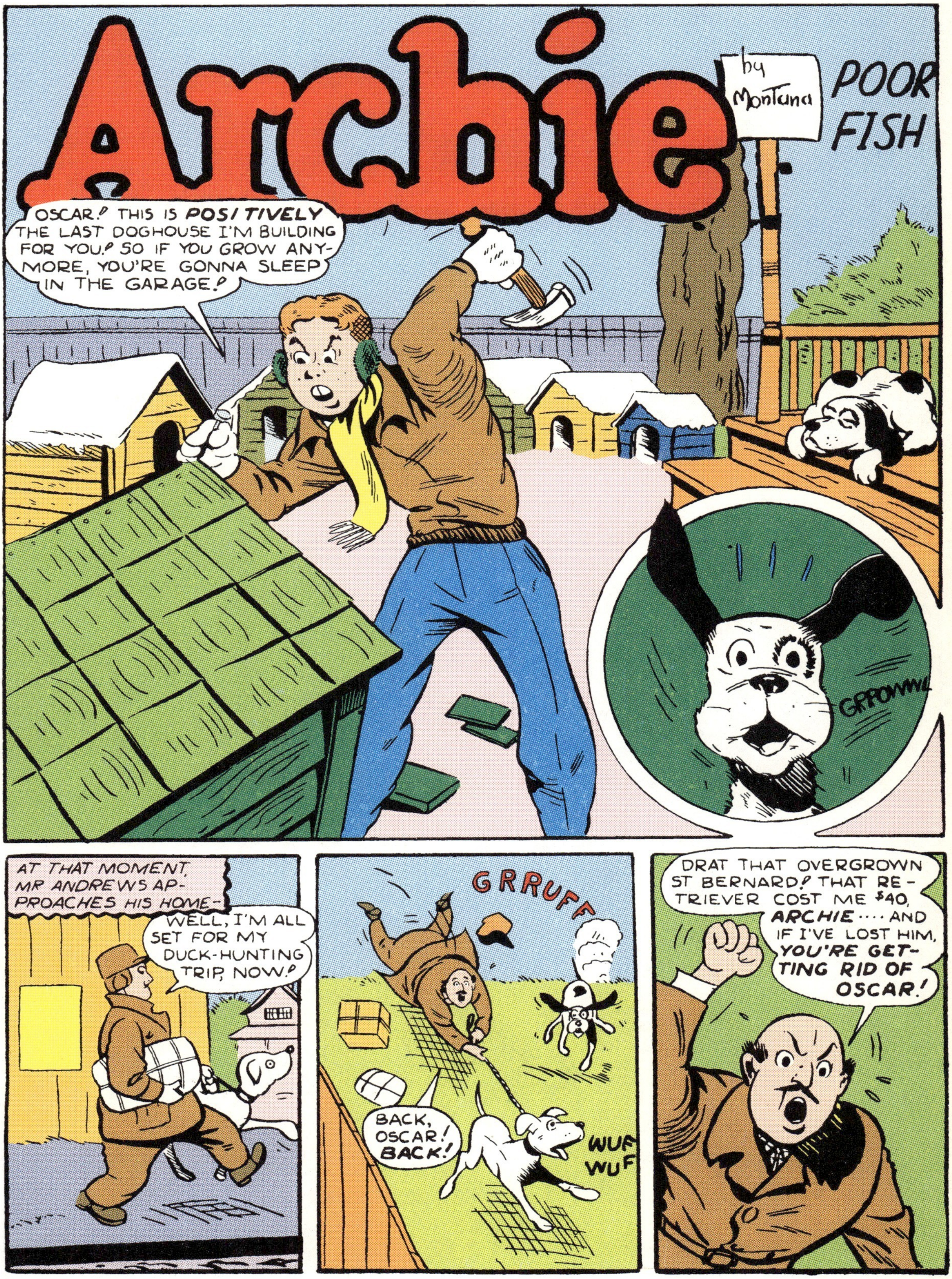
Archie
by MonTana
POOR FISH
OSCAR! THIS IS POSITIVELY THE LAST DOGHOUSE I'M BUILDING FOR YOU! SO IF YOU GROW ANY-MORE, YOU'RE GONNA SLEEP IN THE GARAGE!
GRROWWL
AT THAT MOMENT, MR ANDREWS AP-PROACHES HIS HOME-
WELL, I'M ALL SET FOR MY DUCK-HUNTING TRIP, NOW!
GRRUFF
BACK, OSCAR! BACK!
WUF WUF
DRAT THAT OVERGROWN ST BERNARD! THAT RE-TRIEVER COST ME $40, ARCHIE.... AND IF I'VE LOST HIM, YOU'RE GET-TING RID OF OSCAR!

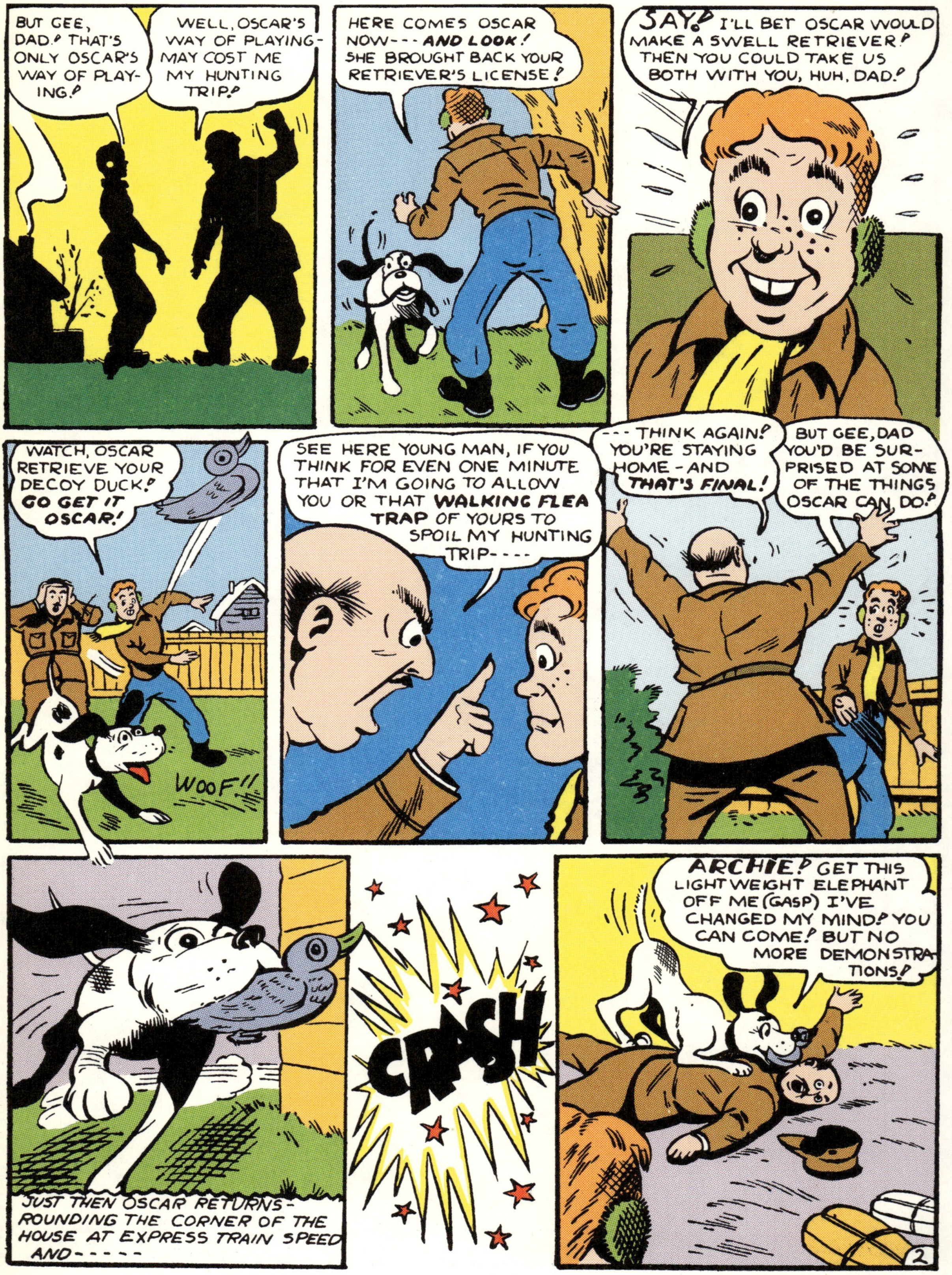

BUT GEE, DAD! THAT'S ONLY OSCAR'S WAY OF PLAY-ING!
WELL, OSCAR'S WAY OF PLAYING-MAY COST ME MY HUNTING TRIP!
HERE COMES OSCAR NOW--- AND LOOK! SHE BROUGHT BACK YOUR RETRIEVER'S LICENSE!
SAY! I'LL BET OSCAR WOULD MAKE A SWELL RETRIEVER! THEN YOU COULD TAKE US BOTH WITH YOU, HUH, DAD!
WATCH, OSCAR RETRIEVE YOUR DECOY DUCK! GO GET IT OSCAR!
WOOF!!
SEE HERE YOUNG MAN, IF YOU THINK FOR EVEN ONE MINUTE THAT I'M GOING TO ALLOW YOU OR THAT WALKING FLEA TRAP OF YOURS TO SPOIL MY HUNTING TRIP---
---THINK AGAIN! YOU'RE STAYING HOME - AND THAT'S FINAL!
BUT GEE, DAD YOU'D BE SUR-PRISED AT SOME OF THE THINGS OSCAR CAN DO!
JUST THEN OSCAR RETURNS- ROUNDING THE CORNER OF THE HOUSE AT EXPRESS TRAIN SPEED AND-----
CRASH
ARCHIE! GET THIS LIGHTWEIGHT ELEPHANT OFF ME (GASP) I'VE CHANGED MY MIND! YOU CAN COME! BUT NO MORE DEMONSTRA-TIONS!
2

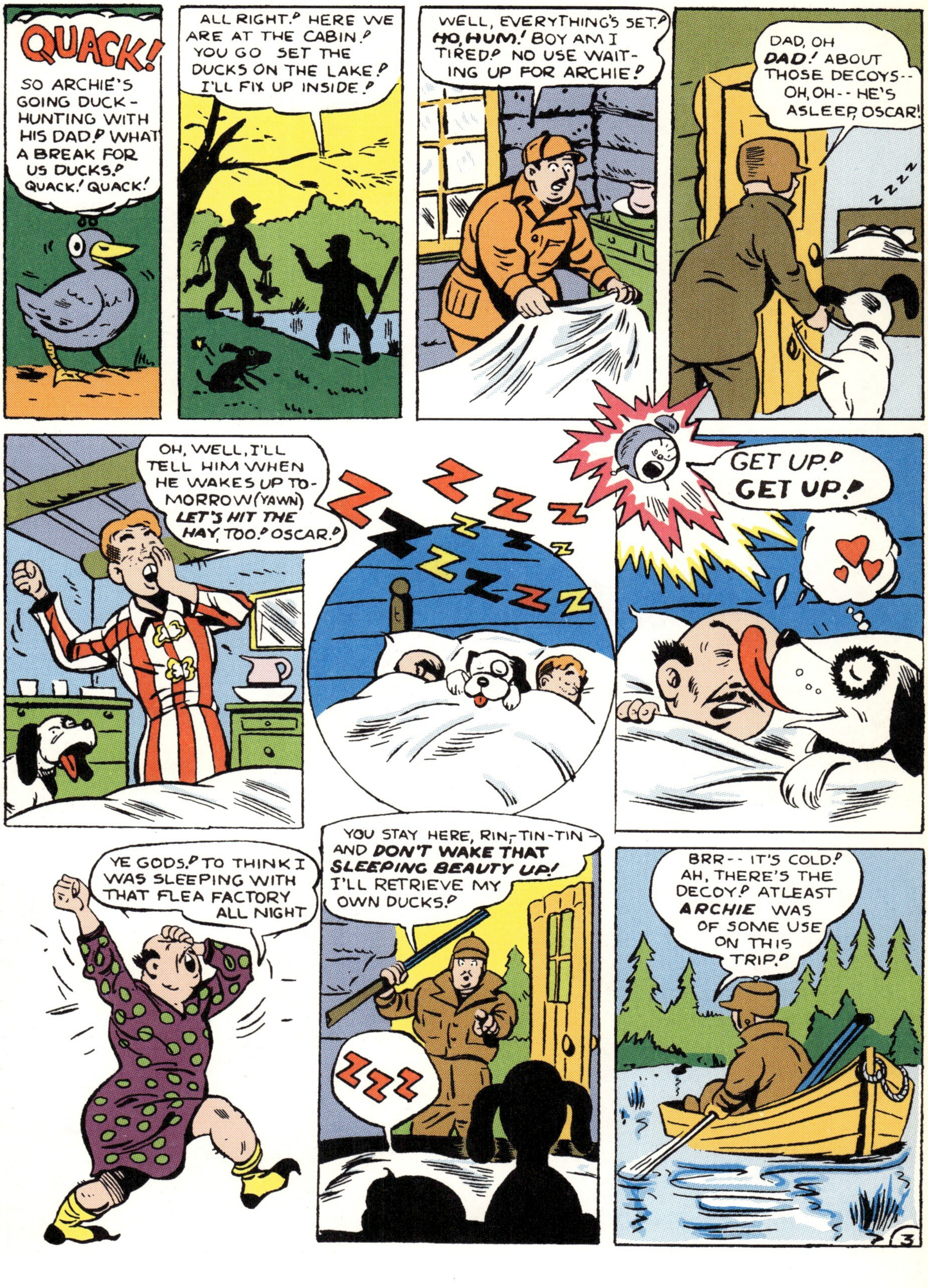
QUACK!
SO ARCHIE'S GOING DUCK-HUNTING WITH HIS DAD! WHAT A BREAK FOR US DUCKS! QUACK! QUACK!
ALL RIGHT! HERE WE ARE AT THE CABIN! YOU GO SET THE DUCKS ON THE LAKE! I'LL FIX UP INSIDE!
WELL, EVERYTHING'S SET! HO, HUM! BOY AM I TIRED! NO USE WAITING UP FOR ARCHIE!
DAD, OH DAD! ABOUT THOSE DECOYS-- OH, OH-- HE'S ASLEEP, OSCAR!
OH, WELL, I'LL TELL HIM WHEN HE WAKES UP TOMORROW (YAWN) LET'S HIT THE HAY, TOO! OSCAR!
GET UP! GET UP!
YE GODS! TO THINK I WAS SLEEPING WITH THAT FLEA FACTORY ALL NIGHT
YOU STAY HERE, RIN-TIN-TIN AND DON'T WAKE THAT SLEEPING BEAUTY UP! I'LL RETRIEVE MY OWN DUCKS!
BRR-- IT'S COLD! AH, THERE'S THE DECOY! ATLEAST ARCHIE WAS OF SOME USE ON THIS TRIP!
3

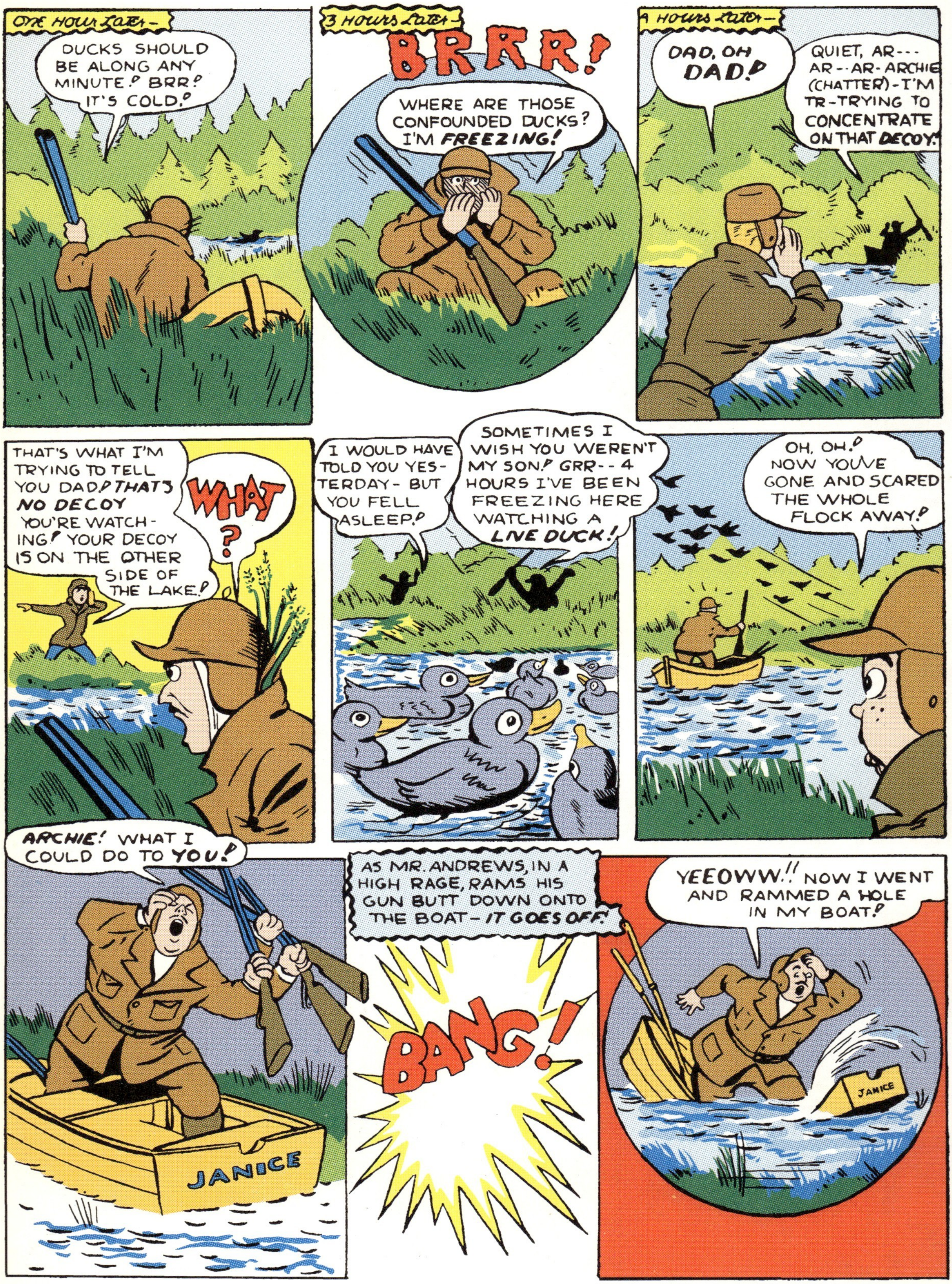
One Hour Later—
DUCKS SHOULD BE ALONG ANY MINUTE! BRR! IT'S COLD!
3 Hours Later—
BRRR!
WHERE ARE THOSE CONFOUNDED DUCKS? I'M FREEZING!
4 Hours Later—
DAD, OH DAD!
QUIET, AR--- AR--AR-ARCHIE (CHATTER)-I'M TR-TRYING TO CONCENTRATE ON THAT DECOY!
THAT'S WHAT I'M TRYING TO TELL YOU DAD! THAT'S NO DECOY YOU'RE WATCHING! YOUR DECOY IS ON THE OTHER SIDE OF THE LAKE!
WHAT ?
I WOULD HAVE TOLD YOU YES-TERDAY- BUT YOU FELL ASLEEP!
SOMETIMES I WISH YOU WEREN'T MY SON! GRR--4 HOURS I'VE BEEN FREEZING HERE WATCHING A LIVE DUCK!
OH, OH! NOW YOU'VE GONE AND SCARED THE WHOLE FLOCK AWAY!
ARCHIE! WHAT I COULD DO TO YOU!
JANICE
AS MR. ANDREWS, IN A HIGH RAGE, RAMS HIS GUN BUTT DOWN ONTO THE BOAT- IT GOES OFF!
BANG!
YEEOWW!! NOW I WENT AND RAMMED A HOLE IN MY BOAT!
JANICE

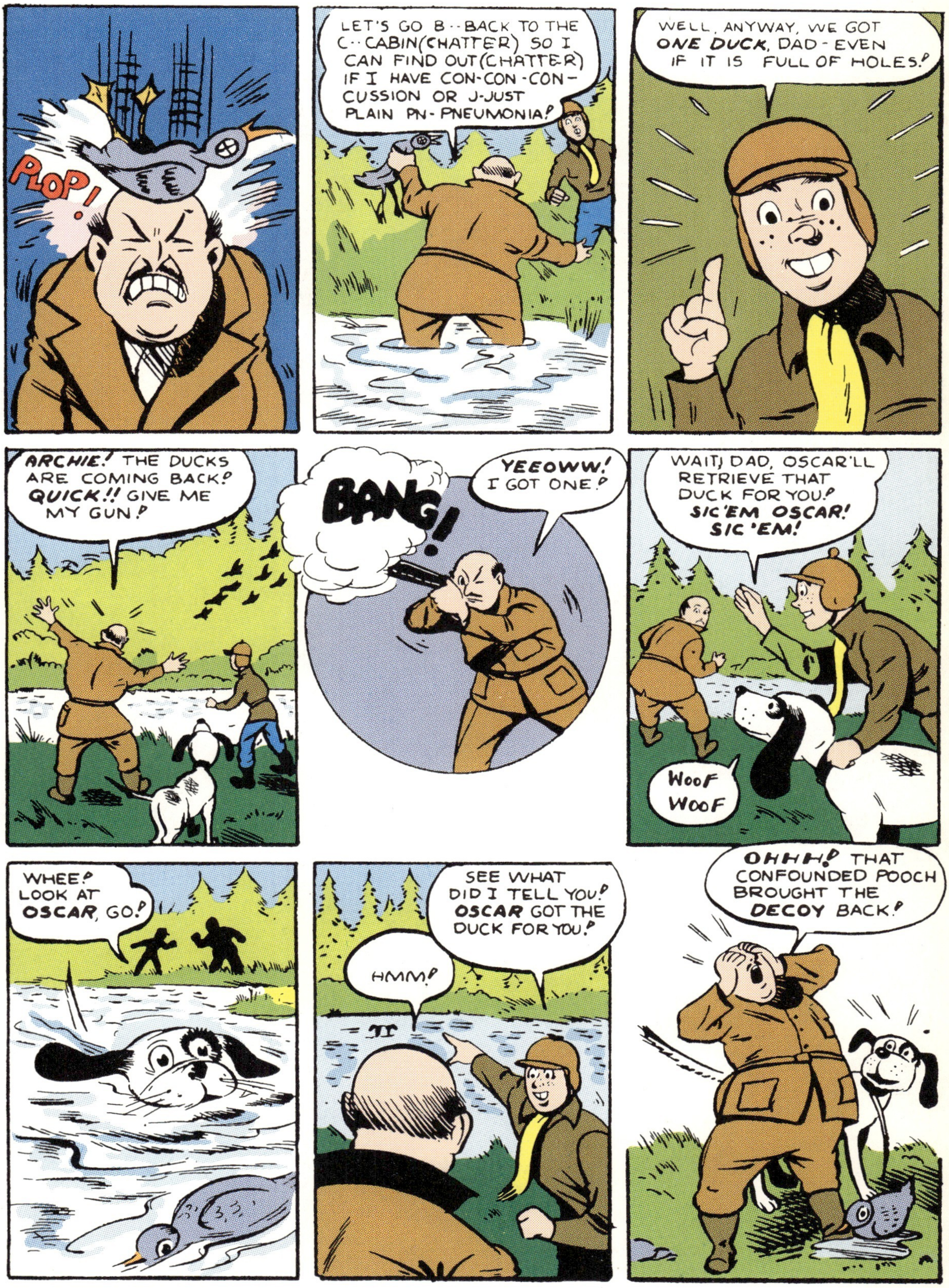
PLOP!
LET'S GO B--BACK TO THE C--CABIN(CHATTER) SO I CAN FIND OUT(CHATTER) IF I HAVE CON-CON-CON-CUSSION OR J-JUST PLAIN PN-PNEUMONIA!
WELL, ANYWAY, WE GOT ONE DUCK, DAD - EVEN IF IT IS FULL OF HOLES!
ARCHIE! THE DUCKS ARE COMING BACK! QUICK!! GIVE ME MY GUN!
BANG!
YEEOWW! I GOT ONE!
WAIT, DAD, OSCAR'LL RETRIEVE THAT DUCK FOR YOU! SIC'EM OSCAR! SIC'EM!
WOOF WOOF
WHEE! LOOK AT OSCAR, GO!
SEE WHAT DID I TELL YOU! OSCAR GOT THE DUCK FOR YOU!
HMM!
OHHH! THAT CONFOUNDED POOCH BROUGHT THE DECOY BACK!

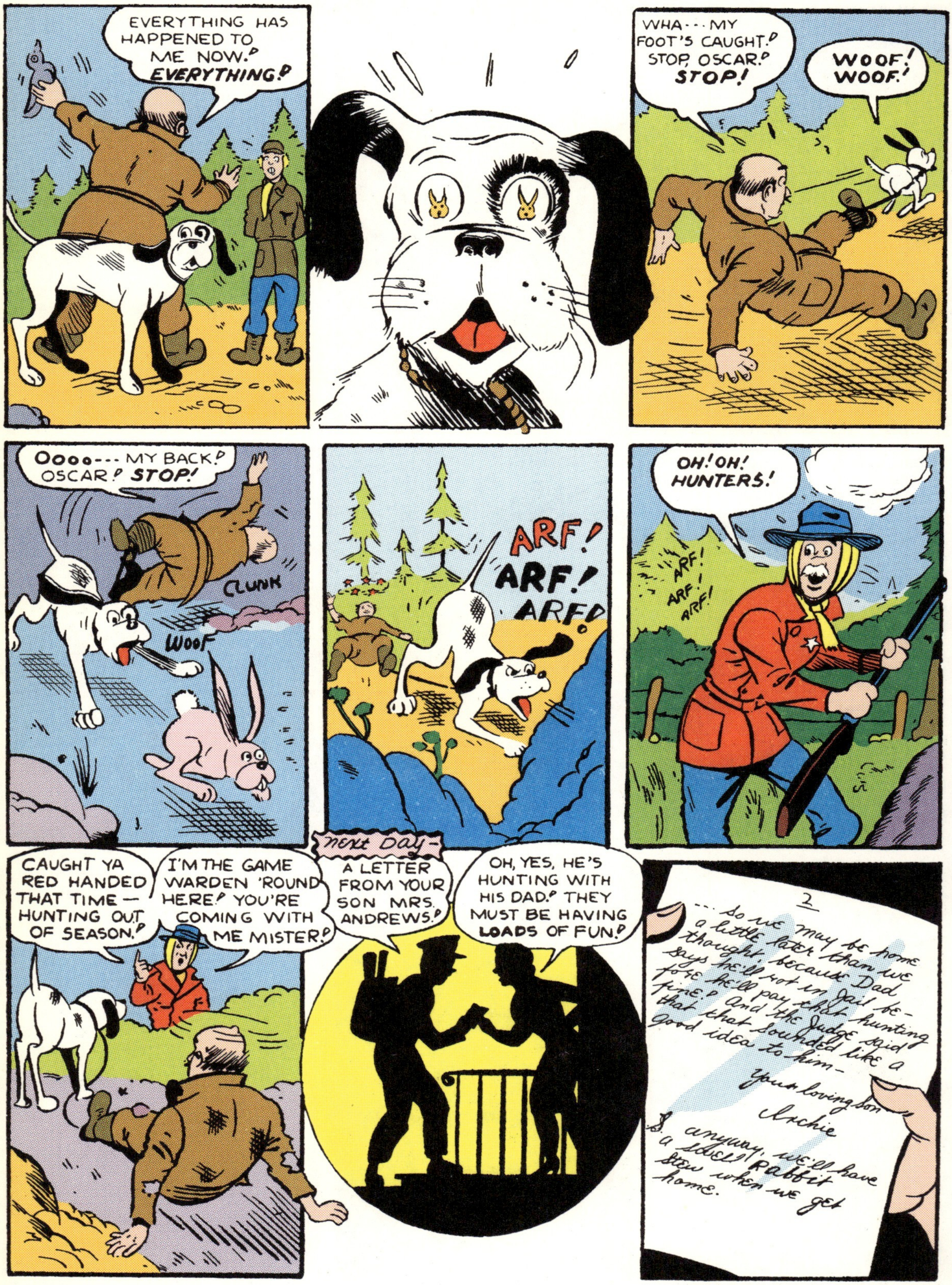
EVERYTHING HAS HAPPENED TO ME NOW. EVERYTHING!
WHA--- MY FOOT'S CAUGHT. STOP, OSCAR. STOP!
WOOF! WOOF!
Oooo--- MY BACK! OSCAR! STOP!
CLUNK
WOOF
ARF! ARF! ARF!
OH! OH! HUNTERS!
ARF! ARF! ARF!
CAUGHT YA RED HANDED THAT TIME — HUNTING OUT OF SEASON.
I'M THE GAME WARDEN 'ROUND HERE! YOU'RE COMING WITH ME MISTER!
next Day-
A LETTER FROM YOUR SON MRS. ANDREWS.
OH, YES, HE'S HUNTING WITH HIS DAD. THEY MUST BE HAVING LOADS OF FUN!
2
... So we may be home a little later than we thought, because Dad says he'll rot in jail before he'll pay that hunting fine! And the Judge said that that sounded like a good idea to him-
Your loving son
Archie
P.S. anyway, we'll have a swell Rabbit stew when we get home.

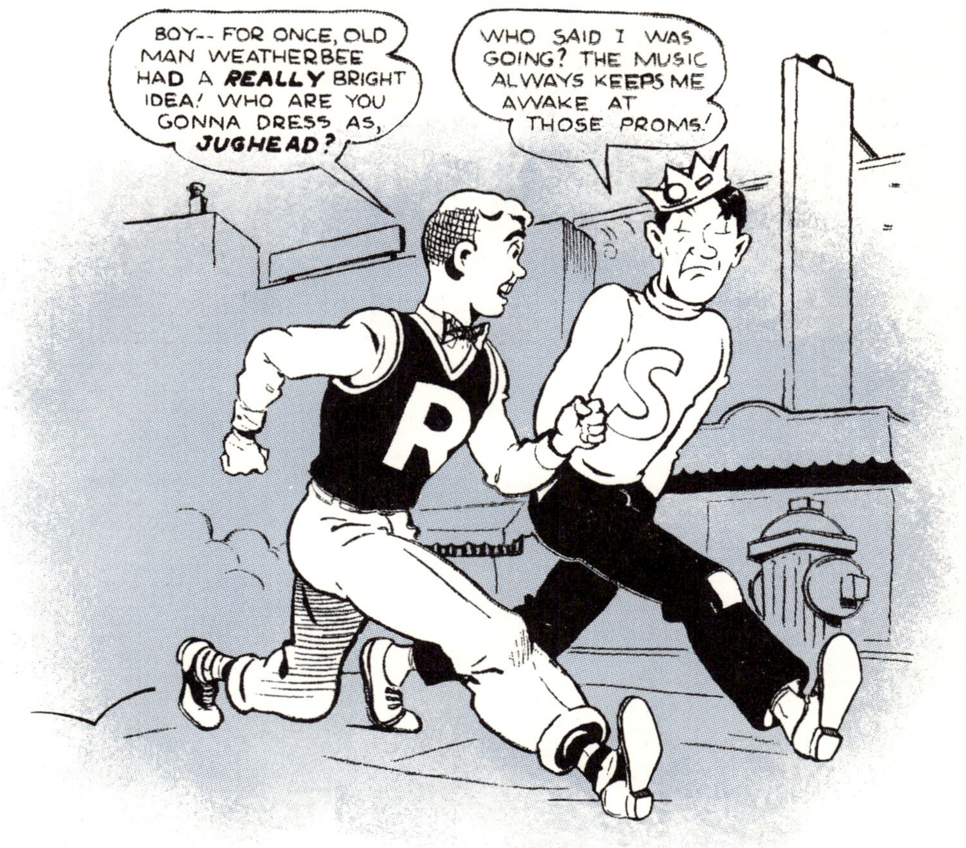
BOY-- FOR ONCE, OLD MAN WEATHERBEE HAD A **REALLY** BRIGHT IDEA! WHO ARE YOU GONNA DRESS AS, **JUGHEAD?**
WHO SAID I WAS GOING? THE MUSIC ALWAYS KEEPS ME AWAKE AT THOSE PROMS!

DARK HORSE ARCHIVES

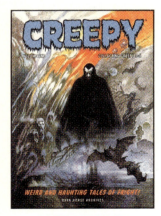

CREEPY ARCHIVES
Volume One
ISBN 978-1-59307-973-4
Volume Two
ISBN 978-1-59582-168-3
Volume Three
ISBN 978-1-59582-259-8
Volume Four
ISBN 978-1-59582-308-3
Volume Five
ISBN 978-1-59582-353-3
Volume Six
ISBN 978-1-59582-354-0
Volume Seven
ISBN 978-1-59582-516-2
Volume Eight
ISBN 978-1-59582-568-1
Volume Nine
ISBN 978-1-59582-693-0
$49.99 each

EERIE ARCHIVES
Volume One
ISBN 978-1-59582-245-1
Volume Two
ISBN 978-1-59582-315-1
Volume Three
ISBN 978-1-59582-369-4
Volume Four
ISBN 978-1-59582-429-5
Volume Five
ISBN 978-1-59582-525-4
Volume Six
ISBN 978-1-59582-569-8
$49.99 each

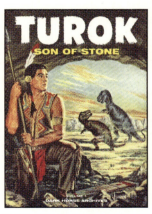

TUROK, SON OF STONE ARCHIVES
Volume One
ISBN 978-1-59582-155-3
Volume Two
ISBN 978-1-59582-275-8
Volume Three
ISBN 978-1-59582-281-9
Volume Four
ISBN 978-1-59582-343-4
Volume Five
ISBN 978-1-59582-442-4
Volume Six
ISBN 978-1-59582-484-4
Volume Seven
ISBN 978-1-59582-565-0
Volume Eight
ISBN 978-1-59582-641-1
$49.99 each

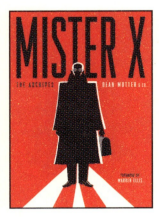

MISTER X: THE ARCHIVES
ISBN 978-1-59582-184-3
$79.99

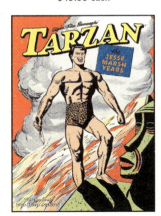

**TARZAN ARCHIVES:
THE JESSE MARSH YEARS**
Volume One
ISBN 978-1-59582-238-3
Volume Two
ISBN 978-1-59582-294-9
Volume Three
ISBN 978-1-59582-379-3
Volume Four
ISBN 978-1-59582-392-2
Volume Five
ISBN 978-1-59582-426-4
Volume Six
ISBN 978-1-59582-497-4
Volume Seven
ISBN 978-1-59582-547-6
Volume Eight
ISBN 978-1-59582-548-3
Volume Nine
ISBN 978-1-59582-649-7
$49.99 each

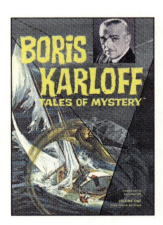

**BORIS KARLOFF TALES OF
MYSTERY ARCHIVES**
Volume One
ISBN 978-1-59582-219-2
Volume Two
ISBN 978-1-59582-428-8
Volume Three
ISBN 978-1-59582-551-3
Volume Four
ISBN 978-1-59582-614-5
Volume Five
ISBN 978-1-59582-615-2
$49.99 each

DARK HORSE COMICS

AVAILABLE AT YOUR LOCAL COMICS SHOP OR BOOKSTORE!

NEMESIS
DARK HORSE ARCHIVES

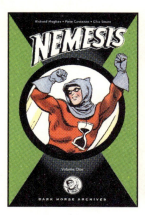

NEMESIS ARCHIVES
ISBN 978-1-59307-986-4
$59.99

Tarzan
DARK HORSE ARCHIVES

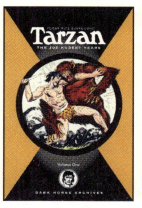

TARZAN ARCHIVES: THE JOE KUBERT YEARS
Volume One
ISBN 978-1-59307-404-3
Volume Two
ISBN 978-1-59307-416-6
Volume Three
ISBN 978-1-59307-417-3
$49.99 each

MAKE WAY FOR the FAT FURY
HERBIE
DARK HORSE ARCHIVES

HERBIE ARCHIVES
Volume One
ISBN 978-1-59307-987-1
Volume Two
ISBN 978-1-59582-216-1
Volume Three
ISBN 978-1-59582-302-1
$49.99 each

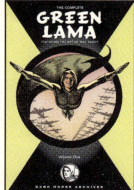

THE COMPLETE
GREEN LAMA
DARK HORSE ARCHIVES

THE COMPLETE GREEN LAMA, FEATURING THE ART OF MAC RABOY
Volume One
ISBN 978-1-59307-942-0
Volume Two
ISBN 978-1-59582-154-6
$49.99 each

SHMOO
DARK HORSE ARCHIVES

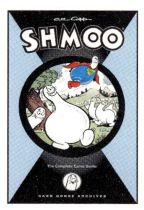

AL CAPP'S COMPLETE SHMOO
ISBN 978-1-59307-901-7
$49.99

Roy Rogers
COMICS
DARK HORSE ARCHIVES

ROY ROGERS ARCHIVES
ISBN 978-1-59307-966-6
$49.99

MAGICMAN
DARK HORSE ARCHIVES

MAGICMAN ARCHIVES
ISBN 978-1-59307-985-7
$59.99

NEXUS
DARK HORSE ARCHIVES

NEXUS ARCHIVES
Volume One
ISBN 978-1-59307-398-5
Volume Two
ISBN 978-1-59307-455-5
Volume Three
ISBN 978-1-59307-495-1
Volume Four
ISBN 978-1-59307-583-5
Volume Five
ISBN 978-1-59307-584-2
Volume Six
ISBN 978-1-59307-791-4
Volume Seven
ISBN 978-1-59307-877-5
Volume Eight
ISBN 978-1-59582-236-9
Volume Nine
ISBN 978-1-59582-313-7
Volume Ten
ISBN 978-1-59582-438-7
Volume Eleven
ISBN 978-1-59582-496-7
Volume Twelve
ISBN 978-1-59582-636-7
$49.99 each

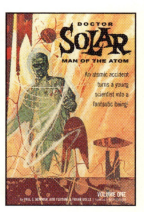

DOCTOR
SOLAR
MAN OF THE ATOM
An atomic accident turns a young scientist into a fantastic being!
VOLUME ONE

DOCTOR SOLAR: MAN OF THE ATOM
Volume One (TPB)
ISBN 978-1-59582-586-5
$19.99
Volume Two (HC)
ISBN 978-1-59307-327-5
Volume Three (HC)
ISBN 978-1-59307-374-9
Volume Four (HC)
ISBN 978-1-59307-825-6
$49.99 each

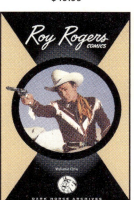

Little Lulu®

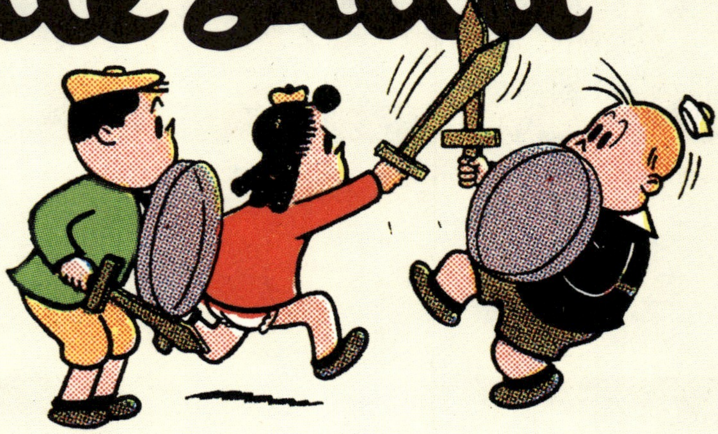

• GIANT-SIZE LITTLE LULU •

Volume 1:
Collects Little Lulu *volumes 1–3*
978-1-59582-502-5 | $24.99

Volume 2:
Collects Little Lulu *volumes 4–6*
978-1-59582-540-7 | $24.99

Volume 3:
Collects Little Lulu *volumes 7–9*
978-1-59582-634-3 | $24.99

• LITTLE LULU •

Volume 10:
All Dressed Up
978-1-59307-534-7 | $9.99

Volume 11:
April Fools
978-1-59307-557-6 | $9.99

Volume 12:
Leave It to Lulu
978-1-59307-620-7 | $9.99

Volume 13:
Too Much Fun
978-1-59307-621-4 | $9.99

Volume 14:
Queen Lulu
978-1-59307-683-2 | $9.99

Volume 15:
The Explorers
978-1-59307-684-9 | $9.99

Volume 16:
A Handy Kid
978-1-59307-685-6 | $10.99

Volume 17:
The Valentine
978-1-59307-686-3 | $10.99

Volume 18:
The Expert
978-1-59307-687-0 | $10.99

• FULL COLOR VOLUMES •

Volume 19:
The Alamo and Other Stories
978-1-59582-293-2 | $14.99

Volume 20:
The Bawlplayers and Other Stories
978-1-59582-364-9 | $14.99

Volume 21:
Miss Feeny's Folly and Other Stories
978-1-59582-365-6 | $14.99

Volume 22:
The Big Dipper Club and Other Stories
978-1-59582-420-2 | $14.99

Volume 23:
The Bogey Snowman and Other Stories
978-1-59582-474-5 | $14.99

Volume 24:
The Space Dolly and Other Stories
978-1-59582-475-2 | $14.99

Volume 25:
The Burglar-Proof Clubhouse and Other Stories
978-1-59582-539-1 | $14.99

Volume 26:
The Feud and Other Stories
978-1-59582-632-9 | $14.99

AVAILABLE AT YOUR LOCAL COMICS SHOP OR BOOKSTORE!
To find a comics shop in your area, call 1.888.266.4226. For more information or to order direct, visit darkhorse.com or call 1.800.862.0052. Mon.–Fri. 9 A.M. to 5 P.M. Pacific Time. *Prices and availability subject to change without notice.

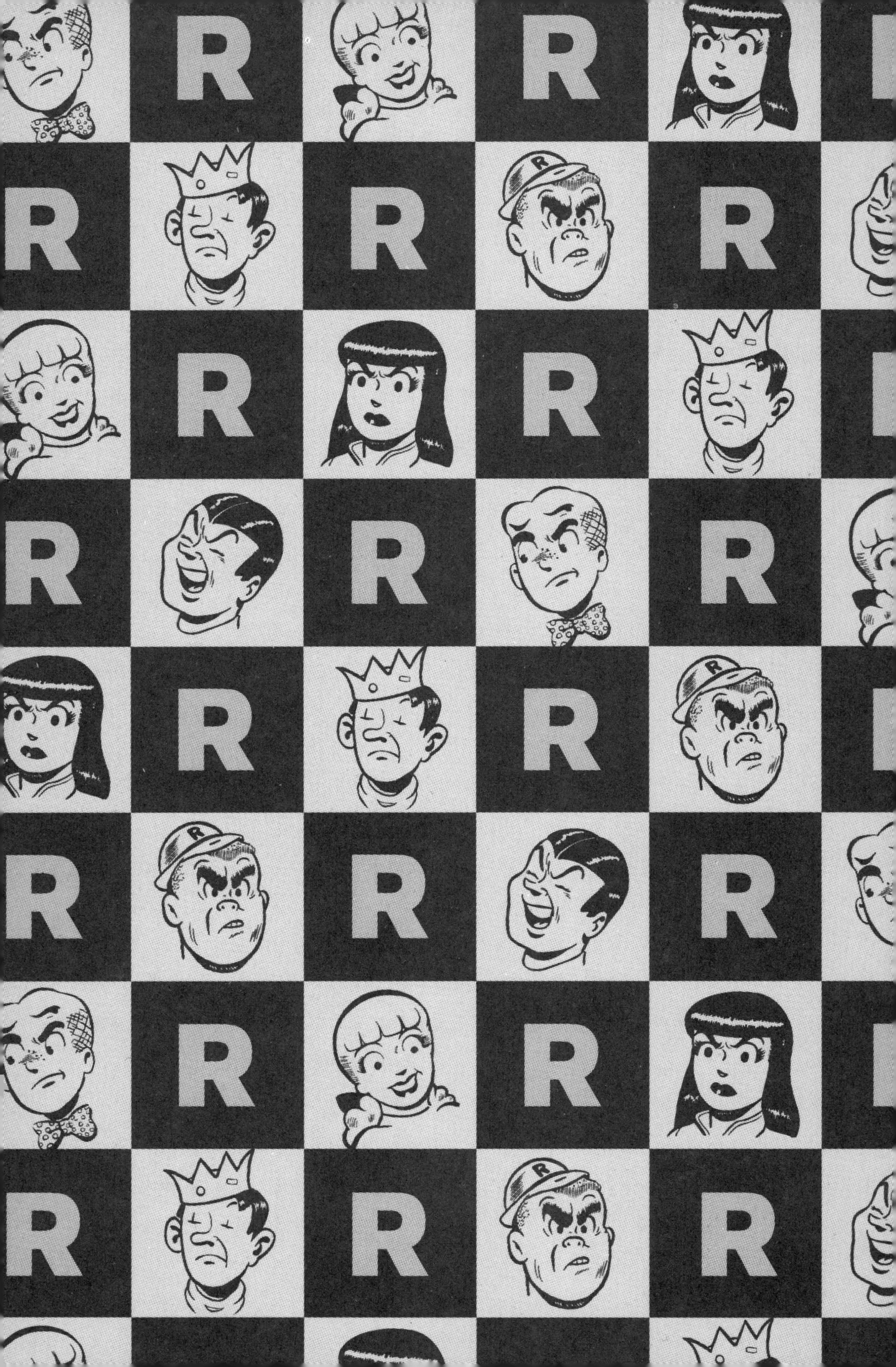